THE
ESSENTIAL
PEIRCE

THE
ESSENTIAL
PEIRCE

Selected Philosophical Writings

VOLUME 2
(1893–1913)

———

edited by the Peirce Edition Project

Nathan Houser, *General Editor*

André De Tienne, *Assistant Editor*

Jonathan R. Eller, *Textual Editor*

Cathy L. Clark, *Editorial Associate*

Albert C. Lewis, *Associate Editor*

D. Bront Davis, *Technical Editor*

Indiana
University
Press

BLOOMINGTON AND INDIANAPOLIS

MANUFACTURED IN THE UNITED STATES OF AMERICA

Library of Congress Cataloging-in-Publication Data

Peirce, Charles S. (Charles Sanders), 1839–1914.
    [Selections. 1998]
    The essential Peirce: selected philosophical writings / edited by
the Peirce Edition Project
    p. cm.
    Includes bibliographical references and index.
    Contents: v. 2. 1893–1913.
    ISBN 0-253-33397-0 (alk. paper). ISBN 0-253-21190-5
(pbk.: alk. paper)
    1. Philosophy.   I. Peirce Edition Project.
II. Title
B945.P4125   1998
191–dc20   91-32113

1 2 3 4 5 02 01 00 99 98

Thou art the unanswered question
  Couldst see thy proper eye
Always it asketh, asketh;
  And each answer is a lie.
                              —Emerson

*Greek Sculpture of the Sphinx, in the British Museum,
as reproduced in the* Century Dictionary

This book
is dedicated to the memory of

MAX H. FISCH

whose legacy of research
made it possible.

PREFACE

This collection of writings by Charles Sanders Peirce provides in a convenient format a selection from his seminal works; one that is sufficiently comprehensive to enable readers to form a relatively complete impression of the main doctrines of his system of philosophy and to study its development. The present volume covers a period of about twenty years, roughly the years Max Fisch called Peirce's *Monist* period—when many of Peirce's philosophical papers were written for Open Court's journal, *The Monist*. If volume size had not been a factor, we would have included other notable philosophical papers, including Peirce's 1900 paper written for *Cosmopolitan*, "Our Senses as Reasoning Machines"; his informative 1902 application to the Carnegie Institution for a grant to enable him to write thirty-six memoirs on logic in which he planned to set out his complete system of philosophy; a more complete representation of his 1898 Cambridge Conference Lectures and his 1903 Lowell Lectures; and the papers, published and unpublished, from the 1905–6 *Monist* series on pragmatism that employ the Existential Graphs in the proof of pragmatism. We believe there is a need for a special volume devoted to Peirce's graphical logic and to writings that are based on the Existential Graphs, and hope to assemble such a volume as a separate publication in the course of preparing the *Writings*. As it is, we have had to exclude many valuable writings, among them most of Peirce's technical papers on mathematics, logic, and science, as well as his many contributions to other disciplines. Given these limitations, readers should bear in mind that Peirce, more than any other classic American philosopher, related his thought to mathematical, logical, and scientific conceptions.* The main selections in this volume are arranged chronologically from 1893 to 1913, beginning with a short paper on synechism and ending with one of Peirce's many unfinished late attempts to record for posterity his final views on the intricacies of reasoning. An appendix follows with excerpts from letters to Victoria Lady Welby and to William James to help fill out the most mature form of Peirce's theory of signs.

The introduction printed in Volume 1 (EP1) provides a summary account of Peirce's philosophy and serves as the general introduction to the present volume. The introduction to Volume 2 deals more fully with some of the key issues that motivated Peirce's thought after 1893. Peirce was fifty-three years old when the first EP2 selection was written in 1893. He would live for another twenty-one years and, during that time, would produce his most fully

---

*Many of Peirce's most significant technical works are available elsewhere: his scientific writings in the annual reports of the U.S. Coast and Geodetic Survey and in the first six volumes of the *Writings of Charles S. Peirce*; his logical writings in volumes 2–4 of the *Collected Papers of Charles Sanders Peirce*; and his mathematical writings in the four volumes of Carolyn Eisele's *New Elements of Mathematics*.

developed theory of signs and many of his most subtle and refined metaphysical theories. It was also during these later years that his interest in pragmatism was rekindled and that, in an attempt to work out a proof of his pragmatism, he put into service his unique system of graphical logic (his Existential Graphs) alongside his categories and his theory of signs. Peirce's interest in the theory of reasoning, a life-long preoccupation, continued unabated throughout these years up to his final days when he seemed to see with exceptional clarity the tension between "safe" but impotent thinking and the creative potency of "unsafe" reasoning. The subject of reasoning along with the related subjects of pragmatism and signs make up the principal themes of the thirty-one papers (plus appendix) that constitute this volume, although to say that may obscure more than it reveals. A reminder from the foreword to EP1 bears repeating: to read Peirce without keeping in mind the growth of his thought is to miss one of its key features, its special vitality. Peirce's writings are signs of a great intellect *in the process* of working its way toward the truth.

Peirce's extant writings—many writings were lost during his itinerant years with the Coast and Geodetic Survey and on several occasions after his death—would fill a hundred volumes the size of this one. A selected edition of some fifty volumes would be necessary to get a comprehensive sense of his work in all of the areas to which he contributed, including mathematics, geodesy, logic, philosophy, lexicology, the natural sciences, history, and psychology. The most ambitious multi-volume edition, *Writings of Charles S. Peirce: A Chronological Edition*, is now underway at the Peirce Edition Project at Indiana University–Purdue University, Indianapolis (IUPUI); thirty volumes are projected (Indiana University Press, 1981–). The first multi-volume edition started to appear some sixty-five years ago when the first of eight volumes of the *Collected Papers* was published (Harvard University Press, 1931–58). Four other major English-language collections have appeared within the last twenty-five years. Peirce's *Contributions to THE NATION* was edited by Kenneth L. Ketner and James E. Cook, in four parts (Texas Tech Press, 1975–88) and his *New Elements of Mathematics*, in three volumes, edited by Carolyn Eisele (Mouton/Humanities Press, 1975–76). A microfiche edition, *Complete Published Works*, was prepared under the general editorship of Ketner and accompanied by a printed *Comprehensive Bibliography* (Johnson Associates, 1977; revised and enlarged, Philosophy Documentation Center, 1986). Carolyn Eisele brought out two volumes of *Historical Perspectives on Peirce's Logic of Science: A History of Science* (Mouton, 1985). Two important series of lectures by Peirce have recently appeared in print: *Reasoning and the Logic of Things: The Cambridge Conference Lectures of 1898*, Kenneth L. Ketner, editor (Harvard University Press, 1992); and *Pragmatism As a Principle and Method of Right Thinking: The 1903 Harvard Lectures on Pragmatism*, Patricia Ann Turrisi, editor (State University of New York Press, 1997). A number of significant translations have also appeared, and more are underway.

The present two-volume collection cannot replace the more comprehensive editions, but it provides an affordable and reliable text that covers the full extent of Peirce's system of philosophy. Its thematic boundaries are more expansive than those of several other one- or two-volume collections, and it is arranged chronologically, in two parts, to preserve the developmental character of Peirce's thought. Of the thirty-one principal selections included in this volume, only six were published during Peirce's lifetime. Of the remaining twenty-five writings, all edited from manuscripts and typescripts, only a few have already appeared in print in the forms given to the texts for the present edition. Special attention has been taken to ensure the integrity of the edited texts, and even though the selections from the last part of EP1 and all of EP2 will be reedited for the critical edition in accordance with the demanding guidelines of the Modern Language Association, we are confident that the volume as a whole is reliable from a textual point of view.

Editorial Policies

The selections in the present collection are printed with a minimum of editorial intrusion in the reading text, although we have used italicized editorial brackets to identify physical problems such as missing or unreadable text, and have indicated, with superscript arabic numerals, where we have contributed annotations. These annotations provide information (including translations) that Peirce himself did not provide. The footnotes, identified by asterisks, daggers, and so on, are Peirce's own. In a few of these footnotes we have provided, in italic brackets, additional information—such as names, dates, page numbers, and references to EP1 or to the *Writings*.

Copy-texts were selected with the standards of the critical edition in mind; they usually represent the most mature surviving forms closest to Peirce's hand. For those few items that Peirce saw through to publication, his final manuscript or typescript is used when it has survived. In such cases, Peirce's identifiable revisions in the publication (and in any surviving proofs or offprints) are emended into the text; variations judged to be typesetting errors or editorial sophistications are rejected. Two of Peirce's five published pieces ("Pearson's *Grammar of Science*" and "What Pragmatism Is") have no surviving pre-publication forms, and are edited directly from the original published text.

In all selections, Peirce's own errors of content are corrected. Where Peirce's punctuation or lack of punctuation might introduce confusion into a sentence, we have emended the punctuation for the convenience of the reader. Ease of reading is more central to the concept of the *Essential Peirce* volumes than to the critical edition, so we have made a number of regularizations to further facilitate reader comprehension. These emendations, which distinguish this edition from the critically-edited *Writings*, can be grouped under three categories of intervention:

(1) For the *Essential Peirce* we have generally regularized Peirce's inconsistencies of spelling, and modernized both his spellings and his word compounds. British spellings, used inconsistently by Peirce (and occasionally imposed by journal editors), are usually americanized. We have retained his

nineteenth-century style of pairing dashes with commas and other punctuation, but we have expanded his abbreviated terms and symbols into finished text. Ordinal numbers and related forms (i.e., "2ndly") are spelled out except in mathematical formulas or contexts. The conjunction "and" replaces his ampersands, "manuscript" replaces "MS," and so on. His abbreviated citations of books, articles, and journals are spelled out; where these appear parenthetically in running text, the bibliographical details are moved to Peirce's accompanying footnote or to the selection's backmatter annotations. Where we have supplied or emended titles, it is noted in the selection's headnote.

(2) Peirce's inconsistent use of single and double quotation marks to identify terms and to offset quotations has been regularized to double quotation marks throughout. In the present volume, single quotation marks are reserved for quotations within quotations. Commas and periods after quoted words or passages are normalized to the American standard form by placement within the closing quotation marks; all other marks of punctuation are placed outside the quotation. Cosmetic changes, such as the italicization of book titles cited by Peirce and the indentation of opening paragraphs, are also silently regularized. Peirce sometimes lists items as a series of single-sentence paragraphs; in general, we have grouped the items of each series together into single paragraphs.

(3) A peculiarity of Peirce's writing is his employment of capital letters for rhetorical emphasis or, more frequently, for words being defined, for class terms used specifically in reference to their place in a classification, for terms denoting "Platonic forms," and for terms of special importance in the discussion at hand. In general, we retain Peirce's capitalizations in these cases, and raise some terms to capitals where he has been inconsistent or erratic; however, where Peirce's capitalization is irregular, and does not reveal any of the patterns identified above, we have regularized to lowercase. Peirce's rhetorical cues sometimes go beyond capitalization—he also occasionally used heavily-inked squared script letters (in contrast to his normal cursive script) to convey special meaning or emphasis. This practice is most evident in his spoken lectures, where he may have intended the heavy printing as a reminder to emphasize a spoken word, or perhaps to write a word or phrase on a chalkboard. We represent these terms or phrases in italics.

Ordinarily, for the present volume, these editing interventions are not listed, but in cases where an intervention seems especially significant or problematic it is noted and discussed in the volume's backmatter annotations. A fuller record of our editorial interventions is available in *The Companion to The Essential Peirce*, which may be accessed through the Peirce Project Home Page (http://www.iupui.edu/~peirce); the *Companion* includes supplementary texts and expanded editorial commentary by the editors, and is expected to undergo frequent modifications.

As indicated above, editorial brackets are used to indicate textual problems. Words appearing in italic brackets indicate that they have been supplied or reconstructed by the editors; word substitutions, as when we emend "that" for "than" or "it" for "is" to correct Peirce's slips of the pen, are emended silently. Text recovered from Peirce's incomplete or accidental manuscript deletions also appears without brackets; authoritative revisions by Peirce in subsequent surviving forms of the text are also emended into the copy-text without brackets. As with other emendations to the copy-text, these cases are recorded in the *Companion*. Omitted sections of text within a selection are indicated by ellipsis points surrounded by editorial brackets to distinguish these excisions from Peirce's own uses of ellipses, which will appear unbracketed. Editorial ellipses are supplied only if we omit text internally; selections that are extracts from larger works are so identified in their headnotes and are not bounded by ellipses.

The headnotes, which appear in old-style type after the title of each item, serve several purposes. They identify each item as a published paper or an unpublished manuscript; provide information on its composition and publication; and characterize its contents, indicating its place in the overall development of Peirce's system of philosophy. Papers published during Peirce's lifetime are identified by a "P" followed by a number keyed to the bibliographic information provided in Kenneth L. Ketner's *Comprehensive Bibliography* (2nd rev. ed., Philosophy Documentation Center, 1986). Unpublished papers are identified by "MS" followed by the number assigned in Richard Robin's *Annotated Catalogue of the Papers of Charles S. Peirce* (University of Massachusetts Press, 1967) and his "The Peirce Papers: A Supplementary Catalogue" (*Transactions of the Charles S. Peirce Society* 7 [1971]: 35–37). Republication (or first publication) in the two major editions is indicated either by a "W" (*Writings of Charles S. Peirce*), followed by volume and page numbers, or by "CP" (*Collected Papers of Charles Sanders Peirce*), followed by volume and paragraph numbers. Republication in some other editions is also noted by the following abbreviations: HP (HPPLS in EP1) (*Historical Perspectives on Peirce's Logic of Science*), NEM (*The New Elements of Mathematics*), CN (Peirce's *Contributions to* THE NATION), RLT (*Reasoning and the Logic of Things*), and HL (*The 1903 Harvard Lectures*, edited by Turrisi). These abbreviations are used extensively in the notes.

We do not provide a list of secondary studies since the number of such works has grown to enormous proportions and the increasing availability of comprehensive bibliographic databases has almost obviated the need for printed bibliographies. The most complete printed listings of secondary studies, through 1982, are in the *Comprehensive Bibliography* and in *The Relevance of Charles Peirce* (The Hegeler Institute, 1983).

Acknowledgments

This volume represents the conclusion of a project begun in 1991 by Nathan Houser and Christian Kloesel. They carried out their plan for a two-volume edition of Peirce's "essential" philosophical writings through the publication of *The Essential Peirce*, Vol. 1 (EP1) and a preliminary selection of writings for EP2. That selection was made with advice from a number of Peirce scholars, including H. William Davenport, Carl R. Hausman, Christopher Hookway, Menno Hulswit, Kenneth L. Ketner, Don D. Roberts, Richard S. Robin, Thomas L. Short, and Shea Zellweger. With supporting grants from IUPUI's School of Liberal Arts, Houser and Kloesel had some selected manuscripts transcribed but were unable to carry out the textual work and editing needed to prepare the writings for publication and the research required for annotations. Early in 1997 the Peirce Edition Project agreed to finish the selection and to undertake the editing for EP2. This decision was taken because all of the writings included in EP2 will also be included in the critical edition, making the preparation of EP2 a reasonable preliminary for the critical edition, and also because it was much desired by Indiana University Press, which has been such a good friend and supporter of the Peirce Edition Project. All royalties for EP2 have been assigned to the Peirce Edition Project.

Among those who have made significant contributions to the preparation of EP2, we would especially like to acknowledge Beth Eccles, who worked in the first stage with Houser and Kloesel, and the second-stage collaborators who helped so much after the work was assumed by the Peirce Project: Leah Cummins, Mary A. Gallagher, Ginger Johnson, Adam Kovach, Matt Lamm, Brian C. McDonald, and Tracie Peterson. We are also grateful for advice and support from Arthur W. Burks and Albert Wertheim, and for assistance from Webb Dordick, Aleta Houser, and Steven Russell. We would like to thank the Prince Charitable Trusts for helping the Peirce Project establish a stronger base of external support. We also want to acknowledge the NEH for their support of the *Writings*, which indirectly but significantly contributed to this work. Deserving of special mention for their support in the preparation of this book are Don L. Cook for his editorial advice, and our colleagues at the Indiana University Press for their encouragement and cooperation; IUPUI's School of Liberal Arts and its Dean, John D. Barlow; and Chancellor Gerald Bepko and Vice Chancellor William B. Plater. We would like to thank Indiana University President Myles Brand for his advice and support. We are grateful to the Harvard University Department of Philosophy and the Houghton Library at Harvard University, the Morris Library at Southern Illinois University, the York University Library, and the Smithsonian Institution, for permission to publish Peirce manuscripts or letters from their holdings.

Indianapolis, 1998

INTRODUCTION

In April 1887 Peirce moved with his second wife, Juliette, from New York City to Milford, Pennsylvania, a small resort town in the upper Poconos. A year and a half later the Peirces moved into a farmhouse two miles northeast of Milford in the direction of Port Jervis, New York. This was to become Peirce's Arisbe, named for a Greek town south of the Hellespont, a colony of Miletus, home of the first philosophers of Greece.[1] The renovation and expansion of the Arisbe house would often preoccupy Peirce during his remaining years. The architectural work of remodeling Arisbe, always with an eye for something vast, would become a living metaphor for his intellectual life.[2]

Starting in the mid-80s with his "Guess at the Riddle," Peirce began to gather his philosophical doctrines together into an integrated system of thought, and with his 1891 *Monist* article, "Architecture of Theories," he began to attend explicitly to the structural integrity of his system as a whole. One of Peirce's main efforts after 1890 was to reestablish pragmatism, not attended to since his 1877–78 "Illustrations," as an integral component of his systematic philosophy. The integrating structure for his mature philosophy would be a much expanded, though never fully completed, theory of signs. Also prominent in Peirce's later writings is a more dominating form of naturalism that ties the development of human reason unambiguously to natural evolution and that takes on clear religious overtones.

The introduction printed in volume 1 (EP1) is the general introduction for *The Essential Peirce* as a whole, but no attempt was made to represent Peirce's intellectual development during his last two decades. This special introduction to volume 2 (EP2) is intended to supplement the general introduction by providing a sketch of this period. Peirce's life continues to resist easy characterization—unless cryptically in the claim that he embodied the general maxim he extolled in his fourth Harvard Lecture (sel. 13): "Never say die." There is no doubt that his life was one of much suffering and many defeats, but he never for long lost sight of his purpose: to do what he could to advance human understanding. He knew his own powers, and he knew the mundane truth that knowledge is advanced through scholarly preparedness, insight, humility, and hard intellectual work; and it was no delusion of grandeur for him to realize that he was poised to make contributions no one else could make. The story of Peirce's struggle to redeem his talents is one of the great personal tragedies of

1. See Max H. Fisch, *Peirce, Semeiotic, and Pragmatism*, K. L. Ketner and C. J. W. Kloesel, eds. (Indiana University Press, 1986), pp. 227–48.

2. Murray G. Murphey, *The Development of Peirce's Philosophy* (Harvard University Press, 1961; Indianapolis: Hackett Publishing Co., 1993), p. 3.

our time, but it cannot be told here.[3] These remarks are intended only to provide a unifying structure for the writings in this collection and a vantage point for surveying the grand expanse of a remarkably rich and complicated mind.

One obstacle to a comprehensive understanding of Peirce's thought is the broad range of his intellectual achievements, covering so many of the human and physical sciences; but added to that is the difficulty of determining to what extent he was influenced by his predecessors and peers. Of course, no one can think in a vacuum—thought must necessarily relate to past thought, just as it must appeal to subsequent thought—so it is never cogent to ask about any thinker whether his or her thought was influenced by previous thinkers, but only how and to what extent. To Peirce, this was obvious. Given his upbringing among mathematicians and experimental scientists he learned early that intellectual progress is always relative to knowledge already gained and that any successful science must be a cooperative endeavor. One of the reasons Peirce is so important for the history of ideas is that he approached philosophy in this way, knowing that if philosophy was ever really to amount to anything it would have to abandon the notion that great ideas arise ex nihilo—that one's ideas are wholly one's own. As a result of this understanding, and of his desire to help move philosophy toward a more mature stage of development, Peirce became a diligent student of the history of ideas and sought to connect his thought with the intellectual currents of the past. He also studied carefully the leading ideas of his own time. His debts are extensive—far too numerous to be cataloged fully here—but it could not be too far wrong to say that Aristotle and Kant were his most influential predecessors, with Plato, Scotus, and perhaps Berkeley coming next, although only on the heels of many others such as Leibniz, Hegel, and Comte. With respect to Peirce's scientific, mathematical, or logical ideas, others have to be added, including, certainly, De Morgan and Boole. When one considers how Peirce's thought was influenced by the ideas of his contemporaries one is hard-pressed to settle on a short list. Peirce was very current in many fields of study, due both to his scientifically informed approach and to the fact that he wrote hundreds of book reviews and newspaper reports on scientific meetings and "picked up" ideas along the way. In logic and mathematics, and even in philosophy, aside from predecessors, the influence of Cayley, Sylvester, Schröder, Kempe, Klein, and especially Cantor stands out. Peirce was also responsive to the writings of his fellow-pragmatists, among whom he included Josiah Royce; but he was more influenced by William James than by any other contemporary. Other contemporaries of note were the philosopher and editor, Paul Carus, and the English semiotician, Victoria Lady Welby, whose work on signs ("significs") led her to Peirce, and whose attentive interest in his semiotic ideas encouraged him to develop his theory of signs more fully than he would have without her.

---

3. Peirce's life was long neglected and is still obscure. The best accounts can be found in: Fisch, *Peirce, Semeiotic, and Pragmatism*; Joseph Brent, *Charles Sanders Peirce: A Life* (Indiana University Press, 1993; revised ed. 1998); and Kenneth Laine Ketner, *His Glassy Essence: An Autobiography of Charles Sanders Peirce* (Vanderbilt University Press, 1998).

Paul Carus (1852–1919) is a special case. Carus, a student of Hermann Grassmann, has been surprisingly neglected by historians, given his remarkable output as a philosopher and his importance as an editor and critic. He wrote scores of books and hundreds of articles (not only on philosophy) and edited over one hundred issues of the *Monist* and over seven hundred issues of the *Open Court*, the two periodical publications of the Open Court Publishing Company.[4] Open Court authors included the classic American quartet, Peirce, James, Royce, and Dewey, and a host of others ranging from Ernst Mach and Bertrand Russell to D. T. Suzuki. Carus was a confirmed monist, as is revealed in the name of his journal, and devoted to the reconciliation of science and religion. He took a special interest in Peirce and for over twenty years, notwithstanding some periods of acrimony, he did more to promote Peirce's philosophy than anyone. Beginning in 1891, Carus published nineteen of Peirce's articles (thirteen in *The Monist* and six in *The Open Court*) and many of Peirce's unpublished writings were intended for Carus. The important role played by Carus in Peirce's later life, in particular the fact that after 1890 Peirce wrote most of his best work for the *Monist*, is what led Max Fisch to call that time Peirce's *Monist* period.

The writings in the present volume begin in 1893 when Peirce was fifty-three years old, only three years into the *Monist* period and one year after his forced resignation from the Coast and Geodetic Survey. He had recently delivered a course of lectures on "The History of Science" at the Lowell Institute in Cambridge and was just bringing to a close—one article prematurely—his influential metaphysical series for the *Monist* (EP1, sels. 21–25). He was at work on "Search for a Method," which was to include a substantially revised version of his 1877–78 "Illustrations of the Logic of Science" (EP1, sels. 7–12), and was about to announce a twelve-volume opus, *The Principles of Philosophy*, possibly inspired by James's recent success with his *Principles of Psychology*. Clearly, the opening writings of the present volume arose in the context of an active and ongoing program of research.

For an intellectual profile of EP2, the separate headnotes to the selections might be read consecutively. Although they were not composed to provide a continuous flow of text, they do give an idea of a thread of intellectual development that ties together the writings in this volume. Obviously it is not possible to capture rich full texts, as most of Peirce's are, in short notes, but sometimes a single strand of connected meaning is all that is needed to precipitate more substantial linkings. Building on the headnotes, bearing in mind some of the biographical structures developed in the general introduction in EP1, and also some of the more significant intellectual events of this later period, the following sketch emerges as one way to trace Peirce's development.

In the first selection, "Immortality in the Light of Synechism," written in 1893, Peirce gave an indication of the significance of the argument for continuity

---

4. Harold Henderson, *Catalyst for Controversy: Paul Carus of Open Court*, (Southern Illinois University Press, 1993). The Open Court Publishing Company was owned by the Chicago industrialist Edward C. Hegeler.

that he had planned for a conclusion to his *Monist* metaphysical series. "I carry the doctrine so far as to maintain that continuity governs the whole domain of experience in every element of it. Accordingly, every proposition, except so far as it relates to an unattainable limit of experience (which I call the Absolute), is to be taken with an indefinite qualification; for a proposition which has no relation whatever to experience is devoid of all meaning." Synechism would guide Peirce's philosophical investigations for the rest of his life. Peirce also signaled his growing conviction that science and religion were closely allied at some deep level.

The following year, in "What is a Sign?" (sel. 2), Peirce explored the relationship between logic and semiotics—even equating reasoning with semiosis. "What is a Sign" is taken from Peirce's unpublished book "How to Reason," also known as "Grand Logic." Elsewhere in that work, Peirce revived the nominalism-realism issue, which he had not dealt with since 1871, and he identified himself, for the first time, as an "extreme" realist.[5] Another year later, in "Of Reasoning in General" (sel. 3), he further developed his semiotic theory of logic elaborating more fully his theory that propositions must always involve two signs, one iconic and the other indexical. These ideas, along with the idea that our success in discovering natural laws is explained by our affinity with nature, would reemerge as key conceptions in Peirce's struggle to rework pragmatism and to account for non-rational human insight. But for a time, he would submerge himself in writing a mathematical textbook called "New Elements of Mathematics,"[6] and also in formal logic, particularly in some elaborate reviews of the recently published volumes of Ernst Schröder's *Vorlesungen über die Algebra der Logik*.[7]

Near the end of 1896 Peirce took what Max Fisch calls his "most decisive single step" in his progress toward an all-encompassing realism: he accepted "the possible" as a "positive universe" and rejected the nominalist view that the possible is merely what we do not know not to be true.[8] Peirce reported this change of mind in January 1897 in his second Schröder review (CP 3.527) and on 18 March wrote to James that he had "reached this truth by studying the question of possible grades of multitude, where I found myself arrested until I could form a whole logic of possibility" (CP 8.308). With his acceptance of real possibilities—which put Peirce in the Aristotelian wing of the realist camp—Peirce had become what Fisch called "a three-category realist," no longer regarding the potential as what the actual makes it to be, and now distinguishing the generality of firsts from the generality of thirds.

Peirce's embrace of what he would come to call "would-be's" marks a watershed that might be said to separate his middle years from the final period of his intellectual life. This change, in conjunction with his attention to the importance

---

5. Fisch, *Peirce, Semeiotic, and Pragmatism*, p. 193

6. Peirce's book was completed but not published in his lifetime. See notes 2–4 to selection 22 (p. 537).

7. Peirce's reviews appeared in the *Nation* and the *Monist;* see P620 (CP 3.425–455), P627 (CN 2:132–33), and P637 (CP 3.456–552).

8. Fisch, *Peirce, Semeiotic, and Pragmatism*, p. 194.

of continuity, would motivate much of the content of his 1898 Cambridge Conferences Lectures. However, the two lectures from that set that are included in the present volume (sels. 4 and 5) were perhaps shaped more by another event: the 1897 appearance of William James's book, *The Will to Believe and Other Essays in Popular Philosophy*. James had dedicated that book "To my old friend, Charles Sanders Peirce, to whose philosophic comradeship in old times and to whose writings in more recent years I owe more incitement and help than I can express or repay." Peirce was touched, and on 13 March wrote a reflective letter to James expressing his appreciation ("it was a truly sweet thing, my dear William"), and pointing out some ways his thinking had been affected by his experience of "the world of misery" which had been disclosed to him. Although rating "higher than ever the individual deed as the only real meaning there is [in] the Concept," he had come to see "more sharply than ever that it is not the mere arbitrary force in the deed but the life it gives to the idea that is valuable." It is not to "mere action as brute exercise of strength" that we should look if we want to find purpose. Peirce praised James's opening essay, "The Will to Believe," especially for its style and lucidity, but he clearly had reservations. James introduced his essay as an illustration of the continuing concern at Harvard for "vital subjects": it is "a defence of our right to adopt a believing attitude in religious matters, in spite of the fact that our merely logical intellect may not have been coerced."[9] A key point is that "our non-intellectual nature" influences our convictions. "Our passional nature," James wrote, "not only lawfully may, but must, decide an option between propositions, whenever it is a genuine option that cannot by its nature be decided on intellectual grounds." It seems evident that in his Cambridge Conferences Lectures Peirce's great interest in the tensions between theory and practice, and his advocacy of "the will to learn" as a prerequisite to actually learning, were stimulated by James's "The Will to Believe." It is noteworthy that from at least that time on, the role of instinct, or sentiment, as a co-participant with reason in the acquisition of knowledge became a key concern for Peirce, and it would not be long until he came to regard ethics and esthetics as epistemically more fundamental than logic.

Less than six months after hearing Peirce's lectures in 1898, William James traveled to California to address (on 26 August) the Philosophical Union at Berkeley.[10] It was in that lecture, entitled "Philosophical Conceptions and Practical Results," that James publicly introduced the word "Pragmatism."[11] James told his auditors that he would have preferred the name "Practicalism" but that he had settled on "Pragmatism" because that was the name Peirce had used in the early 1870s when he first advocated for pragmatism before the

---

9. This and the quotations that follow in this paragraph are from the opening essay of William James, *The Will to Believe and Other Essays in Popular Philosophy* (Longmans Green, 1896; Harvard University Press, 1979).

10. For Fisch's full account see *Peirce, Semeiotic, and Pragmatism*, pp. 283 ff.

11. K. L. Ketner and H. Putnam speculate that James's new-found interest in pragmatism, as well as "Royce's drift toward Peirce's ideas," was a consequence of Peirce's 1898 Cambridge Lectures (RLT 36).

Cambridge Metaphysical Club.[12] James was by this time one of America's most respected intellectuals and his message fell on fertile ground; before long there were a host of pragmatists in the U.S. and abroad. James's acknowledgment of Peirce as the originator of pragmatism increased Peirce's prominence and opened for him an opportunity to bring his distinct views into the growing international debate.[13]

Peirce's second wave of interest in pragmatism is often thought to have started with James's California lecture, but it would be more accurate to say that it began in the early 1890s with the resumption of his research in logic and methodology for his "Critic of Arguments" series for the *Open Court*, and for his books, "Search for a Method" and "How to Reason." If anything, James's 1890 *Principles of Psychology*, especially the treatment of the role of inference in perception, probably had more to do with Peirce's return to pragmatism. But it was also about 1890 when Peirce accepted the reality of actuality, or secondness, and then saw clearly that the individual is to be distinguished from the general. It may have been the logical ramifications of that large step toward a more embracing realism, precipitated by his recognition in the mid-80s of the need for both icons and indices for meaningful reference, that led Peirce to begin to rethink the argument of his 1877–78 "Illustrations." Nevertheless, it surely was the increasing popularity of pragmatism that James had spawned in 1898 that led Peirce to resolve to produce a proof that would distinguish his version of pragmatism from popular versions and sanction his as the "scientific" one.

The nineteenth century, after his Cambridge Conferences Lectures, came to a bad ending for Peirce. Between periods of illness and failures to land employment Peirce must have learned more about misery.[14] But he continued to make intellectual progress. On 17 August 1899 he wrote to Carus that "the true nature of continuity . . . is now quite clear to me." Previously Peirce had been "dominated by Cantor's point of view" and had dismissed Kant's definition unjustly. Now he saw that it is best not to try "to build up a continuum from points as Cantor does."[15] He began the twentieth century thinking about great men of science. On 12 January 1901 he published "The Century's Great Men in Science" in the *New York Evening Post*, noting that "the glory of the nineteenth century has been its science" and asking what it was that has distinguished its great contributors.[16] "Their distinctive characteristic throughout the century, and more and more so in each succeeding generation, has been devotion to the pursuit of truth for truth's sake." He reflected on his own boyhood in

12. Peirce's key anti-foundational arguments had appeared earlier in his 1868 *Journal of Speculative Philosophy* series; EP1, selections 2–4.

13. According to Murray Murphey, James's lecture put Peirce "in an intolerable intellectual position." Peirce could not now disown pragmatism, but neither could he "embrace it without qualification." Peirce had to come forward with his distinct views (*The Development of Peirce's Philosophy*, pp. 358–59).

14. See Brent, *Charles Sanders Peirce: A Life*, ch. 4.

15. Quoted in Eisele's NEM 3:780.

16. This article, as reprinted in the *Annual Report of the Smithsonian Institution for Year Ending June 30, 1900* (Washington, D.C., 1901) is published in Philip P. Wiener, ed., *Charles S. Peirce: Selected Writings* (Dover, 1966), pp. 265–74. Quotations are taken from Wiener's book.

Cambridge and on the leaders of the "scientific generation of Darwin," most of whom had passed through his home: "The word *science* was one often in those men's mouths, and I am quite sure they did not mean by it 'systematized knowledge,' as former ages had defined it, nor anything set down in a book, but, on the contrary, a mode of life; not knowledge, but the devoted, well-considered life-pursuit of knowledge; devotion to Truth—not 'devotion to truth as one sees it,' for that is no devotion to truth at all, but only to party—no, far from that, devotion to the truth that the man is not yet able to see but is striving to obtain." As Peirce's career opportunities dried up he came more and more to regard science and philosophy as devout pursuits.

Fortunately for Peirce, near the end of 1900 James Mark Baldwin hired him to finish the logic definitions after "J" for his *Dictionary of Philosophy and Psychology*. This work occupied much of Peirce's time in 1901, yet he managed to publish about twenty book reviews and to translate seven articles for the Smithsonian. One of the books Peirce reviewed in 1901 was Karl Pearson's *Grammar of Science* (sel. 6). An idea Peirce had put forward in his Cambridge Conferences Lectures, that it is illogical to make one's personal well-being "a matter of overwhelming moment," can be seen to be at work in this review. Peirce objected to Pearson's claim that human conduct should be regulated by Darwinian theory and that social stability is the sole justification of scientific research. The human affinity with nature that Peirce had earlier appealed to to explain our success in discovering natural laws (sel. 3), was here explained as resulting from the fact that the human intellect is an outgrowth of the rationality inherent in nature. This was a further rejection of nominalism, which holds that the rationality in nature arises in human reason. Peirce also rejected Pearson's claim that there are first impressions of sense that serve as the starting point for reasoning, and argues that reasoning begins in percepts, which are products of psychical operations involving three kinds of elements: qualities of feelings, reactions, and generalizing elements.

In 1901 in "Laws of Nature" (sel. 7), Peirce reviewed different conceptions of natural law and argued that the typical conception of scientists is that a law of nature is an objective fact—"much more reliable than any single observation." In remarking on the method scientists employ in their "exhumation" of laws of nature, he briefly described a method of conjecture and testing that he would develop in the following selection, "On the Logic of Drawing History from Ancient Documents." In selection 8, Peirce gave one of his most elaborate accounts of the different kinds of reasoning. He drew a distinction between two kinds of deductive reasoning, corollarial, which draws only those conclusions that can be derived from the analysis and manipulation of the premises as given, and theorematic, which enriches the inference base by adding propositions which were not part of the original premise set—and "which the *thesis* of the theorem does not contemplate" (p. 96). Peirce believed this distinction to be the most important division of deductions, and his most important discovery in the logic of mathematics.[17] He also introduced the crucial point he

17. Fisch, *Peirce, Semeiotic, and Pragmatism*, p. 334

would elaborate in his 1903 Harvard Lectures that "logical criticism cannot go behind *perceptual facts*"—the "first judgments which we make concerning percepts." Logic cannot criticize involuntary processes. Yet these "first judgments" do *represent* their percepts, although "in a very meager way."

By mid-1901 Peirce was ready to draw together the many interesting and diverse results he had been achieving into a major book project. The book was to be on logic, but in addition to reflecting his findings on continuity and modality, and his excitement with his progress on a graphical syntax for formal logic, he would incorporate his new discoveries in semiotics and reflect his growing belief that logic is a normative science. The book would be called "Minute Logic" to reflect the minute thoroughness with which he planned to examine every relevant problem. An early draft of the first chapter (MS 425) began with a section entitled "Logic's Promises" and the opening sentence: "Begin, if you will, by calling logic the theory of the conditions which determine reasonings to be secure." Within a year Peirce had drafted and redrafted hundreds of pages, and had finished four large chapters.[18] In July 1902 he prepared an elaborate application asking the Carnegie Institution, presided over by Daniel C. Gilman, to fund his "Logic" which he had reconceived as a set of thirty-six memoirs. His application ran to forty-five pages in typescript, and remains the best single guide to Peirce's system of thought.[19] Even though Peirce received strong recommendations from a powerful group of supporters, including the President, Theodore Roosevelt, and Andrew Carnegie himself, his project was not funded. On 19 June 1903 Peirce's brother, James Mills (Jem) wrote to William James: "Nobody who is familiar with the history of this affair can doubt that the refusal of the Committee is due to determined personal hostility on the part of certain members of the Committee." The matter had dragged on for so long, though, that by the time the rejection was definite, Peirce had already given his 1903 Harvard Lectures and was preparing for his Lowell Institute series—he would never return to his "Minute Logic." Jem wrote to James again on 23 June about the injustice of the Carnegie decision and thanked James for securing the Harvard Lectures for Charles: "I consider that the set of lectures given this Spring at Cambridge and the promise of the Lowell Lectures have saved him from going to ruin. For his fortunes were so desperate, that he could not much longer have resisted forces tending to destroy his bodily health and break down his mind."

The part of the "Minute Logic" included in EP2 is an excerpt from a chapter on the classification of the sciences. In "On Science and Natural Classes" (sel. 9), Peirce described a "natural class" as one "whose members are the sole offspring and vehicles of one idea," and he explained how ideas can "confer existence upon the individual members of the class"—not by bringing them

18. For an illustration of the logical depth of Peirce's work for this book, see the chapters by Glenn Clark and Shea Zellweger in *Studies in the Logic of Charles Sanders Peirce* (Indiana University Press, 1997).

19. Peirce's application to the Carnegie Institution (L 75) is available electronically on the Peirce-focused website: http://www.door.net/ARISBE/arisbe.htm.

into material existence, but by conferring on them "the power of working out results in this world." Such ideas, Peirce says, when not embodied have a "potential being, a being *in futuro*." This is Peirce's account of final causation, the power that ideas have "of finding or creating their vehicles, and having found them, of conferring upon them the ability to transform the face of the earth." Such is the power, Peirce believes, of the ideas of Truth and Right. It is in this context that he quotes the famous line from William Cullen Bryant, "Truth, crushed to earth, shall rise again."

In following out this thread of connecting ideas we come to what is probably the single most significant time in Peirce's mature life of ideas, his time in Cambridge in 1903 when he gave his famous "Harvard Lectures," just referred to above, followed not long after by his third series of Lowell Lectures. Peirce had paid close attention to the stream of writings on pragmatism that was gaining momentum and he thought the time had come for him to make a case for a more or less definitive core statement. But making his case or, as he saw it, proving his thesis, was a complicated matter requiring the marshaling of support from all areas of his vast system of thought. Further complicating matters was the fact that Peirce's system had gone through many changes since the 1870s. Among the more significant of those changes, some already mentioned above, was his acceptance of the reality of actuality (secondness) and later of possibility (firstness); his realization that human rationality is continuous with an immanent rationality in the natural cosmos; and his new-found conviction that logic is a normative science, epistemically dependent on ethics and esthetics. For Peirce, pragmatism had become a doctrine that conceptions are fundamentally relative to *aims* rather than to action per se as he had held in earlier years. To prove pragmatism, then, called for a basic rethinking within the context of a transformed, and still growing, philosophy. That was the task Peirce set out to perform in his 1903 Harvard and Lowell Lectures, and the program he inaugurated that year would guide him for the rest of his life.

In his Harvard Lectures, Peirce built his case for pragmatism on a new theory of perception, grounded in his theory of categories and on results from phenomenology, esthetics, and ethics (sel. 10). He argued that there is a realm of reality associated with each category and that the reality of thirdness is necessary to explain a mode of influence on external facts that cannot be explained by mechanical action alone (sel. 11). He argued that pragmatism is a logical, or semiotic, thesis concerning the meaning of a particular kind of symbol, the proposition, and explained that propositions are signs that must refer to their objects in two ways: indexically, by means of subjects, and iconically, by means of predicates (sel. 12). The crucial element of Peirce's argument, from the standpoint of his realism, involved the connection between propositional thought and perception. To preserve his realism, Peirce distinguished percepts, which are not propositional, from perceptual judgments, which are propositional, and which are, furthermore, the "first premises" of all our reasonings. The process by which perceptual judgments arise from percepts became a key factor in Peirce's case (sel. 13). But *if* perceptual judgments are the starting points for all intellectual development, then we must be able to perceive generality (sel. 14). Peirce next argued that abduction shades into perception, so that pragmatism may be regarded as the logic of abduction, and, finally, isolated three key points: that nothing is in the intellect that is not first in the senses; that perceptual judgments contain general elements; and that abductive inference shades into perceptual judgment without any sharp line of demarcation (sel. 15). Pragmatism, Peirce showed, follows from these propositions (sel. 16).

According to Fisch,[20] it was in the Harvard Lectures that Peirce, for the first time, made it clear that his realism was opposed to idealism as well as to nominalism. Peirce's new theory of perception embraced the doctrine of immediate perception, to deny which, according to Peirce, "cuts off all possibility of ever cognizing a *relation*." That idea was carried forward into the Lowell Lectures, where Peirce continued with his effort to prove pragmatism, making his best attempt so far, according to Fisch.[21] In "What Makes a Reasoning Sound" (sel. 17), the only lecture from the Lowell series that is included in EP2, Peirce made a strong case for objective grounds for evaluating reasonings and argued that with the right method even "a slight tendency to guess correctly" will assure progress toward the truth.

In conjunction with his Lowell Lectures, Peirce prepared a "Syllabus" to be distributed to his auditors. The first part is "An Outline Classification of the Sciences" (sel. 18), showing the normative sciences—esthetics, ethics, and logic—as constituting the central part of philosophy, and giving the order of epistemic and data-support relationships among the sciences that will guide his subsequent research. In "The Ethics of Terminology" (sel. 19), Peirce paused from his central task to elaborate on an issue that had been troubling him since he began working on logic entries in 1900 for Baldwin's *Dictionary* (and perhaps earlier with his work for the *Century Dictionary*): the unscientific terminology that prevailed in philosophy. Peirce recognized that philosophy could never abandon ordinary language altogether, for it is essential to understanding common conceptions, but philosophical analysis and progress calls for a specialized vocabulary. That was Peirce's strong conviction, and it explains his frequent resort to neologisms.

It may be that the attention Peirce gave to his classification of the sciences, along with his new-found conviction that logic is coextensive with semiotics, provided the impetus for the remaining two parts of the "Syllabus" that are included in EP2. They introduced a shift to an intensive development of his theory of signs along taxonomic lines motivated by his categories. In "Sundry Logical Conceptions" (sel. 20), Peirce introduced the semiotic trichotomy that divides signs according to whether they are interpreted as signs of possibility, fact, or law: rhemes (here called sumisigns), dicisigns, and arguments. That trichotomy was additional to his long-held division of signs according to whether they represent their objects by virtue of similarity, existential connection, or

---

20. Fisch, *Peirce, Semeiotic, and Pragmatism*, p. 195.
21. Fisch, *Peirce, Semeiotic, and Pragmatism*, p. 365.

law: icons, indices, or symbols. In "Nomenclature and Divisions of Triadic Relations" (sel. 21), Peirce introduced another trichotomy that distinguishes signs according to whether, in and of themselves, they are qualities, existents, or laws: qualisigns, sinsigns, and legisigns. With these three trichotomies in place, Peirce was able to identify ten distinct classes of signs. This was the beginning of a rapid development of his formal semiotic theory. There were two other parts of the "Syllabus" that are not included in EP2, one on Peirce's system of Existential Graphs, which Peirce would later choose as the preferred medium for the presentation of his proof of pragmatism, and the other an in-depth treatment of dyadic relations parallel to the treatment of triadic relations found in selection 21.

In the next two selections Peirce shifted his attention from pragmatism and its proof to concentrate more fully on the theory of signs. In "New Elements" (sel. 22), he focused on the abstract mathematical structures necessarily exhibited by sign relations and argued, as he had in "On Science and Natural Classes," that "representations have power to cause real facts" and that "there can be no reality which has not the life of a symbol." And in "Ideas, Stray or Stolen, about Scientific Writing" (sel. 23) Peirce gave one of his most focused accounts of speculative rhetoric, the third branch of his semiotic trivium, which has as its aim to find out "the general secret of rendering signs effective." Peirce made it clear that the range of legitimate semiotic effects (interpretants) includes feelings and physical results, as well as thoughts and other signs. Peirce reiterated a point he had made at least as early as his Harvard Lectures, that nothing can be represented unless it is of the nature of a sign, and he stressed that ideas can only be communicated through their physical effects.

While Peirce was writing about semiotics—and topics outside the scope of this volume (e.g., mathematics and graphical logic)—he had not stopped thinking about pragmatism. On 7 March 1904 he wrote to William James: "The humanistic element of pragmatism is very true and important and impressive; but I do not think that the doctrine can be *proved* in that way. The present generation likes to skip proofs. . . . You and Schiller carry pragmatism too far for me. I don't want to exaggerate it but keep it within the bounds to which the evidences of it are limited." By this time he was already at work on the first article of another series of papers for the *Monist* where he would again take up the proof of pragmatism.

Peirce's third *Monist* series opened with the April 1905 publication of "What Pragmatism Is" (sel. 24). This was to be the first of three papers that would explain in detail Peirce's special brand of pragmatism, give examples of its application, and prove it. Not long into his paper, Peirce paused to deliver a short lesson on philosophical nomenclature—the message being essentially the same as that of selection 19—as a rationale for renaming his form of pragmatism. He chose the name "pragmaticism" as one "ugly enough" to be safe from kidnappers. Peirce lamented that his word "pragmatism" was now met with in the literary journals, "where it gets abused in the merciless way that words have to expect when they fall into literary clutches." He would continue using his new "ugly" word for the rest of the *Monist* series, and as late at 1909 (sel. 30, p. 457) he used "pragmaticism" because, he wrote, James and Schiller had made "pragmatism" imply "the will to believe, the mutability of truth, the soundness of Zeno's refutation of motion, and pluralism generally"; but he would often revert to his original name, indicating that he may not really have wanted to give it up.

After his excursus into philosophical terminology, Peirce examined the presuppositions of pragmaticism with his proof in mind. One key assumption was that all mental development (learning) takes place in the context of a mass of already formed conceptions, and another was that meaning is always virtual. He also argued for the relevance of all three of the categories of being for his pragmaticism: thought (thirdness) can only govern through action (secondness) which, in turn, cannot arise except in feeling (firstness).

The same year, in "Issues of Pragmaticism" (sel. 25), Peirce restated his pragmatic maxim in semiotic terms, along lines suggested in his sixth Harvard Lecture (sel. 15). He identified the meaning that pragmaticism seeks to enunciate as that of symbols rather than of simple conceptions. The thrust of this article was to articulate his forms of critical common-sensism and scholastic realism, which he regarded as consequences (or "issues") of pragmaticism. He extended his realism to include the acceptance of "real vagues" and "real possibilities," and he pointed out that "it is the reality of some possibilities that pragmaticism is most concerned to insist upon." According to Fisch, *pragmaticism* had now become *pragmatism* "purged of the nominalistic dross of its original exposition."[22]

There are a number of manuscript drafts for a third *Monist* article which indicate that Peirce intended to proceed with his proof along lines he would follow in selection 28. In one of those drafts, "The Basis of Pragmaticism in Phaneroscopy" (sel. 26), he began with an argument from the valency of concepts based in his phenomenology (phaneroscopy) and theory of categories. In another, "The Basis of Pragmaticism in the Normative Sciences" (sel. 27), he focused on the normative sciences, especially on his general theory of signs, as the key to the proof. Peirce pointed out that the pragmaticist will grant that the *"summum bonum"* consists in a "continual increase of the embodiment of the idea-potentiality" but insisted that without embodiment in something other than symbols, "the principles of logic show there never could be the least growth in idea-potentiality."

Around this time, Peirce was working intensely on the formal structure and systematic interconnections of semiotic relations. His logic notebook (MS 339) in 1905 and 1906 is rife with semiotic analyses and discoveries giving weight to the idea that it was in the context of his theory of signs that he expected to deliver his promised proof of pragmaticism. But when the third article of the series, "Prolegomena to an Apology for Pragmaticism," finally appeared in October 1906, it turned out to be an explication of his system of logical graphs, the Existential Graphs, instead of the expected proof. Peirce had decided that it

22. Fisch, *Peirce, Semeiotic, and Pragmatism*, p. 195.

was by means of the Existential Graphs that he could most convincingly set out his proof, which was to follow in subsequent articles (although it is significantly previewed in this one). Peirce had decided to use his system of graphs for his proof for three principal reasons: it employed the fewest possible arbitrary conventions for representing propositions, its syntax was iconic, and it facilitated the most complete analysis. Peirce worked for years on the continuation of this series, but he never finished it.

It is not known for certain why Peirce was unable to complete his Existential Graphs-based proof, but it is often supposed to have been a consequence of his failure to reach a satisfactory solution to the problem of continuity.[23] It is clear that Peirce expected his argument for pragmatism to also constitute a proof of synechism (see selection 24, p. 335). So it may have been technical problems involving the logic of continuity that kept Peirce from completing this series of papers. Peirce interrupted his efforts to complete this third *Monist* series with a separate series on "amazing mazes" (two articles of a proposed three were published in 1908–9) in which he developed applications of the Existential Graphs and worked out new definitions of continuity.[24] This mathematical line of thought led Peirce into a number of important technical questions involving probability and modality. By February 1909, Peirce had worked out a matrix method for an extension of the propositional calculus to three values—at least ten years before the similar work of Lukasiewicz and Post.[25] Peirce's acceptance of real possibility had convinced him that the definition of "probability" should include reference to dispositions in addition to frequencies, but even though he tried many alternatives involving the *propensity* view he was never satisfied that he had got it quite right.[26] For Peirce, this was a matter of considerable importance for pragmatism, because one of the great defects he found with his early theory was the nominalistic appeal to a frequency theory of probability. He also gave up the material interpretation of logical implication.[27]

Among the more entangled and confounding sets of manuscripts in the Harvard collection (the manuscripts acquired by the Harvard Philosophy Department after Peirce's death) is one from 1906–7 in which Peirce attempted to compose a more or less popular account of pragmaticism—but again called "pragmatism"—and to give at least a summary proof (MSS 316–22). Nominally, Peirce was composing a "letter to the editor," initially for the *Nation* but later for the *Atlantic*, although Peirce recognized it as a full-fledged article in his correspondence. In the two variants combined in selection 28, Peirce delivered a proof that is probably the one he was intending to give in the

---

23. See Fisch, *Peirce, Semeiotic, and Pragmatism*, p. 365 and Richard S. Robin, "Classical Pragmatism and Pragmatism's Proof" in *The Rule of Reason: The Philosophy of Charles Sanders Peirce*, Jacqueline Brunning and Paul Forster, eds. (University of Toronto Press, 1997), p. 149.

24. Fisch, *Peirce, Semeiotic, and Pragmatism*, p. 196.

25. See Fisch, "Peirce's Triadic Logic" (written with Atwell Turquette) in *Peirce, Semeiotic, and Pragmatism*, pp. 171–83, for details and for further remarks on triadic logic.

26. Fisch, *Peirce, Semeiotic, and Pragmatism*, p. 196.

27. According to Fisch (*Peirce, Semeiotic, and Pragmatism*, p. 196), material (Philonian) implication was Peirce's last nominalist stronghold.

Monist before he decided on a more formal approach using his Existential Graphs. The proof in selection 28 is based on Peirce's theory of signs, beginning with the premiss that every concept and every thought beyond immediate perception is a sign, and concluding with the proposition that a final logical interpretant must be of the nature of a habit. This selection provides an illuminating integration of Peirce's theory of signs, including his mature theories of propositions and inference, with his pragmaticism.

It is evident from the refinement of the theory of signs expressed in his remarkable "letter" that Peirce had not given up work on semiotics when he turned to his Existential Graphs for his *Monist* proof of pragmatism. There may have been a hiatus following his failure to get his "letter" into print, but by August 1908 he was hard at work on the classification of triadic relations (MS 339) and in December he resumed discussion of his theory of signs in correspondence with Lady Welby (sel. 32). Peirce's letters to Lady Welby record, often in summary form, the most advanced theory of signs ever fashioned. The theory as a whole is far too complex to be represented here, although it was lightly sketched in the general introduction in EP1, and a recent book by James Liszka provides an excellent introduction to the system in full.[28] For the thread of intellectual development being pursued here, it is noteworthy that early in 1906 Peirce wrote to Lady Welby that he had found it necessary to distinguish two semiotic objects (immediate and dynamical) and three interpretants (here called "intentional," "effectual," and "communicational"), and he introduced the important conception of the *commens*, which "consists of all that is, and must be, well understood between utterer and interpreter, at the outset, in order that the sign in question should fulfill its function." On 23 December 1908 Peirce defined "sign" as "anything which is so determined by something else, called its Object, and so determines an effect upon a person, which effect I call its Interpretant, that the latter is thereby mediately determined by the former." He immediately added that the only reason he had inserted "upon a person" into his definition was because he despaired of making his broader conception understood. Over the course of the next few days he laid out his "ten main trichotomies of signs" (eight of them had been quietly given in a single remarkable paragraph on pp. 402–3 of selection 28), the tenth one being the division that expresses the three sources of assurance utterances can have: instinct, experience, or form. This tenth trichotomy would occupy Peirce a great deal during his remaining five years. Peirce's correspondence with William James (sel. 33) repeats many of the same semiotic developments recorded in the letters to Lady Welby, but sometimes more perspicuously and always in a different voice. Modal considerations are more evident in the letters to James. As pointed out above, by 1909 Peirce had made deep advances into modal logic and this is reflected in various ways; for example, in Peirce's emphatic statement that the final interpretant consists in the way every mind "would act," not in the way any mind does act, and also in Peirce's division of semiotic objects into may-be's, actualities, and would-be's.

28. James Jakób Liszka, *A General Introduction to the Semeiotic of Charles Sanders Peirce* (Indiana University Press, 1996).

On 9 April 1908 Peirce received a letter from Cassius J. Keyser inviting him to write an article for the *Hibbert Journal*. Peirce replied (10 April), outlining ten alternative topics and asking Keyser to choose one. Peirce had written, as his third alternative: "as I believe the *Hibbert Journal* is favorable to theological discussion, I should willingly treat a little known 'proof' of the Being of God. Properly speaking it is not *itself* a proof, but is a statement of what I believe to be a fact, which fact, if true, shows that a reasonable man by duly weighing certain great truths will inevitably be led to believe in God."[29] Whether it was Keyser or Peirce who chose the third alternative is not clear, but Peirce spent most of the next three months composing "A Neglected Argument for the Reality of God" (sel. 29).

In that paper Peirce examined the attractive force of the idea of God and concluded that humans instinctively gravitate to it. He contended that belief in God is irresistible to anyone who naturally (through musement) comes to contemplate the possibility of God. The "God hypothesis" appears to be a special kind of abduction (he uses "retroduction" instead of "abduction" in this paper). It arises from a human power of guessing that is analogous to the instincts of animals, and because it recommends itself with unusual force we can take "a certain altogether peculiar confidence" in it as a sign of the truth. Peirce called this his "humble argument" but pointed out that it is not a "proof" because the process leading from the idea of God to belief in God is not a reasoned (self-controlled) development of ideas. Peirce was led to make a distinction between "argument" and "argumentation" that he had not explicitly made before: an *argument* is "any process of thought reasonably tending to produce a definite belief" while an *argumentation* is "an argument proceeding upon definitely formulated premisses." An argument, in other words, does not have to be self-controlled. The power of guessing was put forward as "a sort of divinatory power," what Galileo called *il lume naturale*, and appears to have supplanted Ockham's razor in Peirce's methodological arsenal.

As the conclusion of an "argumentation," the "God hypothesis" must pass through the three successive stages of inquiry: retroduction, deduction, and induction. Peirce devoted nearly half the paper to a discussion of these three stages, but ended up giving only the barest sketch of how they apply in this case. Scientific inquiry requires that any hypothesis be verified by putting its implications to the test of actual experience. The difficulty with the "God hypothesis" is that it is so vague—its object so "infinitely incomprehensible"—that it seems to be impossible to draw any definite implications from its supposed truth. This might appear to fall short of the demands of pragmatism, but, on closer look, one finds that after Peirce embraced the reality of possibility he reconceived the idea of "practical consequences." In his Harvard Lectures he had emphasized that the maxim of pragmatism reaches far beyond the *merely practical* and allows for any "flight of imagination," provided only that this imagination "ultimately alights upon a possible practical effect." The practical

---

29. Peirce to C. J. Keyser, 10 April 1908 (Rare Book and Manuscript Library, Columbia University).

effect that Peirce conceived the "God hypothesis" to "alight upon" is "the self-controlled growth of man's conduct of life." Some scholars wonder whether this weakens the pragmatic maxim beyond recovery—whether, in other words, this opens the way for reinstating into our ontologies all sorts of "beings" that Peirce's earlier pragmatism excluded—but that underscores the fundamental issue raised by this article: whether belief *can* have any value for the self-controlled growth of the conduct of life *if* its object is *not* real.

Peirce's probing of the logic of perception and his reflections on the effectiveness of religious belief, probably along with suggestions that arose from his taxonomic investigations in semiotics, led him in his last years to devote a great deal of thought to "the kinds and degrees of assurance that can be afforded by the different ways of reasoning." The related theory is what Peirce meant by "logical critics," the subject of his intended contribution for a book to honor Lady Welby. That paper, "A Sketch of Logical Critics" (sel. 30), is incomplete, but in the part he finished he made the important point that by "reasoning" we mean a "change in thought" that appeals to a relation between our new cognition (the "conclusion") and "an already existing cognition" (the premiss or premisses) to support our assent in the truth of the conclusion. But not all belief acquisition appeals, in any deliberate sense, to previous cognition, as we saw in the case of perceptual judgments and belief in God. Peirce's conclusion was that knowledge is acquired in two ways, by reasoning, of course, but also by experience. Belief acquired through reasoning must be justified by what preceded it in our minds, but belief gained through experience needs no justification.

In the final article in EP2, "An Essay Toward Reasoning in Security and in Uberty" (sel. 31), Peirce carried further his consideration of the benefits afforded by the different kinds of reasoning—although here again the discussion is left incomplete. This paper, written in October 1913, only a few months before his death, might suggest that he was having doubts about the value of pragmatism. But it would be more accurate to conclude that in his later years Peirce's thought gravitated to ideas and concerns that forced him—or *enabled* him—to see the limitations of pragmatism. In 1903 he had proclaimed Pragmatism to be "a wonderfully efficient instrument . . . of signal service in every branch of science" (sel. 10). He had recommended it as advantageous for the conduct of life. Now he saw that the appeal of pragmatism was its contribution to the security of reasoning—but there is a price to pay for security. According to Peirce, reasoning always involves a trade-off between security and uberty (rich suggestiveness; potency). Deductive reasoning provides the most security, but it is austere and almost entirely without evocative power. Abduction, on the other hand, is abundant in its uberty though nearly devoid of security. Peirce had come to see that pragmatism has the limitations that come with choosing security over uberty: "[it] does not bestow a single smile upon beauty, upon moral virtue, or upon abstract truth;—the three things that alone raise Humanity above Animality."

Naturalism had grown into a powerful force in Peirce's thought. He had come to believe that attunement to nature was the key to the advancement of knowledge—as it was for life itself—and he thought that the power to guess nature's ways was one of the great wonders of the cosmos. Just as with animals, whose instinct enables them to "rise far above the general level of their intelligence" in performing their proper functions, so it is with humans, whose proper function, Peirce insisted, is to embody general ideas in art-creations, in utilities, and above all in theoretical cognition. But if attunement to nature is the key to the advancement of knowledge, it is at most a necessary condition; it puts thought on the scent of truth, which, to attain, must be won by skilled reasoning. Peirce remained a logician to the end.

This concludes the thread of development chosen here to draw together the separate papers in EP2, but it is only one of many approaches that could have been taken. Peirce's shift to a graphical syntax for his formal logic, with its corresponding emphasis on the importance of icons for reasoning, led to remarkable results in logic and in philosophy that parallels the course of development outlined above. Alternatively, the evolution of Peirce's theory of signs that is evident throughout EP2 might have been more systematically used to mark movements in Peirce's thought through these years. Or one might have expanded on Fisch's account of Peirce's ever-strengthening commitment to realism—or have followed the shifting influence of major thinkers and scientific discoveries on Peirce's thought. These and other approaches could be turned into useful heuristic guides to Peirce's intellectual life in his final two decades. But the growth of his pragmatism and, in particular, the development of its proof, surely represents a strong current running through the period and for much of it probably best represents Peirce's leading idea.

Something more should be said about Peirce's proof of pragmatism—one of the great puzzles for Peirce scholars. Max Fisch characterized it as "elusive" and Richard Robin says it is "unfinished business."[30] When he first claimed publicly in 1905 to have a proof (sel. 24), he said it was "a proof which seems to the writer to leave no reasonable doubt on the subject." Elsewhere he called it a "strict proof" or "scientific proof." We should not accept the pragmatic maxim, Peirce told the auditors of his second Harvard Lecture (sel. 11), "until it has passed through the fire of a drastic analysis." Peirce literally meant to "prove" pragmatism—but in the sense called for by philosophy. Philosophical proofs seek to prove *truths*, not just *theorems* (they strive to be *sound*, not just *valid*), and must therefore be concerned with establishing the truth of their premises. Only rarely is the deductive form of a philosophical argument in dispute; the crucial questions almost always have to do with the legitimacy and strength of the premises. And as with science generally, establishing the relevance and truth of contingent premises calls for non-deductive forms of reasoning. As a result, proving pragmatism calls for marshaling an appropriate set of assumptions and supportable claims which, as premises, will entail pragmatism as expressed in Peirce's maxim. In his first Harvard Lecture, to add to the "strictness" of the proof, Peirce deliberately expressed his maxim as a theorem:

---

30. Fisch, *Peirce, Semeiotic, and Pragmatism*, p. 363, and Robin, "Classical Pragmatism and Pragmatism's Proof," p. 149.

"Pragmatism is the principle that every theoretical judgment expressible in a sentence in the indicative mood is a confused form of thought whose only meaning, if it has any, lies in its tendency to enforce a corresponding practical maxim expressible as a conditional sentence having its apodosis in the imperative mood." So when Peirce claimed to have a proof of pragmatism, he meant that he could produce what he believed to be a convincing rationale, an argument (or, as he would say in his "Neglected Argument," an argumentation), to demonstrate that the pragmatic maxim, in a given form, strictly follows from a given set of premises, and, furthermore, that each of the premises is either a common assumption or can otherwise be shown to be admissible.

When Peirce's efforts to prove pragmatism are understood to be attempts to provide a convincing rationale or argument for the truth of his maxim, it makes sense to suppose that his first proof began to take shape in the early 1870s when he promoted pragmatism among the members of the Cambridge Metaphysical Club. His first published proof, then, would have been the argument of his "Illustrations." This is the view expressed by Max Fisch[31] and it is strongly supported by Peirce himself in his first Harvard Lecture (sel. 10): "The argument upon which I rested the maxim in my original paper was that belief consists mainly in being deliberately prepared to adopt the formula believed in as the guide to action." This belief, in turn, was carried back to "an original impulse to act consistently, to have a definite intention." But this is a "psychological principle" and by 1903 Peirce no longer thought it "satisfactory to reduce such fundamental things to psychology." Besides, as he wrote in the "additament" to his "Neglected Argument" (sel. 29), "I must confess the argument . . . might with some justice be said to beg the question." We might think of this early proof as the proof based on Peirce's theory of belief.

By 1903 Peirce had devoted a great deal of study to scientific proofs and to epistemic support relationships across sciences. By then he was much better prepared to build a proof of pragmatism, and it is clear that he was thinking of "proof" in a more rigorous sense. In his more technical restatement of his maxim for his Harvard Lectures, pragmatism was restricted to conceptions that can be expressed in sentential form. According to the pragmatic maxim, so stated, the meaning of a theoretical judgment expressible in a sentence in the indicative mood (what was originally expressed as "the object of our conception") lies in its tendency to enforce a corresponding practical maxim that takes the form of a conditional sentence (originally, "our conception of effects that might conceivably have practical bearings"). This is the thesis Peirce set out in 1903 to demonstrate. How did he go about it? Roughly by establishing, first, that all intellectual contents amount to theoretical judgments expressible in indicative sentences and, second, that all such judgments fundamentally appeal to imperative practical conditionals. To support the first part, he established: (1) nothing is in the intellect that was not first in the senses, (2) the process by which sensory stimulation rises to perceptual judgment is not subject to self-control, (3) perceptual judgments cannot be called into question and are the

31. Fisch, *Peirce, Semeiotic, and Pragmatism*, p. 363.

first premisses of all our reasonings, (4) perceptual judgments contain general (i.e. interpretative) elements (as in predicates of propositions), and (5) although literally particular, perceptual judgments entail general propositions. Then Peirce argued that (6) the process which results in perceptual judgments is a quasi-abductive process (depending on intellectual habits) which "interprets" percepts as cases falling under practical conditionals (and, therefore in relation to a purpose). This effectively proved his thesis. We might think of this as Peirce's proof of pragmatism based on his theory of perception.

In "Pragmatism" (sel. 28), Peirce shifted the burden of his proof to his theory of signs. He began by developing his thesis along lines he seemed to initially have had in mind for his *Monist* proof (see selection 26). First he characterized pragmatism as a method of ascertaining the meaning of "intellectual concepts" and he noted that "triadic predicates" are the principal examples (although, in passing, he considered whether there might be non-intellectual triadic relations). He noted that while signs can convey any of three forms of predicates (monadic, dyadic, or triadic), only triadic predicates are properly called "intellectual concepts." Only intellectual concepts convey more than feeling or existential fact, namely the "*would-acts*" of habitual behavior; and no agglomeration of actual happenings can ever completely fill up the meaning of a "would-be." This line of thought (with many steps left out) led Peirce to his thesis, what he called "the kernel of pragmatism" (p. 402): "The *total* meaning of the predication of an intellectual concept consists in affirming that, under all conceivable circumstances of a given kind, the subject of the predication would (or would not) behave in a certain way,—that is, that it either would, or would not, be true that under given experiential circumstances (or under a given proportion of them, taken *as they would occur* in experience) certain facts would exist." He also expressed his thesis in a simpler form: "The whole meaning of an intellectual predicate is that certain kinds of events would happen, once in so often, in the course of experience, under certain kinds of existential circumstances." This is what Peirce set out to prove in 1907.

Peirce's proof, much abbreviated, ran something like this:

1. "Every concept and every thought beyond immediate perception is a sign."
2. The object of a sign is necessarily unexpressed in the sign.
3. The interpretant is the "total proper effect of the sign" and this effect may be emotional, energetic, or logical, but it is the logical interpretant alone that constitutes "the intellectual apprehension of the meaning of a sign."
4. "A sign is anything, of whatsoever mode of being, which mediates between an object and an interpretant; since it is both determined by the object *relatively to the interpretant*, and determines the interpretant *in reference to the object*, in such wise as to cause the interpretant to be determined by the object through the mediation of this 'sign.'"
5. The logical interpretant does not correspond to any kind of object, but is essentially in a relatively future tense, what Peirce calls a "would-be." Thus the logical interpretant must be "general in its possibilities of reference."
6. Therefore, the logical interpretant is of the nature of habit.
7. A concept, proposition, or argument may be a logical interpretant, but not a final logical interpretant. The habit alone, though it may be a sign in some other way, does not call for further interpretation. It calls for action.

8. "The deliberately formed, self-analyzing habit . . . is the *living definition*, the veritable and final logical interpretant."

9. "*Consequently*, the most perfect account of a concept that words can convey will consist in a description of that habit which that concept is calculated to produce. But how otherwise can a habit be described than by a description of the kind of action to which it gives rise, with the specification of the conditions and of the motive?"

This conclusion is virtually a paraphrase of Peirce's thesis, the "kernel of pragmatism," so it completes his proof. We might think of this as the proof from Peirce's theory of signs. On 10 April 1907, Peirce sent Giovanni Papini a similar, though somewhat fuller, outline and explained that "among all scientific proofs with which I am acquainted [this is] the one that seems to me to come nearest to popular apprehension."[32]

When Peirce began his third *Monist* series, represented in EP2 in selections 24–27, he probably had something like the above proof in mind, although perhaps something more wide-ranging. The definition of pragmatism as set out in "What Pragmatism Is" (sel. 24) gives some idea of what he was aiming for: pragmatism, he wrote, is "the theory that a *conception*, that is, the rational purport of a word or other expression, lies exclusively in its conceivable bearing upon the conduct of life; so that, since obviously nothing that might not result from experiment can have any direct bearing upon conduct, if one can define accurately all the conceivable experimental phenomena which the affirmation or denial of a concept could imply, one will have therein a complete definition of the concept, and *there is absolutely nothing more in it*" (332). Peirce pointed out that to prove this thesis it would be necessary to appeal to a wide range of "preliminary propositions." Don D. Roberts has listed seventeen "premises" that he thinks are likely to be among the ones Peirce had in mind, and these include "dismiss make-believes," "logical self-control is a mirror of ethical self-control," "an experiment is an operation of thought," "we do not doubt that we can exert a measure of self-control over our future actions," "a person is not absolutely individual," and "thinking is a kind of dialogue."[33]

Midway through his third *Monist* series, Peirce changed his mind and decided to base his proof on his Existential Graphs. He never completed his graph-based proof, but there are many manuscript pages indicating what he had in mind. In one draft (MS 298) Peirce explained: "You 'catch on,' I hope. I mean, you apprehend in what way the system of Existential Graphs is to furnish a test of the truth or falsity of Pragmaticism. Namely, a sufficient study of the Graphs should show what nature is truly common to all significations of concepts; whereupon a comparison will show whether that nature be or be not the very ilk that Pragmaticism (by the definition of it) avers that it is. . . ."

That proof, as represented in preliminary form in Peirce's 1906 "Prolegomena to an Apology for Pragmaticism" (CP 4.530–72) and in MSS 296–300, is extremely complex. It depends heavily on establishing that the system of

32. Peirce to G. Papini, 10 April 1907 (Papini Archives).
33. Don D. Roberts, "An Introduction to Peirce's Proof of Pragmatism," *Transactions of the Charles S. Peirce Society* 14 (1978), p. 128.

Existential Graphs provides a working model of thought and that experimenting with the Graphs amounts to experimenting with concepts themselves. The sweep of issues addressed in the premises of this proof includes: that the proper objects for investigation in experiments with diagrams are *forms of relation*; that deductive reasoning is no more certain than inductive reasoning when experimentation can be "multiplied at will at no more cost than a summons before the imagination"; that icons have more to do with the living character of truth than either symbols or indices; that reasoning must be chiefly concerned with forms; that diagrams are icons of the forms of relations that constitute their objects; that members of a collection, taken singly, are not as numerous as the relations among them; that there can be no thought without signs and there are no isolated signs; that every logical evolution of thought should be dialogic; and that thought is not necessarily connected with a brain. This is only a sampling. There is little doubt that the full exposition of Peirce's Graphs-based proof would shed considerable light on the complex network of relationships internal to Peirce's system of thought that support pragmatism, but it is not so clear whether its upshot would be to prove pragmatism or to prove that the system of Existential Graphs is a valid normative logic of cognition—*really* a "moving picture of thought" as Peirce once said (CP 4.11).

Most of Peirce's arguments for pragmatism, and there are a number that have not been mentioned, seem to be quite straightforward in setting out what is to be proved—the pragmatic maxim as a carefully stated thesis—and in supplying the assumptions and premises that entail that thesis as conclusion. The intractability of these arguments usually results from their large number of premisses, ranging over vast sweeps of Peirce's system of thought, and from the difficulty involved in establishing the premisses. But the matter is complicated by the fact that many of the involved premises require inductive support, and by apparent promises of inductive confirmation for the pragmatic conclusion, which Peirce thought his readers might hesitate to accept because of the overall complexity of the argument and the novel ideas it involved.[34] An important question emerges: What kind of principle is the pragmatic maxim after all? Is it a logical maxim and a regulative principle, or is it a positive truth that can be treated as a scientific hypothesis calling for inductive confirmation? Peirce's treatment suggests that it is both. But as a positive truth informing us how to construe the meaning of conceptions or propositions—signs with intellectual value—how could the pragmatic maxim be confirmed? In criticizing the argument of his 1877–78 "Illustrations," Peirce disallowed any appeal to psychology, and in any case his classification of the sciences shows that the only positive sciences that can legitimately be appealed to are phenomenology and the prior normative sciences (and parts of logic) on which logical methods must rely. Peirce thought the maxim could be tested by *using* it to analyze familiar intellectual conceptions such as "real," "identity," "sequence," "substance," "time," and "probability," but *only* after he had established that his logical analyses of

34. See, for example, MS 300 and Roberts, "An Introduction to Peirce's Proof of Pragmatism," p. 129, for some elaboration.

those conceptions was neither psychological nor question-begging. That seems to be why he had first to prove that working with his Existential Graphs was "equivalent" to working with conceptions themselves. His proof from the Existential Graphs, then, appears to have been integral to his effort to prove pragmatism inductively. One of the limitations of this approach is that it can never wield demonstrative force, and the argument can always be carried further; but the hope must be that the time will come when further confirmation is beside the point. It is probably this inductive approach that has lent support to the view that Peirce's proof is rather amorphous and perhaps at best a cable with fibers of independent sub-arguments. Overall, it is easy to see why Thompson said that a "real proof" of pragmatism "would amount to a kind of elucidation of most of Peirce's philosophy and formal logic" and why Robin said that "coming to terms with pragmatism's proof" means coming to terms "with the whole Peirce."[35]

When Peirce died in the spring of 1914 he left a lot of important work unfinished. Perhaps most to be regretted is that he was unable to complete his "System of Logic, Considered as Semeiotic," which he hoped would stand for realism in the twentieth century as Mill's *System of Logic* had stood for nominalism in the nineteenth.[36] As it was, he did leave far more than has since been put to good use. More than fifty years ago, the great American social philosopher, Sidney Hook, wrote of Peirce that "he is just as much the philosopher's philosopher [today], just as much the pioneer of a second Copernican revolution in thought (one more genuine than Kant's) as he was when his meteoric genius first flashed across American skies."[37] It is still true that Peirce is mainly a "philosopher's philosopher." But it may turn out that his pioneering work, perhaps especially his later writings so tightly packed with ideas, will bloom at last into the influential legacy that Peirce in hopeful moments imagined would be his bequest to the future. Perhaps this collection, in spite of its limitations, will contribute to that end.

Nathan Houser

35. Manley Thompson, *The Pragmatic Philosophy of C. S. Peirce* (University of Chicago Press, 1953), p. 249. Robin, "Classical Pragmatism and Pragmatism's Proof," p. 150.

36. See MS 640 and NEM 3:875; and Fisch, *Peirce, Semeiotic, and Pragmatism*, p. 196. Many manuscripts from Peirce's last decade develop logic from the standpoint of semiotics but, perhaps, none more fully than MS 693.

37. Quoted from a tribute solicited by Frederic Harold Young and published by him in *Charles Sanders Peirce; America's Greatest Logician and Most Original Philosopher* (privately published, 1946), an address delivered in October 1945 to the Pike County Historical Society in Milford, Pennsylvania.

THE
ESSENTIAL
PEIRCE

1

Immortality in the Light of Synechism

MS 886. [First published in CP 7.565–78. This article, submitted on 4 May 1893, was written for the weekly magazine The Open Court *and was favorably considered for* The Monist, *but was not published because of a misunderstanding between Peirce and their editor, Paul Carus.] In this short and provoking paper, Peirce considers synechism, his doctrine that everything is continuous, and characterizes the stance of the synechist toward various philosophical questions. He applies his doctrine to the question of immortality and finds that it is rash to assume that we only have carnal life. Peirce maintains that synechism is a purely scientific philosophy and predicts that it will help reconcile science and religion.*

The word *synechism* is the English form of the Greek συνεχισμός, from συνεχής, continuous. For two centuries we have been affixing *-ist* and *-ism* to words, in order to note sects which exalt the importance of those elements which the stem-words signify. Thus, *materialism* is the doctrine that matter is everything, *idealism* the doctrine that ideas are everything, *dualism* the philosophy which splits everything in two. In like manner, I have proposed to make *synechism* mean the tendency to regard everything as continuous.*

For many years I have been endeavoring to develop this idea, and have, of late, given some of my results in the *Monist*.[2] I carry the doctrine so far as to maintain that continuity governs the whole domain of experience in every element of it. Accordingly, every proposition, except so far as it relates to an unattainable limit of experience (which I call the Absolute), is to be taken with an indefinite qualification; for a proposition which has no relation whatever to experience is devoid of all meaning.[3]

I propose here, without going into the extremely difficult question of the evidences of this doctrine, to give a specimen of the manner in which it can be applied to religious questions. I cannot here treat in full of the method of its application. It readily yields corollaries which appear at first highly enigmatic; but their meaning is cleared up by a more thoroughgoing application of the principle. This principle is, of course, itself to be understood in a synechistic sense; and, so understood, it in no wise contradicts itself. Consequently, it must lead to definite results, if the deductions are accurately performed.

---

*The Greek word means continuity of parts brought about by surgery.[1]

Thoroughgoing synechism will not permit us to say that the sum of the angles of a triangle exactly equals two right angles, but only that it equals that quantity plus or minus some quantity which is excessively small for all the triangles we can measure. We must not accept the proposition that space has three dimensions as strictly accurate; but can only say that any movements of bodies out of the three dimensions are at most exceedingly minute. We must not say that phenomena are perfectly regular, but only that the degree of their regularity is very high indeed.

There is a famous saying of Parmenides, ἔστι γὰρ εἶναι μηδὲν δ'οὐκ ἔστιν, "being is, and not-being is nothing."[4] This sounds plausible; yet synechism flatly denies it, declaring that being is a matter of more or less, so as to merge insensibly into nothing. How this can be appears when we consider that to say that a thing *is* is to say that in the upshot of intellectual progress it will attain a permanent status in the realm of ideas. Now, as no experiential question can be answered with absolute certainty, so we never can have reason to think that any given idea will either become unshakably established or be forever exploded. But to say that neither of these two events will come to pass definitively is to say that the object has an imperfect and qualified existence. Surely, no reader will suppose that this principle is intended to apply only to some phenomena and not to others,—only, for instance, to the little province of matter and not to the rest of the great empire of ideas. Nor must it be understood only of phenomena to the exclusion of their underlying substrates. Synechism certainly has no concern with any incognizable; but it will not admit a sharp sundering of phenomena from substrates. That which underlies a phenomenon and determines it, thereby is, itself, in a measure, a phenomenon.

Synechism, even in its less stalwart forms, can never abide dualism, properly so called. It does not wish to exterminate the conception of twoness, nor can any of these philosophic cranks who preach crusades against this or that fundamental conception find the slightest comfort in this doctrine. But dualism in its broadest legitimate meaning as the philosophy which performs its analyses with an axe, leaving, as the ultimate elements, unrelated chunks of being, this is most hostile to synechism. In particular, the synechist will not admit that physical and psychical phenomena are entirely distinct,—whether as belonging to different categories of substance, or as entirely separate sides of one shield,—but will insist that all phenomena are of one character, though some are more mental and spontaneous, others more material and regular. Still, all alike present that mixture of freedom and constraint, which allows them to be, nay, makes them to be teleological, or purposive.

Nor must any synechist say, "I am altogether myself, and not at all you." If you embrace synechism, you must abjure this metaphysics of wickedness. In the first place, your neighbors are, in a measure, yourself, and in far greater measure than, without deep studies in psychology, you would believe. Really, the selfhood you like to attribute to yourself is, for the most part, the vulgarest delusion of vanity. In the second place, all men who resemble you and are in analogous circumstances are, in a measure, yourself, though not quite in the same way in which your neighbors are you.

There is still another direction in which the barbaric conception of personal identity must be broadened. A Brahmanical hymn begins as follows: "I am that pure and infinite Self, who am bliss, eternal, manifest, all-pervading, and who am the substrate of all that owns name and form."[5] This expresses more than humiliation,—the utter swallowing up of the poor individual self in the spirit of prayer. All communication from mind to mind is through continuity of being. A man is capable of having assigned to him a *rôle* in the drama of creation; and so far as he loses himself in that *rôle*,—no matter how humble it may be,—so far he identifies himself with its Author.

Synechism denies that there are any immeasurable differences between phenomena; and by the same token, there can be no immeasurable difference between waking and sleeping. When you sleep, you are not so largely asleep as you fancy that you be.

Synechism refuses to believe that when death comes, even the carnal consciousness ceases quickly. How it is to be, it is hard to say, in the all but entire lack of observational data. Here, as elsewhere, the synechistic oracle is enigmatic. Possibly, the suggestion of that powerful fiction *Dreams of the Dead*, recently published,[6] may be the truth.

But, further, synechism recognizes that the carnal consciousness is but a small part of the man. There is, in the second place, the social consciousness, by which a man's spirit is embodied in others, and which continues to live and breathe and have its being very much longer than superficial observers think. Our readers need not be told how superbly this is set forth in Freytag's *Lost Manuscript*.[7]

Nor is this, by any means, all. A man is capable of a spiritual consciousness, which constitutes him one of the eternal verities, which is embodied in the universe as a whole. This as an archetypal idea can never fail; and in the world to come is destined to a special spiritual embodiment.

A friend of mine, in consequence of a fever, totally lost his sense of hearing. He had been very fond of music before his calamity; and, strange to say, even afterwards would love to stand by the piano when a good performer played. "So then," I said to him, "after all you can hear a little." "Absolutely not at all," he replied; "but I can *feel* the music all over my body." "Why," I exclaimed, "how is it possible for a new sense to be developed in a few months!" "It is not a new sense," he answered. "Now that my hearing is gone I can recognize that I always possessed this mode of consciousness, which I formerly, with other people, mistook for hearing." In the same manner, when the carnal consciousness passes away in death, we shall at once perceive that we have had all along a lively spiritual consciousness which we have been confusing with something different.

I have said enough, I think, to show that, though synechism is not religion, but, on the contrary, is a purely scientific philosophy, yet should it become generally accepted, as I confidently anticipate, it may play a part in the onement of religion and science.

2

What Is a Sign?

MS 404. [Published in part in CP 2.281, 285, and 297–302. This work, probably composed early in 1894, was originally the first chapter of a book entitled "The Art of Reasoning," but was then turned into the second chapter of Peirce's multi-volume "How to Reason: A Critick of Arguments" (also known as "Grand Logic").] In this selection Peirce gives an account of signs based on an analysis of conscious experience from the standpoint of his three universal categories. He discusses the three principal kinds of signs—icons, indices, and symbols—and provides many examples. He maintains, as he had earlier, that reasoning must involve all three kinds of signs, and he claims that the art of reasoning is the art of marshalling signs, thus emphasizing the relationship between logic and semiotics.

§1. This is a most necessary question, since all reasoning is an interpretation of signs of some kind. But it is also a very difficult question, calling for deep reflection.[1]

It is necessary to recognize three different states of mind. First, imagine a person in a dreamy state. Let us suppose he is thinking of nothing but a red color. Not thinking about it, either, that is, not asking nor answering any questions about it, not even saying to himself that it pleases him, but just contemplating it, as his fancy brings it up. Perhaps, when he gets tired of the red, he will change it to some other color,—say a turquoise blue,—or a rose-color;—but if he does so, it will be in the play of fancy without any reason and without any compulsion. This is about as near as may be to a state of mind in which something is present, without compulsion and without reason; it is called *Feeling*. Except in a half-waking hour, nobody really is in a state of feeling, pure and simple. But whenever we are awake, something is present to the mind, and what is present, without reference to any compulsion or reason, is feeling.

Second, imagine our dreamer suddenly to hear a loud and prolonged steam whistle. At the instant it begins, he is startled. He instinctively tries to get away; his hands go to his ears. It is not so much that it is unpleasing, but it forces itself so upon him. The instinctive resistance is a necessary part of it: the man would not be sensible his will was borne down, if he had no self-assertion to be borne down. It is the same when we exert ourselves against outer resistance; except for that resistance we should not have anything upon which to exercise strength. This sense of acting and of being acted upon, which is our sense of the reality of things,—both of outward things and of ourselves,—

may be called the sense of Reaction. It does not reside in any one Feeling; it comes upon the breaking of one feeling by another feeling. It essentially involves two things acting upon one another.

Third, let us imagine that our now-awakened dreamer, unable to shut out the piercing sound, jumps up and seeks to make his escape by the door, which we will suppose had been blown to with a bang just as the whistle commenced. But the instant our man opens the door let us say the whistle ceases. Much relieved, he thinks he will return to his seat, and so shuts the door, again. No sooner, however, has he done so than the whistle recommences. He asks himself whether the shutting of the door had anything to do with it; and once more opens the mysterious portal. As he opens it, the sound ceases. He is now in a third state of mind: he is *Thinking.* That is, he is aware of learning, or of going through a process by which a phenomenon is found to be governed by a rule, or has a general knowable way of behaving. He finds that one action is the means, or middle, for bringing about another result. This third state of mind is entirely different from the other two. In the second there was only a sense of brute force; now there is a sense of government by a general rule. In Reaction only two things are involved; but in government there is a third thing which is a means to an end. The very word *means* signifies something which is in the middle between two others. Moreover, this third state of mind, or Thought, is a sense of learning, and learning is the means by which we pass from ignorance to knowledge. As the most rudimentary sense of Reaction involves two states of Feeling, so it will be found that the most rudimentary Thought involves three states of Feeling.

As we advance into the subject, these ideas, which seem hazy at our first glimpse of them, will come to stand out more and more distinctly; and their great importance will also force itself upon our minds.

§2. There are three kinds of interest we may take in a thing. First, we may have a primary interest in it for itself. Second, we may have a secondary interest in it, on account of its reactions with other things. Third, we may have a mediatory interest in it, in so far as it conveys to a mind an idea about a thing. In so far as it does this, it is a *sign*, or representation.

§3. There are three kinds of signs. Firstly, there are *likenesses*, or icons; which serve to convey ideas of the things they represent simply by imitating them. Secondly, there are *indications*, or indices; which show something about things, on account of their being physically connected with them. Such is a guidepost, which points down the road to be taken, or a relative pronoun, which is placed just after the name of the thing intended to be denoted, or a vocative exclamation, as "Hi! there," which acts upon the nerves of the person addressed and forces his attention. Thirdly, there are *symbols*, or general signs, which have become associated with their meanings by usage. Such are most words, and phrases, and speeches, and books, and libraries.

Let us consider the various uses of these three kinds of signs more closely.

§4. *Likenesses.* Photographs, especially instantaneous photographs, are very instructive, because we know that they are in certain respects exactly like the objects they represent. But this resemblance is due to the photographs having been produced under such circumstances that they were physically forced to correspond point by point to nature. In that aspect, then, they belong to the second class of signs, those by physical connection. The case is different, if I surmise that zebras are likely to be obstinate, or otherwise disagreeable animals, because they seem to have a general resemblance to donkeys, and donkeys are self-willed. Here the donkey serves precisely as a probable likeness of the zebra. It is true we suppose that resemblance has a physical cause in heredity; but then, this hereditary affinity is itself only an inference from the likeness between the two animals, and we have not (as in the case of the photograph) any independent knowledge of the circumstances of the production of the two species. Another example of the use of a likeness is the design an artist draws of a statue, pictorial composition, architectural elevation, or piece of decoration, by the contemplation of which he can ascertain whether what he proposes will be beautiful and satisfactory. The question asked is thus answered almost with certainty because it relates to how the artist will himself be affected. The reasoning of mathematicians will be found to turn chiefly upon the use of likenesses, which are the very hinges of the gates of their science. The utility of likenesses to mathematicians consists in their suggesting, in a very precise way, new aspects of supposed states of things. For example, suppose we have a winding curve, with continual points where the curvature changes from clockwise to counter-clockwise and conversely as in figure 1. Let us further suppose that this curve is continued so that it crosses itself at every such point of reversed bending in another such

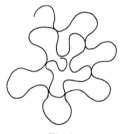

Fig. 1

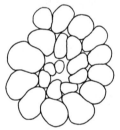

Fig. 2

point. The result appears in figure 2. It may be described as a number of ovals flattened together, as if by pressure. One would not perceive that the first description and the second were equivalent, without the figures. We shall find, when we get further into the subject, that all these different uses of likeness may be brought under one general formula.

In intercommunication, too, likenesses are quite indispensable. Imagine two men who know no common speech, thrown together remote from the rest of the race. They must communicate; but how are they to do so? By imitative sounds, by imitative gestures, and by pictures. These are three kinds of likenesses. It is true that they will also use other signs, finger-pointings, and the like. But, after all, the likenesses will be the only means of describing the qualities of the things and actions which they have in mind. Rudimentary language, when men first began to talk together, must have largely consisted either in directly imitative words, or in conventional names which they attached to pictures. The Egyptian language is an excessively rude one. It was, as far as we know, the earliest to be written; and the writing is all in pictures. Some of these pictures came to stand for sounds,—letters and syllables. But others stand directly for ideas. They are not nouns; they are not verbs; they are just pictorial ideas.

§5. *Indications.* But pictures alone,—pure likenesses,—can never convey the slightest information. Thus, figure 3 suggests a wheel. But it leaves the

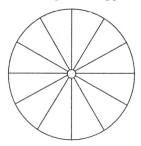

Fig. 3

spectator uncertain whether it is a copy of something actually existing or a mere play of fancy. The same thing is true of general language and of all *symbols.* No combination of words (excluding proper nouns, and in the absence of gestures or other indicative concomitants of speech) can ever convey the slightest information. This may sound paradoxical; but the following imaginary little dialogue will show how true it is:

Two men, *A* and *B*, meet on a country road, when the following conversation ensues.

B. The owner of that house is the richest man in these parts.
A. What house?
B. Why do you not see a house to your right about seven kilometres distant, on a hill?
A. Yes, I think I can descry it.
B. Very well; that is the house.

Thus, *A* has acquired information. But if he walks to a distant village and says "the owner of a house is the richest man in those parts," the remark will refer to nothing, unless he explains to his interlocutor how to proceed from where he is in order to find that district and that house. Without that, he does not indicate what he is talking about. To identify an object, we generally state its place at a stated time; and in every case must show how an experience of it can be connected with the previous experience of the hearer. To state a time, we must reckon from a known epoch,—either the present moment, or the assumed birth of Christ, or something of the sort. When we say the epoch must be known, we mean it must be connected with the hearer's experience.

We also have to reckon in units of time; and there is no way of making known what unit we propose to use except by appealing to the hearer's experience. So no place can be described, except relatively to some known place; and the unit of distance used must be defined by reference to some bar or other object which people can actually use directly or indirectly in measurement. It is true that a map is very useful in designating a place; and a map is a sort of picture. But unless the map carries a mark of a known locality, and the scale of miles, and the points of the compass, it no more shows where a place is than the map in *Gulliver's Travels* shows the location of Brobdingnag.[2] It is true that if a new island were found, say, in the Arctic Seas, its location could be approximately shown on a map which should have no lettering, meridians, nor parallels; for the familiar outlines of Iceland, Nova Zemla, Greenland, etc., serve to indicate the position. In such a case, we should avail ourselves of our knowledge that there is no second place that any being on this earth is likely to make a map of which has outlines like those of the Arctic shores. This experience of the world we live in renders the map something more than a mere *icon* and confers upon it the added characters of an *index*. Thus, it is true that one and the same sign may be at once a likeness and an indication. Still, the offices of these orders of signs are totally different. It may be objected that likenesses as much as indices[3] are founded on experience, that an image of red is meaningless to the color blind, as is that of erotic passion to the child. But these are truly objections which help the distinction; for it is *not* experience, but the *capacity* for experience, which they show is requisite for a likeness; and this is requisite, not in order that the likeness should be interpreted, but in order that it should at all be presented to the sense. Very different is the case of the inexperienced and the experienced person meeting the same man and noticing the same peculiarities, which to the experienced man indicate a whole history, but to the inexperienced reveal nothing.

Let us examine some examples of indications. I see a man with a rolling gait. This is a probable indication that he is a sailor. I see a bowlegged man in corduroys, gaiters, and a jacket. These are probable indications that he is a jockey or something of the sort. A weathercock *indicates* the direction of the wind. A sun-dial or a clock *indicates* the time of day. Geometricians mark letters against the different parts of their diagrams and then use those letters to indicate those parts. Letters are similarly used by lawyers and others. Thus, we may say: If *A* and *B* are married to one another and *C* is their child while *D* is brother of *A*, then *D* is uncle of *C*. Here *A*, *B*, *C*, and *D* fulfill the office of relative pronouns, but are more convenient since they require no special collocation of words. A rap on the door is an indication. Anything which focuses the attention is an indication. Anything which startles us is an indication, in so far as it marks the junction between two portions of experience. Thus a tremendous thunderbolt indicates that *something* considerable happened, though we may not know precisely what the event was. But it may be expected to connect itself with some other experience.

§6. *Symbols*. The word *symbol* has so many meanings that it would be an injury to the language to add a new one. I do not think that the signification I attach to it, that of a conventional sign, or one depending upon habit (acquired or inborn), is so much a new meaning as a return to the original meaning. Etymologically, it should mean a thing thrown together, just as ἔμβολον (embolum) is a thing thrown into something, a bolt, and παράβολον (parabolum) is a thing thrown besides, collateral security, and ὑπόβολον (hypobolum) is a thing thrown underneath, an antenuptial gift. It is usually said that in the word *symbol*, the throwing together is to be understood in the sense of to conjecture; but were that the case, we ought to find that *sometimes*, at least, it meant a conjecture, a meaning for which literature may be searched in vain. But the Greeks used "throw together" *(συμβάλλειν)* very frequently to signify the making of a contract or convention. Now, we do find symbol *(σύμβολον)* early and often used to mean a convention or contract. Aristotle calls a noun a "symbol," that is, a conventional sign.[4] In Greek,[5] a watch-fire is a "symbol," that is, a signal agreed upon; a standard or ensign is a "symbol," a watch-word is a "symbol," a badge is a "symbol"; a church creed is called a symbol, because it serves as a badge or shibboleth; a theatre-ticket is called a "symbol"; any ticket or check entitling one to receive anything is a "symbol." Moreover, any expression of sentiment was called a "symbol." Such were the principal meanings of the word in the original language. The reader will judge whether they suffice to establish my claim that I am not seriously wrenching the word in employing it as I propose to do.

Any ordinary word, as "give," "bird," "marriage," is an example of a symbol. It is *applicable to whatever may be found to realize the idea connected with the word;* it does not, in itself, identify those things. It does not show us a bird, nor enact before our eyes a giving or a marriage, but supposes that we are able to imagine those things, and have associated the word with them.

§7. A regular progression of one, two, three may be remarked in the three orders of signs, Likeness, Index, Symbol. The likeness has no dynamical connection with the object it represents; it simply happens that its qualities resemble those of that object, and excite analogous sensations in the mind for which it is a likeness. But it really stands unconnected with them. The index is physically connected with its object; they make an organic pair. But the interpreting mind has nothing to do with this connection, except remarking it, after it is established. The symbol is connected with its object by virtue of the idea of the symbol-using mind, without which no such connection would exist.

Every physical force reacts between a pair of particles, either of which may serve as an index of the other. On the other hand, we shall find that every intellectual operation involves a triad of symbols.

§8. A symbol, as we have seen, cannot indicate any particular thing; it denotes a kind of thing. Not only that, but it is itself a kind and not a single thing. You can write down the word "star"; but that does not make you the creator of the word, nor if you erase it have you destroyed the word. The word lives in the minds of those who use it. Even if they are all asleep, it exists in their memory. So we may admit, if there be reason to do so, that generals are mere words without at all saying, as Ockham supposed,[6] that they are really individuals.

Symbols grow. They come into being by development out of other signs, particularly from likenesses or from mixed signs partaking of the nature of likenesses and symbols. We think only in signs. These mental signs are of mixed nature; the symbol-parts of them are called concepts. If a man makes a new symbol, it is by thoughts involving concepts. So it is only out of symbols that a new symbol can grow. *Omne symbolum de symbolo.*[7] A symbol, once in being, spreads among the peoples. In use and in experience, its meaning grows. Such words as *force, law, wealth, marriage*, bear for us very different meanings from those they bore to our barbarous ancestors. The symbol may, with Emerson's sphynx,[8] say to man,

Of thine eye I am eyebeam.

In all reasoning, we have to use a mixture of *likenesses, indices*, and *symbols*. We cannot dispense with any of them. The complex whole may be called a *symbol;* for its symbolic, living character is the prevailing one. A metaphor is not always to be despised: though a man may be said to be composed of living tissues, yet portions of his nails, teeth, hair, and bones, which are most necessary to him, have ceased to undergo the metabolic processes which constitute life, and there are liquids in his body which are not alive. Now, we may liken the indices we use in reasoning to the hard parts of the body, and the likenesses we use to the blood: the one holds us stiffly up to the realities, the other with its swift changes supplies the nutriment for the main body of thought.

§9. Suppose a man to reason as follows: The Bible says that Enoch and Elijah were caught up into heaven; then, either the Bible errs, or else it is not strictly true that all men are mortal. What the Bible is, and what the historic world of men is, to which this reasoning relates, must be shown by indices. The reasoner makes some sort of mental diagram by which he sees that his alternative conclusion must be true, if the premise is so; and this diagram is an *icon* or likeness. The rest is symbols; and the whole may be considered as a modified symbol. It is not a dead thing, but carries the mind from one point to another. The art of reasoning is the art of marshalling such signs, and of finding out the truth.

3

Of Reasoning in General

MS 595. [Published in part in CP 2.282, 286–91, 295–96, 435–44, and 7.555–58. This is the first part of a work entitled "Short Logic" that Peirce began in 1895 for Ginn & Co. (who had rejected his lengthy "How to Reason"). This is the only chapter Peirce wrote.] The relationship between logic and semiotics is more deeply examined in this selection. Peirce considers reasoning in a broad context that includes both the process of belief change and the expression of thoughts in language, but he stresses the centrality of signs for reasoning. Here, as in the second selection, he focuses on icons, indices, and symbols, again giving many helpful examples, and applies this classification in his analysis of propositions and inferences. He divides the study of signs into three branches, which he calls the philosophical trivium: *speculative grammar, logic, and speculative rhetoric. Peirce then explains our success in discovering natural laws by our affinity with nature.*

Article 1. *Logic* is the art of reasoning.

The old times saw endless disputes as to whether logic was an *art* or a *science*. It is not worth while even to explain what those words were taken to mean. The present definition, respectable in its antiquity and superficiality, is intended merely to afford a rough preliminary notion of what this treatise is about. This chapter shall tell something more; but the student cannot expect to attain a real comprehension of the nature of logic till after he has gone through the book.

The facts upon which logic is based come mostly within ordinary knowledge; though many escape ordinary notice. The science is largely, not wholly, one of rearrangement.

Article 2. *Reasoning* is the process by which we attain a belief which we regard as the result of previous knowledge.

Some beliefs are results of other knowledge without the believer suspecting it. After a sojourn among young people exclusively, an acquaintance met may seem to have aged more than he really has. This is a case of error. But not all such results are erroneous. A stranger with whom I am dealing may make an impression of being dishonest owing to indications too slight for me to know what they are. Yet the impression may be well founded. Such results are usually set down to "intuition." Though inferential in their nature, they are not exactly *inferences*.

Again, a given belief may be regarded as the effect of another given belief, without our seeming to see clearly why or how. Such a process is usually called an *inference;* but it ought not to be called a *rational inference,* or *reasoning.* A blind force constrains us. Thus, Descartes declares himself obliged to believe that he exists because he remarks that he thinks. Yet he seems to doubt (in that stage of his inquiry) whether everything that thinks exists.

The word *illation* signifies a process of inference. Reasoning, in general, is sometimes called *ratiocination. Argumentation* is the expression of a reasoning. *Argument* may be mental or expressed. The belief to which an inference leads is called the *conclusion,* the beliefs from which it sets out are called the *premises.* (Sometimes written *premisses.*) The fact that the premises necessitate the truth of the conclusion is called the *consequence,* or *following* of the conclusion from the premises.

Article 3. A *Belief* is a state of mind of the nature of a habit, of which the person is aware, and which, if he acts deliberately on a suitable occasion, would induce him to act in a way different from what he might act in the absence of such habit.

Thus, if a man *believes* a straight line to be the shortest distance between two points, then in case he wishes to proceed by the shortest way from one point to another, and thinks he can move in a straight line, he will endeavor to do so. If a man really believes that alcohol is injurious to him, and does not choose to injure himself, but still drinks for the sake of the momentary satisfaction, then he is not acting deliberately. But a habit of which we are not aware, or with which we are not deliberately satisfied, is not a belief.

An act of consciousness in which a person thinks he recognizes a belief is called a *judgment.* The expression of a judgment is called in logic a *proposition.*

Article 4. "The unit of speech is the sentence," says one of the most illustrious of living linguists, the Rev. A. H. Sayce, in the article "Grammar" in the *Encyclopaedia Britannica.*[1] Modern logicians have come to a conclusion analogous to that of modern linguists in holding that the unit of thought is the judgment.

Still, it is as necessary in logic to dissect judgments as it is in grammar to analyze sentences.

Our grammars teach that a perfect sentence consists of a *subject* and *predicate.* There is some truth in that; yet it rather forces the facts to bring all sentences even in the European languages to that form. But Indo-European languages are to all languages what phanerogams are to plants as a whole or vertebrates to animals as a whole, a smallish part though the highest type. Grammarians are children of Procrustes and will make our grammar fit all languages, against the protests of those to whom they are vernacular. In the Eskimo tongue what we call the subject is generally put in the genitive case, and in many languages, except for proper names, words that are distinctly and decidedly nouns are quite exceptional. Still, there is something like a subject and a predicate in most languages; and something of the sort must exist in every logical proposition. In order to be able to understand precisely how this is we must turn our attention to signs.

Article 5. A *sign* is a thing which serves to convey knowledge of some other thing, which it is said to *stand for* or *represent*. This thing is called the *object* of the sign; the idea in the mind that the sign excites, which is a mental sign of the same object, is called an *interpretant* of the sign.

Signs are of three classes, namely, *Icons* (or images), *Indices*, and *Symbols*.

Article 6. An *icon* is a sign which stands for its object because as a thing perceived it excites an idea naturally allied to the idea that object would excite. Most icons, if not all, are *likenesses* of their objects. A photograph is an icon, usually conveying a flood of information. A piece of mimicry may be an auditory icon. A diagram is a kind of icon particularly useful, because it suppresses a quantity of details, and so allows the mind more easily to think of the important features. The figures of geometry are, if accurately drawn, such close likenesses of their objects that they are almost instances of them; but every student of geometry knows that it is not all necessary, nor even useful, to draw them so nicely, since if roughly drawn they still sufficiently resemble their objects in the particulars to which attention has to be drawn. Many diagrams resemble their objects not at all in looks; it is only in respect to the relations of their parts that their likeness consists. Thus, we may show the relation between the different kinds of signs by a brace, thus:

$$\text{Signs} \begin{cases} \text{Icons} \\ \text{Indices} \\ \text{Symbols} \end{cases}$$

This is an icon. But the only respect in which it resembles its object is that the brace shows the classes of *icons*, *indices*, and *symbols* to be related to one another and to the general class of signs, as they really are, in a general way. When, in algebra, we write equations under one another in a regular array, especially when we put resembling letters for corresponding coefficients, the array is an icon. Here is an example:

$$a_1 x + b_1 y = n_1,$$
$$a_2 x + b_2 y = n_2.$$

This is an icon, in that it makes quantities look alike which are in analogous relations to the problem. In fact, every algebraical equation is an icon, in so far as it *exhibits*, by means of the algebraical signs (which are not themselves icons), the relations of the quantities concerned.

It may be questioned whether all icons are likenesses or not. For example, if a drunken man is exhibited in order to show by contrast, the excellence of temperance, this is certainly an *icon*, but whether it is a likeness or not may be doubted. The question seems somewhat trivial.

Article 7. An *index* stands for its object by virtue of a real connection with it, or because it forces the mind to attend to that object. Thus, we say a low barometer with a moist air is an *indication* of rain; that is, we suppose that the forces of nature establish a probable connection between the low barometer with moist air and coming rain. A weathercock is an *indication*, or *index*, of the direction of the wind; because, in the first place, it really takes the selfsame direction as the wind, so that there is a real connection between them, and in the second place, we are so constituted that when we see a weathercock pointing in a certain direction it draws our attention to that direction, and when we see the weathercock veering with the wind, we are forced by the law of mind to think that direction is connected with the wind. The pole star is an *index*, or pointing finger, to show us which way is north. A spirit-level, or a plumb bob, is an *index* of the vertical direction. A yardstick might seem, at first sight, to be an icon of a yard; and so it would be, if it were merely intended to show a yard as near as it can be seen and estimated to be a yard. But the very purpose of the yardstick is to show a yard nearer than it can be estimated by its appearance. This it does in consequence of an accurate mechanical comparison made with the bar in London called the Yard, either the yardstick used, or some one from which it has been copied, having been transported from the Westminster Palace. Thus, it is a real connection which gives the yardstick its value as a representamen; and thus it is an *index*, not a mere *icon*. When a driver, to attract the attention of a foot-passenger and cause him to save himself, calls out "Hi!", so far as this is a significant word, it is, as will be seen below, something more than an index; but so far as it is simply intended to act upon the hearer's nervous system and to rouse him to get out of the way, it is an index, because it is meant to put him in real connection with the object, which is his situation relative to the approaching horse. Suppose two men meet upon a country road and one of them says to the other, "The chimney of that house is on fire." The other looks about him and descries a house with green blinds and a verandah having a smoking chimney. He walks on a few miles and meets a second traveller. Like a Simple Simon he says, "The chimney of that house is on fire." "What house?" asks the other. "Oh, a house with green blinds and a verandah," replies the simpleton. "Where is the house?" asks the stranger. He desires some *index* which shall connect his apprehension with the house meant. Words alone cannot do this. The demonstrative pronouns, "this" and "that," are indices. For they call upon the hearer to use his powers of observation, and so establish a real connection between his mind and the object; and if the demonstrative pronoun does that,—without which its meaning is not understood,—it goes to establish such a connection; and so is an *index*. The relative pronouns, *who* and *which*, demand observational activity in much the same way, only with them the observation has to be directed to the words that have gone before. Lawyers use *A*, *B*, *C*, practically, as very effective relative pronouns. To show how effective they are, we may note that Messrs. Allen and Greenough, in their admirable (though in the edition of 1877 too small) *Latin Grammar*,[2] declare that no conceivable syntax could wholly remove the ambiguity of the following sentence, "*A* replied to *B* that he thought *C* (his brother) more unjust to himself than to his own friend." Now, any lawyer would state that with perfect clearness, by using *A*, *B*, *C* as relatives, thus: *A* replied to *B* that he, $\left\{ \begin{array}{c} A \\ B \end{array} \right\}$, thought *C* (his, $\left\{ \begin{array}{c} A\text{'s} \\ B\text{'s} \end{array} \right\}$, brother) more unjust to himself, $\left\{ \begin{array}{c} A \\ B \\ C \end{array} \right\}$, than to his, $\left\{ \begin{array}{c} A\text{'s} \\ B\text{'s} \\ C\text{'s} \end{array} \right\}$, own friend.* The terminations which in any inflected language are attached to words "governed" by other words, and which serve to show which the governing word is, by repeating what is elsewhere expressed in the same form, are likewise *indices* of the same relative-pronoun character. Any bit of Latin poetry illustrates this, such as the twelve-line sentence beginning, "Jam satis terris."[3] Both in these terminations and in the *A*, *B*, *C*, a likeness is relied upon to carry the attention to the right object. But this does not make them icons, in any important way; for it is of no consequence how the letters *A*, *B*, *C* are shaped or what the terminations are. It is not merely that one occurrence of an *A* is like a previous occurrence that is the important circumstance, but that *there is an understanding [that] like letters shall stand for the same thing*, and this acts as a force carrying the attention from one occurrence of *A* to the previous one. A possessive pronoun is two ways an index, first it indicates the possessor, and, second, it has a modification which syntactically carries the attention to the word denoting the thing possessed.

Some indices are more or less detailed directions for what the hearer is to do in order to place himself in direct experiential or other connection with the thing meant. Thus, the Coast Survey issues "Notices to Mariners," giving the latitude and longitude, four or five bearings of prominent objects, etc., and saying *there* is a rock, or shoal, or buoy, or light-ship. Although there will be other elements in such directions, yet in the main they are indices.

---

*Modern grammars define a pronoun as a word used in place of a noun. That is an ancient doctrine which, exploded early in the thirteenth century, disappeared from the grammars for several hundred years. But the substitute employed was not very clear; and when a barbarous rage against medieval thought broke out, it was swept away. Some recent grammars, as *Allen and Greenough's*, set the matter right again. There is no reason for saying that, *I, thou, that, this*, stand in place of nouns; they indicate things in the directest possible way. It is impossible to express what an assertion refers to except by means of an index. A pronoun is an index. A noun, on the other hand, does not *indicate* the object it denotes; and when a noun is used to show what one is talking about, the experience of the hearer is relied upon to make up for the incapacity of the noun for doing what the pronoun does at once. Thus, a noun is an imperfect substitute for a pronoun. Nouns also serve to help out verbs. A pronoun ought to be defined as *a word which may indicate anything to which the first and second persons have suitable real connections, by calling the attention of the second person to it*. Allen and Greenough say "pronouns indicate some person or thing without either naming or describing." This is correct, refreshingly correct; only it seems better to say what they *do*, and not merely what they *don't*.

Along with such indexical directions of what to do to find the object meant, ought to be classed those pronouns which should be entitled *selective* pronouns, because they inform the hearer how he is to pick out one of the objects intended, but which grammarians call by the very indefinite designation of *indefinite* pronouns. Two varieties of these are particularly important in logic, the *universal selectives*, such as *quivis, quilibet, quisquam, ullus, nullus, nemo, quisque, uterque*, and in English, *any, every, all, no, none, whatever, whoever, everybody, anybody, nobody*. These mean that the hearer is at liberty to select any instance he likes within limits expressed or understood, and the assertion is intended to apply to that one. The other logically important variety consists of the *particular selectives, quis, quispiam, nescio quis, aliquius, quidam*, and in English, *some, something, somebody, a, a certain, some or other, a suitable, one*.

Allied to the above pronouns are such expressions as *all but one, one or two, a few, nearly all, every other one*, etc. Along with pronouns are to be classed adverbs of place and time, etc.

Not very unlike these are, *the first, the last, the seventh, two-thirds of, thousands of*, etc.

Other indexical words are prepositions, and prepositional phrases, such as *on the right* (or *left*) *of*. Right and left cannot be distinguished by any general description. Other prepositions signify relations which *may*, perhaps, be described; but when they refer, as they do oftener than would be supposed, to a situation relative to the observed, or assumed to be experientially known, place and attitude of the speaker relatively to that of the hearer, then the indexical element is the dominant element.*

Article 8. Icons and indices assert nothing. If an icon could be interpreted by a sentence, that sentence must be in a "potential mood," that is, it would merely say, "Suppose a figure has three sides," etc. Were an index so interpreted, the mood must be imperative, or exclamatory, as "See there!" or "Look out!" But the kinds of signs which we are now coming to consider are,

---

*If a logician had to construct a language *de novo*,—which he actually has almost to do,—he would naturally say, I shall need prepositions to express the temporal relations of *before, after*, and *at the same time with*, I shall need prepositions to express the spatial relations of *adjoining, containing, touching*, of *in range with*, of *near to, far from*, of *to the right of, to the left of, above, below, before, behind*, and I shall need prepositions to express motions into and out of these situations. For the rest, I can manage with metaphors. Only if my language is intended for use by people having some great geographical feature related the same way to all of them, as a mountain range, the sea, a great river, it will be desirable to have prepositions signifying situations relatively to that, as *across, seaward*, etc. But when we examine actual languages, it would seem as though they had supplied the place of many of these distinctions by gestures. The Egyptians had no preposition nor demonstrative having any apparent reference to the Nile. Only the Eskimo are so wrapped up in their bearskins that they have demonstratives distinguishing landward, seaward, north, south, east, and west. But examining the cases or prepositions of any actual language we find them a haphazard lot.

by nature, in the "indicative," or, as it should be called, the *declarative* mood.*
Of course, they can go to the expression of any other mood, since we may
declare assertions to be doubtful, or mere interrogations, or imperatively requisite.

A *symbol* is a sign naturally fit to declare that the set of objects, which is
denoted by whatever set of indices may be in certain ways attached to it, is
represented by an icon associated with it. To show what this complicated definition means, let us take as an example of a symbol the word "loveth." Associated with this word is an idea, which is the mental icon of one person loving
another. Now we are to understand that "loveth" occurs in a sentence; for
what it may mean by itself, if it means anything, is not the question. Let the
sentence, then, be "Ezekiel loveth Huldah." Ezekiel and Huldah must, then,
be or contain indices; for without indices it is impossible to designate what
one is talking about. Any mere description would leave it uncertain whether
they were not mere characters in a ballad; but whether they be so or not, indices can designate them. Now the effect of the word "loveth" is that the pair of
objects denoted by the pair of indices, Ezekiel and Huldah, is represented by
the icon, or the image we have in our minds of a lover and his beloved.

The same thing is equally true of every verb in the declarative mood; and
indeed of every verb, for the other moods are merely declarations of a fact
somewhat different from that expressed by the declarative mood.

As for a noun, considering the meaning which it has in the sentence, and
not as standing by itself, it is most conveniently regarded as a portion of a
symbol. Thus, the sentence "every man loves a woman" is equivalent to
"whatever is a man loves something that is a woman." Here "whatever" is a
universal selective index, "is a man" is a symbol, "loves" is a symbol, "something that" is a particular selective index, and "is a woman" is a symbol.

Article 9. The astonishing variety which exists in the syntax of different
languages shows that different men think the same fact in very different
ways. There is no respect in which the constructions of languages differ more
than in regard to the noun. Our Aryan languages are quite peculiar in the distinctness with which nouns are marked off from verbs. When we speak of a
noun, we do not think of what its effect in a sentence may be, but we think of
it as standing alone. Now a common noun *[such]* as "man," standing alone, is

---

*The nomenclature of grammar, like that of logic, is derived chiefly from a late Latin, the
words being transferred from the Greek, the Latin prefix translating the Greek prefix, and the
Latin stem the Greek stem. But while the logical words were chosen with fastidious care, the
grammarians were excessively careless, and none more so than Priscian.[4] The word *indicative* is
one of Priscian's creations. It was evidently intended to translate Aristotle's ἀποφαντική. But this
is precisely equivalent to *declarative* both in signification and according to the rules of transference, *de*, taking the place of ἀπό, as is usual in these artificial formations (*de*monstration for
ἀπόδειξις, etc.), and *clarare* representing φαινειν, to make clear. Perhaps the reason Priscian did
not choose the word *declarativus* was that Appuleius, a great authority on words, had used this in
a somewhat different sense.

certainly an index, but not of the object it denotes. It is an index of the mental object which it calls up. It is the index of an icon; for it denotes whatever there may be which is like that image. [. . .]⁵

There are too many types of speech to allow the insertion here of illustrations of all the different ways in which one and the same fact is thought by different peoples. Sufficient has been said to show the danger of assuming that because a certain way of thinking is natural to us Aryans, therefore, in the absence of any more positive evidence than that no other way occurs to *us*, it is a law of the human mind that man must think in that way. Still more presumptuous would it be to assume on those grounds that a given form of thought belongs to every intelligent being.

Article 10. Thinking a fact in a different way will not alter its value as a premise or as a conclusion. Whether from the judgment, *A*, it is proper to infer the judgment, *C*, depends upon whether or not the fact which *A* expresses could possibly take place without the fact which *C* expresses going along with it. On this connection of *facts* mere thinking can have no effect.

But it is now time to draw attention to three different tasks that are set before teacher and learner of the art of reasoning.

The principal business of logic is to ascertain whether given reasonings are good or bad, strong or weak. In this regard, whether we think our propositions in one form or in another is of no more consequence than whether we express them in English or in German, whether we write them or enunciate them, whether we drawl or gabble. In the eye of logic, two propositions expressing the same fact are *equivalent*, or virtually (at least) identical.

Accordingly, the practice of logicians has always been to adopt certain *canonical forms* in which they require that judgments should be expressed, before the reasonings which involve them are brought before them for examination. In choosing these forms, logicians need not be biased by the usage of any languages nor by the ways in which Aryans, or all the races of this little planet, may employ in their thinking. They will do best to take the forms which are the most convenient for their own purpose of tracing the relationship of dependence between one *fact* and another.

To say whether a given way of thinking is correct or not, it is requisite to consider what facts the thought expresses. To this, then, those who occupy themselves with the art of reasoning must attend. The logician cannot be asked to teach the tongues: it is the business of the philologist to do that. Syntax must explain what facts different forms of expression signify; and the forms of expression undoubtedly follow in the main the ways of thinking. Comparative syntax is a recognized branch of philology; and this must survey the whole ground of different ways of thinking the same fact, so far as they betray themselves in speech. Thus, a very important part of the labor of the art of reasoning is undertaken by the grammarian, and may be severed from logic proper. Every form of thinking must betray itself in some form of expression or go undiscovered. There are undoubtedly numerous other ways of making assertions besides verbal expressions, such as algebra, arithmetical figures, emblems, gesture-language, manners, uniforms, monuments, to mention only *intentional* modes of declaration. Some of these are of the highest importance for reasoning. Philologists have not deemed those sorts of language interesting to them. So, cultivators of the art of reasoning found themselves long ago obliged to institute a *speculative grammar* which should study *modes of signifying*, in general.* It is best regarded as separate from logic proper; for one of these days philologists may take it in hand, for which logicians will thank them.

An art of thinking ought also to recommend such forms of thinking as will most economically serve the purpose of Reason. The doing of this in a well-reasoned way involves a great theory. We shall get some glimpse of this in another chapter.[8] Logicians have done little in this line of study. Yet a number of books, not called logics (for the most part), have made unsystematic explorations into this science. Since this is the general foundation of the art of putting propositions into effective forms, it has been called *speculative rhetoric.*†

The sciences of speculative grammar, logic, and speculative rhetoric may be called the *philosophical trivium.*‡

Article 11. We shall now be able more fully to explain the nature of a proposition. We have seen that a judgment is an act of consciousness in which we recognize a belief, and a belief is an intelligent habit upon which we shall act when occasion presents itself. Of what nature is that recognition? It may come very near action. The muscles may twitch and we may restrain ourselves only by considering that the proper occasion has not arisen. But in general, we *virtually resolve* upon a certain occasion to act as if certain imagined circumstances were perceived. This act which amounts to such a resolve, is a peculiar act of the will whereby we cause an image, or *icon*, to be associated, in a peculiarly strenuous way, with an object represented to us by an *index*. This act itself is represented in the proposition by a *symbol*, and the consciousness of it fulfills the function of a symbol in the judgment. Suppose, for example, I detect a person with whom I have to deal, in an act of dishonesty. I have in my

---

*The *Tractatus de modis significandi sive Grammatica Speculativa* has been regarded by all those who have carefully examined the question, as a genuine work of Duns Scotus.[6] A minute comparison with the works of Siger of Brabant and Michael of Marbais,[7] together with undisputed works of Duns, leaves no reasonable doubt of this. The conjecture that it was written by Albert of Saxony is utterly untenable. It would seem to have been written in 1299 or 1300. Though it clearly sets forth some Scotistic opinions, its greatest merit is the idea of the sciences embodied in the title.

†*Proceedings of the American Academy of Arts and Sciences*, May 14, 1867, vol. VII, p. 295.

‡The Seven Liberal Arts of the Roman Schools of the fourth and fifth centuries (see Davidson's *Aristotle and Ancient Educational Ideals*, App.)[9] were Grammar, Logic, Rhetoric, making up the "*Trivium*," Geometry, Arithmetic, Astronomy, Music, making up the "*Quadrivium*." *Quadrivium* means cross-roads, *trivium* a fork in a road, hence, a public place. The fanciful application to the arts was in familiar use. The word *trivial*, in its Latin form, was used meaning commonplace long before the application to arts was heard of; but in modern languages the adjective does not occur until after the rage against scholasticism must have influenced the associations of the word.

mind something like a "composite photograph" of all the persons that I have known and read of that have had that character;[10] and at the instant I make the discovery concerning that person, who is distinguished from others for me by certain indications, upon that index, at that moment, down goes the stamp of RASCAL, to remain indefinitely.

A proposition *asserts* something. That assertion is performed by the symbol which stands for the act of consciousness. That which accounts for *assertion* seeming so different from other sorts of signification is its *volitional* character.

Every assertion is an assertion that two different signs have the same object. If we ask why it should have that *dual* character, the answer is that volition involves an action and reaction. The consequences of this duality are found not only in the analysis of propositions, but also in their classification.

It is impossible to find a proposition so simple as not to have reference to two signs. Take, for instance, "it rains." Here the icon is the mental composite photograph of all the rainy days the thinker has experienced. The index is all whereby he distinguishes *that day*, as it is placed in his experience. The symbol is the mental act whereby he stamps that day as rainy.

The traditional logic divides propositions into the *categorical*, or incomplex, and the *hypothetical*, or complex. Very many logics of this century, in place of the hypothetical in the sense of complex, put the *conditional* (now often called the *hypothetical*) and the *disjunctive*, throwing out other kinds of complex propositions for no good reason, probably because of a fancy for triads. The categorical proposition, according to the usual variety of the traditional doctrine, is made up of two names called its *terms*, namely its *subject* and *predicate*, as principal parts; in addition to which it has a *copula*, the verb *is*. The doctrine of subject, predicate, and copula is so far true that it may be retained, with corrections, and so far false that it is doubtful whether it is expedient to retain the phraseology. It cannot be disputed that a proposition *can* be so analyzed, and with certain modifications, it is the most convenient analysis for the purposes of logic. The categorical proposition of traditional logic follows the Aryan syntax and is like this: "man is mortal." The grammatical subject is the logical *subject*. The grammatical predicate is replaced by *is* followed by a name, which is the logical *predicate*. The subject contains the whole or a part of the *index*, which gives it its peculiar thing-like character as subject, while the predicate involves the *icon*, which gives it its peculiar ideal character as predicate. The *copula* is the *symbol*.

The traditional analysis answers its purpose well enough in the simplest kind of reasonings, which alone the traditional logic considers. But in order properly to exhibit the relation between premises and conclusion of mathematical reasonings, it is necessary to recognize that in most cases the *subject-index* is compound, and consists of a *set* of indices. Thus, in the proposition, "*A* sells *B* to *C* for the price *D*," *A*, *B*, *C*, *D* form a set of four indices. The symbol "___ sells ___ to ___ for the price ___" refers to a mental icon, or idea, of the act of sale, and declares that this image represents the *set A, B, C, D*, considered as attached to that icon, *A* as seller, *C* as buyer, *B* as object sold, and *D* as price. If we call *A, B, C, D* four *subjects* of the proposition and "___ sells ___ to ___ for the price ___" as *predicate*, we represent the logical relation well enough, but we abandon the Aryan syntax.

It may be asked, Why may not an assertion identify the objects of any two signs whatever, as two indices? Why should it be limited to declaring the object of an *index* to be represented by an *icon?* The answer is that an assertion *may* identify the objects of any two signs whatever; yet in every case this will amount to declaring that an *index*, or set of indices, is represented by an *icon*. For instance, let the proposition be, that that William *Lamare*, the author of the book *Correctorium fratris Thomae* is really the William *Ware* who was the teacher of Duns Scotus.[11] Here the objects of two indices are identified. But this is logically equivalent to the assertion that the icon of identity, that is, the mental composite image of two aspects of one and the same thing, represents the objects of the set of indices William *Mare* and William *Ware*.* We are not, indeed, absolutely forced to regard one of the signs as an *icon* in any case; but this is a very convenient way of taking account of certain properties of inferences. It happens, too, to have some secondary advantages, such as that of agreeing with our natural metaphysics, and with our feeling in regard to subject and predicate.

As the index may be complex, so also may the icon. For instance, taking the universal selective index, *everything*, we may have an icon which is composed alternatively of two, a sort of composite of two icons, in the same way that any image is a "composite photograph" of innumerable particulars. Even what is called an "instantaneous photograph," taken with a camera, is a composite of the effects of intervals of exposure more numerous by far than the sands of the sea. Take an absolute instant during the exposure and the composite represents *this* among other conditions. Now, the two alternative icons are combined like that. We have an icon of this alternation, a composite of all the alternative cases we have thought of. The symbol asserts that one or other of those icons represents the universally selected index. Let one of the alternative icons be the idea of what is not a man, the other the idea of what is mortal. Then, the proposition will be: Take anything you please, and it will either not be a man or will be mortal. Two signs so conjoined are said to be *aggregated*, or *disjunctively connected*, or *alternatively conjoined*. Take another example. Let the index be particularly selective. Let an icon be so compounded of two icons that in each variation of it both those icons are conjoined. For instance, let one be an *icon* of a Chinese, the other of a woman. Then, the combined *icon* will be an icon of a Chinese woman. Thus, the proposition will be, Something can be so selected as to be at once a Chinese and a woman. Two signs so conjoined are said to be *combined*, or *conjunctively*

*That *Marra* and *Warra* were really the same cannot be positively asserted; but the hypothesis suits the known facts remarkably well, except for two differences of names, which is perhaps not an insuperable obstacle.

connected, or *simultaneously conjoined.* The matter of compound icons will have to be more fully considered in another chapter.[12]

Article 12. It is now time to examine more carefully the nature of *inference,* or the conscious and controlled adoption of a belief as a consequence of other knowledge. The first step of inference usually consists in bringing together certain propositions which we believe to be true, but which, supposing the inference to be a new one, we have hitherto not considered together, or not as united in the same way. This step is called *colligation.* The compound assertion resulting from colligation is a *conjunctive proposition,* that is, it is a proposition with a composite icon, as well as usually with a composite index. Colligation is a very important part of reasoning, calling for genius perhaps more than any other part of the process. Many logicians refuse the name of reasoning to an inferential act of which colligation forms no part. Such an inferential act they call an *immediate inference.* This term may be accepted; but although colligation certainly gives a higher intellectuality to inference, yet its importance is exaggerated when it is represented to be of more account than the conscious control of the operation. The latter ought to determine the title of *reasoning.*

An inference, then, may have but a single premise, or several premises may be united by colligation. In the latter case, they form, when colligated, one conjunctive proposition. But even if there be but one premise, the icon of that proposition is always more or less complex. The next step of inference to be considered consists in the contemplation of that complex icon, the fixation of the attention upon a certain feature of it, and the obliteration of the rest of it, so as to produce a new icon.

If the question is asked in what the processes of contemplation and of fixation of the attention consist, this question being psychological, it is necessary, before answering it, to describe some phenomena of the mind. As psychological, not logical, facts, they can only be briefly stated here, without the evidence on which their truth rests. Suffice it to say, on that head, that they are not hastily adopted, but result from an exact discussion of special experiments. It must be premised that the word *feeling* is used throughout this book to denote that which is supposed to be immediately, and at one instant, present to consciousness. The words "supposed to be" are here inserted because we cannot directly observe what is instantaneously present to consciousness. To speak of no other hindrance, before we can get attention focused upon what is immediately present, instead of upon the practical or emotional aspects which had been interesting us, the idea has gone by, and the memory of it represents it transformed and worked up in the process of thought. We infer, however, from what we can observe, that feeling is subject to degrees. That is to say, besides the *objective intensity,* which distinguishes a loud sound from a faint one, there is a *subjective intensity,* which distinguishes a lively consciousness of the sound from a dull consciousness of it. Though the two intensities are apt to go together, yet it may happen that a person recalls the tick of a watch most intensely, at the same time that he hardly can recall the sound of an explosion, which, so far as he does remember it, he remembers as very loud. For example, suppose a person lying awake in bed in perfect darkness is endeavoring to recall an aunt of his early childhood, and is trying to remember, what he scarce *can* remember, how an explosion he heard really sounded. Suppose that, while he is so occupied, he suddenly hears a watch ticking, although, so far as he knows, there is no watch in the room. He pricks up his ears; he tries again to make out the ticking. He hears it no more; but he remembers it most vividly. One cause of this intensity is the recency of the ticking; another is the interest he has in it. The intensity itself belongs to the feeling, and does not consist in the strength of the association. In thinking of the long past explosion, an *allowance* is made in the estimation of its loudness for the remoteness of the sensation. But that allowance is not a merely intellectual one; it affects the feeling. Dim as the feeling is, it is the feeling of a very loud sound. Lively as the other feeling is, it is the feeling of a very faint sound.

Feelings of such low subjective intensity as usually to pass unnoticed act upon one another, undergo transformations in a thinking process, and excite emotions and voluntary actions, just as lively feelings do. But they do those things more slowly, as a rule, and less decidedly than they would do if they were livelier. Moreover, other things being equal, the ideas of which we are little conscious are little under direct control. This, however, needs qualification. A feeling forced upon the mind through the senses, so as to bear down the power of the will, is almost always of a high grade of subjective intensity. We shall soon see why it should be so. But when a feeling is *not* thus forced upon us, it is the more manageable the livelier it is. Everybody knows that it is much easier to trace out suppositions about things interesting than about things uninteresting, when, at least, the interest is not so immediate as to force us to leave off scheming and commence acting.

There are certain combinations of feelings which are specially *interesting*,—that is, they are strongly suggestive of thought. *What* combinations are interesting? Answer: those which are very near a reaction between mind and body, whether in sense, in the action of the glands, in contractions of involuntary muscles, in voluntary outward acts, or in inward acts by which one part of the nerves discharge in an extraordinary manner upon another. The interesting combination of ideas, when formed, increases rapidly in subjective intensity for a short time; although later, after habits are formed, it is less intense for being interesting.

The action of thought is all the time going on, not merely in that part of consciousness which thrusts itself upon attention, but also in those parts that are deeply shaded and of which we are too little conscious to be much affected by what takes place there. But when, in the uncontrolled play of that part of thought, an interesting combination occurs, its subjective intensity increases for a short time with great rapidity. This is the phenomenon which constitutes the fixation of the attention. As for contemplation, that consists in using our self-control to seclude us from the forcible intrusion of other thoughts and in dwelling upon the interesting bearings of what may lie hidden in the icon, with a view of causing its subjective intensity to increase.

Thus, then, it is that the complex icon suggests another that is a feature of it. Whenever one thing suggests another, both are together in the mind for an instant. In the present case, this conjunction is specially interesting, and in its turn suggests that the one necessarily involves the other. A few mental experiments,—or even a single one, so expert do we become at this kind of experimental inquiry,—satisfies the mind that the one icon would at all times involve the other, that is, suggest it in a special way, into which we shall soon inquire. Hence, the mind is not only led from believing the premises to judge the conclusion true, but it further attaches to this judgment another that *every* proposition *like* the premise, that is having an icon like it, *would* involve, and compel acceptance, of a proposition related to it as the conclusion then drawn is related to that premise. Thus we see, what is most important, that every inference is thought /of/, at the time of drawing it, as one of a possible class of inferences. In the case of a rational inference, we *see*, in an icon which represents the dependence of the icon of the conclusion upon the icon of the premise, about what that class of inferences is, although as the outlines of icons are always more or less vague, there is always more or less of vagueness in our conception of that class of inferences.

There is no other element of inference essentially different from those which have been mentioned. It is true that changes generally take place in the indices as well as in the icon of the premise. Some indices may be dropped out. Some may be identified. The order of selections may sometimes be changed. But these all take place substantially in the same manner in which a feature of the icon attracts attention and must be justified in the inference by experiments upon icons.

It thus appears that all knowledge comes to us by observation. A part is forced upon us from without and seems to result from Nature's mind; a part comes from the depths of the mind as seen from within, which by an egotistical anacoluthon we call *our* mind.

The three essential elements of inference are, then, colligation, observation, and the judgment that /what/ we observe in the colligated data follows a rule.

Article 13. There is a great distinction between reasoning which depends upon the laws of the inner world and reasoning which depends upon the laws of the outer world.

We observe the outer world and seem to catch the idea of a given line of phenomena. In this way, we have so well detected the nature of the regularity in the motions of the stars that we can make very accurate predictions about them. This we certainly never could do even approximately if there were not an affinity between our mind and Nature's. But even granting that affinity, since it is only here and there that we catch an idea, and that, doubtless, only imperfectly, we never can be *sure* that our predictions will be verified. In fact, we are so very far from sure, that the imperfection of our knowledge attracts our attention markedly.

Unscientific people have a very imperfect sense of the grades of assurance that attach to scientific propositions. The first inferences a scientific man makes are very uncertain. Not infrequently, if their value were to be rated simply on the basis of the chances in favor of their being strictly true, they would be worth much less than nothing; for they are much more likely to prove false than true. But knowledge must begin somewhere as well as it can. Those inferences are not valueless, because scientific inquiry does not rest upon them, but goes forward until it refutes them; and in refuting them gains indications of what theory it is that ought to be tried next. Thus, suppose a quantity of inscriptions to be found in a wholly unknown mode of writing and in an unknown tongue. To find out what that writing means, we have to begin with some guess. We should naturally make the most likely guess we possibly could; and that is an inference. Yet it is considerably more likely to be wrong than right. Still, it has to be *tried*. By the time it is satisfactorily refuted, we shall be perhaps in condition to make another guess. But no matter how far science goes, those inferences which are uppermost in the mind of the investigator are very uncertain. They are on probation. They must have a fair trial and not be condemned till proved false beyond all reasonable doubt; and the moment that proof is reached, the investigator must be ready to abandon them without the slightest tenderness toward them. Thus, the scientific inquirer has to be always ready at a moment to abandon summarily all the theories to the study of which he has been devoting perhaps many years. Take, for example, the case of those who have made the study of telepathy the business of their lives. Notwithstanding all that was to be said in favor of the theory, those men must, if they were coldly logical, have foreseen when they staked their fortunes upon that hypothesis, that the chances were that it would prove to be unfounded. Nevertheless, on they marched, a forlorn hope attacking a terrible problem; and if they are good scientific men, they must be ready any day to come forward and declare that the evidence now is, the whole thing is a delusion. A degree of heroism is required to maintain that attitude, which is all the more sublime that the mass of mankind, instead of praising such recantation, will look upon it as utterly contemptible.

But reasoning based upon the laws of the inner world is not thus uncertain. It is called *demonstrative reasoning*, or *demonstration*. For instance, if you add up a column of five hundred figures, you get the sum total by mathematical reasoning. It is said to be absolutely certain that your result will be correct. This is an exaggeration. We have seen that it depends upon observation; and observation is always subject to error. But experimentation is so handy upon creations of our own imagination. The trials can so quickly and at so little cost be repeated; and doing it very frequently we get to be so extremely expert at it, that the probability of error is reduced to a point at which those people who only make dual distinctions, and who class questions into those of which we *positively know* the answers and those of which we *guess* the answers, prefer to class our knowledge of such inferences as positive certainty. In truth, positive certainty is unattainable by man. Are you *sure* twice two are four? Not at all. A certain *percentage* of the human race are insane and subject to illusions. It may be you are one of them, and that your idea that twice two is four is a lunatic notion, and your seeming recollection that other people think so, the baseless fabric of a vision.[13] Or twice two may ordinarily be *five*, but when anybody counts it up, that may have the effect of temporarily reducing it to *four.*

Nevertheless, there is undoubtedly a great distinction between inferences resting on merely inward observation, which a moderate amount of attention can put beyond all reasonable doubt, and inferences based upon our attempts to catch the regularities of Nature, essays in which we can never hope to attain more than a somewhat close approach to the truth, and whose surmised regularities we can hardly be much surprised to find are only quite exceptionally even at all near the veritable law. This is the great distinction of *demonstrative* and *experiential* reasoning. Of these two kinds of reasoning the demonstrative, depending upon inward observation and inward regularities, has to be studied first.

The remark that reasoning consists in the observation of an icon will be found equally important in the theory and the practice of reasoning.

4

Philosophy and the Conduct of Life

MS 437. [Published in CP 1.616–48, in part, and in RLT 105–22. Delivered on 10 February, this was the first of eight Cambridge Conferences Lectures Peirce gave in February and March 1898.] Peirce objects here to "the Hellenic tendency to mingle philosophy with practice" and argues that true scientific investigation must not be conducted with the question of utility in mind. The purpose of philosophy is not to win adherents and to improve their lives. Peirce makes a telling distinction between matters of vital importance and the selfless advancement of knowledge, and argues that, for the former, reason is a poor substitute for sentiment and instinct while, for the latter, reason is key. The upshot is that belief has no place in science but is what must guide action in practical affairs.

The early Greek philosopher, such as we read about in Diogenes Laertius, is certainly one of the most amusing curiosities of the whole human menagerie. It seems to have been demanded of him that his conduct should be in marked contrast with the dictates of ordinary common sense. Had he behaved as other men are supposed to do, his fellow-citizens would have thought his philosophy had not taught him much. I know that historians possessed of "higher criticism" deny all the ridiculous anecdotes about the Hellenic sages.[1] These scholars seem to think that logic is a question of literary taste, and their refined perceptions refuse to accept those narratives. But in truth even were taste carried to a point of delicacy exceeding that of the German professor,—which he would think was pushing it quite into that realm of imaginary quantities which lies on the other side of infinity,—it still would not weigh as logic, which is a matter of strict mathematical demonstration wherein opinion is of no weight at all. Now scientific logic cannot approve that historical method which leads to the absolute and confident denial of all the positive testimony that is extant, the moment that testimony deviates from the preconceived ideas of the historian.[2] The story about Thales falling into the ditch while pointing out the different stars to the old woman is told by Plato about two centuries later.[3] But Dr. Edouard Zeller says he knows better, and pronounces the occurrence quite impossible.[4] Were you to point out that the anecdote only attributes to Thales a character common to almost all mathematicians, this would afford him a new opportunity of applying his favorite argument of objection, that the story is "too probable." So the assertion of half a dozen classical writers that Democritus was always laughing and Heraclitus always weeping "proclaims itself," says Zeller, "an idle fabrication,"[5] notwithstanding the support it receives from the fragments. Even Zeller admits that Diogenes of Sinope was a trifle eccentric.[6] Being a contemporary of Aristotle and one of the best known men of Greece, his history cannot well be denied even by Zeller, who has to content himself with averring that the stories are "grossly exaggerated."[7] There was no other philosopher whose conduct according to all testimony was quite so extravagant as that of Pyrrho.[8] The accounts of him seem to come direct from a writing of his devoted pupil, Timon of Phlius,[9] and some of our authorities, of whom there are a dozen, profess to use this book. Yet Zeller and the critics do not believe them; and Brandis[10] objects that the citizens of Elis would not have chosen a half insane man high priest,—as if symptoms of that kind would not have particularly recommended him for a divine office. That fashion of writing history is I hope now at last passing away. However, disbelieve the stories if you will; you cannot refuse to admit that they show what kind of a man the narrators expected a philosopher to be,—if they were imaginary legends, all the more so. Now those narrators are a cloud of the sanest and soberest minds of Antiquity,— Plato, Aristotle, Cicero, Seneca, Pliny, Plutarch, Lucian, Elian, and so forth. The Greeks expected philosophy to affect life,—not by any slow process of percolation of forms, as *we* may expect that researches into differential equations, stellar photometry, the taxonomy of echinoderms, and the like, will ultimately affect the conduct of life,—but forthwith in the person and soul of the philosopher himself rendering him different from ordinary men in his views of right conduct. So little did they separate philosophy from esthetic and moral culture that the *docti furor arduus Lucreti*[11] could clothe an elaborate *cosmogony* in noble verse, for the express purpose of influencing men's lives; and Plato tells us in many places how inextricably he considers the study of Dialectic to be bound up with virtuous living.[12] Aristotle, on the other hand, set this matter right. Aristotle was not much of a Greek. That he was of full Greek blood is not likely. That he was not altogether a Greek-minded man is manifest. Though he belonged to the school of Plato, yet when he went there he was already a student, perhaps a personal pupil, of Democritus, himself another Thracian; and during his first years in Athens he cannot have had much intercourse with Plato, who was away at Syracuse a large part of the time. Above all, Aristotle was an Asclepiades,[13] that is to say, he belonged to a line every man of whom since the heroic age had, as a child, received a finished training in the dissecting-room. Aristotle was a thorough-paced scientific man such as we see nowadays, except for this, that he ranged over all knowledge. As a man of scientific instinct, he classed metaphysics, in which I doubt not he included logic, as a matter of course, among the sciences,—sciences in *our* sense, I mean, what *he* called theoretical sciences,—along with mathematics and natural science,—natural science embracing what we call the physical sciences and the psychical sciences, generally. This theoretical science was for him one thing, animated by one spirit and having knowledge of theory as its ultimate end and aim. Aesthetic studies were of a radically different kind; while morals, and all that relates to the conduct of life, formed a *third* department of intellectual activity, radically foreign in its nature and idea from both the other two. Now, Gentlemen, it behooves me, at the outset of this course, to confess to you that in this respect I stand before you an Aristotelian and a scientific man, condemning with the whole strength of conviction the Hellenic tendency to mingle Philosophy and Practice.

There are sciences, of course, many of whose results are almost immediately applicable to human life, such as physiology and chemistry. But the true scientific investigator completely loses sight of the utility of what he is about. It never enters his mind. Do you think that the physiologist who cuts up a dog reflects, while doing so, that he may be saving a human life? Nonsense. If he did, it would spoil him for a scientific man; and *then* the vivisection would become a crime. However, in physiology and in chemistry, the man whose brain is occupied with utilities, though he will not do much for science, may do a great deal for human life. But in philosophy, touching as it does upon matters which are, and ought to be, sacred to us, the investigator who does not stand aloof from all intent to make practical applications, will not only obstruct the advance of the pure science, but what is infinitely worse, he will endanger his own moral integrity and that of his readers.

In my opinion, the present infantile condition of philosophy,—for as long as earnest and industrious students of it are able to come to agreement upon scarce a single principle, I do not see how it can be considered as otherwise than in its infancy,—is due to the fact that during this century it has chiefly been pursued by men who have not been nurtured in dissecting-rooms and other laboratories, and who consequently have not been animated by the true scientific Eros, but who have on the contrary come from theological seminaries, and have consequently been inflamed with a desire to amend the lives of themselves and others, a spirit no doubt more important than the love of science, for men in average situations, but radically unfitting them for the task of scientific investigation. And it is precisely because of this utterly unsettled and uncertain condition of philosophy at present, that I regard any practical applications of it to Religion and Conduct as exceedingly dangerous. I have not one word to say against the Philosophy of Religion or of Ethics in general or in particular. I only say that for the present it is all far too dubious to warrant risking any human life upon it. I do not say that Philosophical Science should not ultimately influence Religion and Morality; I only say that it should be allowed to do so only with secular slowness and the most conservative caution.

Now I may be utterly wrong in all this, and I do not propose to argue the question. I do not ask you to go with me. But to avoid any possible misapprehension, I am bound honestly to declare that I do not hold forth the slightest promise that I have any philosophical wares to offer you which will make you either better men or more successful men.

It is particularly needful that I should say this owing to a singular hybrid character which you will detect in these lectures. I was asked in December to prepare a course of lectures upon my views of philosophy. I accordingly set to work to draw up in eight lectures an outline of one branch of philosophy, namely, Objective Logic.[14] But just as I was finishing one lecture, word came that you would expect to be addressed on Topics of Vital Importance, and that it would be as well to make the lectures detached.[15] I thereupon threw aside what I had written[16] and began again to prepare the same number of homilies on intellectual ethics and economics. They were wretched things; and I was glad enough to learn, when three-quarters of my task was done, that it would be desirable that as much as possible should be said of certain philosophical questions, other subjects being put in the background.[17] At that time, however, it was too late to write a course which should set before you what I should have greatly desired to submit to your judgment. I could only patch up some fragments partly philosophical and partly practical. Thus, you will find me part of the time offering you Detached Ideas upon Topics of Vital Importance, while part of the time I shall be presenting philosophical considerations, in which you will be able to feel an undercurrent toward that Logic of Things concerning which I shall have an opportunity to interject scarce one overt word.

I shall have a good deal to say about right reasoning; and in default of better, I had reckoned *that* as a Topic of Vital Importance. But I do not know that the theory of reasoning is quite vitally important. That it is absolutely essential in metaphysics, I am as sure as I am of any truth of philosophy. But in the conduct of life, we have to distinguish everyday affairs and great crises. In the great decisions, I do not believe it is safe to trust to individual reason. In everyday business, reasoning is tolerably successful; but I am inclined to think that it is done as well without the aid of theory as with it. A *logica utens*, like the analytical mechanics resident in the billiard player's nerves, best fulfills familiar uses.

In metaphysics, however, it is not so, at all; and the reason is obvious. The truths that the metaphysician infers can be brought to the test of experience, if at all, only in a department of experience quite foreign from that which furnishes his premises. Thus a metaphysician who infers anything about a life beyond the grave can never find out for certain that his inference is false until he has gone out of the metaphysical business, at his present stand, at least. The consequence is that unless the metaphysician is a most thorough master of formal logic,—and especially of the inductive side of the logic of relatives, immeasurably more important and difficult than all the rest of formal logic put together,—he will inevitably fall into the practice of deciding upon the validity of reasonings in the same manner in which, for example, the practical politician decides as to the weight that ought to be allowed to different considerations, that is to say, by the impressions those reasonings make upon his mind, only with this stupendous difference, that the one man's impressions are the resultant of long experiential training, while with such training the other man is altogether unacquainted. The metaphysician who adopts a metaphysical reasoning because he is impressed that it is sound, might just as well, or better, adopt his conclusions directly because he is impressed that they are true, in the good old style of Descartes and of Plato. To convince yourself of the extent to which this way of working actually vitiates philosophy, just look at the dealings of the metaphysicians with Zeno's objections to motion. They are simply at the mercy of the adroit Italian. For this reason, then, if for no other, the metaphysician who is not prepared to grapple with all the difficulties of modern exact logic had better put up his shutters and go out of the trade. Unless he will do one or the other, I tell him to his conscience that he is not the genuine, honest, earnest, resolute, energetic, industrious, and accomplished doubter that it is his duty to be.

But this is not all, nor half. For after all, metaphysical reasonings, such as they have hitherto been, have been simple enough for the most part. It is the metaphysical concepts which it is difficult to apprehend. Now the metaphysical conceptions, as I need not waste words to show, are merely adapted from those of formal logic, and therefore can only be apprehended in the light of a minutely accurate and thoroughgoing system of formal logic.

But in practical affairs, in matters of vital importance, it is very easy to exaggerate the importance of ratiocination. Man is so vain of his power of reason! It seems impossible for him to see himself in this respect, as he himself would see himself if he could duplicate himself and observe himself with a critical eye. Those whom we are so fond of referring to as the "lower animals" reason very little. Now I beg you to observe that those beings very rarely commit a *mistake*, while we _____! We employ twelve good men and true to decide a question, we lay the facts before them with the greatest care, the "perfection of human reason" presides over the presentment, they hear, they go out and deliberate, they come to a unanimous opinion, and it is generally admitted that the parties to the suit might almost as well have tossed up a penny to decide! Such is man's glory!

The mental qualities we most admire in all human beings except our several selves are the maiden's delicacy, the mother's devotion, manly courage, and other inheritances that have come to us from the biped who did not yet speak; while the characters that are most contemptible take their origin in reasoning. The very fact that everybody so ridiculously overrates his own reasoning is sufficient to show how superficial the faculty is. For you do not hear the courageous man vaunt his own courage, or the modest woman boast of her modesty, or the really loyal plume themselves on their honesty. What they *are* vain about is always some *insignificant* gift of beauty or of skill.

It is the instincts, the sentiments, that make the substance of the soul. Cognition is only its surface, its locus of contact with what is external to it.

Do you ask me to prove this? If so, you must be a rationalist, indeed. I can prove it,—but only by assuming a logical principle of the demonstration of which I shall give a hint in the next lecture.[18] When people ask me to prove a proposition in philosophy I am often obliged to reply that it is a corollary from the logic of relatives. Then certain men say, I should like exceedingly to look into this logic of relatives; you must write out an exposition of it. The next day I bring them a manuscript. But when they see that it is full of *A*, *B*, and *C*, they never look at it again. Such men,—oh, well.[19] Reasoning is of three kinds. The first is necessary, but it only professes to give us information concerning the matter of our own hypotheses, and distinctly declares that if we want to know anything else, we must go elsewhere. The second depends upon probabilities. The only cases in which it pretends to be of value is where we have, like an insurance company, an endless multitude of insignificant risks. Wherever a vital interest is at stake, it clearly says, "Don't ask me." The third kind of reasoning tries what *il lume naturale*, which lit the footsteps of Galileo, can do. It is really an appeal to instinct. Thus reason, for all the frills it customarily wears, in vital crises, comes down upon its marrow-bones to beg the succor of instinct.

Reason is of its very essence egotistical. In many matters it acts the fly on the wheel.[20] Do not doubt that the bee thinks it has a good reason for making the end of its cell as it does. But I should be very much surprised to learn that its reason had solved that problem of isoperimetry that its instinct has solved. Men many times fancy that they act from reason when, in point of fact, the reasons they attribute to themselves are nothing but excuses which unconscious instinct invents to satisfy the teasing "why's" of the *ego*. The extent of this self-delusion is such as to render philosophical rationalism a farce.

Reason, then, appeals to sentiment in the last resort. Sentiment, on its side, feels itself to be the man. That is my simple apology for philosophical sentimentalism.

Sentimentalism implies conservatism; and it is of the essence of conservatism to refuse to push any practical principle to its extreme limits,—including the principle of conservatism itself. We do not say that sentiment is *never* to be influenced by reason, nor that under no circumstances would we advocate radical reforms. We only say that the man who would allow his religious life to be wounded by any sudden acceptance of a philosophy of religion or who would precipitately change his code of morals, at the dictate of a philosophy of ethics,—who would, let us say, hastily practice incest,—is a man whom we should consider *unwise*. The regnant system of sexual rules is an instinctive or sentimental induction summarizing the experience of all our race. That it is abstractly and absolutely infallible we do not pretend; but that it is practically infallible for the individual,—which is the only clear sense the word "infallibility" will bear,—in that he ought to obey it and not his individual reason, *that* we do maintain.

I would not allow to sentiment or instinct any weight whatsoever in theoretical matters, not the slightest. Right sentiment does not demand any such weight; and right reason would emphatically repudiate the claim, if it were made. True, we are driven oftentimes in science to try the suggestions of instinct; but we only *try* them, we compare them with experience, we hold ourselves ready to throw them overboard at a moment's notice from experience. If I allow the supremacy of sentiment in human affairs, I do so at the dictation of reason itself; and equally at the dictation of sentiment, in theoretical matters I refuse to allow sentiment any weight whatever. Hence, I hold that what is properly and usually called *belief,* that is, the adoption of a proposition as a κτῆμα εἰς ἀεί, to use the energetic phrase of Dr. Carus,[21] has no place in science at all. We *believe* the proposition we are ready to act upon. *Full belief* is willingness to act upon the proposition in vital crises, *opinion* is willingness to act upon it in relatively insignificant affairs. But pure science has nothing at all to do with *action.* The propositions it accepts, it merely writes in the list of premises it proposes to use. Nothing is *vital* for science; nothing can be. Its accepted propositions, therefore, are but opinions at most; and the whole list is provisional. The scientific man is not in the least wedded to his conclusions. He risks nothing upon them. He stands ready to abandon one or all as soon as experience opposes them. Some of them, I grant, he is in the habit of calling *established truths;* but that merely means propositions to which no competent man today demurs. It seems probable that any given proposition of that sort will remain for a long time upon the list of propositions to be admitted. Still, it may be refuted tomorrow; and if so, the scientific man will be glad to have got rid of an error. There is thus no proposition at all in science which answers to the conception of belief.

But in vital matters, it is quite otherwise. We must act in such matters; and the principle upon which we are willing to act is a *belief.*

Thus, pure theoretical knowledge, or science, has nothing directly to say concerning practical matters, and nothing even applicable at all to vital crises. Theory is applicable to minor practical affairs; but matters of vital importance must be left to sentiment, that is, to instinct.

Now there are two conceivable ways in which right sentiment might treat such terrible crises; on the one hand, it might be that while human instincts are not so detailed and featured as those of the dumb animals yet they might be sufficient to guide us in the *greatest* concerns without any aid from reason, while on the other hand, sentiment might act to bring the vital crises under the domain of reason by rising under such circumstances to such a height of self-abnegation as to render the situation insignificant. In point of fact, we observe that a healthy natural human nature does act in both these ways.

The instincts of those animals whose instincts are remarkable present the character of being chiefly, if not altogether, directed to the preservation of the stock and of benefitting the individual very little, if at all, except so far as he may happen as a possible procreator to be a potential public functionary. Such, therefore, is the description of instinct that we ought to expect to find in man, in regard to vital matters; and so we do. It is not necessary to enumerate the facts of human life which show this, because it is too plain. It is to be remarked, however, that individuals who have passed the reproductive period, are more useful to the propagation of the human race than to any other. For they amass wealth, and teach prudence, they keep the peace, they are friends of the little ones, and they inculcate all the sexual duties and virtues. Such instinct does, as a matter of course, prompt us, in all vital crises, to look upon our individual lives as small matters. It is no extraordinary pitch of virtue to do so; it is the character of every man or woman who is not despicable. Somebody during the Reign of Terror said: "Tout le monde croit qu'il est difficile de mourir. Je le crois comme les autres. Cependant je vois que quand on est là chacun s'en tire."[22] It is less characteristic of the woman because her life is more important to the stock, and her immolation less useful.

Having thus shown how much less vitally important reason is than instinct, I next desire to point out how exceedingly desirable, not to say indispensable, it is, for the successful march of discovery in philosophy and in science generally, that practical utilities, whether low or high, should be PUT OUT OF SIGHT by the investigator.

The point of view of utility is always a narrow point of view. How much more we should know of chemistry today if the most practically important bodies had not received excessive attention; and how much *less* we should know, if the rare elements and the compounds which only exist at low temperatures had received only the *share* of attention to which their *utility* entitled them.

It is notoriously true that into whatever you do not put your whole heart and soul, in that you will not have much success. Now, the two masters, *theory* and *practice*, you cannot serve. That perfect balance of attention which is requisite for observing the system of things is utterly lost if human desires intervene, and all the more so the higher and holier those desires may be.

In addition to that, in philosophy we have prejudices so potent that it is impossible to keep one's *sang-froid* if we allow ourselves to dwell upon them at all.

It is far better to let philosophy follow perfectly untrammeled a scientific method, *predetermined* in advance of knowing to what it will lead. If that course be honestly and scrupulously carried out, the results reached, even if they be not altogether true, even if they be grossly mistaken, cannot but be highly serviceable for the ultimate discovery of truth. Meantime, sentiment can say "Oh well, philosophical science has not by any means said its last word yet; and meantime I will continue to believe *so and so.*"

No doubt a large proportion of those who now busy themselves with philosophy will lose all interest in it as soon as it is forbidden to look upon it as susceptible of practical applications. We who continue to pursue the theory must bid adieu to them. But so we must in any department of pure science. And though we regret to lose their company, it is infinitely better that men devoid of genuine scientific curiosity should not barricade the road of science with empty books and embarrassing assumptions.

I *repeat* that a great many people think they shape their lives according to reason, when it is really just the other way. But as for the man who should in truth allow his moral conduct to be vitally changed by an ethical theory, or his religious life by a philosophy of religion, I should need a strong word to express my view of his unwisdom.

I would classify the sciences upon the general principle set forth by Auguste Comte, that is, in the order of abstractness of their objects, so that each science may largely rest for its principles upon those above it in the scale while drawing its data in part from those below it.[23] At their head I would place Mathematics, for this irrefutable reason, that it is the only one of the sciences which does not concern itself to inquire what the actual facts are, but studies hypotheses exclusively. It is merely because it did not become clear to mathematicians themselves before modern times that they do study nothing but hypotheses without as pure mathematicians caring at all how the actual facts may be,—a principle perfectly established today,—that Plato and Aristotle and the whole host of philosophers made Philosophy more abstract than Mathematics. But there is this criticism to be made upon almost all philosophic systems beginning with Plato's Doctrine of Ideas. Plato before he went to Socrates had been a student of the Heraclitean Cratylus. And the consequence of that accidental circumstance is that almost every philosopher from that day to this has been infected with one of the two great errors of Heraclitus, namely with the notion that Continuity implies Transitoriness.[24] The things of this world, that seem so transitory to philosophers, are *not* continuous. They are composed of discrete atoms, no doubt Boscovichian points.[25] The really continuous things, Space, and Time, and Law, are eternal. The dialogue of the *Sophistes*, lately shown to belong to Plato's last period,[26]— when he had, as Aristotle tells us,[27] abandoned Ideas and put Numbers in place of them,—this dialogue, I say, gives reasons for abandoning the Theory of Ideas which imply that Plato himself had come to see, if not that the Eternal Essences are continuous, at least, that there is an order of affinity among them, such as there is among Numbers. Thus, at last, the Platonic Ideas became Mathematical Essences, not possessed of Actual Existence but only of a Potential Being quite as *Real*, and his maturest philosophy became welded into mathematics.

Next under Mathematics I would place Philosophy, which has the following characteristics: *first*, it differs from mathematics in being a search for real truth; *second*, it consequently draws upon experience for premises and not merely, like mathematics,—for suggestions; *third*, it differs from the special sciences in not confining itself to the reality of existence, but also to the reality of potential being; *fourth*, the phenomena which it uses as premises, are not special facts, observable with a microscope or telescope, or which require trained faculties of observation to detect, but they are those universal phenomena which saturate all experience through and through so that they cannot escape us; *fifth*, in consequence at once of the universality of the phenomena upon which philosophy draws for premises, and also of its extending its theories to potential being, the conclusions of metaphysics have a certain necessity,—by which I do not mean that we cannot help accepting them, or a necessity of form,—I mean a necessity of matter, in that they inform us not merely how the things are but how from the very nature of being they *must* be.

Philosophy seems to consist of two parts, Logic and Metaphysics. I exclude Ethics, for two reasons.[28] In the first place, as the science of the end and aim of life, [ethics] seems to be exclusively psychical, and therefore to be confined to a special department of experience, while philosophy studies experience in its universal characteristics. In the second place, in seeking to define the proper aim of life, ethics seems to me to rank with the arts, or rather with the theories of the arts, which of all theoretical sciences I regard as the most concrete, while what I mean by philosophy is the most abstract of all the real sciences.

Logic is the science of thought, not merely of thought as a psychical phenomenon but of thought in general, its general laws and kinds. Metaphysics is the science of being, not merely as given in physical experience, but of being in general, its laws and types. Of the two branches of philosophy, logic is somewhat more affiliated to psychics, metaphysics to physics.

As I have already said, it seems to me one of the least doubtful of propositions that metaphysics must take as the guide of its every step the theory of logic.

On the other hand, I hold that logic is guided by mathematics, in a sense which is not true of any other science. Every science has its mathematical part, in which certain results of the special science are assumed as mathematical hypotheses. But it is not merely in this way that logic is mathematical. It *is* mathematical in that way, and to a far greater extent than any other science; but besides that it takes the proceedings of mathematics in all their generality and founds upon them logical principles.

All necessary reasoning is strictly speaking mathematical reasoning, that is to say, it is performed by *observing* something equivalent to a mathematical diagram; but mathematical reasoning *par excellence* consists in those peculiarly intricate kinds of reasoning which belong to the logic of relatives. The most peculiarly mathematical of these are reasonings about continuity of which geometrical topics, or topology, and the theory of functions offer examples. In my eighth lecture I shall hope to make clear my reasons for thinking that metaphysics will never make any real advance until it avails itself of mathematics of this kind.[29]

Metaphysics recognizes an inner and an outer world, a world of time and a world of space. The special sciences, all that follow after Metaphysics divide themselves into Psychics and Physics. In each of these branches of inquiry, there are first, Nomological Sciences which formulate the laws of psychology on the one hand, of dynamics on the other. Next there are Classificatory Sciences, such as linguistics and anthropology on the psychical side, chemistry on the physical side. The aim of these sciences is from the known laws made out by the nomological investigations, and the fundamental differences which are mathematically possible, to deduce all the properties of the different classes of mental products on the one hand, of kinds of matter on the other hand. Finally there are the Descriptive Sciences in Psychics and Physics. History generally speaking on the psychical side, geology, astronomy, geography, hydrology, meterology, etc. on the physical side. The aim of these sciences is to explain special phenomena by showing that they are the results of the general laws ascertained by the Nomological Sciences applied to the special kinds discovered by the Classificatory Sciences together with certain accidental arrangements. Last of all Psychics and Physics reunite in the Applied Sciences or Arts. Of these I have made a list not at all intended to be exhaustive but only to serve as examples from which to get some idea of the relations of these sorts of science. This list contains upwards of three hundred different sciences ranging from such general psychical sciences as ethics, religion, law, to gold beating, cooking, charcoal burning, and so forth.

It has been an unfortunate accident of our century that philosophy has come to be set off from the other sciences as if it were foreign and almost hostile to them. In the early years of the century, men like Hegel fancied that their philosophical methods were so strong that they could afford to rather emphasize the contrast. They fancied they were able to run the inductive sciences down, to outstrip them altogether. They had been educated in theological seminaries and they only knew natural science in a popular way from the outside. Pride must have a fall, generally involving more or less injustice; and the natural result of this Hegelian arrogance has been a mistaken notion that metaphysics, in general, not this or that system of it, but all metaphysics, is necessarily idle, subjective, and illogical stuff. This is a very serious accusation. It is not to be treated lightly on the one side or the other. The question is, can we find anything in metaphysics, not which shall contrast with other science now put beyond all peradventure, but falling in with it as in inward harmony with it, obeying its logic, and serving its turn?

Having thus presented to you a schedule of all the sciences, a very imperfect one, I dare say, but such a schedule as my acquaintance with the different branches of science enables me to draw up, we come to the question, what is the general upshot of all these sciences, what do they all come to? Now in minor particulars I am hostile to Plato. I think it most unfortunate that he should in his most brilliant works have eviscerated his Ideas of those two elements which especially render ideas valuable. But in regard to the general conception of what the ultimate purpose and importance of science consists in, no philosopher who ever lived, ever brought that out more clearly than this early scientific philosopher. Aristotle justly finds fault with Plato in many respects. But all his criticisms leave unscathed Plato's definitive philosophy, which results from the correction of that error of Heraclitus which consisted in holding the Continuous to be Transitory and also from making the Being of the Idea potential. Aristotle for example justly complains that of the four kinds of causes Plato only recognizes the two internal ones, Form and Matter, and loses sight of the two external ones, the Efficient Cause and the End.[30] Though in regard to final causes this is scarcely just, it is more than just, in another respect. For not only does Plato only recognize internal causes, but he does not even recognize Matter as anything positive. He makes it mere negation, mere non-Being, or Emptiness, forgetting or perhaps not knowing that that which produces positive effects must have a positive nature. Although Plato's whole philosophy is a philosophy of Thirdness,—that is to say, it is a philosophy which attributes everything to an action which rightly analyzed has Thirdness for its capital and chief constituent,—he himself only recognizes duality, and makes himself an apostle of Dichotomy,— which is a misunderstanding of himself. To overlook second causes is only a special case of the common fault of all metaphysicians that they overlook the Logic of Relatives. But when he neglects external causes, it is Secondness itself that he is overlooking. This self-misunderstanding, this failure to recognize his own conceptions, marks Plato throughout. It is a characteristic of the man that he sees much deeper into the nature of things than he does into the nature of his own philosophy, and it is a trait to which we cannot altogether refuse our esteem.

If you ask me why I drag in the name of Plato so often in this lecture on the relation of philosophy to the conduct of life, I reply that it is because Plato, who upon many subjects is at once more in the wrong and yet more in the right than other philosophers, upon this question outdoes himself in this double *rôle*. There is no philosopher of any age who mixes poetry with philosophy with such effrontery as Plato. Is Robert Browning within a mile of doing so? As for our philosophic poets, so called, Alexander Pope, Fulke Greville (Baron Brooke of Beauchamp Court), Sir John Davies,[31] I am sure nobody ought to complain that they mingle too much sentiment with their philosophy. They do not err more in regard to the practicality of philosophy than the majority of prose philosophers. Plato, on the other hand, is more extravagant than anybody else in this respect. Only having committed the error of making the value and motive to philosophy consist mainly in its moral influence, he surprises his reader by balancing this error by the opposite one of making the whole end and aim of human life to consist in making the acquaintance of pure ideas. In saying that one of these errors counterbalances the other, I do not mean that taken together they do justice at all to those who live simple lives without at all thinking of philosophy, or that they give any just view of right conduct even for the philosopher. For undoubtedly each person ought to select some definite duty that clearly lies before him and is well within his power as the special task of his life. But what I mean is that the two propositions taken together do express a correct view of the ultimate end of philosophy and of science in general.

As a general proposition, the history of science shows every science growing into a more abstract science, one higher in our scale.

The art of medicine grew from the Egyptian book of formulas into physiology.[32] The study of the steam engine gave birth to modern thermodynamics. Such is the historical fact. The steam engine made mechanical precision possible and needful. Mechanical precision rendered modern observational precision possible, and developed it. Now every scientific development is due to some new means of improved observation. So much for the tendency of the arts. Can any man with a soul deny that the development of pure science is the great end of the arts? Not indeed for the individual man. He uses them, just as /he/ uses the deer, which I yesterday saw out of my window; and just as in writing this lecture I am burning great logs in a fireplace. But we are barbarians to treat the deer and the forest trees in that fashion. They have ends of their own, not related to my individual stomach or skin. So, too, man looks upon the arts from his selfish point of view. But they, too, like the beasts and the trees, are living organisms, none the less so for being parasitic to man's mind; and their manifest internal destiny is to grow into pure sciences.

Next consider the descriptive sciences. The proverb that history is philosophy teaching by examples,[33] is another way of saying that the descriptive science of history tends to grow into a classificatory science of kinds of events of which the events of history are specimens. In like manner astronomy under the hands of Sir William Herschel rose from the *tiers état* of a descriptive science to the rank of a classificatory science.[34] Physical geography is more or less following the same course. So likewise is geology. Galton, de Candolle, and others have endeavored to elevate biography into a classificatory science.[35]

Next look at the classificatory sciences. Linguistics is becoming more and more nomological. Anthropology is tending that same way. On the physical side of the schedule, zoology and botany have made long strides toward nomology during the last half century. The wonderful law of Mendeléeff and the development of Williamson's ideas go toward accomplishing the same result for chemistry.[36] To become nomological is manifestly the destiny of such sciences.

Now let us proceed to the nomological sciences, general psychics, or psychology, on the one hand, general physics on the other. Both of these branches are surely developing into parts of metaphysics. That is their aim. We are far enough from that goal yet. Nevertheless, all the world plainly sees it before us in distance, "sparkling in the monstrous hill."[37]

Metaphysics in its turn is gradually and surely taking on the character of a logic. And finally logic seems destined to become more and more converted into mathematics.

Thus, all the sciences are slowly but surely converging to that center. There is a lesson there.[38]

And now whither is mathematics tending? Mathematics is based wholly upon hypotheses, which would seem to be entirely arbitrary. It is very rare, too, to find a mathematical investigator who covers the whole field. Cayley evidently made it a point to do so, as far as he could; and yet, for all that marvellous insight which produced his famous "Sixth Memoir on Quantics" with its theory of the Absolute and the doctrine that geometrical metrics was only a special case of geometrical optics, or optical geometry, which produced his

"Memoir on Matrices,"and his "Memoir on Abstract Geometry," he showed himself downright stupid about multiple algebra and about quaternions, and he did nothing important either in geometrical topics, or topical geometry, or in the theory of numbers proper.[39] Even he, therefore, was unable to embrace the whole of mathematics. Even Klein, whose studies have brought the most widely separated subjects into connection, has his limitations.[40] The host of men, who achieve the bulk of each year's new discoveries, are mostly confined to narrow ranges. For that reason you would expect the arbitrary hypotheses of the different mathematicians to shoot out in every direction into the boundless void of arbitrariness. But you do not find any such thing. On the contrary, what you find is that men working in fields as remote from one another as the African diamond fields are from the Klondike, reproduce the same forms of novel hypothesis. Riemann had apparently never heard of his contemporary Listing.[41] The latter was a naturalistic geometer, occupied with the shapes of leaves and birds' nests, while the former was working upon analytical functions. And yet that which seems the most arbitrary in the ideas created by the two men, is one and the same form. This phenomenon is not an isolated one; it characterizes the mathematics of our times, as is, indeed, well known. All this crowd of creators of forms for which the real world affords no parallel, each man arbitrarily following his own sweet will, are, as we now begin to discern, gradually uncovering one great cosmos of forms, a world of potential being. The pure mathematician himself feels that this is so. He is not indeed in the habit of publishing any of his sentiments nor even his generalizations. The fashion in mathematics is to print nothing but demonstrations, and the reader is left to divine the workings of the man's mind from the sequence of those demonstrations. But if you enjoy the good fortune of talking with a number of mathematicians of a high order, you will find that the typical Pure Mathematician is a sort of Platonist. Only, he is [a] Platonist who corrects the Heraclitean error that the Eternal is not Continuous. The Eternal is for him a world, a cosmos, in which the universe of actual existence is nothing but an arbitrary locus. The end that Pure Mathematics is pursuing is to discover that real potential world.

Once you become inflated with that idea, *vital importance* seems to be a very low kind of importance, indeed.

But such ideas are only suitable to regulate another life than this. Here we are in this workaday world, little creatures, mere cells in a social organism itself a poor and little thing enough, and we must look to see what little and definite task circumstances have set before our little strength to do. The performance of that task will require us to draw upon all our powers, reason included. And in the doing of it we should chiefly depend not upon that department of the soul which is most superficial and fallible,—I mean our reason,—but upon that department that is deep and sure,—which is instinct. Instinct is capable of development and growth,—though by a movement which is slow in the proportion in which it is vital; and this development takes place upon lines which are altogether parallel to those of reasoning. And just as reasoning springs from experience, so the development of sentiment arises from the soul's inward and outward experiences. Not only is it of the same nature as the development of cognition; but it chiefly takes place through the instrumentality of cognition. The soul's deeper parts can only be reached through its surface. In this way the eternal forms, that mathematics and philosophy and the other sciences make us acquainted with, will by slow percolation gradually reach the very core of one's being; and will come to influence our lives; and this they will do, not because they involve truths of merely vital importance, but because they are ideal and eternal verities.

5

The First Rule of Logic

MSS 442, 825. [Published in CP 5.574–89 and 7.135–40 (in part), and in RLT 165–80. Delivered on 21 February 1898, this is the fourth Cambridge Conferences Lecture. William James, who had read it a month earlier, told Peirce it was "a model of what a popular lecture ought to be" and implored him "on bended knees to give it first," but Peirce rewrote his first lecture instead and kept this one, much revised, as his fourth.] Peirce considers the role of observation in deduction, induction, and retroduction, and compares the three kinds of reasoning with respect to their self-correcting properties and their usefulness for supporting belief. He puts forward the rule that "in order to learn you must desire to learn," and contrasts, if only implicitly, his "Will to Learn" with the "Will to Believe" that had been expounded the previous year by William James. Peirce claims that American universities have been "miserably insignificant" because they have been institutions for teaching, not for learning. In this lecture, Peirce returns to the distinction between matters of vital importance, which James extolled, and matters of importance for science.

Certain methods of mathematical computation correct themselves; so that if an error be committed, it is only necessary to keep right on, and it will be corrected in the end. For instance, I want to extract the cube root of 2. The true answer is 1.25992105…. The rule is as follows:

Form a column of numbers, which for the sake of brevity we may call the A's. The first three A's are any three numbers taken at will. To form a new A, add the last two A's, triple the sum, add to this sum the last A but two, and set down the result as the next A. Now any A, the lower in the column the better, divided by the following A gives a fraction which increased by 1 is approximately $\sqrt[3]{2}$ *[see table 1]*.

You see the error committed in the second computation, though it seemed to multiply itself greatly, became substantially corrected in the end.

If you sit down to solve *ten* ordinary linear equations between ten unknown quantities, you will receive materials for a commentary upon the infallibility of mathematical processes. For you will almost infallibly get a wrong solution. I take it as a matter of course that you are not an expert professional computer. He will proceed according to a method which will correct his errors if he makes any.

Table 1

Correct Computation				Erroneous Computation		
	Sum of two	Triple			Sum of two	Triple
1				1		
0				0		
1	1	3		1	1	3
4	5	15		4	5	15
15	19	57		*Error!* 16	20	60
58	73	219		61	77	231
223	281	843		235	296	888
858	1081	3243		904	1139	3417
3301	4159	12477		3478	4382	13146
12700				13381		

$$1\frac{3301}{12700} = 1.2599213 \qquad 1\frac{3478}{13381} = 1.2599208$$

$$Error = +.0000002+ \qquad\qquad Error = -.0000002+$$

This calls to mind one of the most wonderful features of reasoning and one of the most important philosophemes in the doctrine of science, of which however you will search in vain for any mention in any book I can think of, namely, that reasoning tends to correct itself, and the more so the more wisely its plan is laid. Nay, it not only corrects its conclusions, it even corrects its premises. The theory of Aristotle is that a necessary conclusion is just equally as certain as its premises, while a probable conclusion somewhat less so.[1] Hence, he was driven to his strange distinction between what is better known to Nature and what is better known to us. But were every probable inference less certain than its premises, science, which piles inference upon inference, often quite deeply, would soon be in a bad way. Every astronomer, however, is familiar with the fact that the catalogue place of a fundamental star, which is the result of elaborate reasoning, is far more accurate than any of the observations from which it was deduced.

That induction tends to correct itself, is obvious enough. When a man undertakes to construct a table of mortality upon the basis of the Census, he is engaged in an inductive inquiry. And lo, the very first thing that he will discover from the figures, if he did not know it before, is that those figures are very seriously vitiated by their falsity. The young find it to their advantage to be thought older than they are, and the old to be thought younger than they are. The number of young men who are just twenty-one is altogether in excess of those who are twenty, although in all other cases the ages expressed in round numbers are in great excess. Now the operation of inferring a law in a succession of observed numbers is, broadly speaking, inductive; and therefore we see that a properly conducted inductive research corrects its own premises.

That the same thing may be true of a deductive inquiry our arithmetical example has shown. *Theoretically*, I grant you, there is no possibility of error in necessary reasoning. But to speak thus "theoretically," is to use language in a Pickwickian sense.[2] In practice and in fact, mathematics is not exempt from that liability to error that affects everything that man does. Strictly speaking, it is not certain that twice two is four. If on an average in every thousand figures obtained by addition by the average man there be one error, and if a thousand million men have each added 2 to 2 ten thousand times, there is still a possibility that they have all committed the same error of addition every time. If everything were fairly taken into account, I do not suppose that twice two is four is more certain than Edmund Gurney held the existence of veridical phantasms of the dying or dead to be.[3] Deductive inquiry, then, has its errors; and it corrects them, too. But it is by no means so sure, or at least so swift to do this as is inductive science. A celebrated error in the *Mécanique Céleste* concerning the amount of theoretical acceleration of the moon's mean motion deceived the whole world of astronomy for more than half a century.[4] Errors of reasoning in the first book of Euclid's *Elements*, the logic of which book was for two thousand years subjected to more careful criticism than any other piece of reasoning without exception ever was or probably ever will be, only became known after the non-Euclidean geometry had been developed. The certainty of mathematical reasoning, however, lies in this, that once an error is suspected, the whole world is speedily in accord about it.

As for retroductive inquiries, or the explanatory sciences, such as geology, evolution, and the like, they always have been and always must be theatres of controversy. These controversies do get settled, after a time, in the minds of candid inquirers; though it does not always happen that the protagonists themselves are able to assent to the justice of the decision. Nor is the general verdict always logical or just.

So it appears that this marvellous self-correcting property of Reason, which Hegel made so much of, belongs to every sort of science, although it appears as essential, intrinsic, and inevitable only in the highest type of reasoning, which is induction. But the logic of relatives shows that the other types of reasoning, deduction and retroduction, are not so thoroughly unlike induction as they might be thought, and as deduction, at least, always has been thought to be. Stuart Mill, alone among the older logicians, in his analysis of the *Pons Asinorum* came very near to the view which the logic of relatives forces us to take.[5] Namely, in the logic of relatives, treated let us say, in order to fix our ideas, by means of those existential graphs of which I gave a slight sketch in the last lecture, [we] begin a deduction by writing down all the premises.[6] Those different premises are then brought into one field of assertion, that is, are *colligated*, as Whewell would say,[7] or joined into one copulative proposition. Thereupon, we proceed attentively to observe the graph. It is just as much an operation of *observation* as is the observation of bees.[8] This observation leads us to make an *experiment* upon the graph. Namely, we first duplicate portions of it; and then we erase portions of it, that is, we put out of sight part of the assertion in order to see what the rest of it is. We observe the result of this experiment, and that is our deductive conclusion. Precisely those three things are all that enter into the experiment of any deduction,— colligation, iteration, erasure. The rest of the process consists of observing the result. It is not, however, in every deduction that all the three possible elements of the experiment take place. In particular, in ordinary syllogism the iteration may be said to be absent. And that is the reason that ordinary syllogism can be worked by a machine.[9] There is but one conclusion of any consequence to be drawn by ordinary syllogism from given premises. Hence it is that we fall into the habit of talking of *the* conclusion. But in the logic of relatives there are conclusions of different orders, depending upon how much iteration takes place. What is *the* conclusion deducible from the very simple first principles of number? It is ridiculous to speak of *the* conclusion. *The* conclusion is no less than the aggregate of all the theorems of higher arithmetic that have been discovered or that ever will be discovered. Now let us turn to induction. This mode of reasoning also begins by a colligation. In fact it was precisely the colligation that gave induction its name, ἐπανάγωγή with Socrates, συναγωγή with Plato, ἐπαγωγή with Aristotle.[10] It must by the rule of predesignation be a deliberate experiment. In ordinary induction we proceed to observe something about each instance. Relative induction is illustrated by the process of making out the law of the arrangement of the scales of a pine cone. It is necessary to mark a scale taken as an instance, and counting in certain directions to come back to that marked scale. This double observation of the same instance corresponds to iteration in deduction. Finally, we erase the particular instances and leave the class or system sampled directly connected with the characters, relative or otherwise, which have been found in the sample of it.

We see, then, that induction and deduction are after all not so very unlike. It is true that in induction we commonly make many experiments and in deduction only one. Yet this is not always the case. The chemist contents himself with a single experiment to establish any qualitative fact. True, he does this because he knows that there is such a uniformity in the behavior of chemical bodies that another experiment would be a mere repetition of the first in every respect. But it is precisely such a knowledge of a uniformity that leads the mathematician to content himself with one experiment. The inexperienced student in mathematics will mentally perform a number of geometrical experiments which the veteran would regard as superfluous before he will permit himself to come to a general conclusion. For example, if the question is, how many rays can cut four rays fixed in space, the experienced mathematician will content himself with imagining that two of the fixed rays intersect and that the other two likewise intersect. He will see, then, that there is one ray through the two intersections and another along the intersection of the two planes of pairs of intersecting fixed rays, and will unhesitatingly declare thereupon that but two rays can cut four fixed rays, unless the fixed rays are so situated that an infinite multitude of rays will cut them all. But I dare say many of you would want to experiment with other arrangements of the four fixed rays, before making any confident pronouncement. A friend of mine who seemed to have difficulties in adding up her accounts was once counselled to add each column five times and adopt the mean of the different results. It is evident that when we run a column of figures down as well as up, as a check, or when we review a demonstration in order to look out for any possible flaw in the reasoning, we are acting precisely as when in an induction we enlarge our sample for the sake of the self-correcting effect of induction.

As for retroduction, it is itself an experiment. A retroductive research is an experimental research; and when we look upon induction and deduction from the point of view of experiment and observation, we are merely tracing in those types of reasoning their affinity to retroduction. It begins always with colligation, of course, of a variety of separately observed facts about the subject of the hypothesis. How remarkable it is, by the way, that the entire army of logicians from Zeno to Whately should have left it to this mineralogist to point out colligation as a generally essential step in reasoning. But, then, Whewell was a most admirable reasoner, who is underestimated simply because he stands detached both from the main current of philosophy and from that of science. It is worth the journey to the Rheingau, simply for the lesson in reasoning that one learns by reading upon the spot that remarkable work modestly thrown into the form of *Notes on German Churches*.[11] As for the *History of Inductive Sciences*[12], it comes as near to standing for what Dr. Carus calls a κτῆμα εἰς ἀεί[13] as anything in philosophy can do. Mill's *Logic* was written to refute this book. I certainly would not have Mill's *Logic* lost, false as it is to the theory of inductive reasoning; but the contrast between Whewell's deep acquaintance with the springs of science and Mill's exterior survey is well shown by the circumstance that whatever scientific reasonings Whewell has praised have been more and more confirmed by time while every one of the examples which Mill picked out as choice specimens of successful inductions in his first edition have long been utterly exploded.[14] To return to retroduction, then, it begins with colligation. Something corresponding to iteration may or may not take place. And then comes an observation. Not, however, an external observation of the objects as in induction, nor yet an observation made upon the parts of a diagram, as in deduction; but for all that just as truly an observation. For what is observation? What is experience? It is the enforced element in the history of our lives. It is that which we are constrained to be conscious of by an occult force residing in an object which we contemplate. The act of observation is the deliberate yielding of ourselves to that *force majeure*,—an early surrender at discretion, due to our foreseeing that we must, whatever we do, be borne down by that power, at last. Now the surrender which we make in retroduction is a surrender to the insistence of an idea. The hypothesis, as the Frenchman says, *c'est plus fort que moi*. It is irresistible; it is imperative. We must throw open our gates and admit it, at any rate for the time being. I have been reading Alexandre Dumas's charming *Impressions de voyage*.[15] It is full of slips of the pen. He says Pisa when he means Florence, Lorenzo when he means the Old Cosimo, the eighteenth century when he means the thirteenth, six hundred years when he means five hundred. The new word comes to me and is substituted just as if I had seen it. For it makes sense; and what I see printed does not. Finally, retroduction lets slip out of attention the special characters involved in its premises, because they are virtually contained in the hypothesis which it has been led to presume. But as our study of the subject of the hypothesis grows deeper, that hypothesis will be sure gradually to take another color, little by little to receive modifications, corrections, amplifications, even in case no catastrophe befalls it.[16]

Thus it is that inquiry of every type, fully carried out, has the vital power of self-correction and of growth. This is a property so deeply saturating its inmost nature that it may truly be said that there is but one thing needful for learning the truth, and that is a hearty and active desire to learn what is true. If you really want to learn the truth, you will, by however devious a path, be surely led into the way of truth, at last. No matter how erroneous your ideas of the method may be at first, you will be forced at length to correct them so long as your activity is moved by that sincere desire. Nay, no matter if you only half desire it, at first, that desire would at length conquer all others, could experience continue long enough. But the more veraciously truth is desired at the outset, the shorter by centuries will the road to it be.

In order to demonstrate that this is so, it is necessary to note what is essentially involved in the Will to Learn. The first thing that the Will to Learn supposes is a dissatisfaction with one's present state of opinion. There lies the secret of why it is that our American universities are so miserably insignificant. What have they done for the advance of civilization? What is the great idea or where is /the/ single great man who can truly be said to be the product of an American university? The English universities, rotting with sloth as they always have, have nevertheless in the past given birth to Locke and to Newton, and in our time to Cayley, Sylvester, and Clifford.[17] The German universities have been the light of the whole world. The medieval University of Bologna gave Europe its system of law. The University of Paris, and that despised scholasticism took Abelard and made him into Descartes. The reason was that they were institutions of learning while ours are institutions for teaching. In order that a man's whole heart may be in teaching he must be thoroughly imbued with the vital importance and absolute truth of what he has to teach; while in order that he may have any measure of success in learning he must be penetrated with a sense of the unsatisfactoriness of his present condition of knowledge. The two attitudes are almost irreconcilable. But just as it is not the self-righteous man who brings multitudes to a sense of sin, but the man who is most deeply conscious that he is himself a sinner, and it is only by a sense of sin that men can escape its thraldom; so it is not the man who thinks he knows it all that can bring other men to feel their need of learning, and it is only a deep sense that one is miserably ignorant that can spur one on in the toilsome path of learning. That is why, to my very humble apprehension, it cannot but seem that those admirable pedagogical methods for which the American teacher is distinguished are of little more consequence than the cut of his coat, that they surely are as nothing compared with that fever for learning that must consume the soul of the man who is to infect others with the same apparent malady. Let me say that of the present condition of Harvard I really know nothing at all except that I know the leaders of the department of philosophy to be all true scholars, particularly marked by eagerness to learn and freedom from dogmatism. And in every age, it can only be the philosophy of that age, such as it may be, which can animate the special sciences to any work that shall really carry forward the human mind to some new and valuable truth. Because the valuable truth is not the detached one, but the one that goes toward enlarging the system of what is already known.

The inductive method springs directly out of dissatisfaction with existing knowledge. The great rule of predesignation which must guide it is as much as to say that an induction to be valid must be prompted by a definite doubt or at least an interrogation; and what is such an interrogation but first, a sense that we do not know something, second, a desire to know it, and third, an effort,—implying a willingness to labor,—for the sake of seeing how the truth may really be. If that interrogation inspires you, you will be sure to examine the instances; while if it does not, you will pass them by without attention.[18]

Upon this first, and in one sense this sole, rule of reason, that in order to learn you must desire to learn and in so desiring not be satisfied with what you already incline to think, there follows one corollary which itself deserves to be inscribed upon every wall of the city of philosophy,

Do not block the way of inquiry.

Although it is better to be methodical in our investigations, and to consider the Economics of Research,[19] yet there is no positive sin against logic in *trying* any theory which may come into our heads, so long as it is adopted in such a sense as to permit the investigation to go on unimpeded and undiscouraged. On the other hand, to set up a philosophy which barricades the road of further advance toward the truth is the one unpardonable offense in reasoning, as it is also the one to which metaphysicians have in all ages shown themselves the most addicted.

Let me call your attention to four familiar shapes in which this venomous error assails our knowledge:

The first is the shape of absolute assertion. That we can be sure of nothing in science is an ancient truth. The Academy taught it.[20] Yet science has been infested with over-confident assertion, especially on the part of the third-rate and fourth-rate men, who have been more concerned with teaching than with learning, at all times. No doubt some of the geometries still teach as a self-evident truth the proposition that if two straight lines in one plane meet a third straight line so as to make the sum of the internal angles on one side less than two right angles, those two lines will meet on that side if sufficiently prolonged. Euclid, who[se] logic was more careful, only reckoned this proposition as a *Postulate*, or arbitrary hypothesis. Yet even he places among his axioms the proposition that a part is less than its whole, and falls into several conflicts with our most modern geometry in consequence. But why need we stop to consider cases where some subtilty of thought is required to see that the assertion is not warranted when every book which applies philosophy to the conduct of life lays down as positive certainty propositions which it is quite as easy to doubt as to believe.

The second bar which philosophers often set up across the roadway of inquiry lies in maintaining that this, that, and the other never can be known. When Auguste Comte was pressed to specify any matter of positive fact to the knowledge of which no man could by any possibility attain, he instanced the knowledge of the chemical composition of the fixed stars; and you may see his answer set down in the *Philosophie positive*.[21] But the ink was scarcely dry upon the printed page before the spectroscope was discovered and that which he had deemed absolutely unknowable was well on the way of getting ascertained. It is easy enough to mention a question the answer to which is not known to me today. But to aver that that answer will not be known tomorrow is somewhat risky; for oftentimes it is precisely the least expected truth which is turned up under the ploughshare of research. And when it comes to positive assertion that the truth never will be found out, that, in the light of the history of our time, seems to me more hazardous than the venture of Andrée.[22]

The third philosophical stratagem for cutting off inquiry consists in maintaining that this, that, or the other element of science is basic, ultimate, independent of aught else, and utterly inexplicable,—not so much from any defect in our knowing as because there is nothing beneath it to know. The only type of reasoning by which such a conclusion could possibly be reached is *retroduction*. Now nothing justifies a retroductive inference except its affording an explanation of the facts. It is, however, no explanation at all of a fact to pronounce it *inexplicable*. That therefore is a conclusion which no reasoning can ever justify or excuse.

The last philosophical obstacle to the advance of knowledge which I intend to mention is the holding that this or that law or truth has found its last and perfect formulation,—and especially that the ordinary and usual course of nature never can be broken through. "Stones do not fall from heaven" said Laplace, although they had been falling upon inhabited ground every day from the earliest times. But there is no kind of inference which can lend the slightest probability to any such absolute denial of an unusual phenomenon.

I repeat that I know nothing about the Harvard of today, but one of the things which I hope to learn during my stay in Cambridge is the answer to this question, whether the Commonwealth of Massachusetts has set up this University to the end that such young men as can come here may receive a fine education and may thus be able to earn handsome incomes, and have a canvas-back and a bottle of Clos de Vougeot for dinner,—whether this is what she is driving at,—or whether it is, that, knowing that all America looks largely to sons of Massachusetts for the solutions of the most urgent problems of each generation, she hopes that in this place something may be studied out which shall be of service in the solutions of those problems. In short, I hope to find out whether Harvard is an educational establishment or whether it is an institution for learning what is not yet thoroughly known, whether it is for the benefit of the individual students or whether it is for the good of the country and for the speedier elevation of man into that rational animal of *[which]* he is the embryonic form.

There is one thing that I am sure a Harvard education cannot fail to do, because it did that much even in my time and for a very insouciant student, I mean that it cannot fail to disabuse the student of the popular notion that modern science is so very great a thing as to be commensurate with Nature and indeed to constitute of itself some account of the universe, and to show him that it is yet, what it appeared to Isaac Newton to be,[23] a child's collection of pebbles gathered upon the beach,—the vast ocean of Being lying there unsounded.

It is not merely that in all our gropings we bump up against problems which we cannot imagine how to attack: *[of]* why space should have but three dimensions, if it really has but three; *[of]* why the Listing numbers[24] which define its shape should all equal one, if they really do, or why some of them should be zero, as Listing himself and many geometers think they are, if that be the truth; of why forces should determine the second derivative of the space rather than the third or fourth; of why matter should consist of about seventy distinct kinds, and all those of each kind apparently exactly alike, and these different kinds having masses nearly in arithmetical progression and yet not exactly so; of why atoms should attract one another at a distance in peculiar ways, if they really do, or if not what produced such vortices, and what gave the vortices such peculiar laws of attraction; of how or by what kind of influence matter came to be sifted out, so that the different kinds occur in considerable aggregations; of why certain motions of the atoms of certain kinds of protoplasm are accompanied by sensation, and so on through the whole list. These things do indeed show us how superficial our science still is; but its littleness is made even more manifest when we consider within how narrow a range all our inquiries have hitherto lain. The instincts connected with the need of nutrition have furnished all animals with some virtual knowledge of space and of force, and made them applied physicists. The instincts connected with sexual reproduction have furnished all animals at all like ourselves with some virtual comprehension of the minds of other animals of their kind, so that they are applied psychists. Now not only our accomplished science, but even our scientific questions have been pretty exclusively limited to the development of those two branches of natural knowledge. There may for aught we know be a thousand other kinds of relationship which have as much to do with connecting phenomena and leading from one to another, as dynamical and social relationships have. Astrology, magic, ghosts, prophecies, serve as suggestions of what such relationships might be.

Not only is our knowledge thus limited in scope, but it is even more important that we should thoroughly realize that the very best of what we, humanly speaking, know, /we know/ only in an uncertain and inexact way.[25] In favor of pure mathematics we must, indeed, make an exception. It is true that even that does not reach certainty with mathematical exactitude. But then the theorems of pure mathematics, take them, as Captain Cuttle would do,[26] "by and large," are without doubt exactly and certainly true, for all purposes except that of logical theory. Pure mathematics, however, is no science of existing things. It is a mere science of hypotheses. It is consistent with itself; and if there is nothing else to which it professes to conform, it perfectly fulfils its promise and its purpose. Certainly, you will not find in any modern book of pure mathematics any further profession than that. But mathematicians are not in the habit of setting down statements they are not prepared to prove; and it may very well be that they generally entertain a somewhat different idea of their science. All the great mathematicians whom I have happened to know very well were Platonists, and I have little doubt that if the contributors to the leading mathematical journals were polled, it would be found that there were among them a larger proportion of Platonists than among any other class of scientific men. I believe the great majority of them would regard the formation of such conceptions as that of imaginary quantity and that of Riemann surfaces as mathematical achievements, and *that*, considering those hypotheses not as mere instruments for investigating real quantity, but in themselves. They would rank them as having a much higher value than anything in the *Arabian Nights*, for example. Yet why should they do so, if those hypotheses are pure fictions? There is certainly something to which modern mathematical conceptions strive to conform, be it no more than an artistic ideal. And the true question is whether they fulfil their endeavor with any greater success than other human works. If it be only beauty that is aimed at, then mathematical hypotheses must be ranked as something similar but inferior to the Alhambra decorations,—as pretty but soulless. If on the other hand they are essays at the portrayal of a Platonic world, then we can only say that they are so exceedingly slight and fragmentary as hardly to enable us to understand their drift and not at all to find room for any application of the conception of accuracy.

So much for the certainty of deductive science. As to induction it is, upon the face of it, merely probable and approximate, and it is only when it is confined to finite and denumeral collections that it attains even that grade of perfection. It only infers the value of a ratio and therefore when applied to any natural class which is conceived to be more than denumeral, no amount of inductive evidence can ever give us the *slightest reason*,—no, would not justify the very slightest inclination to believe,—that an inductive law was without exception. Indeed, every sane mind will readily enough admit that this is so as soon as a law is made clearly to appear as a pure induction and nothing more. Nobody would dream of contending that because the sun has risen and set every day so far, that afforded any reason at all for supposing that it would go on doing so to all eternity. But when I say that there is not the very slightest reason for thinking that no material atoms ever go out of existence or come into existence, there I fail to carry the average man with me; and I suppose the reason is that he dimly conceives that there is some reason other than the pure and simple induction for holding matter to be ingenerable and indestructible. For it is plain that if it be a mere question of our weighings or other experiences, all that appears is that not more than one atom in a million or ten million becomes annihilated before the deficiency of mass is pretty certain to be balanced by another atom's being created. Now when we are speaking of atoms, a million or ten million is an excessively minute quantity. So that as far as purely inductive evidence is concerned we are very very far from being entitled to think that matter is absolutely permanent. If you put the question to a physicist his reply will probably be, as it certainly ought to be, that physicists only deal with such phenomena as they can either directly or indirectly observe, or are likely to become able to observe until there is some great revolution in science, and to that he will very likely add that any limitation upon the permanence of matter would be a purely gratuitous hypothesis without anything whatever to support it. Now this last part of the physicist's reply is, in regard to the order of considerations which he has in mind, excellent good sense. But from an absolute point of view, I think it leaves something out of account. Do you believe that the fortune of the Rothschilds will endure forever? Certainly not; because although they may be safe enough as far as the ordinary causes go which engulf fortunes, yet there is always a chance of some revolution or catastrophe which may destroy all property. And no matter how little that chance may be, as far as this decade or this generation goes, yet in limitless decades and generations, it is pretty sure that the pitcher will get broken, at last. There is no danger, however slight, which in an indefinite multitude of occasions does [not] come as near to absolute certainty as probability can come. The existence of the human race, we may be as good as sure, will come to an end at last. For not to speak of the gradual operation of causes of which we know, the action of the tides, the resisting medium, the dissipation of energy, there is all the time a certain danger that the earth may be struck by a meteor or wandering star so large as to ruin it, or by some poisonous gas. That a purely gratuitous hypothesis should turn out to be true is, indeed, something so exceedingly improbable that we cannot be appreciably wrong in calling it zero. Still, the chance that out of an infinite multitude of gratuitous hypotheses an infinitesimal proportion, which may itself be an infinite multitude, should turn out to be true, is zero multiplied by infinity, which is absolutely indeterminate. That is to say we simply know nothing whatever about it. Now that any single atom should be annihilated is a gratuitous hypothesis. But there are, we may suppose, an infinite multitude of atoms, and a similar hypothesis may be made for each. And thus we return to my original statement that as to whether any finite number or even an infinite number of atoms are annihilated *per* year, that is something of which we are simply in a state of blank ignorance, unless we have found out some method of reasoning altogether superior to induction. If, therefore, we should detect any general phenomenon of nature which could very well be explained, not by supposing any definite breach of the laws of nature, for that would be no explanation at all, but by supposing that a continual breach of all the laws of nature, every day and every second, was itself one of the laws or habitudes of nature, there would be no power in induction to offer the slightest logical objection to that theory. But as long as we /are/ aware of no such general phenomena tending to show such continual inexactitude in law, then we must remain absolutely without any rational opinion upon the matter *pro* or *con*.

There are various ways in which the natural cocksuredness and conceit of man struggles to escape such confession of total ignorance. But they seem to be all quite futile. One of the commonest and at the same time the silliest is the argument /that/ God would for this or that excellent reason never act in such an irregular manner. I think all the men who talk like that must be near-sighted. For to suppose that any man who could see the moving clouds and survey a wide expanse of landscape and note its wonderful complexity, and consider how unimaginably small it all was in comparison to the whole face of the globe, not to speak of the millions of orbs in space, and who would not presume to predict what move Morphy or Steinitz might make in so simple a thing as a game of chess,[27] should undertake to say what God would do, would seem to impeach his sanity. But if instead of its being a God, after whose image we are made, and whom we can, therefore, begin to understand, it were some metaphysical principle of Being, even more incomprehensible, whose action the man pretended to compute, that would seem to be a pitch of absurdity one degree higher yet.

Passing to retroduction, this type of reasoning cannot logically justify any belief at all, if we understand by belief the holding of a proposition as a definitive conclusion. It is here to be remarked that the word hypothesis is often extended to cases where it has no proper application.[28] People talk of a hypothesis where there is a *vera causa*. But in such cases the inference is not hypothetic but inductive. A *vera causa* is a state of things known to be present and known partially at least to explain the phenomena, but not known to explain them with quantitative precision. Thus, when seeing ordinary bodies round us accelerated toward the earth's center and seeing also the moon, which both in its *albedo* and its volcanic appearance altogether resembles stone, to be likewise accelerated toward the earth, and when finding these two accelerations are in the inverse duplicate ratios of their distances from that center, we conclude that their nature, whatever it may be, is the same, we are inferring an analogy, which is a type of inference having all the strength of induction and more, besides. For the sake of simplicity, I have said nothing about it in these lectures; but I am here forced to make that remark. Moreover, when we consider that all that we infer about the gravitation of the Moon is a continuity between the terrestrial and lunar phenomena, a continuity which is found throughout physics, and when we add to that the analogies of electrical and magnetical attractions, both of which vary inversely as the square of the distance, we plainly recognize here one of the strongest arguments of which science affords any example. Newton was entirely in the right when he said, *Hypotheses non fingo*.[29] It is they who have criticized the dictum whose logic is at fault. They are attributing an obscure psychological signification to *force*, or *vis insita*, which in physics only connotes a regularity among accelerations. Thus inferences concerning *verae causae* are inductions not retroductions, and of course have only such uncertainty and inexactitude as belong to induction.

When I say that a retroductive inference is not a matter for belief at all, I encounter the difficulty that there are certain inferences which scientifically considered are undoubtedly hypotheses and yet which practically are perfectly certain. Such for instance is the inference that Napoleon Bonaparte really lived at about the beginning of this century, a hypothesis which we adopt for the purpose of explaining the concordant testimony of a hundred memoirs, the public records of history, tradition, and numberless monuments and relics. It would surely be downright insanity to entertain a doubt about Napoleon's existence. A still better example is that of the translations of the cuneiform inscriptions which began in mere guesses, in which their authors could have had no real confidence. Yet by piling new conjectures upon former conjectures apparently verified, this science has gone on to produce under our very eyes a result so bound together by the agreement of the readings with one another, with other history, and with known facts of linguistics, that we are unwilling any longer to apply the word *theory* to it. You will ask me how I can reconcile such facts as these with my dictum that hypothesis is not a matter for belief. In order to answer this question I must first examine such inferences in their scientific aspect and afterwards in their practical aspect. The only end of science, as such, is to learn the lesson that the universe has to teach it. In induction it simply surrenders itself to the force of facts. But it finds, at once,—I am partially inverting the historical order, in order to state the process in its logical order,—it finds I say that this is not enough. It is driven in desperation to call upon its inward sympathy with nature, its instinct for aid, just as we find Galileo at the dawn of modern science making his appeal to *il lume naturale*. But insofar as it does this, the solid ground of fact fails it. It feels from that moment that its position is only provisional. It must then find confirmations or else shift its footing. Even if it does find confirmations, they are only partial. It still is not standing upon the bedrock of fact. It is walking upon a bog, and can only say, this ground seems to hold for the present. Here I will stay till it begins to give way.[30] Moreover, in all its progress, science vaguely feels that it is only learning a lesson. The value of *facts* to *it*, lies only in this, that they belong to Nature; and Nature is something great, and beautiful, and sacred, and eternal, and real,—the object of its worship and its aspiration. It therein takes an entirely different attitude toward facts from that which Practice takes. For Practice, facts are the arbitrary forces with which it has to reckon and to wrestle. Science, when it comes to understand itself, regards facts as merely the vehicle of eternal truth, while for Practice they remain the obstacles which it has to turn, the enemy of which it is determined to get the better. Science, feeling that there is an arbitrary element in its theories, still continues its studies confident that so it will gradually become more and more purified from the dross of subjectivity; but Practice requires something to go upon, and it will be no consolation to it to know that it is on the path to objective truth,—the actual truth it must have, or when it cannot attain certainty must at least have high probability, that is, must know that though a few of its ventures may fail the bulk of them will succeed. Hence the hypothesis which answers the purpose of theory may be perfectly worthless for Art. After a while, as Science progresses, it comes upon more solid ground. It is now entitled to reflect, this ground has held a long time without showing signs of yielding. I may hope that it will continue to hold for a great while longer. This reflection, however, is quite aside from the purpose of Science. It does not modify its procedure in the least degree. It is extra-scientific. For Practice, however, it is vitally important, quite altering the situation. As Practice apprehends it, the conclusion no longer rests upon mere retroduction, it is inductively supported. For a large sample has now been drawn from the entire collection of occasions in which the theory comes into comparison with fact, and an overwhelming proportion, in fact all the cases that have presented themselves, have been found to bear out the theory. And so, says Practice, I can safely presume that so it will be with the great bulk of the cases in which I shall go upon the theory, especially as they will closely resemble those which have been well tried. In other words there is now reason to believe in the theory, for belief is the willingness to risk a great deal upon a proposition. But this belief is no concern of science which has nothing at stake on any temporal venture, but is in pursuit of eternal verities, not semblances to truth, and looks upon this pursuit, not as the work of one man's life, but as that of generation after generation, indefinitely. Thus those retroductive inferences which at length acquire such high degrees of certainty, so far as they are so probable are not pure retroductions and do not belong to science, as such, while so far as they are scientific and are pure retroductions have no true probability and are not matters for belief. We call them in science established truths, that is, they are propositions into which the economy of endeavor prescribes that for the time being further inquiry shall cease.[31]

An eminent religious teacher, Dr. Carus, seems to think that I do not regard with sufficient horror the doctrine that the conception of truth is ambiguous. For in an article in which he holds up several other of my moral failings to public reprobation,[32] he caps the climax by saying that I admire Duns Scotus who was a man who held that a proposition might be false in philosophy yet true in religion, and names the volumes and pages in the works of Duns Scotus of two passages, which the reader infers would enunciate that position. One of the pages is substantially blank and the other contains nothing remotely bearing on the subject. Duns Scotus may possibly have said something of the kind; but if he did I cannot imagine where it can be hidden away. This however I do know, that that doctrine was the distinguishing tenet of the followers of Averrhoes. Now I know of but one place in all my reading of Duns in which he speaks unkindly of any opponent, and that one is where he alludes to Averrhoes as "Iste damnatus Averroes."[33] This hardly looks as if he followed him in his main position. But whether the word truth has two meanings or not, I certainly do think that *holding for true* is of two kinds; the one is that practical holding for true which alone is entitled to the name of Belief, while the other is that acceptance of a proposition which in the intention of pure science remains always provisional. To adhere to a proposition in an absolutely definitive manner, supposing that by this is merely meant that the believer has personally wedded his fate to it, is something which in practical concerns, say for instance in matters of right and wrong, we sometimes cannot and ought not to avoid; but to do so in science amounts simply to not wishing to learn. Now he who does not wish to learn cuts himself off from science altogether.

6

Pearson's Grammar of Science

P 802: Popular Science Monthly *58 (January 1901):296–306. [Published in CP 8.132–52. The complete title includes the subtitle: "Annotations on the First Three Chapters" (but some remarks are made on the fourth chapter as well). Peirce first wrote this piece for* The Psychological Review.*]* *In this review, Peirce objects to Pearson's claim that human conduct should be regulated by Darwinian theory, and to the related view that social stability is the sole justification of scientific research. Peirce holds that these doctrines lead to bad ethics and bad science. "I must confess that I belong to that class of scallawags who propose, with God's help, to look the truth in the face, whether doing so be conducive to the interests of society or not." The man of science should be motivated by the majesty of truth, "as that to which, sooner or later, every knee must bow." Against Pearson's nominalistic claim that the rationality inherent in nature owes its origin to the human intellect, Peirce argues that it is the human mind that is determined by the rationality in nature. Peirce also rejects Pearson's claim that there are first impressions of sense that serve as the starting point of reasoning, and argues that reasoning begins in percepts, which are products of psychical operations involving three kinds of elements: qualities of feelings, reactions, and generalizing elements.*

If any follower of Dr. Pearson[1] thinks that in the observations I am about to make I am not sufficiently respectful to his master, I can assure him that without a high opinion of his powers I should not have taken the trouble to make these annotations, and without a higher opinion still, I should not have used the bluntness which becomes the impersonal discussions of mathematicians.

An introductory chapter of ethical content sounds the dominant note of the book. The author opens with the declaration that our conduct ought to be regulated by the Darwinian theory. Since that theory is an attempt to show how natural causes tend to impart to stocks of animals and plants characters which, in the long run, promote reproduction and thus insure the continuance of those stocks, it would seem that making Darwinism the guide of conduct ought to mean that the continuance of the race is to be taken as the *summum bonum*, and *Multiplicamini* as the epitome of the moral law.[2] Professor Pearson, however, understands the matter a little differently, expressing himself thus: "The sole reason [for encouraging] any form of human activity . . . lies in this: [its] existence tends to promote the welfare of human society, to increase social happiness, or to strengthen social stability. In the spirit of the age we are bound to question the value of science; to ask in what way it increases the happiness of mankind or promotes social efficiency."[3]

The second of these two statements omits the phrase, "the welfare of human society," which conveys no definite meaning; and we may, therefore, regard it as a mere diluent, adding nothing to the essence of what is laid down. Strict adhesion to Darwinian principles would preclude the admission of the "happiness of mankind" as an ultimate aim. For on those principles everything is directed to the continuance of the stock, and the individual is utterly of no account, except in so far as he is an agent of reproduction. Now there is no other happiness of mankind than the happiness of individual men. We must, therefore, regard this clause as logically deleterious to the purity of the doctrine. As to "social stability," we all know very well what ideas this phrase is intended to convey to English apprehensions;[4] and it must be admitted that Darwinism, generalized in due measure, may apply to English society the same principles that Darwin applied to breeds. A family in which the standards of that society are not traditional will go under and die out, and thus "social stability" tends to be maintained.

But against the doctrine that social stability is the sole justification of scientific research, whether this doctrine be adulterated or not with the utilitarian clause, I have to object, first, that it is historically false, in that it does not accord with the predominant sentiment of scientific men; second, that it is bad ethics; and, third, that its propagation would retard the progress of science.

Professor Pearson does not, indeed, pretend that that which effectually animates the labors of scientific men is any desire "to strengthen social stability." Such a proposition would be too grotesque. Yet if it was his business, in treating of the grammar of science, to set forth the legitimate motive to research,—as he has deemed it to be,—it was certainly also his business, especially in view of the splendid successes of science, to show what has, in fact, moved such men. They have, at all events, not been inspired by a wish either to "support social stability" or, in the main, to increase the sum of men's pleasures. The man of science has received a deep impression of the majesty of truth, as that to which, sooner or later, every knee must bow. He has further found that his own mind is sufficiently akin to that truth, to enable him, on condition of submissive observation, to interpret it in some measure. As he gradually becomes better and better acquainted with the character of cosmical truth, and learns that human reason is its issue and can be brought step by step into accord with it, he conceives a passion for its fuller revelation. He is keenly aware of his own ignorance, and knows that personally he can make but small steps in discovery. Yet, small as they are, he deems them precious; and he hopes that by conscientiously pursuing the methods of science he may erect a foundation upon which his successors may climb higher. This, for him, is what makes life worth living and what makes the human race worth perpetuation. The very being of law, general truth, reason,—call it what you will,—consists in its expressing itself in a cosmos and in intellects which reflect it,[5] and in doing this progressively; and that which makes progressive creation worth doing,—so the researcher comes to feel,—is precisely the reason, the law, the general truth for the sake of which it takes place.

Such, I believe, as a matter of fact, is the motive which effectually works in the man of science. That granted, we have next to inquire which motive is the more rational, the one just described or that which Professor Pearson recommends. The ethical textbooks offer us classifications of human motives. But for our present purpose it will suffice to pass in rapid review some of the more prominent ethical classes of motives.[6]

A man may act with reference only to the momentary occasion, either from unrestrained desire, or from preference for one desideratum over another, or from provision against future desires, or from persuasion, or from imitative instinct, or from dread of blame, or in awed obedience to an instant command; or he may act according to some general rule restricted to his own wishes, such as the pursuit of pleasure, or self-preservation, or goodwill toward an acquaintance, or attachment to home and surroundings, or conformity to the customs of his tribe, or reverence for a law; or, becoming a moralist, he may aim at bringing about an ideal state of things definitely conceived, such as one in which everybody attends exclusively to his own business and interest (individualism), or in which the maximum total pleasure of all beings capable of pleasure is attained (utilitarianism), or in which altruistic sentiments universally prevail (altruism), or in which his community is placed out of all danger (patriotism), or in which the ways of nature are as little modified as possible (naturalism); or he may aim at hastening some result not otherwise known in advance than as that, whatever it may turn out to be, to which some process seeming to him good must inevitably lead, such as whatever the dictates of the human heart may approve (sentimentalism), or whatever would result from every man's duly weighing, before action, the advantages of his every purpose (to which I will attach the nonce-name *entelism*, distinguishing it and others below by italics), or whatever the historical evolution of public sentiment may decree (*historicism*), or whatever the operation of cosmical causes may be destined to bring about (evolutionism); or he may be devoted to truth, and may be determined to do nothing not pronounced reasonable, either by his own cogitations (rationalism), or by public discussion (dialecticism), or by crucial experiment; or he may feel that the only thing really worth striving for is the generalizing or assimilating elements in truth, and that either as the sole object in which the mind can ultimately recognize its veritable aim (educationalism), or that which alone is destined to gain universal sway (pancratism); or, finally, he may be filled with the idea that the only reason that can reasonably be admitted as ultimate is that living reason for the sake of which the psychical and physical universe is in process of creation (*religionism*).

This list of ethical classes of motives may, it is hoped, serve as a tolerable sample upon which to base reflections upon the acceptability as ultimate of different kinds of human motives; and it makes no pretension to any higher value. The enumeration has been so ordered as to bring into view the various degrees of generality of motives. It would conduce to our purpose, however, to compare them in other respects. Thus, we might arrange them in reference to the degree to which an impulse of dependence enters into them, from express obedience, generalized obedience, conformity to an external exemplar, action for the sake of an object regarded as external, the adoption of a motive centering on something which is partially opposed to what is present, the balancing of one consideration against another, until we reach such motives as unrestrained desire, the pursuit of pleasure, individualism, sentimentalism, rationalism, educationalism, religionism, in which the element of otherness is reduced to a minimum. Again, we might arrange the classes of motives according to the degree in which immediate qualities of feeling appear in them, from unrestrained desire, through desire present but restrained, action for self, action for pleasure generalized beyond self, motives involving a retro-consciousness of self in outward things, the personification of the community, to such motives as direct obedience, reverence, naturalism, evolutionism, experimentalism, pancratism, religionism, in which the element of self-feeling is reduced to a minimum. But the important thing is to make ourselves thoroughly acquainted, as far as possible from the inside, with a variety of human motives ranging over the whole field of ethics.

I will not go further into ethics than simply to remark that all motives that are directed toward pleasure or self-satisfaction, of however high a type, will be pronounced by every experienced person to be inevitably destined to miss the satisfaction at which they aim. This is true even of the highest of such motives, that which Josiah Royce develops in his *World and Individual*.[7] On the other hand, every motive involving dependence on some other leads us to ask for some ulterior reason. The only desirable object which is quite satisfactory in itself without any ulterior reason for desiring it, is the reasonable itself. I do not mean to put this forward as a demonstration; because, like all demonstrations about such matters, it would be a mere quibble, a sheaf of fallacies. I maintain simply that it is an experiential truth.

The only ethically sound motive is the most general one; and the motive that actually inspires the man of science, if not quite that, is very near to it,—nearer, I venture to believe, than that of any other equally common type of humanity. On the other hand, Professor Pearson's aim, "the stability of society," which is nothing but a narrow British patriotism, prompts the *cui bono* at once. I am willing to grant that England has been for two or three centuries a most precious factor of human development. But there were and are *reasons* for this. To demand that man should aim at the stability of British society, or of society at large, or the perpetuation of the race, as an *ultimate* end, is too much. The human species will be extirpated sometime; and when the time comes the universe will, no doubt, be well rid of it. Professor Pearson's ethics are not at all improved by being adulterated with utilitarianism, which is a lower motive still. Utilitarianism is one of the few theoretical motives which has unquestionably had an extremely beneficial influence. But the greatest happiness of the greatest number, as expounded by Bentham, resolves itself into merely superinducing the quality of pleasure upon men's immediate feelings. Now, if the pursuit of pleasure is not a satisfactory ultimate motive for me, why should I enslave myself to procuring it for others? Leslie Stephen's book[8] was far from uttering the last word upon ethics; but it is difficult to comprehend how anybody who has read it reflectively can continue to hold the mixed doctrine that no action is to be encouraged for any other reason than that it either tends to the stability of society or to general happiness.

Ethics, as such, is extraneous to a Grammar of Science; but it is a serious fault in such a book to inculcate reasons for scientific research the acceptance of which must tend to lower the character of such research. Science is, upon the whole, at present in a very healthy condition. It would not remain so if the motives of scientific men were lowered. The worst feature of the present state of things is that the great majority of the members of many scientific societies, and a large part of others, are men whose chief interest in science is as a means of gaining money, and who have a contempt, or half-contempt, for pure science. Now, to declare that the sole reason for scientific research is the good of society is to encourage those pseudo-scientists to claim, and the general public to admit, that they, who deal with the applications of knowledge, are the true men of science, and that the theoreticians are little better than idlers.

In Chapter II, entitled "The Facts of Science," we find that the "stability of society" is not only to regulate our conduct, but, also, that our opinions have to be squared to it. In Section 10 we are told that we must not believe a certain purely theoretical proposition because it is "anti-social" to do so, and because to do so "is opposed to the interests of society." As to the "canons of legitimate inference" themselves, that are laid down by Professor Pearson, I have no great objection to them. They certainly involve important truths. They are excessively vague and capable of being twisted to support illogical opinions, as they are twisted by their author, and they leave much ground uncovered. But I will not pursue these objections. I do say, however, that truth is truth, whether it is opposed to the interests of society to admit it or not,—and that the notion that we must deny what it is not conducive to the stability of British society to affirm is the mainspring of the mendacity and hypocrisy which Englishmen so commonly regard as virtues. I must confess that I belong to that class of scallawags who purpose, with God's help, to look the truth in the face, whether doing so be conducive to the interests of society or not. Moreover, if I should ever attack that excessively difficult problem, "What is for the true interest of society?" I should feel that I stood in need of a great deal of help from the science of legitimate inference; and, therefore, to avoid running round a circle, I will endeavor to base my theory of legitimate inference upon something less questionable,—as well as more germane to the subject,—than the true interest of society.

The remainder of this chapter on the "Facts of Science" is taken up with a theory of cognition, in which the author falls into the too common error of confounding psychology with logic. He will have it that knowledge is built up out of sense-impressions,—a correct enough statement of a conclusion of psychology. Understood, however, as Professor Pearson understands and applies it, as a statement of the nature of our logical data, of "the facts of science," it is altogether incorrect. He tells us that each of us is like the operator at a central telephone office, shut out from the external world, of which he is informed only by sense-impressions. Not at all! Few things are more completely hidden from my observation than those hypothetical elements of thought which the psychologist finds reason to pronounce "immediate," in his sense. But the starting point of all our reasoning is not in those sense-impressions, but in our percepts. When we first wake up to the fact that we are thinking beings and can exercise some control over our reasonings, we have to set out upon our intellectual travels from the home where we already find ourselves. Now, this home is the parish of percepts. It is not inside our skulls, either, but out in the open. It is the external world that we directly observe. What passes within we only know as it is mirrored in external objects. In a certain sense, there is such a thing as introspection; but it consists in an interpretation of phenomena presenting themselves as external percepts. We first see blue and red things. It is quite a discovery when we find the eye has anything to do with them, and a discovery still more recondite when we learn that there is an *ego* behind the eye, to which these qualities properly belong. Our logically initial data are percepts. Those percepts are undoubtedly purely psychical, altogether of the nature of thought. They involve three kinds of psychical elements: their qualities of feelings, their reaction against my will, and their generalizing or associating element. But all that we find out afterward. I see an inkstand on the table: that is a percept. Moving my head, I get a different percept of the inkstand. It coalesces with the other. What I call the inkstand is a generalized percept, a quasi-inference from percepts, perhaps I might say a composite photograph of percepts. In this psychical product is involved an element of resistance to me, which I am obscurely conscious of from the first.[9] Subsequently, when I accept the hypothesis of an inward subject for my thoughts, I yield to that consciousness of resistance and admit the inkstand to the standing of an external object. Still later, I may call this in question. But as soon as I do that, I find that the inkstand appears there in spite of me. If I turn away my eyes, other witnesses will tell me that it still remains. If we all leave the room and dismiss the matter from our thoughts, still a photographic camera would show the inkstand still there, with the same roundness, polish and transparency, and with the same opaque liquid within. Thus, or otherwise, I confirm myself in the opinion that its characters are what they are, and persist at every opportunity in revealing themselves, regardless of what you, or I, or any man, or generation of men, may think that they are.[10] That conclusion to which I find myself driven, struggle against it as I may, I briefly express by saying that the inkstand is a *real* thing. Of course, in being real and external, it does not in the least cease to be a purely psychical product, a generalized percept, like everything of which I can take any sort of cognizance.

It might not be a very serious error to say that the facts of science are sense-impressions, did it not lead to dire confusion upon other points. We see this in Chapter III,[11] in whose long meanderings through irrelevant subjects, in the endeavor to make out that there is no rational element in nature, and that the rational element of natural laws is imported into them by the minds of their discoverers, it would be impossible for the author to lose sight entirely of the bearing of the question which he himself has distinctly formulated, if he were not laboring with the confusing effects of his notion that the data of science are the sense-impressions. It does not occur to him that he is laboring to prove that the mind has a marvelous power of creating an element absolutely supernatural,—a power that would go far toward establishing a dualism quite antagonistic to the spirit of his philosophy. He evidently imagines that those who believe in the reality of law, or the rational element in nature, fail to apprehend that the data of science are of a psychical nature. He even devotes a section to proving that natural law does not belong to things-in-themselves, as if it were possible to find any philosopher who ever thought it did. Certainly, Kant, who first decked out philosophy with these chaste ornaments of things-in-themselves, was not of that opinion; nor could anybody well hold it after what he wrote. In point of fact, it is not Professor Pearson's opponents but he himself who has not thoroughly assimilated the truth that everything we can in any way take cognizance of is purely mental. This is betrayed in many little ways, as, for instance, when he makes his answer to the question, whether the law of gravitation ruled the motion of the planets before Newton was born, to turn upon the circumstance that the law of gravitation is a formula expressive of the motion of the planets "in terms of a purely mental conception," as if there could be a conception of anything not purely mental. Repeatedly, when he has proved the content of an idea to be mental, he seems to think he has proved its object to be of human origin. He goes to no end of trouble to prove, in various ways, what his opponent would have granted with the utmost cheerfulness at the outset, that laws of nature are rational; and, having got so far, he seems to think nothing more is requisite than to seize a logical maxim as a leaping pole and lightly skip to the conclusion that the laws of nature are of human provenance. If he had thoroughly accepted the truth that all realities, as well as all figments, are alike of purely mental composition, he would have seen that the question was, not whether natural law is of an intellectual nature or not, but whether it is of the number of those intellectual objects that are destined ultimately to be exploded from the spectacle of our universe, or whether, as far as we can judge, it has the stuff to stand its ground in spite of all attacks. In other words, is there anything that is really and truly a law of nature, or are all pretended laws of nature figments, in which latter case, all natural science is a delusion, and the writing of a grammar of science a very idle pastime?

Professor Pearson's theory of natural law is characterized by a singular vagueness and by a defect so glaring as to remind one of the second book of the *Novum Organum*[12] or of some strong chess-player whose attention has been so riveted upon a part of the board that a fatal danger has, as it were, been held upon the blind-spot of his mental retina. The manner in which the current of thought passes from the woods into the open plain and back again into the woods, over and over again, betrays the amount of labor that has been expended upon the chapter. The author calls attention to the sifting action both of our perceptive and of our reflective faculties. I think that I myself extracted from that vein of thought pretty much all that is valuable in reference to the regularity of nature in the *Popular Science Monthly* for June, 1878.[13] I there remarked that the degree to which nature seems to present a general regularity depends upon the fact that the regularities in it are of interest and importance to us, while the irregularities are without practical use or significance; and in the same article I endeavored to show that it is impossible to conceive of nature's being markedly less regular, taking it "by and large," than it actually is. But I am confident, from having repeatedly returned to that line of thought that it is impossible legitimately to deduce from any such considerations the unreality of natural law. "As a pure suggestion and nothing more," toward the end of the chapter, after his whole plea has been put in, Dr. Pearson brings forward the idea that a transcendental operation of the perceptive faculty may reject a mass of sensation altogether and arrange the rest in place and time, and that to this the laws in nature may be attributable,—a notion to which Kant undoubtedly leaned at one time. The mere emission of such a theory, after his argument has been fully set forth, almost amounts to a confession of failure to prove his proposition. Granting, by way of waiver, that such a theory is intelligible and is more than a nonsensical juxtaposition of terms, so far from helping Professor Pearson's contention at all, the acceptance of it would at once decide the case against him, as every student of the *Critic of the Pure Reason* will at once perceive. For the theory sets the rationality in nature upon a rock perfectly impregnable by you, me or any company of men.

Although that theory is only problematically put forth by Professor Pearson, yet at the very outset of his argumentation he insists upon the relativity of regularity to our faculties, as if that were in some way pertinent to the question. "Our law of tides," he says, "could have no meaning for a blind worm on the shore, for whom the moon had no existence."[14] Quite so; but would that truism in any manner help to prove that the moon was a figment and no reality? On the contrary, it could only help to show that there may be more things in heaven and earth than your philosophy has dreamed of.[15] Now the *moon*, on the one hand, and the *law of the tides*, on the other, stand in entirely analogous positions relatively to the remark, which can no more help to prove the unreality of the one than of the other. So, too, the final decisive stroke of the whole argumentation consists in urging substantially the same idea in the terrible shape of a syllogism, which the reader may examine in Section 11. I will make no comment upon it.

Professor Pearson's argumentation rests upon three legs. The first is the fact that both our perceptive and our reflective faculties reject part of what is presented to them, and "sort out" the rest. Upon that, I remark that our minds are not, and cannot be, positively mendacious. To suppose them so is to misunderstand what we all mean by truth and reality. Our eyes tell us that some things in nature are red and others blue; and so they really are. For the real world is the world of insistent generalized percepts. It is true that the best physical idea which we can at present fit to the real world, has nothing but longer and shorter waves to correspond to red and blue. But this is evidently owing to the acknowledged circumstance that the physical theory is to the last degree incomplete, if not to its being, no doubt, in some measure, errone-ous. For surely the completed theory will have to account for the extraordi-nary contrast between red and blue. In a word, it is the business of a physical theory to account for the percepts; and it would be absurd to accuse the per-cepts,—that is to say, the facts,—of mendacity because they do not square with the theory.

The second leg of the argumentation is that the mind projects its worked-over impressions into an object, and then projects into that object the com-parisons, etc., that are the results of its own work. I admit, of course, that errors and delusions are everyday phenomena, and hallucinations not rare. We have just three means at our command for detecting any unreality, that is, lack of insistency, in a notion. First, many ideas yield at once to a direct effort of the will. We call them *fancies*. Secondly, we can call in other witnesses, including ourselves under new conditions. Sometimes dialectic disputation will dispel an error. At any rate, it may be voted down so overwhelmingly as to convince even the person whom it affects. Thirdly, the last resort is prediction and experimentation. Note that these two are equally essential parts of this method, which Professor Pearson keeps,—I had almost said sedulously,—out of sight in his discussion of the rationality of nature. He only alludes to it when he comes to his transcendental "pure suggestion." Nothing is more notorious than that this method of prediction and experimentation has proved the master key to science; and yet, in Chapter IV,[16] Professor Pearson tries to persuade us that prediction is no part of science, which must only describe sense-impressions. (A sense-impression cannot be described.) He does not say that he would permit generalization of the facts. He ought not to do so, since generalization inevitably involves prediction.

The third leg of the argumentation is that human beings are so much alike that what one man perceives and infers, another man will be likely to perceive and infer. This is a recognized weakness of the second of the above methods. It is by no means sufficient to destroy that method, but along with other defects it does render resort to the third method imperative. When I see Dr. Pearson passing over without notice the first and third of the only three pos-sible ways of distinguishing whether the rationality of nature is real or not, and giving a lame excuse for reversing the verdict of the second, so that his decision seems to spring from antecedent predilection, I cannot recommend his procedure as affording such an exemplar of the logic of science as one might expect to find in a grammar of science.

An ignorant sailor on a desert island lights in some way upon the idea of the parallelogram of forces, and sets to work making experiments to see whether the actions of bodies conform to that formula. He finds that they do so, as nearly as he can observe, in many trials invariably. He wonders why inanimate things should thus conform to a widely general intellectual formula. Just then, a disciple of Professor Pearson lands on the island and the sailor asks him what he thinks about it. "It is very simple," says the disciple, "you see you made the formula and then you projected it into the phenomena." *Sailor:* What are the phenomena? *Pearsonist:* The motions of the stones you experimented with. *Sailor:* But I could not tell until afterward whether the stones had acted according to the rule or not. *Pearsonist:* That makes no difference. You made the rule by looking at some stones, and all stones are alike. *Sailor:* But those I used were very unlike, and I want to know what made them all move exactly according to one rule. *Pearsonist:* Well, maybe your mind is not in time, and so you made all the things behave the same way at all times. Mind, I don't say it is so; but it may be. *Sailor:* Is that all you know about it? Why not say the stones are made to move as they do by something *like* my mind?

When the disciple gets home, he consults Dr. Pearson. "Why," says Dr. Pearson, "you must not deny that the facts are really concatenated; only there is no rationality about that." "Dear me," says the disciple, "then there really is a concatenation that makes all the component accelerations of all the bodies scattered through space conform to the formula that Newton, or Lami, or Varignon invented?" "Well, the formula is the device of one of those men, and it conforms to the facts." "To the facts its inventor knew, and also to those he only predicted?" "As for prediction, it is unscientific business." "Still the prediction and the facts predicted agree." "Yes." "Then," says the disciple, "it appears to me that there really is in nature something extremely like action in conformity with a highly general intellectual principle." "Perhaps so," I suppose Dr. Pearson would say, "but nothing in the least like rationality." "Oh," says the disciple, "I thought rationality was conformity to a widely general principle."

7

Laws of Nature

MS and TS from the Smithsonian Institution Library (doc. 3804.10).
[Published in Philip P. Wiener's Charles S. Peirce: Selected Writings,
pp. 289–321. From a longer paper, "Hume on Miracles and Laws of Na-
ture," and eventually retitled "The Laws of Nature and Hume's Argu-
ment against Miracles," written at the end of May 1901 at the invitation
of Samuel P. Langley, Secretary of the Smithsonian Institution. After
many revisions, Langley declined to publish it.] Peirce aims here to explain
to non-specialists what laws of nature are and how they have been con-
ceived—his foil being the nominalist conception typical of Hume's thought
and of modern empiricism. Every genuine law of nature is an objective
generalization from observations and must support verifiable predictions
about future observations. Subjective generalizations put forward as laws
of nature cannot pass the test of predictability. In explaining how predict-
ability is possible, Peirce introduces a theme that will come to dominate his
later thought: "Must we not say that . . . there is an energizing reason-
ableness that shapes phenomena in some sense, and that this same working
reasonableness has molded the reason of man into something like its own
image?" Peirce points out that his evolutionary conception of law is that of
the scientific man, claiming that the reliability of laws of nature leads sci-
entists to accept them as facts, "almost to be called [things] of power," al-
though with the caveat that any such law might be falsified.

I. What is a Law of Nature?

This phrase is used by physicists pretty vaguely and capriciously, in several respects. It is felt to be particularly appropriate as the designation of a physical truth of a widely general kind, exact in its definition, and found to be true without exception, to a high degree of precision. Yet there are truths of this description to which the title is refused; while others, special, rough in their statement, merely approximate in their truth, even subject to out-and-out exceptions, are nevertheless, so called.

But there are two common characters of all the truths called laws of nature. The first of these characters is that every such law is a generalization from a collection of results of observations *gathered* upon the principle that the observing was done so well as to conform to outward conditions; but not *selected* with any regard to what the results themselves were found to be;—a harvest or a gleaning of the fruit of known seed, not culled or select, but fairly representative.

The second character is that a law of nature is neither a mere chance coincidence among the observations on which it has been based, nor is it a subjective generalization, but is of such a nature that from it can be drawn an endless series of prophecies, or predictions, respecting other observations not among those on which the law was based; and experiment shall verify those prophecies, though perhaps not absolutely (which would be the ideal of a law of nature), yet in the main. Nor is a proposition termed a "law of nature" until its predictive power has been tried and proved so thoroughly that no real doubt of it remains. But the expression "subjective generalization" calls for explanation. Augustus De Morgan very simply demonstrated[1] that, taking any selection of observations whatever, propositions without number can always be found which shall be strictly true of all those observations (and it may be added that they may be propositions not going beyond the matter of the observations), and yet no one of them [is] likely to be true of any other observations which the same principle of selection might add to the collection. Such a generalization, a mere fabrication of ingenuity, which I term a subjective generalization, is often proposed by an amateur in science as an induction. "Bode's law" was a subjective generalization.[2] Let the artificers of such false inductions dare to set up predictions upon them, and the first blast of nature's verity will bring them down, houses of cards that they are.

So then, I do not think a better definition of a *law of nature* can be given than this: it is a prognostic generalization of observations.

This said, the question is instantly started, How can the reason of a man attain to prognosis?

How shall we answer? Must we not say that the fact that he can so attain proves that there is an energizing reasonableness that shapes phenomena in some sense, and that this same working reasonableness has moulded the reason of man into something like its own image? These questions must remain for the reader to decide to his own satisfaction.

II. *What conception of a Law of Nature was entertained in England in Hume's day, not by those who wrote upon the subject, but by the silent mass of educated men?*

In Hume's day, more than at other times, the great mass of educated Englishmen were grossly "practical." They did not waste thought upon anything not pretty directly concerning their own comfort, security, or amusement. They went to church, because doing so set a good example to the people, and so tended to maintain the supremacy of the upper classes. That was commonly regarded among university graduates as the chief function of the church; and consequently, anything that tended to weaken the church awoke in such men horror and dread.*

The small remainder who really had any philosophical opinions, and yet did not write, were divided among three different ways of thinking. The Scotistic opinion, which had ruled the universities before the Reformation, had,

*For a picture of Oxford in 1721, see Amhurst's *Terrae Filius*.[3]

in Hume's day, quite disappeared. That opinion, it is necessary to remember, had been that, in addition to Actual Existence, there are various modes of Imperfect Being, all of them varieties of Being *in futuro*,—which we talk of when we say that "Christmas *really is* coming";—and in one of those modes of being, it was held that there really was something, which we of today should call a "law of nature," but which in the Latin language is simply a "nature"; and the Being *in futuro* of this law of nature was held to *consist in* this, that future events would conform to it. The theoretical element in that opinion lay precisely in the supposition that that which the ordinary course of things is bound (if not hindered) to bring about, already has a Germinal Being. That was no scholastic invention: it was the very heart of Aristotle's philosophy. But in Hume's day, nobody any longer believed in any such thing as that.

The oldest opinion rife at that time was that of the Ockhamists, which was developed in the first half of the fourteenth century, and has had a very strong following in England from that day even to our own, without yet betraying any great signs of enfeeblement. This opinion is that there is but one mode of Being, that of individual objects or facts; and that this is sufficient to explain everything, provided it be borne in mind that among such objects are included *signs*, that among signs there are *general* signs, i.e., signs applicable each to more than a single object, and that among such general signs are included the different individual *conceptions* of the mind. This theory opens a labyrinthine controversy, full of pitfalls, which ninety-nine readers out of every hundred lack the patience to thread to the last; so that they finally leap the hedge and decide the question according to their personal predilections. I will simply aver, from having analyzed the whole argument, that the Ockhamists are forced to say of a law of nature that it is a similarity between phenomena, which similarity consists in the fact that somebody *thinks* the phenomena similar. But when they are asked why *future* phenomena conform to the law, they are apt to evade the question as long as they can. Held to it, they have their choice between three replies.

The reply which the stricter Ockhamists usually give is that the conformity of future observations to inductive predictions is an "ultimate fact." They mostly endeavor to generalize this reply, so that, as they phrase it, it is the "uniformity of nature," or something of the sort, that is the ultimate fact. Such a generalization is inherently vague; and besides, a general fact has, for them, no being at all except as somebody's thought about its particulars; so that there seems to be no inaccuracy in saying that they make each fulfillment of a prognostication an "ultimate," that is to say, an utterly inexplicable, fact. But they cannot, and do not, maintain that the fulfillment of the prophecy is *self-evidently* an ultimate fact. Indeed, the Ockhamists are justly very chary of admitting "self-evidence." No, they admit that the "ultimacy" of the prognostication is their *theory* of it. But at this point, Logic puts in a demurrer. For the only possible logical justification that a theory can have, must be that it furnishes a rational explanation of the relation between the observed facts; while to say that a relation between observations is an "ultimate fact" is nothing more than another way of saying that it is *not susceptible* of rational explanation. That, one would think, ought to put this first answer out of court, at once.

There remain two other possible answers, though neither is much in the Ockhamistic taste. To the question how true prognostication was possible, an answer sometimes given in Hume's time was that it was rendered so "by the courteous revelations of spirits." If these were finite spirits, as some of the Cambridge men thought, one does not see how they could prognosticate better than their superior, redeemed man.

Finally, a quite common answer was that prognostications come true because God chooses so to govern the universe that they may come true. I term this style of explanation, that things happen as they do because God chooses that they shall so happen, "explanation *à la turque.*" It is a right handy contrivance for explaining all past, present, and future phenomena, without stirring from one's sofa, in one brief sentence which no monotheist can deny. Some may think it a disadvantage in this theory that it refuses to lend itself to any definite prediction, for all its making of prediction such a simple matter. But then, it so escapes all danger of refutation. Ockhamists do not commonly attach much importance to prediction, anyway, and often seem to hate to hear it talked about.

Under the head of Ockhamists, I mean to include, first, Hobbes, more extreme than Ockham himself; then Berkeley, Hume, the Mills, etc.; then Locke and many others less decidedly of this turn of thought. But the truth is that all modern philosophy is more or less tainted with this malady.

Another philosophy which had some currency in England in Hume's time was the theory of a "plastic nature," that is to say, a slightly intelligent agent, intermediate between the Creator and the universe, God's factotum, which attended to the ordinary routine of administration of the universe.[4] This theory was so much out of date that I should not have mentioned it were it not that I suspect it aided considerably in bringing into vogue the phrase "law of nature" in England, an expression which the sectaries of the plastic nature might very naturally, and in fact early did, employ. One of them, for example, Lord Brooke, in a work published in 1633, but "written in his youth and familiar exercise with Sir Philip Sidney," has the following:[5]

> And where the progresse was to finde the cause
> First by effects out, now her regresse should
> Forme Art directly under *Natures Lawes*,
> And all effects so in their causes mould
> > As fraile Man lively, without Schoole of smart,
> > Might see Successes comming in an Art.

Here, "Nature's laws" are nothing but prognostic generalizations of observations. However, a stray poetical example does not argue much.

Another philosophy, famous even in England, was that of Descartes, who made all connections between events to be due solely to the direct intervention of the Deity. In short, he held the explanation *à la turque* to be the only true one. It followed that if we can attain any prognoses, this is because the Deity has chosen somehow to make the order of events in some measure comprehensible to us. But the conclusion which Descartes *held* to be deducible, for he it was who set that fashion of loose reasoning to which all subsequent metaphysicians have so religiously conformed, went a good deal further; for from the bare thought "I think, and so I exist," he professed to demonstrate that whatever appears to us clear and distinct must be true;—another of those modern conveniences by which Descartes rendered philosophizing so reposeful! Meantime, one might expect that Descartes's opinion would lead to his calling prognostic generalizations of observations by the name of "laws of nature"; and so, accordingly we read, in his *Principia Philosophiae*, published in 1644: "Moreover, from this same immutability of God, certain rules, or Laws of Nature, can be known, which are the secondary and particular causes of the different movements which we observe in bodies."* It will be observed that Descartes does not acknowledge that his laws of nature are generalizations from experience, although they are prognostic. He was as extreme in attributing almost the whole achievement of science to the light of reason as the Ockhamists are in altogether denying it any part in that achievement.

The branch of philosophy in which the Britain of Hume's time really takes a distinguished place was ethics. The great light at the time Hume's argument was published was Hutcheson.[6] Hume considered his own greatest work to be his *Principles of Morals* (1751), which merely modified Hutcheson's doctrine. The book which reading Englishmen were talking most about when Hume's argument appeared was Wollaston's *Religion of Nature*.[7] It had gone, I believe, through seven editions. Its main doctrine was that all vice is, at bottom, lying; and the one virtue, truthfulness. But as far as I am aware, there is little in all that literature to illuminate the problem we have before us.

In asking what speculations were passing in the minds of men who lived near two centuries ago, and never set pen to paper, I found myself before a pretty enigma. Still, having made my little research (all too hasty, I confess), I ought, at least, to know more about the matter than the average man. Now, however, I have to take up a question where I can only rely on personal observation within an area of acquaintance very likely no wider than my reader's,—perhaps less so. The question lies across my path, however, not to be avoided. I must briefly consider it.

---

*Atque ex eadem immutabilitate Dei, regulae quaedam, sive leges naturae cognosci possunt, quae sunt causae secundariae et particulares diversorum motuum, quos in singulis corporibus advertimus. Pars II, xxxvii.

III. What conception of laws of nature is entertained today by the generality of educated men?

I should say, most commonly, the same Ockhamistic conception which was commonest in Hume's time; for most men whom I meet, when they refer to such matters, talk the language of Mill's *Logic*. In particular, the explanation of prognosis most common is that it is rendered possible by the uniformity of nature, which is an "ultimate fact." This adapts itself well to the atheistic opinion which has always been common among Ockhamists,—more so, perhaps, about 1870 than at any other time.

Today, the idea uppermost in most minds is Evolution. In their genuine nature, no two things could be more hostile than the idea of evolution and that individualism upon which Ockham erected his philosophy. But this hostility has not yet made itself obvious; so that the lion cub and the lamb still lie down together in one mind, until a certain one of them shall have become more mature. Whatever in the philosophies of our day (as far as we need consider them) is not Ockhamism is evolutionism of one kind or another; and every evolutionism must in its evolution eventually restore that rejected idea of law as a reasonableness energizing in the world (no matter through what mechanism of natural selection or otherwise) which belonged to the essentially evolutionary metaphysics of Aristotle, as well as to the scholastic modifications of it by Aquinas and Scotus.* To this wing of philosophy belongs,

---

*The acute reader (and it has become known to me that the Smithsonian Reports number among their readers men who, though they be children in scientific methods, yet surpass the average of the great scientists in the precision and vigor of their thought) will ask what I mean by a "reasonableness energizing in the world." I do not define the reasonable as that which accords with men's natural ways of thinking, when corrected by careful consideration; although it is a *fact* that men's natural ways of thinking are more or less reasonable. I had best explain myself by degrees. By reasonableness, I mean, in the first place, such unity as reason apprehends,—say, generality. "Humph! By generality I suppose you mean that different events resemble one another." Not quite: let me distinguish. The green shade over my lamp, the foliage I see through the window, the emerald on my companion's finger, have a resemblance. It consists in an impression I get on comparing those and other things, and exists by virtue of their being as they are. But if a man's whole life is animated by a desire to become rich, there is a general character in all his actions, which is not caused by, but is formative of, his behavior. "Do you mean then that there is a purpose in nature?" I am not insisting that it is a purpose; but it is the law that shapes the event, not a chance resemblance between the events that constitutes the law. "But are you so ignorant as not to know that generality only belongs to the figments of the mind?" That would seem to be my condition. If you will have it that generality takes its origin in mind alone, that is beside the question. But if things can only be *understood* as generalized, generalized they really and truly *are*; for no idea can be attached to a reality essentially incognizable. However, Generality, as commonly understood is not the whole of my "reasonableness." It includes *Continuity*, of which indeed, Generality is but a cruder form. Nor is this all. We refuse to call a design reasonable unless it be feasible. There are certain ideas which have a character which our reason can in some measure appreciate but which it by no means creates, which character insures their sooner or later getting realized. What machinery may be requisite for this I do not now ask. But the laws of nature have, I suppose, been brought about in some way; and if so, it would seem that they were of such a nature as inevitably to realize themselves. These, then, are the naked abstract characters that must be recognized in the "reasonableness"

too, that theory of Gassendi which the present writer endeavored, a few years ago, to reawaken (in a perfected form),[8] and of which, for the sake of the evolutionary conception of law which it illustrates, may here be inserted a description by an opponent of it, which was published in 1678:

> But because men may yet be puzzled with the universality and constancy of this regularity, and its long continuance through so many ages, that there are no records at all of the contrary any where to be found; the atomic Atheist further adds, that the senseless atoms, playing and toying up and down, without any care or thought, and from eternity trying all manner of tricks, conclusions and experiments, were at length (they know not how) taught, and by the necessity of things themselves, as it were, driven, to a certain kind of trade of artificialness and methodicalness; so that though their motions were at first all casual and fortuitous, yet in length of time they became orderly and artificial, and governed by a certain *law*, they contracting as it were upon themselves, by long practice and experience, a kind of habit of moving regularly (Cudworth's *True Intellectual System of the Universe*).[9]

IV. What is the conception of law entertained today by typical scientific men?

It does not belong to the function of a scientific man to ascertain the metaphysical essence of laws of nature. On the contrary, that task calls for talents widely different from those which he requires. Still, the metaphysician's account of law ought to be in harmony with the practice of the scientific man in discovering the laws; and in the mind of the typical scientific man, untroubled by dabbling with metaphysical theories, there will grow up a notion of law rooted in his own practice.

The scientific man finds himself confronted by phenomena which he seeks to generalize or to explain. His first attempts to do this, though they will be suggested by the phenomena, can yet, after all, be reckoned but mere conjectures; albeit, unless there be something like inspiration in them, he never could make a successful step. Of those conjectures,—to make a long matter short,—he selects one to be tested. In this choice, he ought to be governed solely by considerations of economy. If, for example, the prospect is that a good many hypotheses to account for any one set of facts, will probably have to be taken up and rejected in succession, and if it so happens that, among these hypotheses, one that is unlikely to be true can probably be disposed of by a single easy experiment, it may be excellent economy to begin by taking up that. In this part of his work, the scientist can learn something from the businessman's wisdom. At last, however, a hypothesis will have been provisionally adopted, on probation; and now, the effort ought to be to search out the most unlikely necessary consequence of it that can be thought of, and that

---

of a law of nature. Whether or no it be a legitimate presumption from those characters that nature has an intelligent author, I certainly do not see how the abstraction could, better than in that statement, be clothed in the concrete forms which many minds require, or how they could better be connected with appropriate sentiments.

is among those that are readily capable of being brought to the test of experiment. The experiment is made. If the prediction from the hypothesis fails, its failure may be so utter as to be conclusive; or, maybe, nothing more than an alteration of the defective theory need be undertaken. If, notwithstanding its unlikelihood, the prediction be verified, and if the same thing happen again and again, although each time the most unlikely of the (convenient) predictions has been tried, one begins to doff one's cap to the rising star that nature herself seems to favor.

The scientific man certainly looks upon a law, if it really *be* a law, as a matter of fact as objective as fact can be. The only way in which, to the scientist's apprehension, a newly recognized law differs from a fact directly observed is, that he is, perhaps, not quite sure that it *is* a law. Ultimately, the law becomes for him much *more* reliable than any single observation. It now begins to stand before the scientific man, the hardest of hard facts, by no means a fabrication of his,—his exhumation rather,—almost to be called a thing of power; although, even now, it might conceivably be brought to naught by a sufficient array of new observations; and, indeed, the presumption is that the time will come when it will have to be reformed, or perhaps even superseded.

8

On the Logic of Drawing History from Ancient Documents, Especially from Testimonies

MS 690. [Published in CP 7.164–231 and HP 2:705–62. Only the first half of the document is printed here. It was written in October and November 1901, with the financial support of Francis Lathrop, whose secretary had the manuscript typed. Peirce made a number of revisions in the typescript, and the present text, transcribed from the manuscript, incorporates those revisions.] In this monograph, Peirce argues that even though Hume's method of balancing the veracity of a witness against the improbability of his narrative may be defended in certain cases, it is not generally applicable and is rarely used by historians. The probabilities generally relied on by historians are subjective— "mere expressions of their preconceived notions"—and are completely unreliable. Peirce claims that what is needed for scientific history is a method that does not turn on either estimates of probability or degrees of belief. He recommends the general method of experimental science. Peirce gives a sustained discussion of the logic of science, outlining many nuances of the different kinds of reasoning, including two types of deduction (corollarial and theorematic) and three types of induction. Peirce gives a detailed account of the economic and other factors that must be brought to bear on the selection of historical hypotheses.

Ancient history is drawn partly from documents and partly from monuments. The last generation has afforded so many examples of the refutation by archeology of the conclusions of the critics of documents as to suggest the question whether the whole logical procedure of the latter class of students has not been radically wrong. The purpose of the present paper is to show that this is the case; that the logical theory upon which the critics proceed is as bad as logic can be; to set forth and defend the true logical method of treating ancient historical documents; and to set this new theory in a clear light by applying it to two or three examples, including a case where the testimonies are comparatively strong and another where the testimony is at best very feeble.[1]

The theory of the logic of testimony which forms the basis of the procedure of historical critics today is, I suppose, old. But it can only have taken a distinct form when the doctrine of probabilities was developed in the early years of the eighteenth century. A popular statement of it was, I believe, first given by Hume, in his essay on miracles, in 1748.[2] Hume's statement is, mathematically considered, excessively crude. It seems evident that he had been reading either De Moivre's *Doctrine of Chances* (first edition, 1718; second enlarged edition, 1738) or De Montmort's *Essai d'analyse sur les jeux de hazard* (1708; second edition, 1713). For Jacob Bernoulli's posthumous *Ars conjectandi* (1713) would have been beyond him.[3] Whatever work he read he did not understand. Yet in a confused and untenable form, he put forth ideas of his own of considerable value. I may restate Hume's doctrine, correcting such errors as are not inseparable from it, as follows. When a reputable witness makes, or witnesses make, an assertion which experience renders highly improbable, or when there are other independent arguments in its favor, each independent argument *pro* or *con* produces a certain impression upon the mind of the wise man, dependent for its quantity upon the frequency with which arguments of those kinds lead to the truth, and the algebraical sum of these impressions is the resultant impression that measures the wise man's state of opinion on the whole. For example, if there are a number of independent arguments, *pro*, such that, in general, such arguments lead to the truth, p_1 times, p_2 times, p_3 times, etc., respectively, for every q_1 times, q_2 times, q_3 times, etc., that they lead to error; and if there are arguments *con*, which lead to the truth q_5 times, q_6 times, q_7 times, etc., for every p_5 times, p_6 times, p_7 times, etc., that they lead to error, then the probability that the arguments *pro* all lead to the truth, and the arguments *con* all lead to error will be

$$\frac{p_1}{p_1+q_1} \cdot \frac{p_2}{p_2+q_2} \cdot \frac{p_3}{p_3+q_3} \cdot \text{etc.} \times \frac{p_5}{p_5+q_5} \cdot \frac{p_6}{p_6+q_6} \cdot \frac{p_7}{p_7+q_7} \cdot \text{etc.}$$

and the probability that all the arguments *pro* lead to error while all the arguments *con* lead to truth, will be

$$\frac{q_1}{p_1+q_1} \cdot \frac{q_2}{p_2+q_2} \cdot \frac{q_3}{p_3+q_3} \cdot \text{etc.} \times \frac{q_5}{p_5+q_5} \cdot \frac{q_6}{p_6+q_6} \cdot \frac{q_7}{p_7+q_7} \cdot \text{etc.}$$

But one or other of these two alternatives must be the case; so that the *odds* or ratio of favorable to unfavorable probability, on the whole is simply

$$\frac{p_1 \cdot p_2 \cdot p_3 \cdot \text{etc.} \cdot p_5 \cdot p_6 \cdot p_7 \cdot \text{etc.}}{q_1 \cdot q_2 \cdot q_3 \cdot \text{etc.} \cdot q_5 \cdot q_6 \cdot q_7 \cdot \text{etc.}}.$$

Now if we suppose that the impression made on the mind of the wise man is proportional to the logarithm of the *odds* as its exciting cause, then the total impression will be

$$\log\!\left(\frac{p_1}{q_1}\cdot\frac{p_2}{q_2}\cdot\frac{p_3}{q_3}\cdot\text{etc.}\times\frac{p_5}{q_5}\cdot\frac{p_6}{q_6}\cdot\frac{p_7}{q_7}\cdot\text{etc.}\right)$$

$$=\log\frac{p_1}{q_1}+\log\frac{p_2}{q_2}+\log\frac{p_3}{q_3}+\text{etc.}+\log\frac{p_5}{q_5}+\log\frac{p_6}{q_6}+\log\frac{p_7}{q_7}+\text{etc.}$$

This is *Hume's Theory Improved*, by merely being disembarrassed of blunders. If we strip the mathematics from it, we have the simple *theory of balancing likelihoods*, which is the theory that Hume undertook to elaborate and to render scientific. It really hardly differs from *Hume's Theory Improved* except in its vagueness. At any rate, it involves the notion that the different arguments have likelihoods, that they are quantities upon an algebraical scale, and that they are to be combined as independent summands.

Now the practice of those modern German critics of ancient history whose works I have read,[4] particularly those who treat of the history of philosophy, and whose methods are generally extolled, is based upon the theory of balancing likelihoods. In so far as their general logical method departs from that of Hume, it is only less refined. The principal difference between Hume and them is that the word "Proof" is continually in their mouths, a word which Hume scrupulously avoided in speaking of the minor facts of ancient history. He recognized the question as purely one of probabilities. They seem to be discontented with mere probability; and are always in search of an argument that something "must" be. The necessity which enters into the conclusion of such an argument as part of its subject matter is confounded by them with the necessity of a mathematical demonstration, in the conclusion of which the word "must" does not frequently occur. Now since it happens ten times that we can argue that testimony *must* be false to every once that we can argue that it *must* be true, it naturally follows, and is a fact, that these critics show far greater favor to views which reject all the historical evidence in our possession than they do to views which are based on some part of the evidence. "That, however, is not *proved*," is their usual comment upon any such hypothesis. Another particular in which they depart from Hume is in applying to history generally the canon of Bentley concerning the criticism of texts, that, in general, the more difficult reading is to be preferred.[5] In like manner, they hold that that narrative which was least likely to be invented, owing to its improbability, is to be preferred. They are thus provided with two defenses against historical testimony. If the story told appears to them in any degree unlikely, they reject it without scruple; while if there is no taint of improbability in it, it will fall under the heavier accusation of being too probable; and in this way, they preserve a noble freedom in manufacturing history to suit their subjective impressions.

I now propose to show some weighty reasons for holding that the theory of balancing likelihoods, however it may be worked out, and though there are, undoubtedly, special cases where it ought to be followed, is nevertheless, as a general method of treating ancient documents, a bad one. In cases where objective and somewhat definite probabilities can be attributed to all the different arguments on both sides, and where they are, as arguments, independent of one another, it seems to be incontestable that Hume's method improved is sound. [. . .][6]

Thus, when the essential conditions are fulfilled, this method is perfectly correct. Nor is it requisite that they should be fulfilled with any exactitude. A rough approximation is sufficient to give the conclusion some value. But the further from fulfillment the conditions are, the further from any scientific value is the conclusion; and with sufficient time and space I would undertake to show that, in reference to ancient history, they are, in a large majority of those cases in which there is any room for two opinions, so far from fulfillment, that it not only becomes utter nonsense to talk of "proof" and "perfect demonstration,"—phrases perpetually in the mouths of the critics,—but, were there no better way of investigation, this method, taken as the general and regular method of treating questions of ancient history, must sink it in all its details to the rank of idle surmise. In this paper, however, I shall only give an outline of what this argument would be, because it is here not my principal object to refute the method now prevalent, but to expound a different logical theory, and to show what method of study results from it.

Let it be clearly understood, then, that what I attack is the method of deciding questions of fact by weighing, that is by algebraically adding, the feelings of approval produced in the mind by the different testimonies and other arguments pertinent to the case. I acknowledge that this method is supported, under abstract conditions, by the doctrine of chances, and that there are cases in which it is useful. But I maintain that those conditions are not often even roughly fulfilled in questions of ancient history; so that in those investigations it commonly has no value worth consideration.

Let us first make sure that we take proper account of everything that can be urged in favor of the method. Now, as far as I am aware, beyond its foundation in the doctrine of chances,—the argument which was stated with such consummate skill by Hume,—there are only two things to be said in favor of this method.

The first is that every science must develop its own method out of the natural reason of man; and that is the very way in which this method has been developed. Balancing reasons *pro* and *con* is the natural procedure of every man. No man can avoid doing so continually; and if he could, he would only have trained himself to the observance of rules having no foundation in reason. For reason is nothing but man's natural way of thinking, carefully and consistently observed.

The remaining argument in favor of this method is that the only alternatives are that of using this method and that of swallowing uncriticized all the incredible tales with which ancient history abounds.

This last argument need not detain us; because I shall in this paper develop a different method, which, instead *[of]* being less critical than that of balancing likelihoods, is much more so. But I repeat that I do not maintain that the ordinary method is never to be employed, but that its use should be restricted to exceptional cases, instead of being made the regular and standard procedure.

Now as to this method's being natural, I admit that there is some foundation for that. There is no kind of fallacious reasoning to which mankind is liable for which as much as that might not be said. But I appeal to modern psychologists to support me in the assertion that it is not at all natural for men to employ this method as a usual procedure. On the contrary, the natural thing is to believe anything that one may hear said, until it is found that that assumption leads to difficulties; and when it is found to lead to difficulties, the most natural impulse is to make further inquiries, to cross-examine, etc. The occasions when we naturally balance reasons *pro* and *con* mostly relate to what we prefer to do, not to questions of fact. But, in the next place, I demur to the principle that what is natural is necessarily reasonable. It is one of the consequences of German preeminence in science and philosophy, which I hope will not last much longer, that subjective ways of deciding questions are, at this time, far too highly esteemed. Logic itself is made a pure question of feeling by Sigwart, whose treatise is now more in vogue than any other.[7] The Anglo-Saxon mind will never assent to that. I am sorry to say that it has been only too true that, under the German lead, the methods of reasoning in the different branches of science and philosophy have been left to grow up pretty much as they naturally would; and sooner or later, no doubt, natural tendencies do bring them right; but that result would be brought about much more quickly if methods were subjected to a more continual and strict criticism from exact logic; and what I mean by this, I must hope that this very paper may illustrate.

Passing now to the objections to the method of balancing likelihoods in the study of ancient history, the most obvious, perhaps, although not the most important, is that the different testimonies and other arguments are not commonly even in a rough sense independent, as the only rational basis for the method requires that they should be. Circumstantial evidences are, no doubt, often sufficiently independent; but direct testimony seldom is so. The same circumstances which lead one witness into error are likely to operate to deceive another. Nor does this want of independence always lead them into agreement. It may, frequently, be the cause of disagreement. Conflict of testimony in the vast majority of cases is *not* principally a mere chance result, as the theory supposes it to be. That concordance of testimony commonly has some other cause than its mere tendency to truth, is too obvious to need saying. The method of balancing likelihoods not only supposes that the testimonies are independent but also that each of them is independent of the antecedent probability of the story; and since it is far more difficult to make allowance for a violation of this requirement than of that of the independence of the testimonies, it becomes a much more serious matter. But how very remote from the real state of things it is to suppose that the narration of an ancient event is independent of the likelihood of the story told! Roughly speaking, it may be said that all detached stories of Greece and Rome were told chiefly because the writer had something marvellous to recount; so that we may almost say that ancient history is simply the narrative of all the unlikely events that happened during the centuries it covers. It is evident that this circumstance in itself almost destroys the legitimate weight of any argument from the antecedent improbability, unless that improbability is so great as to render the story absolutely incredible. Examples are useful at this point. It is well known that three ancient authorities[8] give the story that Pythagoras had a golden thigh; and the custom of modern critics is simply to pass it by, hardly mentioned. Now had any historian asserted that the thigh of Pythagoras was of metallic gold to the center while his lower leg and foot were solid flesh, that would unquestionably have been a case in which the method under consideration might very properly have been employed to reject the testimony. I may mention, however, that one of the authorities affords an illustration of the opposite kind of influence of antecedent probability upon the matter of testimony. For when Diogenes Laertius softens the story as he does,[9] it is, in my opinion, in order to avoid extreme improbability. As another example, let us take a story the extreme improbability of which has caused almost, if not quite, every modern critic to overrule the testimony of a baker's dozen of the greatest authorities that antiquity can boast.[10] This story is that the mathematician Thales once stumbled and fell into a ditch while he was showing an old woman the constellations. Zeller, one of the few modern writers who so much as condescends to show reasons for almost giving Aristotle, Plato, Cicero, and all the rest the lie, says that it is utterly incredible that Thales should have been such an impracticable theorist.[11] Considering that pretty much all we know about the personality of Thales is that the Greeks considered him as the first of the wise men, and that eccentricity was, according to the Greek conception, essential to the character of a philosopher, that reason of Zeller's shows a wonderful depth of psychological insight. Of all the modern mathematicians whom I have known, there have been perhaps not over one in five, of whom I should not hesitate to believe such a thing. But I should like to know how the story ever came to be so generally stated, both by ancient writers, and by all modern writers until the days of modern criticism, if it is not that the whole thing, both Thales stumbling and /the/ old woman's and Zeller's contempt for him for doing so, is too richly true to human nature. If it is not historical, it must surely have been its extreme antecedent likelihood which caused so many authorities to assert that it was true. Many more examples are needed in order to show how very far ancient testimony is from being independent of the antecedent probability of its matter. But I leave this point, in order to hasten to another which is more important.

The theory of probabilities has been called the logic of the modern exact sciences; and it is known to be the basis of the vast business of insurance; and therefore when a literary man learns that the method which he has been pursuing has the sanction of such a great mathematical doctrine, he begins to feel that he is a very scientific person. I notice that this sense of personal scientificality is far more developed in men who write second-hand commentaries on ancient authors than it is in the Faradays, the Helmholtzes, and the Mendeléefs. It is, therefore, well to point out to such persons that the word *probability*, taken in the sense in which the insurance business uses it, means a well-founded statistical generalization. Nor are probabilities assumed in the exact sciences without either a statistical basis or else a thoroughly criticized assurance that no serious error can result. But if by "probability" be meant the degree to which a hypothesis in regard to what happened in ancient Greece recommends itself to a professor in a German university town, then there is no mathematical theory of probabilities which will withstand the artillery of modern mathematical criticism. A probability, in that sense, is nothing but the degree to which a hypothesis accords with one's preconceived notions; and its value depends entirely upon how those notions have been formed, and upon how much objectivity they can lay a solid claim to. If a man brings me a collection of sphygmograph tracings accompanied with notes of the circumstances under which they were taken, and tells me that he thinks they prove that the pulse of a man is affected by the mental state of another man on the other side of a brick wall, I confess that his hypothesis is so contrary to my preconceived notions that I shall not easily be persuaded to interrupt my work to make a study of the case. But those preconceived notions I hold to have a far more solid basis than those which ordinarily influence historical critics to pronounce an ancient narrative improbable. Yet even so, it is only my practical conduct which I allow to be influenced by that improbability. My action has to be decided, one way or the other, and without loss of time; and "rough and ready" is unavoidably the character of the majority of practical decisions. But were I once to undertake the study of the sphygmograph tracings, I would endeavor to get to the bottom of the question, without reference to my preconceived notions. For preconceived notions are only a fit basis for applications of science, not for science itself.

Thus everything that is put into one pan of the balance in weighing historical probabilities is utterly uncertain. Yet, if possible, what goes into the other pan is worse still. This consists of the "credibilities" of the testimonies. The inappropriateness of the application of the conception of probability here is striking. In playing a game, say with dice, there is this good reason for the calculation of chances, that any one face turns up as often as any other, quite independently of the result of any other throw, and the cause of the die turning up any particular face at any particular throw is quite beyond our powers of analysis. It is probably due to the combination of many little influences. In like manner, in insurance, though the cause of any one man's death might be ascertained, yet that would have no relation to the purposes of insurance, and why it is that out of a thousand men insured at the age of thirty, just so many will die each year afterward, is a question not to be answered, except that it is due to the cooperation of many causes. It is this which makes the calculation of chances appropriate. So, in making astronomical observations, why it is that out of a thousand observations, just so many will have just such an amount of error, can only be answered by saying that it is due to the summation of many small effects. But now on the other hand, take a question of history. We do not care to know how many times a witness would report a given fact correctly, because he reports that fact but once. If he misstates the matter, there is no cooperation of myriad causes. It is, on the contrary, due to some one cause which, if it cannot often be ascertained with certainty, can at any rate be very plausibly guessed in most cases, if the circumstances are closely inquired into; and it is most pertinent to the business of the historical critic to consider how a mistake, if mistake there be, might credibly have arisen. A mere general ratio of true statements to false would be utterly insufficient for his purpose, even if it really existed. But it does not exist. In the case of the die, we know that one throw in every six will bring up an ace in the future as it has done in the past; and so it is with insurance, and with the errors of observations. However complex the causes, that simple law *will be* followed, we are sure. But nothing of the kind is true in the case of a witness. His new statements, if he makes any, will necessarily relate to different topics from his old ones, which he has exhausted; and his personal relation to them will be different. There is, therefore, no arguing from what his credibility was in one case, to what it will be in another, as there would be if the error were a sum due to the recurrence of myriad small effects. There thus neither is any such quantity as a real, general, and predictive truthfulness of a witness; nor if there were, would it answer the purposes of the historian to deal with it. For he does not want to know merely how many of a witness's statements out of a hundred are wrong; but just which ones of them are wrong.

This objection goes vastly deeper and is vastly weightier than that based on the want of independence of the arguments. Yet even this objection is downright insignificant as compared with the principal one, which I now proceed to state, although I have already hinted at it.

All mathematical reasoning, even though it relates to probability, is of the nature of necessary reasoning. All necessary reasoning consists of tracing out what is virtually asserted in the assumed premises.[12] While some of these may be new observations, yet the principal ones relate to states of things not capable of being directly observed. As has often been said, especially since Kant, such reasoning really does not amplify our positive knowledge, although it may render our understanding of our own assumptions more perfect. It is the kind of reasoning proper for any application of science. For example, it is by such reasoning that, assuming the law of gravitation to have been scientifically established, we go on to predict the time and place of an eclipse of the sun. Or, if our desire is to rectify our theory of the moon, we may do so by comparing such predictions, regarded as conditional, with observations. If, in making the correction, we assume that there can be no error discoverable by these observations except in the values of one or two constants employed, the correction is, by a mere application of principles assumed, made to be already scientifically established; and although it will be called a contribution to science, it leaves the framework of the theory untouched, and merely consists in incorporating the new observations into the places provided for them in our existing assumptions, so that there really is, in the logician's sense, no enlargement of our knowledge, but merely an arrangement or preservation of the systematization of knowledge already established. In applying observations to the fundamental correction of a theory, as Kepler applied Tycho's observations to the correction of the crude Copernican system,[13] a kind of reasoning comes in which is not purely mathematical demonstration. If I remember rightly, there were only three points in the orbit of Mars,—I am sure there were only about three or four,—where Kepler ascertained the position of Mars in space by positive triangulation. Even those triangulations involved hypothetical elements, such as the assumption that the orbit was the same at every revolution, which might very well not have been true; and even had they been absolutely positive, they were altogether inadequate to determining the form of the orbit. These, therefore, as well as all the other items of his argument, were merely of this nature, that all simpler theories having been proved inadequate, all the predictions which could be based upon the theory of the elliptical orbit were verified by the observations well within the limits of possible, and even of not apparently unlikely, error. This was not mathematical demonstration; and all the subsequent work upon the solar system has merely multiplied and made more precise the same kind of proof, but has not changed its character. It is not now mathematical demonstration any more than it was then. Empirical science can never be enlarged by mathematical demonstration or any other kind of necessary reasoning; although when nomological science has advanced to a certain point, a mathematical theory can be based upon it which will be useful, not only for nomological science itself, but also for the classificatory and descriptive sciences which depend upon it.

Now ancient history occupies a place among the psychical sciences somewhat analogous to that of astronomy among the physical sciences. The one is a description of what is distant in the world of mind, as the other is a description of what is distant in the world of matter; and curiously enough, or significantly enough, an ancient alliance exists between the two sciences through chronology. Yet the amount of aid which physical astronomy can derive from mathematics is quite moderate, notwithstanding the mathematical perfection of nomological physics. Anybody can convince himself that the reasoning of physical astronomy is not of a demonstrative kind by simply running over any textbook of the subject. But the science of nomological psychics,—psychology, as we call it,—is still far too backward to afford any distinguished aid to history; and consequently, the demonstrative part of rightly reasoned history exclusive of mere chronology must, for a long time, remain very small. History, however, is as much more worthy than astronomy of being studied scientifically as mind is more worthy of our attention than matter. The use we should desire to make of ancient history is to *learn* from the study of it, and not to carry our preconceived notions into it, until they can be put upon a much more scientific basis than at present they can. Consequently, the staple of our reasoning in ancient history should not be of the demonstrative kind, as it is, as long as it remains, at best, an application of the mathematical doctrine of chances. If somebody replies that in weighing arguments *pro* and *con* critics make no use of the mathematical calculus of probabilities, the rejoinder will be that their proceeding only differs from that by its greater vagueness, and that a vague and inexact use of probabilities has no logical advantage over a more critical employment of them. If it is said that, as far as possible, the critics avoid likelihoods, and aim at positive certainty, the answer will be that they endeavor to do this by the employment of apodictic arguments, which only mark a still less exact grade of the same kind of demonstrative reasoning. Fully to appreciate the force of this argument one must have a well-matured comprehension of the logic of science; but when it is fairly apprehended, it cannot but be deemed quite conclusive.

Nevertheless, there still remains a further objection to the method of balancing likelihoods in the study of ancient history which is worthy of attention even after what has been said. We all know that as soon as a hypothesis has been settled upon as preferable to others, the next business in order is to commence deducing from it whatever experiential predictions are extremest and most unlikely among those deducible from it, in order to subject them to the test of experiment, and thus either quite to refute the hypothesis or make such corrections of it as may be called for by the experiments; and the hypothesis must ultimately stand or fall by the result of such experiments. Now what is true of any single hypothesis should equally hold good for any method of constructing many hypotheses. It, too, should have its consequences experimentally tested, and must stand or fall by the ultimate result. Now within the last half of the nineteenth century the merits of the procedure of the historical critics has been many times subjected to the test of archeological exploration; and what has been the result? I have not the necessary knowledge myself to sum it up in a magisterial manner; but from what I have casually heard about the relation of Egyptian exploration to the critics' previous opinion of Manetho and even of Herodotus, about the explorations in the Troad and in Mycenae, and much else, I gather that on the whole, it has been shown that the critics were found to be more or less fundamentally wrong in nearly every case, and in particular that their fashion of throwing all the positive evidence overboard in favor of their notions of what was likely, stands condemned by those tests. If this be so, it is no slight modification, but a complete revolution, of their logic which is called for; because, considering their great learning and competence, and the absolute confidence which they attached to their conclusions as perfectly ineluctable, there is no middle course between pronouncing those men to have been a pack of charlatans and concluding that their method was wrong in principle. If it were not so, their pretensions to scientific determinacy of those conclusions would have been simply disgraceful.

Having thus outlined the argument for the timeliness of a new logical theory of the proper method of dealing with ancient testimonies, I proceed to show how the question appears from the point of view of the "Minute Logic" of which I am a defender.[14]

I could not present the reason which has the greatest weight to my own mind, so that it should be convincing, unless I were to write a paper more than fifteen times the length of this one. That has to be foregone. Meantime, the secondary considerations that remain will be strong enough to maintain the position successfully.[15]

To begin with, let me say that I propose to confine myself exclusively to the consideration of the proper *scientific* procedure concerning the documents in question. I do not propose to touch upon the question of miracles in so far as it is a practical religious question for an individual man.[16] This is not from timidity or any indisposition to express myself, could I have my whole say; but it is because it would expand this paper beyond all bounds of convenience in all respects. A practical belief is what a man proposes to go upon. A decision is more or less pressing. What ought it to be? That must depend upon what the purpose of his action is. What, then, is the purpose of a man? That is the question of pure ethics, a very great question which must be disposed of before the logic of practical belief can be entered upon to any good effect. With science it is entirely different. A problem started today may not reach any scientific solution for generations. The man who begins the inquiry does not expect to learn, in this life, what conclusion it is to which his labors are tending. Strictly speaking, the inquiry never will be completely closed. Even without any logical method at all, the gradual accumulation of knowledge might probably ultimately bring a sufficient solution. Consequently, the object of a logical method is to bring about more speedily and at less expense the result which is destined, in any case, ultimately to be reached, but which, even with the best logic, will not probably come in our day. Really the word "belief" is out of place in the vocabulary of science. If an engineer or other practical man takes a scientific result, and makes it the basis for action, it is he who converts it into a belief. In pure science, it is merely the formula reached in the existing state of scientific progress. The question of what rules scientific inference ought to follow in order to accelerate the progress of science to the utmost is a comparatively simple one, and may be treated by itself. The question of how a given man, with not much time to give to the subject, had best proceed to form his hasty decision, involves other very serious difficulties, which make it a distinct inquiry. The former question, taken by itself, will be enough for the present communication.

I have said that in order to determine what the logic of the individual man should be, it would be necessary to consider what his purpose was. The same remark applies to the logic of science. It is easier to determine the purpose of science. It does not involve opening the question of ethics. Yet it is not a perfectly simple matter, either. Several definitions of the purpose of science that I have met with made it the business of science to ascertain that certain things were so, to reach foregone conclusions. Nothing could be more contrary to the spirit of science. Science seeks to discover whatever there may be that is true.

I am inclined to think that even single perceptual facts are of intrinsic value in its eyes, although their value in themselves is so small that one cannot be quite sure that there is any. But every truth which will prevent a future fact of perception from surprising us, which will give the means of predicting it, or the means of conditionally predicting what would be perceived were anybody to be in a situation to perceive it, this is, beyond doubt, that which science values. Although some will contradict me, I am bound to say that, as I conceive the matter, science will value these truths for themselves, and not merely as useful. Mathematics appears to me to be a science, as much as any science, although it may not contain all the ingredients of the complete idea of a science. But it is a science, as far as it goes; the spirit and purpose of the mathematician are acknowledged by other scientific men to be substantially the same as their own. Yet the greater part of the propositions of mathematics do not correspond to any perceptual facts that are regarded as even being possible. The diagonal of the square is incommensurable with its side; but how could perception ever distinguish between the commensurable and the incommensurable? The mathematical interest of the imaginary inflections of plane curves is quite as great as that of the real inflections. Yet we cannot say that the scientific man's interest is in mere ideas, like a poet's or a musician's. Indeed, we may go so far as to say that he cares for nothing which could not conceivably come to have a bearing on some practical question. Whether a magnitude is commensurable or not has a practical bearing on the mathematician's action. On the other hand, it cannot be said that there is any kind of proportion between the scientific interest of a fact and its probability of becoming practically interesting. So far is that from being the case, that, although we are taught in many ways the lesson of the Petersburg problem,[17]—so stupidly obscured by the extraneous consideration of moral expectation,—the lesson that we utterly neglect minute probabilities, yet for all that, facts whose probabilities of ever becoming practical are next to nothing are still regarded with keen scientific interest, not only by scientific men, but even by a large public. Here, then, are the facts to be reconciled in order to determine what the purpose of science, what scientific interest, consists in. First, every truth which affords the means of predicting what would be perceived under any conceivable conditions is scientifically interesting; and nothing which has no conceivable bearing upon practice is so, unless it be the perceptual facts themselves. But, second, the scientific interest does not lie in the application of those truths for the sake of such predictions. Nor, thirdly, is it true that the scientific interest is a mere poetical interest in the ideas as images; but solid truth, or reality, is demanded, though not necessarily existential reality. Carefully comparing these three conditions, we find ourselves forced to conclude that scientific interest lies in finding what we roughly call generality or rationality or law to be true, independently of whether you and I and any generations of men think it to be so or not. I might enunciate and prove this with more accuracy and evidence; but since I am not now undertaking to present the subject with the strictest method, I think what I have said will answer my purpose.

But, however this question be argued, it is one of those concerning which

A man convinced against his will
Is of his own opinion still,[18]

(a current corruption worth dozens of distiches such as its original.) The dry light of intelligence is manifestly not sufficient to determine a great purpose: the whole man goes into it. So the fact that logic depends upon such a question is sufficient to account for the endless disputes of which logic is still the theatre.

Confining ourselves to science, inference, in the broadest sense, is coextensive with the deliberate adoption, in any measure, of an assertion as true. For deliberation implies that the adoption is voluntary; and so consequently, the observation of perceptual facts that are forced upon us in experience is excluded. General principles, on the other hand, if deliberately adopted, must have been subjected to criticism; and any criticism of them that can be called scientific and that results in their acceptance must involve an argument in favor of their truth. My statement was that an inference, in the broadest sense, is a deliberate adoption, *in any measure*, of an assertion as true. The phrase "in any measure" is not as clear as might be wished. "Measure," here translates *modus*. The modes of acceptance of an assertion that are traditionally recognized are the necessary, the possible, and the contingent. But we shall learn more accurately, as our inquiry proceeds, how the different measures of acceptance are to be enumerated and defined. Then, as to the word "true," I may be asked what this means. Now the different sciences deal with different kinds of truth; mathematical truth is one thing, ethical truth is another, the actually existing state of the universe is a third; but all these different conceptions have in common something very marked and clear. We all hope that the different scientific inquiries in which we are severally engaged are going ultimately to lead to some definitely established conclusion, which conclusion we endeavor to anticipate in some measure. Agreement with that ultimate proposition that we look forward to,—agreement with that, whatever it may turn out to be, is the scientific truth.

Perhaps there will here be no harm in indulging in a little diagrammatic psychology after the manner of the old writers' discussions concerning the *primum cognitum;* for however worthless it may be as psychology, it is not a bad way to get orientated in our logic. No man can recall the time when he had not yet begun a theory of the universe, when any particular course of things was so little expected that nothing could surprise him, even though it startled him. The first surprise would naturally be the first thing that would offer sufficient handle for memory to draw it forth from the general background. It was something new. Of course, nothing can appear as definitely new without being contrasted with a background of the old. At this, the infantile scientific impulse,—what becomes developed later into various kinds of intelligence, but we will call it the scientific impulse because it is science that we are now endeavoring to get a general notion of,—this infantile scientific impulse must strive to reconcile the new to the old. The first new feature of this first surprise is, for example, that it is a surprise; and the only way of accounting for that is that there had been before an expectation. Thus it is that all knowledge begins by the discovery that there has been an erroneous expectation of which we had before hardly been conscious. Each branch of science begins with a new phenomenon which violates a sort of negative subconscious expectation, like the frog's legs of Signora Galvani.[19]

What, then, is that element of a phenomenon that renders it surprising, in the sense that an explanation for it is demanded? *Par excellence*, it is irregularity, says Dr. Paul Carus, in substance.[20] I cannot but think that there is a faulty analysis, here. Nobody is surprised that the trees in a forest do not form a regular pattern, or asks for any explanation of such a fact. So, irregularity does not prompt us to ask for an explanation. Nor can it be said that it is because the explanation is obvious; for there is, on the contrary, no explanation to be given, except that there is no particular reason why there should be a regular pattern; or rather that there is no sufficient reason; because there must be a tendency for large trees to grow where there is most room, which tendency, if it were strong enough and undisturbed enough, would produce a regular pattern. I mention this to show that, so far is mere irregularity a motive for demanding an explanation, that, even when there is a slight reason for expecting a regularity and we find irregularity, we do not ask for an explanation, whereas if it were an equally unexpected *regularity* that we had met with, we certainly should have asked for an explanation. I am, for reasons similar to this, as well as for others, confident that mere irregularity, where no definite regularity is expected, creates no surprise nor excites any curiosity. Why should it, when irregularity is the overwhelmingly preponderant rule of experience, and regularity only the strange exception? In what a state of amazement should I pass my life, if I were to wonder why there was no regularity connecting days upon which I receive an even number of letters by mail and nights on which I notice an even number of shooting stars! But who would seek explanations for irregularities like that?

Let me not, however, be understood to make the strength of an emotion of surprise the measure of a logical need for explanation. The emotion is merely the instinctive indication of the logical situation. It is evolution (φύσις) that has provided us with the emotion. The situation is what we have to study.

Before dismissing irregularity, I may note, as aiding to clear the matter up, that a breach of an existing regularity always stimulates a demand for an explanation; but where, having expected regularity, we only find irregularity without any breach of regularity, we are only induced to revise our reasons for expecting anything. Irregularity, be it noted, cannot be expected, as such. For an expectation is, in every case, founded upon some regularity. For the same reason, merely not finding regularity where no particular regularity was expected, occasions no surprise.

In order to define the circumstances under which a scientific explanation is really needed, the best way is to ask in what way explanation subserves the purpose of science. We shall then see what the evil situation is which it remedies, or what the need is which it may be expected to supply. Now what an explanation of a phenomenon does is to supply a proposition which, if it had been known to be true before the phenomenon presented itself, would have rendered that phenomenon predictable, if not with certainty, at least as something very likely to occur. It thus renders that phenomenon rational, that is, makes it a logical consequence, necessary or probable. Consequently, if without any particular explanation, a phenomenon is such as must have occurred, there is no room at all for explanation. If the phenomenon is such as need not have occurred on the special occasion, but must occur on occasions differing in no discoverable and exactly assignable pertinent respect from the special occasion on which the phenomenon in question actually occurs, still there is nothing for explanation to do, until it is ascertained in what respects, if any, the individual occasion differs from those other occasions. For example, I throw a die, and it turns up ace. Now I know already that this die will turn up ace once in six times; and I am persuaded that it would be hopeless to attempt, at present, to find any pertinent conditions fulfilled on this occasion which are not fulfilled every time the die is thrown. Hence, no proposed explanation of the die's turning up an ace can be in order, unless we can discover some peculiar and pertinent feature about the present occasion. Why should my lottery ticket have drawn a blank, and somebody else's a prize? No explanation is called for. The question is silly.

Let us now pass to the case of a phenomenon in which, apart from a particular explanation, there was antecedently no reason for expecting it, and as little for expecting it not to happen. Suppose, for example, that on the day of the Lisbon earthquake[21] the brightest new star had appeared in the heavens. There might possibly have been some explanation for this; but there would have been no motive for searching for one. To have done so would, indeed, have been a foolish proceeding, for reasons we need not now consider.

Thus, the only case in which this method of investigation, namely, by the study of how an explanation can further the purpose of science, leads to the conclusion that an explanation is positively called for, is the case in which a phenomenon presents itself which, without some special explanation, there would be reason to expect would *not* present itself; and the logical demand for an explanation is the greater, the stronger the reason for expecting it not to occur was.

Since it is never prudent to rely upon reasoning that is largely deductive without a check upon its accuracy, especially where the conclusion is disputed, as this is, I will select a few examples calculated to refute it, if it is to be refuted, and examine its application to them. First, suppose the phenomenon observed consists simply in irregularity; then, if there were no ground for anticipating any particular regularity, there is simply nothing to explain (irregularity being the prevailing character of experience generally). This agrees with our natural judgment. But if we anticipated a regularity, and find simple irregularity, but no *breach* of regularity,—as for example if we were to expect that an attentive observation of a forest would show something like a pattern,—then there is nothing to explain except the singular fact that we should have anticipated something that has not been realized. Here, by our theory, there is need of an explanation, not of an objective, but of a subjective phenomenon (pardon the jargon,—slang jargon, at that). This again agrees with our natural judgment; for in such a case we straightway commence reviewing our logic to find how our error is to be explained.

Streetcars are famous *ateliers* for speculative modelling. Detained there, with no business to occupy him, one sets to scrutinizing the people opposite, and to working up biographies to fit them. I see a woman of forty. Her countenance is so sinister as scarcely to be matched among a thousand, almost to the border of insanity, yet with a grimace of amiability that few even of her sex are sufficiently trained to command:—along with it, those two ugly lines, right and left of the compressed lips, chronicling years of severe discipline. An expression of servility and hypocrisy there is, too abject for a domestic; while a certain low, yet not quite vulgar, kind of education that is evinced, together with a taste in dress neither gross nor meretricious, but still by no means elevated, bespeak companionship with something superior, beyond any mere contact as of a maid with her mistress. The whole combination, although not striking at first glance, is seen upon close inspection to be a very unusual one. Here our theory declares an explanation is called for; and I should not be long in guessing that the woman was an ex-nun.

In this last case, the emotion of surprise is not felt, because the cognitive part of the mind must be uppermost in order to recognize the rarity of the phenomenon. There are cases in which the most familiar of facts seem to call for explanation. I am myself, for example, fond of urging that no theory of space can be satisfactory which does not explain why it should have three dimensions. Perhaps all will not agree with me on this point. They will say, it must have some number of dimensions; why not three as well as any number? Or I may be asked what number of dimensions I should expect space to have. My reply is, that if I did not know what number of dimensions space really had, and was obliged to investigate the question as we usually investigate scientific questions, by trying successive hypotheses until I found one that experiment would not refute, I should soon see that one dimension would not be sufficient, and I should try two as giving, not only the simplest, but by far the most comprehensible, of continua. I should guess that it was similar to the field of imaginary quantity. When that was refuted, I should pass to the next most comprehensible continuum, that of the field of real quaternions, quadridimensional space. Although the reasons for those numbers are not at all apodictic, yet I should, I am sure, be much surprised to learn that its dimensionality was three, which is so much more difficult to conceive than four. No doubt, it may be said that rationality has nothing to do with the question; and I have to confess that the fact that space has three dimensions has the air, at least, of proving that rationality has, in fact, nothing to do with it. But if it has not, still it seems to me that three is a number one would decidedly not expect. For triads mostly have some connection with Rationality; while things that are not governed by Rational considerations very seldom have three elements. I say all this, because it seems to me that this is almost a crucial instance for my theory of what it is that demands explanation. For, to the majority of minds, who would not definitely expect one number of dimensions rather than another, the fact that space has three dimensions does not seem to call for any particular explanation. That this is the fact seems to be proved by the circumstance that, of all the philosophers who have elaborated theories of space, hardly one has paid the smallest attention to the number of its dimensions, or regarded it as at all significant. But in me we have an instance of a mind to which it does seem that this feature of space calls for some definite explanation; and this same mind we find differs from the others in that it would decidedly have expected antecedently some other number. Certainly, my theory of what it is that demands explanation appears to be remarkably verified in this instance.

It is singular that there are not many logicians who attempt to define the circumstances which render an explanation of a phenomenon desirable or urgent. The majority of them seem tacitly to assume that any one fact calls for explanation as much as any other. Mr. Venn, however, in his *Empirical Logic*,[22] states, without much discussion, that it is the *isolation* of a fact that creates the need of an explanation. This approaches pretty close to my opinion, since the work of reason consists in finding connections between facts. Still, the distinctions between the two doctrines are manifold, too. All facts are more or less connected and more or less separated; so that Mr. Venn ought to say, and probably would say, that all facts call for explanation more or less. According to me, however, the demand for explanation is a more definite demand. All conceivable facts are divisible into those which, upon examination, would be found to call for explanation and those which would not. For if any fact would call for explanation, then if that which was ascertained in the consequent investigation was no more nor less than the falsity of that supposed fact, this latter would not call for explanation. Although I have not bestowed upon Mr. Venn's whole volume the minute study which it merits, so that I may be mistaken, I think I can account for this discrepancy. Mr. Venn belongs to a school which considers the logical process as starting at the percepts, if not at impressions of sense. Mr. Venn is himself so candid and so acute that he may perhaps have seen the error of this. But supposing that he has followed his school, the discrepancy between him and me would easily be accounted for, because there can be no doubt that every *percept* does involve elements that call for explanation. But I maintain that logical criticism cannot go behind *perceptual facts*, which are the first judgments which we make concerning percepts. A perceptual fact is therefore an abstract affair. Each such fact covers only certain features of the percept. I look at an object and think that it seems white. That is my judgment of the object perceived, my judgment concerning the percept, but not the percept itself; and it is idle to attempt to criticize, by any logic, that part of the performance of the intellect which draws that judgment from the percept, for the excellent reason that it is involuntary and cannot be prevented or corrected. Such a fact, which represents the percept in a very meagre way, although it is, in itself, a relatively isolated fact,—as isolated as any fact can be,—nevertheless does not, in itself, call for any explanation. On the contrary, it can only do that when it has been connected with other facts which taken by themselves would justify an expectation of the contrary of this fact. For example, if we should find that this object which seemed white, in the first place *was* white, and then that it was a crow, and finally that all the crows known were black, then the fact of this seeming and really being white would require explanation. It might be an albino, or it might be some new species or variety of crow. But perhaps it will be insisted that this thing's appearing white *does* call for an explanation;—that we want to know the cause of its being white. To this I reply that it has always been agreed that the tendency of the understanding was merely toward synthesis, or unification. Now no fact could possibly be more unified and simple than the fact that this is white, taken in itself. It would seem, therefore, that, if we consider this fact isolated from all others, it completely accomplishes the tendency of reason. To find a cause for the whiteness would only be to complicate our conception of the matter; and I never heard it suggested that intelligence *per se* demands complexity and multiplicity. But I suspect that when Mr. Venn speaks of *isolation*, he is thinking of there being other facts from which the given fact is separated; and that it is not *isolation* that he means, but *separation*. Now separation is itself a kind of connection; so that if that be his meaning, the state of things which calls for explanation is a connection which is not satisfactory to the mind. In that case, it is incumbent on Mr. Venn to explain himself more precisely, and to say in what respect it is unsatisfactory. If he were to say, "unsatisfactory in being contrary to what ought to be expected," he would come to my position, precisely.

Further light on the question may be obtained by considering the different types of explanation, of which Mr. Venn admits three after Mill, although he says of the third that it is to be received with reserve. I so far agree with him in this, that I think if the second type is accurately defined, it will be seen to include the third as a special and not important variety. The others I fully accept, though with my own definitions of them. I will take the example of each which Mr. Venn has himself proposed. In illustration of the first type, he says: "We notice a plant that is flagging on a hot summer day:

next morning it stands up again fresh and green. 'Why has it revived in the morning?'—'Oh they always do.'"[23] One may smile at the *naïveté* of this; and certainly, it is not an explanation in the proper sense of the word. Still, its general function is the same as that of explanation; namely, it renders the fact a conclusion, necessary or probable, from what is already well known. It might be called a *regularization*, explanation and regularization being the two types of *rationalization*. The regularization, stated in full, would be,

> Plants of a certain class usually revive in the morning;
> This plant belongs to that class;
> ∴ This plant might be expected to revive in the morning.

Now it is true that the effect of the regularization is that the fact observed is less isolated than before; but the purpose of the regularization is, I think, much more accurately said to be to show that it might have been expected, had the facts been fully known. That the demand for regularization is due to the contrary being expected is shown by the fact that when that contrary expectation is very strong indeed, a regularization which even leaves the event quite improbable will in great measure satisfy the mind. When my father, Benjamin Peirce, stated (as Leverrier himself also did, at first) that the planet discovered by Galle was not that predicted by Leverrier,[24] people generally, who imagined that, in the absence of any prediction, the entire sphere of the heavens might have had to be swept to find the planet, asked, "How, then, was it that Galle found it in the very telescopic field in which Leverrier located his planet?" This was a challenge for a regularization; to which the response was that Galle's planet was about fifty minutes of longitude distant from Leverrier's place, and that this would occur by pure chance once in two hundred times. It was, therefore, about as extraordinary as that a given man of seventy-five should live to be a hundred. But the popular notion was that its probability was as one square degree is to the surface of the sphere, or as one to 41,254. It is plain that the partial satisfaction which such a regularization affords is due to the great diminution of the unexpectedness.

The other type of demand for explanation is exemplified by Mr. Venn by the question, "Why is it so difficult to walk on ice?" He gives several supposed attempts at explanation; but the one he pronounces satisfactory is, "Because, owing to the absence of friction, there is no horizontal reaction to the impulse of the feet,"[25] which, except for the misuse of the word impulse, is correct, but I fear not very perspicuous to anybody who really needed the explanation. If we endeavor to place ourselves into the shoes of such a person, we must imagine ourselves noticing how easy it looks to skate upon ice, and to have remarked some such fact as that if a wagon receives a push from the land to the ice, it moves with the utmost ease on the ice. All these hazy ideas about the ice surface jostle one another in the mind in a perplexing way. It is, therefore, not the simple fact that ice is hard to walk on which creates the demand for an explanation: it is, on the contrary, a puzzling complexus of facts. Tell a man who never saw ice that frozen water is very hard to walk on, and he may ask whether the feet stick to it, or put other questions in order to figure for himself what you mean; but as long as the fact is apprehended by him as a simple one, he will no more ask why it should be so than a common man asks why lead should be heavy. The fact is entirely sufficient as long as it is simple and isolated. It is when the difficulty of walking on ice is compared with the extraordinary distance that a ball can be bowled upon it, or with such other facts as would naturally lead one to expect that ice would be particularly easy to walk on, that a scientific explanation is sought. This is shown by the rarity of the inquiry why it is tiresome to walk on sand. Everybody knows that it is hard to make a vehicle go over sand; and so it seems, to minds in the state of ignorance supposed, to be quite natural that walking on sand should be tiresome; and thus no explanation is asked for, although, in other respects, the question is so similar to that about ice. An isolated fact is precisely what a demand for an explanation proper never refers to; it always applies to some fact connected with other facts which seem to render it improbable.

I think I have now said enough to show that my theory that that which makes the need, in science, of an explanation or, in general, of any rationalization of any fact, is that, without such rationalization, the contrary of the fact would be anticipated, so that reason and experience would be at variance, contrary to the purpose of science, is correct;—or as nearly so as we can make any theory of the matter, at present. I will add, however, one more argument. Mr. Venn has felt the need of accounting for that desire of getting rid of isolated facts, to which he attributes the demand for an explanation; and he does so by remarking that isolated facts are dangerous.[26] Now how, I should be glad to know, are isolated facts dangerous? The only way in which they would appear to be so, and it is the only way which Mr. Venn points out, is that in their presence we do not know what to expect. But if this is so, getting rid of the isolation of facts is not, after all, the ultimate motive of seeking an explanation; but on the contrary, an ulterior purpose has reference to expectation. And what is this condition described as being full of risk, of not knowing what to expect? It is not a mere negation of all expectation,—the state of mind in which a man takes his Sunday afternoon's stroll. It is a state in which a man seems to have ground for expecting certain things, and yet has evidence that those expectations may be falsified. Now this precisely describes the conditions under which according to my theory rationalization is called for. It may, however, be objected that if we are to go back to the ultimate motive for explanation, I should have asked what the danger is to which error would expose us. I reply that were I investigating the practical logic of the individual man, then, as I have already remarked, the question of pure ethics would have to be taken up, namely, the question "What can a man deliberately accept as his ultimate purpose?" But restricting myself, as I do, to scientific reasoning, I need not go behind the recognized purpose of science, which stops at knowledge.

Accepting the conclusion that an explanation is needed when facts contrary to what we should expect emerge, it follows that the explanation must be such a proposition as would lead to the prediction of the observed facts, either as necessary consequences or at least as very probable under the circumstances. A hypothesis, then, has to be adopted, which is likely in itself, and renders the facts likely. This step of adopting a hypothesis as being suggested by the facts, is what I call *abduction*. I reckon it as a form of inference, however problematical the hypothesis may be held. What are to be the logical rules to which we are to conform in taking this step? There would be no logic in imposing rules, and saying that they *ought* to be followed, until it is made out that the purpose of hypothesis requires them. Accordingly, it appears that the early scientists, Thales, Anaximander, and their brethren, seemed to think the work of science was done when a likely hypothesis was suggested. I applaud their sound logical instinct for that. Even Plato, in the *Timaeus* and elsewhere, does not hesitate roundly to assert the truth of anything, if it seems to render the world reasonable, and this same procedure, in a more refined modification, is the essence of modern historical criticism. It is all right as long as it is not found to interfere with the usefulness of the hypothesis. Aristotle departs a little from that method. His physical hypotheses are equally unfounded; but he always adds a "perhaps." That, I take it, was because Aristotle had been a great reader of other philosophers, and it had struck him that there are various inconsistent ways of explaining the same facts. Ultimately, the circumstance that a hypothesis, although it may lead us to expect some facts to be as they are, may in the future lead us to erroneous expectations about other facts,—this circumstance, which anybody must have admitted as soon as it was brought home to him, was brought home to scientific men so forcibly, first in astronomy, and then in other sciences, that it became axiomatical that a hypothesis adopted by abduction could only be adopted on probation, and must be tested.

When this is duly recognized, the first thing that will be done, as soon as a hypothesis has been adopted, will be to trace out its necessary and probable experiential consequences. This step is *deduction*. Here I may notice a rule of abduction much insisted upon by Auguste Comte, to the effect that metaphysical hypotheses should be excluded; and by a metaphysical hypothesis he means, as he tells us, a hypothesis which has no experiential consequences.[27] I suppose a partially metaphysical hypothesis would be one that had, among its consequences, some not relating to possible experience; and that from those Comte would wish us to tear away the metaphysical part. I have no particular objection to Comte's rule. Indeed, I think it would obviously be fully justified by a consideration of the purposes of hypothesis. Only, I beg to remark that its positive utility is limited by the circumstance that such *[a]* thing as a hypothesis which is either wholly or partially metaphysical cannot be constructed. I may be asked what I should say to the proposition that

> The warranted genuine Snark has a taste
> Which is meagre and hollow, but crisp;
> Like a coat that is rather too tight in the waist,
> With a flavor of Will-o-the-wisp.[28]

I reply that it is not a metaphysical proposition, because it is no proposition at all, but only an imitation proposition. For a proposition is a sign separately indicating what it is a sign of; and analysis shows that this amounts to saying that it represents that an image is similar to something to which actual experience forces the attention. Consequently a proposition cannot predicate a character not capable of sensuous presentation; nor can it refer to anything with which experience does not connect us. A metaphysical proposition, in Comte's sense, would, therefore, be a grammatical arrangement of words simulating a proposition, but in fact, not a proposition, because destitute of meaning. Comte's use of the word "metaphysical," in a sense which makes it synonymous with nonsense, simply marks the nominalistic tendency of Comte's time, from which he was unable to free himself, although the general tendency of his philosophy is rather opposed to it. However, be that as it may. The entire meaning of a hypothesis lies in its conditional experiential predictions; if all its predictions are true, the hypothesis is wholly true.

This appears to be in harmony with Kant's view of deduction, namely, that it merely explicates what is implicitly asserted in the premisses.[29] This is what is called a half-truth. Deductions are of two kinds, which I call *corollarial* and *theorematic*. The corollarial are those reasonings by which all corollaries and the majority of what are called theorems are deduced; the theorematic are those by which the major theorems are deduced. If you take the thesis of a corollary, i.e., the proposition to be proved, and carefully analyze its meaning, by substituting for each term its definition, you will find that its truth follows, in a straightforward manner, from previous propositions similarly analyzed. But when it comes to proving a major theorem, you will very often find you have need of a *lemma*, which is a demonstrable proposition about something outside the subject of inquiry; and even if a lemma does not have to be demonstrated, it is necessary to introduce the definition of something which the *thesis* of the theorem does not contemplate. In the most remarkable cases, this is some abstraction; that is to say, a subject whose existence *consists* in some fact about other things. Such, for example, are operations considered as in themselves subject to operation: *lines*, which are nothing but descriptions of the motion of a particle, considered as being themselves movable; *collections*; *numbers*; and the like. When the reform of mathematical reasoning now going on is complete,[30] it will be seen that every such supposition ought to be supported by a proper postulate. At any rate, Kant himself ought to admit, and would admit if he were alive today, that the conclusion of reasoning of this kind, although it is strictly deductive, does not flow from definitions alone, but that postulates are requisite for it.

Deduction, of course, relates exclusively to an ideal state of things. A hypothesis presents such an ideal state of things, and asserts that it is the icon, or analogue of an experience.

Having, then, by means of deduction, drawn from a hypothesis predictions as to what the results of experiment will be, we proceed to test the hypothesis by making the experiments and comparing those predictions with the actual results of experiment. Experiment is very expensive business, in money, in time, and in thought; so that it will be a saving of expense to begin with that positive prediction from the hypothesis which seems least likely to be verified. For a single experiment may absolutely refute the most valuable of hypotheses, while a hypothesis must be a trifling one indeed if a single experiment could establish it. When, however, we find that prediction after prediction, notwithstanding a preference for putting the most unlikely ones to the test, is verified by experiment, whether without modification or with a merely quantitative modification, we begin to accord to the hypothesis a standing among scientific results. This sort of inference it is, from experiments testing predictions based on a hypothesis, that is alone properly entitled to be called *induction*.

I may as well say that arguments which I cannot now stop to set forth ought to remove all doubt that, accepting the term "induction" in this sense, the critical distinction, that is, the distinction in respect to the nature of their validity between deduction and induction, consists in this. Namely, deduction professes to show that certain admitted facts could not exist, even in an ideal world constructed for the purpose, either without the existence of the very fact concluded, or without the occurrence of this fact in the long run in that proportion of cases of the fulfillment of certain objective conditions in which it is concluded that it will occur, or in other words, without its having the concluded objective probability. In either case, deductive reasoning is necessary reasoning, although, in the latter case, its subject matter is probability. Induction, on the other hand, is not justified by any relation between the facts stated in the premises and the fact stated in the conclusion; and it does not infer that the latter fact is either necessary or objectively probable. But the justification of its conclusion is that that conclusion is reached by a method which, steadily persisted in, must lead to true knowledge in the long run of cases of its application, whether to the existing world or to any imaginable world whatsoever. Deduction cannot make any such claim as this, since it does not lead to any positive knowledge at all, but only traces out the ideal consequences of hypotheses.

It is desirable to consider a large range of inductions, with a view to distinguishing accurately between induction and abduction, which have generally been much confounded. I will, therefore, mention that, in the present state of my studies, I think I recognize three distinct genera of induction. I somewhat hesitate to publish this division; but it might take more years than I have to live to render it as satisfactory as I could wish. It is not that there seems to be any very serious want of clearness in it, or that the reasons for maintaining it are wanting in conclusiveness, or that I have any particular reason to doubt either the conclusion or the correctness of the reasoning; but it is simply that the factor of safety is too small. I have not so thoroughly considered the subject as to be quite secure against possible oversights of one kind or another, nor have I collected a sufficient surplus of proofs so that they will hold even though oversights there be. Consequently, I am not yet willing to incorporate this division with the body of results of this investigation. But with this warning, I now state the division.

The first genus of induction is where we judge what approximate proportion of the members of a collection have a predesignate character by a sample drawn under one or other of the following three conditions, forming three species of this genus. First, the sample may be a *random* one, an expression to which I attach a peculiar meaning. Namely, I mean by a random sample, a sample drawn from the whole class by a method which if it were applied over and over again would in the long run draw any one possible collection of the members of the whole collection sampled as often as any other collection of the same size, and would produce them in any one order as often as in any other. In this peculiar sense of the term *random sample*, it is only from a finite collection that a random sample can be drawn. And here it will be well to call to mind the exact meanings of a few terms relating to multitudes. By a *collection*,[31] I mean an individual object whose actual presence in any part of experience consists in the actual presence of certain other individual objects called its *members*, so that if one of them were absent, the same collection would not be present, and these members are such that any part of them might logically be present or absent irrespectively of the presence or absence of any others; and the truth of any predication concerning a collection consists in the truth of a corresponding predication concerning whatever members it may possess, so that taking any universal proposition whatever, there is a collection having for its only members whatever independent objects there may be of which that proposition makes any given affirmation. Thus, if I say "All men are mortal," there is a collection consisting of whatever men there may be. If I say "All the men in Mars are mortal," there is a collection of all the men in Mars. If there actually are no men in Mars, this collection has no actual existence; but it remains a collection, just the same. According to the definition, in *Nothing* there is the essence of a collection, but not the actual existence. Some persons to whom this is said will be in a hurry to interject that that which has no existence has no being, and some will go so far as to insist that every collection, in the sense defined, is a fiction. For my part, I am convinced that it is idle to introduce metaphysics into logic, and, therefore, I do not care whether these persons are right or wrong. Plainly, every object of direct perception is a collection. But all I ask is to be allowed to use words in the senses clearly defined by me, including the words *essence* and *existence*. Having thus defined a collection, I call attention in passing to the circumstance that a time, as ordinarily conceived, is not a collection of instants, nor a line of points, but any instant when present is a part of time and instants with their relations may be conceived as constituting time, and therefore I will use the word *aggregate* in such a sense that time may be said to be an aggregate of instants and any collection to be an aggregate also. Confining myself to collections, however, I say that any one collection, say the collection of the A's is *at least as small as* any other collection, say the collection of the B's, or, in other words, that the A's are *at least as few as* the B's, if and only if, there is some relation ρ such that every A is in the relation ρ to some B to which no other A is in the relation ρ. Of course, I use the terms *as great as* and *as many as* as correlative to *as small as* and *as few as*. I say that one collection is *equal* to another, if and only if, each of the two is at least as small as the other; and if one collection is as small as another but the latter is not as small as the former, the former is said to be *smaller than* the latter, and the latter *greater than* the former. I use the term *multitude* to express that character of any collection which consists in its being as small as whatever collections it is as small as, and being as great as whatever collections it is as great as. The multitude of every collection is either *enumerable* or finite, *denumeral* or indefinite, *abnumerable* or transfinite. The scientific definitions of these terms were, I believe, first given by me in 1881; but Dedekind gave, perhaps independently, in 1888, substantially the same definition of a finite multitude.[32] An *enumerable* multitude is the multitude of a collection, say the A's, if and only if, no matter what relation ρ may be, either it is not true that every A is in the relation ρ to some A to which no other A stands in the relation ρ, or else to every A some one A, and no other, stands in the relation ρ. This is as much as to say that the A's form a non-enumerable, or infinite, collection if and only if there be some relation ρ such that every A stands in the relation ρ to an A to which no other A stands in the relation ρ, although there is an A of which it is not true that any A stands in the relation ρ while no other A does so. Now according to our definition of the relation of being as small as, this is the same as to say that a collection, say the A's, is non-enumerable or infinite, if and only if the entire collection of A's is as small as a collection of A's from which some A is excluded; and this again is obviously identical with Dedekind's definition of an infinite collection which is that a collection is infinite if and only if the whole of it is as small as some part of it not the whole. But a more readily intelligible definition, coming to the same thing, is to say that an enumerable multitude is a multitude less than that of all the finite whole numbers. The *denumeral* multitude, for there is but one, is the multitude of a collection, say the A's, if and only if there is a relation, say σ, and an A, say A_0, such that every A stands in the relation σ to some A to which no other A stands in this relation, and no A stands in the relation σ to A_0, and taking any predicate P whatever, either every A has this character P, or A_0 does not possess the character P, or there is an A having the character P which is not in the relation σ to any A that has the character P. This comes to the same thing as saying that the denumeral multitude is the multitude of the finite whole numbers. Every denumeral collection is numerable; that is to every member of it a separate ordinal number may be assigned; and this may be done in such a way as to exhaust the entire collection of finite whole numbers. Every denumeral collection, therefore, either has an order or may receive an order. A denumeral collection being taken in a certain order may be said to have a finite ratio to another taken in a given order, but, taken in another order, the ratio will be different. Thus taking the whole numbers in their natural order, one half of them are even; but they may be taken in such an order that only every third is even; as

$$1, 3, 2, 5, 7, 4, 9, 11, 6, 13, 15, 8, 17, 19, 10, \text{ etc.}$$

This series being indefinitely extended, no even number will be repeated nor will any odd number be repeated. For every number of the form $2N$ will be in the $3N$ place and every odd number of the form $4M + N$ where N is plus or minus 1 will be in the $3M + N$ place. To show that the whole is no more numerous than a part, or all the numbers than the even numbers, it suffices to write down

$$
\begin{array}{ccccccccc}
1 & 2 & 3 & 4 & 5 & 6 & 7 & 8 & 9, \text{ etc.} \\
2 & 4 & 6 & 8 & 10 & 12 & 14 & 16 & 18, \text{ etc.}
\end{array}
$$

Of course, there is no number without a double, and each double is an even number. An *abnumerable** multitude is one of a denumeral succession of multitudes greater than the denumeral multitude; each of these being the multitude of the different possible collections of members of a collection of the next lower abnumerable multitude. I have proved that there is no multitude greater than every abnumerable multitude; and it seems to follow from a theorem of Cantor's about ordinal numbers that there is no multitude intermediate between two abnumerable multitudes.† It will, therefore, suffice to define an abnumerable multitude as a multitude greater than that of all the finite whole numbers. If there is room on a line for any multitude of points, however great, a genuine continuity implies, then, that the aggregate of points on a line is too great to form a collection: the points lose their identity; or rather, they never had any numerical identity, for the reason that they are only possibilities, and therefore are essentially general. They only become individual when they are separately marked on the line; and however many be separately marked, there is room to mark more in any multitude.

Returning to the first genus of induction, it now becomes plain that a random sample, in the exact sense defined, can only be drawn from a finite collection. For the definition contains the phrase "the long run." Now what is meant by "the long run"? The phrase is only used in saying that the ratio of frequency of an event has such and such a value in the long run. The meaning is that if the occasion referred to upon which the event might happen were to recur indefinitely, and if tallies were to be kept of the occurrences and the non-occurrences, then the ratio of the one number to the other, as the occasions went on, would indefinitely converge toward a definite limit.

---

*"Ultranumerable" would be a better word than abnumerable. Cantor's word is "abzählbar."

† I can now positively demonstrate that there is no such intermediate number; but it is not so clear to me that there are no multitudes greater than the "abnumerable."

The word "converge" is here used in a different sense from that which is usual in mathematics. The common definition is that a series of values x_1, x_2, x_3, etc., converges toward a limiting value x, provided, after any discrepancy ε has been named, it is possible to find one of the members of the series x_v, such that, for every value of n greater than v, $(x_v - x_n)^2 < \varepsilon^2$.[33] This ought to be called *definite* convergence. No such member x_v can, in the indefinite convergence with which we have to do, be fixed in advance of the experiment. Nevertheless, there will be some such value.

Such being the nature of a long run, we see that the idea of a random sample supposes that in a denumeral series of trials all possible samples of the class sampled are to be capable of being drawn, and that in every possible order *inter se*. But all possible orders in which all possible samples, however small, could be drawn from a denumeral collection would be abnumerable, and therefore not to be completed in a long run. It follows that it is only a finite or enumerable class from which a random sample in the sense of the definition can be drawn. It is, indeed, evident that one cannot take even a single whole number at random; for a whole number taken at random would be infinitely more likely to be larger than any predesignate number than not.

Let us now consider another species of the first genus of induction. It had better be mentioned, by the way, that no multitude not enumerable is increased by being multiplied by itself; so that a denumeral collection of denumeral collections makes up a denumeral collection of the members of the latter collections. Let us now suppose that we are about to sample a denumeral collection in order to ascertain the proportionate frequency with which its members have a certain character designated in advance of the examination. Usually, there is no sense in speaking of a definite finite proportion of a denumeral collection; but I am going to suppose that this collection has an order which gives it a sense. The sample is to be drawn under the guidance of a precept under which we can enlarge any sample drawn indefinitely, and can also draw an indefinite number of samples. Now I shall suppose that in some way, no matter how, we become assured that a relation exists between four correlates, to wit, the predesignate character, the precept of sampling, the collection sampled, and the future course of experience, this relation being such that, in the long run, the distribution of the predesignate character in samples drawn under the precept will be the same as if they had been drawn strictly at random from an indefinitely large finite collection composing all our future experience of members of the same collection. Then, as before, we can infer inductively the proportional frequency of that character in future experiences of members of the same collection; and the induction must approximate indefinitely, though irregularly, to the true proportion. As an example, take a certain die. All the falls of it shall form the denumeral collection. In future experience this die will probably be thrown a very large but finite number of times. Let me sample the throws in order to find out (since it may be loaded or badly made) with what relative frequency it will turn up an ace. My precept shall be to throw it from the dice box after shaking, replace it, and go on in the same way. I will not stop to inquire how I know that my sample throws will, as far as the distribution of aces is concerned, be determined as if they had been drawn strictly at random among all future throws, because this question has, at this stage, no relevancy, and would only divert our minds from our point. And besides, the elements of the difficulty will find their solution in questions we have presently to take up.

Perhaps we may reckon, as a third species under the first genus of induction, those cases in which we find a denumeral series in an objective order of succession, and wish to know what the law of occurrence of a certain character among its members is, without at the outset so much as knowing whether it has any definite frequency in the long run or not. As an example, I will make a very slight examination of the occurrence of the figure five in the endless decimal that would express the value of π. Since the enormous labor has been performed of calculating this number to over seven hundred places, it seems a pity that no use whatever should be made of it. An instructor having a class in probabilities might very well give out as an exercise the examination of the calculated figures with a view to drawing such inferences as might be drawn by the doctrine of chances. I shall confine myself to illustrating this sort of induction by beginning an inquiry whether the figure five occurs in a purely chance way. I do not know why I chose this particular figure: I did so before I looked at the value of π. Taking the first 700 places, I separate them into the first 350 and the second 350. If these are quasi-random samples of the whole and all the figures occur equally often, there ought not to be far from 35 fives in each set. The odds that the number will fall in the thirties are about 2 to 1. The odds that it will fall between 28 and 42 *exclusive* is just 3 to 1. We find, in fact, that there are 33 fives in the first 350 and 28 in the second 350. Since the odds against this are only about 2 to 1, we conclude that the *fives*, and presumably the other figures, either occur by chance or very nearly so. It would, however, perhaps not be surprising if they were to occur with a little more approach to regularity than if they were purely fortuitous. Therefore, as a further illustration of this kind of induction, I have counted the number of fives in each of the seventy sets of ten successive figures. In these seventy sets, the normal number of those having 1 five should be 27½.[34] But we suspect there will be more owing to the fives coming a little more regularly than merely by chance. We will ask then what is the probability that there will be no more than 32 tens containing just 1 five. It is about ⅚; but the actual number of such tens is 33. There is, therefore, a doubtful indication of such regularity.

These are all the species I can mention of this first type of induction, in which we ascertain the value of a ratio and are morally certain to approximate to it indefinitely in the long run for each problem. By "morally certain," I mean that the probability of that event is 1. Of course, there is a difference between probability 1 and absolute certainty. In like manner, "bare possibility" should mean the possibility of that whose probability is zero. It is barely possible that a well-made pair of dice should turn up doublets every time they were thrown: it is a conceivable chance, though morally certain not to happen. But that a pair of dice will not turn up *sevens* is absolutely certain; it is not possible.

The second genus of induction comprises those cases in which the inductive method if persisted in will certainly in time correct any error that it may have led us into; but it will not do so gradually, inasmuch as it is not quantitative;—not but that it may relate to quantity, but it is not a quantitative induction. It does not discover a ratio of frequency. The first species under this genus is where the collection to be sampled is an objective series of which some members have been experienced, while the rest remain to be experienced, and we simply conclude that future experience will be like the past. We may take Quetelet's well-known example of the ancient Greek who, never having heard of the flux and reflux of the ocean, should have wandered to the shores of the Bay of Biscay and should have there seen the tide rise for m successive half-days.[35] I need hardly say that I utterly reject the doctrine that there is any consequent definite probability that the event will happen during the next half-day. That doctrine has been absolutely disproved. If the Greek's conclusion is that the tide rises about once every half-day, it is an induction of the first genus, second species. He may say that the indication is that the frequency is somewhere between $(m - \frac{1}{2})/m$ and $(m + \frac{1}{2})/m$ although this is only a rough approximation. He may, thence, deduce the conclusion that a tide will not be wanting in the following m half-days, although he ought not to risk much upon it. Beyond that it cannot be said that the quantitative induction warrants such a prediction. But if the Greek had seen the tide rise just often enough to suggest to him that it would rise every half-day forever, and had proposed then to make observations to test this hypothesis, had done so, and finding the predictions successful, had provisionally accepted the theory that the tide would never cease to rise every half-day, there would be just this justification for this conclusion, that it was the result of a method which, if it be persisted in, must correct its result if it were wrong. For if the tide was going to skip a half-day, he must discover it, if he continued his observations long enough. This degree of justification and no more he would have whether he made a dozen trials, or half a dozen, or three, or two, or one only, or even none at all. The argument would have precisely the same justification in either case. The method would infallibly correct itself, provided he continued this series of experiments; but not if he dropped it and subsequently commenced another series, as would be the case with quantitative induction. For this induction, not being quantitative, does not conclude that the probability of the tides rising is 1; but that it rises every half-day without exception. It has nothing to do with probabilities or improbabilities; and if the series of observations skips a single day, that day may be the very day of the exceptional fact. This kind of induction further differs from quantitative induction, inasmuch as there is no probable indication in advance, if its conclusion is to break down; so that, as long as it does not break down, there is nothing to be said but that no reason appears as yet for giving up the hypothesis. It gives, therefore, but a very slight and merely negative support to the hypothesis. It is a proper answer enough to gratuitous hypotheses. It is impossible to avoid making some use of it for that purpose. But it must be set down as the weakest possible of inductive arguments. I have confined myself to cases in which the series of occasions considered is objective. But I am unable to perceive that there is any intrinsic logical distinction between these cases and those in which the series results from our own subdivision of a continuum. It might, for example, be suggested that the action of gravitation may be intermittent, either with a very short period, or without any definite period. In that case, a body moving for a considerable time would show merely the average acceleration; but two molecules might, during the interval of their encounter, either undergo no acceleration, so that it would be as if there were no encounter, or they might undergo accelerations many times that of average gravitation; and this might account for there seeming to be greater attraction at small distances than the law of average gravitation would account for. Moreover, greater masses moving slower than smaller ones, a periodic relation between atomic weights and attractions of atoms might be expected. Now, as a test of that hypothesis, it might be proposed to shorten the period of a pendulum more and more, and try to observe some irregularities of its amplitudes. If we found that, as far as we could go, say with pendulums oscillating fifty times a second, there were no observable irregularities of amplitude, and were to infer that there was no intermittency of gravitation, I am unable to see that the argument would differ from the argument that the tide will rise on every half-day forever, because it has been seen to do so on several successive half-days. It is true that this latter argument is weakened by the consideration that states of things not universal usually come to an end, while the other is strengthened by the consideration that time, being continuous, it is reasonable to suppose that, in sufficiently short intervals, there will be no further variation of any given phenomenon. But both of these are extraneous considerations. As far as the mere argument that what has not been found need not be expected is concerned, there seems to be no logical distinction between them. Let us consider one more example. By means of a well-constructed color box, two adjacent rectangles are illuminated, each with nearly homogeneous violet light, of the same apparent luminosity; the one of a wavelength of about 404 millimicrons, the other of 402 millimicrons, and the observer who knows only what he sees, is asked which is the redder. He says he sees no difference. But the operator insists upon his deciding for one or the other; and with reluctance he names one, as it seems to him quite at random. However, the experiment having been repeated several hundred times, it is found that in each set of a hundred answers, a decided majority makes the more refrangible the redder. Now then, what if we proceed to infer from this that there is no such thing as a *Differenz-Schwelle*,[36] but that no matter how small the difference of excitations a sufficient number of answers would betray a difference of sensation? The only justification for this would be that it is the result of a method that, persisted in, must eventually correct any error that it leads us into. I may mention, that the argument that there is no *Differenz-Schwelle* is, in reality, stronger than this. But a negative induction of this sort, a refusal to expect what is contrary to experience, will rightly be resorted to when gratuitous objections are raised to any induction.

I seem to recognize a third genus of inductions where we draw a sample of an aggregate which cannot be considered as a collection, since it does not consist of units capable of being either counted or measured, however roughly, and where probability therefore cannot enter, but where we can draw the distinction of much and little, so that we can conceive of measurement being established; and where we may expect that any error into which the sampling will lead us, though it may not be corrected by a mere enlargement of the sample, or even by drawing other similar samples, yet must be brought to light, and that gradually, by persistence in the same general method. This kind of reasoning may be described in slightly different terms by saying that it tests a hypothesis by sampling the possible predictions that may be based upon it. Predictions are not units; for they may be more or less detailed. One can say roughly that one is more significant than another; but no approach to actual weighing of their significance can, in most cases, be made. Consequently, we cannot say that a collection of predictions drawn from a hypothesis constitutes a strictly random sample of all that can be drawn. Sometimes we can say that it appears to constitute a very fair, or even a severe, sample of the possible predictions; while in other cases, we cannot even say that, but only that it comprises all the predictions which we can as yet draw and put to the test. Those two classes of cases may be taken as constituting two species under this genus. We cannot ordinarily hope that our hypothesis will pass through the fire of induction, absolutely unmodified. Consequently, we ought not to conclude that it is absolutely correct, but only that it very much resembles the truth. In so far as further induction will modify it, as it must be expected that it will do, if it is not to meet with downright refutation, it can hardly fail that the modification should come about gradually. We shall first find facts, reconcilable yet unexpected. These will be discovered in greater volume, until they show that a modification of the theory is necessary. The familiar history of the kinetical theory of gases well illustrates this. It began with a number of spheres almost infinitesimally small occasionally colliding. It was afterward so far modified that the forces between the spheres, instead of merely separating them, were mainly attractive, that the molecules were not spheres, but systems, and that the part of space within which their motions are free is appreciably less than the entire volume of the gas. There was no new hypothetical element in these modifications. They were partly merely quantitative, and partly such as to make the formal hypothesis represent better what was really supposed to be the case, but which had been simplified for mathematical simplicity. There was, besides, an important modification which was imposed by mathematical necessity. So far as these modifications were introduced in order to bring the hypothesis into better accord with the facts, they were indicated and suspected long before the need of them became quite apparent; so that this genus of induction shares with the first the advantage that where the inductive conclusion errs, it will be but slightly, and the discovery, instead of being shot like a bolt out of the blue, creeps upon us as a dawning day.

The reasonings of science are for the most part complex. Their parts are so put together as to increase their strength. Our attention has been confined to the elements out of which scientific argumentations are built up. We have now passed in review all the logically distinct forms of pure induction. It has been seen that one and all are mere processes for testing hypotheses already in hand. The induction adds nothing. At the very most it corrects the value of a ratio or slightly modifies a hypothesis in a way which had already been contemplated as possible.

Abduction, on the other hand, is merely preparatory. It is the first step of scientific reasoning, as induction is the concluding step. Nothing has so much contributed to present chaotic or erroneous ideas of the logic of science as failure to distinguish the essentially different characters of different elements of scientific reasoning; and one of the worst of these confusions, as well as one of the commonest, consists in regarding abduction and induction taken together (often mixed also with deduction), as a simple argument. Abduction and induction have, to be sure, this common feature, that both lead to the acceptance of a hypothesis because observed facts are such as would necessarily or probably result as consequences of that hypothesis. But for all that, they are the opposite poles of reason, the one the most ineffective, the other the most effective of arguments. The method of either is the very reverse of the other's. Abduction makes its start from the facts, without, at the outset, having any particular theory in view, though it is motived by the feeling that a theory is needed to explain the surprising facts. Induction makes its start from a hypothesis which seems to recommend itself, without at the outset having any particular facts in view, though it feels the need of facts to support the theory. Abduction seeks a theory. Induction seeks for facts. In abduction the consideration of the facts suggests the hypothesis. In induction the study of the hypothesis suggests the experiments which bring to light the very facts to which the hypothesis had pointed. The mode of suggestion by which, in abduction, the facts suggest the hypothesis is by *resemblance*,—the resemblance of the facts to the consequences of the hypothesis. The mode of suggestion by which in induction the hypothesis suggests the facts is by *contiguity*,—familiar knowledge that the conditions of the hypothesis can be realized in certain experimental ways.

I now proceed to consider what principles should guide us in abduction, or the process of choosing a hypothesis. Underlying all such principles there is a fundamental and primary abduction, a hypothesis which we must embrace at the outset, however destitute of evidentiary support it may be. That hypothesis is that the facts in hand admit of rationalization, and of rationalization by us. That we must hope they do, for the same reason that a general who has to capture a position, or see his country ruined, must go on the hypothesis that there is some way in which he can and shall capture it. We must be animated by that hope concerning the problem we have in hand, whether we extend it to a general postulate covering all facts, or not. Now, that the matter of no new truth can come from induction or from deduction, we have seen. It can only come from abduction; and abduction is, after all, nothing but guessing. We are therefore bound to hope that, although the possible explanations of our facts may be strictly innumerable, yet our mind will be able in some finite number of guesses, to guess the sole true explanation of them. *That* we are bound to assume, independently of any evidence that it is true. Animated by that hope, we are to proceed to the construction of a hypothesis.

Now the only way to discover the principles upon which anything ought to be constructed is to consider what is to be done with the constructed thing after it is constructed. That which is to be done with the hypothesis is to trace out its consequences by deduction, to compare them with results of experiment by induction, and to discard the hypothesis, and try another, as soon as the first has been refuted, as it presumably will be. How long it will be before we light upon the hypothesis which shall resist all tests we cannot tell; but we hope we shall do so, at last. In view of this prospect, it is plain that three considerations should determine our choice of a hypothesis. In the first place, it must be capable of being subjected to experimental testing. It must consist of experiential consequences with only so much logical cement as is needed to render them rational. In the second place, the hypothesis must be such that it will explain the surprising facts we have before us which it is the whole motive of our inquiry to rationalize. This explanation may consist in making the observed facts natural chance results, as the kinetical theory of gases explains facts; or it may render the facts necessary, and in the latter case as implicitly asserting them or as the ground for a mathematical demonstration of their truth. In the third place, quite as necessary a consideration as either of those I have mentioned, in view of the fact that the true hypothesis is only one out of innumerable possible false ones, in view, too, of the enormous expensiveness of experimentation in money, time, energy, and thought, is the consideration of economy. Now economy, in general, depends upon three kinds of factors: cost; the value of the thing proposed, in itself; and its effect upon other projects. Under the head of cost, if a hypothesis can be put to the test of experiment with very little expense of any kind, that should be regarded as a recommendation for giving it precedence in the inductive procedure. For even if it be barely admissible for other reasons, still it may clear the ground to have disposed of it. In the beginning of the wonderful reasonings by which the cuneiform inscriptions were made legible, one or two hypotheses which were never considered likely were taken up and soon refuted with great advantage. Under the head of value, we must place those considerations which tend toward an expectation that a given hypothesis may be true. These are of two kinds, the purely instinctive and the reasoned. In regard to instinctive considerations, I have already pointed out that it is a primary hypothesis underlying all abduction that the human mind is akin to the truth in the sense that in a finite number of guesses it will light upon the correct hypothesis. Now inductive experience supports that hypothesis in a remarkable measure. For if there were no tendency of that kind, if, when a surprising phenomenon presented itself in our laboratory, we had to make random shots at the determining conditions, trying such hypotheses as that the aspect of the planets had something to do with it, or what the dowager empress had been doing just five hours previously, if such hypotheses had as good a chance of being true as those which seem marked by good sense, then we never could have made any progress in science at all. But that we have made solid gains in knowledge is indisputable; and moreover, the history of science proves that when the phenomena were properly analyzed, upon fundamental points, at least, it has seldom been necessary to try more than two or three hypotheses made by clear genius before the right one was found. I have heard it said that Kepler tried nineteen orbits for Mars before he hit upon the right one; but in the first place, I cannot admit that that is a fair description of his elaborate series of inductions, and in the second place the subject of the hypothesis was not of the fundamental class. We cannot go so far as to say that high human intelligence is more often right than wrong in its guesses; but we can say that, after due analysis, and unswerved by prepossessions, it has been, and no doubt will be, not very many times more likely to be wrong than right. As we advance further and further into science, the aid that we can derive from the natural light of reason becomes, no doubt, less and less; but still science will cease to progress if ever we shall reach the point where there is no longer an infinite saving of expense in experimentation to be effected by care that our hypotheses are such as naturally recommend themselves to the mind, and make upon us the impression of simplicity,—which here means facility of comprehension by the human mind,—of aptness, of reasonableness, of good sense. For the existence of a natural instinct for truth is, after all, the sheet anchor of science. From the instinctive, we pass to reasoned marks of truth in the hypothesis. Of course, if we know any positive facts which render a given hypothesis objectively probable, they recommend it for inductive testing. When this is not the case, but the hypothesis seems to us likely or unlikely, this likelihood is an indication that the hypothesis accords or disaccords with our preconceived ideas; and since those ideas are presumably based upon some experience, it follows that, other things being equal, there will be, in the long run, some economy in giving the hypothesis a place in the order of precedence in accordance with this indication. But experience must be our chart in economical navigation; and experience shows that likelihoods are treacherous guides. Nothing has caused so much waste of time and means, in all sorts of researches, as inquirers' becoming so wedded to certain likelihoods as to forget all the other factors of the economy of research; so that, unless it be very solidly grounded, likelihood is far better disregarded, or nearly so; and even when it seems solidly grounded, it should be proceeded upon with a cautious tread, with an eye to other considerations, and a recollection of the disasters it has caused.

The third category of factors of economy, those arising from the relation of what is proposed to other projects, is especially important in abduction, because very rarely can we positively expect a given hypothesis to prove entirely satisfactory, and we must always consider what will happen when the hypothesis proposed breaks down. The qualities which these considerations induce us to value in a hypothesis are three, which I may entitle Caution, Breadth, and Incomplexity. In respect to caution, the game of twenty questions is instructive. In this game, one party thinks of some individual object, real or fictitious, which is well known to all educated people. The other party is entitled to answers to any twenty interrogatories they propound which can be answered by *Yes* or *No*, and are then to guess what was thought of, if they can. If the questioning is skillful, the object will invariably be guessed; but if the questioners allow themselves to be led astray by the will-o-the-wisp of any prepossession, they will almost as infallibly come to grief. The uniform success of good questioners is based upon the circumstance that the entire collection of individual objects well known to all the world does not amount to a million. If, therefore, each question could exactly bisect the possibilities, so that *yes* and *no* were equally probable, the right object could be identified among a collection numbering 2^{20}. Now the logarithm of 2 being 0.30103, that of its twentieth power is 6.0206, which is the logarithm of about 1,000,000 $(1 + .02 \times 2.3)(1 + .0006 \times 2.3)$ or over one million and forty-seven thousand, or more than the entire number of objects from which the selection has been made. Thus, twenty skillful hypotheses will ascertain what two hundred thousand stupid ones might fail to do. The secret of the business lies in the caution which breaks a hypothesis up into its smallest logical components, and only risks one of them at a time. What a world of futile controversy and of confused experimentation might have been saved if this principle had guided investigations into the theory of light! The ancient and medieval notion was that sight starts from the eye, is shot to the object from which it is reflected, and returned to the eye. This idea had, no doubt, been entirely given up before Römer showed that it took light a quarter of an hour to traverse the earth's orbit,[37] a discovery which would have refuted it by the experiment of opening the closed eyes and looking at the stars. The next point in order was to ascertain of what the ray of light consisted. But this not being answerable by *yes* or *no*, the first question should have been "Is the ray homogeneous along its length?" Diffraction showed that it was not so. That being established, the next question should have been "Is the ray homogeneous on all sides?" Had that question been put to experiment, polarization must have been speedily discovered; and the same sort of procedure would have developed the whole theory with a gain of half a century.

Correlative to the quality of caution is that of breadth. For when we break the hypothesis into elementary parts, we may, and should, inquire how far the same explanation accounts for the same phenomenon when it appears in other subjects. For example, the kinetical theory of gases, although it was originally proposed with a view merely to explaining the law of Boyle,[38] never attracted much attention, nor was there any good reason why it should, until the conservation of energy was brought to light, and it was found that the kinetical theory would account, in a remarkably satisfactory way, for non-conservative phenomena. It accounts for those phenomena, so far as it does account for them, by representing that they are results of chance, or, if you please, of the law of high numbers; for it is remarkable that chance operates in one way and not in the opposite way. Under those circumstances, the economical consideration which we now have in view, would recommend that we at once inquire into non-conservative phenomena, generally, in order to see whether the same sort of explanation is equally admissible in all cases, or whether we are thus led to some broad category of conditions under which non-conservative phenomena appear, or whether there are several distinct ways in which they are brought about. For great economy must result in whichever way this question is answered, provided it can be answered at not too great an expense. Thus, if we find that there are several explanations of non-conservative phenomena, we have only to trace out their several consequences, and we shall have criteria for distinguishing them; while if we find there is but one cause, we at once reach a wide generalization which will save repetitious work. It is, therefore, good economy, other things being equal, to make our hypotheses as broad as possible. But, of course, one consideration has to be balanced against another.

There still remains one more economic consideration in reference to a hypothesis; namely, that it may give a good "leave," as the billiard players say. If it does not suit the facts, still the comparison with the facts may be instructive with reference to the next hypothesis. For example, I might be inclined to surmise that an observable quantity y was such a function of a quantity x, determined by the conditions of experiments, as to be expressible in the form $y = a + bx^2$. Still, as I am not sure of this, perhaps it would be wise first to try how well the experiments could be satisfied by $y = cx$ because the residuals will be more readily interpretable in the latter case. As a provisional hypothesis, it will, for this reason, other considerations apart, be better to assume something very simple, even though we imagine that by complicating the hypothesis it could be brought nearer the truth. Let us suppose, for example, that I wished to find some mathematical relation between the atomic weights and the succession of chemical elements according to Mendeléef's system. In point of fact, I hardly think that the time has yet come when it is worth while to take up that question for its own sake. The discoveries of Gallium,

Germanium, and Scandium have proved that there is some truth in one part of Mendeléef's theory; but the non-discovery of hecamagnesium inclines me, I must say, to think that Chromium and Magnesium are exceptional elements; and it seems to me that the groups, unless it be the extreme ones, are founded on pretty superficial characters. And if we are to separate all elements into what Mendeléef calls groups, it seems to me that the rare earths seem to afford symptoms that an additional group must be admitted, say perhaps between the group of Zinc and the group of Gallium. However, if we are to retain Mendeléef's system, let us suppose, as a first rough approximation to the truth, that, in the absence of disturbing conditions of which we know nothing, the atomic weights of the elements would increase from $K = 39$ by 2 ½ units at each step. Even if it is of little service to chemistry it will, at least, serve as a tolerable illustration of the point of logic we have under consideration to compare the numbers required by this hypothesis with the numbers found. The latter depend upon the purity of the materials, of which the sole and insufficient guarantee is that atomic weights of material from different sources and subjected to different chemical operations agree. The following table *[p. 112]* shows the comparison.[39]

There are sixteen consecutive elements undiscovered, according to Mendeléef's theory.[40] Those that we know of the same groups, that is those in the table just above and just below the vacant spaces, may very well be contaminated with the unknown elements. The twenty-four first, not open to this suspicion, mostly differ from our calculation by not more than 1. Those just above the missing elements have on the average atomic weights 2 units too great, those just below are on the average about ½ a unit too small. Thus, this very incomplex and even rough hypothesis has done for us what a more elaborate one would almost surely have failed to do, namely, it has brought to light an indication that all the elements from Ruthenium up are probably largely contaminated with undiscovered elements, which contaminations have mostly atomic weights between 146 and 182, but are partly of large atomic weights, say from 211 up. Since this perturbation is largest in Tellurium and Barium, we should naturally look in these elements, especially, for admixtures of substances of higher atomic weight.[41] In Tellurium they have been sought, in vain; yet one cannot say that the negative has been rendered altogether improbable. In Barium, on the other hand, there are indications of something of the sort, though whether it is sufficient to account for the large atomic weight, it is impossible to decide at present. I will not say that the hypothesis merits much attention, for the reason that it rests upon the acceptance of Mendeléef's arrangement, and that arrangement is itself in considerable doubt.

Having now passed in review all the elements of merit of an hypothesis, I ought, in regular procedure, to consider the general principles of synthesis of these elements. But I think that that would delay us to no advantage; for once it is granted that the elements I have enumerated are the points to consider,

Table 1

Element	K	Ca	Sc	Ti	V	Cr	Mn	Fe	Co	Ni	Cu	Zn	Ga	Ge	As	Se	Br	Kr
Calc	39	$41\frac{1}{2}$	44	$46\frac{1}{2}$	49	$51\frac{1}{2}$	54	$56\frac{1}{2}$	59	$61'\frac{1}{2}$	64	$66\frac{1}{2}$	69	$71\frac{1}{2}$	74	$76\frac{1}{2}$	79	$81\frac{1}{2}$
Obs	39.1	40.0	44	48.2	51.4	52.1	55.0	55.9	59.0	58.7	63.6	65.4	70.0	72.5	75.0	79.2	80.0	81.6
O – C	+0	$-1\frac{1}{2}$	0	$+1\frac{1}{2}$	$+2\frac{1}{2}$	$+\frac{1}{2}$	+1	$-\frac{1}{2}$	0	-3	$-\frac{1}{2}$	-1	+1	+1	+1	$+2\frac{1}{2}$	+1	+0

Element	Rb	Sr	Y	Zr	Nb	Mo		Ru	Rh	Pd	Ag	Cd	In	Sn	Sb	Te	I	Xe
Calc	84	$86\frac{1}{2}$	89	$91\frac{1}{2}$	94	$96\frac{1}{2}$	99	$101\frac{1}{2}$	104	$106\frac{1}{2}$	109	$111\frac{1}{2}$	114	$116\frac{1}{2}$	119	$121\frac{1}{2}$	124	$126\frac{1}{2}$
Obs	85.4	87.7	89.0	90.6	94	96.0	—	101.7	103.0	106.5	107.9	112.3	114	119.0	120.0	127.5	126.8	128.0
O – C	$+1\frac{1}{2}$	+1	0	-1	0	$-\frac{1}{2}$	—	+0	-1	0	-1	+1	0	$+2\frac{1}{2}$	+1	+6	+3	$+1\frac{1}{2}$

Element	Cs	Ba	La	Ce	Pr	Nd												
Calc	129	$131\frac{1}{2}$	134	$136\frac{1}{2}$	139	$141\frac{1}{2}$	144	$146\frac{1}{2}$	149	$151\frac{1}{2}$	154	$156\frac{1}{2}$	159	$161\frac{1}{2}$	164	$166\frac{1}{2}$	169	$171\frac{1}{2}$
Obs	132.9	137.4	138.5	140	140.5	143.6	—	—	—	—	—	—	—	—	—	—	—	—
O – C	+4	+6	$+4\frac{1}{2}$	$+3\frac{1}{2}$	$+1\frac{1}{2}$	+2	—	—	—	—	—	—	—	—	—	—	—	—

Element					Ta	W		Os	Ir	Pt	Au	Hg	Tl	Pb	Bi			
Calc	174	$176\frac{1}{2}$	179	$181\frac{1}{2}$	184	$186\frac{1}{2}$	189	$191\frac{1}{2}$	194	$196\frac{1}{2}$	199	$201\frac{1}{2}$	204	$206\frac{1}{2}$	209	$211\frac{1}{2}$	214	$216\frac{1}{2}$
Obs	—	—	—	—	183	184	—	190.8	193.0	195.2	197.3	200.0	204.2	206.9	208	—	—	—
O – C	—	—	—	—	-1	$-2\frac{1}{2}$	—	$-\frac{1}{2}$	-1	$-1\frac{1}{2}$	$-1\frac{1}{2}$	$-1\frac{1}{2}$	0	$+\frac{1}{2}$	-1	—	—	—

the mode in which they are to be combined in the case of ancient history is too obvious for dispute. The elements are as follows:

Experiential character of the hypothesis

Its explaining all the facts
- as natural concomitants
- as Deductions
  - Corollarial
  - Theorematic

Economical considerations
- Cheapness
- Intrinsic Value
  - Naturalness
  - Likelihood
- Relation of Hypotheses
  - Caution
  - Breadth
  - Incomplexity

In the case of ancient history, the facts to be explained are, in part, of the nature of monuments, among which are to be reckoned the manuscripts; but the greater part of the facts are documentary; that is, they are assertions and virtual assertions which we read either in the manuscripts or upon inscriptions. This latter class of facts is so much in excess that ancient history may be said to consist in the interpretation of testimonies, occasionally supported or refuted by the indirect evidence of the monuments.

Now the first rule which we should set up is that our hypothesis ought to explain *all* the related facts. It is not sufficient to say that testimony is not true; it is our business to explain how it came to be such as it is.

The second rule is that our first hypothesis should be that the principal testimonies are true; and this hypothesis should not be abandoned until it is conclusively refuted. No practice is more wasteful than that of abandoning a hypothesis once taken up, until it becomes evident that it is quite untenable. An excellent method in the great majority of those cases in which it is applicable and in which it leads to any unequivocal results is to give precedence to that hypothesis which reposes upon a deep and primary instinct, such as is the instinct to believe testimony, without which human society could not exist. There is no surer mark of inexperience in dealing with witnesses than a tendency to believe they are falsifying, without any definite, objective, and strong reason for the suspicion. But especially in ancient history, where the only facts we have are, in most cases, testimonies, the extremely bad economy of supposing those testimonies false, before we have first thoroughly tried the hypothesis that they are true, and have found it quite inadmissible, is so obvious, that it is difficult to repress a certain contempt for the reasoning powers of those critics who are given to this procedure.

The third rule will be that probabilities that are strictly objective and at the same time very great, although they can never be absolutely conclusive, ought nevertheless to influence our preference for one hypothesis over another; but slight probabilities, even if objective, are not worth consideration; and merely subjective likelihoods should be disregarded altogether. For they are merely expressions of our preconceived notions. Now one of the main purposes of studying history ought to be to free us from the tyranny of our preconceived notions.

The fourth rule will be that we should split up a hypothesis into its items as much as possible, so as to test each one singly.

The fifth rule will be that when we are in doubt which of two hypotheses ought to have precedence, we should try whether, by enlarging the field of facts which they are to explain, a good reason will not appear for giving one of them a decided preference over the other.

The sixth rule will be that if the work of testing a particular hypothesis will have substantially or largely to be done in any case, in the process of testing another hypothesis, that circumstance should, other things being equal, give this hypothesis which thus involves little or no extra expense, a preference over another which would require special work of no value except for testing it.

A hypothesis having been adopted on probation, the process of testing it will consist, not in examining the facts, in order to see how well they accord with the hypothesis, but on the contrary in examining such of the probable consequences of the hypothesis as would be capable of direct verification, especially those consequences which would be very unlikely or surprising in case the hypothesis were not true. It is not easy to enumerate the different kinds of consequences; but among them may be that the hypothesis would render the present existence of a monument probable, or would result in giving a known monument a certain character; that if it were true, certain ancient documents ought to contain some allusion to it; that if it is misstated by some authority not considered in the selection of the hypothesis, that misstatement would be likely to be of a certain kind; that if the hypothesis is true, and an assertion or allusion found in an ancient work is to be explained by the author's knowing it to be true, he must have had certain other knowledge, etc. When the hypothesis has sustained a testing as severe as the present state of our knowledge of the particular branch of history to which it belongs renders imperative, it will be admitted provisionally into the list of our present historical results, subject of course to reconsideration along with all those other results when we are in a condition to insist upon a higher grade of security.

9

On Science and Natural Classes

MS 427. [Published in CP 1.203–37. Written in February 1902, this selection comes from Chapter II of Peirce's projected book, "Minute Logic."] In this selection, excerpted from a broader discussion on logic and the classification of sciences, Peirce discusses his theory of natural classes and classification, and presents his conception of science. The problem of natural classes had been of interest to Peirce from early in his career, when he was concerned with distinguishing his views from those of J. S. Mill, but here he refines his views by giving final causation a prominent role in his theory. Natural classes are defined by final causes, though not necessarily by purposes. Peirce then characterizes science as "a living thing," not the collection of "systematized knowledge on the shelves." Science is what scientists do; it "consists in actually drawing the bow upon truth with intentness in the eye, with energy in the arm." Peirce argues that the divisions of science that have grown out of its practice are natural classes.

When the best method of doing a thing is in doubt, one of the best aids toward getting set upon the right path is to consider what need of doing it there is.[1] This is axiomatic. Since, then, logic teaches us how to attain truth, the need of a systematic doctrine of logic will best appear by considering its relation to the different sciences, which are the different departments of the endeavor to attain the truth, and by considering the relations of these different endeavors to one another, particularly with reference to the aid that they afford one another. This is the need to us of the inquiry I propose here to enter upon, that of the natural classification of the sciences.

Many have been the attempts at a general classification of the sciences. Dr. Richardson's little book upon the subject* is quite incomplete, only enumerating 146 systems. They are naturally many, because not only are their purposes various, but their conceptions of a science are divergent, and their notions of what classification is are still more so. Many of these schemes introduce sciences which nobody ever heard of; so that they seem to aim at classifying, not actually existent sciences, but possible sciences. A somewhat presumptuous undertaking is that of classifying the science of the remote future. On the other hand, if classifications are to be restricted to sciences actually existing at the time the classifications are made, the classifications

---

Classification. By Ernest Cushing Richardson, 1901.[2]

certainly ought to differ from age to age. If Plato's classification was satisfactory in his day, it cannot be good today; and if it be good now, the inference will be that it was bad when he proposed it.

This business of classifying sciences is not one to be undertaken precipitately or off-hand. That is plain. We should not begin the execution of the
task until we have well considered, first, what classification is; and secondly,
what science is.

NATURE OF
NATURAL
CLASSIFICATION.
What mode of classifying anything is to be preferred depends entirely
upon what use the classification is to be put to. For example, the alphabetic
arrangement is certainly the best for the index of a book; and readers will
never cease to curse the writer,—a German most likely,—who offers an
elaborate index *raisonné* as a substitute for an alphabetical arrangement. Yet
no arrangement can be worse than an alphabetical one for any more rational purpose. The 146 systems mentioned above as dealt with in Dr. Richardson's book do not include classifications for the purpose of reference to a
library of which he adds a separate catalogue of 173 systems. The 146, like
the classification which we desire, were given as having each a scientific
value,—as being *the* one true and natural classification. The first question,
then, that it seems well to consider (remembering that classification is one
of the topics of logic to be dealt with more scientifically in its proper place,
and that I can here only skim the surface of it) is, What is meant by a true
and natural class? A great many logicians say there is no such thing; and,
what is strange, even many students of taxonomic sciences not only follow
this opinion, but allow it a great part in determining the conclusions of botany and zoology. The cause of their holding this opinion has two factors;
firstly, that they attach a metaphysical signification to the term *natural* or
real class, and secondly, that they have embraced a system of metaphysics
which allows them to believe in no such thing as that which they have
defined a real or natural class to be. Far be it from me to wish to close any
avenue by which truth may be arrived at; and if botanists and zoologists
come to the conclusion that botany and zoology must rest upon metaphysics, I have not a word of objection to make. Only I can tell them that metaphysics is a most difficult science, presenting more pitfalls for the unin-
formed than almost any, which a mere amateur at it would be foolish to
fancy that he could escape. Therefore, if botany and zoology must perforce
rest upon metaphysics, by all means let this metaphysics be recognized as an
explicit branch of those sciences, and be treated in a thoroughgoing and scientific manner. Having devoted many years to it, I am entitled to my opinion upon a metaphysical question, although it may be a mistaken one; and
my opinion is that it is a shallow and sciolistic metaphysics which declares a
"real class," in the sense which those writers attach to the term, to be an
impossible thing. At the same time, I am unable to see any need at all in positive science for considering such metaphysically real classes. To my apprehension the business of classification has no concern with them, but only

with true and natural classes, in another and a purely experiential sense. For example, if I were to attempt to classify the arts, which I shall not do, I should have to recognize, as one of them, the art of illumination, and should have occasion to remark that lamps form a true, real, and natural class, because every lamp has been made and has come into being as a result of an aim common and peculiar to all lamps. A *class*, of course, is the total of whatever objects there may be in the universe which are of a certain description. What if we try taking the term "natural" or "real class" to mean a class of which all the members owe their existence as members of the class to a common final cause? This is somewhat vague; but it is better to allow a term like this to remain vague, until we see our way to rational precision. In the case of lamps, we know what that cause is: that instinct which enables us to distinguish human productions and to divine their purpose informs us of this with a degree of certainty which it were futile to hope that any science should surpass. But in the case of natural classes the final cause remains occult. Perhaps, since phrases retain their sway over men's minds long after their meaning has evaporated, it may be that some reader, even at this day, remains imbued with the old notion that there are no final causes in nature; in which case, natural selection, and every form of evolution, would be false. For evolution is nothing more nor less than the working out of a definite end. A final cause may be conceived to operate without having been the purpose of any mind: that supposed phenomenon goes by the name of *fate*. The doctrine of evolution refrains from pronouncing whether forms are simply fated or whether they are providential; but that definite ends are worked out none of us today any longer deny. Our eyes have been opened; and the evidence is too overwhelming. In regard to natural objects, however, it may be said, in general, that we do not know precisely what their final causes are. But need that prevent us from ascertaining whether or not there is a common cause by virtue of which those things that have the essential characters of the class are enabled to exist? The manner of distribution of the class-character will show, with a high degree of certainty, whether or not it is determinative of existence. Take, for example, the class of animals that have legs. The use of legs is clear to us, having them ourselves. But if we pass the animal kingdom in review, we see that in the majority of branches there are no such organs of locomotion; while in the others they are present throughout some whole classes, are absent throughout others; and in still others are sometimes present, sometimes absent. With such a distribution, this mode of locomotion may be so connected with the possibility of a form, that two animals of the same order could not differ in respect to using legs; but it is evident that animals having legs do not form a natural group; for they are not separated from all others in any other important particular. We thus get a tolerably clear idea of what a natural class is: it will amply suffice for our present purpose; though we can hardly hope that it will turn out to be logically accurate. We also see that, when an object has

DISTRIBUTIO
OF CHARACTI
IN A CLASS.

been made with a purpose, as is, of course, the case with the sciences, no classes can be more fundamental nor broader than those which are defined

DESIRE
ALWAYS
GENERAL.

by the purpose. A purpose is an operative desire. Now a desire is always general; that is, it is always some *kind* of thing or event which is desired; at least, until the element of will, which is always exercised upon an individual object upon an individual occasion, becomes so predominant as to overrule the generalizing character of desire. Thus, desires create classes, and extremely broad classes. But desires become, in the pursuit of them, more specific. Let us revert, for example, to lamps. We desire, in the first instance, merely economical illumination. But we remark that that may be carried out by combustion, where there is a chemical process kindling itself, or heat may be supplied from without in electric lighting, or it may be stored up, as in phosphorescence. These three ways of carrying out our main purpose constitute subsidiary purposes.* So if we decide upon electric lighting, the question will be between incandescent and arc lighting. If we decide upon combustion, the burning matter may itself become incandescent, or its heat may serve to render another more suitable thing incandescent, as in the Welsbach burner.[4] Here is a complication which will ordinarily be advantageous, since by not making the same thing fulfill the two functions of supplying heat to produce incandescence and of incandescing upon being heated, there is more freedom to choose things suitable to the two functions. This is a good example of that sort of natural class which Agassiz called an order; that is, a class created by a useful complication of a general plan.

DESIRE
ALWAYS
VAGUE.

Closely connected with the fact that every desire is general, are two other facts which must be taken into account in considering purposive classes. The first of these is that a desire is always more or less variable, or vague. For example, a man wants an economical lamp. Then if he burns oil in it, he will endeavor to burn that oil which gives him sufficient light at the lowest cost. But another man, who lives a little further from the source of supply of that oil and a little nearer the source of a different oil, may find that different oil to be the better for him. So it is with the desires of one individual. The same man who prefers veal to pork as a general thing, may think that an occasional spare rib is better than having cold boiled veal every day of his life. In short, variety is the spice of life for the individual, and practically still more so for a large number of individuals; and as far as we can compare Nature's ways with ours, she seems to be even more given to variety than we. These three cases may be very different on their subjective side; but for purposes of classification they are equivalent.

DESIRE
ALWAYS HAS
LONGITUDE.

But not only is desire *general* and *vague,* or indeterminate, it has besides a certain *longitude,* or third dimension. By this I mean that while a certain ideal state of things might most perfectly satisfy a desire, yet a situation

---

*I am here influenced by the *Essay on Classification* of L. Agassiz, whose pupil I was for a few months.[3]

somewhat differing from that will be far better than nothing; and in general, when a state is not too far from the ideal state, the nearer it approaches that state the better. Moreover, the situation of things most satisfactory to one desire is almost never the situation most satisfactory to another. A brighter lamp than that I use would, perhaps, be more agreeable to my eyes; but it would be less so to my pocket, to my lungs, and to my sense of heat. Accordingly, a compromise is struck; and since all the desires concerned are somewhat vague, the result is that the objects actually will cluster about certain middling qualities, some being removed this way, some that way, and at greater and greater removes fewer and fewer objects will be so determined. Thus, clustering distributions will characterize purposive classes.

One consequence of this deserves particular notice, since it will concern us a good deal in our classification of the sciences, and yet is quite usually overlooked and assumed not [to] be as it is. Namely, it follows that it may be quite impossible to draw a sharp line of demarcation between two classes, although they are real and natural classes in strictest truth. Namely, this will happen when the form about which the individuals of one class cluster is not so unlike the form about which individuals of another class cluster but that variations from each middling form may precisely agree. In such a case, we may know in regard to any intermediate form what proportion of the objects of that form had one purpose and what proportion the other; but unless we have some supplementary information we cannot tell which ones had one purpose and which the other. The reader may be disposed to suspect that this is merely a mathematician's fancy, and that no such case would be likely ever to occur. But he may be assured that such occurrences are far from being rare. In order to satisfy him that this state of things does occur, I will mention an incontestable instance of it;—incontestable, at least, by any fair mind competent to deal with the problem. Professor Flinders Petrie,[5] whose reasoning powers I had admired long before his other great scientific qualities had been proved, among which his great exactitude and circumspection as a metrologist concerns us here, exhumed, at the ancient trading town of Naucratis, no less than 158 balance-weights having the Egyptian *ket* as their unit.* The great majority of them are of basalt and syenite, material so unchangeable that the corrections needed to bring them to their original values are small. I shall deal only with 144 of them from each of which Mr. Petrie has calculated the value of the *ket* to a tenth of a troy grain. Since these values range all the way from 137 to 152 grains, it is evident that the weights were intended to be copies of several different standards, probably four or five; for there would be no use of a balance, if one could detect the errors of the balance-weights by simply "hefting" them, and comparing them with one's memory of the standard weight. Considering that these weights are small, and were therefore used for weighing costly or even precious matter, our knowledge of the practice of

NATURAL CLASSES NOT ALWAYS DEFINITELY DISTINGUISHED.

THE KETS OF NAUCRATIS.

---

*Egyptian Exploration Fund. *Third Memoir*, pp. 75–76.

weighing among the ancients gives us ground for thinking it likely that about half the weights would depart from their virtual standards by more, and about half by less, than, say, 4 or 5 tenths of one per cent, which, upon a ket, would be from half to two-thirds of a grain. Now the whole interval here is 14 ½ grains; and between 136.8 grains to 151.3 grains, there is no case of an interval of more than a third of a grain not represented by any weight among the 144. To a person thoroughly familiar with the theory of errors this shows that there must be four or five different standards to which different ones aim to conform. [. . .][6]

FINAL
CAUSATION.
I hope this long digression[7] (which will be referred to with some interest when we come to study the theory of errors) will not have caused the reader to forget that we were engaged in tracing out some of the consequences of understanding the term "natural" or "real class" to mean a class the existence of whose members is due to a common and peculiar final cause. It is, as I was saying, a widespread error to think that a "final cause" is necessarily a purpose. A purpose is merely that form of final cause which is most familiar to our experience. The signification of the phrase "final cause" must be determined by its use in the statement of Aristotle that all causation divides into two grand branches, the efficient, or forceful; and the ideal, or final.[8] If we are to conserve the truth of that statement, we must understand by final causation that mode of bringing facts about according to which a general description of result is made to come about, quite irrespective of any compulsion for it to come about in this or that particular way; although the means may be adapted to the end. The general result may be brought about at one time in one way, and at another time in another way. Final causation does not determine in what particular way it is to be brought about, but only that the result shall have a certain general character. Efficient causation, on the other hand, is a compulsion determined by the particular condition of things, and is a compulsion acting to make that situation begin to change in a perfectly determinate way; and what the general character of the result may be in no way concerns the efficient causation. For example, I shoot at an eagle on the wing; and since my purpose,—a special sort of final, or ideal, cause,—is to hit the bird, I do not shoot directly at it, but a little ahead of it, making allowance for the change of place by the time the bullet gets to that distance. So far, it is an affair of final causation. But after the bullet leaves the rifle, the affair is turned over to the stupid efficient causation, and should the eagle make a swoop in another direction, the bullet does not swerve in the least, efficient causation having no regard whatsoever for results, but simply obeying orders blindly. It is true that the force of the bullet conforms to a law; and the law is something general. But for that very reason the law is not a force. For force is compulsion; and compulsion is *hic et nunc*. It is either that or it is no compulsion. Law, without force to carry it out, would be a court without a sheriff; and all its dicta would be vaporings. Thus, the relation of law, as a cause, to the action of force, as its

effect, is final, or ideal, causation, not efficient causation. The relation is somewhat similar to that of my pulling the hair trigger of my rifle; when the cartridge explodes with a force of its own, and off goes the bullet in blind obedience to perform the special instantaneous beginning of an act that it is, each instant, compelled to commence. It is a vehicle of compulsion *hic et nunc*, receiving and transmitting it; while I receive and transmit ideal influence, of which I am a vehicle. When we speak of an "idea," or "notion," or "conception of the mind," we are most usually thinking,—or trying to think,—of an idea abstracted from all efficiency. But a court without a sheriff, or the means of creating one, would not be a court at all; and did it ever occur to you, my reader, that an idea without efficiency is something equally absurd and unthinkable? Imagine such an idea if you can! Have you done so? Well, where did you get this idea? If it was communicated to you *viva voce* from another person, it must have had efficiency enough to get the particles of air vibrating. If you read it in a newspaper, it had set a monstrous printing press in motion. If you thought it out yourself, it had caused something to happen in your brain. And again, how do you know that you did have the idea when this discussion began a few lines above, unless it had efficiency to make some record on the brain? The court cannot be imagined without a sheriff. Final causality cannot be imagined without efficient causality; but no whit the less on that account are their modes of action polar contraries. The sheriff would still have his fist, even if there were no court; but an efficient cause, detached from a final cause in the form of a law, would not even possess efficiency: it might exert itself, and something might follow *post hoc*, but not *propter hoc*; for *propter* implies potential regularity. Now without law there is no regularity; and without the influence of ideas there is no potentiality.

The light of these reflections brings out into distinct view characters of our definition of a real class which we might otherwise have overlooked or misinterpreted. Every class has its definition, which is an idea; but it is not every class where the *existence*, that is, the occurrence in the universe, of its members is due to the active causality of the defining idea of the class. That circumstance makes the epithet *natural* particularly appropriate to the class. The word *natura* evidently must originally have meant *birth*; although even in the oldest Latin it very seldom bears that meaning. There is, however, a certain subconscious memory of that meaning in many phrases; just as with words from φύσις, there is the idea of springing forth, or a more vegetable-like production, without so much reference to a progenitor. Things, it may be, φύεται spontaneously; but *nature* is an inheritance. Heredity, of which so much has been said since 1860, is not a force but a law, although, like other laws, it doubtless avails itself of forces.[9] But it is essential that the offspring shall have a *general* resemblance to the parent, not that this general resemblance happens to result from this or that blind and particular action. No doubt, there is some blind efficient causation; but it is not that which

A NATURAL CLASS, WHAT?

constitutes the heredity, but, on the contrary, the general resemblance. So, then, those naturalists are right who hold that the action of evolution in reproduction produces *real* classes, as by the very force of the words it produces *natural* classes. In considering the classification of sciences, however, we have no need of penetrating the mysteries of biological development; for the generation here is of ideas by ideas,—unless one is to say, with many logicians, that ideas arise from the consideration of facts in which there are no such ideas, nor any ideas. That opinion is a superficial one, allied on one side of it, to the notion that the only final cause is a purpose. So, those logicians imagine that an idea has to be connected with a brain, or has to inhere in a "soul." This is preposterous: the idea does not belong to the soul; it is the soul that belongs to the idea. The soul does for the idea just what the cellulose does for the Beauty of the rose; that is to say, it affords it opportunity. It is the court-sheriff, the arm of the law.

THE POWER OF IDEAS.

I fear I may be producing the impression of talking at random. It is that I wish the reader to "catch on" to my conception, my point of view; and just as one cannot make a man see that a thing is red, or is beautiful, or is touching, by describing redness, beauty, or pathos, but can only point to something else that is red, beautiful, or pathetic, and say, "Look here too for something like that there," so if the reader has not been in the habit of conceiving ideas as I conceive them, I can only cast a sort of dragnet into his experience and hope that it may fish up some instance in which he shall have had a similar conception. Do you think, reader, that it is a positive fact that

Truth, crushed to earth, shall rise again;[10]

or do you think that this, being poetry, is only a pretty fiction? Do you think that, notwithstanding the horrible wickedness of every mortal wight, the idea of right and wrong is nevertheless the greatest power on this earth, to which every knee must sooner or later bow or be broken down; or do you think that this is another notion at which common sense should smile? Even if you are of the negative opinion, still you must acknowledge that the affirmative is intelligible. Here, then, are two instances of ideas which either have, or are believed to have, life, the power of bringing things to pass, here below. Perhaps you may object that right and wrong are only a power because there are, or will be, powerful men who are disposed to make them so; just as they might take it into their heads to make tulip-fancying, or Freemasonry, or Volapük[11] a power. But you must acknowledge that this is not the position of those on the affirmative side. On the contrary, they hold that it is the idea which will create its defenders, and render them powerful. They will say that if it be that Freemasonry or its foe, the Papacy, ever pass away,—as perhaps either may,—it will be precisely because they are ideas devoid of inherent, incorruptible vitality, and not at all because they have been unsupplied with stalwart defenders. Thus, whether you accept the opinion or not, you must see that it is a perfectly intelligible opinion that ideas are not all mere creations of this or that mind, but on the contrary have a power of finding or creating their vehicles, and having found them, of conferring upon them the ability to transform the face of the earth. If you ask what mode of being is supposed to belong to an idea that is in no mind, the reply will come that undoubtedly the idea must be embodied (or ensouled; it is all one) in order to attain complete being, and that if, at any moment, it should happen that an idea,—say that of physical decency,—was quite unconceived by any living being, then its mode of being (supposing that it was not altogether dead) would consist precisely in this, namely, that it was about to receive embodiment (or ensoulment) and to work in the world. This would be a mere potential being, a being *in futuro;* but it would not be the utter nothingness which would befall matter (or spirit) if it were to be deprived of the governance of ideas, and thus were to have no regularity in its action, so that throughout no fraction of a second could it steadily act in any general way. For matter would thus not only not actually exist; but it would not have even a potential existence; since potentiality is an affair of ideas. It would be just downright Nothing.

It so happens that I myself believe in the eternal life of the ideas Truth and Right. I need not, however, insist upon that for my present purpose, and have only spoken of them in order to make my meaning clear. What I do insist upon is not now the infinite vitality of those particular ideas, but that every idea has in some measure, in the same sense that those are supposed to have it in unlimited measure, the power to work out physical and psychical results. They have life, generative life.

That it is so is a matter of experiential fact. But whether it is so or not is not a question to be settled by producing a microscope or telescope or any recondite observations of any kind. Its evidence stares us all in the face every hour of our lives. Nor is any ingenious reasoning needed to make it plain. If one does not see it, it is for the same reason that some men have not a sense of sin; and there is nothing for it but to be born again and become as a little child. If you do not see it, you have to look upon the world with new eyes.

I may be asked what I mean by the objects of *[a]* class *deriving their existence* from an idea. Do I mean that the idea calls new matter into existence? Certainly not. That would be pure intellectualism, which denies that blind force is an element of experience distinct from rationality, or logical force. I believe that to be a great error; but I need not stop to disprove it now, for those who entertain it will be on my side in regard to classification. But it will be urged that if that is not my meaning, then the idea merely confers upon the members of the class its character; and since every class has a defining character, any one class is as "natural" or "real" as another, if that term be taken in the sense I give to it. I cannot, however, quite admit that. Whether or not every class is or is not more or less a natural class is a question which may be worth consideration; but I do not think that the relation

HOW EXISTENCE MAY BE DERIVED FROM IDEAS.

of the idea to the members of the natural class is simply that it is applicable to them as a predicate, as it is to every class equally. What I mean by the idea's conferring existence upon the individual members of the class is that it confers upon them the power of working out results in this world, that it confers upon them, that is to say, organic existence, or, in one word, life. The existence of an individual man is a totally different thing from the existence of the matter which at any given instant happens to compose him, and which is incessantly passing in and out. A man is a wave, but not a vortex.[12] Even the existence of the vortex, though it does happen to contain, while it lasts, always the same particles, is a very different thing from the existence of those particles. Neither does the existence of wave or vortex consist merely in the fact that something is true of whatever particles compose them; although it is inseparably bound up with that fact. Let me not be understood as proposing any new definitions of a vortex and a wave. What I mean is this. Take a corpse: dissect it more perfectly than it ever was dissected. Take out the whole system of blood vessels entire, as we see them figured in the books. Treat the whole systems of spinal and sympathetic nerves, the alimentary canal with its adjuvants, the muscular system, the osseous system, in the same way. Hang these all in a cabinet so that from a

A DEFINITION IS AN AFFAIR OF EFFICIENCY.

certain point of view each appears superposed over the others in its proper place. That would be a singularly instructive specimen. But to call it a man would be what nobody would for an instant do or dream. Now the best definition that ever was framed is, at best, but a similar dissection. It will not really work in the world as the object defined will. It will enable us to see how the thing works, in so far as it shows the efficient causation. The final causation, which is what characterizes the *definitum*, it leaves out of account. We make smoke rings. We make one pass through another, and perform various experiments, which give us an imperfect idea, yet some idea, of what a vortex really is. *How* all these things happen can be traced out from the definition. But the *rôle* that vortices really play in the universe,—no insignificant one, if all matter is built of them,—the real life of them, depends upon the idea of them, which simply finds its opportunity in those circum-

NEW STATE-MENT OF THE DISTINCTION OF FINALITY AND EFFICIENCY.

stances that are enumerated in the definition.[13] Efficient causation is that kind of causation whereby the parts compose the whole; final causation is that kind of causation whereby the whole calls out its parts. Final causation without efficient causation is helpless: mere calling for parts is what a Hotspur,[14] or any man, may do; but they will not come without efficient causation. Efficient causation without final causation, however, is worse than helpless, by far; it is mere chaos; and chaos is not even so much as chaos, without final causation: it is blank nothing.

The writer of a book can do nothing but set down the items of his thought. For the living thought, itself, in its entirety, the reader has to dig into his own soul. I think I have done my part, as well as I can. I am sorry to have left the reader an irksome chore before him. But he will find it worth the doing.

So then, a natural class being a family whose members are the sole off-spring and vehicles of one idea, from which they derive their peculiar fac-ulty, to classify by abstract definitions is simply a sure means of avoiding a natural classification. I am not decrying definitions. I have a lively sense of their great value in science. I only say that it should not be by means of def-initions that one should seek to find natural classes. When the classes have been found, then it is proper to try to define them; and one may even, with great caution and reserve, allow the definitions to lead us to turn back and see whether our classes ought not to have their boundaries differently drawn. After all, boundary lines in some cases can only be artificial, although the classes are natural, as we saw in the case of the *kets*. When one can lay one's finger upon the purpose to which a class of things owes its ori-gin, then indeed abstract definition may formulate that purpose. But when one cannot do that, but one can trace the genesis of a class and ascertain how several have been derived by different lines of descent from one less special-ized form, this is the best route toward an understanding of what the natural classes are. This is true even in biology: it is much more clearly so when the objects generated are, like sciences, themselves of the nature of ideas.

There are cases where we are quite in the dark, alike concerning the cre-ating purpose and concerning the genesis of things, but where we find a sys-tem of classes connected with a system of abstract ideas,—most frequently numbers,—and that in such a manner as to give us reason to guess that those ideas in some way, usually obscure, determine the possibilities of the things. For example, chemical compounds, generally,—or, at least, the more decidedly characterized of them, including, it would seem, the so-called elements,—seem to belong to types, so that, to take a single example, chlorates $KClO_3$, manganates $KMnO_3$, bromates $KBrO_3$, rutheniates $KRuO_3$, iodates KIO_3, behave chemically in strikingly analogous ways.[15] That this sort of argument for the existence of natural classes,—I mean the argument drawn from types, that is, from a connection between the things and a system of formal ideas,—may be much stronger and more direct than one might expect to find it, is shown by the circumstance that ideas them-selves,—and are they not the easiest of all things to classify naturally, with assured truth?—can be classified on no other grounds than this, except in a few exceptional cases. Even in those few cases, this method would seem to be the safest. For example, in pure mathematics, almost all the classification reposes on the relations of the forms classified to numbers or other multi-tudes. Thus, in topical geometry, figures are classified according to the whole numbers attached to their *choresis, cyclosis, periphraxis, apeiresis,* etc.[16] As for the exceptions, such as the classes of hessians, jacobians, invariants, vectors, etc., they all depend upon types, too, although upon types of a dif-ferent kind. It is plain that it must be so; and all the natural classes of logic will be found to have the same character.

There are two remarks more about natural classification which, though they are commonplace enough, cannot decently be passed by

NATURAL CLASSIFICATION DOES NOT PROCEED BY DEFINITION.

CLASSIFICATION ACCORDING TO FINAL CAUSES.

CLASSIFICATION BY TYPES.

CLASSIFICATION BY RULING NUMBERS.

CLASSES DETERMINED BY EXAMPLES, NOT BY DEFINITIONS.

without recognition. They have both just been virtually said, but they had better be more explicitly expressed and put in a light in which their bearing upon the practice of classification shall be plain. The descriptive definition of a natural class, according to what I have been saying, is not the essence of it. It is only an enumeration of tests by which the class may be recognized in any one of its members. A description of a natural class must be founded upon samples of it or typical examples. Possibly a zoologist or a botanist may have so definite a conception of what a species is that a single type-specimen may enable him to say whether a form of which he finds a specimen belongs to the same species or not. But it will be much safer to have a large number of individual specimens before him, from which he may get an idea of the amount and kind of individual or geographical variation to which the given species is subject. In proportion as the category of the class is higher, the greater will be the need of a multiplicity of examples. True, a naturalist may be so familiar with what a Genus is, what a Family is, what an Order is, what a Class is, that if you were to show him a new specimen of a hitherto unknown Class, he could, with that single specimen before him, sit down and write out definitions, not only of its Class, but also of its Order, of its Family, and of its Genus, as well as of its Species. Such a feat would display marvellous familiarity with what those Categories /mean/ in botany and in zoology; but intellectually it would be a performance of no high order, and the less so the greater the certainty of the conclusion. Generalization, broad, luminous, and solid, must enter into an intellectual performance in order to command much admiration. Such generalization, which teaches a new and clear lesson upon the truth of which reliance can be placed, requires to be drawn from many specimens. We shall endeavor, in that way, to define each class, that is, to enumerate characters which are absolutely decisive as to whether a given individual does or does not belong to the class. But it may be, as our *kets* show, that this is altogether out of the question; and the fact that two classes merge is no proof that they are not truly distinct natural classes.

NATURAL
CLASSIFICATION
ESSENTIALLY
A STUDY OF
GENESIS.

For they may, nevertheless, be genealogically distinct, just as no degree of resemblance between two men is proof positive that they are brothers. Now genealogical classification, among those objects of which the genesis is genealogical, is the classification we can most certainly rely /upon/ as being natural. No harm will be done if, in those cases, we *define* the natural classification as the genealogical classification; or, at least, that we make the genealogical character one of the essential characters of a natural classification. It cannot be more; because if we had before us ranged in ancestral order all the intermediate forms through which the human stock has passed in developing from non-man into man, it is plain that other considerations would be necessary in determining (if it admitted of determination) at what point in the series the forms begin to merit the name of human. The sciences are, in part, produced each from others. Thus, spectroscopic astronomy has for its parents, astronomy, chemistry, and optics. But this is not the whole genesis nor the principal part of the genesis of any broad and definite science. It has its own peculiar problem springing from an idea. That geometry derived its birth from land surveying is the tradition, which is borne out by the tradition that it took its origin in Egypt where the yearly floods must have rendered accurate surveying of special importance. Moreover, the wonderful accuracy of the dimensions of the great pyramid exhibits a degree of skill in laying out ground which could only have been attained by great intellectual activity; and this activity could hardly fail to lead to some beginnings of geometry. We may, therefore, accept with considerable confidence the tradition involved in the very name of geometry. Speaking in a broad, rough way, it may be said that the sciences have grown out of the useful arts, or out of arts supposed to be useful. Astronomy out of astrology; physiology, taking medicine as a halfway, out of magic; chemistry out of alchemy; thermotics from the steam engine, etc. Among the theoretical sciences, while some of the most abstract have sprung straight from the concretest arts, there is nevertheless a well-marked tendency for a science to be first descriptive, later classificatory, and lastly to embrace all classes in one law. The classificatory stage may be skipped. Yet in the truer order of development, the generation proceeds quite in the other direction. Men may and do begin to study the different kinds of animals and plants before they know anything of the general laws of physiology. But they cannot attain any true understanding of taxonomic biology until they can be guided by the discoveries of the physiologists. Till then the study of mollusks will be nothing but conchology. On the other hand the physiologist may be aided by a fact or two here and there drawn from taxonomic biology; but he asks but little, and that little not very urgently, of anything that the taxonomist can tell him and that he could not find out for himself. All natural classification is then essentially, we may almost say, an attempt to find out the true genesis of the objects classified. But by genesis must be understood not the efficient action which produces the whole by producing the parts, but the final action which produces the parts because they are needed to make the whole. Genesis is production from ideas. It may be difficult to understand how this is true in the biological world, though there is proof enough that it is so. But in regard to science it is a proposition easily enough intelligible. A science is defined by its problem; and its problem is clearly formulated on the basis of abstracter science.

This is all I intended to say here concerning classification, in general.

Having found the natural classes of the objects to be classified, we shall then use the same methods,—probably, in most cases, the third,—in order to discover the natural classes of those classes that we have found. Is this the whole business of classification? No serious student can hold it to be so. The classes found have to be defined, naturally if possible, but if not, then at least conveniently for the purposes of science. They have not only to be

CLASSIFICATORY SCIENCE MORE THAN TAXONOMY.

defined but described, a story without an end. This applies, of course, not merely to the species or immediate classes of the objects described, but to the higher orders of classes. There may also be between the different classes relations, each of which appertains just as much to the description of any one of the set of classes to which it belongs as to any other.

CATEGORIES OF NATURAL CLASSIFICATION.

In regard to the higher orders of classes, so far as concerns animals, Louis Agassiz thought that he was able to characterize in general terms the different categories of classes which zoologists talk of. That is, he undertook to say what sort of characters distinguish *branches* from branches, *classes* from classes, *orders* from orders, *families* from families, *genera* from genera, and *species* from species. His general classification of animals has passed away; and few naturalists attach much importance to his characterizations of the categories. Yet they are the outcome of deep study, and it is a merit of them that they involve no attempt at hard abstract accuracy of statement. How can he have been so long immersed in the study of nature without some truth sticking to him? I will just set down his vague definitions and allow myself to be vaguely influenced by them, so far as I find anything in the facts that answers to his descriptions. Although I am an ignoramus in biology, I ought by this time to recognize metaphysics when I meet with it; and it is apparent to me that those biologists whose views of classification are most opposite to those of Agassiz are saturated with metaphysics in its dangerous form,—i.e., the unconscious form,—to such an extent that what they say upon this subject is rather the expression of a traditionally absorbed fourteenth-century metaphysics than of scientific observation.

It would be useless for our purpose to copy the definitions of Agassiz* had he not expressed them in the briefest terms, as follows:[17] *Branches* are characterized by the plan of structure; *Classes*, by the manner in which that plan is executed, as far as ways and means are concerned ("Structure is the watchword for the recognition of classes."); *Orders*, by the degrees of complication of that structure ("The leading idea . . . is that of a definite rank among them."); *Families*, by their form, as determined by structure ("When we see new animals, does not the first glance, that is, the first impression made upon us by their form, give us a very correct idea of their nearest relationship? . . . So form is characteristic of families; . . . I do not mean the mere outline, but form as determined by structure."); *Genera*, by the details of the execution in special parts; *Species*, by the relations of individuals to one another and to the world in which they live, as well as by the proportions of their parts, their ornamentation, etc.

ALL CLASSIFICATION IS GOVERNED BY IDEAS.

All classification, whether artificial or natural, is the arrangement of objects according to ideas. A natural classification is the arrangement of them according to those ideas from which their existence results. No greater merit can a taxonomist have than that of having his eyes open to the

---

Essay on Classification, 4th, 1857, p. 170. The reader will perceive by the date, that these ideas were put forth at a somewhat inauspicious moment.

ideas in nature; no more deplorable blindness can afflict him than that of not seeing that there are ideas in nature which determine the existence of objects. The definitions of Agassiz will, at least, do us the service of directing our attention to the supreme importance of bearing in mind the final cause of objects in finding out their own natural classifications.

So much in regard to classification. Now if we are to classify the sciences, it is highly desirable that we should begin with a definite notion of what we mean by a science; and in view of what has been said of natural classification, it is plainly important that our notion of science should be a notion of science as it lives and not a mere abstract definition. Let us remember that science is a pursuit of living men, and that its most marked characteristic is that, when it is genuine, it is in an incessant state of metabolism and growth. If we resort to a dictionary, we shall be told that it is systematized knowledge. Most of the classifications of the sciences have been classifications of systematized and established knowledge,—which is nothing but the exudation of living science;—as if plants were to be classified according to the characters of their gums. Some of the classifications do even worse than that, by taking science in the sense attached by the ancient Greeks, especially Aristotle, to the word ἐπιστήμη. A person can take no right view of the relation of ancient to modern science unless he clearly apprehends the difference between what the Greeks meant by ἐπιστήμη and what we mean by knowledge. The best translation of ἐπιστήμη is "comprehension." It is the ability to define a thing in such a manner that all its properties shall be corollaries from its definition. Now it may be that we shall ultimately be able to do that, say for light or electricity. On the other hand, it may equally turn out that it forever remains as impossible as it certainly is to define number in such a way that Fermat's and Wilson's theorems[18] should be simple corollaries from the definition.* But, at any rate, the Greek conception of knowledge was all wrong in that they thought that one must advance in direct attack upon this ἐπιστήμη; and attached little value to any knowledge that did not manifestly tend to that. To look upon science in that point of view in one's classification is to throw modern science into confusion.

Another fault of many classifications,—or if not a fault, it is at least a purpose very different from that which I should be bold enough to attempt,—is that they are classifications not of science as it exists, but of systematized knowledge such as the classifier hopes may some time exist. I do not believe it is possible to have that intimate acquaintance with the science of the indefinite future that the discovery of the real and natural classification of it would require. At any rate, I will make no such attempt, except in one department, and there only partially and timidly.

*I do not mean to deny that those theorems are deducible from the definition. All that is here being urged turns on the falsity of the old notion that all deduction is corollarial deduction.

Let us look upon science,—the science of today,—as a living thing. What characterizes it generally, from this point of view, is that the thoroughly established truths are labelled and put upon the shelves of each scientist's mind, where they can be at hand when there is occasion to use them,—arranged, therefore, to suit his special convenience,—while science itself,—the living process,—is busied mainly with conjectures, which are either getting framed or getting tested. When that systematized knowledge on the shelves is used, it is used almost exactly as a manufacturer or practicing physician might use it; that is to say, it is merely applied. If it ever becomes the object of science, it is because in the advance of science, the moment has come when it must undergo a process of purification or of transformation.

A MAN OF
SCIENCE
DEFINED. A scientific man is likely in the course of a long life to pick up a pretty extensive acquaintance with the results of science; but in many branches, this is so little necessary that one will meet with men of the most deserved renown in science who will tell you that, beyond their own little nooks, they hardly know anything of what others have done. Sylvester[19] always used to say that he knew very little mathematics: true, he seemed to know more than he thought he did. In various branches of science, some of the most eminent men first took up those subjects as mere pastimes, knowing little or nothing of the accumulations of knowledge. So it was with the astronomer Lockyer;[20] so it has been with many naturalists. Now, did those men gradually become men of science as their stores of knowledge increased, or was there an epoch in their lives, before which they were amateurs and after which they were scientists? I believe that the answer is that, like any other regeneration, the metamorphosis is commonly sudden, though sometimes slow. When it is sudden, what is it that constitutes the transformation? It is their being seized with a great desire to learn the truth, and their going to work with all their might by a well-considered method to gratify that desire. The man who is working in the right way to learn something not already known is recognized by all men of science as one of themselves, no matter how little he is informed. It would be monstrous to say that Ptolemy, Archimedes, Eratosthenes, and Posidonius, were not scientific men because their knowledge was comparatively small. The life of science is in the desire to learn. If this desire is not pure, but is mingled with a desire to prove the truth of a definite opinion, or of a general mode of conceiving of things, it will almost inevitably lead to the adoption of a faulty method; and *in so far,* such men, among whom many have been looked upon in their day as great lights, are not genuine men of science; though it would be foul injustice to exclude them absolutely from that class. So if a man pursues a futile method through neglect to inform himself of effective methods, he is no scientific man; he has not been moved by an intelligently sincere and effective desire to learn. But if a man simply fails to inform himself of previous work which would have facilitated his own, although he is to blame, it would be too

harsh to say that he has violated the essential principles of science. If a man pursues a method which, though very bad, is the best that the state of intellectual development of his time or the state of the particular science he pursues would enable a man to take,—I mean, for example, such men as Lavater, Paracelsus and the earlier alchemists, the author of the first chapter of Genesis, and the old metaphysicians,—we perhaps cannot call them scientific men, while perhaps we ought to do so. Opinions would differ about this. They are, at any rate, entitled to an honorable place in the vestibule of science. A pretty wild play of the imagination is, it cannot be doubted, an inevitable, and probably even a useful, prelude to science proper. For my part, if these men really had an effective rage to learn the very truth, and did what they did as the best way they knew, or could know, to find it out, I could not bring myself to deny them the title. The difficulty is that one of the things that coheres to that undeveloped state of intelligence is precisely a very imperfect and impure thirst for truth. Paracelsus and the alchemists were rank charlatans seeking for gold more than for truth. The metaphysicians were not only pedants and pretenders, but they were trying to establish foregone conclusions. These are the traits which deprive those men of the title scientist, although we ought to entertain a high respect for them as mortals go; because they could no more escape the corruptness of their aims than they could the deficiencies of their knowledge. Science consists in actually drawing the bow upon truth, with intentness in the eye, with energy in the arm.

Such being the essence of science, it is obvious that its first offspring will be men,—men whose whole lives are devoted to it. By such devotion each of them acquires a training in making some particular kind of observations and experiments.* He will thus live in quite a different world,—quite a different aggregate of experience,—from unscientific men, and even from scientific men pursuing other lines of work than his. He naturally converses with, and reads the writings of, those who, having the same experience, have ideas interpretable into his own. This society develops conceptions of its own. Bring together two men from widely different departments,—say a bacteriologist and an astronomer,—and they will hardly know what to say to one another; for neither has seen the world in which the other lives. True, both use optical instruments; but the qualities striven for in a telescopic objective are of no consequence in a microscopical objective; and all the subsidiary parts of telescope and microscope are constructed on principles utterly foreign to one another,—except their stiffness.

Here, then, are natural classes of sciences all sorted out for us in nature itself, so long as we limit our classification to actually recognized sciences.

THE TRUE CLASSIFICATION OF SCIENCE MUST BE A TRUE CLASSIFICATION OF THE LIVES OF SCIENTIFIC MEN.

*Unfortunately, his acquisition of books, instruments, laboratory, etc., depends upon qualifications in which the man of science is usually rather wanting,—as wealth, diplomacy, popularity as a teacher,—so that he is less likely to be provided with them than are men less qualified to use them for the advancement of science.

We have only to look over the list of scientific periodicals and the list of scientific societies to find the Families of science ready named. I call such classes Families because Agassiz tells us that it is the Family which strikes the observer at first glance. To make out the genera and especially the species, closer examination is requisite; while the knowledge of orders, classes, and branches calls for a broader acquaintance with science.[21]

10

The Maxim of Pragmatism

MS 301. [Published in CP 5.14–40 and in HL 104–21. This lecture, delivered on 26 March 1903, was left untitled.] This is the first in a series of seven lectures, delivered at Harvard from March through May, 1903, in which Peirce sought to build a case for pragmatism by examining its pros and cons. He also wanted to distinguish his pragmatism from other, more popular, versions. These are the lectures that William James characterized as "flashes of brilliant light relieved against Cimmerian darkness!" In Lecture I, Peirce considers the utility of the pragmatic maxim and claims that its usefulness does not constitute a proof of its truth—it must pass "through the fire of drastic analysis." Peirce outlines the steps he will take to support his version of pragmatism. He rejects his earlier appeal to facts of psychology and points out that if pragmatism teaches that what we think is to be understood in terms of what we are prepared to do, then the doctrine of how we ought to think (logic) must be a branch of the doctrine of what we deliberately choose to do (ethics). But what we choose to do depends on what we are prepared to admire, which brings us to esthetics. An examination of pragmatism, therefore, involves all three of the normative sciences: logic, ethics, and esthetics. But first we must consider phenomenology, the science that deals with phenomena objectively and isolates the universal categories that pervade all our experience.

Ladies and Gentlemen:

A certain maxim of Logic which I have called Pragmatism has recommended itself to me for divers reasons and on sundry considerations. Having taken it as my guide in most of my thought, I find that as the years of my knowledge of it lengthen, my sense of the importance of it presses upon me more and more. If it is only true, it is certainly a wonderfully efficient instrument. It is not to philosophy only that it is applicable. I have found it of signal service in every branch of science that I have studied. My want of skill in practical affairs does not prevent me from perceiving the advantage of being well imbued with pragmatism in the conduct of life.

Yet I am free to confess that objections to this way of thinking have forced themselves upon me and have been found more formidable the further my plummet has been dropped into the abyss of philosophy, and the closer my questioning at each new attempt to fathom its depths.

I propose, then, to submit to your judgment in half a dozen lectures an examination of the *pros* and *cons* of pragmatism by means of which I hope to show you the result of allowing to both *pros* and *cons* their full legitimate values. With more time I would gladly follow up the guiding thread so caught up and go on to ascertain what are the veritable conclusions, or at least the genera of veritable conclusions to which a carefully rectified pragmatism will truly lead. If you find what I say acceptable you will have learned something worth your while. If you can refute me, the gain will be chiefly on my side; but even in that event, I anticipate your acknowledging, when I take my leave of you, that the discussion has not been without profit; and in future years I am confident that you will recur to these thoughts and find that you have more to thank me for than you could understand at first.

I suppose I may take it for granted that you all know what *pragmatism* is. I have met with a number of definitions of it lately, against none of which I am much disposed to raise any violent protest.[1] Yet to say exactly what pragmatism is describes pretty well what you and I have to puzzle out together.

We must start with some rough approximation of it, and I am inclined to think that the shape in which I first stated it will be the most useful one to adopt as matter to work upon, chiefly because it is the form most personal to your lecturer, and /on/ which for that reason he can discourse most intelligently. Besides, pragmatism and personality are more or less of the same kidney.

I sent forth my statement in January 1878; and for about twenty years never heard from it again.[2] I let fly my dove; and that dove has never come back to me to this very day. But of late quite a brood of young ones have been fluttering about, from the feathers of which I might fancy that mine had found a brood. To speak plainly, a considerable number of philosophers have lately written as they might have written in case they had been reading either what I wrote but were ashamed to confess it, or had been reading something that some reader of mine had written. For they seem quite disposed to adopt my term *pragmatism*.[3]

I shouldn't wonder if they were ashamed of me. What could be more humiliating than to confess that one has learned anything of a logician? But for my part I am delighted to find myself sharing the opinions of so brilliant a company. The new pragmatists seem to be distinguished for their terse, vivid, and concrete style of expression together with a certain buoyancy of tone as if they were conscious of carrying about them the master key to all the secrets of metaphysics.

Every metaphysician is supposed to have some radical fault to find with every other, and I cannot find any direr fault with the new pragmatists than that they are *lively*. In order to be deep it is requisite to be dull.

On their side, one of the faults that I think they might find with me is that I make pragmatism to be a mere maxim of logic instead of a sublime principle of speculative philosophy.

In order to be admitted to better philosophical standing I have endeavored to put pragmatism as I understand it into the form of a philosophical theorem. I have not succeeded any better than this: Pragmatism is the principle that every theoretical judgment expressible in a sentence in the indicative mood is a confused form of thought whose only meaning, if it has any, lies in its tendency to enforce a corresponding practical maxim expressible as a conditional sentence having its apodosis in the imperative mood.

But the Maxim of Pragmatism, as I originally stated it,* is as follows:

> Consider what effects that might conceivably have practical bearings we conceive the object of our conception to have: then, our conception of those effects is the whole of our conceptions of the object.†

The utility of the maxim, provided it is only true, appears in a sufficient light in the original article. I will here add a few examples which were not given in that paper.

There are many problems connected with probabilities which are subject to doubt. One of them, for example, is this: Suppose an infinitely large company of infinitely rich men sit down to play against an infinitely rich bank at a game of chance, at which neither side has any advantage, each one betting a franc against a franc at each bet. Suppose that each player continues to play until he has netted a gain of one franc and then retires, surrendering his place to a new player.

The chance that a player will ultimately net a gain of a franc may be calculated as follows:

Let x_l be a player's chance, if he were to continue playing indefinitely, of ever netting a gain of l francs.

But after he has netted a gain of 1 franc, his chance of doing which is x_1, he is no richer than before, since he is infinitely rich. Consequently his chance of winning the second franc, after he has won the first, is the same as his chance of winning the first franc. That is, it is x_1 and his chance of winning both is $x_2 = (x_1)^2$. And so in general $x_l = (x_1)^l$.

Now his chance of netting a gain of 1 franc, x_1, is the sum of the chances of the two ways in which it may come about; namely, by first winning the first bet of which the chance is ½, and by first losing the first bet and then netting a

---

Revue Philosophique VII, pp. 47, 48 and *Popular Science Monthly* XII, p. 293 *[EP1:132]*.

† *[The original French version, with a preliminary passage, appears here as Peirce included it in his lecture text.]* Pour développer le sens d'une pensée, il faut donc simplement déterminer quelles habitudes elle produit, car le sens d'une chose consiste simplement dans les habitudes qu'elle implique. Le caractère d'une habitude dépend de la façon dont elle peut nous faire agir non pas seulement dans telle circonstance probable, mais dans toute circonstance possible, si improbable qu'elle puisse être. Ce qu'est une habitude dépend de ces deux points: quand et comment elle fait agir. Pour le premier point: quand? tout stimulant à l'action dérive d'une perception; pour le second point: comment? le but de toute action est d'amener au résultat sensible. Nous atteignons ainsi le tangible et le pratique comme base de toute différence de pensée, si subtile qu'elle puisse être. . . . [4]

Considérer quels sont les effets pratiques que nous pensons pouvoir être produits par l'objet de notre conception. La conception de tous ces effets est la conception complète de l'objet.[5]

gain of 2 francs of which the chance is $\frac{1}{2}x_1^2$.

Therefore

$$x_1 = \frac{1}{2} + \frac{1}{2}x_1^2$$

$$\text{or} \quad x_1^2 - 2x_1 + 1 = 0$$

$$\text{or} \quad (x_1 - 1)^2 = 0$$

But if the square of a number is zero, the number itself is zero.

Therefore

$$x_1 - 1 = 0$$

$$\text{or} \quad x_1 = 1$$

If so it must be certain that *every* player would win his franc and would retire.

Consequently there would be a continual outflow of money from the bank. And yet, since the game is an even one, the banker would not net any loss. How is this paradox to be explained?

The theory of probabilities is full of paradoxes and puzzles. Let us, then, apply the maxim of pragmatism to the solution of them.

In order to do this, we must ask, *What is meant by saying that the probability of an event has a certain value, p?* According to the maxim of pragmatism, then, we must ask what practical difference it can make whether the value is p or something else. Then we must ask how are probabilities applied to practical affairs. The answer is that the great business of insurance depends upon it. Probability is used in insurance to determine how much must be paid on a certain risk to make it safe to pay a certain sum if the event insured against should occur. Then, we must ask how can it be safe to engage to pay a large sum if an uncertain event occurs. The answer is that the insurance company does a very large business and is able to ascertain pretty closely out of a thousand risks of a given description how many in any one year will be losses. The business problem is this. The number of policies of a certain description that can be sold in a year will depend on the price set up on them. Let p be that price, and let n be the number that can be sold at that price, so that the larger p is, the smaller n will be. Now n being a large number a certain proportion q of these policies, qn in all, will be losses during the year; and if l be the loss on each, qnl will be the total loss. Then what the insurance company has to do is to set p at such a figure that $pn - qln$ or $(p - ql)n$ shall reach its maximum possible value.

The solution of this equation is

$$p = ql + \frac{\partial p}{\partial n}n$$

where $\dfrac{\partial p}{\partial n}$ is the amount by which the price would have to be lowered in order to sell one policy more. Of course if the price were raised instead of lowered just one policy fewer would be sold.

For then by so lowering *[the price,]* the profit from being

$$(p - ql)n$$

would be changed to

$$\left(p - ql - \frac{\partial p}{\partial n}\right)(n + 1)$$

that is, to

$$(p - ql)n + p - ql - \frac{\partial p}{\partial n}(n + 1)$$

and this being less than before

$$ql + \frac{\partial p}{\partial n}(n + 1) > p$$

and by raising it, the change would be to

$$\left(p - ql + \frac{\partial p}{\partial n}\right)(n - 1)$$

that is, to

$$(p - ql)n - p + ql + \frac{\partial p}{\partial n}(n - 1)$$

and this being less than before

$$p > ql + \frac{\partial p}{\partial n}(n - 1)$$

So since p is intermediate between

$$ql + \frac{\partial p}{\partial n}n + \frac{\partial p}{\partial n}$$

and $$ql + \frac{\partial p}{\partial n}n - \frac{\partial p}{\partial n}$$

and $\frac{\partial p}{\partial n}$ is very small, it must be very close to the truth to write

$$p = ql + \frac{\partial p}{\partial n}n$$

This is the problem of insurance. Now in order that probability may have any bearing on this problem, it is obvious that it must be of the nature of a *real fact* and not a mere *state of mind*. For facts only enter into the solution of the problem of insurance. And this fact must evidently be a fact of statistics.

Without now going into certain reasons of detail that I should enter into if I were lecturing on probabilities, it must be that probability is a *statistical ratio* and further in order to satisfy still more special conditions, it is convenient, for the class of problems to which insurance belongs, to make it the statistical ratio of the number of experiential occurrences of a specific kind to the number of experiential occurrences of a generic kind, in the long run.

In order, then, that probability should mean anything, it will be requisite to specify to what *species* of event it refers and to what *genus* of event it refers.

It also refers to a *long run*, that is, to an indefinitely long series of occurrences taken together in the order of their occurrence in possible experience.

In this view of the matter, we note, to begin with, that a given species of event considered as belonging to a given genus of events does not necessarily have any definite probability. Because the probability is the ratio of one infinite multitude to another. Now infinity divided by infinity is altogether indeterminate, except in special cases.

It is very easy to give examples of events that have no definite probability. If a person agrees [to] toss up a cent again and again forever and, beginning as soon as the first head turns up, whenever two heads are separated by any odd number of tails in the succession of throws, pay 2 to that power in cents provided that whenever the two successive heads are separated by any even number of throws he receives 2 to that power in cents,* it is impossible to say what the probability will be that he comes out a winner.

In half of the cases after the first head, the next throw will be a head and he will receive $(-2)^0 = 1$ cent, which, since it happens half the time, will be in the long run a winning of $\frac{1}{2}$ a cent per head thrown.

But in half of the other half [of] the cases, that is, in a quarter of all the cases, one tail will intervene and he will have to receive $(-2)^1 = -2$ cents, i.e., he will have to pay 2 cents, which happening a quarter of the time will make an average loss of $\frac{1}{2}$ a cent per head thrown.

But in half the remaining quarter of the cases, i.e., one eighth of all the cases, two tails will intervene, and he will receive $(-2)^2 = 4$ cents, which happening once every eight times, will be worth $\frac{1}{2}$ a cent per head thrown and so on; so that his account in the long run will be

$$\tfrac{1}{2} - \tfrac{1}{2} + \tfrac{1}{2} - \tfrac{1}{2} + \tfrac{1}{2} - \tfrac{1}{2} + \tfrac{1}{2} - \tfrac{1}{2} \text{ ad infinitum,}$$

the sum of which may be $\frac{1}{2}$ or may be *zero*. Or rather it is quite indeterminate.

If instead of being paid $(-2)^n$ when n is the number of intervening tails, he were paid $(-2)^{n^2}$ the result would be that he would probably either win or lose enormously without there being any definite probability that it would be winning rather than losing.

I think I may recommend this game with confidence to gamblers as being the most frightful ruin yet invented; and a little cheating would do everything in it.

Now let us revert to our original problem[6] and consider the state of things after every other bet. After the second,

G|G a quarter of the players will have gained, gone out, and been replaced by players who have gained and gone out so that a number of francs equal to half the number of seats will have been paid out by the bank

---

* He receives $(-2)^n$ cents if n tails intervene between two successive heads.

G|L a quarter of the players will have gained and gone out and been replaced by players who have lost, making the bank even

L|G a quarter of the players will have lost and then gained, making the bank and them even

L|L a quarter of the players will have lost twice, making a gain to the bank of half as many francs as there are seats at the table.

The bank then will be where it was. Players to the number of three quarters of the seats will have netted their franc each; but players to the number of a quarter of the seats will have lost two francs each and another equal number one franc each, just paying for the gains of those who have retired.

That is the way it will happen every time. Just before the fifth bet of the player at the table, ⅜ will have lost nothing, ¼ will have lost one franc, ¼ two francs, ¹⁄₁₆ three francs and ¹⁄₁₆ four francs. Thus some will always have lost a good deal. Those who sit at the table will among them always have paid just what those who have gone out have carried away.

But it will be asked, How then can it happen that *all* gain? I reply that I never said all would gain, I only said the probability was 1 that any one would ultimately gain his franc. But does not probability 1 mean certainty? Not at all, it only means that the ratio of the number of those who ultimately gain to the total number is 1. Since the number of seats at the table is infinite, the ratio of the number of those who never gain to the number of seats may be zero and yet they may be infinitely numerous. So that probabilities 1 and 0 are very far from corresponding to certainty *pro* and *con*.

If I were to go into practical matters, the advantage of pragmatism, of looking at the substantial practical issue, would be still more apparent. But here pragmatism is generally practiced by successful men. In fact, the genus of efficient men is mainly distinguished from the inefficient precisely by this.

There is no doubt, then, that pragmatism opens a very easy road to the solution of an immense variety of questions. But it does not at all follow from that that it is true. On the contrary, one may very properly entertain a suspicion of any method which so resolves the most difficult questions into easy problems. No doubt Ockham's razor is logically sound. A hypothesis should be stripped of every feature which is in no wise called for to furnish an explanation of observed facts. *Entia non sunt multiplicanda praeter necessitatem;*[7] only we may very well doubt whether a very simple hypothesis can contain every factor that is necessary. Certain it is that most hypotheses which at first seemed to unite great simplicity with entire sufficiency have had to be greatly complicated in the further progress of science.

What is the *proof* that the possible practical consequences of a concept constitute the sum total of the concept? The argument upon which I rested the maxim in my original paper was that *belief* consists mainly in being deliberately prepared to adopt the formula believed in as the guide to action.

If this be in truth the nature of belief, then undoubtedly the proposition believed in can itself be nothing but a maxim of conduct. That, I believe, is quite evident.

But *how do we know* that belief is nothing but the deliberate preparedness to act according to the formula believed?

My original article carried this back to a psychological principle. The conception of truth according to me was developed out of an original impulse to act consistently, to have a definite intention. But in the first place, this was not very clearly made out, and in the second place, I do not think it satisfactory to reduce such fundamental things to facts of psychology. For man could alter his nature, or his environment would alter it if he did not voluntarily do so, if the impulse were not what was advantageous or fitting. Why has evolution made man's mind to be so constructed? That is the question we must nowadays ask, and all attempts to ground the fundamentals of logic on psychology are seen to be essentially shallow.

The question of the nature of belief, or in other words the question of what the true logical analysis of the act of judgment is, is the question upon which logicians of late years have chiefly concentrated their energies. Is the pragmatistic answer satisfactory?

Do we not all perceive that *judgment* is something closely allied to *assertion?* That is the view that ordinary speech entertains. A man or woman will be heard to use the phrase "I says to myself." That is, *judgment* is held to be either no more than an *assertion to oneself* or at any rate something very like that.

Now it is a fairly easy problem to analyze the nature of *assertion*. To find an easily dissected example, we shall naturally take a case where the assertive element is magnified,—a very formal assertion, such as an affidavit. Here a man goes before a notary or magistrate and takes such action that if what he says is not true, evil consequences will be visited upon him, and this he does with a view to thus causing other men to be affected just as they would if the proposition sworn to had presented itself to them as a perceptual fact.

We thus see that the act of assertion is an act of a totally different nature from the act of apprehending the meaning of the proposition and we cannot expect that any analysis of what assertion is or any analysis of what *judgment* or *belief* is, if that act is at all allied to assertion, should throw any light at all on the widely different question of what the apprehension of the meaning of a proposition is.

What is the difference between making an *assertion* and *laying a wager?* Both are acts whereby the agent deliberately subjects himself to evil consequences if a certain proposition is not true. Only when he offers to bet he hopes the other man will make himself responsible in the same way for the truth of the contrary proposition; while when he makes an *assertion* he always (or almost always) wishes the man to whom he makes it to be led to do what he does. Accordingly, in our vernacular "I will bet so and so" is the phrase expressive of a private opinion which one does not expect others to share, while "You bet_____" is a form of assertion intended to cause another to follow suit.

Such then seems at least in a preliminary glance at the matter to be a satisfactory account of assertion. Now let us pass to judgment and belief. There can, of course, be no question that a man will act in accordance with his belief so far as his belief has any practical consequences. The only doubt is whether this is *all* that belief is, whether belief is a mere nullity so far as it does not influence conduct. What possible effect upon conduct can it have, for example, to believe that the diagonal of a square is incommensurable with the side? Name a discrepancy ε no matter how small, and the diagonal differs from a rational quantity by much less than that. Professor Newcomb[8] in his calculus and all mathematicians of his rather antiquated fashion think that they have proved two quantities to be equal when they have proved that they differ by less than any assignable quantity. I once tried hard to make Newcomb say whether the diagonal of the square differed from a rational fraction of the side or not; but he saw what I was driving at and would not answer. The proposition that the diagonal is incommensurable has stood in the textbooks from time immemorial without ever being assailed and I am sure that the most modern type of mathematician holds to it most decidedly. Yet it seems quite absurd to say that there is any objective practical difference between commensurable and incommensurable.[9]

Of course you can say if you like that the act of expressing a quantity as a rational fraction is a piece of conduct and that it is in itself a *practical* difference that one kind of quantity can be so expressed and the other not. But a thinker must be shallow indeed if he does not see that to admit a species of practicality that consists in one's conduct about words and modes of expression is at once to break down all the bars against the nonsense that pragmatism is designed to exclude.

What the pragmatist has his pragmatism for is to be able to say, Here is a definition and it does not differ at all from your confusedly apprehended conception because there is no *practical* difference. But what is to prevent his opponent from replying that there is a practical difference which consists in his recognizing one as his conception and not the other, that is, one is expressible in a way in which the other is not expressible?

Pragmatism is completely volatilized if you admit that sort of practicality.

It must be understood that all I am now attempting to show is that Pragmatism is apparently a matter of such great probable concern, and at the same time so much doubt hangs over its legitimacy, that it will be well worth our while to make a methodical, scientific, and thorough examination of the whole question, so as to make sure of our ground, and obtain some secure method for such a preliminary filtration of questions as pragmatism professes to furnish.

Let us, then, enter upon this inquiry. But before doing so let us mark out the proposed course of it. That should always be done in such cases, even if circumstances subsequently require the plan to be modified, as they usually will.

Although our inquiry is to be an inquiry into truth, whatever the truth may turn out to be, and therefore of course is not to be influenced by any liking for pragmatism or any pride in it as an American doctrine, yet still we do not come to this inquiry any more than anybody comes to any inquiry in that blank state that the lawyers pretend to insist upon as desirable; though I give them credit for enough common sense to know better.

We have some reason already to think there is some truth in pragmatism although we also have some reason to think that there is something wrong with it. For unless both branches of this statement were true we should do wrong to waste time and energy upon the inquiry we are undertaking.

I will, therefore, presume that there is enough truth in it to render a preliminary glance at ethics desirable. For if, as pragmatism teaches us, what we think is to be interpreted in terms of what we are prepared to do, then surely *logic*, or the doctrine of what we ought to think, must be an application of the doctrine of what we deliberately choose to do, which is Ethics.

But we cannot get any clue to the secret of Ethics,—a most entrancing field of thought but sown broadcast with pitfalls,—until we have first made up our formula for what it is that we are prepared to admire. I do not care what doctrine of ethics be embraced, it will always be so. Suppose for example our maxim of ethics to be Pearson's that all our action ought to be directed toward the perpetuation of the biological stock to which we belong.[10] Then the question will arise, On what principle should it be deemed such a fine thing for this stock to survive,—or a fine thing at all? Is there nothing in the world or *in posse* that would be admirable *per se* except copulation and swarming? Is swarming a fine thing at all apart from any results that it may lead to? The course of thought will follow a parallel line if we consider Marshall's ethical maxim: "Act to restrain the impulses which demand immediate reaction, in order that the impulse-order determined by the existence of impulses of less strength, but of wider significance, may have full weight in the guidance of your life."[11] Although I have not as clear an apprehension as I could wish of the philosophy of this very close, but too technical, thinker, yet I presume that he would not be among those who would object to making Ethics dependent upon Esthetics. Certainly, this maxim which I have just read to you from his latest book supposes that it is a fine thing for an impulse to have its way, but yet not an equally fine thing for one impulse to have its way and for another impulse to have its way. There is a preference which depends upon the *significance* of impulses, whatever that may mean. It supposes that there is some ideal state of things which regardless of how it should be brought about and independently of any ulterior reason whatsoever, is held to be good or fine.

In short, ethics must rest upon a doctrine which without at all considering what our conduct is to be, divides ideally possible states of things into two classes, those that would be admirable and those that would be unadmirable, and undertakes to define precisely what it is that constitutes the admirableness of an ideal. Its problem is to determine by analysis what it is that one ought deliberately to admire *per se* in itself regardless of what it may lead to and regardless of its bearings upon human conduct. I call that inquiry *Esthetics*, because it is generally said that the three normative sciences are logic, ethics, and esthetics, being the three doctrines that distinguish [the] good and the bad, *Logic* in regard to representations of truth, *Ethics* in regard to efforts of will, and *Esthetics* in objects considered simply in their presentation. Now that third normative science can I think be no other than that which I have described. It is evidently the basic normative science upon which as a foundation the doctrine of ethics must be reared to be surmounted in its turn by the doctrine of logic.

But before we can attack any normative science, any science which proposes to separate the sheep from the goats, it is plain that there must be a preliminary inquiry which shall justify the attempt to establish such dualism. This must be a science that does *not* draw any distinction of good and bad in any sense whatever, but just contemplates phenomena as they are, simply opens its eyes and describes what it sees. Not what it sees in the real as distinguished from figment,—not regarding any such dichotomy,—but simply describing the object, as a phenomenon, and stating what it finds in all phenomena alike. This is the science which Hegel made his starting point, under the name of the *Phänomenologie des Geistes,*—although he considered it in a fatally narrow spirit, since he restricted himself to what *actually* forces itself on the mind and so colored his whole philosophy with the ignoration of the distinction of essence and existence and so gave it the nominalistic and I might say in a certain sense the *pragmatoidal* character in which the worst of the Hegelian errors have their origin. I will so far follow Hegel as to call this science *Phenomenology* although I will not restrict it to the observation and analysis of *experience* but extend it to describing all the features that are common to whatever is *experienced* or might conceivably be experienced or become an object of study in any way direct or indirect.

Hegel was quite right in holding that it was the business of this science to bring out and make clear the *Categories* or fundamental modes. He was also right in holding that these *categories* are of two kinds, the Universal Categories, all of which apply to everything, and the series of categories consisting of phases of evolution.

As to these latter, I am satisfied that Hegel has not approximated to any correct catalogue of them. It may be that here and there, in the long wanderings of his *Encyclopaedia* he has been a little warmed by the truth.[12] But in all its main features his catalogue is utterly wrong, according to me. I have made long and arduous studies of this matter, but I have not been able to draw up any catalogue that satisfies me. My studies, if they are ever published, will I believe be found helpful to future students of this most difficult problem; but in these lectures I shall have little to say on that subject. The case is quite different with the three Universal Categories, which Hegel, by the way, does not look upon as Categories at all, or at least he does not call them so, but as three stages of thinking.[13] In regard to these, it appears to me that Hegel is so nearly right that my own doctrine might very well be taken for a variety of

Hegelianism, although in point of fact it was determined in my mind by considerations entirely foreign to Hegel, at a time when my attitude toward Hegelianism was one of contempt. There was no influence upon me from Hegel unless it was of so occult a kind as to entirely escape my ken; and if there was such an occult influence, it strikes me as about as good an argument for the essential truth of the doctrine, as is the coincidence that Hegel and I arrived in quite independent ways substantially to the same result.

This science of phenomenology, then, must be taken as the basis upon which normative science is to be erected, and accordingly must claim our first attention.

This science of phenomenology is in my view the most primal of all the positive sciences. That is, it is not based, as to its principles, upon any other *positive science*. By a *positive science* I mean an inquiry which seeks for *positive* knowledge, that is, for such knowledge as may conveniently be expressed in a *categorical proposition*. Logic and the other normative sciences, although they ask, not what *is* but what *ought to be*, nevertheless are positive sciences since it is by asserting positive, categorical truth that they are able to show that what they call good really is so; and the right reason, right effort, and right being of which they treat derive that character from positive categorical fact.

Perhaps you will ask me whether it is possible to conceive of a science which should not aim to declare that something is positively or categorically true. I reply that it is not only possible to conceive of such a science, but that such science exists and flourishes, and phenomenology, which does not depend upon any other *positive science*, nevertheless must, if it is to be properly grounded, be made to depend upon the Conditional or Hypothetical Science of *Pure Mathematics*, whose only aim is to discover not how things actually are, but how they might be supposed to be, if not in our universe, then in some other. A phenomenology which does not reckon with pure mathematics, a science hardly come to years of discretion when Hegel wrote, will be the same pitiful clubfooted affair that Hegel produced.

11

On Phenomenology

MSS 305, 306. [Published in CP 5.41–56, 59–65 (in part) and in HL 150–65. These two manuscripts together form the version of the text that Peirce most likely used to deliver his second Harvard lecture on 2 April 1903.] Peirce remarks near the beginning of this lecture that "my purpose this evening is to call your attention to certain questions of phenomenology upon the answers to which, whatever they may be, our final conclusion concerning pragmatism must repose at last." He goes on to clarify the nature of phenomenology (later called phaneroscopy), whose goal is to isolate the universal categories of experience. Peirce has found these to be, first, the quality of feeling, second, the element of struggle or reaction in experience or consciousness, and third, an intellectual element that seems much like representation or a sense of learning. He believes that this third element is necessary to explain a mode of influence on external facts that cannot be explained by mechanical action alone and he thinks that the idea of evolution requires this element. Near the end of this lecture Peirce remarks that "what the true definition of Pragmatism may be, I find it very hard to say; but in my nature it is a sort of instinctive attraction for living facts."

I[1]

Ladies and Gentlemen:

The last lecture was devoted to an introductory glance at Pragmatism, considered as the maxim that the entire meaning and significance of any conception lies in its *conceivably* practical bearings,—not certainly altogether in consequences that would influence our conduct so far as we can foresee our future circumstances but which in *conceivable* circumstances would go to determine how we should deliberately act, and how we should act in a practical way and not merely how we should act as affirming or denying the conception to be cleared up.

It was shown that this maxim would be so supremely important an aid to thought, provided only it be true, that it is well worth a good deal of earnest inquiry to ascertain whether or not it can be maintained in the sense in which I originally proposed it,[2] or if not whether it is capable of rectification, so as still to leave it a maxim that can be worked. At the same time objections apparently so redoubtable presented themselves against admitting the truth of it, that it certainly ought not to be accepted until it has passed through the fire of a drastic analysis.

For example, mathematicians never would confess that it means nothing to say that the diagonal of a square is incommensurable with its side, and yet how could the distinction of commensurable and incommensurable ever become practical, in view of the fact that the diagonal of a square differs from some rational fraction of the side by less than any previously assigned quantity? Nor would this difficulty be diminished by one iota if instead of *practical* consequences we were to modify the maxim so as to make it relate to *experiential* consequences. That is quite evident.

I invite you, then, this evening to begin with me a searching examination of the nature of what we call the *meaning* or *significance* of any phrase or conception.

An examination of mathematical conceptions, such as *commensurability*, *continuity*, *infinity*, and the like, might be expected to throw some light upon our problem. But the whole subject of mathematics is only one of a number of highly pertinent topics that I shall be forced to pass over in silence owing to my being restricted to six lectures of an hour each.[3]

Pure mathematics differs from the positive sciences in not making any categorical assertions, but only saying what would be true in case certain hypotheses were true, and not undertaking to be in the least responsible for there being anything in nature corresponding to its hypotheses, whether exactly or approximately. The positive sciences do undertake to assert what the characters of the experiential facts are. But among these positive sciences, Philosophy, as I shall use this word, and use it without any serious rupture with general usage, is distinguished from all the special theoretical sciences, whether they belong to the great Physical wing or to the great Psychical wing of special science, that is, whether they be inquiries into dynamics, physics, chemistry, physiology, anatomy, astronomy, geology, etc., or whether they be inquiries into psychology, anthropology, linguistics, history, etc.—Philosophy, I say, is distinguished from all of these by the circumstance that it does not undertake to make any special observations or to obtain any perceptions of a novel description. Microscopes and telescopes, voyages and exhumations, clairvoyants and witnesses of exceptional experience are substantially superfluous for the purposes of philosophy. It contents itself with a more attentive scrutiny and comparison of the facts of everyday life, such as present themselves to every adult and sane person, and for the most part in every day and hour of his waking life. The reason why a natural classification so draws the line between Philosophy, as *cenóscopy (κοινοσκοπία)* and Special Science, as *idioscopy (ἰδιοσκοπία)*,—to follow Jeremy Bentham's terminology,[4]—is that a very widely different bent of genius is required for the analytical work of philosophy and for the observational work of special science.

More than six lectures would be required merely to set forth in the tersest manner the reasons which have convinced me that Philosophy ought to be regarded as having three principal divisions. Its principal utility, although by no means its only utility, is to furnish a *Weltanschauung*, or conception of the universe, as a basis for the special sciences. Metaphysics is the final branch of philosophical inquiry whose business it is to work this out. But metaphysics must rest upon normative science. That was the judgment of two at least of the most influential of all philosophers, Aristotle and Kant; and Descartes, though he had studied the question less deeply, was of the same opinion. What is meant by a normative science I cannot now stop to explain. It is a theoretical not a practical science, although it is closely connected with practice. It is a positive science and not a mathematical science although its reasoning is mostly mathematical. We may say roughly that a normative science is the research into the theory of the distinction between what is good and what is bad; in the realm of cognition, in the realm of action, and in the realm of feeling, this theory being founded upon certain matters of fact that are open to the daily and hourly observation of every man and woman. Normative science is the central great department of philosophy. The initial great department of philosophy is phenomenology whose task it is to make out what are the elements of appearance that present themselves to us every hour and every minute whether we are pursuing earnest investigations, or are undergoing the strangest vicissitudes of experience, or are dreamily listening to the tales of Scheherazade.[5]

My purpose this evening is to call your attention to certain questions of phenomenology upon the answers to which, whatever they may be, our final conclusion concerning pragmatism must mainly repose at last.

Be it understood, then, that what we have to do, as students of phenomenology, is simply to open our mental eyes and look well at the phenomenon and say what are the characteristics that are never wanting in it, whether that phenomenon be something that outward experience forces upon our attention, or whether it be the wildest of dreams, or whether it be the most abstract and general of the conclusions of science. The faculties which we must endeavor to gather for this work are three. The first and foremost is that rare faculty, the faculty of seeing what stares one in the face, just as it presents itself, unreplaced by any interpretation, unsophisticated by any allowance for this or for that supposed modifying circumstance. This is the faculty of the artist who sees for example the apparent colors of nature as they appear. When the ground is covered by snow on which the sun shines brightly except where shadows fall, if you ask any ordinary man what its color appears to be, he will tell you white, pure white, whiter in the sunlight, a little greyish in the shadow. But that is not what is before his eyes that he is describing; it is his theory of what *ought* to be seen. The artist will tell him that the shadows are not grey but a dull blue and that the snow in the sunshine is of a rich yellow. That artist's observational power is what is most wanted in the study of phenomenology. The second faculty we must strive to arm ourselves with is a resolute discrimination which fastens itself like a bulldog upon the particular feature that we are studying, follows it wherever it may lurk, and detects it beneath all its disguises. The third faculty we shall need is the generalizing power of the mathematician who produces the abstract formula that comprehends the very essence of the feature under examination purified from all admixture of extraneous and irrelevant accompaniments.

A very moderate exercise of this third faculty suffices to show us that the word *Category* bears substantially the same meaning with all philosophers. For Aristotle, for Kant, and for Hegel, a category is an element of phenomena of the first rank of generality. It naturally follows that the categories are few in number, just as the chemical elements are. The business of phenomenology is to draw up a catalogue of categories and prove its sufficiency and freedom from redundancies, to make out the characteristics of each category, and to show the relations of each to the others. I find that there are at least two distinct orders of categories, which I call the particular and the universal.[6] The particular categories form a series, or set of series, only one of each series being present, or at least predominant in any one phenomenon. The universal categories, on the other hand, belong to every phenomenon, one being perhaps more prominent in one aspect of that phenomenon than another but all of them belonging to every phenomenon. I am not very well satisfied with this description of the two orders of categories, but I am pretty well satisfied that there are two orders. I do not recognize them in Aristotle, unless the predicaments and the predicables are the two orders.[7] But in Kant we have Unity, Plurality, and Totality not all present at once; Reality, Negation, and Limitation not all present at once; Inherence, Causation, and Reaction not all present at once; Possibility, Necessity, and Actuality not all present at once. On the other hand, Kant's four greater categories, Quantity, Quality, Relation and Modality form what I should recognize as Kant's Universal Categories.[8] In Hegel his long list which gives the divisions of his *Encyclopedia* are his Particular Categories. His three stages of thought, although he does not apply the word *category* to them, are what I should call Hegel's Universal Categories.[9] My intention this evening is to limit myself to the Universal, or Short List of Categories, and I may say, at once, that I consider Hegel's three stages as being, roughly speaking, the correct list of Universal Categories. I regard the fact that I reached the same result as he did by a process as unlike his as possible, at a time when my attitude toward him was rather one of contempt than of awe, and without being influenced by him in any discernible way however slightly, as being a not inconsiderable argument in favor of the correctness of the list. For if I am mistaken in thinking that my thought was uninfluenced by his, it would seem to follow that that thought was of a quality which gave it a secret power, that would in itself argue pretty strongly for its truth.

Although I am going to confine myself to these three categories, yet you will understand that in an hour's lecture, in what remains of the hour, it will be quite beyond my power either to treat them at all exhaustively, or to make my points as convincingly as I could do if I were less hurried by my desire to get back to my proper subject of pragmatism, or even to give you a perfectly clear notion of what I conceive these three categories to be. What I should like to do would be to take up each category in turn and firstly, point it out to you clearly in the phenomenon, secondly to show what different shapes and aspects it takes and make their characteristics clear, thirdly, to put it before you in the most naked and rational form and show how this describes it in all its protean changes, fourthly to prove to you that it is an element of the phenomenon that must by no means be ignored, and fifthly to make it positively certain that the category is irreducible to any other or mixture of others. These five points being made with reference to each of the three categories I would drop the keystone into my arch by demonstrating that no fourth category could possibly be added to the list, and then I could go on to the moral of the whole story by showing how the chief conflicts between the different warring marshals of metaphysics arise entirely from the endeavor of each to omit from his account of the universe some one or even some two of the three Universal Categories, so that there are, as a historical fact, just seven systems, the true one giving due regard to all three categories A B C; three others that recognize two each, and three that recognize but one each.[10]

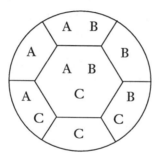

We should thus begin to get a glimmer of light upon the question of pragmatism. But you can readily see, even without knowing how intricate some of these sixteen points would necessarily be, that I could not possibly touch upon so many in one lecture and that it would be equally impossible to give more than one lecture to this extremely general question in a discussion of so special a matter as that of the merits of pragmatism. I can only touch lightly on a few of the points and leave the rest for your own meditations.

When anything is present to the mind, what is the very first and simplest character to be noted in it, in every case, no matter how little elevated the object may be? Certainly, it is its *presentness*. So far Hegel is quite right. Immediacy is his word. To say, however, that presentness, presentness as it is present, present presentness, is *abstract*, is Pure Being, is a falsity so glaring, that one can only say that Hegel's theory that the abstract is more primitive than the concrete blinded his eyes to what stood before them. Go out under the blue dome of heaven and look at what is present as it appears to the artist's eye. The poetic mood approaches the state in which the present appears as it is present. Is poetry so abstract and colorless? The present is just what it is regardless of the absent, regardless of past and future. It is such as it is, utterly ignoring anything else. Consequently, it cannot be *abstracted* (which is what Hegel means by the abstract) for the abstracted is what the concrete, which gives it whatever being it has, makes it to be. The present, being such as it is while utterly ignoring everything else, is *positively* such as it is. Imagine, if you please, a consciousness in which there is no comparison, no relation, no recognized multiplicity (since parts would be other than the whole), no change, no imagination of any modification of what is positively there, no reflexion,—nothing but a simple positive character. Such a consciousness might be just an odor, say a smell of attar; or it might be one infinite dead ache; it might be the hearing of [a] piercing eternal whistle. In short, any simple and positive quality of feeling would be something which our description fits,—that it is such as it is quite regardless of anything else. The quality of feeling is the true psychical representative of the first category of the immediate as it is in its immediacy, of the present in its direct positive presentness. Qualities of feeling show myriad-fold variety, far beyond what the psychologists admit. This variety however is in them only in so far as they are compared and gathered into collections. But as they are in their presentness, each is sole and unique; and all the others are absolute nothingness to it,—or rather much less than nothingness, for not even a recognition as absent things or as fictions is accorded to them. The first category, then, is Quality of Feeling, or whatever is such as it is positively and regardless of aught else.

The next simplest feature that is common to all that comes before the mind, and consequently, the second category, is the element of *Struggle*. It is convenient enough, although by no means necessary, to study this, at first, in a psychological instance. Imagine yourself making a strong muscular effort, say that of pressing with all your might against a half-open door. Obviously, there is a sense of resistance. There could not be effort without an equal resistance any more than there could be a resistance without an equal effort that it resists. Action and reaction are equal. If you find that the door is pushed open in spite of you, you will say that it was the person on the other side that acted and you that resisted, while if you succeed in pushing the door to, you will say that it was you who acted and the other person that resisted. In general, we call the one that succeeds by means of his effort the *agent* and the one that fails the *patient*. But as far as the element of Struggle is concerned, there is no difference between being an agent and being a patient. It is the result that decides; but what it is that is deemed to be the result for the purpose of this distinction is a detail into which we need not enter. If while you are walking quietly along the sidewalk a man carrying a ladder suddenly pokes you violently with it in the back of the head and walks on without noticing what he has done, your impression probably will be that he struck you with great violence and that you made not the slightest resistance; although in fact you must have resisted with a force equal to that of the blow. Of course, it will be understood that I am not using force in the modern sense of a moving force but in the sense of Newton's *actio;*[11] but I must warn you that I have not time to notice such trifles. In like manner, if in pitch darkness a tremendous flash of lightning suddenly comes, you are ready [to] admit having received a shock and being acted upon, but that you reacted you may be inclined to deny. You certainly did so, however, and are conscious of having done so. The sense of shock is as much a sense of resisting as of being acted upon. So it is when anything strikes the senses. The outward excitation succeeds in producing its effect on you, while you in turn produce no discernible effect on it; and therefore you call it the agent, and overlook your own part in the reaction. On the other hand, in reading a geometrical demonstration, if you draw the figure in your imagination instead of on paper, it is so easy to add to your image whatever subsidiary line is wanted, that it seems to you that you have acted on the image without the image having offered any resistance. That it is not so, however, is easily shown. For unless that image had a certain power of persisting such as it is and resisting metamorphosis, and if you were not sensible of strength of persistence, you never could be sure that the construction you are dealing with at one stage of the demonstration was the same that you had before your mind at an earlier stage. The main distinction between the Inner and the Outer Worlds is that inner objects promptly take any modifications we wish, while outer objects are hard facts that no man can make to be other than they are. Yet tremendous as this distinction is, it is after all only relative. Inner objects do offer a certain degree of resistance and outer objects are susceptible of being modified in some measure by sufficient exertion intelligently directed.

Two very serious doubts arise concerning this category of struggle which I should be able completely to set to rest, I think, with only a little more time. But as it is, I can only suggest lines of reflection which, if you perseveringly follow out, ought to bring you to the same result to which they have brought me.

The first of these doubts is whether this element of struggle is anything more than a very special kind of phenomenon, and withal an anthropomorphic conception and therefore not scientifically true.

The other doubt is whether the idea of Struggle is a simple and irresolvable element of the phenomenon; and in opposition to its being so, two contrary parties will enter into a sort of [alliance] without remarking how deeply they are at variance with one another. One of these parties will be composed of those philosophers who understand themselves as wishing to reduce everything in the phenomenon to qualities of feeling.[12] They will appear in the arena of psychology and will declare that there is absolutely no such thing as a specific sense of effort. There is nothing, they will say, but feelings excited upon muscular contraction, feelings which they may or may not be disposed to say have their immediate excitations within the muscles. The other party will be composed of those philosophers who say that there can be only one absolute and only one irreducible element, and since *Noῦς*[13] is such an element, *Noῦς* is really the only thoroughly clear idea there is. These philosophers will take a sort of pragmatistic stand. They will maintain that to say that one thing acts upon another, absolutely the only thing that can be meant is that there is a *law* according to which under all circumstances of a certain general description certain phenomena will result; and therefore to speak of one thing as acting upon another *hic et nunc* regardless of uniformity, regardless of what will happen on all occasions, is simple nonsense.

In the course of considering the second objection, the universality of the element of struggle will get brought to light without any special arguments to that end.[14] But as to its being unscientific because anthropomorphic, that is an objection of a very shallow kind, that arises from prejudices based upon much too narrow considerations. "Anthropomorphic" is what pretty much all conceptions are at bottom; otherwise other roots for the words in which to express them than the old Aryan roots would have to be found. And in regard to any preference for one kind of theory over another, it is well to remember that every single truth of science is due to the affinity of the human soul to the soul of the universe, imperfect as that affinity no doubt is. To say, therefore, that a conception is one natural to man, which comes to just about the same thing as to say that it is anthropomorphic, is as high a recommendation as one could give to it in the eyes of an Exact Logician. I would not have anybody accept any doctrine of logic simply because minute and thorough criticism has resulted in making me perfectly confident of its truth. But I will not allow this scruple to prevent my saying that for my part,—who am characterized in some of the books as a Sceptic in philosophy and have even been called a modern Hume,[15]—I have after long years of the severest examination become fully satisfied that, other things being equal, an anthropomorphic conception, whether it makes the best nucleus for a scientific working hypothesis or not, is far more likely to be approximately true than one that is not anthropomorphic. Suppose, for example, it is a question between accepting *Telepathy* or *Spiritualism*.[16] The former I dare say is the preferable working hypothesis because it can be more readily subjected to experimental investigation. But as long as there is no reason for believing it except phenomena that Spiritualism is equally competent to explain, I think Spiritualism is much the more likely to be approximately true, as being the more anthropomorphic and natural idea; and in like manner, as between an old-fashioned God and a modern patent Absolute, recommend me to the anthropomorphic conception if it is a question of which is the more likely to be about the truth.[17]

As for the double-headed objection, I will first glance at that branch of it that rests upon the idea that the conception of action involves the notion of law or uniformity so that to talk of a reaction regardless of anything but the two individual reacting objects is nonsense. As to that, I should say that a law of nature left to itself would be quite analogous to a court without a sheriff. A court in that predicament might probably be able to induce some citizen to act as sheriff; but until it had so provided itself with an officer who, unlike itself, could not discourse authoritatively but who could put forth the strong arm, its law might be the perfection of human reason but would remain mere fireworks, *brutum fulmen*.[18] Just so, let a law of nature,—say the law of gravitation,—

remain a mere uniformity,—a mere formula establishing a relation between terms,—and what in the world should induce a stone, which is not a term nor a concept but just a plain thing, to act in conformity to that uniformity? All other stones may have done so, and this stone too on former occasions, and it would break the uniformity for it not to do so now. But what of that? There is no use talking reason to a stone. It is deaf and it has no reason. I should ask the objector whether he was a nominalist or a scholastic realist. If he is a nominalist he holds that laws are mere generals, that is, formulae relating to mere terms; and ordinary good sense ought to force him to acknowledge that there are real connections between individual things regardless of mere formulae. Now any real connection whatsoever between individual things involves a reaction between them in the sense of this category. The objector may, however, take somewhat stronger ground by confessing himself to be a scholastic realist, holding that generals may be real. A law of nature, then, will be regarded by him as having a sort of *esse in futuro*. That is to say they will have a present reality which consists in the fact that events *will* happen according to the formulation of those laws. It would seem futile for me to attempt to reply that when, for example, I make a great effort to lift a heavy weight and perhaps am unable to stir it from the ground, there really is a struggle on this occasion regardless of what happens on other occasions; because the objector would simply admit that on such an occasion I have a quality of feeling which I call a feeling of effort, but he would urge that the only thing which makes this designation appropriate to the feeling is the regularity of connection between this feeling and certain notions of matter.

This is a position well enough taken to merit a very respectful reply. But before going into that reply, there is an observation which I should like to lay before the candid objector. Your argument against this category of Struggle is that a struggle regardless of law is not *intelligible*. Yet you have just admitted that my so-called sense of effort involves a peculiar quality of feeling. Now a quality of feeling is not intelligible, either. Nothing can be less so. One can *feel* it, but to comprehend it or express it in a general formula is out of the question. So it appears that unintelligibility does not suffice to destroy or refute a Category. Indeed, if you are to accept scholastic realism, you would seem to be almost bound to admit that Noῦς, or intelligibility, is itself a category; and in that case far from non-intelligibility's refuting a category, intelligibility would do so,—that is, would prove that a conception could not be a category distinct from the category of Noῦς, or intelligibility. If it be objected that the unintelligibility of a Quality of Feeling is of a merely privative kind quite different from the aggressive and brutal anti-intelligibility of action regardless of law, the rejoinder will be that if intelligibility be a category, it is not surprising but rather inevitable that other categories should be in different relations to this one.

But without beating longer round the bush, let us come to close quarters. Experience is our only teacher. Far be it from me to enunciate any doctrine of a *tabula rasa*.[19] For as I said a few minutes ago, there manifestly is not one drop of principle in the whole vast reservoir of established scientific theory that has sprung from any other source than the power of the human mind to *originate* ideas that are true. But this power, for all it has accomplished, is so feeble that as ideas flow from their springs in the soul, the truths are almost drowned in a flood of false notions; and that which experience does is gradually, and by a sort of fractionation, to precipitate and filter off the false ideas, eliminating them and letting the truth pour on in its mighty current.

But precisely how does this action of experience take place? It takes place by a series of surprises. There is no need of going into details. At one time a ship is sailing along in the trades over a smooth sea, the navigator having no more positive expectation than that of the usual monotony of such a voyage,—when suddenly she strikes upon a rock. The majority of discoveries, however, have been the result of experimentation. Now no man makes an experiment without being more or less inclined to think that an interesting result will ensue; for experiments are much too costly of physical and psychical energy to be undertaken at random and aimlessly. And naturally nothing can possibly be learned from an experiment that turns out just as was anticipated. It is by surprises that experience teaches all she deigns to teach us.

In all the works on pedagogy that ever I read,—and they have been many, big, and heavy,—I don't remember that any one has advocated a system of teaching by practical jokes, mostly cruel. That, however, describes the method of our great teacher, Experience. She says,

> Open your mouth and shut your eyes
> And I'll give you something to make you wise;

and thereupon she keeps her promise, and seems to take her pay in the fun of tormenting us.

The phenomenon of surprise in itself is highly instructive in reference to this category because of the emphasis it puts upon a mode of consciousness which can be detected in all perception, namely, a double consciousness at once of an *ego* and a *non-ego*, directly acting upon each other. Understand me well. My appeal is to observation,—observation that each of you must make for himself.

The question is what the *phenomenon* is. We make no vain pretense of going beneath phenomena. We merely ask, What is the content of the Percept?[20] Everybody should be competent to answer that of himself. Examine the Percept in the particularly marked case in which it comes as a surprise. Your mind was filled /with/ an imaginary object that was expected. At the moment when it was expected the vividness of the representation is exalted, and suddenly when it should come something quite different comes instead. I ask you whether at that instant of surprise there is not a double consciousness, on the one hand of an Ego, which is simply the expected idea suddenly broken off, on the other hand of the Non-Ego, which is the Strange Intruder, in his abrupt entrance.

The whole question is what the *perceptual facts* are, as given in direct perceptual judgments. By a perceptual judgment, I mean a judgment asserting in propositional form what a character of a percept directly present to the mind is. The percept of course is not itself a judgment, nor can a judgment in any degree resemble a percept. It is as unlike it as the printed letters in a book where a Madonna of Murillo[21] is described are unlike the picture itself. You may adopt any theory that seems to you acceptable as to the psychological operations by which perceptual judgments are formed. For our present purpose it makes no difference what that theory is. All that I insist upon is that those operations, whatever they may be, are utterly beyond our control and will go on whether we are pleased with them or not. Now I say that taking the word "criticize" in the sense it bears in philosophy, that of apportioning praise and blame, it is perfectly idle to criticize anything over which you can exercise no sort of control. You may wisely criticize a reasoning, because the reasoner, in the light of your criticism, will certainly go over his reasoning again and correct it if your blame of it was just. But to pronounce an involuntary operation of the mind *good* or *bad*, has no more sense than to pronounce the proportion of weights in which hydrogen and chlorine combine, that of 1 to 35.11, to be *good* or *bad*. I said it was idle; but in point of fact "nonsensical" would have been an apter word.

If, therefore, our careful direct interpretation of perception, and more emphatically of such perception as involves surprise, is that the perception represents two objects reacting upon one another, that is not only a decision from which there is no appeal, but it is downright nonsense to dispute the fact that in perception two objects really do so react upon one another.

That, of course, is the doctrine of Immediate Perception which is upheld by Reid, Kant, and all dualists who understand the true nature of dualism, and the denial of which led Cartesians to the utterly absurd theory of divine assistance[22] upon which the preestablished harmony of Leibniz is but a slight improvement. Every philosopher who denies the doctrine of Immediate Perception,—including idealists of every stripe,—by that denial cuts off all possibility of ever cognizing a *relation*. Nor will he better his position by declaring that all relations are illusive appearances, since it is not merely true knowledge of them that he has cut off but every mode of cognitive representation of them.[23]

II

Thus far, gentlemen, I have been insisting very strenuously upon what the most vulgar common sense has every disposition to assent to and only ingenious philosophers have been able to deceive themselves about. But now I come to a category which only a more refined form of common sense is prepared willingly to allow, the category which of the three is the chief burden of Hegel's song, a category toward which the studies of the new logico-mathematicians, Georg Cantor, and the like are steadily pointing,[24] but to which no modern writer of any stripe, unless it be some obscure student like myself, has ever done anything approaching to justice. I wish most earnestly that instead of a few minutes I could give six lectures in opening up to you some of the most striking paths of thought to which this conception will lead any man who pursues it in a spirit of exact criticism.

There never was a sounder logical maxim of scientific procedure than Ockham's razor: *Entia non sunt multiplicanda praeter necessitatem.* That is to say: Before you try a complicated hypothesis, you should make quite sure that no simplification of it will explain the facts equally well. No matter if it takes fifty generations of arduous experimentation to explode the simpler hypothesis, and no matter how incredible it may seem that that simpler hypothesis should suffice, still, fifty generations are nothing in the life of science, which has all time before it, and in the long run, say in some thousands of generations, time will be economized by proceeding in an orderly manner, and by making it an invariable rule to try the simpler hypothesis first. Indeed, one can never be sure that the simpler hypothesis is not the true one, after all, until its cause has been fought out to the bitter end. But you will mark the limitation of my approval of Ockham's razor. It is a sound maxim of *scientific procedure.* If the question be what one ought to *Believe,* the logic of the situation must take other factors into account. Speaking strictly, *Belief* is out of place in pure theoretical science, which has nothing nearer to it than the establishment of doctrines, and only the provisional establishment of them, at that. Compared with living *Belief* it is nothing but a ghost. If the captain [of] a vessel on a lee shore in a terrific storm finds himself in a critical position in which he must instantly either put his wheel to port acting on one hypothesis, or put his wheel to starboard acting on the contrary hypothesis, and his vessel will infallibly be dashed to pieces if he decides the question wrongly, Ockham's razor is not worth the stout belief of any common seaman. For stout belief *may* happen to save the ship, while *Entia non sunt multiplicanda praeter necessitatem* would be only a stupid way of spelling Shipwreck. Now in matters of real practical concern we are all in something like the situation of that sea captain.

Philosophy, as I understand the word, is a positive theoretical science, and a science in an early stage of development. As such it has no more to do with belief than any other science. Indeed, I am bound to confess that it is at present in so unsettled a condition, that if the ordinary theorems of molecular physics and of archeology are but the ghosts of beliefs, then to my mind the doctrines of the philosophers are little better than the ghosts of ghosts. I know this is an extremely heretical opinion. The followers of Haeckel are completely in accord with the followers of Hegel in holding that what they call philosophy is a practical science and the best of guides in the formation of what they take to be Religious Beliefs.[25] I simply note the divergence, and pass on to an unquestionable fact; namely, the fact that all modern philosophy is built upon Ockhamism, by which I mean that it is all nominalistic and that it adopts nominalism because of Ockham's razor. And there is no form of modern philosophy of which this is more essentially true than the philosophy of Hegel. But it is not modern philosophers only who are nominalists. The nominalistic *Weltanschauung* has become incorporated into what I will venture to call the very flesh and blood of the average modern mind.

The third category of which I come now to speak is precisely that whose reality is denied by nominalism. For although nominalism is not credited with any extraordinarily lofty appreciation of the powers of the human soul, yet it attributes to it a power of originating a kind of ideas the like of which Omnipotence has failed to create as objects,[26] and those general conceptions which men will never cease to consider the glory of the human intellect must, according to any consistent nominalism, be entirely wanting in the mind of Deity. Leibniz, the modern nominalist *par excellence*, will not admit that God has the faculty of Reason; and it seems impossible to avoid that conclusion upon nominalistic principles.[27]

But it is not in Nominalism alone that modern thought has attributed to the human mind the miraculous power of originating a category of thought that has no counterpart at all in Heaven or Earth. Already in that strangely influential hodge-podge, the salad of Cartesianism, the doctrine stands out very emphatically that the only force is the force of impact, which clearly belongs to the category of Reaction, and ever since Newton's *Principia* began to affect the general thought of Europe through the sympathetic spirit of Voltaire, there has been a disposition to deny any kind of action except purely mechanical action. The Corpuscular Philosophy of Boyle,[28]—although the pious Boyle did not himself recognize its character,—was bound to come to that in the last resort; and the idea constantly gained strength throughout the eighteenth century and the nineteenth until the doctrine of the Conservation of Energy,[29] generalized rather loosely by philosophers, led to the theory of psychophysical parallelism[30] against which there has only of recent years been any very sensible and widespread revolt. Psychophysical parallelism is merely the doctrine that mechanical action explains all the real facts, except that these facts have an internal aspect which is a little obscure and a little shadowy.

To my way of regarding philosophy, all this movement was perfectly good scientific procedure. For the simpler hypothesis which excluded the influence of ideas upon matter had to be tried and persevered in until it was thoroughly exploded. But I believe that now, at least at any time for the last thirty years, it has been apparent to every man who sufficiently considered the subject that there is a mode of influence upon external facts which cannot be resolved into mere mechanical action, so that henceforward it will be a grave error of scientific philosophy to overlook the universal presence in the phenomenon of this third category. Indeed, from the moment that the Idea of Evolution took possession of the minds of men, the pure corpuscular philosophy together with nominalism had had their doom pronounced. I grew up in Cambridge and was about twenty-one when the *Origin of Species* appeared.[31] There was then living here a thinker who left no remains from which one could now gather what an educative influence his was upon the minds of all of us who enjoyed his intimacy, Mr. Chauncey Wright.[32] He had at first been a Hamiltonian but had early passed over into the warmest advocacy of the nominalism of John Stuart Mill; and being a mathematician at a time when dynamics was regarded as the loftiest branch of mathematics, he was also inclined to regard nature from a strictly mechanical point of view. But his interests were wide and he was also a student of Gray.[33] I was away surveying in the wilds of Louisiana when Darwin's great work appeared, and though I learned by letters of the immense sensation it had created, I did not return until early in the following summer when I found Wright all enthusiasm for Darwin, whose doctrines appeared to him as a sort of supplement to those of Mill. I remember well that I then made a remark to him which, although he did not assent to it, evidently impressed him enough to perplex him. The remark was that these ideas of development had more vitality by far than any of his other favorite conceptions and that though they might at that moment be in his mind like a little vine clinging to the tree of Associationalism,[34] yet after a time that vine would inevitably kill the tree. He asked me why I said that and I replied that the reason was that Mill's doctrine was nothing but a metaphysical point of view to which Darwin's, which was nourished by positive observation, must be deadly. Ten or fifteen years later, when Agnosticism was all the go, I prognosticated a short life for it, as philosophies run, for a similar reason. What the true definition of Pragmatism may be, I find it very hard to say; but in my nature it is a sort of instinctive attraction for living facts.

All nature abounds in proofs of other influences than merely mechanical action even in the physical world. They crowd in upon us at the rate of several every minute. And my observation of men has led me to this little generalization. Speaking only of men who really think for themselves and not of mere reporters, I have not found that it is the men whose lives are mostly passed within the four walls of a physical laboratory who are most inclined to be satisfied with a purely mechanical metaphysics. On the contrary, the more clearly they understand how physical forces work the more incredible it seems to them that such action should explain what happens out of doors. A larger proportion of materialists and agnostics is to be found among the thinking physiologists and other naturalists, and the largest proportion of all among those who derive their ideas of physical science from reading popular books. These last, the Spencers, the Youmans,[35] and the like, seem to be possessed with the idea that science has got the universe pretty well ciphered down to a fine point; while the Faradays and Newtons seem to themselves like children who have picked up a few pretty pebbles upon the ocean beach. But most of us seem to find it difficult to recognize the greatness and wonder of things familiar to us. As the prophet is not without honor save /in his own country,/[36] so it is also with phenomena. Point out to the ordinary man evidence however conclusive of other influence than physical action in things he sees every day, and he will say "Well, *I* don't see as that frog has got any pints about him that's any diffunt from any other frog."[37] For that reason we welcome instances perhaps of less real cogency but which have the merit of being rare and strange. Such, for example, are the right-handed and left-handed screw-structures of the molecules of those bodies which are said to be "optically active." Of every such substance there are two varieties, or as the chemists call them, two modifications, one of which twists a ray of light that passes through it to the right and the other by an exactly equal amount to the left. All the ordinary physical properties of the right-handed and left-handed modifications are identical. Only certain faces of their crystals, often very minute, are differently placed. No chemical process can ever transmute the one modification into the other. And their ordinary chemical behavior is absolutely the same, so that no strictly chemical process can separate them if they are once mixed. Only, the chemical action of one optically active substance upon another is different if they both twist the ray the same way from what it is if they twist the ray different ways. There are certain living organisms which feed on one modification and destroy it while leaving the other one untouched. This is presumably due to such organisms containing in their substance, possibly in very minute proportion, some optically active body. Now I maintain that the original segregation of levo-molecules, or molecules with a left-handed twist, from dextro-molecules, or molecules with a right-handed twist, is absolutely incapable of mechanical explanation. Of course you may suppose that in the original nebula at the very formation of the world, right-handed quartz was collected into one place while left-handed quartz was collected into another place. But to suppose that is *ipso facto* to suppose that that segregation was a phenomenon without any mechanical explanation. The three laws of motion draw no dynamical distinction between right-handed and left-handed screws, and a mechanical explanation is an explanation founded on the three laws of motion. There, then, is a physical phenomenon absolutely inexplicable by mechanical action. This single instance suffices to overthrow the corpuscular philosophy.

12

The Categories Defended

MS 308. [Published in CP 5.66–81, 88–92 (in part) and in HL 167–88. This is the third Harvard lecture, delivered on 9 April 1903.] In this lecture Peirce goes into more detail concerning the nature of his categories and uses them to distinguish three kinds of signs: icons, indices, and symbols. He analyzes in particular one type of symbol, the proposition, which always refers to its object in two ways: indexically, by means of its subject, and iconically, by means of its predicate. Peirce defends his categories against the view he attributes to A. B. Kempe that Thirdness is not required to express the relations of mathematics, and he argues for the independence of Firstness, Secondness, and Thirdness.

I

Ladies and Gentlemen:

Category the First is the Idea of that which is such as it is regardless of anything else. That is to say, it is a *Quality* of Feeling.

Category the Second is the Idea of that which is such as it is as being Second to some First, regardless of anything else and in particular regardless of any *law*, although it may conform to a law. That is to say, it is *Reaction* as an element of the Phenomenon.

Category the Third is the Idea of that which is such as it is as being a Third, or Medium, between a Second and its First. That is to say, it is *Representation* as an element of the Phenomenon.

A mere complication of Category the Third, involving no idea essentially different, will give the idea of something which is such as it is by virtue of its relations to any multitude, enumerable, denumeral, or abnumerable[1] or even to any supermultitude of correlates; so that this Category suffices of itself to give the conception of True Continuity, than which no conception yet discovered is higher.

Category the First, owing to its Extremely Rudimentary character, is not susceptible of any degenerate or weakened modification.

Category the Second has a *Degenerate* Form, in which there is Secondness indeed, but a weak or Secondary Secondness that is not in the pair in its own quality, but belongs to it only in a certain respect. Moreover, this degeneracy need not be absolute but may be only approximative. Thus a genus characterized by Reaction will by the determination of its essential character split into two species, one a species where the secondness is strong, the other a species where the secondness is weak, and the strong species will subdivide into two that will be similarly related, without any corresponding subdivision of the weak species. For example, Psychological Reaction splits into Willing, where the Secondness is strong, and Sensation, where it is weak; and Willing again subdivides into Active Willing and Inhibitive Willing, to which last dichotomy nothing in Sensation corresponds. But it must be confessed that subdivision, as such, involves something more than the second category.

Category the Third exhibits two different ways of Degeneracy, where the irreducible idea of Plurality, as distinguished from Duality, is present indeed but in maimed conditions. The First degree of Degeneracy is found in an Irrational Plurality which, as it exists, in contradistinction from the form of its representation, is a mere complication of duality. We have just had an example of this in the idea of Subdivision. In pure Secondness, the reacting correlates are, as I showed in the last lecture, *Singulars*, and as such are *Individuals*, not capable of further division.[2] Consequently, the conception of Subdivision, say by repeated dichotomy, certainly involves a sort of Thirdness, but it is a thirdness that is conceived to consist in a second secondness.

The most degenerate Thirdness is where we conceive a mere Quality of Feeling, or Firstness, to represent itself to itself as Representation. Such, for example, would be Pure Self-Consciousness, which might be roughly described as a mere feeling that has a dark instinct of being a germ of thought. This sounds nonsensical, I grant. Yet something can be done toward rendering it comprehensible.

I remember a lady's averring that her father had heard a minister, of what complexion she did not say, open a prayer as follows: "O Thou, All-sufficient, Self-sufficient, Insufficient God." Now pure Self-consciousness is Self-sufficient, and if it is also regarded as All-sufficient, it would seem to follow that it must be Insufficient. I ought to apologize for introducing such buffoonery into serious lectures.[3] I do so because I seriously believe that a bit of fun helps thought and tends to keep it pragmatical.

Imagine that upon the soil of a country that has a single boundary line, thus ⊜ and not ⊜ ⊜ or ⊚, there lies a map of that same country. This map may distort the different provinces of the country to any extent.

But I shall suppose that it represents every part of the country that has a single boundary by a part of the map that has a single boundary; that every part is represented as bounded by such parts as it really is bounded by, that every point of the country is represented by a single point of the map, and that every point of the map represents a single point in the country. Let us further suppose that this map is infinitely minute in its representation so that there is no speck on[4] any grain of sand in the country that could not be seen represented upon the map if we were to examine it under a sufficiently high magnifying power. Since, then, everything on the soil of the country is shown on the map, and since the map lies on the soil of the country, the map itself will be portrayed in the map, and in this map of the map everything on the soil of the country can be discerned, including the map itself with the map of the map within its boundary. Thus there will be within the map a map of the map, and within that a map of the map of the map and so on *ad infinitum*. These maps being each within the preceding ones of the series, there will be a point contained in all of them, and this will be the map of itself. Each map which directly or indirectly represents the country is itself mapped, in the next, that is, is in the next, is represented to be a map of the country. In other words each map is *interpreted* as such in the next. We may therefore say that each is a representation of the country *to* the next map; and that point that is in all the maps is in itself the representation of nothing but itself and to nothing but it itself. It is therefore the precise analogue of pure self-consciousness. As such it is *self-sufficient*. It is saved from being insufficient, that is, as no representation at all, by the circumstance that it is not *all-sufficient*, that is, is not a complete representation but is only a point upon a continuous map.

I dare say you may have heard something like this before from Professor Royce; but if so, you will remark an important divergency.[5] The idea itself belongs neither to him nor to me, and was used by me in this connection thirty years ago.[6]

The relatively degenerate forms of the Third category do not fall into a catena, like those of the Second. What we find is this. Taking any class in whose essential idea the predominant element is Thirdness, or Representation, the self-development of that essential idea,—which development, let me say, is not to be compassed by any amount of mere "hard thinking," but only by an elaborate process founded upon experience and reason combined,— results in a *trichotomy* giving rise to three subclasses, or genera, involving respectively a relatively genuine thirdness, a relatively reactional thirdness or thirdness of the lesser degree of degeneracy, and a relatively qualitative thirdness or thirdness of the last degeneracy [see figure 1].[7] This last may subdi-

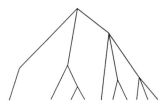

Fig. 1

vide, and its species may even be governed by the three categories, but it will not subdivide in the manner which we are considering by the essential determinations of its conception. The genus corresponding to the lesser degree of degeneracy, the reactionally degenerate genus, will subdivide after the manner of the second category forming a catena, while the genus of relatively genuine Thirdness will subdivide by trichotomy just like that from which it resulted. Only as the division proceeds, the subdivisions become harder and harder to discern. The representamen, for example, divides by trichotomy into the general sign, or *symbol*, the *index*, and the *icon*. An *icon* is a representamen which fulfills the function of a representamen by virtue of a character which it possesses in itself, and would possess just the same though its object did not exist. Thus, the statue of a centaur is not, it is true, a representamen if there be no such thing as a centaur. Still, if it represents a centaur, it is by virtue of its shape; and this shape it will have, just as much, whether there be a centaur or not. An *index* is a representamen which fulfills the function of a representamen by virtue of a character which it could not have if its object did not exist, but which it will continue to have just the same whether it be interpreted as a representamen or not. For instance, an old-fashioned hygrometer is an *index*. For it is so contrived as to have a physical reaction with dryness and moisture in the air, so that the little man will come out if it is wet, and this would happen just the same if the use of the instrument should be entirely forgotten, so that it ceased actually to convey any information. A *symbol* is a representamen which fulfills its function regardless of any similarity or analogy with its object and equally regardless of any *factual* connection therewith, but solely and simply because it will be interpreted to be a representamen. Such for example is any general word, sentence, or book.

Of these three genera of representamens the *Icon* is the Qualitatively Degenerate, the *Index* the Reactionally degenerate, while the *Symbol* is the relatively genuine genus.

Now the *Icon* may undoubtedly be divided according to the categories but the mere completeness of the notion of the *icon* does not imperatively call for any such division. For a pure icon does not draw any distinction between itself and its object. It represents whatever it may represent, and, whatever it is like, it in so far is. It is an affair of suchness only.

It is quite otherwise with the *Index*. Here is a reactional sign, which is such by virtue of a real connection with its object. Then the question arises, is this dual character in the index so that it has two elements, by virtue of the one serving as a substitute for the particular object it does, while the other is an involved *icon* that represents the representamen itself regarded as a quality of the object,—or is there really no such dual character in the index, so that it merely denotes whatever object it happens to be really connected with just as the icon represents whatever object it happens really to resemble? Of the former, the relatively genuine form of index, the hygrometer is an example. Its connection with the weather is dualistic, so that by an involved *icon*, it actually conveys information. On the other hand any mere landmark by which a particular thing may be recognized because it is as a matter of fact associated with that thing, a proper name without signification, a pointing finger, is a degenerate index. Horatio Greenough, who designed Bunker Hill Monument, tells us in his book that he meant it to say simply "Here!" It just stands on that ground and plainly is not movable. So if we are looking for the battlefield, it will tell us whither to direct our steps.[8]

The *Symbol*, or relatively genuine form of Representamen, divides by trichotomy into the Term, the Proposition, and the Argument. The term corresponds to the icon and to the degenerate index. It does excite an icon in the imagination. The proposition conveys definite information like the genuine index, by having two parts of which the function of the one is to indicate the object meant while that of the other is to represent the representamen by exciting an icon of its quality. The argument is a representamen which does not leave the interpretant to be determined as it may by the person to whom the symbol is addressed; but separately represents what is the interpreting representation that it is intended to determine. This interpreting representation is, of course, the conclusion. It would be interesting to push these illustrations further; but I can linger nowhere. As soon as a subject begins to be interesting I am obliged to pass on to another.

II[9]

The three categories furnish an artificial classification of all possible systems of metaphysics which is certainly not without its utility. The scheme is shown in figure 2. It depends upon what ones of the three categories each system admits as important metaphysico-cosmical elements.

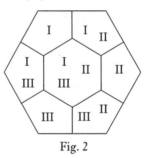

Fig. 2

One very naturally and properly endeavors to give an account of the universe with the fewest and simplest possible categories: *Praedicamenta non sunt multiplicanda praeter necessitatem.* We ought therefore to admire and extol the efforts of Condillac[10] and the Associationalists to explain everything by means of qualities of feeling.

If, however, this turns out to be a failure, the next most admirable hypothesis is that of the corpuscularians, Helmholtz and the like, who would like to explain everything by means of mechanical force, which they do not distinguish from individual reaction. That again failing, the doctrine of Hegel, who regards Category the Third as the only true one, is to be commended. For in the Hegelian system the other two are only introduced in order to be *aufgehoben.* All the categories of Hegel's list from Pure Being up appear to me very manifestly to involve Thirdness, although he does not appear to recognize it, so immersed is he in this category. All three of those simplest systems having worked themselves out into absurdity, it is natural next in accordance with the maxim of Parsimony[11] to try explanations of the Universe based on the recognition of two only of the Categories. The more moderate nominalists who nevertheless apply the epithet *mere* to thought and to representamens may be said to admit Categories First and Second and to deny the Third. The Berkeleyans for whom there are but two kinds of entities,—souls, or centers of determinable thought, and ideas in the souls, these ideas being regarded as pure statical entities, little or nothing else than Qualities of Feeling,—seem to admit Categories First and Third and to deny Secondness, which they wish to replace by Divine Creative Influence, which certainly has all the flavor of Thirdness. So far as one can make out any intelligible aim in that singular hodgepodge, the Cartesian metaphysics, it seems to have been to admit Categories Second and Third as fundamental and to deny the First. Otherwise, I do not know to whom we can attribute this opinion which certainly does not seem to be less acceptable and attractive than several others. But there are other philosophies which seem to do full justice to Categories Second and Third and to minimize the First, and among these perhaps Spinoza and Kant are to be included.

III

I desire in the first place to defend the three Categories as the three irreducible and only constituents of thought, leaving aside for the present the question of the parts they play in the economy of the Universe.

In regard to the First, however, I trust I said enough in the last lecture. I will not return to that.

As to Category the Second, if I were asked to say of what indisputable advantage to philosophy the exact study of the logic of relations had been, and if in answering the question I considered only the manner in which it presents itself to my own mind, I should unhesitatingly mention, as its first and most unquestionable service, that it had put, in the minds of every student of it, the Category of Reaction entirely beyond all doubt as an irreducible element of thought.

And yet the lamented Schröder, in the introduction to his first volume, written, it is true, as is evident enough throughout that and the second volume, before he had very thoroughly studied the logic of relations, appears to me, although probably without fully perceiving the bearing of his doctrine, to take ground quite inconsistent with such recognition of Category the Second.[12] I shall seize this opportunity to enter my protest against the position to which I allude, that position being in my opinion fatal to any sound pragmatistic conceptions. In that introduction Schröder proclaims himself a follower of Sigwart[13] in regard to the fundamentals of logic; and expressly says that he dissents from my opinions because of the reasons that Sigwart has given. I entertain a relatively high respect for Sigwart, such respect as I entertain for Rollin as a historian, Buffon as a naturalist, Priestley as a chemist, and Biot as a physicist.[14] I would go so far as to pronounce him one of the most critical and exact of the inexact logicians. The particular point now in question is this. I had said that the question of whether a reasoning is sound or not is purely a question of *fact;* namely the fact whether or not such premisses as those of whatever argument might be under criticism could be true while the conclusion was false, in case it was proposed as a necessary reasoning,— and in case of probable reasoning /there is/ some analogous question of *fact* corresponding to the pretensions of the argument. I thus, you will /have/ perceived, referred the matter to the Category of Reaction, to which the conceptions of existence and fact chiefly belong. But Schröder dissents from this because Sigwart has said that the question whether a given inference is logical or not must in the last resort come down to a question of how we feel,—a question of logical *Gefühl,* to use his own expression, which is to refer truth to the category of Quality of Feeling. This he undertakes to demonstrate. For, he says, if any other criterion be employed, the correctness of this criterion has to be established by reasoning; and in this reasoning that is thus antecedent to the establishment of any rational criterion there is nothing else upon which we can rely but *Gefühl,* so that *Gefühl* is that to which any other criterion must make its ultimate appeal as its ground. Good, say I. This is the sort of reasoning that advances philosophy,—a good square, explicit, and tangible fallacy, that can be squarely met and definitively refuted. What makes it the more valuable is that it is a form of argument of wide applicability in philosophy. It is on a quite similar principle that the hedonist says that the question of what is good morals and what bad must in the last resort come down to a question of feeling pleasure or pain. For, he urges, whatever we desire we take satisfaction in; and if we did not take satisfaction in it, we should not desire it. Thus the only thing we ever can desire is gratification, or pleasure; and all deliberate action must be performed with a view to enjoyment. So too every idealist sets out with an analogous argument, although he may probably shift his ground insensibly as he proceeds further. But at first he will say: When I perceive anything I am conscious; and when I am conscious of anything I am immediately conscious of something, and it is through that immediate consciousness that I become conscious of whatever is in my consciousness. Consequently, all that I learn from perception is that I have a feeling, together with whatever I infer from that as a premiss.

A single answer will suffice for all such argumentation. What they all assume to be necessary is, on the contrary, impossible. No desire can possibly desire its own gratification; no judgment can judge itself to be true; no reasoning can conclude itself to be sound. For the contrary positions stand on one ground and must stand or fall together, so that to refute one is to refute all. Take, then, the question of whether a judgment judges itself to be true. Unquestionably if one judgment does so, every judgment does so. I myself formerly gave something like the following argument to prove that every judgment does so. Consider the proposition:

This proposition is not true.

This is certainly a proposition. Hence by the definition of a proposition it is either true or not. But suppose it involves no falsity. Then it will follow that it is not true and does involve falsity, thus reducing that hypothesis to absurdity. The proposition is therefore not only false but absurd and self-contradictory. But all that it explicitly asserts is that it is not true. There is certainly no contradiction in saying that it is not true: it is the very conclusion we have come to. Consequently, the only way in which it can involve contradiction is by expressing at the same time the assertion that it is true. We must therefore conclude that every proposition, in the very propositional form itself, expresses the assertion of its own truth.

That may sound forcible, but it is a huge *petitio principii*. For if no proposition asserts its own truth, none asserts its own falsity; and since this asserts nothing else, it would under that hypothesis assert nothing at all and therefore not be a proposition. And if it is not a proposition the whole argument falls to the ground. Now hear an argument on the other side of the question. If a proposition asserts its own truth, it asserts something about itself; and indeed, manifestly the whole question is whether or not a proposition does assert anything about itself. If it asserts anything about itself and about its assertion, it certainly asserts that it asserts what it does assert. But if that be the case, these two propositions

It rains.
I assert that it rains.

are one and the same proposition, or if not, the second forms a part of what the first asserts. But now consider the precise denials of the two. They are

It does not rain.
I do not assert that it rains.

Manifestly the second denial asserts much less than the other. Consequently the proposition which it denies asserts much more than the other. It appears, therefore, that the proposition "It rains" does not itself assert that I assert it rains; but when I utter the proposition "It rains" I afford you the evidence of your senses that I assert it rains. This appears to me unanswerable, and it was this argument which called my attention to the fallacy of my former reasoning.

Suppose two witnesses A and B to have been examined, but by the law of evidence almost their whole testimony has been struck out except only this:

A testifies that B's testimony is true.
B testifies that A's testimony is false.

Common sense would certainly declare that nothing whatever was testified to. But I cannot admit that judgments of common sense should have the slightest weight in scientific logic, whose duty it is to criticize common sense and correct it.

But I have another argument of a pragmatistic kind. Although Aristotle defines a proposition as a symbol that is either true or false,[15] that is not properly the definition of it. However, waiving the question of propriety, I have a right to use the term *proposition* for the nonce in the sense of a symbol which separately indicates its object. Then the principle that every proposition is either true or false becomes either an *axiom* or a *theorem*. But we cannot admit axioms in these days. Why then should the principle be accepted? To say that every proposition is either true or false is to say that whatever the predicate, X, of a proposition may be, its subject S is either X or not X. But this is the principle of Excluded Middle, and the principle of excluded middle, as we saw in the last lecture, merely defines individuality.[16] That is, to say that the principle of excluded middle applies to S is no more than to say that S, the subject of the proposition, is an individual. But how can that be? We know very well that universal propositions have general subjects of which the principle of excluded middle is [not] true. That is, it is not true that "all men are either tall or not tall." The logic of relatives furnishes the solution, by showing that propositions usually have several subjects, that one of these subjects is the so-called Universe of Discourse, that as a general rule a proposition refers to several Universes of Discourse, the chief of which are Singulars, and that all propositions whatsoever refer to one common universe,—the Universal Universe or aggregate of all Singulars, which in ordinary language we denominate the Truth. The analysis of the logic of relations shows that such is the fact, and by the aid of the categories we can easily see why it should be so. A proposition is a symbol which separately INDICATES its object, and the representation in the proposition of that object is called the *subject* of the proposition. Now to INDICATE is to represent in the manner in which an index represents. But an index is a representamen which is such by virtue of standing in a genuine reaction with its object; while a singular is nothing but a genuine reacting object. It does not follow that the subject of a proposition must literally be an index, although it *indicates* the object of the representamen in a manner like the mode of representation of an index. It may be a precept by following which a singular could be found. Take for example the proposition:

Some woman is adored by every Catholic.

This means that a well-disposed person with sufficient means could find an index whose object should be a woman such that allowing an ill-disposed person to select an index whose object should be a Catholic, that Catholic would adore that woman.

Thus the subject of a proposition if not an index is a precept prescribing the conditions under which an index is to be had.

Consequently, though the subject need not be individual, the object to which the subject of a proposition applies must be the object of a possible index and as such it must be such as it is independently of any representamen or other Third. That is to say it must be *real*.

Consequently, it is impossible that a proposition should relate to itself as its object, since as long as it has not yet been enunciated it possesses characters which are not independent of how they may be represented to be.

It is, therefore, quite impossible that a proposition should assert its own truth, or what comes to the same thing, that a desire should desire its own gratification, or that an argument should conclude its own cogency, excepting only in that sense in which a point may map itself to itself, namely, as a special case under a general representation.

Consequently, when Sigwart tells me that in reasoning about a logical criterion I have to *rely* upon a feeling of logicality, he puts the cart before the horse in an utterly impossible way. He supposes that I first *feel* that a certain inference *would* gratify my sense of logicality and then proceed to draw it. But I beg to tell him that in no case whatever is it possible to *feel* what *would* happen. We *reason* about what *would* happen and we feel what *has* happened. We first draw the inference and having drawn it, if we turn our attention to our feelings we become cognizant of a sense of satisfaction. But when we have drawn the inference we have already believed in it and are satisfied, and if we become aware that the inference gives us pleasure, that is a subsequent experience upon contemplating what has happened, and it does not so much as furnish a good reason for renewed confidence in the inference, except so far as the feeling may be a sign that we should draw the same inference every time, and that it is not a mere aberration of mind.

Logic is the criticism of conscious thought, altogether analogous to moral self-control; and just as self-control never can be absolute but always must leave something uncontrolled and unchecked to act by primary impulse, so logical criticism never can be absolute but always must leave something uncriticized and unchecked. But to argue from this that logical criticism is mere feeling, would be like arguing in the other case that the only ground of morality is mere impulse.

Besides, if Sigwart's reasoning is good for anything at all, it goes to prove what he in fact deduces from it and founds his logic upon, namely that sound logic *consists* in the gratification of a feeling, which not only amounts to denying the distinction of truth and falsehood but would necessitate the admission that because my refutation of his position is entirely satisfactory to me and titillates my logical *Gefühl* in the most agreeable manner, therefore this refutation is, *ipso facto*, sound logic.

Were the Holy Father in Rome to take it into his head to use his Infallibility to command the Faithful, under pain of excommunication, to believe everything that any Protestant ever had said or ever should say, he would put himself into a position very much like that *[which]* Sigwart assumes in reducing logicality to a Quality of Feeling.

IV

The irreducibility of the idea of Thirdness appears to me to be evidently proved in the Logic of Relations. Yet Mr. A. B. Kempe, formerly president of the London Mathematical Society, who has made an important contribution to a part of the Logic of Relations in his "Memoir on the Theory of Mathematical Forms" in the *Philosophical Transactions* for 1886,[17] plainly does not share my opinion and without directly mentioning me calls attention to certain phenomena whose interest to his mind evidently is that he regards them as refuting the irreducibility of Thirdness. This objection springing, as it does, from exact analysis, should command my most serious consideration.

In order to expound Mr. Kempe's opinion I must define a few technical terms. In ordinary logical analysis such as is required in the algebraical or other purely formal treatment, it is sufficient to consider Category the Second as a two-sided element in the phenomenon, a *Reaction*, involving two objects which are differently related to one another, but having no general distinctive characters. In like manner Category the Third in the same analysis is regarded as a triadic element of the phenomenon without there being any reason for putting one of the triad of singulars which may be concerned in it as the First, rather than either of the others, nor any one as specially Second or Third. There are other purposes, however, for which it is necessary to conceive that in a reaction the first object *[is distinguished]* from the second by a general character common to all *firsts*, all *seconds* having their general character; and similarly in all triadic facts distinctive general characters are to be attributed to the First, the Second, and the Third of the three objects concerned. If two singulars A and B react upon one another, the action of A upon B and the action of B upon A are absolutely the same element of the phenomenon. Nevertheless, ordinary language makes the distinction of *agent* and *patient*, which, indeed, in the languages that are familiar to us is given great prominence; and this is the case with the majority of the languages of all families, as well as the Procrustean bed imposed by the grammarians allows us to make out their real character. But in all families, languages are found in which little or nothing is made of the distinction. In Gaelic, for example, the usual form of expression places what we should call the subject in an oblique case,—the genitive, in that language, but in some languages it is rather an ablative or an instrumental case. This distinction of agent and patient is sometimes useful even in philosophy. That is, a formal distinction is drawn between the action of A on B and the action of B on A although they are really the same fact. In the action of A on B, the patient B is conceived to be affected by A while the agent A is unaffected by B. A is modified in the action so far as to be in an active state; but this is conceived to be a certain Quality that the agent takes on during the action in which Quality the patient in no way participates, while the patient, on the other hand, takes on a relative character which can neither exist nor be conceived to exist except as correlative to an agent. That is the distinction of agent and patient. So in a triadic fact, say, for example

$$A \text{ gives } B \text{ to } C$$

we make no distinction in the ordinary logic of relations between the *subject nominative*, the *direct object*, and the *indirect object*. We say that the proposition has three *logical subjects*. We regard it as a mere affair of English grammar that there are six ways of expressing this:

A gives *B* to *C*
B enriches *C* at expense of *A*
C thanks *A* for *B*

A benefits *C* with *B*
C receives *B* from *A*
B leaves *A* for *C*

These six sentences express one and the same indivisible phenomenon. Nevertheless, just as /in/ conceiving of two reacting objects we may introduce the metaphysical distinction of *agent* and *patient*, so we may metaphysically distinguish the functions of the three objects denoted by the *subject nominative*, the *direct object*, and the *indirect object*. The *subject nominative* denotes that one of the three objects which in the triadic fact merely assumes a non-relative character of activity. The *direct object* is that object which in the triadic fact receives a character relative to that agent, being the *patient* of its action, while the *indirect object* receives a character which can neither exist nor be conceived to exist without the cooperation of the other two. When I call Category the Third the Category of Representation in which there is a Represented Object, a Representamen, and an Interpretant, I recognize that distinction. This mode of distinction is, indeed, *germane* to Thirdness, while it is *alien* to Secondness. That is to say, *agent* and *patient* as they are by themselves in their duality are not distinguished as agent and patient. The distinction lies in the mode of representing them in my mind, which is a Third. Thus there is an inherent Thirdness in this mode of distinction. But a *triadic* fact is in all cases an intellectual fact. Take *giving* for example. The mere transfer of an object which *A* sets down and *C* takes up does not constitute giving. There must be a transfer of *ownership* and ownership is a matter of Law, an intellectual fact. You now begin to see how the conception of representation is so peculiarly fit to typify the category of Thirdness. The object represented is supposed not to be affected by the representation. That is essential to the idea of representation. The Representamen is affected by /the/ Object but is not otherwise modified in the operation of representation. It is either qualitatively the double of the object in the Icon, or it is a patient on which the object really acts, in the Index; or it is intellectually linked to the object in such a way as to be mentally excited by that object, in the Symbol.

It is desirable that you should understand clearly the distinction between the Genuine and the Degenerate Index. The Genuine Index represents the duality between the representamen and its object. As a whole it stands for the object; but a *part* or element of it represents /it/ as being the Representamen, by being an *Icon* or analogue of the object in some way; and by virtue of that duality, it conveys information about the object. The simplest example of a genuine index would be, say, a telescopic image of a double star. This is not an *icon* simply, because an *icon* is a representamen which represents its object solely by virtue of its similarity to it, as a drawing of a triangle represents a mathematical triangle. But the mere appearance of the telescopic image of a double star does not proclaim itself to be similar to the star itself. It is because we have set the circles of the equatorial so that the field must by physical compulsion contain the image of that star that it represents that star, and by that means we know that the image must be an icon of the star, and information is conveyed. Such is the genuine or informational index.

A Degenerate Index is a representamen which represents a single object because it is *factually* connected with it, but which conveys no information whatever. Such, for example, are the letters attached to a geometrical or other diagram. A *proper name* is substantially the same thing; for although in this case the connection of the sign with its object happens to be a purely mental association, yet that circumstance is of no importance in the functioning of the representamen. The use of letters as indices is not confined to mathematics. Lawyers particularly often discuss cases in which *A* contracts with *B* to do something. These letters are convenient substitutes for relative pronouns. A relative, demonstrative, or personal pronoun comes very near to being a mere index, if it be not accurately so. It is far more correct so to define it than to say that a pronoun is a word placed instead of a noun. It would be nearer right to say that a common noun, when subject nominative, is a word put in place of a pronoun. A degenerate index may be called a *Monstrative* Index, in contradistinction to an *Informational* or Genuine Index.

A *proposition* is a symbol which like the informational index has a special part to represent the representamen, while the whole or another special part represents the object. The part which represents the *representamen* and which excites an *icon* in the imagination, is the Predicate. The part which indicates the object or set of objects of the representamen is called the Subject or Subjects, in grammar the subject nominative, and the objects, each of which can be replaced by a Proper Name or other *Monstrative Index* without the proposition's ceasing thereby to be a proposition. How much shall be embraced in the predicate and how many subjects shall be recognized depends, for the ordinary analyses of logic, upon what mode of analysis will answer the purpose in hand. If from a proposition we strike out a part and leave its place blank, this part being such that a monstrative index being put in its place, the symbol will again become a proposition, the part which remains after such erasure will be a predicate of the kind which I call a *monad*. Here are examples:

$$\text{\_\_\_\_\_ gives } B \text{ to } C$$
$$A \text{ gives \_\_\_\_\_ to } C$$
$$A \text{ gives } B \text{ to \_\_\_\_\_}$$

If two blanks remain, I call the predicate a *dyad*. Such are

$$\text{\_\_\_\_\_ gives \_\_\_\_\_ to } C$$
$$\text{\_\_\_\_\_ gives } B \text{ to \_\_\_\_\_}$$
$$A \text{ gives \_\_\_\_\_ to \_\_\_\_\_}$$

If there are more than two blanks, I call the predicate a *polyad*. The entire proposition may be regarded as a predicate, the circumstances under which it is uttered, the person who utters it, and all the surroundings constituting a monstrative index which will be the subject. I term an entire proposition without a blank when it is considered as a predicate a *medad*, from μηδέν. Every proposition whatever has the *Universe of Discourse* for one of its subjects and all propositions have one Subject in common which we call the *Truth*. It is the aggregate of all realities, what the Hegelians call the *Absolute*.

Thus, to include more in the predicate than need be included is merely not to carry logical analysis as far as it might be carried: it does not affect its accuracy. But to include anything in a subject which might be separated from it and left in the predicate is a positive fault of analysis. To say for example that "All men" is the subject of the proposition "All men are mortal" is incorrect. The true analysis is that "Anything" is the subject and "_____ is mortal or else not a man" is the predicate. So in "Some cat is blue-eyed" the subject is not "some cat" but "something," the predicate being "_____ is a blue-eyed cat." "Something" means that sufficient knowledge would enable us to replace the "something" by a monstrative index and still keep the proposition true. "Anything" means that the interpreter of the proposition is free to replace the "anything" by such monstrative index as he will, and still the proposition will be true. Logicians confine themselves, apart /from/ monstrative indices themselves, to "Anything" and "Something," two descriptions of what monstrative index may replace the subject, the one description *vague*, the other *general*. No others are required since such subjects, "All but one," "All but two," "Almost all," "Two thirds of the occasions that present themselves in experience," and the like are capable of logical analysis.

Everybody who has studied logic is aware that the only *formal* fallacies which ordinary logic detects are confusions between "Anything" and "Something." The same thing remains true in the logic of relatives except that we now meet with fallacies owing to confusions about the order of succession of "Anything" and "Something" as if one should carelessly substitute for the proposition "Every man is born of some woman" the proposition "There is some woman of whom every man is born."

Now in mathematics as it has been developed, all such confusions are next to impossible for the reason that mathematicians confine their studies almost exclusively to hypotheses which present only systems of relationship that are perfectly regular or as nearly so as the nature of things allows. I could give you some amusing instances of confusions between some and all in actual mathematical treatises; but they are rare. Practically, the mathematician confines himself to the study of relations among sets of hypothetical singulars.

Now Mr. Kempe considers only mathematical relationships in that sense, that is, considers only relations between single objects. Moreover, he further limits himself to relationships among enumerable sets of singulars, although mathematicians are incessantly considering denumeral or endless sets, and very often sets still more multitudinous. So confining his studies, Mr. Kempe finds that all the relationships he meets with can be represented by graphs composed of dots of various colors connected by lines. For example, the relations between ten rays of the ten-ray theorem of Optical Geometry, which von Staudt demonstrated so beautifully, and which are shown in this figure,[18]

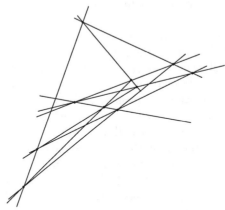

Fig. 3

are represented by Kempe in a graph substantially like *[*figure 4*]*:[19]

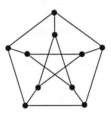

Fig. 4

Now Mr. Kempe seems to think that because his graphs are composed of but two kinds of elements, the spots of various colors and the lines, therefore a third category is not called for. To mathematical minds this will probably seem a formidable objection. It seemed so to me when I read it, I confess. But I will give three answers to it, each sufficient to completely reverse its force.

The first reply is that it is not true that Mr. Kempe's graphs only contain two kinds of elements. It no doubt seems at first glance that the dots of various colors represent Qualities, and the lines Reactions; and one then looks in vain for anything corresponding to Thirdness. The lines which are all drawn between pairs of points no doubt do in truth embody the Category of Duality. And in confirmation of this, it is to be remarked that the lines really dichotomize into two kinds, although Kempe draws but one kind. For *non-connection* is itself a species of connection. Thus in the graph to which I have called your attention, the pairs of lines between which there are no dots are the pairs which intersect at the ten significant points of the theorem.

But the spots, each of which ties together any number of lines and always many either of the written kind or of the unwritten, far from representing the Category of Unity, plainly embody the Category of Plurality,—the Third Category,—and it is the Surface upon which the graph is written as *one* whole which in its Unity represents the Category of Unity. So that it appears that three kinds of elements are needed for his graphs, which therefore vindicate the third category instead of refuting it as they were supposed to do.[20]

My other two answers to Kempe which would be works of supererogation must be left unperformed. I will just mention their nature. Answer number two would have consisted in the remark that Kempe does not represent in his graphs any entire system of real mathematical relationships. For example, his graph of the ten-ray theorem fails to show what triplets of rays are copunctual. This is still more strikingly the case with the nine-ray theorem, of which

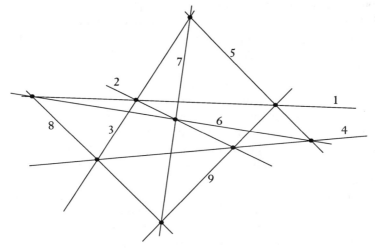

Fig. 5

[figure 5] is the geometrical figure and *[figure 6]* the graph drawn as Kempe has drawn *[it]*,[21] than of the ten-ray theorem. In short, he has simply omitted from consideration all triadic relations and then points triumphantly to the fact that he has nothing to represent Thirdness, as if that proved there was no such irreducible conception. But if his graphs were modified so as to exhibit the copunctual rays and collinear points, the triadic character of his spots would come out very clearly.

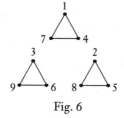

Fig. 6

Answer number three is that Kempe not only fails altogether to represent general relations, but simply gives an icon. His graphs never express *propositions*, far less *necessary consequences*. Now I invented and developed a good many years ago such a modification of Kempe's method of representation as was required to make it really express everything in mathematics. I inserted a slight sketch of it into Baldwin's *Dictionary*. It has never been published otherwise.[22] In consequence of my great interest in the working of that system, my studies of it had always followed that line and, until I came to write this lecture, it had never occurred to me to examine it in respect to its relation to the categories. On doing so, I found the three Categories copiously illustrated in the system. But what was still more interesting, a certain fault in the system, by no means of a fatal kind but still a vexatious inelegance which I had often remarked but could see no way of remedying, now, when looked upon from the point of view of the categories, appeared in a new and stronger light than ever before, showing me not only how to remedy the defect that I had seen, but opening my eyes to new possibilities of perfectionment that I had never dreamed of. I wish I could present all this to you, for it is very beautiful and interesting as well *[as]* very instructive; but it would require several lectures and lead me quite away from Pragmatism.

It is certainly hard to believe, until one is forced to the belief, that a conception so obtrusively complex as Thirdness is should be an irreducible unanalyzable conception. What, one naturally exclaims, does this man think to convince us that a conception is complex and simple, at the same time! I might answer this by drawing a distinction. It is complex in the sense that different features may be discriminated in it, but the peculiar idea of *complexity* that it contains, although it has complexity as its object, is an unanalyzable idea. Of what is the conception of *complexity* built up? Produce it by construction without using any idea which involves it if you can.

The best way of satisfying oneself whether Thirdness is elementary or not,—at least, it would be the best way for me, who had in the first place a natural aptitude for logical analysis which has been in constant training all my life long,—and I rather think it would be the best way for anybody provided he ruminates over his analysis, returns to it again and again, and criticizes it severely and sincerely, until he reaches a complete insight into the analysis,— the best way, I say, is to take the idea of representation, say the idea of the fact that the object, A, is represented in the representation, B, so as to determine the interpretation, C,—to take this idea and endeavor to state what it consists in without introducing the idea of Thirdness at all if possible, or if you find that impossible, to see what is the minimum or most degenerate form of Thirdness which will answer the purpose.

Then, having exercised yourself on that problem, take another idea in which, according to my views, Thirdness takes a more degenerate form. Try your hand at a logical analysis of the fact that A gives B to C.

Then pass to a case in which Thirdness takes a still more degenerate form, as for example the idea of "A and B." What is at once A and B involves the idea of three variables. Putting it mathematically, it is $z = xy$ which is the equation of the simpler of the two hyperboloids, the two-sheeted one as it is called.[23]

Whoever wishes to train his logical powers will find those problems furnish capital exercize; and whoever wishes to get a just conception of the universe will find that the solutions of those problems have a more intimate connection with that conception than he could suspect in advance.

V

I have thus far been intent on repelling attacks upon the categories which should consist in maintaining that the idea of Reaction can be reduced to that of Quality of Feeling and the idea of Representation to those of Reaction and Quality of Feeling taken together. But meantime may not the enemy have stolen upon my rear, and shall I not suddenly find myself exposed to an attack which shall run as follows:

We fully admit that you have proved, until we begin to doubt it, that Secondness is not involved in Firstness nor Thirdness in Secondness and Firstness. But you have entirely failed to prove that Firstness, Secondness, and Thirdness are independent ideas for the obvious reason that it is as plain as the nose on your face that the idea of a triplet involves the idea of pairs, and the idea of a pair the idea of units. Consequently, Thirdness is the one and sole category. This is substantially the idea of Hegel; and unquestionably it contains a truth.

Not only does Thirdness suppose and involve the ideas of Secondness and Firstness, but never will it be possible to find any Secondness or Firstness in the phenomenon that is not accompanied by Thirdness.

If the Hegelians confined themselves to that position they would find a hearty friend in my doctrine.

But they do not. Hegel is possessed with the idea that the Absolute is One. Three absolutes he would regard as a ludicrous contradiction *in adjecto*. Consequently, he wishes to make out that the three categories have not their several independent and irrefutable standings in thought. *Firstness* and *Secondness* must somehow be *aufgehoben*. But it is not true. They are in no way refuted nor refutable. Thirdness it is true involves Secondness and Firstness, in a sense. That is to say, if you have the idea of Thirdness you must have had the ideas of Secondness and Firstness to build upon. But what is required for the idea of a genuine Thirdness is an independent solid Secondness and not a Secondness that is a mere corollary of an unfounded and inconceivable Thirdness; and a similar remark may be made in reference to Firstness.

Let the Universe be an evolution of Pure Reason if you will. Yet if while you are walking in the street reflecting upon how everything is the pure distillate of Reason, a man carrying a heavy pole suddenly pokes you in the small of the back, you may think there is something in the Universe that Pure Reason fails to account for; and when you look at the color *red* and ask yourself how Pure Reason could make *red* to have that utterly inexpressible and irrational positive quality it has, you will be perhaps disposed to think that Quality and Reaction have their independent standings in the Universe.

VI

So far I have only considered whether or not the categories must be admitted as so many independent constituents of thought. In my next lecture I shall have to examine whether they all three have their place among the realities of nature and constitute all there is in nature.

I confess I wonder how any philosopher can say "Oh, *Thirdness* merely exists in thought. There is no such thing in reality." You do know I am enough of a sceptic to be unwilling to believe in the miraculous power he attributes to the mind of originating a category the like of which God could not put into the realities, and which the Divine Mind would seem not to have been able to conceive. Still, those philosophers will reply that this may be fine talk but it certainly is not argument; and I must confess that it is not. So in the next lecture the categories must be defended as realities.

13

The Seven Systems of Metaphysics

MS 309. [Published in CP 5.77n, 93–111, 114–18, 1.314–16, 5.119, 111–13, 57–58; also in HL 189–203. This is the fourth Harvard lecture, delivered on 16 April 1903.] Here Peirce uses his doctrine of categories to characterize seven systems of metaphysics: Nihilism, Individualism, Hegelianism, Cartesianism, Berkeleyanism, Nominalism, and Kantianism. The systems are distinguished by which categories are admitted "as important metaphysico-cosmical elements." Peirce regards these seven systems, and variants of them, as exemplifying the full scope of metaphysics. Peirce aligns himself with the seventh system, arguing for the reality of all three categories and claiming that each is really operative in nature. He argues that perceptual judgements are the first premises of all our reasonings, that symbols influence events in the way natural laws do, and that the universe is a great symbol "working out its conclusions in living realities." He strongly recommends a version of the fundamental "ethical" maxim: never say die.

I[1]

Ladies and Gentlemen:

Pragmatism is a maxim of logic; and logic can gain not the slightest support from metaphysics. Nevertheless, I am going this evening to break the strict development of our subject by lecturing to you on metaphysics. My reason for doing so is that I desire to familiarize you with the three categories before proceeding further in my main argument.

To treat the three categories simply as three units, regardless of their distinctiveness and of their essential correlations, will be a crude procedure from which no useful approximation to the truth of Nature were to be expected.

But when it is *not* the truth of Nature that we aim to represent, but all the aberrations of the philosophers in their illogical and helter-skelter rummagings after a just conception of the world, nothing perhaps could be better than to suppose every conceivable combination of the categories, rational or irrational, to have emerged during the history of metaphysics.

Grant me that the three categories of Firstness, Secondness, and Thirdness, or Quality, Reaction, and Representation, have in truth the enormous importance for thought that I attribute to them, and it would seem that no division of theories of metaphysics could surpass in importance a division based upon the consideration of what ones of the three categories each of the different metaphysical systems has fully admitted as real constituents of nature.

It is, at any rate, a hypothesis easy to try; and the exact logic of hypothesis allots great weight to that consideration. There will be then these seven possible classes.

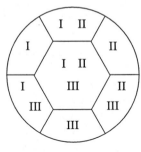

Fig. 1

 I Nihilism, so-called, and Idealistic Sensualism.
 II Strict individualism. The doctrine of Lutoslawski and his unpronounceable master.[2]
 III Hegelianism of all shades.
 II III Cartesianism of all kinds, Leibnizianism, Spinozism and the metaphysics of the physicists of today.
 I III Berkeleyanism.
 I II Ordinary Nominalism.
 I II III The metaphysics that recognizes all the categories may need at once to be subdivided. But I shall not stop to consider its subdivision. It embraces Kantism,—Reid's philosophy and the Platonic philosophy of which Aristotelianism is a special development.

A great variety of thinkers call themselves Aristotelians, even the Hegelians, on the strength of special agreements. No modern philosophy or very little[3] has any real right to the title. I should call myself an Aristotelian of the scholastic wing, approaching Scotism, but going much further in the direction of scholastic realism.

The doctrine of Aristotle is distinguished from substantially all modern philosophy[4] by its recognition of at least two grades of being. That is, besides *actual reactive existence*, Aristotle recognizes a germinal being, an *esse in potentia* or I like to call it an *esse in futuro*. In places Aristotle has glimpses of a distinction between ἐνέργεια and ἐντελέχεια.[5]

Hegel's whole doctrine of *Wesen*,[6] the most labored and the most unsuccessful part of his work, is an attempt to work out something similar. But the truth is that Hegel agrees with all other modern philosophers in recognizing no other mode of being than being *in actu*.

If I had eternity at my disposal in place of an hour, I would take up successively all the six kinds of metaphysics which fail to recognize the *reality* of all the categories and would point out the fatal defect of each.

Within my hour I cannot even promise to sketch some one of the arguments for the reality of each of the three categories. I will take them up in the order of their importance for what is to follow, in view of the opinions to which I imagine you mostly incline. I will say something, first, in favor of the Reality of Thirdness; and then put in a few words a defense of real Firstness. After that, if a few minutes remain to me, I shall have something of considerable interest to add in favor of Secondness. But if not, I shall have to let that go undefended.

II. *[*The Reality of Thirdness*]*

1. I proceed to argue that *Thirdness* is operative in Nature. Suppose we attack the question experimentally. Here is a stone. Now I place that stone where there will be no obstacle between it and the floor, and I will predict with confidence that as soon as I let go my hold upon the stone it will fall to the floor. I will prove that I can make a correct prediction by actual trial if you like. But I see by your faces that you all think it will be a very silly experiment. Why so? Because you all know very well that I *can* predict what will happen, and that the fact will verify my prediction.

But *how can* I know what is going to happen? You certainly do not think that is by clairvoyance, as if the future event by its existential reactiveness could affect me directly, as in an *experience* of it, as an event scarcely past might affect me. You know very well that there is nothing of the sort in this case. Still, it remains true that I *do know* that that stone will drop, as a *fact*, as soon as I let go my hold. If I *truly know* anything, that which I know must be *real*. It would be quite absurd to say that I could be enabled to know how events are going to be determined over which I can exercise no more control than I shall be able to exercise over this stone after it shall have left my hand, that I can so peer in the future merely on the strength of any acquaintance with any pure fiction.

I know that this stone will fall if it is let go, because experience has convinced me that objects of this kind always do fall; and if anyone present has any doubt on the subject, I should be happy to try the experiment, and I will bet him a hundred to one on the result.

But the general proposition that all solid bodies fall in the absence of any upward forces or pressure, this formula, I say, is of the nature of a representation. Our nominalistic friends would be the last to dispute that. They will go so far as to say that it is a *mere* representation,—the word *mere* meaning that to be represented and really to be are two very different things; and that this formula has no being except a being represented. It certainly is of the nature of a representation. That is undeniable, I grant. And it is equally undeniable that that which is of the nature of a representation is not *ipso facto* real. In that respect there is a great contrast between an object of reaction and an object of representation. Whatever reacts IS *ipso facto* real. But an object of representation is not *ipso facto* real. If I were to predict that on my letting go of the stone it would fly up in the air, that would be mere fiction; and the proof that it was so would be obtained by simply trying the experiment. That is clear. On the other hand, and by the same token, the fact that I *know* that this stone will fall to the floor when I let it go, as you all must confess, if you are not blinded by theory, that I *do know*,—and none of you cares to take up my bet, I notice,—is the proof that the formula, or uniformity, as furnishing a safe basis for prediction, is, or if you like it better, *corresponds to*, a reality.

Possibly at this point somebody may raise an objection, and say: You admit that *[it]* is one thing really to be and another to be represented; and you further admit that it is of the nature of the law of nature to be represented. Then it follows that it has not the mode of being of a reality. My answer to this would be that it rests upon an ambiguity. When I say that the general proposition as to what will happen whenever a certain condition may be fulfilled is of the nature of a representation, I mean that it refers to experiences *in futuro* which I do not know are all of them experienced and never can know have been all experienced. But when I say that really to be is different from being represented, I mean that what really is ultimately consists in what shall be forced upon us in experience, that there is an element of brute compulsion in fact, and that fact is not a mere question of reasonableness. Thus, if I say, "I shall wind up my watch every day as long as I live," I never can have a positive experience which *certainly* covers all that is here promised, because I never shall know for certain that my last day has come. But what the real fact will be does not depend upon what I represent, but upon what the experiential reactions shall be.

My assertion that I shall wind up my watch every day of my life may turn out to accord with facts, even though I be the most irregular of persons, by my dying before nightfall. If we call that being true by chance, here is a case of a *general proposition* being entirely true in all its generality by chance.

Every general proposition is limited to a finite number of occasions in which it might conceivably be falsified, supposing that it is an assertion confined to what human beings may experience; and consequently it is conceivable that, although it should be true without exception, it should still only be by chance that it turns out true.

But if I see a man who is very regular in his habits and am led to offer to wager that that man will not miss winding his watch for the next month, you have your choice between two alternative hypotheses only: first, you may suppose that *some principle* or *cause* is *really* operative to *make* him wind his watch daily, which *active principle* may have more or less strength; or, second, you may suppose that it is mere chance that his actions have hitherto been regular; and in that case, that regularity in the past affords you not the slightest reason for expecting its continuance in the future, any more than, if he had thrown sixes three times running, *that* event would render it either more or less likely that his next throw would show sixes.

It is the same with the operations of nature. With overwhelming uniformity, in our past experience, direct and indirect, stones left free to fall have fallen. Thereupon two hypotheses only are open to us. Either: first, the uniformity with which those stones have fallen has been due to mere chance and affords no ground whatever, not the slightest, for any expectation that the next stone that shall be let go will fall; or, second, the uniformity with which stones have fallen has been due to *some active general principle*, in which case it would be a strange coincidence that it should cease to act at the moment my prediction was based upon it.

That position, gentlemen, will sustain criticism. It is irrefragable.

Of course, every sane man will adopt the latter hypothesis. If he could doubt it in the case of the stone,—which he can't,—and I may as well drop the stone once for all,—I told you so!—if anybody doubts this still, a thousand other such inductive predictions are getting verified every day, and he will have to suppose every one of them to be merely fortuitous in order reasonably to escape the conclusion that **general principles are really operative in nature**. That is the doctrine of scholastic realism.

2. You may, perhaps, ask me how I connect generality with Thirdness. Various different replies, each fully satisfactory, may be made to that inquiry. The old definition of a general is *Generale est quod natum aptum est dici de multis.*[7] This recognizes that the general is essentially *predicative* and therefore of the nature of a representamen. And by following out that path of suggestion we should obtain a good reply to the inquiry.

In another respect, however, the definition represents a very degenerate sort of generality. None of the scholastic logics fails to explain that *sol* is a general term; because although there happens to be but one sun yet the term *sol aptum natum est dici de multis*. But that is most inadequately expressed. If *sol* is apt to be predicated of *many*, it is apt to be predicated of any multitude however great, and since there is no maximum multitude, those objects of which it is fit to be predicated form an aggregate that exceeds all multitude. Take any two possible objects that might be called *suns* and however much alike they may be, any multitude whatsoever of intermediate suns are alternatively possible and therefore, as before, these intermediate possible suns transcend all multitude. In short, the idea of a general involves the idea of possible variations which no multitude of existent things could exhaust but would leave between any two not merely *many* possibilities, but possibilities absolutely beyond all multitude.

Now Thirdness is nothing but the character of an object which embodies Betweenness or Mediation in its simplest and most rudimentary form; and I use it as the name of that element of the phenomenon which is predominant wherever Mediation is predominant, and which reaches its fullness in Representation.

Thirdness as I use the term is only a synonym for Representation, to which I prefer the less colored term because its suggestions are not so narrow and special as those of the word Representation. Now it is proper to say that a general principle that is operative in the real world is of the essential nature of a representation and of a symbol because its *modus operandi* is the same as that by which *words* produce physical effects. Nobody can deny that words do produce such effects. Take, for example, that sentence of Patrick Henry which, at the time of our revolution, was repeated by every man to his neighbor: "Three millions of people, armed in the holy cause of Liberty, and in such a country as we possess, are invincible against any force that the enemy can bring against us."[8]

Those words present this character of the general law of nature, that they might have produced effects indefinitely transcending any that circumstances allowed them to produce. It might, for example, have happened that some American schoolboy, sailing as a passenger in the Pacific Ocean, should have idly written down those words on a slip of paper. The paper might have been tossed overboard and might have been picked up by some Tagala on a beach of the island of Luzon; and if he had had them translated to him they might easily have passed from mouth to mouth there as they did in this country, and with similar effect.

Words then do produce physical effects. It is madness to deny it. The very denial of it involves a belief in it; and nobody can consistently fail to acknowledge it until he sinks to a complete mental paresis.

But *how* do they produce their effect? They certainly do not, in their character as symbols, *directly* react upon matter. Such action as they have is merely logical. It is not even psychological. It is merely that one symbol would justify another. However, suppose that first difficulty to have been surmounted, and that they do act upon actual thoughts. That thoughts act on the physical world and *conversely*, is one of the most familiar of facts. Those who deny it are persons with whom theories are stronger than facts. But how thoughts act on things, it is impossible for us, in the present state of our knowledge, so much as to make any very promising guess; although, as I will show you presently, a guess can be made which suffices to show that the problem is not beyond all hope of ultimate solution.

All this is equally true of the manner in which the laws of nature influence matter. A law is in itself nothing but a general formula or symbol. An existing thing is simply a blind reacting thing, to which not merely all generality, but even all representation, is utterly foreign. The general formula may logically determine another, less broadly general. But it will be of its essential nature general, and its being narrower does not in the least constitute any participation in the reacting character of the thing. Here we have that great problem of the *principle of individuation*[9] which the scholastic doctors after a century of the closest possible analysis were obliged to confess was quite incomprehensible to them. Analogy suggests that the laws of nature are ideas or resolutions in the mind of some vast consciousness, who, whether supreme or subordinate, is a Deity relatively to us. I do not approve of mixing up Religion and Philosophy; but as a purely philosophical hypothesis, that has the advantage of being supported by analogy. Yet I cannot clearly see that beyond that support to the imagination it is of any particular scientific service.

All philosophers must in future study the mathematico-logical doctrine of multitude.[10] We now have no difficulty in reasoning with mathematical accuracy about infinity. I regret that I cannot include it in these lectures, but I should be happy if any of you could find time for them, to give two or three lectures on that subject.[11] However, what I have now to say will require no more understanding of the subject than is requisite to solve the little *quibble* of Achilles and the Tortoise. That I may presume you see through clearly.

Let us consider for example the spiral[12] whose equation is

$$\theta = \frac{1}{\log(P-r) - \log(r-Q)}$$

It is obvious that the real values of θ will be those for which the value of r is less than P and greater than Q. Suppose we write $r = \rho P + (1 - \rho)Q$ where (ρ varies from 0 to 1).

$$P - r = (1 - \rho)(P - Q) \qquad \log(P - r) = \log(1 - \rho) + \log(P - Q)$$

$$r - Q = \rho(P - Q) \qquad \log(r - Q) = \log\rho + \log(P - Q)$$

$$\log(P - r) - \log(r - Q) = \log(1 - \rho) - \log\rho = \log\left(\frac{1}{\rho} - 1\right)$$

The spiral[13] will start outwards and wind round an endless series of times asymptotic to a circle of radius $(P + Q)/2$ which it is within and then, leaving the circle, will depart from [it] still winding outwards and finally stop again.

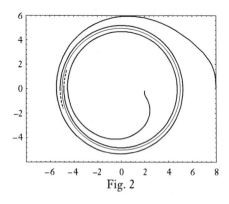

Fig. 2

Surely nobody who has ever considered Achilles and the Tortoise can imagine any difficulty in supposing that after having made an endless succession of turns inside the circle it goes on outside the circle.

Now let the increasing value of r represent the variable of time.

Let each revolution round the origin represent some kind of operation, those within the circle $r = (P + Q)/2$ to be operations of thought following logically upon one another, those exterior to the circle representing operations of matter under mechanical laws.

The only difficulty is to imagine an endless series of operations taking place in a finite time. But that is no more than happens to Achilles and the Tortoise.

Here then *thought* directly influences nothing but thought and *matter* is directly acted upon only by matter and yet mind is represented as acting upon matter without any *tertium quid* or if we had supposed that the flow of time was in the direction of the shortening radius vector, it would be matter that acted on mind.

This shows that the supposition that thought acts directly only on thought and matter directly only on matter does not in the least interfere with the mutual action of matter and thought. Only it is requisite to suppose that in speaking of matter acting on matter and mind on mind we have adopted a mode of analysis of the phenomenon which requires us to suppose an infinite series, just as in Achilles and the Tortoise.

Perhaps I shall not confuse the subject too much if I suggest that if the atoms of ordinary matter are vortices in a medium, and if that medium is composed of atoms each of which is a vortex in another medium and so on *ad infinitum*, then if energy is transformed from one to another and the increasing velocity is such as the relative velocities of sound and light would suggest, the whole infinite series might well be run through in a fraction of a second.

That no doubt is a wild hypothesis enough. But perhaps it may help to show that there is no contradiction in the idea of *symbols* influencing the *blind reactions* and the reverse.

Let us now consider [the reality of firstness.]

III. The Reality of Firstness

The popular metaphysics of today, at least among those who are influenced by physical conceptions, no doubt is that Qualities do not act in nature, and have no being except in consciousness.

My judgment, as a logician, is that the hypothesis of the older physicists is scientifically the preferable one still. It is presumably not sufficient; but the indications are that it is by the comparison of that hypothesis with the facts that we are likely the soonest to find out what hypothesis deserves to be tried next, and those who have endeavored to correct it have modified it in too many particulars at once, thereby violating the Maxim of Parsimony.

That hypothesis is that atomicules all alike act mechanically upon one another according to one fixed law of force. This recognizes Thirdness as real not only in recognizing the reality of Law but also in recognizing the reality of Space and Time. For all these physicists, although they may hold with

Leibniz that Space and Time are mere relations, not Substance as Newton thought, and *that*, whether they are supposed with Kant to be forms of intuition or not, nevertheless agree in making Space and Time to be phenomenally Real. I ought to add that they, further, make highly degenerate Thirdness to be real in supposing the atomicules to be immensely multitudinous. They hold Secondness, too, in the form of Reaction to be real. But as for Qualities, they are supposed to be in consciousness merely, with nothing in the real thing to correspond to them except mere degrees of more or less. Now all Quantity they will say (perhaps not always thinking quite clearly) involves just three elements: Number, Standard Unit, and an Origin. Number they may very well admit to be an affair of Thirdness. At any rate, it involves no real Quality. The Standard Unit is an affair of Reaction. If it be a standard of length, the metre used has to be transported,—that very reacting object has to be transported,—to the *Pavillon de Breteuil* and put into reaction with an object kept there. So it is with the standard of mass. And the standard of time has to be put into reaction with the heavens as a reacting object. As for the Origin that would be the affair of each person's individual consciousness, apart from the Thirdness and Secondness that it may involve. A punctual origin refers to his simpler consciousness, a *plane* origin refers to the median of his body as he stands facing *Polaris*, or to the feeling of the difference between his right and his left hand, which would be an affair of *Thirdness*.[14]

As for Hertz's hypothesis of Mechanics,[15] coming from such a man it is certainly my duty to examine it thoroughly. But I have to confess that hitherto I have not found the energy to do more than glance at it. He wishes to get rid of *accelerations* by supposing that in some occult way particles are subject to *absolute constraints*,—as if they slid along through rigid tubes. I can see no reason for that hypothesis except a desire to suppress Thirdness, which appears to me to be evidently impossible. He will only suppress it in one place to find it emerging at another place.

I have looked more closely into Poincaré's views of the logic of physics and in my opinion Boltzmann has the best of the argument. Only Boltzmann is not a logician and the question is a question of logic. Poincaré would have us write down the equations of hydrodynamics and stop there.[16] This I declare to be contrary to demonstrated principles of logic. It is an error analogous to that of *agnosticism*. It is a species of agnosticism,—a recommendation that a certain line of inquiry be entirely abandoned. If reason could be proved to be at war with itself, it would no doubt be well enough to give up reasoning altogether, and simply accept what opinions suit our fancy, or convenience, or seem likely to advance our interests,—a method which may be said to be the prevalent one in regard to philosophy, the world over. But it is absolutely impossible that reason ever should be proved to be at war with itself. Such a thing cannot be imagined, for a distinction would very shortly [be] drawn. The argument would be an attempt to dam up an unceasing flow. The flood would be arrested for a time, but the head of water behind it would rise higher and higher,—and finally the right *distinction* would allow it to flow on at first in a mighty burst and ultimately with its former quiet. Let me recommend this Logical Maxim to you:

> Never allow yourself to think that any definite problem is incapable of being solved to any assignable degree of perfection.

The likelihood is that it will be solved long before you could have dreamed it possible. Think of Auguste Comte, who, when asked to name any thing that could never be found out, instanced the chemical composition of the fixed stars;[17] and almost before his book became known to the world at large, the first steps had been taken in spectral analysis. But you must not suppose that the maxim has no more solid basis than historical induction. It rests on the consideration of the nature of reasoning. When I speak of reasoning I conceive experimentation to be a part of it. But it is sufficient to say that my maxim is a special case of the general maxim, *Never say die*, which is an ethical principle of the most fundamental character.

These different metaphysical conceptions of the younger physicists do not differ from that of the older physicists in respect to making Qualities to be mere illusions. But when one considers the matter from a *logical* point of view the notion that qualities are illusions and play no part in the real universe shows itself to be a peculiarly *unfounded* opinion.

Reasoning cannot possibly be divorced from *logic;* because whenever a man reasons he thinks that he is drawing a conclusion such as would be justified in every analogous case. He therefore cannot really *infer* without having a notion of a class of possible inferences, all of which are logically *good.* That distinction of *good* and *bad* he always has in mind when he infers. Logic proper is the *critics* of arguments, the pronouncing them to be good or bad. There are, as I am prepared to maintain, operations of the mind which are logically exactly analogous to inferences excepting only that they are unconscious and therefore uncontrollable and therefore not subject to criticism. But that makes all the difference in the world; for *inference* is essentially deliberate and self-controlled. Any operation which cannot be controlled, any conclusion which is not abandoned, not merely as soon as *criticism* has pronounced against it, but in the very act of pronouncing that decree, is not of the nature of rational inference,—is not reasoning. Reasoning as deliberate is essentially critical, and it is idle to criticize as good or bad that which cannot be controlled. Reasoning essentially involves *self-control;* so that the *logica utens*[18] is a particular species of morality. Logical goodness and badness, which we shall find is simply the distinction of *Truth* and *Falsity* in general, amounts, in the last analysis, to nothing but a particular application of the real general distinction of Moral Goodness and Badness, or Righteousness and Wickedness.[19]

To criticize as logically sound or unsound an operation of thought that cannot be controlled is not less ridiculous than it would be to pronounce the growth of your hair to be morally good or bad. The ridiculousness in both cases consists in the fact that such a critical judgment may be *pretended* but cannot really be performed in clear thought, for on analysis it will be found absurd.

I am quite aware that this position is open to two serious objections which I have not time to discuss, but which I have carefully considered and refuted. The first is that this is making logic a question of psychology. But this I deny. Logic does rest on certain facts of experience among which are facts about men, but not upon any theory about the human mind or any theory to explain facts. The other objection is that *if* the distinction [of] Good and Bad Logic is a special case of [the distinction of] Good and Bad Morals, by the same token the distinction of Good and Bad Morals is a special case of the distinction [of] Esthetic Goodness and Badness. Now to admit this is not only to admit hedonism, which no man in his senses and not blinded by theory or something worse can admit, but it [is] also [to seek the origin of] the essentially Dualistic distinction of Good and Bad,—which is manifestly an affair of Category the Second,— in Esthetic Feeling which belongs to Category the First.

This last objection deceived me for many years. The reply to it involves a very important point which I shall have to postpone to the next lecture. When it first presented itself to me, all I knew of ethics was derived from the study of Jouffroy under Dr. Walker, of Kant, and of a wooden treatise by Whewell;[20] and I was led by this objection to a line of thought which brought me to regard ethics as a mere art, or applied science, and not a pure normative science at all. But when beginning in 1883 I came to read the works of the great moralists,[21] whose great fertility of thought I found in wonderful contrast to the sterility of the logicians, I was forced to recognize the dependence of Logic upon Ethics; and then took refuge in the idea that there was no science of esthetics, that because *de gustibus non est disputandum*, therefore, there is no esthetic *truth* and *falsity* or generally valid goodness and badness. But I did not remain of this opinion long. I soon came to see that this whole objection rests upon a fundamental misconception. To say that morality, in the last resort, comes to an esthetic judgment is *not* hedonism,—but is directly opposed to hedonism. In the next place every pronouncement between Good and Bad certainly comes under Category the Second; and for that reason such pronouncement comes out in the voice of conscience with an absoluteness of duality which we do not find even in logic; and although I am still a perfect ignoramus in esthetics, I venture to think that the esthetic state of mind is purest when perfectly naïve without any critical pronouncement, and that the esthetic critic founds his judgments upon the result of throwing himself back into such a pure naïve state,—and the best critic is the man who has trained himself to do this the most perfectly.

It is a great mistake to suppose that the phenomena of pleasure and pain are mainly phenomena of feeling. Examine *pain*, which would seem to be a good deal more positive than *pleasure*. I am unable to recognize with confidence any quality of feeling common to all *pains;* and if I cannot I am sure it cannot be an easy thing for anybody. For I have gone through a systematic course of training in recognizing my feelings. I have worked with intensity for so many hours a day every day for long years to train myself to this; and it is a training which I would recommend to all of you. The artist has such a training; but most of his effort goes to reproducing in one form or another what he sees or hears, which is in every art a very complicated trade; while I have striven simply to see what it is that I see. That this limitation of the task is a great advantage is proved to me by finding that the great majority of artists are extremely narrow. Their esthetic appreciations are narrow; and this comes from their only having the power of recognizing the qualities of their percepts in certain directions.

But the majority of those who opine that pain is a quality of feeling are not even artists; and even among those who are artists there are extremely few who are *artists in pain*. But the truth is that there are certain states of mind, especially among states of mind in which Feeling has a large share, which we have an impulse to get rid of. That is the obvious phenomenon; and the ordinary theory is that this impulse is excited by a quality of feeling common to all those states,—a theory which is supported by the fact that this impulse is particularly energetic in regard to states in which Feeling is the predominant element. Now whether this be true or false, it is a *theory*. It is not the fact that any such common quality in all pains is readily to be recognized.

At any rate, while the whole phenomenon of pain and the whole phenomenon of pleasure are phenomena that arise within the universe of states of mind and attain no great prominence except when they concern states of mind in which Feeling is predominant, yet these phenomena themselves do not mainly consist in any common Feeling-quality of Pleasure or any common Feeling-quality of Pain, even if there are such Qualities of Feeling; but they mainly consist (Pain) in a Struggle to give a state of mind its *quietus*, and (Pleasure) in a peculiar mode of consciousness allied to the consciousness of *making a generalization*, in which not Feeling, but rather Cognition, is the principal constituent. This may be hard to make out as regards the lower pleasures, but they do not concern the argument we are considering. It is esthetic enjoyment which concerns us; and ignorant as I am of Art, I have a fair share of capacity for esthetic enjoyment, and it seems to me that while in esthetic enjoyment we attend to the totality of Feeling,—and especially to the total resultant Quality of Feeling presented in the work of art we are contemplating,—yet it is a sort of intellectual sympathy, a sense that here is a feeling that one can comprehend, a reasonable feeling. I do not succeed in saying exactly what it is, but it is a consciousness belonging to the category of Representation though representing something in the Category of Quality of Feeling.

In that view of the matter, the objection to the doctrine that the distinction [of] Moral Approval and Disapproval [is] ultimately only a species [of] the distinction of Esthetic Approval and Disapproval seems to be answered.

It appears, then, that, *Logica utens* consisting in self-control, the distinction of logical goodness and badness must begin where control of the processes of cognition begins; and any object that antecedes the distinction, if it has to be named either good or bad, must be named *good*. For since no fault can be found with it, it must be taken at its own valuation. Goodness is a colorless quality, a mere absence of badness. Before our first parents had eaten of the fruit of the tree of knowledge of good and evil, of course, they were innocent.[22]

Where then in the process of cognition does the possibility of controlling it begin? Certainly not before the *percept* is formed.

Even after the percept is formed there is an operation which seems to me to be quite uncontrollable. It is that of judging what it is that the person perceives. A judgment is an act of formation of a mental proposition combined with an adoption of it or act of assent to it. A percept on the other hand is an image or moving picture or other exhibition. The *perceptual judgment*, that is, the first judgment of a person as to what is before his senses, bears no more resemblance to the percept than the figure I am going to draw is like a man.

I do not see that it is possible to exercise any control over that operation or to subject it to criticism. If we can criticize it at all, as far as I can see, that criticism would be limited to performing it again and seeing whether with closer attention we get the same result. But when we so perform it again, paying now closer attention, the percept is presumably not such as it was before. I do not see what other means we have of knowing whether it is the same as it was before or not, except by comparing the former perceptual judgment and the later one. I should utterly distrust any other method of ascertaining what the character of the percept was. Consequently, until I am better advised, I shall consider the *perceptual judgment* to be utterly beyond control. Should I be wrong in this, the *Percept*, at all events, would seem to be so. It follows, then, that our perceptual judgments are the first premises of all our reasonings and that they cannot be called in question. All our other judgments are so many theories whose only justification is that they have been and will be borne out by perceptual judgments. But the perceptual judgments declare one thing to be blue, another yellow,—one sound to be that of "A," another that of "U," another that of "I." These are the Qualities of Feeling which the physicists say are mere illusions because there is no room for them in their theories. If the facts won't agree with the theory, so much the worse for them. They are *bad facts*. This sounds to me childish, I confess. It is like an infant that beats an inanimate object that hurts it. Indeed, this is true of all fault-finding with others than oneself and those for whose conduct one is responsible. Reprobation is a silly form of idleness.

But peradventure I shall be asked whether I do not admit that there is any such thing as an illusion or hallucination. Oh, yes;[23] there was a certain great painter who happens to be out of fashion today, especially in this longitude,—so I will not mention his name, which is sacred to me, to be exposed to your ribaldry.[24] But I will only say that a man more absolutely free from all affectation, charlatanry, or *réclame* never walked this earth. I was on intimate terms with him. His easel was in front of a great curtain. One day he had begun a new picture and I observed that he had let down another curtain of a different color from the one I was familiar with. I asked him why; and he explained to me that he always saw the picture he was about to paint on the curtain by the side of the easel and for the picture now in hand the new background suited him better. I myself am so utterly destitute of any such hallucinatory imagination that I was astonished. But I know very well that he was entertaining no idea of selling any pictures at that time, and it would have been wildly absurd to suppose that he was talking to me for effect.

For years I used to frequent artists a good deal; and his is not the only case I have known of hallucinatory imaginations at the beck and call of these ποιηται. Of course, the man knows that such obedient spectres are not real experiences, because experience is that which forces itself upon him, will-he nill-he.

Hallucinations proper,—obsessional hallucinations,—will *not* down at one's bidding, and people who are subject to them are accustomed to sound the people who are with them in order to ascertain whether the object before them has a being independent of their disease or not. There are also social hallucinations. I think I have been present at such a *séance*, but my companion was requested to retire as a sceptic and I chose to accompany him although I seemed to be decidedly a *persona grata* until I confessed myself to be at least as sceptical as he.[25] In such a case, a photographic camera or other instrument might be of service.

Of course, everybody admits and must admit that these apparitions are entities,—*entia*; the question is whether these *entia* belong to the class of realities or not, that is, whether they are such as they are independently of any collection of singular representations that they are so, or whether their mode of being depends upon abnormal conditions. But as for the entire universe of Qualities which the physicist would pronounce Illusory, there is not the smallest shade of just suspicion resting upon their normality. On the contrary, there is considerable evidence that colors, for example, and sounds have the same character for all mankind. Philosophers, who very properly call all things into question, have asked whether we have any reason to suppose that red looks to one eye as it does to another. I answer[26] that slight differences there may be, but the books tell of a man blind from birth who remarked that he imagined that *red* was something like the *blare* of a trumpet. He had collected that notion from hearing ordinary people converse together about colors, and since I was not born to be one of those whom he had heard converse, the fact that I can see a certain analogy shows me not only that my feeling of redness is something like the feelings of the persons whom he had heard talk but also that his feeling of a trumpet's blare was very much like mine. I am confident that the bull and I feel much alike at the sight of a red rag. As for the senses of my dog, I must confess that they seem very unlike my own, but when I reflect to how small a degree he thinks of visual images, and of how *smells* play a part in his thoughts and imaginations analogous to the part played by *sights* in mine, I cease to be surprised that the perfume of roses or of orange flowers does not attract his attention at all and that the effluvia that interest him so much, when at all perceptible to me, are simply unpleasant. He does not think of smells as sources of pleasure and disgust but as sources of information, just as I do not think of blue as a nauseating color, nor of red as a maddening one. I know very well that my dog's musical feelings are quite similar to mine though they agitate him more than they do me. He has the same emotions of affection as I, though they are far more moving in his case. You would never persuade me that my horse and I do not sympathize, or that the canary bird that takes such delight in joking with me does not feel with me and I with him; and this instinctive confidence of mine that it is so, is to my mind evidence that it really is so. My metaphysical friend who asks whether we can ever enter into one another's feelings,—and one particular sceptic whom I have in mind is a most exceptionally sympathetic person, whose doubts are born of her intense interest in her friends,—might just as well ask me whether I am sure that red looked to me yesterday as it does today and that memory is not playing me false. I know experimentally that sensations do vary slightly even from hour to hour; but in the main the evidence is ample that they are common to all beings whose senses are sufficiently developed.

I hear you say: "All that is not *fact*; it is poetry." Nonsense! Bad poetry is false, I grant; but nothing is truer than true poetry. And let me tell the scientific men that the artists are much finer and more accurate observers than they are, except of the special minutiae that the scientific man is looking for.

I hear you say: "This smacks too much of an anthropomorphic conception." I reply that every scientific explanation of a natural phenomenon is a hypothesis that there is something in nature to which the human reason is analogous; and that it really is so, all the successes of science in its applications to human convenience are witnesses. They proclaim that truth over the length and breadth of the modern world. In the light of those successes of science, to my mind there is a degree of baseness in denying our birthright as children of God and in shamefacedly slinking away from anthropomorphic conceptions of the Universe.

Therefore, if you ask me what part Qualities can play in the economy of the Universe, I shall reply that the Universe is a vast representamen, a great symbol of God's purpose, working out its conclusions in living realities. Now every symbol must have, organically attached to it, its Indices of Reactions and its Icons of Qualities; and such part as these reactions and these qualities play in an argument, that they of course play in the Universe, that Universe being precisely an argument. In the little bit that you or I can make out of this huge demonstration, our perceptual judgments are the premisses *for us* and these perceptual judgments have icons as their predicates, in which *icons* Qualities are immediately presented. But what is first for us is not first in nature. The premisses of Nature's own process are all the independent uncaused elements of fact that go to make up the variety of nature, which the necessitarian supposes to have been all in existence from the foundation of the world, but which the Tychist supposes are continually receiving new accretions. Those premisses of nature, however, though they are not the *perceptual facts* that are premisses to us, nevertheless must resemble them in being premisses. We can only imagine what they are by comparing them with the premisses for us. As premisses they must involve Qualities.

Now as to their function in the economy of the Universe,—the Universe as an argument is necessarily a great work of art, a great poem,—for every fine argument is a poem and a symphony,—just as every true poem is a sound argument. But let us compare it rather with a painting,—with an impressionist seashore piece,[27]—then every Quality in a premiss is one of the elementary colored particles of the painting; they are all meant to go together to make up the intended Quality that belongs to the whole as whole. That total effect is beyond our ken; but we can appreciate in some measure the resultant Quality of parts of the whole,—which Qualities result from the combinations of elementary Qualities that belong to the premisses.

But I shall endeavor to make this clearer in the next lecture.[28]

IV. The Reality of Secondness

Now I have only time to indicate in the slightest manner what I should reply to the argument against the reality of Secondness which I mentioned in the second lecture.

The only form in which this objection is really formidable is one in which Firstness and Thirdness are admitted to be real,—that is, *Feelings* and *Laws* of the succession of feelings; but it is maintained that to say that one thing acts upon another is merely to say that there is a certain law of succession of Feelings.

Of the various answers that might be made to this objection, the easiest that occurs to me, though by no means the most instructive, runs as follows:

We all admit that *Experience* is our great Teacher; and Dame Experience practices a pedagogic method which springs from her own affable and complacent nature. Her favorite way of teaching is by means of practical jokes,—the more cruel the better. To describe it more exactly, Experience invariably teaches by means of *surprises*. This statement could be defended in all its length and breadth; but for the purposes of the argument it is sufficient that you should admit that it is largely true.

Now when a man is surprised he knows that he is surprised. Now comes a dilemma. Does he know he is surprised by direct perception or by inference? First try the hypothesis that it is by inference. This theory would be that a person (who must be supposed old enough to have acquired self-consciousness) on becoming conscious of that peculiar quality of feeling which unquestionably belongs to all surprise, is induced by some reason to attribute this feeling to himself. It is, however, a patent fact that we never, *in the first instance*, attribute a Quality of feeling to ourselves. We first attribute it to a *non-ego* and only come to attribute it to ourselves when irrefragable reasons compel us to do so. Therefore, the theory would have to be that the man first pronounces the surprising object a *wonder*, and upon reflection convinces himself that it is only a wonder in the sense that he is *surprised*. That would have to be the theory. But it is in conflict with the facts which are that a man is more or less placidly *expecting* one result, and suddenly finds something in contrast to that forcing itself upon his recognition. A duality is thus forced upon him: on the one hand, his expectation which he had been attributing to Nature, but which he is now compelled to attribute to some mere inner world, and on the other hand, a strong new phenomenon which shoves that expectation into the background and occupies its place. The old expectation, which is [what he] was familiar with, is his inner world, or *ego*. The new phenomenon, the stranger, is from the exterior world or *non-ego*. He does not conclude that he *must* be surprised because the object is so *marvellous*. But on the contrary, it is because of the duality presenting itself as such, that he [is] led by generalization to a conception of a quality of marvellousness.

Try, then, the other alternative that it is by direct perception, that is, in a direct perceptual judgment, that a man knows that he is surprised. The perceptual judgment, however, certainly does not represent that it is he himself who has played a little trick upon himself. A man cannot startle himself by jumping up with an exclamation of *Boo!* Nor could the perceptual judgment have represented anything so out of nature. The perceptual judgment, then, can only be that it is the *non-ego*, something over against the *ego* and bearing it down, [that] is what has surprised him. But if that be so, this direct perception presents an *ego* to which the smashed expectation belonged, and the *non-ego*, the sadder and wiser man, to which the new phenomenon belongs.

Now, as I said before, it is idle and indeed really impossible, to criticize perceptual facts as *false*. You can only criticize interpretations of them. So long as you admit that perception really does represent two objects to us, an *ego* and a *non-ego*,—a past self that turns out to be a *mere* self and a self that is to be faithful to the Truth in the future,—as long as you admit that this is represented in the very perceptual fact, that is final. Nothing remains but to accept it as experience.

Such acceptance I ought to point out involves an acceptance of that doctrine of Immediate Perception which was advocated by Reid, Kant, etc.

14

The Three Normative Sciences

MS 312. [Published in CP 5.120–50 and in HL 205–20. Untitled by Peirce, this fifth Harvard lecture was delivered on 30 April 1903.] Peirce reviews his classification of the sciences, especially the normative sciences: esthetics, ethics, and logic. He argues that reasoning is a form of action and is thus subject to ethical considerations; in particular, it is subject to the need for self-control. The logically good, Peirce says, is a species of the morally good, and the morally good is itself a species of the esthetically good. Now the esthetically good involves the choice of aims, or purposes. Pragmatism comes back in at this point, for pragmatism involves the conception of actions relative to aims. Peirce continues his lecture by considering different types of reasoning or argumentation with respect to their logical goodness, and concludes by claiming that although we have neither immediate consciousness nor direct experience of generality, nevertheless we perceive generality: it "pours in" with our perceptual judgments.

Ladies and Gentlemen:[1]

I have already explained[2] that by Philosophy I mean that department of Positive Science, or Science of Fact, which does not busy itself with gathering facts, but merely with learning what can be learned from that experience which presses in upon every one of us daily and hourly. It does not gather new facts, because it does not need them, and also because new general facts cannot be firmly established without the assumption of a metaphysical doctrine; and this, in turn, requires the cooperation of every department of philosophy; so that such new facts, however striking they may be, afford weaker support to philosophy by far than that *common experience* which nobody doubts or can doubt, and which nobody ever even *pretended* to doubt except as a consequence of a belief in that experience so entire and perfect that it failed to be conscious of itself, just as an American who has never been abroad fails to perceive the characteristics of Americans; just as a writer is unaware of the peculiarities of his own style; just as none of us can see himself as others see him.

Now I am going to make a series of assertions which will sound wild; for I cannot stop to argue them, although I cannot omit them if I am to set the supports of pragmatism in their true light.

Philosophy has three grand divisions. The first is Phenomenology, which simply contemplates the Universal Phenomenon, and discerns its ubiquitous elements, Firstness, Secondness, and Thirdness, together perhaps with other series of categories. The second grand division is Normative Science, which investigates the universal and necessary laws of the relation of Phenomena to *Ends*, that is, perhaps, to Truth, Right, and Beauty. The third grand division is Metaphysics, which endeavors to comprehend the Reality of Phenomena. Now Reality is an affair of Thirdness as Thirdness, that is, in its mediation between Secondness and Firstness. Most, if not all *[of]* you, are, I doubt not, Nominalists; and I beg you will not take offense at a truth which is just as plain and undeniable to me as is the truth that children do not understand human life. To be a nominalist consists in the undeveloped state in one's mind of the apprehension of Thirdness as Thirdness. The remedy for it consists in allowing ideas of human life to play a greater part in one's philosophy. Metaphysics is the science of Reality. Reality consists in regularity. Real regularity is active law. Active law is efficient reasonableness, or in other words is truly reasonable reasonableness. Reasonable reasonableness is Thirdness as Thirdness.

So then the division of Philosophy into these three grand departments, whose distinctness can be established without stopping to consider the contents of Phenomenology, that is, without asking what the true categories may be, turns out to be a division according to Firstness, Secondness, and Thirdness, and is thus one of the very numerous phenomena I have met with which confirm this list of categories.

For Phenomenology treats of the universal Qualities of Phenomena in their immediate phenomenal character, in themselves as phenomena. It, thus, treats of Phenomena in their Firstness.

Normative Science treats of the laws of the relation of phenomena to ends, that is, it treats of Phenomena in their Secondness.

Metaphysics, as I have just remarked, treats of Phenomena in their Thirdness.

If, then, Normative Science does not seem to be sufficiently described by saying that it treats of phenomena in their Secondness, this is an indication that our conception of Normative Science is too narrow; and I had come to the conclusion that this is true of even the best modes of conceiving Normative Science which have achieved any renown many years before I recognized the proper division of philosophy.

I wish I could talk for an hour to you concerning the true conception of Normative Science. But I shall only be able to make a few negative assertions which, even if they were proved, would not go far toward developing that conception. Normative Science is not a skill, nor is it an investigation conducted with a view to the production of skill. Coriolis wrote a book on the Analytic Mechanics of the Game of Billiards.[3] If that book does not help people in the least degree to play billiards, that is nothing against it. The book is only intended to be pure theory. In like manner, if Normative Science does not in the least tend to the development of skill, its value as Normative Science remains the same. It is purely theoretical. Of course there *are* practical sciences of reasoning and investigation, of the conduct of life, and of the production of works of art. They *correspond* to the Normative Sciences, and may be probably expected to receive aid from them. But they are not integrant parts of these sciences; and the reason that they are not so, thank you, is no mere formalism, but is this, that it will be in general quite *different men*, and two knots of men not apt to consort the one with the other, who will conduct the two kinds of inquiry. Nor again is Normative Science a *special* science, that is, one of those sciences that discover new phenomena. It is not even aided in any appreciable degree by any such science, and let me say that it is no more by psychology than by any other special science. If we were to place six lots each of seven coffee beans in one pan of an equal armed balance, and forty-two coffee beans in the other pan, and were to find on trial that the two loads nearly balanced one another, this observation might be regarded as adding in some excessively slight measure to the certainty of the proposition that six times seven make forty-two; because it is conceivable that this proposition should be a mistake due to some peculiar insanity affecting the whole human race; and the experiment may possibly evade the effects of that insanity supposing that we are affected with it. In like manner, *and in just about the same degree*, the facts that men for the most part show a natural disposition to approve nearly the same arguments that logic approves, nearly the same acts that ethics approves, and nearly the same works of art that esthetics approves, may be regarded as tending to support the conclusions of logic, ethics, and esthetics. But such support is perfectly insignificant; and when it comes to a particular case, to urge that anything is sound and good logically, morally, or esthetically, for no better reason than that men have a natural tendency to think so, I care not how strong and imperious that tendency may be, is as pernicious a fallacy as ever was. Of course it is quite a different thing for a man to acknowledge that he cannot perceive that he doubts what he does not appreciably doubt.

In one of the ways I have indicated, especially the last, normative science is by the majority of writers of the present day ranked too low in the scale of the sciences. On the other hand, some students of exact logic rank *that* normative science, at least, *too high*, by virtually treating it as on a par with pure mathematics. There are three excellent reasons any one of which ought to rescue them from the error of this opinion. In the first place, the hypotheses from which the deductions of normative science proceed are *intended to conform* to positive truth of fact and those deductions derive their interest from that circumstance almost exclusively; while the hypotheses of pure mathematics are purely ideal in intention, and their interest is purely intellectual. But in the second place, the procedure of the normative sciences is *not purely deductive*, as that of mathematics is, nor even principally so. Their peculiar analyses of familiar phenomena, analyses which ought to be guided by the facts of phenomenology in a manner in which mathematics is not at all guided, separate normative science from mathematics quite radically. In the third place, there is a most intimate and essential element of normative science which is still *more* proper to it, and that is its *peculiar appreciations*, to which nothing at all in the phenomena, in themselves, corresponds. These appreciations relate to the conformity of phenomena *to ends* which are not immanent within those phenomena.

There are sundry other widely spread misconceptions of the nature of normative science. One of these is that the chief, if not the only problem of normative science is to say what is *good* and what *bad*, logically, ethically, and esthetically; or what degree of goodness a given description of phenomenon attains.

Were this the case, normative science would be, in a certain sense, *mathematical*, since it would deal entirely with a question of *quantity*. But I am strongly inclined to think that this view will not sustain critical examination. Logic classifies arguments, and in doing so recognizes different *kinds* of truth. In ethics, too, *qualities* of good are admitted by the great majority of moralists. As for esthetics, in that field qualitative differences appear to be so prominent that, abstracted from them, it is impossible to say that there is any appearance which is not esthetically good. Vulgarity and pretension, themselves, may appear quite delicious in their perfection, if we can once conquer our squeamishness about them, a squeamishness which results from a contemplation of them as possible qualities of our own handiwork,—but that is a *moral* and not an *esthetic* way of considering them. I hardly need remind you that goodness, whether esthetic, moral, or logical, may either be *negative*,—consisting in freedom from fault,—or *quantitative*,— consisting in the degree to which it attains. But in an inquiry such as we are now engaged upon negative goodness is the important thing.

A subtle and almost ineradicable narrowness in the conception of normative science runs through almost all modern philosophy in making it relate exclusively to the human mind. The beautiful is conceived to be relative to human taste, right and wrong concern human conduct alone, logic deals with human reasoning. Now in the truest sense these sciences certainly are indeed sciences of mind. Only, modern philosophy has never been able quite to shake off the Cartesian idea of the mind, as something that "resides,"— such is the term,—in the pineal gland.[4] Everybody laughs at this nowadays, and yet everybody continues to think of mind in this same general way, as something within this person or that, belonging to him and correlative to the real world. A whole course of lectures would be required to expose this error. I can only hint that if you reflect upon it without being dominated by preconceived ideas, you will soon begin to perceive that it is a very narrow view of mind. I should think it must appear so to anybody who was sufficiently soaked in the *Critic of the Pure Reason*.

I cannot linger more upon the general conception of normative science. I must come down to the particular normative sciences. These are now commonly said to be logic, ethics, and esthetics. Formerly only logic and ethics were reckoned as such. A few logicians refuse to recognize any other normative science than their own. My own opinions of ethics and esthetics are far less matured than my logical opinions. It is only since 1883 that I have numbered ethics among my special studies; and until about four years ago, I was not prepared to affirm that ethics was a normative science.[5] As for esthetics, although the first year of my study of philosophy was devoted to this branch exclusively,[6] yet I have since then so completely neglected it that I do not feel entitled to have any confident opinions about it. I am inclined to think that there is such a normative science; but I feel by no means sure even of that.

Supposing, however, that normative science divides into esthetics, ethics, and logic, then it is easily perceived, from my standpoint, that this division is governed by the three categories. For normative science in general being the science of the laws of conformity of things to ends, esthetics considers those things whose ends are to embody qualities of feeling, ethics those things whose ends lie in action, and logic those things whose end is to represent something.

Just at this point we begin to get upon the trail of the secret of pragmatism, after a long and apparently aimless beating about the bush. Let us glance at the relations of these three sciences to one another. Whatever opinion be entertained in regard to the scope of logic, it will be generally agreed that the heart of it lies in the classification and critic of arguments. Now it is peculiar to the nature of argument that no argument can exist without being referred to some special class of arguments. The act of inference consists in the thought that the inferred conclusion is true because *in any analogous case* an analogous conclusion *would be true.* Thus, logic is coeval with reasoning. Whoever reasons *ipso facto* virtually holds a logical doctrine, his *logica utens.* This classification is not a mere qualification of the argument. It essentially involves an *approval* of it,—a *qualitative approval.* Now such self-approval supposes *self-control.* Not that we regard our approval as *itself* a voluntary act, but that we hold the act of inference which we approve to be voluntary. That is, if we did not approve, we should not infer. There are mental operations which are as completely beyond our control as the growth of our hair. To approve or disapprove of *them* would be idle. But when we institute an experiment to test a theory, or when we imagine an extra line to be inserted in a geometrical diagram in order to determine a question in geometry, these are *voluntary acts* which our logic, whether it be of the natural or the scientific sort, *approves.* Now, *the approval of a voluntary act* is a *moral* approval. *Ethics is the study of what ends of action we are deliberately prepared to adopt.* That is right action which is in conformity to ends which we are prepared deliberately to adopt. That is all there *can be* in the notion of righteousness, as it seems to me. The righteous man is the man who controls his passions, and makes them conform to such ends as he is prepared deliberately to adopt as *ultimate.* If it were in the nature of a man to be perfectly satisfied to make his personal comfort his ultimate aim, no more blame would attach to him for doing so than attaches to a hog for behaving in the same way. A logical reasoner is a reasoner who exercises great self-control in his intellectual operations; and therefore the logically good is simply a particular species of the morally good. Ethics,—the genuine normative science of ethics, as contradistinguished from that branch of anthropology which in our day often passes under the name of ethics,—this genuine ethics is the normative science *par excellence,* because an *end,*—the essential object of normative science,—is germane to a voluntary act in a primary way in which it is germane to nothing else. For that reason I have some lingering doubt as to there being any true normative science of the beautiful. On the other hand, an ultimate end of action *deliberately* adopted,—that is to say, *reasonably* adopted,—must be a state of things that *reasonably recommends itself in itself* aside from any ulterior consideration. It must be an *admirable ideal,* having the only kind of goodness that such an ideal *can* have, namely, esthetic goodness. From this point of view the morally good appears as a particular species of the esthetically good.

If this line of thought be sound, the morally good will be the esthetically good specially determined by a peculiar superadded element; and the logically good will be the morally good specially determined by a special superadded element. Now it will be admitted to be, at least, very likely that in order to correct or to vindicate the maxim of pragmatism, we must find out precisely what the logically good consists in; and it would appear from what has been said that in order to analyze the nature of the logically good we must first gain clear apprehensions of the nature of the esthetically good and especially that of the morally good.

So then, incompetent as I am to it, I find the task imposed upon me of defining the esthetically good,—a work which so many philosophical artists have made as many attempts at performing. In the light of the doctrine of categories I should say that an object, to be esthetically good, must have a multitude of parts so related to one another as to impart a positive simple immediate quality to their totality; and whatever does this is, in so far, esthetically good, no matter what the particular quality of the total may be. If that quality be such as to nauseate us, to scare us, or otherwise to disturb us to the point of throwing us out of the mood of esthetic enjoyment, out of the mood of simply contemplating the embodiment of the quality,—just, for example, as the Alps affected the people of old times, when the state of civilization was such that an impression of great power was inseparably associated with lively apprehension and terror,—then the object remains nonetheless esthetically good, although people in our condition are incapacitated from a calm esthetic contemplation of it.

This suggestion must go for what it may be worth, which I dare say may be very little. If it be correct, it will follow that there is no such thing as positive esthetic badness; and since by goodness we chiefly in this discussion mean merely the absence of badness, or faultlessness, there will be no such thing as esthetic goodness. All there will be will be various esthetic qualities, that is, simple qualities of totalities not capable of full embodiment in the parts, which qualities may be more decided and strong in one case than in another.

But the very reduction of the intensity may be an esthetic quality; nay, it *will* be so; and I am seriously inclined to doubt there being any distinction of pure esthetic betterness and worseness. My notion would be that there are innumerable varieties of esthetic quality, but no purely esthetic grade of excellence.

But the instant that an esthetic ideal is proposed as an ultimate end of action, at that instant a categorical imperative pronounces for or against it. Kant, as you know, proposes to allow that categorical imperative to stand unchallenged,—an eternal pronouncement.[7] His position is in extreme disfavor now, and not without reason. Yet I cannot think very highly of the logic of the ordinary attempts at refuting it. The whole question is whether or not this categorical imperative be beyond control. If this voice of conscience is unsupported by ulterior reasons, is it not simply an insistent irrational howl, the hooting of an owl which we may disregard if we can? *Why should* we pay any more attention to it than we would to the barking of a cur? If we *cannot* disregard conscience, all homilies and moral maxims are perfectly idle. But if it can be disregarded, it is, in one sense, not beyond control. It leaves us free to control ourselves. So then, it appears to me that any aim whatever which can be consistently pursued becomes, as soon as it is unfalteringly adopted, beyond all possible criticism, except the quite impertinent criticism of outsiders. An aim which *cannot* be adopted and consistently pursued is a bad aim. It cannot properly be called an *ultimate aim* at all. The only moral evil is not to have an ultimate aim.

Accordingly the problem of ethics is to ascertain what end is possible. It might be thoughtlessly supposed that *special science* could aid in this ascertainment. But that would rest on a misconception of the nature of an absolute aim, which is what *would* be pursued under all possible circumstances,—that is, even though the contingent facts ascertained by special sciences were entirely different from what they are. Nor, on the other hand, must the definition of such [an] aim be reduced to a mere formalism.

The importance of the matter for pragmatism is obvious. For if the meaning of a symbol consists in *how* it might cause us to act, it is plain that this "how" cannot refer to the description of mechanical motions that it might cause, but must intend to refer to a description of the action as having this or that *aim*. In order to understand pragmatism, therefore, well enough to subject it to intelligent criticism, it is incumbent upon us to inquire what an ultimate aim, capable of being pursued in an indefinitely prolonged course of action, can be.

The deduction of this is somewhat intricate, on account of the number of points which have to be taken into account; and of course I cannot go into details. In order that the aim should be immutable under all circumstances, without which it will not be an ultimate aim, it is requisite that it should accord with a free development of the agent's own esthetic quality. At the same time it is requisite that it should not ultimately tend to be disturbed by the reactions upon the agent of that outward world which is supposed in the very idea of action. It is plain that these two conditions can be fulfilled at once only if it happens that the esthetic quality toward which the agent's free development tends and that of the ultimate action of experience upon him are parts of one esthetic total. Whether or not this is really so, is a metaphysical question which it does not fall within the scope of normative science to answer. If it is *not* so, the aim is essentially *unattainable*. But just as in playing a hand of whist, when only three tricks remain to be played, the rule is to assume that the cards are so distributed that the odd trick can be made, so the rule of ethics will be to adhere to the only possible absolute aim, and to hope that it will prove attainable. Meantime, it is comforting to know that all experience is favorable to that assumption.

The ground is now cleared for the analysis of logical goodness, or the goodness of representation. There is a special variety of esthetic goodness that may belong to a representamen, namely, *expressiveness*. There is also a special moral goodness of representations, namely, *veracity*. But besides this there is a peculiar mode [of] goodness which is logical. What this consists in we have to inquire.

The mode of being of a representamen is such that it is capable of repetition. Take, for example, any proverb. "Evil communications corrupt good manners." Every time this is written or spoken in English, Greek, or any other language, and every time it is thought of, it is one and the same representamen. It is the same with a diagram or picture. It is the same with a physical sign or symptom. If two weathercocks are different signs, it is only in so far as they refer to different parts of the air. A representamen which should have a unique embodiment, incapable of repetition, would not be a representamen, but a part of the very fact represented. This repetitory character of the representamen involves as a consequence that it is essential to a representamen that it should contribute to the determination of another representamen distinct from itself. For in what sense would it be true that a representamen was repeated if it were not capable of determining some different representamen? "Evil communications corrupt good manners" and φθείρουσιν ἤθη χρήσθ᾽ ὁμιλίαι κακαί are one and the same representamen.[8] They are so, however, only so far as they are represented as being so; and it is one thing to say that "Evil communications corrupt good manners" and quite a different thing to say that "Evil communications corrupt good manners" and φθείρουσιν ἤθη χρήσθ᾽ὁμιλίαι κακαί are two expressions of the same proverb. Thus every representamen must be capable of contributing to the determination of a representamen different from itself. Every conclusion from premisses is an instance in point; and what would be a representamen that was not capable of contributing to any ulterior conclusion? I call a representamen which is determined by another representamen an *interpretant* of the latter. Every representamen is related or is capable of being related to a reacting thing, its object, and every representamen embodies, in some sense, some quality, which may be called its *signification*, what in the case of a common name J. S. Mill calls its *connotation*, a particularly objectionable expression.[9]

A representamen is either a *rhema*, a *proposition*, or an *argument*. An *argument* is a representamen which separately shows what interpretant it is intended to determine. A *proposition* is a representamen which is not an argument, but which separately indicates what object it is intended to represent. A *rhema* is a simple representation without such separate part.

Esthetic goodness, or *expressiveness*, may be possessed, and in some degree must be possessed, by any kind of representamen,—rhema, proposition, or argument.

Moral goodness, or *veracity*, may be possessed by a proposition or by an argument, but cannot be possessed by a rhema. A mental judgment or inference must possess some degree of veracity.

As to logical goodness, or *truth*, the statements in the books are faulty; and it is highly important for our inquiry that they should be corrected. The books distinguish between *logical truth*, which some of them rightly confine to arguments that do not promise more than they perform, and *material truth*, which belongs to propositions, being that which veracity aims to be; and this is conceived to be a higher grade of truth than mere logical truth. I would correct this conception as follows. In the first place, all our knowledge rests upon perceptual judgments. These are necessarily veracious, in greater or less degree according to the effort made, but there is no meaning in saying that they have any other truth than veracity, since a perceptual judgment can never be repeated. At most we can say of a perceptual judgment that its relation to other perceptual judgments is such as to permit a simple theory of the facts. Thus I may judge that I see a clean white surface. But a moment later I may question whether the surface really was clean, and may look again more sharply. If this second more veracious judgment still asserts that I see a clean surface, the theory of the facts will be simpler than if, at my second look, I discern that the surface is soiled. Still, even in this last case, I have no right to say that my first *percept* was that of a soiled surface. I absolutely have no testimony concerning it, except my perceptual judgment, and although that was careless and had no high degree of veracity, still I have to accept the only evidence in my possession. Now consider any other judgment I may make. That is a conclusion of inferences ultimately based on perceptual judgments, and since these are indisputable, all the truth which my judgment can have must consist in the logical correctness of those inferences. Or I may argue the matter in another way. To say that a proposition is false is not veracious unless the speaker has found out that it is false. Confining ourselves, therefore, to veracious propositions, to say that a proposition is false and that it has been *found* to be false are equivalent, in the sense of being necessarily either both true or both false. Consequently, to say that a proposition is *perhaps* false is the same as to say that it will *perhaps* be found out to be false. Hence to deny one of these is to deny the other. To say that a proposition is certainly true means simply that it never can be found out to be false, or in other words that it is derived by logically correct arguments from veracious perceptual judgments. Consequently, the only difference between material truth and the logical correctness of argumentation is that the *latter* refers to a single line of argument and the *former* to all the arguments which could have a given proposition or its denial as their conclusion.

Let me say to you that this reasoning needs to be scrutinized with the severest and minutest logical criticism, because pragmatism largely depends upon it.

It appears, then, that logical goodness is simply the excellence of argument;—its negative, and more fundamental, goodness being its soundness and weight, its really having the force that it pretends to have and that force being great, while its quantitative goodness consists in the degree in which it advances our knowledge. In what then does the soundness of argument consist?

In order to answer that question it is necessary to recognize three radically different kinds of arguments which I signalized in 1867[10] and which had been recognized by the logicians of the eighteenth century, although those logicians quite pardonably failed to recognize the inferential character of one of them. Indeed, I suppose that the three were given by Aristotle in the *Prior Analytics*, although the unfortunate illegibility of a single word in his manuscript and its replacement by a wrong word by his first editor, the stupid [Apellicon],[11] has completely altered the sense of the chapter on Abduction. At any rate, even if my conjecture is wrong, and the text must stand as it is, still Aristotle, in that chapter on Abduction, was even in that case evidently groping for that mode of inference which I call by the otherwise quite useless name of Abduction,—a word which is only employed in logic to translate the [ἀπαγωγή] of that chapter.

These three kinds of reasoning are Abduction, Induction, and Deduction. Deduction is the only necessary reasoning. It is the reasoning of mathematics. It starts from a hypothesis, the truth or falsity of which has nothing to do with the reasoning; and of course its conclusions are equally ideal. The ordinary use of the doctrine of chances is necessary reasoning, although it is reasoning concerning probabilities. Induction is the experimental testing of a theory. The justification of it is that, although the conclusion at any stage of the investigation may be more or less erroneous, yet the further application of the same method must correct the error. The only thing that induction accomplishes is to determine the value of a quantity. It sets out with a theory and it measures the degree of concordance of that theory with fact. It never can originate any idea whatever. No more can deduction. All the ideas of science come to it by the way of abduction. Abduction consists in studying facts and devising a theory to explain them. Its only justification is that if we are ever to understand things at all, it must be in that way.[12]

Concerning the relations of these three modes of inference to the categories and concerning certain other details, my opinions, I confess, have wavered. These points are of such a nature that only the closest students of what I have written would remark the discrepancies. Such a student might infer that I have been given to expressing myself without due consideration; but in fact I have never, in any philosophical writing,—barring anonymous contributions to newspapers,—made any statement which was not based on at least half a dozen attempts in writing to subject the whole question to a very far more minute and critical examination than could be attempted in print, these attempts being made quite independently of one another, at intervals of many months, but subsequently compared together with the most careful criticism, and being themselves based upon at least two briefs of the state of the question, covering its whole literature, as far as known to me, and carrying the criticism in the strictest logical form to its extreme beginnings, without leaving any loopholes that I was able to discern with my utmost pains, these two briefs being made at an interval of a year or more and as independently as possible, although they were subsequently minutely compared, amended, and reduced to one.[13] My waverings, therefore, have never been due to haste. They may argue stupidity. But I can at least claim that they prove one quality in my favor. That is that so far from my being wedded to opinions as being my own, I have shown rather a decided distrust of any opinion of which I have been an advocate. This perhaps ought to give a slight additional weight to those opinions in which I have never wavered,—although I need not say that the notion of any weight of authority being attached to opinions in philosophy or in science is utterly illogical and unscientific. Among these opinions which I have constantly maintained is this, that while abductive and inductive reasoning are utterly irreducible, either to the other or to deduction, or deduction to either of them, yet the only *rationale* of these methods is essentially deductive or necessary. If then we can state wherein the validity of deductive reasoning lies, we shall have defined the foundation of logical goodness of whatever kind.

Now all necessary reasoning, whether it be good or bad, is of the nature of mathematical reasoning. The philosophers are fond of boasting of the pure conceptual character of their reasoning. The more conceptual it is, the nearer it approaches to verbiage. I am not speaking from surmise. My analyses of reasoning surpass in thoroughness all that has ever been done in print, whether in words or in symbols,—all that De Morgan, Dedekind, Schröder, Peano, Russell, and others have ever done,—to such a degree as to remind one of the difference between a pencil sketch of a scene and a photograph of it. To say that I analyze the passage from the premisses to the conclusion of a syllogism in Barbara into seven or eight distinct inferential steps gives but a very inadequate idea of the thoroughness of my analysis.[14] Let any responsible person pledge himself to go through the matter and dig it out, point by point, and he shall receive the manuscript. It is on the basis of such analysis that I declare that all necessary reasoning, be it the merest verbiage of the theologians, so far as there is any semblance of necessity in it, is mathematical reasoning. Now mathematical reasoning is diagrammatic. This is as true of algebra as of geometry. But in order to discern the features of diagrammatic reasoning, it is requisite to begin with examples that are not too simple. In simple cases, the essential features are so nearly obliterated that they can only be discerned when one knows what to look for. But beginning with suitable examples and thence proceeding to others, one finds that the diagram itself in its individuality is not what the reasoning is concerned with. I will take an example which recommends itself only by its consideration requiring but a moment. A line abuts upon an ordinary point of another line forming two angles.

The sum of these angles is proved by Legendre to be equal to the sum of two right angles by erecting a perpendicular to the second line in the plane of the two and through the point of abuttal.

This perpendicular must lie in the one angle or the other. The pupil is supposed to *see* that. He sees it only in a special case, but he is supposed to perceive that it will be so in any case. The more careful logician may demonstrate that it must fall in one angle or the other; but this demonstration will only consist in substituting a different diagram in place of Legendre's figure. But in any case, either in the new diagram or else, and more usually, in passing from one diagram to the other, the interpreter of the argumentation will be supposed to *see* something which will present this little difficulty for the theory of vision, that it is of a *general nature*. Mr. Mill's disciples will say that this proves that geometrical reasoning is inductive. I do not wish to speak disparagingly of Mill's treatment of the *Pons Asinorum*[15] because it penetrates further into the logic of the subject than anybody had penetrated before. Only it does not quite touch bottom. As for such general perceptions being inductive, I might treat the question from a technical standpoint and show that the essential characters of induction are wanting. But besides the interminable length, such a way of dealing with the matter would hardly meet the point. It is better to remark that the "uniformity of nature" is not in question, and that there is no way of applying that principle to supporting the mathematical reasoning that will not enable me to give a precisely analogous instance in every essential particular except that it will be a fallacy that no good mathematician could overlook. If you admit the principle that logic stops where self-control stops, you will find yourself obliged to admit that a *perceptual fact*, a logical origin, may involve generality. This can be shown for ordinary generality. But if you have already convinced yourself that continuity is generality, it will be somewhat easier to show that a perceptual fact may involve continuity than that it can involve non-relative generality.

If you object that there can be no immediate consciousness of generality, I grant that. If you add that one can have no direct experience of the general, I grant that as well. Generality, Thirdness, pours in upon us in our very perceptual judgments, and all reasoning, so far as it depends on necessary reasoning, that is to say, mathematical reasoning, turns upon the perception of generality and continuity at every step.

15

The Nature of Meaning

MSS 314, 316. [Published in CP 5.151–79 (in part), and in HL 221–39. This is the sixth Harvard lecture, delivered on 7 May 1903.] Peirce sets out from his concluding claim in Lecture V, that perceptual judgments involve generality. He gives a sustained discussion of the different kinds of reasoning—deduction, induction, and abduction—and discusses other logical conceptions relevant to the question of the nature of meaning. He will use "meaning" technically, he says, to "denote the intended interpretant of a symbol." He then considers the role of perception in the acquisition of knowledge and the relation of perception to reasoning. Peirce claims that "every single item" of established scientific theory is the result of abduction but that the human faculty of "divining the ways of nature" is not subject to self-control. He argues that perception and abduction shade into one another and claims that pragmatism is the logic of abduction.

I

Ladies and Gentlemen:

I was remarking at the end of my last lecture that perceptual judgments involve generality. What is the general? The Aristotelian definition is good enough. It is ὅ ἐπὶ πλειόνων πέφυκε κατηγορεῖσθαι.*[1] When logic was studied in a scientific spirit of exactitude it was recognized on all hands that all ordinary judgments contain a predicate and that this predicate is general. There seemed to be some exceptions of which the only noticeable ones were expository judgments such as *Tully is Cicero.* But the Logic of Relations has now reduced logic to order, and it is seen that a proposition may have any number of subjects but can have but one predicate which is invariably general. Such a proposition as *Tully is Cicero* predicates the general relation of identity of Tully and Cicero. Consequently, it is now clear that if there be any perceptual judgment, or proposition directly expressive of and resulting from the quality of a present percept, or sense-image, that judgment must involve generality in its predicate.

That which is not general is singular; and the singular is that which reacts. The being of a singular may consist in the being of other singulars which are its parts. Thus heaven and earth is a singular; and its being consists in the being of heaven and the being of earth, each of which reacts and is therefore a

---

*["That which is by its nature predicated of a number of things,"] *De Interpretatione* VII.

singular forming a part of heaven and earth. If I had denied that every perceptual judgment refers as to its subject to a singular, and that singular actually reacting upon the mind in forming the judgment, actually reacting too upon the mind in interpreting the judgment, I should have uttered an absurdity. For every proposition whatsoever refers as to its subject to a singular actually reacting upon the utterer of it and actually reacting upon the interpreter of it. All propositions relate to the same ever-reacting singular; namely, to the totality of all real objects. It is true that when the Arabian romancer tells us that there was a lady named Scheherazade, he does not mean to be understood as speaking of the world of outward realities, and there is a great deal of fiction in what he is talking about.[2] For the *fictive* is that whose characters depend upon what characters somebody attributes to it; and the story is, of course, the mere creation of the poet's thought. Nevertheless, once he has imagined Scheherazade and made her young, beautiful, and endowed with a gift of spinning stories, it becomes a real fact that so he has imagined her, which fact he cannot destroy by pretending or thinking that he imagined her to be otherwise. What he wishes us to understand is what he might have expressed in plain prose by saying, "I have imagined a lady, Scheherazade by name, young, beautiful and a tireless teller of tales, and I am going on to imagine what tales she told." This would have been a plain expression of professed fact relating to the sum total of realities.

As I said before, propositions usually have more subjects than one; and almost every proposition, if not quite every one, has one or more singular subjects, to which some propositions do not relate. These are the special parts of /the/ Universe of all Truth to which the given proposition especially refers. It is a characteristic of perceptual judgments that each of them relates to some singular to which no other proposition relates directly, but, if it relates to it at all, /it/ does so by relating to that perceptual judgment. When we express a proposition in words we leave most of its singular subjects unexpressed; for the circumstances of the enunciation sufficiently show what subject is intended, and words, owing to their usual generality, are not well adapted to designating singulars. The pronoun, which may be defined as a part of speech intended to fulfill the function of an index, is never intelligible taken by itself apart from the circumstances of its utterance; and the noun, which may be defined as a part of speech put in place of a pronoun, is always liable to be equivocal.

A subject need not be singular. If it is not so, then when the proposition is expressed in the canonical form used by logicians, this subject will present one or other of two imperfections:

On the one hand it may be *indesignative*, so that the proposition means that a singular of the universe might replace this subject while the truth was preserved, while failing to designate what singular that is; as when we say "*Some* calf has five legs."

Or on the other hand, the subject may be *hypothetical*, that is, may allow any singular to be substituted for it that fulfills certain conditions without guaranteeing that there is any singular which fulfills those conditions; as when we say "Any salamander could live in fire," or "Any man who should be stronger than Samson could do all that Samson did."

A subject which has neither of these two imperfections is a *singular* subject referring to an existing singular collection in its entirety.

If a proposition has two or more subjects of which one is *indesignative* and the other *hypothetical*, then it makes a difference in what order the replacement by singulars is asserted to be possible. It is, for example, one thing to assert that "Any Catholic there may be adores some woman or other" and quite another thing to assert that "There is some woman whom any Catholic adores." If the first general subject is indesignative, the proposition is called particular. If the first general subject is hypothetical, the proposition is called universal.

A particular proposition asserts the existence of something of a given description. A universal proposition merely asserts the non-existence of anything of a given description.

Had I, therefore, asserted that a perceptual judgment could be a universal proposition I should have fallen into rank absurdity. For reaction is existence and the perceptual judgment is the cognitive product of a reaction.

But as from the particular proposition that "There is some woman whom any Catholic you can find will adore," we can with certainty infer the universal proposition that "Any Catholic you can find will adore some woman or other," so if a perceptual judgment involves any general elements, as it certainly does, the presumption is that a universal proposition can be necessarily deduced from it.

In saying that perceptual judgments involve general elements I certainly never intended to be understood as enunciating any proposition in psychology. For my principles absolutely debar me from making the least use of psychology in logic. I am confined entirely to the unquestionable facts of everyday experience, together with what can be deduced from them. All that I can mean by a perceptual judgment is a judgment absolutely forced upon my acceptance and that by a process which I am utterly unable to control and consequently am unable to criticize. Nor can I pretend to absolute certainty about any matter of fact. If with the closest scrutiny I am able to give, a judgment appears to have the characters I have described, I must reckon it among perceptual judgments until I am better advised. Now consider the judgment that one event *C appears to be* subsequent to another event *A*. Certainly, I may have inferred this; because I may have remarked that *C* was subsequent to a third event *B* which was itself subsequent to *A*. But then these premises are judgments of the same description. It does not seem possible that I can have performed an infinite series of acts of criticism each of which must require a distinct effort. The case is quite different from that of Achilles and the tortoise because Achilles does not require to make an infinite series of distinct efforts. It therefore appears that I must have made some judgment that one event *appeared to be* subsequent to another without that judgment having been inferred from any premiss, without any *controlled and criticized* action of reasoning. If this be so, it is a perceptual judgment in the only sense that the logician can recognize. But from that proposition that one event Z is subsequent to another event, Y, I can at once deduce by necessary reasoning a universal proposition. Namely, the definition of the relation of apparent subsequence is well known, or sufficiently so for our purpose. Z will appear to be subsequent to Y if and only if Z appears to stand in a peculiar relation, R, to Y such that nothing can stand in the relation R to itself, and if, furthermore, whatever event, X, there may be to which Y stands in the relation R to that same X, Z also stands in the relation R. This being implied in the meaning of subsequence, concerning which there is no room for doubt, it easily follows that whatever is subsequent to C is subsequent to anything, A, to which C is subsequent, which is a universal proposition.

Thus my assertion at the end of the last lecture appears to be most amply justified. Thirdness pours in upon us through every avenue of sense.

II

We may now profitably ask ourselves what logical goodness is. We have seen that any kind of goodness consists in the adaptation of its subject to its *end*. One might set this down as a truism. Verily, it is scarcely more, although circumstances may have prevented it being clearly apprehended.

If you call this utilitarianism, I shall not be ashamed of the title. For I do not know what other system of philosophy has wrought so much good in the world as that same utilitarianism. Bentham may be a shallow logician;[3] but such truths as he saw he saw most nobly. As for the vulgar utilitarian, his fault does not lie in his pressing too much the question of what would be the good of this or that. On the contrary his fault is that he never presses the question half far enough, or rather he never really raises the question at all. He simply rests in his present desires as if desire were beyond all dialectic. He wants, perhaps, to go to heaven. But he forgets to ask what would be the good of his going to heaven. He would be happy, there, he thinks. But that is a mere word. It is no real answer to the question.

Our question is, What is the use of thinking? We have already remarked that it is the argument alone which is the primary and direct subject of logical goodness and badness. We have therefore to ask what the end of argumentation is, what it ultimately leads to.

The Germans, whose tendency is to look at everything subjectively and to exaggerate the element of Firstness, maintain that the object is simply to satisfy one's logical feeling and that the goodness of reasoning consists in that esthetic satisfaction alone.[4] This might do if we were gods and not subject to the force of experience.

Or if the force of experience were mere blind compulsion, and we were utter foreigners in the world, then again we might as well think to please ourselves; because we then never could make our thoughts conform to that mere Secondness.

But the saving truth is that there is a Thirdness in experience, an element of Reasonableness to which we can train our own reason to conform more and more. If this were not the case there could be no such thing as logical goodness or badness; and therefore we need not wait until it is proved that there is a reason operative in experience to which our own can approximate. We should at once hope that it is so, since in that hope lies the only possibility of any knowledge.

Reasoning is of three types, Deduction, Induction, and Abduction. In deduction, or necessary reasoning, we set out from a hypothetical state of things which we define in certain abstracted respects. Among the characters to which we pay no attention in this mode of argument is whether or not the hypothesis of our premises conforms more or less to the state of things in the outward world. We consider this hypothetical state of things and are led to conclude that, however it may be with the universe in other respects, wherever and whenever the hypothesis may be realized, something else not explicitly supposed in that hypothesis will be true invariably. Our inference is valid if and only if there really is such a relation between the state of things supposed in the premises and the state of things stated in the conclusion. Whether this really be so or not is a question of reality, and has nothing at all to do with how we may be inclined to think. If a given person is unable to see the connection, the argument is nonetheless valid, provided that relation of real facts really subsists. If the entire human race were unable to see the connection, the argument would be nonetheless sound, although it would not be humanly clear. Let us see precisely how we assure ourselves of the reality of the connection. Here, as everywhere throughout logic, the study of relatives has been of the greatest service. The simple syllogisms which are alone considered by the old inexact logicians are such very rudimentary forms that it is practically impossible to discern in them the essential features of deductive inference until our attention has been called to these features in higher forms of deduction. All necessary reasoning without exception is diagrammatic. That is, we construct an icon of our hypothetical state of things and proceed to observe it. This observation leads us to suspect that something is true, which we may or may not be able to formulate with precision, and we proceed to inquire whether it is true or not. For this purpose it is necessary to form a plan of investigation and this is the most difficult part of the whole operation. We not only have to select the features of the diagram which it will be pertinent to pay attention to, but it is also of great importance to return again and again to certain features. Otherwise, although our conclusions may be correct they will not be the particular conclusions at which we are aiming. But the greatest point of art consists in the introduction of suitable *abstractions*. By this I mean such a transformation of our diagrams that characters of one diagram may appear in another as things. A familiar example is where in analysis we treat operations as themselves the subject of operations. Let me say that it would make a grand life-study to give an account of this operation of planning a mathematical demonstration. Sundry sporadic maxims are afloat among mathematicians and several meritorious books have been written upon the subject, but nothing broad and masterly. With the modern reformed mathematics and with my own and other logical results as a basis such a theory of the plan of demonstration is no longer a superhuman task. Having thus determined the plan of the reasoning, we proceed to the reasoning itself, and this I have ascertained can be reduced to three kinds of steps.[5] The first consists in copulating separate propositions into one compound proposition. The second consists in omitting something from a proposition without possibility of introducing error. The third consists in inserting something into a proposition without introducing error.

You can see precisely what these elementary steps of inference are in Baldwin's *Dictionary* under "Symbolic Logic."[6] As a specimen of what they are like, you may take this:

> *A* is a bay horse,
> Therefore, *A* is a horse.

If one asks oneself how one knows that this is certain, one is likely to reply that one imagines a bay horse and on contemplating the image one sees that it is a horse. But that only applies to the single image. How large a horse did this image represent? Would it be the same with a horse of very different size? How old was the horse represented to be? Was his tail docked? Would it be so if he had the blind-staggers, and if so, are you sure it would be so whatever of the numerous diseases of the horse afflicted him? We are perfectly certain that none of those circumstances could affect the question in the least. It is easy enough to formulate reasons by the dozen; but the difficulty is that they are one and all far less evident than the original inference. I do not see that the logician can do better than to say that he *perceives* that when a copulative proposition is given, such as

> *A* is a horse and *A* has a bay color,

any member of the copulation may be omitted without changing the proposition from true to false. In a psychological sense I am willing to take the word of the psychologist if he says that such a general truth cannot be *perceived*. But what better can we do in logic?

Somebody may answer that the copulative proposition contains the conjunction "and" or something equivalent, and that the very *meaning* of this "and" is that the entire copulation is true if and only if each of the members is singly true; so that it is involved in the very *meaning* of the copulative proposition that any member may be dropped.

To this I assent with all my heart. But after all, what does it amount to? It is another way of saying that what we call the *meaning* of a proposition embraces every obvious necessary deduction from it. Considered as the beginning of an analysis of what the meaning of the word "meaning" is, it is a valuable remark. But I ask how it helps us to understand our passing from an accepted judgment A to another judgment C of which we not only feel equally confident but in point of fact *are* equally sure, barring a possible blunder which could be corrected as soon as attention was called to it, barring another equivalent blunder?

To this the advocate of the explanation by the conception of "meaning" may reply: that is *meant* which is intended or purposed; that a judgment is a voluntary act, and our intention is not to employ the form of the judgment A except to the interpretation of images to which judgments corresponding in form to C can be applied.

Perhaps it may reconcile the psychologist to the admission of perceptual judgments involving generality to be told that they are perceptual judgments concerning our own purposes. I certainly think that the certainty of pure mathematics and of all necessary reasoning is due to the circumstance that it relates to objects which are the creations of our own minds, and that mathematical knowledge is to be classed along with knowledge of our own purposes. When we meet with a surprising result in pure mathematics, as we so often do, because a loose reasoning had led us to suppose it impossible, this is essentially the same sort of phenomenon as when in pursuing a purpose we are led to do something that we are quite surprised to find ourselves doing, as being contrary, or apparently contrary, to some weaker purpose.

But if it is supposed that any such considerations afford any logical justification of primary logical principles I must say that, on the contrary, at the very best they *beg the question* by assuming premisses far less certain than the conclusion to be established.

A generation and a half of evolutionary fashions in philosophy has not sufficed entirely to extinguish the fire of admiration for John Stuart Mill,—that very strong but philistine philosopher whose inconsistencies fitted him so well to be the leader of a popular school,—and consequently there will still be those who propose to explain the general principles of formal logic, which are now fully shown to be mathematical principles, by means of induction. Anybody who holds to that view today may be assumed to have a very loose notion of induction; so that all he really means is that the general principles in question are derived from images of the imagination by a process which is, roughly speaking, analogous to induction. Understanding him in that way, I heartily agree with him. But he must not expect me in 1903 to have anything more than a historical admiration for conceptions of induction which shed a brilliant light upon the subject in 1843. Induction is so manifestly inadequate to account for the certainty of these principles that it would be a waste of time to discuss such a theory.

However, it is now time for me to pass to the consideration of Inductive Reasoning. When I say that by inductive reasoning I mean a course of experimental investigation, I do not understand experiment in the narrow sense of an operation by which one varies the conditions of a phenomenon almost as one pleases. We often hear students of sciences which are not in this narrow sense experimental lamenting that in their departments they are debarred from this aid. No doubt there is much justice in this lament; and yet those persons are by no means debarred from pursuing the same logical method precisely although not with the same freedom and facility. An experiment, says Stöckhardt, in his excellent *School of Chemistry*,[7] is a question put to nature. Like any interrogatory it is based on a supposition. If that supposition be correct, a certain sensible result is to be expected under certain circumstances which can be created or at any rate are to be met with. The question is, Will this be the result? If Nature replies "No!" the experimenter has gained an important piece of knowledge. If Nature says "Yes," the experimenter's ideas remain just as they were, only somewhat more deeply engrained. If Nature says "Yes" to the first twenty questions although they were so devised as to render that answer as surprising as possible, the experimenter will be confident that he is on the right track, since 2 to the 20th power exceeds a million. Laplace was of the opinion that the affirmative experiments impart a definite probability to the theory; and that doctrine is taught in most books on probability to this day, although it leads to the most ridiculous results, and is inherently self-contradictory. It rests on a very confused notion of what probability is. Probability applies to the question whether a specified kind of event will occur when certain predetermined conditions are fulfilled; and it is the ratio of the number of times in the long run in which that specified result would follow upon the fulfillment of those conditions to the total number of times on which those conditions were fulfilled in the course of experience. It essentially refers to a course of experience or at least of real events; because mere possibilities are not capable of being counted. You can, for example, ask what the probability is that a given kind of object will be red, provided you define red sufficiently. It is simply the ratio of the number of objects of that kind that are red to the total number of objects of that kind. But to ask in the abstract what the probability is that a shade of color will be red is nonsense, because shades of color are not individuals capable of being counted. You can ask what the probability is that the next chemical element to be discovered will have an atomic weight exceeding a hundred. But you cannot ask what the probability is that the law of universal attraction should be that of the inverse square until you can attach some meaning to statistics of the characters of possible universes. When Leibniz said that this world is the best that was possible he may have had some glimmer of meaning, but when Quetelet says that if a phenomenon has been observed on m occasions the probability that it will occur on the $(m+1)$th occasion is $(m+1)/(m+2)$, he is talking downright nonsense.[8] Mr. F. Y. Edgeworth asserts that of all theories that are started one half are correct.[9] That is not nonsense, but it is ridiculously false. For of theories that have enough to recommend them to be seriously discussed, there are more than two on the average to each general phenomenon to be explained. Poincaré, on the other hand, seems to think that all theories are wrong, and that it is only a question of how wrong they are.[10]

Induction consists in starting from a theory, deducing from it predictions of phenomena, and observing those phenomena in order to see *how nearly* they agree with the theory. The justification for believing that an experiential theory which has been subjected to a number of experimental tests will be in the near future sustained about as well by further such tests as it has hitherto been, is that by steadily pursuing that method we must in the long run find out how the matter really stands. The reason that we must do so is that our theory, if it be admissible even as a theory, simply consists in supposing that such experiments will in the long run have results of a certain character. But I must not be understood as meaning that experience can be exhausted, or that any approach to exhaustion can be made. What I mean is that if there be a series of objects, say crosses and circles, this series having a beginning but no end, then whatever may be the arrangement or want of arrangement of these crosses and circles in the entire endless series must be discoverable to an indefinite degree of approximation by examining a sufficient finite number of successive ones beginning at the beginning of the series. This is a theorem capable of strict demonstration. The principle of the demonstration is that whatever has no end can have no mode of being other than that of a law, and therefore whatever general character it may have must be describable, but the only way of describing an endless series is by stating explicitly or implicitly the law of the succession of one term upon another. But every such term has a finite ordinal place from the beginning and therefore, if it presents any regularity for all finite successions from the beginning, it presents the same regularity throughout. Thus the validity of induction depends upon the necessary relation between the general and the singular. It is precisely this which is the support of pragmatism.

Concerning the validity of abductive inference, there is little to be said, although that little is pertinent to the problem we have in hand.

Abduction is the process of forming an explanatory hypothesis. It is the only logical operation which introduces any new idea; for induction does nothing but determine a value and deduction merely evolves the necessary consequences of a pure hypothesis.

Deduction proves that something *must* be, Induction shows that something *actually is* operative, Abduction merely suggests that something *may be*.

Its only justification is that from its suggestion deduction can draw a prediction which can be tested by induction and that, if we are ever to learn anything or to understand phenomena at all, it must be by abduction that this is to be brought about.

No reason whatsoever can be given for it, as far as I can discover; and it needs no reason, since it merely offers suggestions.

A man must be downright crazy to deny that science has made many true discoveries. But every single item of scientific theory which stands established today has been due to abduction.

But how is it that all this truth has ever been lit up by a process in which there is no compulsiveness nor tendency toward compulsiveness? Is it by chance? Consider the multitude of theories that might have been suggested. A physicist comes across some new phenomenon in his laboratory. How does he know but /that/ the conjunctions of the planets have something to do with it, or that it is not perhaps because the dowager empress of China has at that same time a year ago chanced to pronounce some word of mystical power, or some invisible *Jinny* may be present. Think of what trillions of trillions of hypotheses might be made of which one only is true; and yet after two or three or at the very most a dozen guesses, the physicist hits pretty nearly on the correct hypothesis. By chance he would not have been likely to do so in the whole time that has elapsed since the earth was solidified. You may tell me that astrological and magical hypotheses were resorted to at first and that it is only by degrees that we have learned certain general laws of nature in conse-quence of which the physicist seeks for the explanation of his phenomenon within the four walls of his laboratory. But when you look at the matter more narrowly, the matter is not to be accounted for in any considerable measure in that way. Take a broad view of the matter. Man has not been engaged upon scientific problems for over twenty thousand years or so. But put it at ten times that if you like. But that is not a hundred thousandth part of the time that he might have been expected to have been searching for his first scientific theory.

You may produce this or that excellent psychological account of the mat-ter. But let me tell you that all the psychology in the world will leave the logi-cal problem just where it was. I might occupy hours in developing that point. I must pass it by.

You may say that evolution accounts for the thing. I don't doubt it is evolu-tion. But as for explaining evolution by chance, there has not been time enough.

However man may have acquired his faculty of divining the ways of Nature, it has certainly not been by a self-controlled and critical logic. Even now he cannot give any exact reason for his best guesses. It appears to me that the cleanest statement we can make of the logical situation,—the freest from all questionable admixture,—is to say that man has a certain Insight, not strong enough to be oftener right than wrong, but strong enough not to be overwhelmingly more often wrong than right, into the Thirdnesses, the gen-eral elements, of Nature. An Insight, I call it, because it is to be referred to the same general class of operations to which Perceptive Judgments belong.[11] This Faculty is at the same time of the general nature of Instinct, resembling the instincts of the animals in its so far surpassing the general powers of our reason and for its directing us as if we were in possession of facts that are entirely beyond the reach of our senses. It resembles instinct too in its small liability to error; for though it goes wrong oftener than right, yet the relative frequency with which it is right is on the whole the most wonderful thing in our constitution.

One little remark and I will drop this topic. If you ask an investigator why he does not try this or that wild theory, he will say, "It does not seem *reasonable*." It is curious that we seldom use this word where the strict logic of our procedure is clearly seen. We do [not] say that a mathematical error is not reasonable. We call that opinion reasonable whose only support is instinct.

III

Let us now come to the question of the maxim of Pragmatism. The maxim runs as follows: "Consider what effects that might conceivably have practical bearings we conceive the object of our conception to have. Then, our conception of these effects is the whole of our conception of the object."

We have already seen some reason to hold that the idea of *meaning* is such as to involve some reference to a *purpose*. But Meaning is attributed to representamens alone, and the only kind of representamen which has a definite professed purpose is an "argument." The professed purpose of an argument is to determine an acceptance of its conclusion, and it quite accords with general usage to call the conclusion of an argument its meaning. But I may remark that the word *meaning* has not hitherto been recognized as a technical term of logic, and in proposing it as such, which I have a right to do since I have a new conception to express, that of the conclusion of an argument as its intended interpretant, I should have a recognized right slightly to warp the acceptation of the word "meaning," so as to fit it for the expression of a scientific conception. It seems natural to use the word *meaning* to denote the intended interpretant of a symbol.

I may presume that you are all familiar with Kant's reiterated insistence that necessary reasoning does nothing but explicate the *meaning* of its premisses.[12] Now Kant's conception of the nature of necessary reasoning is clearly shown by the logic of relations to be utterly mistaken, and his distinction between analytic and synthetic judgments, which he otherwise and better terms *explicatory (erläuternde)* and *ampliative (erweiternde)* judgments, which is based on that conception, is so utterly confused that it is difficult or impossible to do anything with it. But, nevertheless, I think we shall do very well to accept Kant's dictum that necessary reasoning is merely explicatory of the meaning of the terms of the premisses, only reversing the use to be made of it. Namely, instead of adopting the conception of meaning from the Wolffian logicians,[13] as he does, and making use of this dictum to express what necessary reasoning can do, about which he was utterly mistaken, we shall do well to understand necessary reasoning as mathematics, as the logic of relations compels us to understand it, and to use the dictum that necessary reasoning only explicates the meanings of the terms of the premises to fix our ideas as to what we shall understand by the *meaning* of a term.

Kant and the logicians with whose writings he was alone acquainted,—he was far from being a thorough student of logic, notwithstanding his great natural power as a logician,—consistently neglected the logic of relations; and the consequence was that the only account they were in condition to give of the meaning of a term, its "signification" as they called it, was that it was composed of all the terms which could be essentially predicated of that term. Consequently, either the analysis of the signification must be capable of being pushed on further and further, without limit,—an opinion which Kant expresses in a well-known passage but which he did not develop,[14]—or, what was more usual, one ultimately reached certain absolutely simple conceptions such as Being, Quality, Relation, Agency, Freedom, etc., which were regarded as absolutely incapable of definition and of being in the highest degree luminous and clear. It is marvellous what a following this opinion that those excessively abstracted conceptions were in themselves in the highest degree simple and facile obtained, notwithstanding its repugnancy to good sense. One of the many important services which the logic of relations has rendered has been that of showing that these so-called simple conceptions, notwithstanding their being unaffected by the particular kind of combination recognized in non-relative logic, are nevertheless capable of analysis in consequence of their implying various modes of relationship. For example, no conceptions are simpler than those of Firstness, Secondness, and Thirdness; but this has not prevented my defining them, and that in a most effective manner, since all the assertions I have made concerning them have been deduced from those definitions.

Another effect of the neglect of the logic of relations was that Kant imagined that all necessary reasoning was of the type of a syllogism in Barbara.[15] Nothing could be more ridiculously in conflict with well-known facts. For had that been the case, any person with a good logical head would be able instantly to see whether a given conclusion followed from given premises or not; and moreover the number of conclusions from a small number of premises would be very moderate. Now it is true that when Kant wrote, Legendre and Gauss[16] had not shown what a countless multitude of theorems are deducible from the very few premises of arithmetic. I suppose we must excuse him, therefore, for not knowing this. But it is difficult to understand what the state of mind on this point could have been of logicians who were at the same time mathematicians, such as Euler, Lambert, and Ploucquet.[17] Euler invented the logical diagrams which go under his name,[18]—for the claims that have been made in favor of predecessors may be set down as baseless,—and Lambert used an equivalent system. Now I need not say that both of these men were mathematicians of great power. One is simply astounded that they should seem to say that all the reasonings of mathematics could be represented in any such ways. One may suppose that Euler never paid much attention to logic. But Lambert wrote a large book in two volumes on the subject, and a pretty superficial affair it is.[19] One has a difficulty in realizing that the author of it was the same man who came so near to the discovery of the non-Euclidean geometry. The logic of relatives is now able to exhibit in strict logical form the reasoning of mathematics. You will find an example of it,—although too simple a one to put all the features into prominence,—in that chapter of Schröder's logic in which he remodels the reasoning of Dedekind in his brochure, *Was sind und was sollen die Zahlen?*,[20] and if it be objected that this analysis was chiefly the work of Dedekind who did not employ the machinery of the logic of relations, I reply that Dedekind's whole book is nothing but an elaboration of a paper published by me several years previously in the *American Journal of Mathematics*,[21] which paper was the direct result of my logical studies. These analyses show that although most of the steps of the reasoning have considerable resemblance to Barbara, yet the difference of effect is very great indeed.

On the whole, then, if by the *meaning* of a term, proposition, or argument, we understand the entire general intended interpretant, then the meaning of an argument is explicit. It is its conclusion, while the meaning of a proposition or term is all that that proposition or term could contribute to the conclusion of a demonstrative argument. But while this analysis will be found useful, it is by no means sufficient to cut off all nonsense or to enable us to judge of the maxim of pragmatism. What we need is an account of the *ultimate* meaning of a term. To this problem we have to address ourselves.

IV

Let us ask then what the *end* of a term is. It is plain that no use can be made of it until it is introduced into a proposition; and when it is introduced into the proposition it must form the predicate or some predicative constituent of the predicate. For the subjects of a proposition merely fulfill the function of indices and involve no general conception whatever, while a term is essentially general, although it may involve indexical constituents.

In order to make this matter clear, which is more important than it seems at first blush, I had better explain what I mean by a term. And here I suppose I shall have to devote a minute or two to a most insignificant distinction between a *term* and a *rhema*. Whenever I speak of a *term* I always mean a *rhema*. The difference is that a term is the equivalent of a common noun and cannot form the predicate of a proposition unless a verb is inserted, while a rhema contains a verb within itself. Thus, "butcher" is a term, "is a butcher" is a rhema, and so is "slaughters." In primitive languages there is strictly no such thing as a common noun. Old Egyptian and Arabic are instances. What proves this is that if in those languages one wishes to say "Smith is a butcher" and one feels the need of inserting something between "Smith" and "butcher," instead of feeling that a verb is needed, it will be a *pronoun* that will be inserted. In

Arabic one will say "Smith *he* butcher." No verb is ever introduced unless a definite meaning is attached to it, as in "Became Smith butcher" or "Remains Smith butcher" or "Continues Smith butcher" and in Egyptian the word *pu*, which is often translated "is," is unquestionably a relative or originally a demonstrative pronoun. Indeed even in Greek a verb is not necessary in a sentence, and though Aristotle sometimes makes the verb a separate part of the proposition in accordance with one mode of expression in the Greek language, he does not usually do so; so that what modern and medieval logicians called the *copula* of a proposition never received a name until the time of Abelard.[22] Nothing can be more preposterous than to base that *grammatica speculativa* which forms the first part of logic upon the usages of language. But it is a fault which seems so ineradicable among most writers, especially in English, that I think it worthwhile to point out that the common noun, instead of being a necessary part of speech, is nothing but a late development chiefly restricted to that small and extremely peculiar family of languages which happens to be the most familiar to us.

Imagine that certain parts of a proposition are erased, so that it is no longer a proposition but a *blank form* of a proposition containing one or more *blanks*, all which blanks are such that if they are all filled with demonstrative pronouns or proper names, the result will be a proposition. Then such a blank form of proposition is a *rhema*, or as I am accustomed to call it, a *term*. For I regard the distinction between a *rhema* and a *term* as too insignificant for notice. For example:

> Every man loves _____
> _____ prefers some woman to _____

are *rhemata* or *terms*. A rhema containing one blank I call a *monad*, that containing two a *dyad*, etc. An entire proposition I term a *medad*, from μηδέν.[23]

Since nothing is essential to a term except its containing at least one blank, it is plain that this blank form may contain demonstrative pronouns or proper names, that is, indicative words.[24] Thus,

> _____ prefers some woman to Victoria

is a term or rhema.

Indeed the question arises whether it is possible to have a term which does *not* implicitly involve an index. If the logic of relatives is neglected, this question cannot arise, because in non-relative logic a term can only be analyzed into terms more abstracted and general than itself, while an index always denotes a reacting singular. The only logical terms which are in perfect strictness singular are the subjects of perceptual judgments and of what I may call volitional judgments which immediately precede action. It is convenient to regard such names as Theodore Roosevelt and Rudyard Kipling as singulars. They denote persons who we may roughly say are equally known to you and to me. However, my knowledge of Theodore Roosevelt or of Rudyard

Kipling is a little different from yours. I have rather hazy recollections of having perceived a very young man at the club,[25] in which perceptions there was a direct consciousness of a reaction, and I remember we used to say, "That young Theodore Roosevelt is going to be an important personage." I recollect to have perceived that name many times in the newspapers and to have talked about the person referred to with his neighbors and relatives; and I recollect later perceiving in the White House a person who seemed to be the President, and who talked as if he were acquainted with me. These circumstances have led me semi-instinctively to suppose that one person preserving an identity through the continuity of space, time, character, memory, etc., has been one singular connected with all these phenomena; and though I have not made any formal induction to test this theory, yet my impression is that I am in possession of *[an]* abundance of facts that would support such an induction quite irresistibly. In a similar way I have no doubt that the phenomena which may have presented themselves to you, together with many more that persons whom I know well must recollect, all unite to support the hypothesis that there is one singular Theodore Roosevelt quite unmistakable for a phantom or for any other man than himself. In each of my own perceptions, if my memory does not deceive me, there was a decided double consciousness or direct consciousness of reaction, and I have abundance of reason to think it was so with your perceptions and with those of all his acquaintances whom I know or have heard of. The notion that all those reacting singulars were in the relation of personal identity to one another, and that their separate singularities consist in a connection to one singular, the collection of them all, this notion is an element of Thirdness abductively connected with them. We may express the matter by saying that all these singular percepts were aspects or parts of one collective singular which may include non-perceptual parts for aught we are now prepared to say.

It is plain that our knowledge of the majority of general conceptions comes about in a manner altogether analogous to our knowledge of an individual person. Take, for example, the general idea of *dog*. I have had many perceptual experiences with which this word *dog* is associated and have ample reason to believe that others have had such experiences. These are all experiences of a singular,—the singular collection of all dogs, the race of dogs, which, according to the doctrine of germ-plasm, is just as much one thing as a single dog is one thing. I do not mean to say that the theory of germ-plasm has any logical connection with the matter; but only that it aids those whose logical training has been neglected,—as it seems to me it is neglected in this university,—to perceive that a class is an individual. In how many books, even recent books, have I seen Claude Bernard[26] praised for having enunciated a great doctrine of physiology in saying, "Disease is not an entity; it is nothing but an assemblage of symptoms." Now this is not a physiological doctrine at all. It is nothing but a logical doctrine and a doctrine of false logic. But in the light of the positive discoveries of Pasteur and Koch, considered in connection with the theories of Weismann,[27] we see that, as far as zymotic diseases are concerned, they are just as much a thing as the ocean is a thing. And indeed if Claude Bernard had not had his mind filled with bad metaphysics, he would have seen that an assemblage of symptoms was not only an entity but necessarily a concrete thing; whereupon he might have set himself to work very usefully to obtain some further acquaintance with that thing.

To return to the dog. My perceptual judgments of percepts of dogs have contained sundry general elements and these I have generalized by abductions chiefly, with small doses of induction, and have thus acquired some general ideas of dogs' ways, of the laws of caninity, some of them invariable so far as I have observed, such as his frequent napping, others merely usual, such as his way of circling when he is preparing to take a nap. These are laws of perceptual judgments, and so beyond all doubt are the great majority of our general notions. It is not evident that this is not the case with all general notions. If, therefore, anybody maintains that there are any general notions which are not given in the perceptual judgments, it is fair to demand that he should prove it by close reasoning and not expect us to accept unsupported assertions to that effect nor to assent to it without something better than vague remarks to convince us that it is so. Yet this is what the nominalistic reasoner is continually doing. He would persuade us that the mind,—that is to say our opinions,—are filled with notions wholly unlike anything in the real world. Now the real world is the world of percepts, concerning which perceptual judgments are our only witnesses. When I ask him how he proves this, he produces an argument which according to my logic is manifestly fallacious. He insists that it is sound, because it excites in him a certain feeling, although in me it excites no such feeling. The curious thing is that he frequently will betray by his conduct that he does not believe in the conclusion to which his reasoning should lead, or even frankly confesses this. So that our two systems of logic differ in that the one recommends certain forms of argument which lead from true premises to false conclusions, because they produce a feeling of satisfaction in one man's breast though not in another's, while the other system does not judge of arguments by the feelings they produce but by whether or not they could lead to contradictory conclusions. If a color-blind man were to endeavor to persuade me that I had no such sensation as that of redness, I could readily understand how he might imagine that he could bring me round to his opinion, but I, being able to put myself in his shoes, should never imagine that I could convince him of his mistake as long as his only standard was his own feelings.

I do not think it is possible fully to comprehend the problem of the merits of pragmatism without recognizing these three truths:[28] *first*, that there are no conceptions which are not given to us in perceptual judgments, so that we may say that all our ideas are perceptual ideas. This sounds like sensationalism. But in order to maintain this position, it is necessary to recognize, *second*, that perceptual judgments contain elements of generality, so that Thirdness is directly perceived; and finally, I think it of great importance to recognize, *third*, that the abductive faculty, whereby we divine the secrets of nature, is, as we may say, a shading off, a gradation of that which in its highest perfection we call perception.

But while, to my apprehension, it is only in the light of those three doctrines that the true characteristics of pragmatism are fully displayed, yet even without them we shall be brought, although less clearly and forcibly, to nearly the same opinion.

Granting that there may be some general concepts which are not perceptual, that is, not elements of perceptual judgments, these may make a kind of music in the soul, or they may in some mysterious way subserve some end; but in order to be of any *cognitive* service, it is plain that they must enter into propositions. For cognition proper is true, or at any rate is either true or false, and it is propositions alone that are either true or false. But the only form in which a general can enter into a proposition is either as predicate or predicative constituent of the predicate or as subject. But a general subject is either an indesignate individual or a quodlibetical individual[29] of the universe to which no descriptive character is attached. It is therefore not what we mean by a concept. It involves merely directions as to what one is to do to find an individual such as is intended, without at all describing that individual. The general concept therefore must be the predicate or an element of the predicate of the nature of a predicate.

Now there are two questions to be asked concerning such a proposition. The first is, What ground can there be for assenting to it? and the second is, What knowledge does it convey supposing it to be accepted?

As to the first question, What ground can there be for assenting to the proposition?, it is obvious that a proposition not assented to has no cognitive value whatever. But nobody will or can assent to a proposition without supposing himself to have sufficient logical reason for doing so, unless a blind force compels him to believe it. But this last cannot be the case with such a proposition as we are considering, whose predicate is not wholly perceptual, for the reason that however the psychologist might class such a compulsory judgment, for the logician it would be perceptual, perception being for the logician simply what experience,—that is, the succession of what happens to him,—forces him to admit immediately and without any reason. This judgment, then, must be inferred. How can it be inferred? Plainly only by abduction, because abduction is the only process by which a new element can be introduced into thought, and it is expressly supposed that we have to do here with that judgment in which the conception in question first makes its appearance. You now see what I meant when in speaking of abduction I said that the little that was to be said of the logic of it was highly pertinent to our problem; for we now see that the true doctrine concerning Pragmatism whatever it may be is nothing else than the true Logic of Abduction.

It is now generally admitted, and it is the result of my own logical analysis, that the true maxim of abduction is that which Auguste Comte endeavored to formulate when he said that any hypothesis might be admissible if and only if it was verifiable.[30] Whatever Comte himself meant by verifiable, which is not very clear, it certainly ought not to be understood to mean verifiable by direct observation, since that would cut off all history as an inadmissible hypothesis. But what must and should be meant is that the hypothesis must be capable of verification by induction. Now induction, or experimental inquiry, consists in comparing perceptual predictions deduced from a theory with the facts of perception predicted, and in taking the measure of agreement observed as the provisional and approximative, or probametric,[31] measure of the general agreement of the theory with fact.

It thus appears that a conception can only be admitted into a hypothesis in so far as its possible consequences would be of a perceptual nature; which agrees with my original maxim of pragmatism as far as it goes.

16

Pragmatism as the Logic of Abduction

MS 315. [Published in CP 5.180–212 (in part) and in HL 241–56). Untitled by Peirce, this is the last of the seven Harvard lectures, delivered on 14 May 1903.] This lecture was added so that Peirce could extend his remarks about the relation of pragmatism to abduction. He elaborates in particular on three key points raised in the sixth lecture: (1) that nothing is in the intellect that is not first in the senses, (2) that perceptual judgments contain general elements, and (3) that abductive inference shades into perceptual judgment without any sharp line of demarcation between them. Pragmatism follows from these propositions. Peirce reiterates that the function of pragmatism is to help us identify unclear ideas and comprehend difficult ones. It is in this lecture that Peirce delivers his famous dictum: "The elements of every concept enter into logical thought at the gate of perception and make their exit at the gate of purposive action; and whatever cannot show its passports at both those two gates is to be arrested as unauthorized by reason." In developing these ideas, Peirce emphasizes that in making every conception equivalent to a conception of "conceivable practical effects," the maxim of pragmatism reaches far beyond the merely practical and allows for any "flight of imagination," provided only that this imagination "ultimately alights upon a possible practical effect."

I

Ladies and Gentlemen:

I am impelled to express my sense of gratitude at your kind interest in coming to listen to an extra lecture at this busy season of the year. I shall feel myself under an obligation to make a special endeavor to say something germinative.

At the end of my last lecture I had just enunciated three propositions which seem to me to give to pragmatism its peculiar character. In order to be able to refer to them briefly this evening, I will call them for the nonce my *cotary* propositions. *Cōs, cōtis* is a whetstone.[1] They appear to me to put the edge on the maxim of pragmatism.

These *cotary* propositions are as follows:

First, *Nihil est in intellectu quin prius fuerit in sensu.*[2] I take this in a sense somewhat different from that which Aristotle intended.[3] By *intellectus*, I understand the *meaning* of any representation in any kind of cognition, virtual, symbolic, or whatever it may be. Berkeley and nominalists of his stripe deny that we have any idea at all of a triangle in general, which is neither equilateral, isosceles, nor scalene.[4] But they cannot deny that there are propositions about triangles in general, which propositions are either true or false; and as long as that is the case, whether we have an *idea* of a triangle in some psychological sense or not, I do not, as a logician, care. We have an *intellectus*, a meaning, of which the triangle in general is an element. As for the other term, *in sensu*, that I take in the sense of in a *perceptual judgment*, the starting-point or first premiss of all critical and controlled thinking. I will state presently what I conceive to be the evidence of the truth of this first cotary proposition. But I prefer to begin by recalling to you what all three of them are.

The second is that perceptual judgments contain general elements, so that universal propositions are deducible from them in the manner in which the logic of relations shows that particular propositions usually, not to say invariably, allow universal propositions to be necessarily inferred from them. This I sufficiently argued in my last lecture. This evening I shall take the truth of it for granted.

The third cotary proposition is that abductive inference shades into perceptual judgment without any sharp line of demarcation between them; or in other words our first premisses, the perceptual judgments, are to be regarded as an extreme case of abductive inferences, from which they differ in being absolutely beyond criticism. The abductive suggestion comes to us like a flash.[5] It is an act of *insight*, although of extremely fallible insight. It is true that the different elements of the hypothesis were in our minds before; but it is the idea of putting together what we had never before dreamed of putting together which flashes the new suggestion before our contemplation.

On its side, the perceptive judgment is the result of a process, although of a process not sufficiently conscious to be controlled, or to state it more truly, not controllable and therefore not fully conscious. If we were to subject this subconscious process to logical analysis we should find that it terminated in what that analysis would represent as an abductive inference resting on the result of a similar process which a similar logical analysis would represent to be terminated by a similar abductive inference, and so on *ad infinitum*. This analysis would be precisely analogous to that which the sophism of Achilles and the tortoise applies to the chase of the tortoise by Achilles, and it would fail to represent the real process for the same reason. Namely, just as Achilles does not have to make the series of distinct endeavors which he is represented as making, so this process of forming the perceptual judgment, because it is subconscious and so not amenable to logical criticism, does not have to make separate acts of inference but performs its act in one continuous process.

II

I have already put in my brief in favor of my second cotary proposition, and in what I am about to say I shall treat that as already sufficiently proved. In arguing it I avoided all resort to anything like special phenomena, upon which I do not think that philosophy ought to rest, at all. Still, there is no harm in using special observations merely in an abductive way to throw a light upon doctrines otherwise established, and to aid the mind in grasping them; and there are some phenomena which, I think, do aid us to see what is meant by asserting that perceptual judgments contain general elements and which will also naturally lead up to a consideration of the third cotary proposition.

I will show you a figure which I remember my father drawing in one of his lectures.[6] I do not remember what it was supposed to show; but I cannot imagine what else it could have been but my cotary proposition number two. If so, in maintaining that proposition I am substantially treading in his footprints, though he would doubtless have put the proposition into a shape very different from mine. Here is the figure (though I cannot draw it as skillfully as he did). It consists of a serpentine line.[7] But when it is completely drawn, it

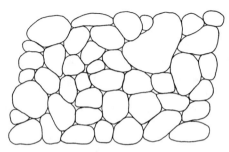

Fig.1

appears to be a stone wall. The point is that there are two ways of conceiving the matter. Both, I beg you to remark, are *general ways of classing the line*, general classes under which the line is subsumed. But the very decided preference of our perception for one mode of classing the percept shows that this classification is contained in the perceptual judgment. So it is with that well-known unshaded outline figure of a pair of steps seen in perspective.[8] We seem at first to be looking at the steps from above; but some unconscious part of the mind seems to tire of putting that construction upon it and suddenly we seem to see the steps from below, and so the perceptive judgment and the percept itself seem to keep shifting from one general aspect to the other and back again.

In all such visual illusions, of which two or three dozen are well known, the most striking thing is that a certain theory of interpretation of the figure has all the appearance of being given in perception. The first time it is shown to us, it seems as completely beyond the control of rational criticism as any percept is; but after many repetitions of the now familiar experiment, the illusion wears off, becoming first less decided, and ultimately ceasing completely. This shows that these phenomena are true connecting links between abductions and perceptions.

If the percept or perceptual judgment were of a nature entirely unrelated to abduction, one would expect that the percept would be entirely free from any characters that are proper to *interpretations*, while it can hardly fail to have such characters if it be merely a continuous series of what discretely and consciously performed would be abductions. We have here then almost a crucial test of my third cotary proposition. Now, then, how is the fact? The fact is that it is not necessary to go beyond ordinary observations of common life to find a variety of widely different ways in which perception is interpretative.

The whole series of hypnotic phenomena, of which so many fall within the realm of ordinary everyday observation,—such as our waking up at the hour we wish to wake much nearer than our waking selves could guess it,—involve the fact that we perceive what we are adjusted for interpreting though it be far less perceptible than any express effort could enable us to perceive; while that to the interpretation of which our adjustments are not fitted, we fail to perceive although it exceed in intensity what we should perceive with the utmost ease if we cared at all for its interpretation. It is a marvel to me that the clock in my study strikes every half hour in the most audible manner, and yet I never hear it. I should not know at all whether the striking part were going, unless it is out of order and strikes the wrong hour. If it does that, I am pretty sure to hear it. Another familiar fact is that we perceive, or seem to perceive, objects differently from how they really are, accommodating them to their manifest intention. Proofreaders get high salaries because ordinary people miss seeing misprints, their eyes correcting them. We can repeat the *sense* of a conversation but we are often quite mistaken as to what words were uttered. Some politicians think it a clever thing to convey an idea which they carefully abstain from stating in words. The result is that a reporter is ready to swear quite sincerely that a politician said something to him which the politician was most careful not to say.

I should tire you if I dwelt further on anything so familiar, especially to every psychological student, as the interpretativeness of the perceptive judgment. It is plainly nothing but the extremest case of Abductive Judgment.

If this third cotary proposition be admitted, the second, that the perceptual judgment contains general elements, must be admitted; and as for the first, that all general elements are given in perception, that loses most of its significance. For if a general element were given otherwise than in the perceptual judgment, it could only first appear in an abductive suggestion, and that is now seen to amount substantially to the same thing. I not only opine, however, that every general element of every hypothesis, however wild or sophisticated it may be, [is] given somewhere in perception, but I will venture so far as to assert that every general *form* of putting concepts together is, in its elements, given in perception. In order to decide whether this be so or not, it is necessary to form a clear notion of the precise difference between abductive judgment and the perceptual judgment which is its limiting case. The only symptom by which the two can be distinguished is that we cannot form the least conception of what it would be to deny the perceptual judgment. If I judge a perceptual image to be red, I can conceive of another man's not having that same percept. I can also conceive of his having this percept but never having thought whether it was red or not. I can conceive that while colors are among his sensations he shall never have had his attention directed to them. Or I can conceive that instead of redness a somewhat different conception should arise in his mind, that he should, for example, judge that this percept has a warmth of color. I can imagine that the redness of my percept is excessively faint and dim so that one can hardly make sure of whether it is red or not. But that any man should have a percept similar to mine and should ask himself the question whether this percept be *red*, which would imply that he had already judged *some* percept to be red, and that he should, upon careful attention to this percept, pronounce it to be decidedly and clearly *not* red, when I judge it to be prominently red, *that* I cannot comprehend at all. An abductive suggestion, however, is something whose truth *can* be questioned or even denied.

We thus come to the *test of inconceivability* as the only means of distinguishing between an abduction and a perceptual judgment. Now I fully assent to all that Stuart Mill so forcibly said in his *Examination of Hamilton* as to the utter untrustworthiness of the test of inconceivability.[9] That which is inconceivable to us today, may prove tomorrow to be conceivable and even probable; so that we never can be absolutely sure that a judgment is perceptual and not abductive; and this may seem to constitute a difficulty in the way of satisfying ourselves that the first cotary proposition is true.[10] At the same time, this difficulty will appear less serious when we remark that in regard to the vast majority of propositions of which men are in the habit of saying that their falsity is inconceivable, when we put the question in this form, "Is this directly perceived?", it will readily be proved that it is not perceived. For example, a man might say, "If I were to face precisely east and walk straight forward sixty steps and were then to turn to the right precisely through a right angle and were to walk straight forward fifty steps and then were to turn to the right precisely through a right angle and were to walk straight forward fifty steps and then were to turn to the right precisely through a right angle and were to walk straight forward until I was on the point of crossing my first path, I directly perceive that I should have to turn precisely through a right angle in order to walk over my previous path." A man, I say, might say that, but I should say to him, "You have, no doubt, been supposing that you would be walking on a level surface, although you did not explicitly say so. But it has probably not occurred to you that a level surface may have any shape whatever, according to the distribution of attracting masses. If you were facing due east on the earth's surface and were to walk straight forward along the path of minimum length, when you had walked sixty paces you would no longer be facing due east but a little to the south of east, so that what you have been saying you perceived would not be the fact. Now then you wish to suppose you were walking on a plane surface. But what do you mean by a plane surface? If you mean one upon which what you are saying would be true, then of course, it is an identical proposition to say that it would be as you say. But if by a plane you mean a surface which, turned upside down, could be brought into exact coincidence with its former position throughout, then you must acknowledge that you do not evidently perceive any connection between this particular property of a plane surface and the property of a surface on which four right angles should make the quadrilateral close precisely."

In ways more or less like this, the class of cases in which abductions may be mistaken for perceptions can be considerably narrowed. Nevertheless, it must be acknowledged that this class of cases, however it may be restricted, is not thus eliminated. It may therefore very likely be objected that doubt must perforce on this account hang over my first cotary proposition that every general element of thought is given in perceptive judgment. This objection, however, involves a logical fallacy. No doubt in regard to the first cotary proposition follows as a necessary consequence of the possibility that what are really abductions have been mistaken for perceptions. For the question is whether that which really is an abductive result can contain elements foreign to its premisses. It must be remembered that abduction, although it is very little hampered by logical rules, nevertheless is logical inference, asserting its conclusion only problematically or conjecturally it is true, but nevertheless having a perfectly definite logical form.

Long before I first classed abduction as an inference it was recognized by logicians that the operation of adopting an explanatory hypothesis,—which is just what abduction is,—was subject to certain conditions. Namely, the hypothesis cannot be admitted, even as a hypothesis, unless it be supposed that it would account for the facts or some of them. The form of inference therefore is this:

> The surprising fact, C, is observed;
> But if A were true, C would be a matter of course.
> Hence, there is reason to suspect that A is true.

Thus, A cannot be abductively inferred, or if you prefer the expression, cannot be abductively conjectured, until its entire contents is already present in the premiss, "If A were true, C would be a matter of course."

Whether this be a correct account of the matter or not, the mere suggestion of it as a possibility shows that the bare fact that abductions may be mistaken for perceptions does not necessarily affect the force of an argument to show [that] quite new conceptions cannot be obtained from abduction.

But when the account just given of abduction is proposed as a proof that all conceptions must be given substantially in perception, three objections will be started.[11] Namely, in the first place, it may be said that even if this be the normative form of abduction, the form to which abduction *ought* to conform, yet it may be that new conceptions arise in a manner which puts the rules of logic at defiance. In the second place, waiving this objection, it may be said that the argument would prove too much; for if it were valid, it would follow that no hypothesis could be so fantastic as not to have presented itself entire in experience. In the third place, it may be said that granting that the abductive conclusion "*A* is true" rests upon the premiss "If *A* is true, *C* is true," still it would be contrary to common knowledge to assert that the antecedents of all conditional judgments are given in perception, and thus it remains almost certain that some conceptions have a different origin.

In answer to the first of these objections, it is to be remarked that it is only in Deduction that there is no difference between a *valid* argument and a *strong* one. An argument is valid if it possesses the sort of strength that it professes and tends toward the establishment of the conclusion in the way in which it pretends to do this. But the question of its strength does not concern the comparison of the due effect of the argument with its pretensions, but simply [rests] upon how great its due effect is. An argument is nonetheless logical for being weak, provided it does not pretend to a strength that it does not possess. It is, I suppose, in view of this that the best modern logicians outside the English school never say a word about fallacies. They assume that there is no such thing as an argument illogical in itself. An argument is fallacious only so far as it is mistakenly, though not illogically, inferred to have professed what it did not perform. Perhaps it may be said that if all our reasonings conform to the laws of logic, this is, at any rate, nothing but a proposition in psychology which my principles ought to forbid my recognizing. But I do not offer it as a principle of psychology only. For a principle of psychology is a contingent truth, while this, as I contend, is a necessary truth. Namely, if a fallacy involves nothing in its conclusion which was not in its premisses, that is, nothing that was not in any previous knowledge that aided in suggesting it, then the forms of logic will invariably and necessarily enable us logically to account for it as due to a mistake arising from the use of a logical but weak argumentation. In most cases it is due to an abduction. The conclusion of an abduction is problematic or conjectural, but is not necessarily at the weakest grade of surmise, and what we call assertoric judgments are, accurately, problematic judgments of a high grade of hopefulness. There is therefore no difficulty in maintaining that fallacies are merely due to mistakes which are logically valid, though weak, argumentations. If, however, a fallacy contains something in the conclusion which was not in the premisses at all, that is, was in no previous knowledge or none that influenced the result, then again a mistake due as before to weak inference has been committed; only in this case the mistake consists in taking that to be an inference which, in respect to this new element, is not an inference, at all. That part of the conclusion which inserts the wholly new element can be separated from the rest with which it has no logical connection nor appearance of logical connection. The first emergence of this new element into consciousness must be regarded as a perceptive judgment. We are irresistibly led to judge that we are conscious of it. But the connection of this perception with other elements must be an ordinary logical inference, subject to error like all inference.

As for the second objection that, according to my account of abduction, every hypothesis, however fantastic, must have presented itself entire in perception, I have only to say that this could only arise in a mind entirely unpracticed in the logic of relations, and apparently quite oblivious of any other mode of inference than abduction. Deduction accomplishes first the simple colligation of different perceptive judgments into a copulative whole, and then, with or without the aid of other modes of inference, is quite capable of so transforming this copulative proposition so as to bring certain of its parts into more intimate connection.

But the third objection is the really serious one; in it lies the whole nodus of the question and its full refutation would be quite a treatise. If the antecedent is not given in a perceptive judgment, then it must first emerge in the conclusion of an inference. At this point we are obliged to draw the distinction between the matter and the logical form. With the aid of the logic of relations it would be easy to show that the entire logical matter of a conclusion must in any mode of inference be contained, piecemeal, in the premisses. Ultimately therefore it must come from the uncontrolled part of the mind, because a series of controlled acts must have a first. But as to the logical *form*, it would be, at any rate, extremely difficult to dispose of it in the same way. An induction, for example, concludes *[in]* a ratio of frequency; but there is nothing about any such ratio in the single instances on which it is based. Where do the conceptions of deductive necessity, of inductive probability, of abductive expectability come from? Where does the conception of inference itself come from? That is the only difficulty. But self-control is the character which distinguishes reasoning from the processes by which perceptual judgments are formed, and self-control of any kind is purely *inhibitory*. It originates nothing.

Therefore it cannot be in the act of adoption of an inference, in the pronouncing of it to be reasonable, that the formal conceptions in question can first emerge. It must be in the first perceiving that so one might conceivably reason. And what is the nature of that? I see that I have instinctively described the phenomenon as a "perceiving." I do not wish to argue from words; but a word may furnish a valuable suggestion. What can our first acquaintance with an inference, when it is not yet adopted, be but a perception,—a perception of the world of ideas? In the first suggestion of it the inference must be thought of as an inference, because when it is adopted there is always the thought that so one might reason in a whole class of cases. But the mere act of inhibition cannot introduce this conception. The inference must, then, be thought of as an inference in the first suggestion of it. Now when an inference is thought of *as* an inference, the conception of inference becomes a part of the *matter* of thought. Therefore, the same argument which we used in regard to matter in general applies to the conception of inference. But I am prepared to show in detail, and indeed virtually have shown, that all the forms of logic can be reduced to combinations of the conception of inference, the conception of otherness, and the conception of a character. These are obviously simply forms of Thirdness, Secondness, and Firstness of which the last two are unquestionably given in perception. Consequently the whole logical form of thought is so given in its elements.

III

It appears to me, then, that my three cotary propositions are satisfactorily grounded. Nevertheless, since others may not regard them as so certain as I myself do, I propose in the first instance to disregard them, and to show that, even if they are put aside as doubtful, a maxim practically little differing in most of its applications from that of pragmatism ought to be acknowledged and followed; and after this has been done, I will show how the recognition of the cotary propositions will affect the matter.[12]

I have argued in several of my early papers that there are but three essentially different modes of reasoning: Deduction, Induction, and Abduction. I may mention in particular papers in the *Proceedings of the American Academy of Arts and Sciences* for April and May 1867.[13] I must say, however, that it would be very easy to misunderstand those arguments. I did not at first fully comprehend them myself. I cannot restate the matter tonight, although I am very desirous of doing so, for I could now put it in a much clearer light. I have already explained to you briefly what these three modes of inference, Deduction, Induction, and Abduction, are. I ought to say that when I described induction as the experimental testing of a hypothesis, I was not thinking of experimentation in the narrow sense in which it is confined to cases in which we ourselves deliberately create the peculiar conditions under which we desire to study a phenomenon. I mean to extend it to every case in which, having ascertained by deduction that a theory would lead us to anticipate under certain circumstances phenomena contrary to what we should expect if the theory were *not* true, we examine the cases of that sort to see how far those predictions are borne out.

If you carefully consider the question of pragmatism you will see that it is nothing else than the question of the logic of abduction. That is, pragmatism proposes a certain maxim which, if sound, must render needless any further rule as to the admissibility of hypotheses to rank as hypotheses, that is to say, as explanations of phenomena held as hopeful suggestions; and furthermore, this is *all* that the maxim of pragmatism really pretends to do, at least so far as it is confined to logic, and is not understood as a proposition in psychology. For the maxim of pragmatism is that a conception can have no logical effect or import differing from that of a second conception except so far as, taken in connection with other conceptions and intentions, it might conceivably modify our practical conduct differently from that second conception. Now it is indisputable that no rule of abduction would be admitted by *any* philosopher which should prohibit on any formalistic grounds any inquiry as to how we ought in consistency to shape our practical conduct. Therefore, a maxim which looks only to possibly practical considerations will not need any supplement in order to exclude any hypotheses as inadmissible. What hypothesis it admits all philosophers would agree ought to be admitted. On the other hand, if it be true that nothing but such considerations has any logical effect or import whatever, it is plain that the maxim of pragmatism cannot cut off any kind of hypothesis which ought to be admitted. Thus, the maxim of pragmatism, if true, fully *covers* the entire logic of abduction. It remains to inquire whether this maxim may not have some *further* logical effect. If so, it must in some way affect inductive or deductive inference. But that pragmatism cannot interfere with induction is evident; because induction simply teaches us what we have to expect as a result of experimentation, and it is plain that any such expectation *may* conceivably concern practical conduct. In a certain sense it *must* affect *deduction*. Anything which gives a rule to abduction and so puts a limit upon admissible hypotheses will cut down *the premisses* of deduction, and thereby will render a *reductio ad absurdum* and other equivalent forms of deduction possible which would not otherwise have been possible. But here three remarks may be made. First, to affect the *premisses* of deduction is not to affect the logic of deduction. For in the process of deduction itself no conception is introduced to which pragmatism could be supposed to object except the act of abstraction. Concerning that, I have only time to say that pragmatism ought not to object to it. Secondly, no effect of pragmatism which *is consequent upon its effect on abduction* can go to show that pragmatism is anything more than a doctrine concerning the logic of abduction. Thirdly, if pragmatism is the doctrine that every conception is a conception of conceivable practical effects, it makes conception reach far beyond the practical. It allows any flight of imagination, provided this imagination ultimately alights upon a possible practical effect, and thus many hypotheses may seem at first glance to be excluded by the pragmatical maxim that are not really so excluded.

IV

Admitting, then, that the question of pragmatism is the question of Abduction, let us consider it under that form. What is good abduction? What should an explanatory hypothesis be to be worthy to rank as a hypothesis? Of course, it must explain the facts. But what other conditions ought it to fulfill to be good? The question of the goodness of anything is whether that thing fulfills its end. What, then, is the end of an explanatory hypothesis? Its end is, through subjection to the test of experiment, to lead to the avoidance of all surprise and to the establishment of a habit of positive expectation that shall not be disappointed. Any hypothesis, therefore, may be admissible, in the absence of any special reasons to the contrary, provided it be capable of experimental verification, and only in so far as it is capable of such verification. This is approximately the doctrine of pragmatism. But just here a broad question opens out before us. What are we to understand by experimental verification? The answer to that involves the whole logic of induction. Let me point out to you the different opinions which we actually find men holding today,—perhaps not consistently, but thinking that they hold them, —upon this subject.

In the first place, we find men who maintain that no hypothesis ought to be admitted, even as a hypothesis, any further than its truth or its falsity is *capable* of being directly perceived. This, as well as I can make out, is what was in the mind of Auguste Comte,[14] who is generally assumed to have first formulated this maxim. Of course, this maxim of abduction supposes that, as people say, we "are to believe only what we actually see"; and there are well-known writers, and writers of no little intellectual force, who maintain that it is unscientific to make predictions,—unscientific, therefore, to expect anything. One ought to restrict one's opinions to what one actually perceives. I need hardly say that that position cannot be consistently maintained. It refutes itself; for it is *itself* an opinion relating to more than is actually in the field of momentary perception.

In the second place, there are those who hold that a theory which has sustained a number of experimental tests may be expected to sustain a number of other similar tests, and to have a general approximate truth, the justification of this being that this kind of inference must prove correct in the long run, as I explained in a previous lecture.[15] But these logicians refuse to admit that we can ever have a right to conclude definitely that a hypothesis is *exactly* true, that is, that it should be able to sustain experimental tests in endless series; for, they urge, no hypothesis can be subjected to an endless series of tests. They are willing we should say that a theory is true, because, all our ideas being more or less vague and approximate, what we mean by saying that a theory is true can only be that it is very near true. But they will not allow us to say that anything put forth as an anticipation of experience should assert exactitude, because exactitude in experience would imply experiences in endless series, which is impossible.

In the third place, the great body of scientific men hold that it is too much to say that induction must be restricted to that for which there can be *positive* experimental evidence. They urge that the rationale of induction, as it is understood by logicians of the second group themselves, entitles us to hold a theory provided it be such that, if it involve any falsity, experiment must some day detect that falsity. We, therefore, have a right, they will say, to infer that something *never* will happen, provided it be of such a nature that it could not occur without being detected.

I wish to avoid in the present lecture *arguing* any such points, because the substance of all sound argumentation about pragmatism, has, as I conceive it, been already given in previous lectures, and there is no end to the forms in which it might be stated. I must, however, except from this statement the logical principles which I intend to state in tomorrow evening's lecture on multitude and continuity;[16] and for the sake of making the relation clear between this third position and the fourth and fifth, I must anticipate a little what I shall further explain tomorrow.

What ought persons who hold this third position to say to the Achilles sophism? Or rather this is not precisely what I wish to inquire, but rather what would they be obliged to say as to Achilles overtaking the tortoise, Achilles and the tortoise being geometrical points, supposing that our only knowledge was derived inductively from observations of the relative positions of Achilles and the tortoise at those stages of the progress that the sophism supposes, and supposing that Achilles really moves twice as fast as the tortoise? They ought to say that *if* it could not happen that Achilles, in one of those stages of his progress, should at length reach a certain finite distance behind the tortoise which he would be unable to halve, *without our learning that fact*, then we should have a right to conclude that he could halve *every* distance and consequently that he could make his distance behind the tortoise less than *all* fractions having a power of two for the denominator. Therefore unless those logicians were to suppose a distance less than any measurable distance, which would be contrary to their principles, they would be obliged to say that Achilles could reduce his distance behind the tortoise to *zero*.

The reason why it would be contrary to their principles to admit any distance less than a measurable distance, is that their way of supporting induction implies that they differ from the logicians of the second class, in that these third-class logicians admit that we can infer a proposition implying an infinite multitude and therefore implying the reality of the infinite multitude itself, while their mode of justifying induction would exclude every infinite multitude except the lowest grade, that of the multitude of all integer numbers. Because with reference to a greater multitude than that, it would not be true that what did not occur in a finite ordinal place in a series could not occur anywhere within the infinite series,—which is the only reason they admit for the inductive conclusion.

But now let us look at something else that those logicians would be obliged to admit. Namely, suppose any regular polygon to have all its vertices joined by straight radii to its center. Then if there were any particular finite number of sides for a regular polygon with radii so drawn, which had the singular property that it should be impossible to bisect all the angles by new radii equal to the others and, by connecting the extremities of each new radius to those of the two adjacent old radii, to make a new polygon of double the number of angles,—if, I say, there were any *finite number* of sides for which this could not

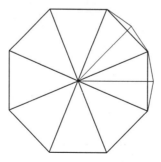

Fig. 2

be done,—it may be admitted that we should be able to find it out. The question I am asking supposes arbitrarily that they admit that. Therefore, these logicians of the third class would have to admit that all such polygons could so have their sides doubled and that consequently there would be a polygon of an infinite multitude of sides which could be, on their principles, nothing else than the circle. But it is easily proved that the perimeter of that polygon, that is, the circumference of the circle, would be incommensurable, so that an incommensurable measure is real and thence it easily follows that all such lengths are real or possible. But these exceed in multitude the only multitude those logicians admit. Without any geometry, the same result could be reached, supposing only that we have an indefinitely bisectible quantity.[17]

We are thus led to a fourth opinion very common among mathematicians, who generally hold that any one irrational real quantity,—say of length, for example,—whether algebraical or transcendental in its general expression, is just as possible and admissible as any rational quantity, but who generally reason that if the distance between two points is less than any assignable quantity, that is, less than any finite quantity, then it is nothing at all. If that be the case, it is possible for us to conceive, with mathematical precision, a state of things in favor of whose actual reality there would seem to be no possible sound argument, however weak. For example, we can conceive that the diagonal of a square is incommensurable with its side.[18] That is to say, if you first name any length commensurable with the side, the diagonal will differ from that by a finite quantity (and a commensurable quantity), yet however accurately we may measure the diagonal of an apparent square, there will always be a limit to our accuracy and the measure will always be commensurable. So we never could have any reason to think it otherwise. Moreover if there be, as they seem to hold, no other points on a line than such as are at distances assignable to an indefinite approximation, it will follow that if a line has an extremity, that extreme point may be conceived to be taken away, so as to leave the line without any extremity while leaving all the other points just as they were. In that case, all the points stand discrete and separate; and the line might be torn apart at any number of places without disturbing the relations of the points to one another. Each point has, on that view, its own independent existence, and there can be no merging of one into another. There is no continuity of points in the sense in which continuity implies generality.[19]

In the fifth place it may be held that we can be justified in inferring true generality, true continuity. But I do not see in what way we ever can be justified in doing so unless we admit the cotary propositions, and in particular that such continuity is given in perception, that is, that whatever the underlying psychical process may be, we seem to perceive a genuine flow of time, such that instants melt into one another without separate individuality.

It would not be necessary for me to deny a psychical theory which should make this to be illusory in such sense as there can be in saying that anything beyond all logical criticism is illusory, but I confess I should strongly suspect that such a psychological theory involved a logical inconsistency; and at best it could do nothing at all toward solving the logical question.

V

There are two functions which we may properly require that pragmatism should perform; or if not pragmatism, whatever the true doctrine of the Logic of Abduction may be ought to do these two services.

Namely, it ought, in the first place, to give us an expeditious riddance of all ideas essentially unclear. In the second place, it ought to lend support [to], and help to render distinct, ideas essentially clear but more or less difficult of apprehension; and in particular, it ought to take a satisfactory attitude toward the element of Thirdness.

Of these two offices of pragmatism, there is at the present day not so crying a need of the first as there was a quarter of a century ago when I enunciated the maxim. The state of logical thought is very much improved. Thirty years ago, when in consequence of my study of the logic of relations I told philosophers that all conceptions ought to be defined, with the sole exception of the familiar concrete conceptions of everyday life, my opinion was considered in every school to be utterly incomprehensible.[20] The doctrine then was, as it remains in nineteen out of every score of logical treatises that are appearing in these days, that there is no way of defining a term except by enumerating all its universal predicates, each of which is more abstracted and general than the term defined. So unless this process can go on endlessly, which was a doctrine little followed, the explication of a concept must stop at such ideas as Pure Being, Agency, Substance, and the like, which were held to be ideas so perfectly simple that no explanation whatever could be given of them. This grotesque doctrine was shattered by the logic of relations, which showed that the simplest conceptions, such as Quality, Relation, Self-consciousness, could be defined, and that such definitions would be of the greatest service in dealing with them.[21] By this time, although few really study the logic of relations, one seldom meets with a philosopher who continues to think the most general relations are particularly simple in any except a technical sense; and of course, the only alternative is to regard as the simplest the practically applied notions of familiar life. We should hardly find today a man of Kirchhoff's rank in science saying that we know exactly what energy *does* but what energy *is* we do not know in the least.[22] For the answer would be that energy being a term in a dynamical equation, if we know how to apply that equation, we thereby know what energy is, although we may suspect that there is some more fundamental law underlying the laws of motion.

In the present situation of philosophy, it is far more important that Thirdness should be adequately dealt with by our logical maxim of abduction. The urgent pertinence of the question of Thirdness, at this moment of the break-up of agnostic calm, when we see that the chief difference between philosophers is in regard to the extent to which they allow elements of Thirdness a place in their theories, is too plain to be insisted upon.

I shall take it for granted that, as far as *thought* goes, I have sufficiently shown that Thirdness is an element not reducible to Secondness and Firstness. But even if so much be granted, three attitudes may be taken: *first*, that Thirdness, though an element of the mental phenomenon, ought not to be admitted into a theory of the real, because it is not experimentally verifiable; *second*, that Thirdness is experimentally verifiable, that is, is inferable by induction, although it cannot be directly perceived; *third*, that it is directly perceived, from which the other cotary propositions can hardly be separated.

The man who takes the first position ought to admit no general law as really operative. Above all, therefore, he ought not to admit the law of laws, the law of the uniformity of nature. He ought to abstain from all prediction, however qualified, by a confession of fallibility. But that position can practically not be maintained.

The man who takes the second position will hold Thirdness to be an addition which the operation of induction[23] introduces over and above what its premises in any way contain, and further that this element, though not perceived in experiment, is justified *by* experiment. Then his conception of reality must be such as completely to sunder the real from perception; and the puzzle for him will be why perception should be allowed such authority in regard to what is real.

I do not think that man can consistently hold that there is room in time for an event between any two events separate in time. But even if he could, he would (if he could grasp the reasoning) be forced to acknowledge that the contents of time consists of separate, independent, unchanging states, and nothing else. There would not be even a determinate order of sequence among these states. He might insist that one order of sequence was more readily grasped by us; but nothing more. Every man is fully satisfied that there is such a thing as truth, or he would not ask any question. *That* truth consists in a conformity to something *independent of his thinking it to be so*, or of any man's opinion on that subject. But for the man who holds this second opinion the only reality there could be would be conformity to the ultimate result of inquiry. But there would not be any course of inquiry possible except in the sense that it would be easier for him so *[to]* interpret the phenomenon; and ultimately he would be forced to say that there was no reality at all except that he now at this instant finds a certain way of thinking easier than any other. But that violates the very idea of reality and of truth.

The man who takes the third position and accepts the cotary propositions will hold with firmest of grasps to the recognition that logical criticism is limited to what we can control. In the future we may be able to control more but we must consider what we can now control. Some elements we can control in some limited measure. But the contents of the perceptual judgment cannot be sensibly controlled now, nor is there any rational hope that it ever can be. Concerning that quite uncontrolled part of the mind, logical maxims have as little to do as with the growth of hair and nails. We may be dimly able to see that in part it depends on the accidents of the moment, in part on what is personal or racial, in part [on what] is common to all nicely adjusted organisms whose equilibrium has narrow ranges of stability, in part on whatever is composed of vast collections of independently variable elements, in part on whatever reacts, and in part on whatever has any mode of being. But the sum of it all is that our logically controlled thoughts compose a small part of the mind, the mere blossom of a vast complexus which we may call the instinctive mind in which this man will not say that he has *faith* because that implies the conceivability of distrust, but upon which he builds as the very fact to which it is the whole business of his logic to be true.

That he will have no difficulty with Thirdness is clear enough, because he will hold that the conformity of action to general intentions is as much given in perception as is the element of action itself which cannot really be mentally torn away from such general purposiveness. There can be no doubt that he will allow hypotheses fully all the range they ought to be allowed. The only question will be whether he succeeds in excluding from hypotheses everything unclear and nonsensical. It will be asked whether he will not have a shocking leaning toward anthropomorphic conceptions? I fear I must confess that he will be inclined to see an anthropomorphic, or even a zoomorphic, if not a physiomorphic, element in all our conceptions. But against unclear and nonsensical hypotheses, whatever aegis there may be in pragmatism will be more essentially significant for him than for any other logician for the reason that it is in action that logical energy returns to the uncontrolled and uncriticizable parts of the mind. His maxim will be this:

> The elements of every concept enter into logical thought at the gate of perception and make their exit at the gate of purposive action; and whatever cannot show its passports at both those two gates is to be arrested as unauthorized by reason.

The digestion of such thoughts is slow, ladies and gentlemen; but when you come in the future to reflect upon all that I have said, I am confident you will find the seven hours you have spent in listening to these ideas have not been altogether wasted.

17

What Makes a Reasoning Sound?

MSS 448–449. [Partly published in CP 1.591–610 (MS 440), 7.611–15 and 8.176 (MS 449). Composed at the end of the summer 1903 and delivered on 23 November 1903, this is the first of eight lectures Peirce gave at the Lowell Institute in Boston under the general title "Some Topics of Logic bearing on Questions now Vexed."] In this lecture, Peirce refutes "a malady" that "has broken out in science," namely the idea then in vogue that rationality rests on a feeling of logicality, and that it is futile to try to find an objective distinction between good and bad reasoning. On the contrary, Peirce claims, that distinction is not at all a matter of what we approve of, but is a question of fact. Good reasoning is based on a method that "tends to carry us toward the truth more speedily than we could otherwise progress." Peirce discusses the significance of even a slight tendency to guess correctly, arguing that, given the right method, that is all that is required to assure progress toward the truth. He continues the argument, first made in the Harvard Lectures, that reasoning is a form of controlled conduct, and thus has an ethical dimension. Peirce concludes with a discussion of the scope of logic, which he now equates with semiotics as a whole.

A malady, ladies and gentlemen, has broken out in science. Science is today in splendid vigor, having thrown off its earlier infirmity of dogmatism, and being in most respects in superlative trim. Its new disease is in its very first stage and is confined as yet almost exclusively to certain members that always have been weakly. The symptoms are local. The disorder, however, is, in its nature, not local, but constitutional; and there is a distinct danger of its appearing in parts that are now untouched. There is a certain *craze* in the universities; by which I mean that certain ideas have become rife in the universities by the force of *vogue*, and not by the force of reasoning, whether good or bad. Such a phenomenon may be likened to fever. Science has, at different times, passed through several such ailments,—some of them pretty serious. They ran their course and health came back. The present visitation is more serious, for the reason that it is no mere feverish attack, not a *mere* fashion, but is in great measure the outcome of a principle. Now every principle, once entertained, possesses vitality, until it is notoriously refuted; and even after they have received their death-blows, we have all had occasion to remark how long life may linger in principles whose formulation has been sonorous.

The principle in this case is a false notion about reasoning arising from a confusion of thought; and unfortunately science, at this moment, is ill-fortified against such an invasion, since scientific men of today are, on the average, less armed than their forerunners were with that logical acumen which is necessary to detect a somewhat subtle sophistry. I have kept watch upon the progress of the symptoms for years; and my observations go to show that they are becoming aggravated. I am unable to resist the belief that the canker is bound to spread and to eat deeper. What renders it particularly malignant is a peculiarity of this particular false notion of reasoning which will prevent any refutation of it from receiving any attention. Let this conception of ratiocination once get control, and science must perforce become exceedingly enfeebled; and the only apparent road to recovery will be through its gradually outgrowing the vicious diathesis. Now this gradual resolution, after the vitality of science has been depressed by its morbid condition, must drag through centuries. A very young and ingenuous person might expect that, in a matter of supreme importance, men would give ear to the refutation that only waits to be heard against the false notion of reasoning that is the living bacillus in the infection of science, that they would pay this refutation sufficient attention to see the point of it, which is plain enough. If men only *would* do that, the situation would be saved. But one must indeed be both sanguine and inexperienced to harbor any such hope.

This false notion of reasoning may be weaved into several varieties of fallacies. In outward guise, they differ considerably; nor are they quite identical in texture. I shall only have time to consider one. One tangle of ideas is common to all. I select for examination an argument as little illogical as any of those weaved from this same tangle; and of those as nearly logical I take the simplest. I had intended to present to you a thorough and formal refutation of the fallacy. But after I had written it out,[1] although it seemed clear and convincing, yet I found it too lengthy and dry; and I felt that it would abuse your patience to ask you to follow the minute examination of all possible ways in which the conclusion and the premises might be emended in hopes of finding a loophole of escape from the refutation. I have, therefore, decided simply to describe the phenomena presented in reasoning and then to point out to you how the argument under examination must falsify these facts however it be interpreted. This ought to satisfy you as far as this argument is concerned, and when you meet with other forms of the same tangle you will see for yourselves that they falsify the facts of reasoning in the same way. I had better mention that the argument I shall criticize is open to quite another objection than that which I notice,—and a more obvious one.[2] You may wonder why I pass over it. It is simply because some forms in which the same confusion of thought occurs are not open to this same objection. I only notice the radical objection that is common to all forms.

But you will think it high time I told you what this tangle of ideas of which I have said so much consists in. First let me state the fallacious argument which embodies it. The particular argument which I have chosen to exemplify it leads to a more extreme conclusion than some of the others. It does so because it is less illogical than those others. Its conclusion is that there is no distinction of good and bad reasoning. Although, thus nakedly exhibited, this conclusion might find few to embrace it, yet it is substantially what I might almost say that all Germany believes in today. For example, few nineteenth-century treatises on logic in the German language have a word to say about fallacies. Why not? Because they hold the law of logic to be, like a law of nature, inviolable. Or to state the matter more exactly, enough of them hold to this opinion to set the fashion for the others. *Fashion* is everything among German philosophers, for the simple reason that the professor's livelihood depends on his lectures being in the favored vogue. The fallacious argument itself runs thus:

Every reasoning takes place in some mind. It would not be that mind's reasoning unless it satisfied that mind's feeling of logicality (*logisches Gefühl*). But as long as it does that, nothing can be gained by criticizing the reasoning any further, since there is no other possible sign by which we could know that it was good than that feeling of logicality in the reasoner's mind. For if the reasoning be criticized, that criticism must be conducted by reasoning; and that reasoning, in its turn, must either be accepted because it satisfies the reasoner's feeling of logicality, or else be criticized by further reasoning. He cannot carry through an endless series of reasonings. Therefore, some final reasoning there must be that is adopted on the assumption that a reasoning which satisfies the feeling of logicality is as good as any reasoning can be; and if this be not true, all reasoning is worthless. Consequently, since every reasoning satisfies the reasoner's feeling of logicality, every reasoning is as good as any reasoning can be. That is, there is no distinction of good and bad reasoning.

That is the argument which I pronounce a miserable fallacy. If we extend to arguments a just maxim of our law, every argument must be presumed to be sound until it is proved fallacious. Accordingly, I will refer to this argument as the "defendant argument," and to the writers who adhere to it as the "defendants."

In order to emphasize that confusion which I think so pestilent, and to prevent your minds from being distracted from it to *another* fault in the defendant argument, I put it into parallel with another argument that involves a quite analogous confusion.

Namely, we find in some of the old writers a fallacious argument to prove that there is no distinction of moral right and wrong. The argument runs as follows:

The distinction between a good act and a bad one, if there be any such distinction, lies in the motive. But the only motive a man can have is his own pleasure. No other is thinkable. For if a man desires to act in any way, it is because he takes pleasure in so acting. Otherwise, his action would not be voluntary and deliberate. Thus, there is but one possible motive for action that has any motive; and consequently, the distinction of right and wrong, which would be a distinction between motives, does not exist.

You see the parallelism between the two arguments. Each undertakes to refute a distinction between good and bad; the one in reasoning, the other in endeavor. Each does this by pronouncing something unthinkable; the one, that a man should adopt a conclusion for any other reason than a feeling of logicality, the other that a man should adopt any line of conduct from any other motive than a feeling of pleasure.

My position, in opposition to these arguments, is that it is so far from being true that every desire necessarily desires its own gratification, that, on the contrary, it is impossible that a desire should desire its own gratification; and it is so far from being true that every inference must necessarily be based upon its seeming satisfactory, that it is, on the contrary, impossible that any inference should be based in any degree upon its seeming satisfactory.

I want to lead you to see clearly that the defendants confound two disparate categories, and, having identified objects belonging to these categories, attribute to them a nature belonging to a third category. They confound an efficient agency, whose very existence consists in its acting when and where it is, with a general mental formulation; and as if this were not blunder enough, they call the identified two a feeling. The first blunder is as if a man, being asked what made the Campanile fall in Venice,[3] were to reply that it was the regularity of nature. That is a confusion tolerably common,—the confusion of a decree of a court with the sheriff's strong right arm. But, after having identified these, to call them a *feeling* is, I believe, a mistake peculiar to philosophers. It is something like confusing a living man with the general idea of a man and, having done so, saying that he was constructed of two nasal consonants and a vowel.

Taking up, first, the argument about morals, let us confront it with the facts of the case. The necessitarians tell us that when we act, we act under a necessity that we cannot control. I am inclined to think that this is substantially so. We certainly cannot control our *past* actions, and I fancy it is too late to control what is happening at the very instant present. You cannot prevent what already is. If this be true, it is true that *when we act*, we do act under a necessity that we cannot control. But our *future* actions we can determine in a great measure; can we not? To deny *that* were mere gabble and word-twisting. No matter how bad the argument may be that we can only control future actions by a present action which is itself necessitated, still it would be idle to find fault with it, since it is quite irrelevant. The point is that our future actions will be controlled by present endeavors. That is sufficient. But let us describe the all-familiar phenomena of self-control.

In the first place, then, every man has certain ideals of the general description of conduct that befits a rational animal in his particular station in life, what most accords with his total nature and relations. If you think this statement too vague, I will say, more specifically, that there are three ways in which these ideals usually recommend themselves and justly do so. In the first place, certain kinds of conduct when the man contemplates them have an esthetic quality. He thinks that conduct fine; and though his notion may be coarse or sentimental, yet if so it will alter in time and must tend to be brought into harmony with his nature. At any rate, his taste *is* his taste for the time being: that is all. In the second place, the man endeavors to shape his ideals into consistency with each other, for inconsistency is odious to him. In the third place, he imagines what the consequences of fully carrying out his ideals would be, and asks himself what the esthetic quality of those consequences would be. His ideals, however, have in the main been imbibed in childhood. Still, they have gradually been shaped to his personal nature and to the ideas of his circle of society rather by a continuous process of growth than by any distinct acts of thought. Reflecting upon these ideals, he is led to *intend* to make his own conduct conform at least to a part of them,—to that part in which he thoroughly believes. Next, he usually formulates, however vaguely, certain *rules of conduct*. He can hardly help doing so. Besides, such rules are convenient and serve to minimize the effects [of] future inadvertence, and what are well named the wiles of the devil within him. Reflection upon these rules, as well as upon the general ideals behind them, has a certain effect upon his disposition, so that what he naturally inclines to do becomes modified. Such being his condition, he often foresees that a special occasion is going to arise; thereupon, a certain gathering of his forces will begin to work, and this working of his being will cause him to consider how he will act, and in accordance with his disposition, such as it now is, he is led to form a *resolution* as to how he will act upon that occasion. This resolution is of the nature of a plan, or, as one might almost say, a *diagram*. It is a mental formula always more or less general. Being nothing more than an idea, this resolution does not necessarily influence his conduct. But now he sits down and goes through a process similar to that of impressing a lesson upon his memory, the result of which is that the *resolution*, or mental formula, is converted into a *determination*, by which I mean a really efficient agency, such that if one knows what its special character is, one can *forecast* the man's conduct on the special occasion. One cannot make forecasts that will come true in the majority of trials of them by means of any figment. It must be by means of something true and real. We do not know by what machinery the conversion of a resolution into a determination is brought about. Several hypotheses have been proposed; but they do not much concern us just now. Suffice it to say that the determination, or efficient agency, is something hidden in the depths of our nature. A peculiar quality of feeling accompanies the first steps of the process of forming this impression; but later we have no direct consciousness of it. We may become aware of the disposition, especially if it is pent up. In that case, we shall recognize it by a feeling of *need*, of *desire*. I must notice that a man does not always have an opportunity to form a definite resolution beforehand. But in such cases there are less definite but still well marked determinations of his nature growing out of the general rules of conduct that he has formulated; or in cases [where] no such appropriate rule has been formulated, his ideal of fitting conduct will have produced some disposition. At length, the anticipated occasion actually arises.

In order to fix our ideas, let us suppose a case. In the course of my reflections, I am led to think that it would be well for me to talk to a certain person in a certain way. I resolve that I will do so when we meet. But considering how, in the heat of conversation, I might be led to take a different tone, I proceed to impress the resolution upon my soul; with the result that when the interview takes place, although my thoughts are then occupied with the matter of the talk, and may never revert to my resolution, nevertheless the determination of my being does influence my conduct. All action in accordance with a determination is accompanied by a feeling that is pleasurable; but whether the feeling at any instant is felt as pleasurable in that very instant or whether the recognition of it as pleasurable comes a little later is a question of fact difficult to make sure about. The argument turns on the feeling of pleasure, and therefore it is necessary, in order to judge of it, to get at the facts about that feeling as accurately as we can. In beginning to perform any series of acts which had been determined upon beforehand, there is a certain sense of joy, an anticipation and commencement of a relaxation of the tension of need, which we now become more conscious of than we had been before. In the act itself taking place at any instant, it may be that we are conscious of pleasure; although that is doubtful. Before the series of acts are done, we already begin to review them, and in that review we recognize the pleasurable character of the feelings that accompanied those acts.

To return to my interview, as soon as it is over I begin to review it more carefully and I then ask myself whether my conduct accorded with my resolution. That resolution, as we agreed, was a mental formula. The memory of my action may be roughly described as an image. I contemplate that image and put the question to myself. Shall I say that that image satisfies the stipulations of my resolution, or not? The answer to this question, like the answer to any inward question, is necessarily of the nature of a mental formula. It is accompanied, however, by a certain quality of feeling which is related to the formula itself very much as the color of the ink in which anything is printed is related to the sense of what is printed. And just as we first become aware of the peculiar color of the ink and afterward ask ourselves whether it is agreeable or not, so in formulating the judgment that the image of our conduct does satisfy our previous resolution we are, in the very act of formulation, aware of a certain quality of *feeling*,—the feeling of satisfaction,—and directly afterward recognize that that feeling was pleasurable. But now I may probe deeper into my conduct, and may ask myself whether it accorded with my general intentions. Here again there will be a judgment and a feeling accompanying it, and directly afterward a recognition that that feeling was pleasurable or painful. This judgment, if favorable, will probably afford less intense pleasure than the other; but the feeling of satisfaction which is pleasurable will be different and, as we say, a *deeper* feeling. I may now go still further and ask how the image of my conduct accords with my ideals of conduct fitting to a man like me. Here will follow a new judgment with its accompanying feeling followed by a recognition of the pleasurable or painful character of that feeling. In any or all of these ways a man may criticize his own conduct; and it is essential to remark that it is not mere idle praise or blame such as writers who are not of the wisest often distribute among the personages of history. No indeed! It is approval or disapproval of the only respectable kind, that which will bear fruit in the future. Whether the man is satisfied with himself or dissatisfied, his nature will absorb the lesson like a sponge; and the next time he will tend to do better than he did before. In addition to these three self-criticisms of single series of actions, a man will from time to time review his *ideals*. This process is not a job that man sits down to do and have done with. The experience of life is continually contributing instances more or less illuminative. These are digested first not in the man's consciousness but in the depths of his reasonable being. The results come to consciousness later. But meditation seems to agitate a mass of tendencies and allow them more quickly to settle down so as to be really more conformed to what is fit for the man. Finally, in addition to this personal meditation on the fitness of one's own ideals, which is of a practical nature, there are the purely theoretical studies of the student of ethics who seeks to ascertain, as a matter of curiosity, what the *fitness* of an ideal of conduct consists in, and to deduce from such definition of fitness what conduct ought to be. Opinions differ as to the wholesomeness of this study. It only concerns our present purpose to remark that it is in itself a purely theoretical inquiry, entirely distinct from the business of shaping one's own conduct. Provided that feature of it be not lost sight of, I myself have no doubt that the study is more or less favorable to right living.

I have thus endeavored to describe fully the typical phenomena of controlled action. *They are not every one present in every case.* Thus, as I have already mentioned, there is not always an opportunity to form a resolution. I have specially emphasized the fact that conduct is determined by what precedes it in time, while the recognition of the pleasure it brings follows after the action. Some may opine that this is not true of what is called the pursuit of pleasure; and I admit that there is room for their opinion while I myself incline to think, for example, that the satisfaction of eating a good dinner is never a satisfaction in the present instantaneous state, but always follows after it. I insist, at any rate, that a *feeling*, as a mere appearance, can have no real power in itself to produce any effect whatever, nor however indirectly.

My account of the facts you will observe leaves a man at full liberty, no matter if we grant all that the necessitarians ask. That is, the man *can*, or if you please is *compelled*, to *make his life more reasonable*. What other distinct idea than that, I should be glad to know, can be attached to the word liberty?

Now let us compare the facts I have stated with the argument I am opposing. That argument rests on two main premisses; first, that it is unthinkable that a man should act from any other motive than pleasure, if his act be deliberate; and second, that action with reference to pleasure leaves no room for any distinction of right and wrong.

Let us consider whether this second premiss is really true. What would be requisite in order to destroy the difference between innocent and guilty conduct? The one thing that would do it would be to destroy the faculty of effective self-criticism. As long as that remained, as long as a man compared his conduct with a preconceived standard and that effectively, it need not make much difference if his only *real* motive were pleasure; for it would become disagreeable to him to incur the sting of conscience. But those who deluded themselves with that fallacy were so inattentive to the phenomena that they confused the judgment after the act that that act satisfied or did not satisfy the requirements of a standard with a pleasure or pain accompanying the act itself.

Let us now consider whether the other premiss is true, that it is unthinkable that a man should act deliberately except for the sake of pleasure. What is the element which it is in truth unthinkable that deliberate action should lack? It is simply and solely the determination. Let his determination remain, as it is certainly conceivable that it should remain although the very nerve of pleasure were cut so that the man were perfectly insensible to pleasure and pain, and he will certainly pursue the line of conduct upon which he is intent. The only effect would be to render the man's intentions more inflexible,—an effect, by the way, which we often have occasion to observe in men whose feelings are almost deadened by age or by some derangement of the brain. But those who have reasoned in this fallacious way have confounded together the determination of the man's nature, which is an efficient agency prepared previously to the act, with the comparison of conduct with a standard, which comparison is a general mental formula subsequent to the act, and having identified these two utterly different things, placed them in the act itself as a mere quality of feeling.

Now if we recur to the defendant argument about reasoning, we shall find that it involves the same sort of tangle of ideas. The phenomena of reasoning are, in their general features, parallel to those of moral conduct. For reasoning is essentially thought that is under self-control, just as moral conduct is conduct under self-control. Indeed reasoning *is* a species of controlled conduct and as such necessarily partakes of the essential features of controlled conduct. If you attend to the phenomena of reasoning, although they are not quite so familiar to you as those of morals because there are no clergymen whose business it is to keep them before your minds, you will nevertheless remark, without difficulty, that a person who draws a rational conclusion not only thinks it to be true, but thinks that similar reasoning would be just in every analogous case. If he fails to think this, the inference is not to be called reasoning. It is merely an idea suggested to his mind and which he cannot resist thinking is true. But not having been subjected to any check or control, it is not deliberately approved and is not to be called reasoning. To call it so would be to ignore a distinction which it ill becomes a rational being to overlook. To be sure, every inference forces itself upon us irresistibly. That is to say, it is irresistible at the instant it first suggests itself. Nevertheless, we all have in our minds certain *norms*, or general patterns of right reasoning, and we can compare the inference with one of those and ask ourselves whether it satisfies that rule. I call it a rule, although the formulation may be somewhat vague, because it has the essential character of a rule of being a general formula applicable to particular cases. If we judge our norm of right reason to be satisfied, we get a feeling of approval, and the inference now not only appears as irresistible as it did before, but it will prove far more unshakable by any doubt.

You see at once that we have here all the main elements of moral conduct; the general standard mentally conceived beforehand, the efficient agency in the inward nature, the act, the subsequent comparison of the act with the standard. Examining the phenomena more closely we shall find that not a single element of moral conduct is unrepresented in reasoning. At the same time, the special case naturally has its peculiarities.

Thus, we have a general ideal of sound logic. But we should not naturally describe it as our idea of the kind of reasoning that befits men in our situation. How should we describe it? How,—if we were to say that sound reasoning is such reasoning that in every conceivable state of the universe in which the facts stated in the premises are true, the fact stated in the conclusion will thereby and therein be true? The objection to this statement is that it only covers necessary reasoning, including reasoning about chances. There is other reasoning which is defensible as probable, in the sense that while the conclusion may be more or less erroneous, yet the same procedure diligently persisted in must, in every conceivable universe in which it leads to any result at all, lead to a result indefinitely approximating to the truth. When that is the case, we shall do right to pursue that method, provided we recognize its true character, since our relation to the universe does not permit us to have any necessary knowledge of positive facts. You will observe that in such a case our ideal is shaped by the consideration of our situation relatively to the universe of existences. There are still other operations of the mind to which the name "reasoning" is especially appropriate, although it is not the prevailing habit of speech to call them so. They are conjectures, but rational conjectures, and the justification of them is that unless a man had a tendency to guess right, unless his guesses are better than tossing up a copper, no truth that he does not already virtually possess could ever be disclosed to him, so that he might as well give up all attempt to reason; while if he has any decided tendency to guess right, as he *may* have, then no matter how often he guesses wrong, he will get at the truth at last. These considerations certainly do take into account the man's inward nature as well as his outward relations; so that the ideals of good logic are truly of the same general nature as ideals of fine conduct. We saw that three kinds of considerations go to support ideals of conduct. They were, first, that certain conduct seems fine in itself. Just so, certain conjectures seem likely and easy in themselves. Secondly, we wish our conduct to be consistent. Just so, the ideal necessary reasoning is consistency simply. Third, we consider what the general effect would be of thoroughly carrying out our ideals. Just so, certain ways of reasoning recommend themselves because if persistently carried out they must lead to the truth. The parallelism, you perceive, is almost exact.

There is also such a thing as a general logical *intention*. But it is not emphasized for the reason that the will does not enter so violently into reasoning as it does into moral conduct. I have already mentioned the logical norms, which correspond to moral laws. In taking up any difficult problem of reasoning we formulate to ourselves a logical resolution; but here again, because the will is not at such high tension in reasoning as it often is in self-controlled conduct, these resolutions are not very prominent phenomena. Owing to this circumstance, the efficient determination of our nature, which causes us to reason in each case as we do, has less relation to resolutions than to logical norms. The act itself is, at the instant, irresistible in both cases. But immediately after, it is subjected to self-criticism by comparison with a previous standard, which is always the norm, or *rule*, in the case of reasoning, although in the case of outward conduct we are too often content to compare the act with the resolution. In the case of general conduct, the lesson of satisfaction or dissatisfaction is frequently not much taken to heart and little influences future conduct. But in the case of reasoning an inference which self-criticism disapproves is always instantly annulled, because there is no difficulty in doing this. Finally, all the different feelings which, as we noticed, accompanied the different operations of self-controlled conduct equally accompany those of reasoning, although they are not quite so vivid.

The parallelism is thus perfect. Nor, I repeat, could it fail to be so, if our description of the phenomena of controlled conduct was true, since reasoning is only a special kind of controlled conduct.

Let us now consider the defendant argument. It rests on two premises, to wit: *first*, that it is unthinkable that a conclusion should be drawn for any other reason than that it will be accompanied by a feeling of logicality; *second*, that if all reasoning is determined by our feeling of logicality, there can be no distinction of good and bad reasoning.

But both these premises are false. Even if our reasonings were all determined by a feeling of logicality, still so long as we were able to compare them with *norms* based on the consideration of the relation of our thoughts to facts, in case the norms were not satisfied, our feeling of logicality would instantly be reversed. In no way could the distinction of good and bad reasoning be destroyed short of destroying the power of comparing it, after it was made, with such norms. The truth is that the defendants confound the judgment of satisfaction or dissatisfaction of the norms which is made subsequent to the act of inference with a feeling accompanying that act.

The first premise is still more manifestly false. Nothing can be more monstrous than to say that it is unthinkable that a reasoning should be based on anything but a feeling of logicality which is a part of it. How can an act be caused by a feeling which does not exist until the act exists? Or who ever reasons, "This seems to me true and therefore it must be true"? Yet even this is not adopting the reasoning because that very reasoning seems sound. That is a thing too absurd to be formulated in words. The only thing without which it is unthinkable that reasoning should take place is a determination of one's nature causing it. But the defendants confound this with that feeling in the act which they also confound with the judgment of satisfaction of the norm.

Besides this principal fault of the defendant argument, there is another that I cannot pass over. When it is said that all inference "assumes that what seems to be good reasoning is so," there is an inaccuracy of expression. For an inference assumes nothing but its premises. But if we understand this to mean that no reasoning would be sound unless what seemed to be good reasoning were good reasoning, I reply that according to my description of the phenomena of reasoning, the only fact which the soundness of all reasoning and the truth of all human thought really depends [on] is that a man's conjectures are somewhat better than purely random propositions. The idea that the criticism of the criticism of reasoning involves some new reasoning overlooks the fact that the criticism is sustained by the original inference. "Reasoning," says Hobbes, "is computation,"[4] and although this is extravagant, yet it is quite true that the criticism of the criticism of reasoning simply repeats the process, like adding up a column of figures a second time. It is conceivable that a blunder should be repeated, but after the column has been added, say ten times, and always with the same result, the arithmetician has no longer any discernible doubt to be quieted; and to add the column an eleventh time would be quite purposeless. In a strict theoretical sense, it is not *certain* that twice two are four, since it is conceivable that a blunder that might occur once has occurred every time the addition has been performed.

Now, ladies and gentlemen, I think you will agree that the defendant argument is a thoroughly bad one, and in particular that the question of what is good reasoning and what bad is not a question of whether the mind approves it or not, but is a question of *fact*. A method that tends to carry us toward the truth more speedily than we could otherwise progress is good; a method that has a tendency to carry us away from the truth is utterly bad, whether we naturally approve of it or not.[5]

This great fallacy once overthrown which governs more or less the German logics, what does right reasoning consist in?[6] It consists in such reasoning as shall be conducive to our ultimate aim. What, then, is our ultimate aim? Perhaps it is not necessary that the logician should answer this question. Perhaps it might be possible to deduce the correct rules of reasoning from the mere assumption that we have some ultimate aim. But I cannot see how this could be done. If we had, for example, no other aim than the pleasure of the moment, we should fall back into the same absence of any logic that the fallacious argument would lead to. We should have no ideal of reasoning, and consequently no norm. It seems to me that the logician ought to recognize what our ultimate aim is. It would seem to be the business of the moralist to find this out; and the logician has to accept the teaching of ethics in this regard. But the moralist, as far as I can make it out, merely tells us that we have a power of self-control, that no narrow or selfish aim can ever prove satisfactory, that the only satisfactory aim is the broadest, highest, and most general possible aim; and for any more definite information, as I conceive the matter, he has to refer us to the esthetician whose business it is to say what is the state of things which is most admirable in itself regardless of any ulterior reason. So, then, we appeal to the esthete to tell us what it is that is admirable without any reason for being admirable beyond its inherent character. Why, that, he replies, is the beautiful. Yes, we urge, such is the name that you give to it, but what *is it?* What is this character? If he replies that it consists in a certain quality of feeling, a certain *bliss,* I for one decline altogether to accept the answer as sufficient. I should say to him, My dear Sir, if you can prove to me that this quality of feeling that you speak of does, as a fact, attach to what you call the beautiful, or that which would be admirable without any reason for being so, I am willing enough to believe you; but I cannot without strenuous proof admit that any particular quality of feeling is admirable without a reason. For it is too revolting to be believed unless one is forced to believe it. A fundamental question like this, however practical the issues of it may be, differs entirely from any ordinary practical question, in that whatever is accepted as good in itself must be accepted without compromise. In deciding any special question of conduct it is often quite right to allow weight to different conflicting considerations and calculate their resultant. But it is quite different in regard to that which is to be [the] aim of all endeavor. The object admirable that is admirable *per se* must, no doubt, be general. Every ideal is more or less general. It may be a complicated state of things. But it must be a *single* ideal; it must have *unity,* because it is an idea, and unity is essential to every idea and every ideal. Objects of utterly disparate kinds may, no doubt, be admirable, because some special reason may make each one of them so. But when it comes to the ideal of the admirable, in itself, the very nature of its being is to be a precise idea; and if somebody tells me it is either this, or that, or that other, I say to him, It is clear you have no *idea* of what precisely it is. But an ideal must be capable of being embraced in a unitary idea, or it is no ideal at all. Therefore, there can be no compromises between different considerations here. The admirable ideal cannot be too extremely admirable. The more thoroughly it has whatever character is essential to it, the more admirable it must be. Now what would the doctrine that that which is admirable in itself is a quality of feeling, come to if taken in all its purity and carried to its furthest extreme,—which should be the extreme of admirableness? It would amount to saying that the one ultimately admirable object is the unrestrained gratification of a desire, regardless of what the nature of that desire may be. Now that is too shocking. It would be the doctrine that all the higher modes of consciousness with which we are acquainted in ourselves, such as love and reason, are good only so far as they subserve the lowest of all modes to consciousness. It would be the doctrine that this vast universe of Nature which we contemplate with such awe is good only to produce a certain quality of feeling. Certainly, I must be excused for not admitting that doctrine unless it be proved with the utmost evidence. So, then, what proof is there that it is true? The only reason for it that I have been able to learn is that *gratification, pleasure*, is the only conceivable result that is satisfied with itself; and therefore since we are seeking for that which is *fine* and *admirable* without any reason beyond itself, *pleasure, bliss*, is the only object which can satisfy the conditions. This is a respectable argument. It deserves consideration. Its premiss, that pleasure is the only conceivable result that is perfectly self-satisfied, must be granted. Only, in these days of evolutionary ideas which are traceable to the French Revolution as their instigator, and still further back to Galileo's experiment at [the] leaning tower of Pisa, and still further back to all the stands that have been made by Luther and even by Robert of Lincoln[7] against attempts to bind down human Reason to any prescriptions fixed in advance,—in these days, I say, when these ideas of progress and growth have themselves grown up so as [to] occupy our minds as they now do, how can we be expected [to] allow the assumption to pass that the admirable in itself is any stationary result? The explanation of the circumstance that the only result that is satisfied with itself is a quality of feeling is that reason always looks forward to an endless future and expects endlessly to improve its results. Consider, for a moment, what Reason, as well as we can today conceive it, really is. I do not mean man's faculty which is so called from its embodying in some measure Reason, or Νοῦς, as a something manifesting itself in the mind, in the history of mind's development, and in nature. What is this Reason? In the first place, it is something that never can have been completely embodied. The most insignificant of general ideas always involves conditional predictions or requires for its fulfillment that events should come to pass, and all that ever can have come to pass must fall short of completely fulfilling its requirements. A little example will serve to illustrate what I am saying. Take any general term whatever. I say of a stone that it is *hard*. That means that so long as the stone remains hard, every essay to scratch it by the moderate pressure of a knife will surely fail. To call the stone *hard* is to predict that no matter how often you try the experiment, it will fail every time. That innumerable series of conditional predictions is involved in the meaning of this lowly adjective. Whatever may have been done will not begin to exhaust its meaning. At the same time, the very being of the General, of Reason, is of such a mode that this being *consists* in the Reason's actually governing events. Suppose a piece of carborundum has been made and has subsequently been dissolved in aqua regia without anybody at any time, so far as I know, ever having tried to scratch it with a knife. Undoubtedly, I may have good reason, nevertheless, to call it hard; because some actual fact has occurred such that Reason compels me to call it so, and a general idea of all the facts of the case can only be formed if I do call it so. In this case, my calling it hard is an actual event which is governed by that law of hardness of the piece of carborundum. But if there were no actual fact whatsoever which was meant by saying that the piece of carborundum was hard, there would be not the slightest meaning in the word hard as applied to it. The very being of the General, of Reason, *consists* in its governing individual events. So, then, the essence of Reason is such that its being never can have been completely perfected. It always must be in a state of incipiency, of growth. It is like the character of a man which consists in the ideas that he will conceive and in the efforts that he will make, and which only develops as the occasions actually arise. Yet in all his life long no son of Adam has ever fully manifested what there was in him. So, then, the development of Reason requires as a part of it the occurrence of more individual events than ever can occur. It requires, too, all the coloring of all qualities of feeling, including pleasure in its proper place among the rest. This development of Reason consists, you will observe, in embodiment, that is, in manifestation. The creation of the universe, which did not take place during a certain busy week, in the year 4004 B.C., but is going on today and never will be done, is this very development of Reason. I do not see how one can have a more satisfying ideal of the admirable than the development of Reason so understood. The one thing whose admirableness is not due to an ulterior Reason is Reason itself comprehended in all its fullness, so far as we can comprehend it. Under this conception, the ideal of conduct will be to execute our little function in the operation of the creation by giving a hand toward rendering the world more reasonable whenever, as the slang is, it is "up to us" to do so. In logic, it will be observed that knowledge is reasonableness; and the ideal of reasoning will be to follow such methods as must develop knowledge the most speedily. The logicality of the judgment that a stone cannot be at once hard and not hard does not consist, as Sigwart and other German logicians say it does, in its satisfying our *feeling of logicality*, but consists in its being true; for everything that is true is logical, whether we know it or not. But this we know to be true, not at all by means of any peculiar feeling it excites in us,—we *might* argue from that feeling, it is true, but any feeling may be deranged,—and we know it much more certainly from this, that when we say that it is true that "a stone cannot be at once hard and not hard," what we are talking of is not what interpretation somebody might put upon that assertion, but what we *mean* by it. Now what we mean by "*not*" is "every proposition would be true if it were." By "not hard" we mean "every proposition would be true if it were hard." So to say that "a stone is at once hard and not hard" is to say that if it is hard every proposition is true, and it is hard. Accordingly this would be to assert that every proposition is true,—a super-Hegelian position that directly denies the distinction of truth and falsity, which, we are fully satisfied, exists.

A little book by Victoria Lady Welby has lately appeared entitled *What is Meaning?*[8] The book has sundry merits, among them that of showing that there are three modes of meaning. But the best feature of it is that it presses home the question "What is meaning?" A word has meaning for us in so far as we are able to make use of it in communicating our knowledge to others and in getting at the knowledge that those others seek to communicate to us. That is the lowest grade of meaning. The *meaning* of a word is more fully the sum total of all the conditional predictions which the person who uses it *intends* to make himself responsible for or intends to deny. That conscious or quasi-conscious *intention* in using the word is the second grade of meaning. But besides the consequences to which the person who accepts a word knowingly commits himself to, there is a vast ocean of unforeseen consequences which the acceptance of the word is destined to bring about, not merely consequences of knowing but perhaps revolutions of society. One cannot tell what power there may be in a word or a phrase to change the face of the world; and the sum of those consequences makes up the third grade of meaning.

Let us now consider what the science of logic ought to embrace. Although whatever is true is logical whether we know it to be so or not, yet it is plain that logic cannot embrace all human knowledge. The logician endeavors to assume an attitude as if, as logician, he had no information at all except what everybody must have to reason at all. This, however, is not exactly possible. There is no exactly defined sphere of knowledge such that everybody who reasons must possess the whole of it and need know nothing else. But the logician assumes that the meaning of language is well known between himself and the person to whom he is imparting his doctrine, although that meaning may not be analyzed and all its elements distinctly recognized, but that no other facts are known. Of course, some others must be known; but they are left out of account.

The ultimate purpose of the logician is to make out the theory of how knowledge is advanced. Just as there is a chemical theory of dyeing which is not exactly the art of dyeing, and there is a theory of thermodynamics which is quite different from the art of constructing heat-engines; so *Methodeutic*, which is the last goal of logical study, is the theory of the advancement of knowledge of all kinds. But this theory is not possible until the logician has first examined all the different elementary modes of getting at truth and especially all the different classes of arguments, and has studied their properties so far as these properties concern /the/ power of the arguments as leading to the truth. This part of logic is called *Critic*. But before it is possible to enter upon this business in any rational way, the first thing that is necessary is to examine thoroughly all the ways in which thought can be expressed. For since thought has no being except in so far as it will be embodied, and since the embodiment of thought is a sign, the business of logical critic cannot be undertaken until the whole structure of signs, especially of general signs, has been thoroughly investigated. This is substantially acknowledged by logicians of all schools. But the different schools conceive of the business quite differently. Many logicians conceive that the inquiry trenches largely upon psychology, depends upon what has been observed about the human mind, and would not necessarily be true for other minds. Much of what they say is unquestionably false of many races of mankind. But I, for my part, take little stock in a logic that is not valid for all minds, inasmuch as the logicality of a given argument, as I have said, does not depend on how we think that argument, but upon what the truth is. Other logicians endeavoring to steer clear of psychology, as far as possible, think that this first branch of logic must relate to the possibility of knowledge of the real world and upon the sense in which it is true that the real world can be known. This branch of philosophy, called epistemology, or *Erkenntnislehre*, is necessarily largely metaphysical. But I, for my part, cannot for an instant assent to the proposal to base logic upon metaphysics, inasmuch as I fully agree with Aristotle, Duns Scotus, Kant, and all the profoundest metaphysicians that metaphysics can, on the contrary, have no secure basis except that which the science of logic affords. I, therefore, take a position quite similar to that of the English logicians, beginning with Scotus himself,[9] in regarding this introductory part of logic as nothing but an analysis of what kinds of signs are absolutely essential to the embodiment of thought. I call it, after Scotus, *Speculative Grammar.* I fully agree, however, with a portion of the English school,—a school I may observe which now has a large and most influential and scientific following in Germany,—I agree, I say, with a portion of this school without thereby coming into positive conflict with the others, in thinking that this Speculative Grammar ought not to confine its studies to those conventional signs of which language is composed, but that it will do well to widen its field of view so as to take into consideration also kinds of signs which, not being conventional, are not of the nature of language. In fact, as a point of theory, I am of opinion that we ought not to limit ourselves to signs but ought to take account of certain objects more or less analogous to signs. In practice, however, I have paid little attention to these quasi-signs.

Thus there are, in my view of the subject, three branches of logic: Speculative Grammar, Critic, and Methodeutic.[10]

18

An Outline Classification of the Sciences

MS 478. [Found in CP 1.180–202, this text is the first section of "A Syllabus of Certain Topics of Logic," a large document composed mostly in October 1903 to supplement the Lowell Lectures. The original syllabus contains six sections, of which four are printed here (selections 18–21). Omitted are "Nomenclature and Divisions of Dyadic Relations" (MS 539; CP 3.571–608) and "Existential Graphs: The Conventions" (MS 508; CP 4.394–417). The first two sections and part of the sixth were printed for the audience by the Lowell Institute (Boston: Alfred Mudge & Son, 1903); the selection below is found there pp. 5–9.] This first part of the "Syllabus" is literally, as proclaimed in its title, an outline. In its summary form, it provides an easy guide to Peirce's mature classification of the sciences, with the normative sciences—esthetics, ethics, and logic—constituting the central branch of philosophy. Peirce defines logic as "the science of the general laws of signs," and divides it, as he had in his first 1903 Lowell Lecture (previous selection) into three departments: speculative grammar, critic, and methodeutic. Peirce's subsequent development of semiotics will be built on this classification.

This classification, which aims to base itself on the principal affinities of the objects classified, is concerned not with all possible sciences, nor with so many branches of knowledge, but with sciences in their present condition, as so many businesses of groups of living men. It borrows its idea from Comte's classification; namely, the idea that one science depends upon another for fundamental principles, but does not furnish such principles to that other.[1] It turns out that in most cases the divisions are trichotomic; the First of the three members relating to universal elements or laws, the Second arranging classes of forms and seeking to bring them under universal laws, the Third going into the utmost detail, describing individual phenomena and endeavoring to explain them. But not all the divisions are of this character.

The classification has been carried into great detail; but only its broader divisions are here given.[2]

All science is either (A) *Science of Discovery;* (B) *Science of Review;* or (C) *Practical Science.*[3]

By "science of review" is meant the business of those who occupy themselves with arranging the results of discovery, beginning with digests and going on to endeavor to form a philosophy of science. Such is the nature of Humboldt's *Kosmos,* of Comte's *Philosophie positive,* and of Spencer's *Synthetic Philosophy.*[4] The classification of the sciences belongs to this department.

Science of Discovery is either (I) *Mathematics;* (II) *Philosophy;* or (III) *Idioscopy.*

Mathematics studies what is and what is not logically possible, without making itself responsible for its actual existence. Philosophy is *positive science,* in the sense of discovering what really is true; but it limits itself to so much of truth as can be inferred from common experience. Idioscopy embraces all the special sciences, which are principally occupied with the accumulation of new facts.

Mathematics may be divided into (a) the *Mathematics of Logic;* (b) the *Mathematics of Discrete Series;* (c) the *Mathematics of Continua and Pseudo-continua.*

I shall not carry this division further. Branch (b) has recourse to branch (a) and branch (c) to branch (b).

Philosophy is divided into (a) *Phenomenology;* (b) *Normative Science;* (c) *Metaphysics.*

Phenomenology ascertains and studies the kinds of elements universally present in the phenomenon; meaning by the *phenomenon,* whatever is present at any time to the mind in any way. Normative science distinguishes what ought to be from what ought not to be, and makes many other divisions and arrangements subservient to its primary dualistic distinction. Metaphysics seeks to give an account of the universe of mind and matter. Normative science rests largely on phenomenology and on mathematics; metaphysics on phenomenology and on normative science.

Idioscopy has two wings: (α) the *Physical Sciences;* and (β) the *Psychical,* or Human, *Sciences.*

Psychical sciences borrow principles continually from the physical sciences; the latter very little from the former.

The Physical Sciences are (a) *Nomological,* or General, *Physics;* (b) *Classificatory Physics;* (c) *Descriptive Physics.*

Nomological Physics discovers the ubiquitous phenomena of the physical universe, formulates their laws, and measures their constants. It draws upon metaphysics and upon mathematics for principles. Classificatory Physics describes and classifies physical forms and seeks to explain them by the laws discovered by nomological physics with which it ultimately tends to coalesce. Descriptive Physics describes individual objects,—the Earth and the Heavens,—endeavors to explain their phenomena by the principles of nomological and classificatory physics, and tends ultimately itself to become classificatory.

The Psychical Sciences are (a) *Nomological Psychics,* or Psychology; (b) *Classificatory Psychics,* or Ethnology; (c) *Descriptive Psychics,* or History.

Nomological Psychics discovers the general elements and laws of mental phenomena. It is greatly influenced by phenomenology, by logic, by metaphysics, and by biology (a branch of classificatory physics). Classificatory

Psychics classifies products of mind and endeavors to explain them on psychological principles. At present it is far too much in its infancy (except linguistics, to which reference will be made below) to approach very closely to psychology. It borrows from psychology and from physics. Descriptive Psychics endeavors in the first place to describe individual manifestations of mind, whether they be permanent works or actions; and to that task it joins that of endeavoring to explain them on the principles of psychology and ethnology. It borrows from geography (a branch of descriptive physics), from astronomy (another branch), and from other branches of physical and psychical science.

I now consider the subdivisions of these sciences, so far as they [are] so widely separated as quite to sunder the groups of investigators who today study them.

Phenomenology is, at present, a single study.

Normative Science has three widely separated divisions: (i) *Esthetics;* (ii) *Ethics;* (iii) *Logic.*

Esthetics is the science of ideals, or of that which is objectively admirable without any ulterior reason. I am not well acquainted with this science; but it ought to repose on phenomenology. Ethics, or the science of right and wrong, must appeal to esthetics for aid in determining the *summum bonum*. It is the theory of self-controlled, or deliberate, conduct. Logic is the theory of self-controlled, or deliberate, thought; and as such, must appeal to ethics for its principles. It also depends upon phenomenology and upon mathematics. All thought being performed by means of signs, Logic may be regarded as the science of the general laws of signs. It has three branches: (1) *Speculative Grammar,* or the general theory of the nature and meanings of signs, whether they be icons, indices, or symbols; (2) *Critic,* which classifies arguments and determines the validity and degree of force of each kind; (3) *Methodeutic,* which studies the methods that ought to be pursued in the investigation, in the exposition, and in the application of truth. Each division depends on that which precedes it.

Metaphysics may be divided into (i) *General Metaphysics,* or Ontology; (ii) *Psychical,* or Religious, *Metaphysics,* concerned chiefly with the questions of (1) God, (2) Freedom, (3) Immortality; and (iii) *Physical Metaphysics,* which discusses the real nature of Time, Space, Laws of Nature, Matter, etc. The second and third branches appear, at present, to look upon one another with supreme contempt.

Nomological Physics is divided into (i) *Molar Physics,* Dynamics and Gravitation; (ii) *Molecular Physics,* Elaterics[5] and Thermodynamics; (iii) *Etherial Physics,* Optics and Electrics. Each division has two subdivisions. The dependence of the divisions is well marked.

Classificatory Physics seems, at present, as a matter of fact, to be divided, quite irrationally and most unequally, into (i) *Crystallography;* (ii) *Chemistry;* (iii) *Biology.*

But Crystallography is rather an offshoot from chemistry, to which it furnishes a few facts, but hardly a principle. It is highly mathematical and depends also on elaterics. Biology might be regarded (although, as a matter of fact, no such view is taken) as the chemistry of the albuminoids and of the forms they assume. It is probable that all the differences of races, individuals, and tissues are chemical, at bottom. At any rate, the possible varieties of albuminoids are amply sufficient to account for all the diversity of organic forms.

Pure Chemistry seems, at present, to consist of (1) Physical Chemistry, consisting of the old chemical physics and the modern chemical dynamics; (2) Organic Chemistry, Aliphatic and Aromatic; (3) Inorganic Chemistry, consisting of the doctrine of the elements, their atomic weights, periodicity, etc., and the doctrine of compounds.

Biology is divided into (1) Physiology, and (2) Anatomy. Physiology is closely allied to chemistry and physics. Anatomy is divided into many distinct fields, according to the nature of the forms studied.

Descriptive Physics is divided into (i) *Geognosy*, and (ii) *Astronomy*. Both have various well-known subdivisions.

Psychology is most naturally divided, according to the methods it follows, into (i) *Introspective Psychology*; (ii) *Experimental Psychology*; (iii) *Physiological Psychology*; (iv) *Child Psychology*.

This division only admits those parts of psychology which investigate the general phenomena of mind. Special psychology belongs to classificatory psychics. Both experimental and physiological psychology are dependent upon introspective psychology. But it is hard to say which of them derives most from the other. Child psychology depends on all the others. Psychology is too young a science to have any further living divisions than such as are here admitted.

Classificatory Psychics is divided into (i) *Special Psychology*, itself consisting of (1) Individual Psychology; (2) Psychical Heredity; (3) Abnormal Psychology; (4) Mob Psychology; (5) Race Psychology; (6) Animal Psychology; (ii) *Linguistics*, a vast science, divided according to the families of speech, and cross-divided into (1) Word Linguistics; (2) Grammar; and there should be a comparative science of forms of composition; (iii) *Ethnology*, divided into (1) the Ethnology of Social Developments, customs, laws, religion, and traditions; and (2) the Ethnology of Technology.

Descriptive Psychics is divided into (i) *History* proper, itself divided according to the nature of its data into (1) Monumental History, (2) Ancient History with all other History that is drawn from few and general testimonies, (3) History drawn from a wealth of documents, as Modern History, generally. History has besides two cross-divisions: the one into (1) Political History, (2) History of the Different Sciences, (3) History of Social Developments, religion, law, slavery, manners, etc.; the other according to the different parts of the world and the different peoples whose history is studied; (ii) *Biography*, which at present is rather a mass of lies than a science; (iii) *Criticism*, the study of individual works of mind, itself divided into (1) Literary Criticism, (2) Art Criticism, of which the latter is divided into many departments, as Criticism of Military Operations, Criticism of Architecture, etc.

The classification of Practical Sciences has been elaborated by the author, but will not here be touched upon.[6] No classification of the Sciences of Review has been attempted.

19

The Ethics of Terminology

MS 478. [This is the second section of the 1903 Syllabus (pp. 10–14 of the printed version), published in CP 2.219–26.] Here Peirce argues for a rational approach to scientific terminology, in particular for philosophy. He gives several compelling reasons for wanting this kind of reform, among them that good language is the essence of good thought and that there can be no scientific progress without collaboration. Philosophy finds itself in the odd situation of having to retain popular language as a re-source—part of its purpose being the study of common conceptions—while at the same time requiring a specialized vocabulary for analytical preci-sion. Peirce concludes with seven rules for instituting a scientific terminol-ogy for philosophy. He will appeal to these rules to explain his own use of neologisms.

In order that my use of terms, notations, etc., may be understood, I explain that my conscience imposes upon me the following rules. Were I to make the smallest pretension to dictate the conduct of others in this matter, I should be reproved by [the] first of these rules. Yet if I were to develop the reasons the force of which I feel myself, I presume they would have weight with others.

Those reasons would embrace, in the first place, the consideration that the woof and warp of all thought and all research is symbols, and the life of thought and science is the life inherent in symbols; so that it is wrong to say that a good language is *important* to good thought, merely; for it is of the essence of it. Next would come the consideration of the increasing value of precision of thought as it advances. Thirdly, the progress of science cannot go far except by collaboration; or, to speak more accurately, no mind can take one step without the aid of other minds. Fourthly, the health of the scientific communion requires the most absolute mental freedom. Yet the scientific and philosophical worlds are infested with pedants and pedagogues who are con-tinually endeavoring to set up a sort of magistrature over thoughts and other symbols. It thus becomes one of the first duties of one who sees what the situ-ation is, energetically to resist everything like arbitrary dictation in scientific affairs, and above all, as to the use of terms and notations. At the same time, a general agreement concerning the use of terms and of notations,—not too rigid, yet prevailing with most of the co-workers in regard to most of the sym-bols, to such a degree that there shall be some small number of different sys-tems of expression that have to be mastered,—is indispensable. Consequently, since this is not to be brought about by arbitrary dictation, it must be brought about by the power of rational principles over the conduct of men.

Now what rational principle is there which will be perfectly determinative as to what terms and notations shall be used, and in what senses, and which at the same time possesses the requisite power to influence all right-feeling and thoughtful men?

In order to find the answer to that question, it is necessary to consider, first, what would be the character of an ideal philosophical terminology and system of logical symbols; and, secondly, to inquire what the experience of those branches of science has been that have encountered and conquered great difficulties of nomenclature, etc., in regard to the principles which have proved efficacious, and in regard to unsuccessful methods of attempting to produce uniformity.

As to the ideal to be aimed at, it is, in the first place, desirable for any branch of science that it should have a vocabulary furnishing a family of cognate words for each *scientific* conception, and that each word should have a single exact meaning, unless its different meanings apply to objects of different categories that can never be mistaken for one another. To be sure, this requisite might be understood in a sense which would make it utterly impossible. For every symbol is a living thing, in a very strict sense that is no mere figure of speech. The body of the symbol changes slowly, but its meaning inevitably grows, incorporates new elements and throws off old ones. But the effort of all should be to keep the *essence* of every scientific term unchanged and exact; although absolute exactitude is not so much as conceivable. Every symbol is, in its origin, either an image of the idea signified, or a reminiscence of some individual occurrence, person, or thing, connected with its meaning, or is a metaphor. Terms of the first and third origins will inevitably be applied to different conceptions; but if the conceptions are strictly analogous in their principal suggestions, this is rather helpful than otherwise, provided always that the different meanings are remote from one another, both in themselves and in the occasions of their occurrence. Science is continually gaining new conceptions; and every new *scientific* conception should receive a new word, or better, a new family of cognate words. The duty of supplying this word naturally falls upon the person who introduces the new conception; but it is a duty not to be undertaken without a thorough knowledge of the principles and a large acquaintance with the details and history of the special terminology in which it is to take a place, nor without a sufficient comprehension of the principles of word-formation of the national language, nor without a proper study of the laws of symbols, in general. That there should be two different terms of identical scientific value may or may not be an inconvenience, according to circumstances. Different systems of expression are often of the greatest advantage.

The ideal terminology will differ somewhat for different sciences. The case of philosophy is very peculiar in that it has positive need of popular words in popular senses,—not as its own language (as it has too usually used those words), but as objects of its study. It thus has a peculiar need of a language distinct and detached from common speech, such a language as Aristotle, the scholastics, and Kant endeavored to supply, while Hegel endeavored to destroy it. It is good economy for philosophy to provide itself with a vocabulary so outlandish that loose thinkers shall not be tempted to borrow its words. Kant's adjectives "objective" and "subjective"[1] proved not to be barbarous enough, by half, long to retain their usefulness in philosophy,—even if there had been no other objection to them. The first rule of good taste in writing is to use words whose meanings will not be misunderstood; and if a reader does not know the meaning of the words, it is infinitely better that he should know he does not know it. This is particularly true in logic, which wholly consists, one might almost say, in exactitude of thought.

The sciences which have had to face the most difficult problems of terminology have unquestionably been the classificatory sciences of physics, chemistry, and biology. The nomenclature of chemistry is, on the whole, good. In their dire need, the chemists assembled in congress, and adopted certain rules for forming names of substances. Those names are well known, but they are hardly used. Why not? Because the chemists were not psychologists, and did not know that a congress is one of the most impotent of things, even less influential by far than a dictionary. The problem of the biological taxonomists has, however, been incomparably more difficult; and they have solved it (barring small exceptions) with brilliant success. How did they accomplish this? Not by appealing to the power of congresses, but by appealing to the power of the idea of right and wrong. For only make a man *really see* that a certain line of conduct is wrong, and he *will* make a strong endeavor to do the right thing,—be he thief, gambler, or even a logician or moral philosopher. The biologists simply talked to one another, and made one another see that when a man has introduced a conception into science, it naturally becomes both his privilege and his duty to assign to that conception suitable scientific expressions, and that when a name has been conferred upon a conception by him to whose labors science is indebted for that conception, it becomes the duty of all,—a duty to the discoverer, and a duty to science,—to accept his name, unless it should be of such a nature that the adoption of it would be unwholesome for science; that should the discoverer fail in his duty either by giving no name or an utterly unsuitable one, then, after a reasonable interval, whoever first has occasion to employ a name for that conception must invent a suitable one; and others ought to follow him; but that whoever deliberately uses a word or other symbol in any other sense than that which was conferred upon it by its sole rightful creator commits a shameful offense against the inventor of the symbol and against science, and it becomes the duty of the others to treat the act with contempt and indignation.

As fast as the students of any branch of philosophy educate themselves to a genuine scientific love of truth to the degree to which the scholastic doctors were moved by it, suggestions similar to those above will suggest themselves; and they will consequently form a technical terminology. In logic, a terminology more than passably good has been inherited by us from the scholastics.[2] This scholastic terminology has passed into English speech more than into any other modern tongue, rendering it the most logically exact of any. This has been accompanied by the inconvenience that a considerable number of words and phrases of scientific logic have come to be used with a laxity quite astounding. Who, for example, among the dealers in Quincy Hall[3] who talk of "articles of *prime necessity*," would be able to say what that phrase "prime necessity" strictly means? He could not have sought out a more technical phrase. There are dozens of other loose expressions of the same provenance.

Having thus given some idea of the nature of the reasons which weigh with me, I proceed to state the rules which I find to be binding upon me in this field.

First, to take pains to avoid following any recommendation of an arbitrary nature as to the use of philosophical terminology.

Second, to avoid using words and phrases of vernacular origin as technical terms of philosophy.

Third, to use the scholastic terms in their anglicized forms for philosophical conceptions, so far as they are strictly applicable; and never to use them in other than their proper senses.

Fourth, for ancient philosophical conceptions overlooked by the scholastics, to imitate, as well as I can, the ancient expression.

Fifth, for precise philosophical conceptions introduced into philosophy since the Middle Ages, to use the anglicized form of the original expression, if not positively unsuitable, but only in its precise original sense.

Sixth, for philosophical conceptions which vary by a hair's breadth from those for which suitable terms exist, to invent terms with a due regard for the usages of philosophical terminology and those of the English language, but yet with a distinctly technical appearance. Before proposing a term, notation, or other symbol, to consider maturely whether it perfectly suits the conception and will lend itself to every occasion, whether it interferes with any existing term, and whether it may not create an inconvenience by interfering with the expression of some conception that may hereafter be introduced into philosophy. Having once introduced a symbol, to consider myself almost as much bound by it as if it had been introduced by somebody else; and after others have accepted it, to consider myself more bound to it than anybody else.

Seventh, to regard it as needful to introduce new systems of expression when new connections of importance between conceptions come to be made out, or when such systems can, in any way, positively subserve the purposes of philosophical study.

20

Sundry Logical Conceptions

MS 478 [The third and longest section of the 1903 Syllabus, this text was not printed in the pamphlet for the audience. The subsection entitled "Speculative Grammar" was published in large part in CP 2.274–77, 283–84, 292–94, and 309–31.] Peirce begins here an important extension of his semiotic theory. He presents his doctrine of signs in the context of his more general theory of categories, making use of three kinds of "separation in thought": dissociation, prescission, and discrimination. He remarks that logic, in fulfilling its historical mission to distinguish good from bad reasonings, develops into a general theory of signs, and he reviews the place of logic within his classification of sciences. Peirce then takes up the first department of logic (semiotics), speculative grammar, and, on the basis of his categories, divides signs into two trichotomies: (1) icons, indices, and symbols, and (2) sumisigns (later called rhemes), dicisigns, and arguments. The second trichotomy is here given for the first time. This is followed by a sustained discussion of propositions as signs, and of how they are related to dicisigns and other semiotic constituents. Peirce concludes with a discussion of the class of signs we call "arguments" and surveys how its three types—deduction, induction, and abduction—work together to perform the operation of reasoning.

Phenomenology is that branch of science which is treated in Hegel's *Phänomenologie des Geistes* (a work far too inaccurate to be recommended to any but mature scholars, though perhaps the most profound ever written) in which the author seeks to make out what are the elements, or, if you please, the kinds of elements, that are invariably present in whatever is, in any sense, in mind. According to the present writer, these *universal categories* are three. Since all three are invariably present, a pure idea of any one, absolutely distinct from the others, is impossible; indeed, anything like a satisfactorily clear discrimination of them is a work of long and active meditation. They may be termed *Firstness, Secondness*, and *Thirdness*.

Firstness is that which is such as it is positively and regardless of anything else.

Secondness is that which is as it is in a *second* something's being as it is, regardless of any third.

Thirdness is that whose being consists in its bringing about a secondness. There is no fourthness that does not merely consist in Thirdnesses.

Of these three, Secondness is the easiest to comprehend, being the element that the rough-and-tumble of this world renders most prominent. We talk of *hard* facts. That hardness, that compulsiveness of experience, is Secondness. A door is slightly ajar. You try to open it. Something prevents. You put your shoulder against it, and experience a sense of effort and a sense of resistance. These are not two forms of consciousness; they are two aspects of one two-sided consciousness. It is inconceivable that there should be any effort without resistance, or any resistance without a contrary effort. This double-sided consciousness is Secondness. All consciousness, all being awake, consists in a sense of reaction between *ego* and *non-ego*, although the sense of effort be absent. It is a peculiarity of Secondness that in whatever field it presents itself there are two forms in which it may present itself; and these two forms differ in the Secondness being more thoroughly genuine in the one than in the other. Thus, reaction with a sense of striving, which we regard as brought on by ourselves, is volition. The Secondness there is strong. But in perception there is a sense of reaction without striving, which we think of as belonging to the outward thing. It is, as we may say, a *degenerate** form of Secondness. The idea of Secondness seems here to be unnecessarily imported into the phenomenon, which might have been regarded as a mere dream, or rather as the quality of our being, without being materially different, except in the absence of the element of Secondness. Secondness cannot be thus eliminated from the phenomenon of volition. So both volition and perception can be exercised upon our own consciousness, giving rise to the conception [of] an Internal world,—which is nothing but consciousness with a Secondness imported into it,—and an External world. We not only thus experience Secondness, but we attribute it to outward things; which we regard as so many individual objects, or quasi-selves, reacting on one another. Secondness only is while it actually is. The same thing can never happen twice. As Heraclitus said, one cannot cross the same river twice: ποταμῷ γὰρ οὐκ ἔστιν ἐμβῆναι δὶς τῷ αὐτῷ.[†1]

For an example of Firstness, look at anything red. That redness is positively what it is. Contrast may heighten our consciousness of it; but the redness is not relative to anything; it is absolute, or positive. If one imagines or remembers red, his imagination will be either vivid or dim; but that will not, in the least, affect the quality of the redness, which may be brilliant or dull, in either case. The vividness is the degree of our consciousness of it, its reaction on us. The quality in itself has no vividness or dimness. In itself, then, it cannot be consciousness. It is, indeed, in itself, a mere possibility. Now consciousness is either awake (more or less) or it has no being at all. Possibility,

---

*This term is borrowed from the geometers, who speak of a pair of complanar rays as a "degenerate conic." That is, the idea of their being a conic is unnecessarily imported. [See illustration, p. 545.]

†These cannot be the very words of Heraclitus. But I have taken one of the more epigrammatic of half a dozen versions. The one most likely to be the correct quotation is too tame.

the mode of being of Firstness, is the embryo of being. It is not nothing. It is not existence. We not only have an immediate acquaintance with Firstness in the qualities of feelings and sensations, but we attribute it to outward things. We think that a piece of iron has a quality in it that a piece of brass has not, which *consists* in the steadily continuing *possibility* of its being attracted by a magnet. In fact, it seems undeniable that there really are such possibilities, and that, though they are not existences, they are not *nothing*. They are possibilities, and nothing more. But whether this be admitted or not, it is undeniable that such elements are in the objects as we commonly conceive them; and that is all that concerns phenomenology. Firstness is too simple to have any degenerate form.

Thirdness is found wherever one thing brings about a Secondness between two things. In all such cases, it will be found that Thought plays a part. By thought is meant something like the meaning of a word, which may be "embodied in," that is, may govern, this or that, but is not confined to any existent. Thought is often supposed to be something in consciousness; but on the contrary, it is impossible ever actually to be directly conscious of thought. It is something to which consciousness will conform, as a writing may conform to it. Thought is rather of the nature of a habit, which determines the suchness of that which may come into existence, when it does come into existence. Of such a habit one may be conscious of a symptom; but to speak of being directly conscious of a habit, as such, is nonsense. In a still fuller sense, Thirdness consists in the formation of a habit. In any succession of events that have occurred there must be some kind of regularity. Nay, there must be regularities strictly exceeding all multitude. But as soon as time adds another event to the series, a great part of those regularities will be broken, and soon indefinitely. If, however, there be a regularity that never will be and never would be broken, that has a mode of being consisting in this destiny or determination of the nature of things that the endless future shall conform to it, that is what we call a *law*. Whether any such law be discoverable or not, it is certain we have the idea of such a thing, and should there be such a *law*, it would evidently have a *reality*, *consisting in* the fact that predictions based on it would be borne out by actual events. Nobody can doubt that we know laws upon which we can base predictions to which actual events still in the womb of the future will conform to a marked extent, if not perfectly. To deny reality to such laws is to quibble about words. Many philosophers say they are "mere symbols." Take away the word *mere*, and this is true. They are symbols; and symbols being the only things in the universe that have any importance, the word "mere" is a great impertinence. In short, wherever there is thought there is Thirdness. It is genuine Thirdness that gives thought its characteristic, although Thirdness consists in nothing but one thing's bringing two into a Secondness. In whatever field we find Thirdness, we find it occurring in three forms, whereof two are related to one another somewhat as the degenerate and genuine forms of Secondness, while the third has a living character that the others want.

In order to understand logic, it is necessary to get as clear notions as possible of these three categories and to gain the ability to recognize them in the different conceptions with which logic deals. Although all three are ubiquitous, yet certain kinds of separations may be effected upon them. There are three distinct kinds of separation in thought. They correspond to the three categories. Separation of Firstness, or Primal Separation, called *Dissociation*, consists in imagining one of the two separands without the other. It may be complete or incomplete. Separation of Secondness, or Secundal Separation, called *Precission*,* consists in supposing a state of things in which one element is present without the other, the one being logically possible without the other.[2] Thus, we cannot imagine a sensuous quality without some degree of vividness. But we usually *suppose* that redness, as it is in red things, has no vividness; and it would certainly be impossible to demonstrate that everything red must have a degree of vividness. Separation of Thirdness, or Tertial Separation, called *discrimination*, consists in representing one of the two separands without representing the other. If A can be prescinded from, i.e. supposed without, B, then B can, at least, be discriminated from A.

Further distinctions have to be drawn between the modes of separation in thought, that were not noticed in the writer's paper of 1867.[3] We have, for example, to distinguish between *definite* and *indefinite precission*. For example, Berkeley says that is impossible to suppose a thing (other than a mind) to exist without being known;[4] which is as much as to say that Secondness cannot be prescinded from Thirdness. That is, to speak of existence that never manifests itself in any way, is meaningless. No doubt, he is right, as regards any definite meaning. But if we abstain from attempting to attach any definite idea to existence, there will be nothing inconsistent in the supposition of things acting on one another without any predetermined law whatever. Distinctions might also be drawn between different modes of discrimination.

It is possible to prescind Firstness from Secondness. We can suppose a being whose whole life consists in one unvarying feeling of redness. But it is impossible to prescind Secondness from Firstness. For to suppose two things is to suppose two units; and however colorless and indefinite an object may be, it is something, and therein has Firstness, even if it has nothing recognizable as a quality. Everything must have some non-relative element; and this is its Firstness. So likewise it is possible to prescind Secondness from Thirdness. But Thirdness without Secondness would be absurd.

Among the familiar ideas of logic in which the element of Secondness is predominant, may be mentioned, in the first place, the conception of a *fact*. The easiest definition of a Fact is that it is an abstract element of the real,

---

*It is usually called "abstraction," but since the other name for it, "precission" or "precision," is in good use, while the term "abstraction" is indispensable for another purpose, that of designating the passage from "good" to "goodness," and the like, it is better to restrict it to meaning either this act or its result. Precission may be termed "precisive abstraction," but that phrase is needlessly long.

corresponding to a proposition. But this needlessly introduces the element of Thirdness. It is true the Reality cannot be dissociated from Thirdness; but it can be prescinded from it. For Reality is simply the character of being independent of what is thought concerning the real object; so that Thirdness only enters into it negatively. A Fact may be defined as the Secondness which consists between anything and a possibility, or Firstness, realized in that thing. It may be thought that Possibility involves Thirdness, because the Possible is sometimes defined as that which is not known to be false in some state of information. But, however convenient and unobjectionable that formula may sometimes be, it is an extremely faulty definition. A Possibility and a Firstness are pretty nearly identical. A *mere* possibility is Firstness without Secondness. It may be the Firstness of a Secondness; for Secondness has, in a sense, its Firstness. Another conception in which Secondness is predominant is that of Existence, which is simply the idea of the most genuine Secondness without limitation. Individuality is another conception in which Secondness is the more prominent element, although Firstness, of course, is a constituent of it. It is the Firstness of a most genuine Second.* Compulsion is almost pure Secondness, with just enough Firstness to give it color. One could invent a phrase that would pretty nearly describe it; but it is doubtful whether it ought to be called an analysis of it. On the other hand, *Necessity* is an idea of Thirdness. This word is equivocal: it is here taken in the sense of rational, i.e., general, necessity. It is not a mere denial of Possibility. For Possibility, in the sense of Firstness, is not a subject of denial. The absence of any given possibility is, of course, a possibility; but to leave a character standing and remove from it its possibility is nonsense, unless one means to speak of a representamen of the quality, in which case the element of Thirdness is the predominant one. The idea of Futurity, meaning what affirmatively *will* be, is a conception of Thirdness, for it involves the idea of *certainty*, and certainty is *knowledge*, and knowledge is *representation*. But the idea of what *may* in the future be, is a singular mixture in which possibility seems to predominate. If we discriminate Futurity from certainty and uncertainty the result seems to have no logical interest. That such ideas as those of Law, of Purpose, of Thought, have Thirdness as their dominant element is too evident to be dwelt upon. It is better worth while to remark upon the conception of Life, that Thirdness essentially involves the production of effects in the world of existence;—not by furnishing energy, but by the gradual development of Laws. For it can be said, without dispute, that no sign ever acts as such without producing a physical replica or interpretant sign.

---

*The conceptions of a *First*, improperly called an "object," and of a *Second* should be carefully distinguished from those of Firstness or Secondness, both of which are involved in the conceptions of First and Second. A First is something to which (or, more accurately, to some substitute for which, thus introducing Thirdness) attention may be directed. It thus involves Secondness as well as Firstness; while a Second is a First *considered as* (here comes Thirdness) a subject of a Secondness. An *object* in the proper sense is a Second.

In the ideas of Firstness, Secondness, and Thirdness, the three elements, or *Universal Categories*, appear under their forms of Firstness. They appear under their forms of Secondness in the ideas of Facts of Firstness, or *Qualia*, Facts of Secondness, or Relations, and Facts of Thirdness, or Signs; and under their forms of Thirdness in the ideas of Signs of Firstness, or Feeling, i.e., things of beauty; Signs of Secondness, or Action, i.e., modes of conduct; and Signs of Thirdness, or Thought, i.e., forms of thought.

Phenomenology studies the Categories in their forms of Firstness. It ought to be followed by a science which should study them in a general way as they present themselves throughout common experience. This seems to be approximately, though not exactly, what Hegel intended in his *Encyclopädie*. This study may be termed, in advance of any serious undertaking of it, *Encyclopedeutics*. Then, and only then, should succeed the *Normative Sciences*. This is the received name; but it is not accurately descriptive. It implies that these sciences have, as their only principal end, the general distinction of the *good* and *bad* (ideas in which Secondness and Thirdness are about equally prominent). But this exaggerates the place occupied by these ideas in these sciences, which is a very eminent place in Ethics, but is less so in Logic, and ought to be quite subordinate in Esthetics, since no form is esthetically bad, if regarded from the strictly esthetical point of view, without any idea of adopting the form in conduct. All esthetic disgust is due to defective insight and narrowness of sympathy. The true principal purpose of these sciences is the Classification of possible forms. But this must be founded on a study of the Physiology of those forms, their general elements, parts, and mode of action. Thereupon should follow the Classificatory part, including the general discussion of what is good and what bad; and this should be followed up by a study of the principles that govern the production of such forms.

Ethics must appeal to Esthetics in forming its conception of the *summmum bonum;* and Logic, as the science of controlled thought, which is but a species of controlled conduct, must rest upon the science of such conduct. A Logic which does not recognize its relations to Ethics must be fatally unsound in its Methodeutic, if not in its Critic.

Logic, which began historically, and in each individual still begins, with the wish to distinguish good and bad reasonings, develops into a general theory of signs. Its three departments are the physiological, or *Speculative Grammar;* its classificatory part, judging particularly what reasoning is good and what bad, or *Logical Critic;* and finally, *Methodeutic,* or the principles of the production of valuable courses of research and exposition.

In this syllabus, only Speculative Grammar will be touched upon.

Speculative Grammar

A *Sign,* or *Representamen,* is a First which stands in such a genuine triadic relation to a Second, called its *Object,* as to be capable of determining a Third, called its *Interpretant,* to assume the same triadic relation to its Object in which it stands itself to the same Object. The triadic relation is *genuine*, that is, its three members are bound together by it in a way that does not consist in any complexus of dyadic relations. That is the reason that the Interpretant, or Third, cannot stand in a mere dyadic relation to the Object, but must stand in such a relation to it as the Representamen itself does. Nor can the triadic relation in which the Third stands be merely similar to that in which the First stands, for this would make the relation of the Third to the First a degenerate Secondness merely. The Third must, indeed, stand in such a relation, and thus must be capable of determining a Third of its own; but besides that, it must have a second triadic relation in which the Representamen, or rather the relation thereof to its Object, shall be its own (the Third's) Object, and must be capable of determining a Third to this relation. All this must equally be true of the Third's Thirds and so on endlessly; and this, and more, is involved in the familiar idea of a Sign; and as the term Representamen is here used, nothing more is implied. A *Sign* is a Representamen with a mental Interpretant. Possibly there may be Representamens that are not Signs. Thus, if a sunflower, in turning towards the sun, becomes by that very act fully capable, without further condition, of reproducing a sunflower which turns in precisely corresponding ways toward the sun, and of doing so with the same reproductive power, the sunflower would become a Representamen of the sun. But *thought* is the chief, if not the only, mode of representation.

Representamens are divided by two trichotomies.[5] The first and most fundamental is that any Representamen is either an *Icon*, an *Index*, or a *Symbol*. Namely, while no Representamen actually functions as such until it actually determines an Interpretant, yet it becomes a Representamen as soon as it is fully capable of doing this; and its Representative Quality is not necessarily dependent upon its ever actually determining an Interpretant, nor even upon its actually having an Object.

An *Icon* is a Representamen whose Representative Quality is a Firstness of it as a First. That is, a quality that it has *qua* thing renders it fit to be a Representamen. Thus, anything is fit to be a *substitute* for anything that it is like. (The conception of "substitute" involves that of a purpose, and thus of genuine Thirdness.) Whether there are other kinds of substitutes or not we shall see. A Representamen by Firstness alone can only have a similar Object. Thus, a sign by contrast denotes its object only by virtue of a contrast, or Secondness, between two qualities. A sign by Firstness is an image of its object and, more strictly speaking, can only be an *idea*. For it must produce an Interpretant idea; and an external object excites an idea by a reaction upon the brain. But most strictly speaking, even an idea, except in the sense of a possibility, or Firstness, cannot be an Icon. A possibility alone is an Icon purely by virtue of its quality; and its object can only be a Firstness. But a sign may be *iconic*, that is, may represent its object mainly by its similarity, no matter what its mode of being. If a substantive be wanted, an iconic Representamen may be termed a *hypoicon*. Any material image, as a painting, is largely conventional in its mode of representation; but in itself, without legend or label, it may be called a *hypoicon*. Hypoicons may roughly *[be]* divided according to the mode of Firstness which they partake. Those which partake the simple qualities, or First Firstnesses, are *images;* those which represent the relations, mainly dyadic, or so regarded, of the parts of one thing by analogous relations in their own parts, are *diagrams;* those which represent the representative character of a representamen by representing a parallelism in something else, are *metaphors.*

An *Index,* or *Seme (σῆμα),* is a Representamen whose Representative character consists in its being an individual Second.[6] If the Secondness is an existential relation, the Index is *genuine.* If the Secondness is a reference, the Index is *degenerate.* A genuine Index and its Object must be existent individuals (whether things or facts), and its immediate Interpretant must be of the same character. But since every individual must have characters, it follows that a genuine Index may contain a Firstness, and so an Icon, as a constituent part of it. Any individual is a degenerate Index of its own characters. Examples of Indices are the hand of a clock, and the veering of a weathercock. *Subindices* or *hyposemes* are signs which are rendered such principally by an actual connection with their objects. Thus, a proper name, *[a]* personal, demonstrative, or relative pronoun, or a letter attached to a diagram, denotes what it does owing to a real connection with its object, but none of these is an Index, since it is not an individual.

A *Symbol* is a Representamen whose Representative character consists precisely in its being a rule that will determine its Interpretant. All words, sentences, books, and other conventional signs are Symbols. We speak of writing or pronouncing the word "man"; but it is only a *replica,* or embodiment of the word, that is pronounced or written. The word itself has no existence, although it has a real being, *consisting in* the fact that existents *will* conform to it. It is a general mode of succession of three sounds or representamens of sounds, which becomes a sign only in the fact that a habit, or acquired law, will cause replicas of it to be interpreted as meaning a man or men. The word and its meaning are both general rules; but the word alone of the two prescribes the qualities of its replicas in themselves. Otherwise the "word" and its "meaning" do not differ, unless some special sense be attached to "meaning."

A Symbol is a law, or regularity of the indefinite future. Its Interpretant must be of the same description; and so must be also its complete immediate Object, or meaning.* But a law necessarily governs, or "is embodied in" individuals, and prescribes some of their qualities. Consequently, a constituent of a Symbol may be an Index, and a constituent may be an Icon. A man walking

---

*There are two ways in which a Symbol may have a real existential thing as its real Object. First, the thing may conform to it, whether accidentally or by virtue of the Symbol having the virtue of a growing habit; and secondly, by the Symbol having an Index as a part of itself. But the immediate Object of a Symbol can only be a Symbol, and if it has in its own nature another kind of object, this must be by an *endless series.*

with a child points his arm up into the air and says "There is a balloon." The pointing arm is an essential part of the Symbol without which the latter would convey no information. But if the child asks, "What is a balloon?" and the man replies, "It is something like a great big soap bubble," he makes the image a part of the Symbol. Thus, while the complete Object of a Symbol, that is to say, its meaning, is of the nature of a law, it must *denote* an individual, and must *signify* a character. A *genuine* Symbol is a Symbol that has a general meaning. There are two kinds of degenerate Symbols, the *Singular Symbol* whose Object is an existent individual, and which signifies only such characters as that individual may realize; and the *Abstract Symbol,* whose only Object is a character.

Although the immediate Interpretant of an Index must be an Index, yet since its Object may be the Object of a Singular Symbol, the Index may have such a Symbol for its indirect Interpretant. Even a genuine Symbol may be an imperfect Interpretant of it. So an *Icon* may have a degenerate Index, or an Abstract Symbol, for an indirect Interpretant, and a genuine Index or Symbol for an imperfect Interpretant.

The second trichotomy of representamens[7] is [divided] into: first, simple signs, substitutive signs, or *Sumisigns;* second, double signs, informational signs, quasi-propositions, or *Dicisigns;* third, triple signs, rationally persuasive signs, *arguments,* or *Suadisigns.*

Of these three classes, the one whose nature is, by all odds, the easiest to comprehend, is the second, that of quasi-propositions, despite the fact that the question of the essential nature of the "judgment" is today quite the most vexed of all questions of logic. The truth is that *all* these classes are of very intricate natures; but the problem of the day is needlessly complicated by the attention of most logicians, instead of extending to propositions in general, being confined to "judgments," or acts of mental acceptance of propositions, which not only involve characters additional to those of propositions in general,—characters required to differentiate them as propositions of a particular kind,—but which further involve, beside the mental proposition itself, the peculiar act of assent. The problem is difficult enough, when we merely seek to analyze the essential nature of the *Dicisign,* in general, that is, the kind of sign that *conveys* information, in contradistinction to a sign from which information may be derived.*

The readiest characteristic test showing whether a sign is a Dicisign or not, is that a Dicisign is either true or false, but does not directly furnish reasons for its being so. This shows that a Dicisign must profess to refer or relate to something as having a real being independently of the representation of it as such, and further that this reference or relation must not be shown as rational, but must appear as a blind Secondness. But the only kind of sign whose

---

*To explain the judgment in terms of the "proposition" is to explain it by that which is essentially intelligible. To explain the proposition in terms of the "judgment" is to explain the self-intelligible in terms of a psychical act, which is the most obscure of phenomena or facts.

Object is necessarily existent is the genuine Index. This Index might, indeed, be a part of a Symbol; but in that case the relation would appear as rational. Consequently a Dicisign necessarily represents itself to be a genuine Index, and to be nothing more. At this point let us discard all other considerations, and see what sort of a sign a sign must be that in any way represents itself to be a genuine Index of its Object, and nothing more. Substituting for "represents____to be" a clearer interpretation, the statement is that the Dicisign's Interpretant represents an identity of the Dicisign with a genuine Index of the Dicisign's real Object. That is, the Interpretant represents a real existential relation, or genuine Secondness, as subsisting between the Dicisign and its real Object. But the Interpretant of a Sign can represent no other Object than that of the Sign itself. Hence, this same existential relation must be an Object of the Dicisign, if the latter have any real Object. This represented existential relation, in being an Object of the Dicisign, makes that real Object which is the correlate of this relation also an Object of the Dicisign. This latter Object may be distinguished as the *Primary Object*, the other being termed the *Secondary Object*. The Dicisign, in so far as it is the relate of the existential relation which is the Secondary Object of the Dicisign, can evidently not be the entire Dicisign. It is at once a part of the Object and a part of the Interpretant of the Dicisign. Since the Dicisign is represented in its Interpretant to be an Index of a complexus as such, it must be represented in that same Interpretant to be composed of two parts, corresponding respectively to its Object and to itself. That is to say, in order to understand the Dicisign, it must be regarded as composed of two such parts whether it be in itself so composed or not. It is difficult to see how this can be, unless it really have two such parts; but perhaps this may be possible. Let us consider these two represented parts separately. The part which is represented to represent the Primary Object, since the Dicisign is represented to be an Index of its Object, must be represented as an Index, or some Representamen of an Index, of the Primary Object. The part which is represented to represent a part of the Dicisign, is represented as at once part of the Interpretant and part of the Object. It must, therefore, be represented as such a sort of Representamen (or to represent such a sort) as can have its Object and its Interpretant the same. Now, a *Symbol* cannot even have itself as its Object; for it is a law governing its Object. For example, if I say "This proposition conveys information about itself," or "Let the term *'sphinx'* be a general term to denote any thing of the nature of a symbol that is applicable to every 'sphinx' and to nothing else," I shall talk unadulterated nonsense. But a Representamen mediates between its Interpretant and its Object, and that which cannot be the Object of the Representamen cannot be the Object of the Interpretant. Hence, *a fortiori*, it is impossible that a Symbol should have its Object as its Interpretant. An *Index* can very well represent itself. Thus, every number has a double; and thus the entire collection of even numbers is an Index of the entire collection of numbers, and so this collection of even numbers contains an Index of itself. But it is impossible for an Index to be its own Interpretant, since an Index is nothing but an individual existence in a Secondness with something; and it only becomes an Index by being capable of being represented by some Representamen as being in that relation. Could this Interpretant be itself, there would be no difference between an Index and a Second. An *Icon*, however, is strictly a possibility, involving a possibility, and thus the possibility of its being represented as a possibility is the possibility of the involved possibility. In this kind of Representamen alone, then, the Interpretant may be the Object. Consequently, that constituent of the Dicisign which is represented in the Interpretant as being a part of the Object, must be represented by an Icon or by a Representamen of an Icon. The Dicisign, as it must be understood in order to be understood at all, must contain those two parts. But the Dicisign is represented to be an Index of the Object, in that the latter involves something corresponding to these parts; and it is this Secondness that the Dicisign is represented to be the Index of. Hence the Dicisign must exhibit a connection between these parts of itself, and must represent this connection to correspond to a connection in the Object between the Secundal Primary Object and Firstness indicated by the part corresponding to the Dicisign.

We conclude, then, that, if we have succeeded in threading our way through the maze of these abstractions, a Dicisign, defined as a Representamen whose Interpretant represents it as an Index of its Object, must have the following characters.

First, it must, in order to be understood, be considered as containing two parts. Of these, the one, which may be called the *Subject*, is or represents an Index of a Second existing independently of its being represented, while the other, which may be called the *Predicate*, is or represents an Icon of a Firstness.

Second, these two parts must be represented as connected; and that in such a way that if the Dicisign has any Object, it must be an Index of a Secondness subsisting between the real Object represented in one represented part of the Dicisign to be indicated, and a Firstness represented in the other represented part of the Dicisign to be iconized.

Let us now examine whether these conclusions, together with the assumption from which they proceed, hold good of all signs which profess to convey information without furnishing any rational persuasion of it; and whether they fail alike for all signs which do not convey information as well as for all those which furnish evidence of the truth of their information, or reasons for believing it. If our analysis sustains these tests, we may infer that the definition of the Dicisign on which they are founded, holding, at least, within the sphere of signs, is presumably sound beyond that sphere.

Our definition forbids an Icon to be a Dicisign, since the proper Interpretant of an Icon cannot represent it to be an Index, the Index being essentially more complicated than the Icon. There ought, therefore, to be no informational signs among Icons. We find that, in fact, icons may be of the greatest service in obtaining information,—in geometry, for example;—but still, it is true that an Icon cannot, of itself, convey information, since its Object is whatever there may be which is like the Icon, and is its Object in the measure in which it is like the Icon. All propositions are informational Symbols. Our conclusions do not prevent Dicisigns from being Symbols; but let us begin by examining whether or not our definition and conclusions apply to ordinary propositions. To fix our ideas, let us set down the proposition "Tully has a wart on his nose." That is a proposition, whether it be true or not, whether anybody asserts it or not, and whether anybody assents to it or not. For an act of assertion supposes that, a proposition being formulated, a person performs an act which renders him liable to the penalties of the social law (or, at any rate, those of the moral law) in case it should not be true, unless he has a definite and sufficient excuse; and an act of assent is an act of the mind by which one endeavors to impress the meaning of the proposition upon his disposition, so that it shall govern his conduct, including thought under conduct, this habit being ready to be broken in case reasons should appear for breaking it. Now in performing either of these acts, the proposition is recognized as being a proposition whether the act be performed or not. Nor can a sound objection be grounded on the fact that a proposition is always understood as something that *might be* assented to and asserted.* For our definition of the Dicisign more than recognizes the truth of that in stating that (supposing the proposition to be a Dicisign) the Interpretant of it (that is, the mental representation, or thought, which it tends to determine) represents the proposition to be a genuine Index of a real Object, independent of the representation. For an Index involves the existence of its Object. The definition adds that this Object is a Secondness, or real Fact. That this is true of ordinary "ampliative" propositions, namely, that what they mean to represent is a fact, is beyond question. But as regards explicative propositions, and especially definitions, it may be doubted. If a definition is to be understood as introducing the definitum, so that it means "Let so and so,—the definitum,—mean so and so,—the definition," then it is a proposition in the imperative mood, and consequently, not a proposition; for a proposition is equivalent to a sentence in the indicative mood. The definition is thus only a proposition if the definitum be already known to the interpreter. But in that case it clearly conveys information as to the character of this definitum, which is matter of fact. But take an "analytical," i.e., an explicative, proposition; and to begin with, take the formula "*A* is *A*." If this be intended to state anything about real things, it is quite unintelligible. It must be understood to mean something about symbols; no doubt, that the substantive verb "is" expresses one of those relations that everything bears to itself, like "loves whatever may be loved by." So understood, it conveys information about a symbol. A symbol is not an individual, it

---

*But if anybody prefers a form of analysis which gives more prominence to the unquestionable fact that a proposition is something capable of being assented to and asserted, it is not my intention to make any objection to that. I do not think my analysis does put quite the emphasis on that that it justly might.

is true. But any information about a symbol is information about every replica of it; and a replica is strictly an individual. What information, then, does the proposition "*A* is *A*" furnish concerning this replica? The information is that if the replica be modified so as to bring the same name before it and after it, then the result will be a replica of a proposition which will never be in conflict with any fact. To say that something *never* will be is not to state any real fact; and until some experience occurs,—whether outward experience, or experience of fancies,—which might be an occasion for a conflict with the proposition in question, it does not, to our knowledge, represent any actual Secondness. But as soon as such an occasion does arise, the proposition relates to the single replica that then occurs and to the single experience, and describes the relation between them. Similar remarks apply to every explicative proposition. The proposition "Every phoenix, in rising from its ashes, sings 'Yankee Doodle,'" will be, we may be confident, not in conflict with any experience. If so, it is perfectly true. "Every four-sided triangle is deep blue," is necessarily true, since it is impossible that any experience should conflict with it. But both propositions are meaningless. Equally meaningless is any explicative proposition that is true, unless it be regarded as a proposition about a certain kind of symbol of which a replica actually occurs. If "Man is a biped" be allowed to be an explicative proposition, it means nothing unless there be an occasion in which the name "man" may be applied. If there be such an occasion, in regard to that existential individual event it is said that the term "biped" may be applied to it. That is, on an occasion on which the word "biped" is applied, the result will never be in conflict with any experience, real or imaginary. Thus, every kind of proposition is either meaningless or has a real Secondness as its object. This is a fact that every reader of philosophy should constantly bear in mind, translating every abstractly expressed proposition into its precise meaning in reference to an individual experience. The system of Existential Graphs, which is capable of expressing every proposition as analytically as may be desired, expresses an assertion by actually attaching an individual replica to the individual sheet; and such possible attachment is precisely what the Interpretant of a proposition represents before the proposition is asserted.

Let us now proceed to compare the conclusions from the abstract definition of a Dicisign with the facts about propositions. The first conclusion is that every proposition contains a *Subject* and a *Predicate*, the former representing (or being) an Index of the Primary Object, or Correlate of the relation represented, the latter representing (or being) an Icon of the Dicisign in some respect. Before inquiring whether every proposition has such parts, let us see whether the descriptions given of them are accurate, when there are such parts. The proposition "Cain kills Abel" has two subjects "Cain" and "Abel" and relates as much to the real Object of one of these as to that of the other. But it may be regarded as primarily relating to the Dyad composed of Cain, as first, and of Abel, as second member. This Pair is a single individual object having this relation to Cain and to Abel, that its existence *consists* in the existence of Cain and in the existence of Abel and in nothing more. The Pair, though its existence thus depends on Cain's existence and on Abel's, is, nevertheless, just as truly existent as they severally are. The *Dyad* is not precisely the Pair. The Dyad is a mental diagram consisting of two images of two objects, one existentially connected with one member of the Pair, the other with the other; the one having attached to it, as representing it, a Symbol whose meaning is "First," and the other a Symbol whose meaning is "Second." Thus, this diagram, the Dyad, represents Indices of Cain and Abel, respectively; and thus the Subject conforms to our conclusion. Next consider the Subject of this proposition, "Every man is the son of two parents." This supposes a mental diagram of a pair labelled "First" and "Second," as before (or rather by symbols equivalent to these for the special purpose), but instead of the two units of the diagram being directly considered as Indices of two existent individuals, the Interpretant of the diagram represents that if the interpreter of the whole proposition by an act of the mind actually attaches one of the units of the diagram to any individual man, there will be an existent relation attaching the other unit to a certain pair of individuals of which if the interpreter of the whole proposition attaches one of them specially to that unit, then the predicate will be true of that individual dyad in the order of its members.[8] Of course, it is not meant that the person who sufficiently understands the diagram actually goes through this elaborate process of thought, but only that this is substantially what has to be done, completely and accurately to understand the proposition. The graph of the proposition will afford help in seeing that this is so. Here, as before, the Subject represents the individual dyad, of which the proposition is the Symbol, to be represented by an Index. If the proposition has an abstract subject, as "Redness" or "Justice," it may either be treated, after the style of the scholastics, as an *exponible*, that is, as a proposition whose real construction is disguised by a grammatical trope,[9] or, if this does not afford the true interpretation, the proposition discourses of a universe comprising one replica each of a collection of possible symbols, somewhat indefinite, but embracing all that need be considered. We cannot say "all that are pertinent," since no collection could exhaust the possible pertinent symbols. In the case of a *conditional* proposition,[*] "If it freezes tonight, your roses will be killed," the meaning is that any replica of the proposition "It will freeze tonight" which may be true, coexists with a true replica of the proposition "your roses will be killed." This involves a representation of an Index just as much as does the subject of the proposition "Every rose will be

---

[*]*Conditional* is the right appellation, and not *hypothetical*, if the rules of the author's "Ethics of Philosophical Terminology" are to be followed. The meaning of ὑποθετικός was quite unsettled with the Greeks; but the word seems ultimately to have come to be applied to any compound proposition; and so Appuleius, under Nero, uses the translation *conditionalis*; saying, "Propositionum igitur, perinde ut ipsarum conclusionum, duae species sunt: altera praedicativa, quae etiam simplex est; ut si dicamus, *Qui regnat, beatus est*: altera substitutiva, vel conditionalis, quae etiam composita est; ut si aias: *qui regnat, si sapit, beatus est*. Substituis enim conditionem, qua, nisi sapiens est, not sit beatus."[10] But as early as Boëthius and Cassiodorus, that is, about A.D.

killed." Passing now to the consideration of the Predicate, it is plain enough that the last proposition, or any at all like it, only conveys its signification by exciting in the mind some image or, as it were, a composite photograph of images, like the Firstness meant. This, however, does not squarely meet the question, which is not what our mental constitution causes to happen, but how the predicate represents the Firstness that it signifies.* The predicate is necessarily an Iconic *Sumisign* (which is not always true of the subject) and as such, as we should find by a full analysis of the Sumisign, essentially signifies what it does by representing itself to represent an Icon of it. Without an analysis of the Sumisign this point must remain a little obscure.

We next come to the question whether every proposition has a Subject and a Predicate. It has been shown above that this is true of a Conditional; and it is easily seen that it is equally so of any Disjunctive. Only, an ordinary Disjunctive has such a construction that one mode of analysis of it is as good as another. That is, to say "Either *A* or *B* is true" may equally be regarded as saying "A replica of a symbol is true which is not true if no replica of *A* is true and no replica of *B* is true" or as saying "If a replica of *A* is not true, a replica of *B* is true" or as saying "If a replica of *B* is not true, a replica of *A* is true." These come to the same thing, just as "Some *X* is *Y*," "Some *Y* is *X*," and "Something is both *X* and *Y*" come to the same thing. The most perfectly thorough analysis throws the whole substance of the Dicisign into the Predicate. A copulative proposition even more obviously has a Subject and Predicate. It predicates the genuinely triadic relation of *tri-coexistence*, "*P* and *Q* and *R* coexist." For to say that both *A* and *B* is true is to say that something exists which *tri-coexists* with true replicas of *A* and *B*. Some logical writers are so remarkably biased or dense as to adduce the Latin sentences *fulget* and *lucet* as propositions without any subject.[13] But who cannot see that these words convey no information at all without a reference (which will usually be Indexical, the Index being the common environment of the interlocutors)

500, it was settled that *hypothetica* applies to any compound proposition, and *conditionalis* to a proposition asserting one thing only in case a condition set forth in a separate clause be fulfilled. This was the universally accepted use of the terms throughout the Middle Ages. Therefore, *hypotheticals* should have been divided into *disjunctives* and *copulatives*. They were usually divided into conditionals, disjunctives, and copulatives. But conditionals are really only a special kind of *disjunctives*. To say, "If it freezes tonight, your roses will be killed" is the same as to say, "It either will not freeze, or your roses will tonight be killed." A disjunctive does not exclude the truth of both alternatives, at once.

*Mill's term *connote* is not very accurate. *Connote* properly means to denote along with in a secondary way. Thus, "killer" connotes a living thing killed. When the scholastics said that an adjective *connoted*, they meant it connoted the abstraction named by the corresponding abstract noun. But the ordinary case of an adjective involves no reference to any abstraction. The word *signify* has been the regular technical term since the twelfth century, when John of Salisbury (*Metalogicus*, II, xx) spoke of "quod fere in omnium ore celebre est, aliud scilicet esse quod appellativa [i.e., adjectives] *significant*, et aliud esse quod *nominant*. Nominantur singularia [i.e., existent individual things and facts], sed universalia [i.e., Firstnesses] significantur."[11] See the author's paper of November 13, 1867, in the *Proceedings of the American Academy of Arts and Sciences*,[12] to which he might now add a multitude of instances in support of what is here said concerning *connote* and *signify*.

to the circumstances under which the Firstnesses they signify are asserted to take place?

Finally, our conclusions require that the proposition should have an actual *Syntax*, which is represented to be the Index of those elements of the fact represented that correspond to the Subject and Predicate. This is apparent in all propositions. Since Abelard it has been usual to make this Syntax a third part of the proposition, under the name of the Copula. The historical cause of the emergence of this conception in the twelfth century was, of course, that the Latin of that day did not permit the omission of the verb *est*, which was familiarly, though not invariably, omitted in Greek, and not very uncommonly in classical Latin. In most languages there is no such verb. But it is plain that one does not escape the need of a Syntax by regarding the Copula as a third part of the proposition; and it is simpler to say that it is merely the accidental form that Syntax may take.

It has thus been sufficiently shown that all propositions conform to the definition of the Dicisign and to the corollaries drawn from that definition. A proposition is, in short, a Dicisign that is a Symbol. But an Index, likewise, may be a Dicisign. A man's portrait with a man's name written under it is strictly a proposition, although its syntax is not that of speech, and although the portrait itself not only represents, but is a Hypoicon. But the proper name so nearly approximates to the nature of an Index, that this might suffice to give an idea of an informational Index. A better example is a photograph. The mere print does not, in itself, convey any information. But the fact that it is virtually a section of rays projected from an object *otherwise known*, renders it a *Dicisign*. Every Dicisign, as the system of Existential Graphs fully recognizes, is a further determination of an already known sign of the same object. It is not, perhaps, sufficiently brought out in the present analysis. It will be remarked that this connection of the print, which is the quasi-predicate of the photograph, with the section of the rays, which is the quasi-subject, is the Syntax of the Dicisign; and like the Syntax of the proposition, it is a *fact* concerning the Dicisign considered as a First, that is, in itself, irrespective of its being a sign. Every informational sign thus involves a fact, which is its Syntax. It is quite evident, then, that Index Dicisigns equally accord with the definition and the corollaries.

It will be remarked that this accord, both for propositions and for informational indices, is quite irrespective of their being asserted or assented to. Now in analyses hitherto proposed, it seems to have been thought that if assertion, or at any rate, assent, were omitted, the proposition would be indistinguishable from a compound general term,—that "A man is tall" would then reduce to "A tall man." It therefore becomes important to inquire whether the definition of a Dicisign here found to be applicable to the former (even though it be not "judged") may not be equally applicable to the latter. The answer, however, comes forthwith. Fully to understand and assimilate the symbol "a tall man," it is by no means requisite to understand it to relate, or to profess to relate, to a real Object. Its Interpretant, therefore, does not represent it as a genuine Index; so that the definition of the Dicisign does not apply to it. It is impossible here fully to go into the examination of whether the analysis given does justice to the distinction between propositions and arguments. But it is easy to see that the proposition purports to intend to compel its Interpretant to refer to its real Object, that is, represents itself as an Index, while the argument purports to intend not compulsion, but action by means of comprehensible generals, that is, represents its character to be specially symbolic.

The above is the best analysis the author can, at present, make of the Dicisign. However satisfactory the main points of it may appear, it is not likely, on general principles, to stand without more or less amendment, though it would seem as if it could not but be pretty near to the truth. It is doubtful whether it applies fully to all kinds of propositions. This definition of the Dicisign will naturally lead one to guess that a Sumisign is any Representamen of which the Interpretant represents it as an Icon; and that the Argument, or Suadisign, is a Representamen of which the Interpretant represents it as a Symbol. Close examination encourages the student to believe that this is something like the truth, but so far as it has been carried, excites doubt whether this be the whole story. But /the/ Suadisign and especially the Sumisign, with its want of salient features, are most difficult to analyze with confidence, according to this method, which will not now be pressed further.

Index dicisigns seem to have no important varieties; but propositions are divisible, generally by dichotomy primarily, in various ways. In the first place, according to *Modality* (German *Modalität*, a word, I believe, of Kant's invention)[14] or *Mode* (Latin *modus*, Boëthius), a proposition is either *de inesse* (the phrase used in the *Summulae*,* the highest medieval authority for terms of logic) or *modal* (Latin *modalis*, Abelard). A proposition *de inesse* contemplates only the existing state of things,—existing, that is, in the logical universe of discourse. A modal proposition takes account of a whole range of possibility. According as it asserts something to be true or false throughout the whole range of possibility, it is *necessary* (called by Kant *apodictic*) or *impossible*. According as it asserts something to be true or false within the range of possibility (not expressly including or excluding the existent state of things), it is *possible* (called by Kant *problematic*) or *contingent*. (The terms are all from Boëthius.)

---

*The *Summulae Logicales* of Petrus Hispanus, which Prantl, a writer of little judgment and overrated learning, whose useful History of Logic is full of blunders, misappreciations, and insensate theories, and whose own Billingsgate[15] justifies almost any tone toward him, absurdly maintains that this book was substantially translated from a Greek book, which is manifestly from the Latin. The *Summulae* of Petrus Hispanus are nearly identical with some other contemporary works and evidently show a doctrine which had been taught in the schools from about A.D. 1200. After Boëthius, it is the highest authority for logical terminology, according to the present writer's ethical views.

A subject of a proposition is either *singular, general,* or *abstract (Summulae).* It is singular if it indicates an otherwise known individual. It is general if it describes how an individual is to be selected. A general subject is (as commonly recognized) either *universal* or *particular* (and indefinite). (These last three terms are found in Appuleius,[16] of Nero's time. But a senseless distinction between the indefinite and the particular is by the present writer unnoticed.) There is a complicated doctrine in the books as to the meaning of these terms, some kinds of universals asserting the existence of their subjects. The present writer makes all universals alike in not doing so. Then a *universal* subject is one which indicates that the proposition applies to whatever individual there is in the universe or to whatever there *may be* of a general description without saying that there is any. A *particular* subject is one which does not indicate what individual is intended further than to give a general description of it, but does profess to indicate an existent individual at least. The order in which universal and particular subjects occur is material. Thus, "Some woman is adored by whatever Spaniards may exist," has its first subject "Some woman" particular, and its second "whatever Spaniard may exist" universal. But "Whatever Spaniard may exist adores some woman" has the same subjects in reverse order, and so has a different meaning. It is quite conceivable that a subject should be so described as to be neither universal nor particular; as in *exceptives (Summulae)* as "Every man but one is a sinner." The same may be said of all kinds of numerical propositions, as "Any insect has an even number of legs." But these may be regarded as particular collective subjects. An example of a universal collective subject would be "Any two persons shut up together will quarrel." A collection is logically an individual. The distinction of universal and particular subjects is material, not merely formal; and it seems to be (and was regarded in the middle ages as being) of essentially the same nature as the distinction of necessary and possible propositions.

The distinction of *hypothetical, categorical,* and *relative* propositions is also important. At any rate, the last has some important differences from the others.

The distinction between *affirmative* and *negative* propositions, as applied to ordinary categorical propositions, is purely a matter of form. A process called *infinitation* (used by Abelard, *Opera hactenus Inedita,* and constantly ever since in all Western languages to this day) consisting in prefixing *non-* to a term, converts the proposition from a negative to an *affirmative,* or so-called *infinite* proposition. The difference between a negative and an infinite proposition is no more than that in Latin one may say *non est* or *est non,* without difference of meaning.[17] "Socrates non est mortalis" is the usual form; but "Socrates est non mortalis" can equally be said. It must be remembered that logic has attracted to its study some of the most puerile of writers, and still continues to do so in some measure.

Finally, every proposition is either *true* or *false.* It is false if any proposition could be legitimately deduced from it, without any aid from false propositions, which would conflict with a direct perceptual judgment, could such be had. A proposition is true, if it is not false. Hence, an entirely meaningless form of proposition, if it be called a proposition, at all, is to be classed along with true propositions.

If, from a replica of a proposition, something be erased, such that, if the blank, or blanks, so left were filled, each with a proper name, then the general symbol of which this blank form would be a replica is termed by the present writer a *rheme*. (The word is taken from the use of ῥῆμα in Plato, Aristotle, Dionysius The Thracian, and many others, to denote a verb. The last writer says, Ῥῆμα ἐστὶ λέξις ἄπτωτος, ἐπιδεκτικὴ χρόνων τε καὶ προσώπων καὶ ἀριθμῶν, ἐνέργειαν ἢ πάθος παριστᾶσα.[18] This shows just how far the present writer has warped the original meaning.) A rheme is either a *medad* (a patronymic formed by the writer from μηδέν), a *monad*, a *dyad*, a *triad*, a *polyad*, etc., according as the number of blanks is 0, 1, 2, 3, or more than two.

Any symbol which may be a direct constituent of a proposition is called a *term* (Latin *terminus*, Boëthius).[19] The logicians usually say that a categorical proposition has "two terms," its *subject* and its *predicate*, wherein, by a carelessness of expression, or by copying Aristotle,* they stumble upon the truth. Their usual *doctrine* is (though often not directly stated in one sentence) that such a proposition has three terms, the subject, predicate, and *copula* (Abelard). The correct designation of the subject and predicate, in accord with their doctrine, is the *extremes*, which is translated from the same Greek word as *term* (ὅρος). The ordinary doctrine makes the copula the only verb, and all other terms to be either proper names or general class-names. The present author leaves the *is* as an inseparable part of the class-name; because this gives the simplest and most satisfactory account of the proposition. It happens to be true that in the overwhelming majority of languages there are no general class-names and adjectives that are not conceived as parts of some verb (even when there really is no such verb) and consequently nothing like a copula is required in forming sentences in such languages. The author (though with no pretension to being a linguist) has fumbled the grammars of many languages in the search for a language constructed at all in the way in which the logicians go out of their way to teach that all men think (for even if they do so, that has really nothing to do with logic). The only such tongue that he has succeeded in finding is the Basque, which seems to have but two or three verbs, all the other principal words being conceived as nouns. Every language must have proper names; and there is no verb wrapped up in a proper name. Therefore, there would seem to be a direct suggestion there of a true common noun or adjective. But, notwithstanding that suggestion, almost every family of man thinks of general words as parts of verbs. This seems to refute the logicians' psychology.

---

* Ὅρον δὲ καλῶ εἰς ὃν διαλύεται ἡ πρότασις, οἷον τό τε κατηγορεύμενον καί τὸ καθ' οὗ κατηγορεῖται, says Aristotle, 24b16.[20]

A proper name, when one meets with it for the first time, is existentially connected with some percept or other equivalent individual knowledge of the individual it names. It is *then*, and then only, a genuine Index. The next time one meets with it, one regards it as an Icon of that Index. The habitual acquaintance with it having been acquired, it becomes a Symbol whose Interpretant represents it as an Icon of an Index of the Individual named.

If you look into a textbook of chemistry for a definition of *lithium*, you may be told that it is that element whose atomic weight is 7 very nearly. But if the author has a more logical mind he will tell you that if you search among minerals that are vitreous, translucent, grey or white, very hard, brittle, and insoluble, for one which imparts a crimson tinge to an unluminous flame, this mineral being triturated with lime or witherite rats-bane, and then fused, can be partly dissolved in muriatic acid; and if this solution be evaporated, and the residue be extracted with sulphuric acid, and duly purified, it can be converted by ordinary methods into a chloride, which being obtained in the solid state, fused, and electrolyzed with half a dozen powerful cells, will yield a globule of a pinkish silvery metal that will float on gasolene; and the material of *that* is a specimen of lithium. The peculiarity of this definition,—or rather this precept that is more serviceable than a definition,—is that it tells you what the word lithium denotes by prescribing what you are to *do* in order to gain a perceptual acquaintance with the object of the word. Every subject of a proposition, unless it is either an Index (like the environment of the interlocutors, or something attracting attention in that environment, as the pointing finger of the speaker) or a Subindex (like a proper name, personal pronoun, or demonstrative) must be a *Precept*, or Symbol, not only describing to the Interpreter what is to be done, by him or others or both, in order to obtain an Index of an individual (whether a unit or a single set of units) of which the proposition is represented as meant to be true, but also assigning a designation to that individual, or, if it is a set, to each single unit of the set. Until a better designation is found, such a term may be called a *Precept*. Thus, the Subject of the proposition "Whatever Spaniard there may be adores some woman" may best be regarded as "Take any individual, *A*, in the universe, and then there will be some individual, *B*, in the universe, such that *A* and *B* in this order form a dyad of which what follows is true," the Predicate being, "_____ is either not a Spaniard or else adores a woman that is_____."

Any term fit to be the Subject of a proposition may be termed an *Onome*. A *Categoreumatic Term* (Duns Scotus, but probably earlier) is any term fit to be the Subject or Predicate of a proposition. A *Syncategoreumatic Term* or *Syncathegreuma (Summulae)* is a Symbol going to make up a *Categoreumatic Term*.[21] The copula seems to fall between two stools, being neither categoreumatic nor syncategoreumatic.

Arguments can only be Symbols, not Indices nor Icons. An argument is either a *Deduction*, an *Induction*, or an *Abduction*. [. . .][22]

The whole operation of reasoning begins with *Abduction*, which is now to be described. Its occasion is a *surprise*. That is, some belief, active or passive, formulated or unformulated, has just been broken up. It may be in real experience or it may equally be in pure mathematics, which has its marvels, as nature has. The mind seeks to bring the facts, as modified by the new discovery, into order; that is, to form a general conception embracing them. In some cases, it does this by an act of *generalization*. In other cases, no new law is suggested, but only a peculiar state of facts that will "explain" the surprising phenomenon; and a law already known is recognized as applicable to the suggested hypothesis, so that the phenomenon, under that assumption, would not be surprising, but quite likely, or even would be a necessary result. This synthesis suggesting a new conception or hypothesis, is the Abduction. It is recognized that the phenomena are *like*, i.e. constitute an Icon of, a replica of a general conception, or Symbol. This is not accepted as shown to be *true*, nor even *probable* in the technical sense,—i.e., not probable in such a sense that underwriters could safely make it the basis of business, however multitudinous the cases might be;—but it is shown to be *likely*, in the sense of being some sort of approach to the truth, in an indefinite sense. The conclusion is drawn in the interrogative mood (there is such a mood in Speculative Grammar, whether it occur in any human language or not). This conclusion, which is the Interpretant of the Abduction, represents the Abduction to be a Symbol,—to convey a general concept of the truth,—but not to *assert* it in any measure. The Interpretant represents the Suadisign as a Symbolical Sumisign.

Abduction having performed its work, it is now Deduction's turn. This mode of thought regards the conclusion of the Abduction as a pure dream. For one can reason deductively just the same concerning the so-called imaginaries, that is, the unfounded dreams of mathematicians, as concerning existences. Yet it must be something very different from a dream, in that, either in the hypothesis itself, or in the pre-known truths brought to bear upon it, there must be a *universal* proposition, or Rule. Take the "immediate inference," which is as truly a deduction as any other, from "There is a woman whom any Spaniard there may be adores," to "Any Spaniard there may be stands to some woman or other in the relation of adoring her." This inference may be drawn by a "rule of thumb"; that is, a habit may act to cause a feeling of confidence in the conclusion, without any deliberation or control. This, however, may happen even if the inference is not of the kind termed "immediate" (that is, a deduction from a relatively simple premiss, not a copulative proposition). But such inference, not being self-controlled, is not *Reasoning*. Yet even in that case, the habit is a universal rule in itself, although its operation may be hindered sometimes. But if the inference is drawn deliberately, the reasoner will consider that if the woman can be specified in advance of knowing what Spaniard is to be adduced, it can only make it easier to find such a woman if the Spaniard is fixed upon first; or in some other way, the case will be brought under a known or evident universal truth. Thus, the argument sets out from a law represented to be known actually to hold throughout the universe of the hypothesis, and in the conclusion interprets the effect of this law. As Professor Mitchell* profoundly said, the whole operation virtually consists in *erasure*.

Deduction has two markedly different kinds: *necessary inference* and *inference of a probability*. What is called "probable inference" is not necessarily *probable deduction*, but includes all inference not necessary. Probable deduction is necessary inference concerning probability, in the strict statistical sense. What makes it very distinct from necessary inference proper is that while the latter has no concern with the realization of its hypothesis, and reasons about its premisses as expressing a conceivable state of things, regardless of actual existence, probability, on the other hand, is essentially limited to the *course of experience*. In the realm of Firstness, probability has no meaning. True there is a doctrine of "geometrical probability," but it is only a particular way of viewing problems in geometrical integration. The conception of probability, which is lugged into it, has no particular relevancy to it, further than that it may be suggestive in regard to this problem, as it may in regard to many others. But while probability *supposes* a course of actual experience, this supposition is itself entirely arbitrary, so far as concerns the reasoning.

Deduction produces from the conclusion of Abduction predictions as to what would be found true in experience in case that conclusion were realized. Now comes the work of Induction, which is not to be done while lolling in an easy chair, since it consists in actually going to work and making the experiments, thence going on to settle a general conclusion as to how far the hypothesis holds good.

---

*Because Mitchell happened to be a student under a master at the time he produced his paper "On a New Algebra of Logic,"[23] that work has been spoken of in a tone unfit to be used toward so masterly a performance. Barring the *Analytics* of Aristotle and Boole's *Laws of Thought*, I never read anything else on necessary inference so rich in instructive suggestions. What I have gained from the study of it is inestimable.

21

Nomenclature and Divisions of Triadic Relations, as Far as They Are Determined

MS 540. [This is the fifth section of 1903 Syllabus, first published in CP 2.233–72.] In this well-known essay on signs, Peirce introduces a third semiotic trichotomy (placed first in the logical order of trichotomies)— qualisign, sinsign, legisign—and then generates his famous ten-fold classification of signs. Peirce considers each of the ten classes separately, giving an especially helpful account of the tenth class, the argument (which must also be a symbol and a legisign). He explains his division of arguments into deductions, inductions, and abductions, from the standpoint of his extended semiotic theory, including his division of deduction into two types and of induction into three types. He concludes with a brief reconsideration of his theory of propositions.

The principles and analogies of Phenomenology enable us to describe, in a distant way, what the divisions of triadic relations must be. But until we have met with the different kinds *a posteriori,* and have in that way been led to recognize their importance, the *a priori* descriptions mean little;—not nothing at all, but little. Even after we seem to identify the varieties called for *a priori* with varieties which the experience of reflection leads us to think important, no slight labor is required to make sure that the divisions we have found *a posteriori* are precisely those that have been predicted *a priori.* In most cases, we find that they are not precisely identical, owing to the narrowness of our reflectional experience. It is only after much further arduous analysis that we are able finally to place in the system the conceptions to which experience has led us. In the case of triadic relations, no part of this work has, as yet, been satisfactorily performed, except in some measure for the most important class of triadic relations, those of signs, or representamens, to their objects and interpretants.

Provisionally, we may make a rude division of triadic relations, which, we need not doubt, contains important truth, however imperfectly apprehended, into

Triadic relations of Comparison,
Triadic relations of Performance, and
Triadic relations of Thought.

Triadic relations of Comparison are those which are of the nature of logical possibilities.

Triadic relations of Performance are those which are of the nature of actual facts.

Triadic relations of Thought are those which are of the nature of laws.

We must distinguish between the First, Second, and Third Correlate of any triadic relation.

The First Correlate is that one of the three which is regarded as of the simplest nature, being a mere possibility if any one of the three is of that nature, and not being a law unless all three are of that nature.

The Third Correlate is that one of the three which is regarded as of the most complex nature, being a law if any one of the three is a law, and not being a mere possibility unless all three are of that nature.

The Second Correlate is that one of the three which is regarded as of middling complexity, so that if any two are of the same nature, as to being either mere possibilities, actual existences, or laws, then the Second Correlate is of that same nature, while if the three are all of different natures, the Second Correlate is an actual existence.

Triadic relations are in three ways divisible by trichotomy, according as the First, the Second, or the Third Correlate, respectively, is a mere possibility, an actual existent, or a law. These three trichotomies, taken together, divide all triadic relations into ten classes. These ten classes will have certain subdivisions according as the existent correlates are individual subjects or individual facts, and according as the correlates that are laws are general subjects, general modes of fact, or general modes of law.

There will be besides a second similar division of triadic relations into ten classes, according as the dyadic relations which they constitute between either the First and Second Correlates, or the First and Third, or the Second and Third are of the nature of possibilities, facts, or laws; and these ten classes will be subdivided in different ways.

It may be convenient to collect the ten classes of either set of ten into three groups according as all three of the correlates or dyadic relations, as the case may be, are of different natures, or all are of the same nature, or two are of one nature while the third is of a different nature.

In every genuine Triadic Relation, the First Correlate may be regarded as determining the Third Correlate in some respect; and triadic relations may be divided according as that determination of the Third Correlate is to having some quality, or to being in some existential relation to the Second Correlate, or to being in some relation of thought to the Second for something.

A *Representamen* is the First Correlate of a triadic relation, the Second Correlate being termed its *Object*, and the possible Third Correlate being termed its *Interpretant*, by which triadic relation the possible Interpretant is determined to be the First Correlate of the same triadic relation to the same Object, and for some possible Interpretant.

A *Sign* is a Representamen of which some Interpretant is a cognition of a mind. Signs are the only representamens that have been much studied.

Signs are divisible by three trichotomies: first, according as the sign in itself is a mere quality, is an actual existent, or is a general law; secondly, according as the relation of the sign to its Object consists in the sign's having some character in itself, or in some existential relation to that Object, or in its relation to an Interpretant; thirdly, according as its Interpretant represents it as a sign of possibility, or as a sign of fact, or a sign of reason.

According to the first division, a Sign may be termed a *Qualisign*, a *Sinsign*, or a *Legisign*.[1]

A *Qualisign* is a quality which is a sign. It cannot actually act as a sign until it is embodied; but the embodiment has nothing to do with its character as a sign.

A *Sinsign* (where the syllable *sin* is taken as meaning "being only once," as in *single, simple,* Latin *semel,* etc.) is an actual existent thing or event which is a sign. It can only be so through its qualities; so that it involves a qualisign, or rather, several qualisigns. But these qualisigns are of a peculiar kind and only form a sign through being actually embodied.

A *Legisign* is a law that is a sign. This law is usually established by men. Every conventional sign is a legisign. It is not a single object, but a general type which, it has been agreed, shall be significant. Every legisign signifies through an instance of its application, which may be termed a *Replica* of it. Thus, the word "the" will usually occur from fifteen to twenty-five times on a page. It is in all these occurrences one and the same word, the same legisign. Each single instance of it is a replica. The replica is a sinsign. Thus, every legisign requires sinsigns. But these are not ordinary sinsigns, such as are peculiar occurrences that are regarded as significant. Nor would the replica be significant if it were not for the law which renders it so.

According to the second trichotomy, a Sign may be termed an *Icon*, an *Index*, or a *Symbol*.

An *Icon* is a sign which refers to the Object that it denotes merely by virtue of characters of its own and which it possesses, just the same, whether any such Object actually exists or not. It is true that unless there really is such an Object, the icon does not act [as] a sign; but this has nothing to do with its character as a sign. Anything whatever, be it quality, existent individual, or law, is an icon of anything, in so far as it is like that thing and used as a sign of it.

An *Index* is a sign which refers to the Object that it denotes by virtue of being really affected by that Object. It cannot, therefore, be a qualisign; because qualities are whatever they are independently of anything else. In so far as the index is affected by the Object, it necessarily has some quality in common with the Object, and it is in respect to these that it refers to the Object. It does, therefore, involve a sort of icon, although an icon of a peculiar kind; and it is not the mere resemblance to its Object, even in these respects, which makes it a sign, but it is the actual modification of it by the Object.

A *Symbol* is a sign which refers to the Object that it denotes by virtue of a law, usually an association of general ideas, which operates to cause the Symbol to be interpreted as referring to that Object. It is thus itself a general type or law, that is, is a legisign. As such it acts through a replica. Not only is it general itself, but the Object to which it refers is of a general nature. Now that which is general has its being in the instances which it will determine. There must, therefore, be existent instances of what the symbol denotes, although we must here understand by "existent," existent in the possibly imaginary universe to which the symbol refers. The symbol will indirectly, through the association or other law, be affected by those instances; and thus the symbol will involve a sort of index, although an index of a peculiar kind. It will not, however, be by any means true that the slight effect upon the symbol of those instances accounts for the significant character of the symbol.

According to the third trichotomy, a Sign may be termed a *Rheme*, a *Dicisign* or *Dicent Sign* (that is, a proposition or quasi-proposition), or an *Argument*.

A *Rheme* is a sign which, for its Interpretant, is a sign of qualitative possibility, that is, is understood as representing such and such a kind of possible Object. Any rheme, perhaps, will afford some information; but it is not interpreted as doing so.

A *Dicent Sign* is a sign which, for its Interpretant, is a sign of actual existence. It cannot, therefore, be an icon, which affords no ground for an interpretation of it as referring to actual existence. A Dicisign necessarily involves, as a part of it, a rheme, to describe the fact which it is interpreted as indicating. But this is a peculiar kind of rheme; and while it is essential to the dicisign, it by no means constitutes it.[2]

An *Argument* is a sign which, for its Interpretant, is a sign of law. Or we may say that a Rheme is a sign which is understood to represent its Object in its characters merely; that a Dicisign is a sign which is understood to represent its Object in respect to actual existence; and that an Argument is a sign which is understood to represent its Object in its character as sign. Since these definitions touch upon points at this time much in dispute, a word may be added in defense of them. A question often put is, What is the essence of a Judgment? A judgment is the mental act by which the judger seeks to impress upon himself the truth of a proposition. It is much the same as an act of asserting the proposition, or going before a notary and assuming formal responsibility for its truth, except that those acts are intended to affect others, while the judgment is only intended to affect oneself. However, the logician, as such, cares not what the psychological nature of the act of judging may be. The question for him is, What is the nature of the sort of sign of which a principal variety is called a proposition, which is the matter upon which the act of judging is exercised? The proposition need not be asserted or judged. It may be contemplated as a sign capable of being asserted or denied. This sign itself retains its full meaning whether it be actually asserted or not. The peculiarity of it, therefore, lies in its mode of meaning; and to say this is to say that its peculiarity lies in its relation to its Interpretant. The proposition professes to be really affected by the actual existent or real law to which it refers. The argument makes the same pretension, but that is not the principal pretension of the argument. The rheme makes no such pretension.

The Interpretant of the Argument represents it as an instance of a general class of arguments, which class on the whole will always tend to the truth. It is this law, in some shape, which the argument urges; and this "urging" is the mode of representation proper to arguments. The Argument must, therefore, be a Symbol, or sign whose Object is a general law or type. It must involve a Dicent Symbol, or Proposition, which is termed its *Premiss*; for the Argument can only urge the law by urging it in an instance. This premiss is, however, quite different in force (i.e. in its relation to its Interpretant) from a similar proposition merely asserted; and besides, this is far from being the whole Argument. As for another proposition, called the *Conclusion*, often stated and perhaps required to complete the Argument, it plainly represents the Interpretant, and likewise has a peculiar force, or relation to the Interpretant. There is a difference of opinion among logicians as to whether it forms a part of the Argument or not; and although such opinions have not resulted from an exact analysis of the essence of Argument, they are entitled to weight. The present writer, without being absolutely confident, is strongly inclined to think that the conclusion, although it represents the Interpretant, is essential to the full expression of the Argument. It is usual with logicians to speak of the premisses of an argument, instead of the premiss. But if there are more premisses than one, the first step of the argumentation must be to colligate them into one Copulative Proposition; so that the only simple argument of two premisses is the Argument of Colligation. But even in this case, there are not properly two Premisses. For whenever the mind is in a state ready to assert a proposition, P, it is already in a state of asserting a proposition, O, which the new proposition, P, only further determines; so that it is not P, merely, which comes to be asserted, but OP. In this view of the matter, there is no such thing as an Argument of Colligation. For to say that there is would make every judgment the conclusion of an argument. But if every judgment is to be regarded as the conclusion of an argument, which is, no doubt, an admissible conception, then it is the conclusion of a quite different kind of judgment from a mere Argument of Colligation. Thus, the Argument of Colligation is a form of argument which is introduced into logic merely in order to avoid the necessity of considering the true nature of the argument from which a Copulative Proposition has been derived. For that reason, it seems more proper in general to speak of the "premiss" of an argument than of its "premisses." As to the word *premiss*,—in Latin of the thirteenth Century *praemissa*,—owing to its being so often used in the plural, it has become widely confounded with a totally different word of legal provenance, the "premises," that is, the items of an inventory, etc., and hence buildings enumerated in a deed or lease. It is entirely contrary to good English usage to spell premiss, "premise," and this spelling (whose prevalence is due perhaps to Lord Brougham,[3] or at least chiefly supported by his assistance) simply betrays ignorance of the history of logic, and even of such standard authors as Whately, Watts, etc.[4]

The three trichotomies of signs result together in dividing signs into **Ten Classes of Signs**, of which numerous subdivisions have to be considered. The ten classes are as follows:

First, a Qualisign is any quality in so far as it is a sign. Since a quality is whatever it is positively in itself, a quality can only denote an Object by virtue of some common ingredient or similarity; so that a Qualisign is necessarily an Icon. Further, since a quality is a mere logical possibility it can only be interpreted as a sign of essence, that is, as a Rheme.

Second, an Iconic Sinsign is any object of experience in so far as some quality of it makes it determine the idea of an Object. Being an Icon, and thus a sign by likeness purely, of whatever it may be like, it can only be interpreted as a sign of essence, or Rheme. It will embody a Qualisign.

Third, a Rhematic Indexical Sinsign is any object of direct experience so far as it directs attention to an Object by which its presence is caused. It necessarily involves an Iconic Sinsign of a peculiar kind, yet is quite different since it brings the attention of the interpreter to the very Object denoted.

Fourth, a Dicent Sinsign is any object of direct experience in so far as it is a sign, and, as such, affords information concerning its Object. This it can only do by being really affected by its Object; so that it is necessarily an Index. The only information it can afford is of actual fact. Such a sign must involve an Iconic Sinsign to embody the information and a Rhematic Indexical Sinsign to indicate the Object to which the information refers. But the mode of combination, or *Syntax*, of these two must also be significant.

Fifth, an Iconic Legisign is any general law or type, in so far as it requires each instance of it to embody a definite quality which renders it fit to call up in the mind the idea of a like Object. Being an Icon, it must be a Rheme. Being a Legisign, its mode of being is that of governing single Replicas, each of which will be an Iconic Sinsign of a peculiar kind.

Sixth, a Rhematic Indexical Legisign is any general type or law, however established, which requires each instance of it to be really affected by its Object in such a manner as merely to draw attention to that Object. Each Replica of it will be a Rhematic Indexical Sinsign of a peculiar kind. The Interpretant of a Rhematic Indexical Legisign represents it as an Iconic Legisign; and so it is, in a measure,—but in a very small measure.

Seventh, a Dicent Indexical Legisign is any general type or law, however established, which requires each instance of it to be really affected by its Object in such a manner as to furnish definite information concerning that

Object. It must involve an Iconic Legisign to signify the information and a Rhematic Indexical Legisign to denote the subject of that information. Each Replica of it will be a Dicent Sinsign of a peculiar kind.

Eighth, a Rhematic Symbol, or Symbolic Rheme, is a sign connected with its Object by an association of general ideas in such a way that its Replica calls up an image in the mind which image, owing to certain habits or dispositions of that mind, tends to produce a general concept, and the Replica is interpreted as a sign of an Object that is an instance of that concept. Thus, the Rhematic Symbol either is, or is very like, what the logicians call a general term. The Rhematic Symbol, like any Symbol, is necessarily itself of the nature of a general type, and is thus a Legisign. Its Replica, however, is a Rhematic Indexical Sinsign of a peculiar kind, in that the image it suggests to the mind acts upon a Symbol already in that mind to give rise to a general concept. In this it differs from other Rhematic Indexical Sinsigns, including those which are Replicas of Rhematic Indexical Legisigns. Thus, the demonstrative pronoun "that" is a Legisign, being a general type; but it is not a Symbol, since it does not signify a general concept. Its Replica draws attention to a single Object, and is a Rhematic Indexical Sinsign. A Replica of the word "camel" is likewise a Rhematic Indexical Sinsign, being really affected, through the knowledge of camels, common to the speaker and auditor, by the real camel it denotes, even if this one is not individually known to the auditor; and it is through such real connection that the word "camel" calls up the idea of a camel. The same thing is true of the word "phoenix." For although no phoenix really exists, real descriptions of the phoenix are well known to the speaker and his auditor; and thus the word is really affected by the Object denoted. But not only are the Replicas of Rhematic Symbols very different from ordinary Rhematic Indexical Sinsigns, but so likewise are Replicas of Rhematic Indexical Legisigns. For the thing denoted by "that" has not affected the replica of the word in any such direct and simple manner as that in which, for example, the ring of a telephone bell is affected by the person at the other end who wants to make a communication. The Interpretant of the Rhematic Symbol often represents it as a Rhematic Indexical Legisign; at other times as an Iconic Legisign; and it does in a small measure partake of the nature of both.

Ninth, a Dicent Symbol, or ordinary Proposition, is a sign connected with its Object by an association of general ideas, and acting like a Rhematic Symbol, except that its intended Interpretant represents the Dicent Symbol as being, in respect to what it signifies, really affected by its Object, so that the existence or law which it calls to mind must be actually connected with the indicated Object. Thus, the intended Interpretant looks upon the Dicent Symbol as a Dicent Indexical Legisign; and if it be true, it does partake of this nature, although this does not represent its whole nature. Like the Rhematic Symbol, it is necessarily a Legisign. Like the Dicent Sinsign, it is composite inasmuch as it necessarily involves a Rhematic Symbol (and thus is for its

Interpretant an Iconic Legisign) to express its information and a Rhematic Indexical Legisign to indicate the subject of that information. But its Syntax of these is significant. The Replica of the Dicent Symbol is a Dicent Sinsign of a peculiar kind. This is easily seen to be true when the information the Dicent Symbol conveys is of actual fact. When that information is of a real law, it is not true in the same fullness. For a Dicent Sinsign cannot convey information of law. It is, therefore, true of the Replica of such a Dicent Symbol only in so far as the law has its being in instances.

Tenth, an Argument is a sign whose Interpretant represents its Object as being an ulterior sign through a law, namely, the law that the passage from all such premisses to such conclusions tend to the truth. Manifestly, then, its Object must be general; that is, the Argument must be a Symbol. As a Symbol it must, further, be a Legisign. Its Replica is a Dicent Sinsign.[5]

The affinities of the ten classes are exhibited by arranging their designations in the triangular table here shown, which has heavy boundaries between adjacent squares that are appropriated to classes alike in only one respect. All other adjacent squares pertain to classes alike in two respects. Squares not adjacent pertain to classes alike in one respect only, except that each of the three squares at the vertices of the triangle pertains to a class differing in all three respects from the classes to which the squares along the opposite side of the triangle are appropriated. The lightly printed designations are superfluous.

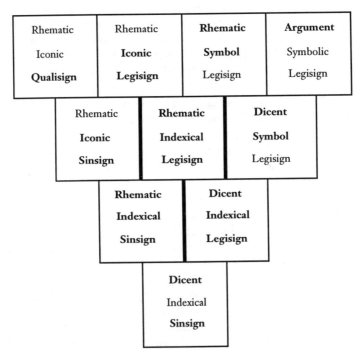

In the course of the above descriptions of the classes, certain subdivisions of some of them have been directly or indirectly referred to. Namely, besides the normal varieties of Sinsigns, Indices, and Dicisigns, there are others which are Replicas of Legisigns, Symbols, and Arguments, respectively. Besides the normal varieties of Qualisigns, Icons, and Rhemes, there are two series of others; to wit, those which are directly involved in Sinsigns, Indices, and Dicisigns, respectively, and also those which are indirectly involved in Legisigns, Symbols, and Arguments, respectively. Thus, the ordinary Dicent Sinsign is exemplified by a weathercock and its veering and by a photograph. The fact that the latter is known to be the effect of the radiations from the object renders it an Index and highly informative. A second variety is a Replica of a Dicent Indexical Legisign. Thus any given street-cry, since its tone and theme identifies the individual, is not a Symbol, but an Indexical Legisign; and any individual instance of it is a Replica of it which is a Dicent Sinsign. A third variety is a Replica of a Proposition. A fourth variety is a Replica of an Argument. Besides the normal variety of the Dicent Indexical Legisign, of which a street-cry is an example, there is a second variety which is that sort of proposition which has the name of a well-known individual as its predicate; as if one is asked "Whose statue is this?" the answer may be, "It is Farragut." The meaning of this answer is a Dicent Indexical Legisign. A third variety may be a premiss of an argument. A Dicent Symbol, or ordinary proposition, in so far as it is a premiss of an argument, takes on a new force, and becomes a second variety of the Dicent Symbol. It would not be worth while to go through all the varieties; but it may be well to consider the varieties of one class more. We may take the Rhematic Indexical Legisign. *The* shout of "Hullo!" is an example of the ordinary variety,—meaning, not an individual shout, but this shout, "Hullo!" in general,—this type of shout. A second variety is a constituent of a Dicent Indexical Legisign; as the word "that" in the reply "That is Farragut." A third variety is a particular application of a Rhematic Symbol; as the exclamation "Hark!" A fourth and fifth variety are in the peculiar force a general word may have in a proposition or argument. It is not impossible that some varieties are here overlooked. It is a nice problem to say to what class a given sign belongs; since all the circumstances of the case have to be considered. But it is seldom requisite to be very accurate; for if one does not locate the sign precisely, one will easily come near enough to its character for any ordinary purpose of logic.

There are other subdivisions of some, at least, of the ten classes which are of greater logical importance. An argument is always understood by its Interpretant to belong to a general class of analogous arguments, which class, as a whole, tends toward the truth. This may happen in three ways, giving rise to a trichotomy of all simple arguments into Deductions, Inductions, and Abductions.

A *Deduction* is an argument whose Interpretant represents that it belongs to a general class of possible arguments precisely analogous which are such that in the long run of experience the greater part of those whose premisses are true will have true conclusions. Deductions are either *Necessary* or *Probable*. Necessary Deductions are those which have nothing to do with any ratio of frequency, but profess (or their Interpretants profess for them) that from true premisses they must invariably produce true conclusions. A Necessary Deduction is a method of producing Dicent Symbols by the study of a diagram. It is either *Corollarial* or *Theorematic*. A Corollarial Deduction is one which represents the conditions of the conclusion in a diagram and finds from the observation of this diagram, as it is, the truth of the conclusion. A Theorematic Deduction is one which, having represented the conditions of the conclusion in a diagram, performs an ingenious experiment upon the diagram, and by the observation of the diagram so modified, ascertains the truth of the conclusion. Probable Deductions, or more accurately Deductions of Probability, are Deductions whose Interpretants represent them to be concerned with ratios of frequency. They are either *Statistical Deductions* or *Probable Deductions proper.* A Statistical Deduction is a Deduction whose Interpretant represents it to reason concerning ratios of frequency, but to reason concerning them with absolute certainty. A Probable Deduction proper is a Deduction whose Interpretant does not represent that its conclusion is certain, but that precisely analogous reasonings would from true premisses produce true conclusions in the majority of cases, in the long run of experience. An *Induction* is a method of forming Dicent Symbols concerning a definite question, of which method the Interpretant does not represent that from true premisses it will yield approximately true results in the majority of instances in the long run of experience, but does represent that if this method be persisted in, it will in the long run yield the truth, or an indefinite approximation to the truth, in regard to every question. An Induction is either a *Pooh-pooh Argument*, or an *Experimental Verification of a general Prediction*, or an *Argument from a Random Sample*. A Pooh-pooh Argument is a method which consists in denying that a general kind of event ever will occur on the ground that it never has occurred. Its justification is that if it be persistently applied on every occasion, it must ultimately be corrected in case it should be wrong, and thus will ultimately reach the true conclusion. A Verification of a general Prediction is a method which consists in finding or making the conditions of the prediction and in concluding that it will be verified about as often as it is experimentally found to be verified. Its justification is that if the Prediction does not tend in the long run to be verified in any approximately determinate proportion of cases, experiment must, in the long run, ascertain this; while if the Prediction will, in the long run, be verified in any determinate, or approximately determinate, proportion of cases, experiment must in the long run, approximately ascertain what that proportion is. An Argument from a Random Sample is a method of ascertaining what proportion of the members of a finite class possess a predesignate, or virtually predesignate, quality, by selecting instances from that class according to a method which will, in the long run, present any instance as often as any other, and concluding that the ratio found for such a sample will hold in the long run. Its justification is evident. An *Abduction* is a method of forming a general prediction without any positive assurance that it will succeed either in the special case or usually, its justification being that it is the only possible hope of regulating our future conduct rationally, and that Induction from past experience gives us strong encouragement to hope that it will be successful in the future.

A Dicent Symbol, or general proposition, is either *Particular* or *Universal.* A Particular Dicent Symbol is represented by its Interpretant to indicate [a] fact of existence; as, "Some swan is black," i.e., there exists a black swan. A Universal Dicent Symbol is represented by its Interpretant to indicate a real law; as "No swan is black," i.e., no amount of research *will ever* discover a black individual among swans. A Dicent Symbol is either *Non-Relative* or *Relative.* A Non-Relative Dicent Symbol is not concerned with the identity of more than one individual. But this must be understood in a particular way, the proposition being first expressed in an exemplar manner. Thus "No swan is black" seems to be concerned with the identity of all swans and all black objects. But it is to be understood that the proposition is to be considered under this form: "Taking any one object in the universe you please, it is either not a swan or is not black." A Relative Dicent Symbol is concerned with the identity of more than one individual, or of what may be more than one, in an exemplar expression; as, "Take any individual, *A*, you please, and thereafter an individual, *B*, can be found, such that if *A* is a city of over a hundred thousand inhabitants, *B* will be a spot on this map corresponding to *A*." Whether a proposition is to be regarded as non-relative or relative depends on what use is to be made of it in argument. But it does not follow that the distinction is merely one of outward guise; for the force of the proposition is different according to the application that is to be made of it. It may here be noted as a matter of correct terminology (according to the views set forth in the second part of this syllabus), that a *Hypothetical Proposition* is any proposition compounded of propositions. The old doctrine is that a hypothetical proposition is either conditional, copulative, or disjunctive. But a conditional is properly a disjunctive proposition. Some propositions may equally well be regarded as copulative or disjunctive. Thus, at once, either Tully or not Cicero and either Cicero or not Tully, is the same as, at once either, Tully and Cicero or not Tully and not Cicero. Any definition may be regarded as a proposition of this sort; and for this reason such propositions might be termed *Definiform*, or *Definitory.* A copulative proposition is naturally allied to a particular proposition, a disjunctive proposition to a universal proposition.

If parts of a proposition be erased so as to leave *blanks* in their places, and if these blanks are of such a nature that if each of them be filled by a proper name the result will be a proposition, then the blank form of proposition which was first produced by the erasures is termed a *rheme.* According as the number of blanks in a rheme is 0, 1, 2, 3, etc., it may be termed a *medad* (from μηδέν, nothing), *monad, dyad, triad*, etc., rheme.

22

New Elements
(Καινὰ στοιχεῖα)

MS 517. [First published in NEM 4:235–63. This document was most probably written in early 1904, as a preface to an intended book on the foundations of mathematics.] Peirce begins with a discussion of "the Euclidean style" he planned to follow in his book. Euclid's Elements *presuppose an understanding of the logical structure of mathematics (geometry) that Peirce, in his "New Elements," wants to explicate. Having recently concluded that the scope of logic should be extended to include all of semiotics, Peirce now wants to work out the semiotic principles that he hopes will shed light on the most abstract science. Building on his work in his 1903 "Syllabus," Peirce deepens his semiotic theory by linking it with the mathematical conception of "degrees of degeneracy." Symbols are taken to be non-degenerate, genuine, signs, while indices are signs degenerate in the first degree and icons are degenerate in the second degree. Symbols must always involve both indices and icons, and indices must always involve icons. Peirce limits his attention to this trichotomy but carries his discussion deeply into epistemology and metaphysics, making such arresting claims as that "representations have power to cause real facts" and that "there can be no reality which has not the life of a symbol." Max Fisch described this paper as Peirce's "best statement so far of his general theory of signs."*

I

I deem it useful to say a few words about this piece.[1] Some years ago I wrote a book entitled "New Elements of Mathematics."[2] It was such a book as a man with considerable natural aptitude for logic and mathematics, who had devoted the best of his time for forty years to the study of the former and all that has been written about it, and had not neglected the latter, was able to write by devoting a year exclusively to it. If the author had been a German, he would have shared the loose ideas of logic that naturally are associated with subjectivism, and consequently could not have written the same book; but had he written it, it would have been in print long ago. As it was, he carried it to three publishers,[3] one of whom had asked him to prepare the book. All of them were very modest men. They did not pretend to know much except about the elements of mathematics. One of them was at that time the publisher of a treatise on geometry which professed to show how to inscribe a regular polygon of any number of sides in a circle by the aid of rule and compasses only. Both the others published treatises on geometry of similar startling pretensions. None of them approved of my book, because it put perspective before metrical geometry, and topical geometry before either. This was the fault of the book; namely, that a publisher who was so well versed in the elements of mathematics was not convinced by it that this arrangement was logical, even though he took the book home with him and glanced at it during the evening. A writer on the logic of mathematics in America must meet American requirements.

Personally, I regret that manuscript has been lost;[4] for it was the record of much close thought. I can never reproduce it, because it was written in the strictest mathematical style, and with advancing years I have lost the power of writing about logic in mathematical style, although in my youth it was natural to me. In losing the power of writing this style, I have equally lost my admiration of it. I beg permission to offer a criticism of the mathematical style in logic.

I say in "logic," because it is only with a view of presenting the logic of the subject that mathematicians employ the Euclidean style. When they are simply intent on the solution of difficult problems they forget all about it. I call it Euclidean because the first book of Euclid's *Elements* is the earliest and the most perfect model of that style. Euclid follows it, in some measure, in his other writings; but it is only in the first book of the *Elements* that it is polished with endless labor and thought. It is easy to see that this style took its origin in the esthetic taste of the Greeks. Everything they did, in literature and in art, shows the predominance of their horror of the "too much." Perhaps this horror was due to the irrepressible activity of Greek minds, and their consequent impatience with useless considerations, together with the expensiveness, at that age in energy of every kind, of the mechanical processes of writing and reading. They took it for granted that the reader would actively think; and the writer's sentences were to serve merely as so many blazes to enable him to follow the track of that writer's thought. The modern book, which I only mention as a foil to the other, in order to be approved, must be approved by a densely stupid and unspeakably indolent young lady as she skims its pages while looking out of the window to be admired. In order to put an idea into such a shape that it cannot fail to be apprehended by her, the first requisite is that it shall fill a certain number of lines, and the second is that not the smallest step shall be left to her own intellectual activity.

The dominating idea of Euclid in writing his first book was plainly that the first elements of geometry can only be comprehended by understanding the logical structure of the doctrine. Yet, in his horror of the too much, he never says a single word about logic from beginning to end. He begins with a couple of dozen "definitions," which are followed by five "postulates," and these by several axioms, or "notions of common sense"; yet he never tells us what a "definition," a "postulate," or a "common notion" is supposed to be; and his meanings in all three cases have been seriously misapprehended. The forty-eight propositions of the book are set forth and arranged in a manner which betrays a profound understanding of their logical relations. Herein is the principal value of the work; today, its only value. Yet this knowledge is so concealed that it requires the same knowledge to detect it.

This profound work is put into the hands of boys who are not Greek, but overfed and logy. They meet with difficulties which they carry to a teacher who is far more incompetent than they, since he knows nothing of the logical structure which is the cryptic subject of the book, and long familiarity has rendered him incapable of perceiving the difficulties which his scholars can, at least, perceive. The old pedagogical method was to thrash the boys till they did understand; and that was tolerably efficient as an antidote to their over-doses of beef. Since that method has been abandoned it has been necessary to abandon the pedagogical use of the book.

II

It is extremely difficult to treat fully and clearly of the logic of mathematics in the Euclidean style, since this strictly requires that not a word should be said about logic. As an exact logician, however, I approve of addressing an actively intelligent reader in the ancient method by means of first, *definitions;* second, *postulates;* third, *axioms;* fourth, *corollaries;* fifth, *diagrams;* sixth, *letters;* seventh, *theorems;* eighth, *scholiums.* This distinction between a *general* proposition (which, if a postulate, is often erroneously called an axiom) and an *indefinite* proposition (to which, if indemonstrable, the word "Postulat" is restricted in German) may also be maintained.

A *definition* is the logical analysis of a predicate in general terms. It has two branches, the one asserting that the definitum is applicable to whatever there may be to which the definition is applicable; the other (which ordinarily has several clauses), that the definition is applicable to whatever there may be to which the definitum is applicable. *A definition does not assert that anything exists.*

A *postulate* is an initial hypothesis in general terms. It may be arbitrarily assumed provided that (the definitions being accepted) it does not conflict with any principle of substantive possibility or with any already adopted postulate. By a principle of substantive possibility, I mean, for example, that it would not be admissible to postulate that there was no relation whatever between two points, or to lay down the proposition that nothing whatever shall be true without exception. For though what this means involves no contradiction, it is in contradiction with the fact that it is itself asserted.

An *axiom* is a self-evident truth, the statement of which is superfluous to the conclusiveness of the reasoning, and which only serves to show a principle involved in the reasoning. It is generally a truth of observation; such as the assertion that something is true.

A *corollary,* as I shall use the word, is an inference drawn in general terms without the use of any construction.*

*At present, *corollary* is not a scientific term. The Latin word, meaning a gratuity, was applied to obvious deductions added by commentators to Euclid's propositions. Those his

A *diagram* is an *icon* or schematic image embodying the meaning of a general predicate; and from the observation of this *icon* we are supposed to construct a new general predicate.

A *letter* is an arbitrary definite designation specially adopted in order to identify a single object of any kind.

A *theorem*, as I shall use the word, is an inference obtained by constructing a diagram according to a general precept, and after modifying it as ingenuity may dictate, observing in it certain relations, and showing that they must subsist in every case, retranslating the proposition into general terms.* A theorem regularly begins with, first, the *general enunciation*. There follows, second, a *precept* for a diagram, in which letters are employed. Then comes, third, the *ecthesis*, which states [that] what it will be sufficient to show must, in every case, be true concerning the diagram. The fourth article is the *subsidiary construction*, by which the diagram is modified in some manner already shown to be possible. The fifth article is the *demonstration*, which traces out the reasons why a certain relation must always subsist between the parts of the diagram. Finally, and sixthly, it is pointed out, by some such expression as Euclid's ὅπερ ἔδει δεῖξαι, or by the usual Q.E.D., or otherwise, that this was all that it was required to show.

A *scholium* is a comment upon the logical structure of the doctrine. This preface is a scholium.

III

1. I now proceed to explain the difference between a *theoretical* and a *practical* proposition, together with the two important parallel distinctions between *definite* and *vague*, and *individual* and *general*, noting, at the same time, some other distinctions connected with these. A *sign* is connected with the "Truth," i.e. the entire Universe of being, or, as some say, the Absolute, in three distinct ways. In the first place, a sign is not a real thing. It is of such a nature as to exist in *replicas*. Look down a printed page, and every *the* you see is the same word, every *e* the same letter. A real thing does not so exist in replica. The being of a sign is merely *being represented*. Now *really being* and *being represented* are very different. Giving to the word *sign* the full scope that reasonably belongs to it for logical purposes, a whole book is a sign; and a translation of it is a replica of the same sign. A whole literature is a sign. The sentence "Roxana was the queen of Alexander" is a sign of Roxana and of Alexander, and though there is a grammatical emphasis on the former, logically the name "Alexander" is as much a *subject* as is the name "Roxana"; and the real persons Roxana and Alexander are *real objects* of the sign. Every sign that

---

proofs compelled them to grant; and they added admissions of the corollaries without requiring proof. I propose to use the word in a definite sense as a term of logic.

*This may exclude some propositions called theorems. But I do not think that mathematicians will object to that, in view of my making a sharp distinction between a corollary and a theorem, and thus furnishing the logic of mathematics with two exact and convenient technical terms in place of vague, unscientific words.

is sufficiently complete refers to sundry real objects. All these objects, even if we are talking of Hamlet's madness, are parts of one and the same Universe of being, the "Truth." But so far as the "Truth" is merely the *object* of a sign, it is merely the Aristotelian *Matter* of it that is so. In addition however to *denoting* objects,[5] every sign sufficiently complete *signifies characters*, or qualities. We have a direct knowledge of real objects in every experiential reaction, whether of *Perception* or of *Exertion* (the one theoretical, the other practical). These are directly *hic et nunc.* But we extend the category, and speak of numberless real objects with which we are not in direct reaction. We have also direct knowledge of qualities in feeling, peripheral and visceral. But we extend this category to numberless characters of which we have no immediate consciousness. All these characters are elements of the "Truth." Every sign signifies the "Truth." But it is only the Aristotelian *Form* of the universe that it signifies. The logician is not concerned with any metaphysical theory; still less, if possible, is the mathematician. But it is highly convenient to express ourselves in terms of a metaphysical theory; and we no more bind ourselves to an acceptance of it than we do when we use substantives such as "humanity," "variety," etc., and speak of them as if they were substances, in the metaphysical sense. But, in the third place, every sign is intended to determine a sign of the same object with the same signification or *meaning*. Any sign, *B*, which a sign, *A*, is fitted so to determine, without violation of its, *A*'s, purpose, that is, in accordance with the "Truth," even though it, *B*, denotes but a part of the objects of the sign, *A*, and signifies but a part of its, *A*'s, characters, I call an *interpretant* of *A*. What we call a "fact" is something having the structure of a proposition, but supposed to be an element of the very universe itself. The purpose of every sign is to express "fact," and by being joined with other signs, to approach as nearly as possible to determining an interpretant which would be the *perfect Truth*, the absolute Truth, and as such (at least, we may use this language) would be the very Universe. Aristotle gropes for a conception of perfection, or *entelechy*, which he never succeeds in making clear. We may adopt the word to mean the very fact, that is, the ideal sign which should be quite perfect, and so identical,—in such identity as a sign may have,—with the very matter denoted united with the very form signified by it. The entelechy of the Universe of being, then, the Universe *qua* fact, will be that Universe in its aspect as a sign, the "Truth" of being. The "Truth," the fact that is not abstracted but complete, is the ultimate interpretant of every sign.

2. Of the two great tasks of humanity, *Theory* and *Practice*, the former sets out from a sign of a real object with which it is *acquainted*, passing from this, as its *matter*, to successive interpretants embodying more and more fully its *form*, wishing ultimately to reach a direct *perception* of the entelechy; while the latter, setting out from a sign signifying a character of which it *has an idea*, passes from this, as its *form*, to successive interpretants realizing more and more precisely its *matter*, hoping ultimately to be able to make a direct *effort*, producing the entelechy. But of these two movements, logic very properly

prefers to take that of Theory as the primary one. It speaks of an *antecedent* as that which, being known, something else, the *consequent*, may *also* be known. In our vernacular, the latter is inaccurately called a *consequence*, a word that the precise terminology of logic reserves for the proposition expressing the relation of any consequent to its antecedent, or for the fact which this proposition expresses. The conception of the relation of antecedent and consequent amounts, therefore, to a confusion of thought between the reference of a sign to its *meaning*, the character which it attributes to its object, and its appeal to an interpretant. But it is the former of these which is the more essential. The knowledge that the sun has always risen about once in each twenty-four hours (sidereal time) is a sign whose object is the sun, and (rightly understood) a part of its signification is the rising of the sun tomorrow morning. The relation of an antecedent to its consequent, in its confusion of the signification with the interpretant, is nothing but a special case of what occurs in all action of one thing upon another, modified so as to be merely an affair of being represented instead of really being. It is the representative action of the sign upon its object. For whenever one thing acts upon another it determines in that other a quality that would not otherwise have been there. In the vernacular we often call an effect a "consequence," because that which really is may correctly be represented; but we should refuse to call a mere logical consequent an "effect," because that which is merely represented, however legitimately, cannot be said really to be. If we speak of an argumentation as "producing a great effect," it is not the interpretant itself, by any means, to which we refer, but only the particular replica of it which is made in the minds of those addressed.

If a sign, *B*, only signifies characters that are elements (or the whole) of the meaning of another sign, *A*, then *B* is said to be a *predicate* (or *essential part*) of *A*. If a sign, *A*, only denotes real objects that are a part or the whole of the objects denoted by another sign, *B*, then *A* is said to be a *subject* (or *substantial part*) of *B*. The totality of the predicates of a sign, and also the totality of the characters it signifies, are indifferently each called its logical *depth*. This is the oldest and most convenient term. Synonyms are the *comprehension* of the Port-Royalists,[6] the *content (Inhalt)* of the Germans, the *force* of De Morgan, the *connotation* of J. S. Mill. (The last is objectionable.) The totality of the subjects, and also, indifferently, the totality of the real objects of a sign, is called the logical *breadth*. This is the oldest and most convenient term. Synonyms are the *extension* of the Port-Royalists (ill-called *extent* by some modern French logicians), the *sphere (Umfang)* of translators from the German, the *scope* of De Morgan, the *denotation* of J. S. Mill.

Besides the logical depth and breadth, I have proposed (in 1867)[7] the terms *information* and *area* to denote the total of fact (true or false) that in a given state of knowledge a sign embodies.

3. Other distinctions depend upon those we have drawn. I have spoken of real relations as reactions. It may be asked how far I mean to say that all real

relations are reactions. It is seldom that one falls upon so fascinating a subject for a train of thought as the analysis of that problem in all its ramifications, mathematical, physical, biological, sociological, psychological, logical, and so round to the mathematical again. The answer cannot be satisfactorily given in a few words; but it lies hidden beneath the obvious truth that any exact necessity is expressible by a general equation; and nothing can be added to one side of a general equation without an equal addition to the other. Logical necessity is the necessity that a sign should be true to a *real* object; and therefore there is *logical* reaction in every real dyadic relation. If *A* is in a real relation to *B*, *B* stands in a logically contrary relation to *A*, that is, in a relation at once converse to and inconsistent with the direct relation. For here we speak not of a vague sign of the relation but of the relation between two individuals, *A* and *B*. This very relation is one in which *A* alone stands to any individual, and it to *B* only. There are, however, *degenerate* dyadic relations,—*degenerate* in the sense in which two coplanar lines form a *degenerate* conic,—where this is not true. Namely, they are individual relations of identity, such as the relation of *A* to *A*. All mere resemblances and relations of reason are of this sort.

Of signs there are two different degenerate forms. But though I give them this disparaging name, they are of the greatest utility, and serve purposes that genuine signs could not. The more degenerate of the two forms (as I look upon it) is the *icon*. This is defined as a sign of which the character that fits it to become a sign of the sort that it is, is simply inherent in it as a quality of it. For example, a geometrical figure drawn on paper may be an *icon* of a triangle or other geometrical form. If one meets a man whose language one does not know and resorts to imitative sounds and gestures, these approach the character of an icon. The reason they are not pure icons is that the purpose of them is emphasized. A pure icon is independent of any purpose. It serves as a sign solely and simply by exhibiting the quality it serves to signify. The relation to its object is a degenerate relation. It asserts nothing. If it conveys information, it is only in the sense in which the object that it is used to represent may be said to convey information. An *icon* can only be a fragment of a completer sign.

The other form of degenerate sign is to be termed an *index*. It is defined as a sign which is fit to serve as such by virtue of being in a real reaction with its object. For example, a weathercock is such a sign. It is fit to be taken as an index of the wind for the reason that it is physically connected with the wind. A weathercock conveys information; but this it does because in facing the very quarter from which the wind blows, it resembles the wind in this respect, and thus has an icon connected with it. In this respect it is not a pure index. A pure index simply forces attention to the object with which it reacts and puts the interpreter into mediate reaction with that object, but conveys no information. As an example, take an exclamation "Oh!" The letters attached to a geometrical figure are another case. Absolutely unexceptionable examples of degenerate forms must not be expected. All that is possible is to give examples which tend sufficiently towards those forms to suggest what is meant. It is remarkable that while neither a pure icon nor a pure index can assert anything, an index which forces something to be an *icon,* as a weathercock does, or which forces us to regard it as an *icon,* as the legend under a portrait does, does make an assertion, and forms a *proposition.* This suggests the true definition of a proposition, which is a question in much dispute at this moment. A proposition is a sign which separately, or independently, indicates its object. No index, however, can be an *argumentation.* It may be what many writers call an *argument;* that is, a basis of argumentation; but an argument in the sense of a sign which separately shows what interpretant it is intended to determine it cannot be.

It will be observed that the icon is very perfect in respect to signification, bringing its interpreter face to face with the very character signified. For this reason, it is the mathematical sign *par excellence.* But in denotation it is wanting. It gives no assurance that any such object as it represents really exists. The index on the other hand does this most perfectly, actually bringing to the interpreter the experience of the very object denoted. But it is quite wanting in signification unless it involves an iconic part.

We now come to the genuine sign, for which I propose the technical designation *symbol,* following a use of that word not infrequent among logicians including Aristotle. A symbol is defined as a sign which is fit to serve as such simply because it will be so interpreted.

To recapitulate,

An icon		it possesses the quality signified.
An index	is a sign fit to be used as such because	it is in real reaction with the object denoted.
A symbol		it determines the interpretant sign.

Language and all abstracted thinking, such as belongs to minds who think in words, is of the symbolic nature. Many words, though strictly symbols, are so far iconic that they are apt to determine iconic interpretants, or as we say, to call up lively images. Such, for example, are those that have a fancied resemblance to sounds associated with their objects; that are *onomatopoetic,* as they say. There are words, which, although symbols, act very much like indices. Such are personal, demonstrative, and relative pronouns, for which A, B, C, etc., are often substituted. A *Proper Name,* also, which denotes a single individual well known to exist by the utterer and interpreter, differs from an index only in that it is a conventional sign. Other words refer indirectly to indices. Such is "*yard,*" which refers to a certain bar in Westminster, and has no meaning unless the interpreter is, directly or indirectly, in physical reaction with that bar. Symbols are particularly remote from the Truth itself. They are abstracted. They neither exhibit the very characters signified as icons do, nor assure us of the reality of their objects, as indices do. Many proverbial sayings express a sense of this weakness; as "Words prove nothing," and the like. Nevertheless, they have a great power of which the degenerate signs are quite destitute. They alone express laws. Nor are they limited to this theoretical use. They serve to bring about reasonableness and law. The words *justice* and *truth*, amid a world that habitually neglects these things and utterly derides the words, are nevertheless among the very greatest powers the world contains. They create defenders and animate them with strength. This is not rhetoric or metaphor: it is a great and solid fact of which it behooves a logician to take account.

A symbol is the only kind of sign which can be an argumentation.*

4. I have already defined an argument as a sign which separately monstrates what its intended interpretant is, and a proposition as a sign which separately indicates /what/ its object is; and we have seen that the icon alone cannot be a proposition while the symbol alone can be an argument. That a sign cannot be an argument without being a proposition is shown by attempting to form such an argument. "Tully, *c'est-à-dire* a Roman," evidently asserts that Tully is a Roman. Why this is so is plain. The interpretant is a sign which denotes that which the sign of which it is interpretant denotes. But, being a symbol, or genuine sign, it has a signification and therefore it represents the object of the principal sign as possessing the characters that it, the interpretant, signifies. It will be observed that an argument is a symbol which separately monstrates (in any way) its *purposed* interpretant. Owing to a symbol being essentially a sign only by virtue of its being interpretable as such, the idea of a purpose is not entirely separable from it. The symbol, by the very definition of it, has an interpretant in view. Its very meaning is intended. Indeed, a purpose is precisely the interpretant of a symbol. But the conclusion of an argument is a specially monstrated interpretant, singled out from among the possible interpretants. It is, therefore, of its nature single, although not necessarily simple. If we erase from an argument every monstration of its special purpose, it becomes a proposition; usually a copulate proposition, composed of several members whose mode of conjunction is of the kind expressed by "and," which the grammarians call a "copulative conjunction." If from a propositional symbol we erase one or more of the parts which separately denote its objects, the remainder is what is called a *rhema*; but I shall take the liberty of calling it a *term*. Thus, from the proposition "Every man is mortal," we erase "Every man," which is shown to be denotative of an object by the circumstance that if it be replaced by an indexical symbol, such as "That" or "Socrates," the symbol is reconverted into a proposition, we get the *rhema* or *term* "_____ is mortal." Most logicians will say that this is not a term. The term, they will say, is "mortal," while I have left the copula "is" standing with it. Now while it is true that one of Aristotle's memoirs[8] dissects a proposition into subject, predicate, and verb, yet as long as Greek was the language which

---

* I commonly call this an argument, for nothing is more false historically than to say that this word has not at all times been used in this sense. Still, the longer word is a little more definite.

logicians had in view, no importance was attached to the substantive verb, "is," because the Greek permits it to be omitted. It was not until the time of Abelard, when Greek was forgotten, and logicians had Latin in mind, that the copula was recognized as a constituent part of the logical proposition. I do not, for my part, regard the usages of language as forming a satisfactory basis for logical doctrine. Logic, for me, is the study of the essential conditions to which signs must conform in order to function as such. How the constitution of the human mind may compel men to think is not the question; and the appeal to language appears to me to be no better than an unsatisfactory method of ascertaining psychological facts that are of no relevancy to logic. But if such appeal is to be made (and logicians generally do make it; in particular their doctrine of the copula appears to rest solely upon this), it would seem that they ought to survey human languages generally and not confine themselves to the small and extremely peculiar group of Aryan speech. Without pretending, myself, to an extensive acquaintance with languages, I am confident that the majority of non-Aryan languages do not ordinarily employ any substantive verb equivalent to "is." Some place a demonstrative or relative pronoun, as if one should say "_____ is a man *that* is translated" for "A man is translated." Others have a word, syllable, or letter, to show that an assertion is intended. I have been led to believe that in very few languages outside the Aryan group is the common noun a well-developed and independent part of speech. Even in the Shemitic languages, which are remarkably similar to the Aryan, common nouns are treated as verbal forms and are quite separated from proper names. The ordinary view of a term, however, supposes it to be a common noun in the fullest sense of the term. It is rather odd that of all the languages which I have examined in a search for some support of this ordinary view, so outlandish a speech as the Basque is the only one I have found that seems to be constructed thoroughly in the manner in which the logicians teach us that every rational being must think.*

What is the difference between "_____ is a man" and "man"? The logicians hold that the essence of the latter lies in a definition describing its characters; which doctrine virtually makes "man" equivalent to "what is a man." It thus differs from "_____ is a man" by the addition of the badly named "indefinite pronoun," *what*. The rhema "_____ is a man" is a fragmentary sign. But "man" is never used alone, and would have no meaning by

---

*While I am on the subject of languages I may take occasion to remark with reference to my treatment of the direct and indirect "objects" of a verb as so many subjects of the proposition, that about nine out [of] every ten languages regularly emphasize one of the subjects, and make it the principal one, by putting it in a special nominative case, or by some equivalent device. The ordinary logicians seem to think that this, too, is a necessity of thought, although one of the living Aryan languages of Europe habitually puts that subject in the genitive which the Latin puts in the nominative. The practice was very likely borrowed from a language similar to the Basque spoken by some progenitors of the Gaels. Some languages employ what is, in effect, an ablative for this purpose. It no doubt is a rhetorical enrichment of a language to have a form "*B* is loved by *A*" in addition to "*A* loves *B*." The language will be still richer if it has a third form in which *A* and *B* are treated as equally the subjects of what is said. But logically, the three are identical.

itself. It is sometimes written upon an object to show the nature of that object; but in such case, the appearance of the object is an index of that object; and the two taken together form a proposition. In respect to being fragmentary, therefore, the two signs are alike. It may be said that "Socrates wise" does not make a sentence in the language at present used in logic, although in Greek it would. But it is important not to forget that no more do "Socrates" and "is wise" make a proposition unless there is something to indicate that they are to be taken as signs of the same object. On the whole, it appears to me that the only difference between my rhema and the "term" of other logicians is that the latter contains no explicit recognition of its own fragmentary nature. But this is as much as to say that logically their meaning is the same; and it is for that reason that I venture to use the old, familiar word "term" to denote the rhema.

It may be asked what is the nature of the sign which joins "Socrates" to "_____ is wise," so as to make the proposition "Socrates is wise." I reply that it is an index. But, it may be objected, an index has for its object a thing *hic et nunc*, while a sign is not such a thing. This is true, if under "thing" we include singular events, which are the only things that are strictly *hic et nunc*. But it is not the two signs "Socrates" and "wise" that are connected, but the *replicas* of them used in the sentence. We do not say that "_____ is wise," as a general sign, is connected specially with Socrates, but only that it is so as here used. The two replicas of the words "Socrates" and "wise" are *hic et nunc*, and their junction is a part of their occurrence *hic et nunc*. They form a pair of reacting things which the index of connection denotes in their present reaction, and not in a general way; although it is possible to generalize the mode of this reaction like any other. There will be no objection to a generalization which shall call the mark of junction a *copula*, provided it be recognized that, in itself, it is not general, but is an *index*. No other kind of sign would answer the purpose; no general verb "is" can express it. For something would have to bring the general sense of that general verb down to the case in hand. An index alone can do this. But how is this index to signify the connection? In the only way in which any index can ever signify anything; by involving an *icon*. The sign itself is a connection. I shall be asked how this applies to Latin, where the parts of the sentence are arranged solely with a view to rhetorical effect. I reply that, nevertheless, it is obvious that in Latin, as in every language, it is the juxtaposition which connects words. Otherwise they might be left in their places in the dictionary. Inflection does a little; but the main work of construction, the whole work of connection, is performed by putting the words together. In Latin much is left to the good sense of the interpreter. That is to say, the common stock of knowledge of utterer and interpreter, called to mind by the words, is a part of the sign. That is more or less the case in all conversation, oral and scriptal. It is, thus, clear that the vital spark of every proposition, the peculiar propositional element of the proposition, is an indexical proposition; an index involving an icon. The rhema, say "_____ loves _____," has blanks which suggest filling; and a concrete actual connection of a subject with each blank monstrates the connection of ideas.

It is the Proposition which forms the main subject of this whole scholium; for the distinctions of *vague* and *distinct, general* and *individual,* are propositional distinctions. I have endeavored to restrain myself from long discussions of terminology. But here we reach a point where a very common terminology overlaps an erroneous conception. Namely those logicians who follow the lead of Germans, instead of treating of propositions, speak of "judgments" *(Urtheile).* They regard a proposition as merely an expression in speech or writing of a judgment. More than one error is involved in this practice. In the first place, a judgment, as they very correctly teach, is a subject of psychology. Since psychologists, nowadays, not only renounce all pretension to knowledge of the *soul,* but also take pains to avoid talking of the *mind,* the latter is at present not a scientific term, at all; and therefore I am not prepared to say that logic does not, as such, treat of the mind. I should like to take mind in such a sense that this could be affirmed; but in any sense in which psychology,—the scientific psychology now recognized,—treats of mind, logic, I maintain, has no concern with it. Without stopping here to discuss this large question, I will say that psychology is a science which makes special observations; and its whole business is to make the phenomena so observed (along with familiar facts allied to those things), definite and comprehensible. Logic is a science little removed from pure mathematics. It cannot be said to make any positive phenomena known, although [it] takes account [of] and rests upon phenomena of daily and hourly experience, which it so analyzes as to bring out recondite truths about them. One might think that a pure mathematician might assume these things as an initial hypothesis and deduce logic from these; but this turns out, upon trial, not to be the case. The logician has to be recurring to reexamination of the phenomena all along the course of his investigations. But logic is all but as far remote from psychology as is pure mathematics. Logic is the study of the essential nature of signs. A sign is something that exists in replicas. Whether the sign "it is raining," or "all pairs of particles of matter have component accelerations toward one another inversely proportional to the square of the distance," happens to have a replica in writing, in oral speech, or in silent thought, is a distinction of the very minutest interest in logic, which is a study, not of replicas, but of signs. But this is not the only, nor the most serious error involved in making logic treat of "judgments" in place of propositions. It involves confounding two things which must be distinguished if a real comprehension of logic is to be attained. A *proposition,* as I have just intimated, is not to be understood as the lingual expression of a judgment. It is, on the contrary, that sign of which the judgment is one replica and the lingual expression another. But a judgment is distinctly *more* than the mere mental replica of a proposition. It not merely *expresses* the proposition, but it goes further and *accepts* it. I grant that the normal use of a proposition is to affirm it; and its chief logical properties relate to what would result in reference to its affirmation. It is, therefore, convenient in logic to express propositions in most cases in the indicative mood. But the proposition in the sentence, "Socrates est sapiens," strictly expressed, is "Socratem sapientem esse."[9] The defense of this position is that in this way we distinguish between a proposition and the assertion of it; and without such distinction it is impossible to get a distinct notion of the nature of the proposition. One and the same proposition may be affirmed, denied, judged, doubted, inwardly inquired into, put as a question, wished, asked for, effectively commanded, taught, or merely expressed, and does not thereby become a different proposition. What is the nature of these operations? The only one that need detain us is affirmation, including judgment, or affirmation to oneself. As an aid in dissecting the constitution of affirmation I shall employ a certain logical magnifying glass that I have often found efficient in such business. Imagine, then, that I write a proposition on a piece of paper, perhaps a number of times, simply as a calligraphic exercise. It is not likely to prove a dangerous amusement. But suppose I afterward carry the paper before a notary public and make affidavit to its contents. That may prove to be a horse of another color. The reason is that this affidavit may be used to determine an assent to the proposition it contains in the minds of judge and jury;—an effect that the paper would not have had if I had not sworn to it. For certain penalties here and hereafter are attached to swearing to a false proposition; and consequently the fact that I have sworn to it will be taken as a negative index that it is not false. This assent in judge and jury's minds may effect in the minds of sheriff and posse a determination to an act of force to the detriment of some innocent man's liberty or property. Now certain ideas of justice and good order are so powerful that the ultimate result may be very bad for me. This is the way that affirmation looks under the microscope; for the only difference between swearing to a proposition and an ordinary affirmation of it, such as logic contemplates, is that in the latter case the penalties are less, and even less certain than those of the law. The reason there are any penalties is, as before, that the affirmation may determine a judgment to the same effect in the mind of the interpreter to his cost. It cannot be that the sole cause of his believing it is that there are such penalties, since two events cannot cause one another, unless they are simultaneous. There must have been, and we well know that there is, a sort of hypnotic disposition to believe what one is told with an air [of] command. It is Grimes's credenciveness, which is the essence of hypnotism.[10] This disposition produced belief; belief produced the penalties; and the knowledge of these strengthens the disposition to believe.

I have discussed the nature of belief in the *Popular Science Monthly* for November 1877.[11] On the whole, we may set down the following definitions:

A *belief* in a proposition is a controlled and contented habit of acting in ways that will be productive of desired results only if the proposition is true.

An *affirmation* is an act of an utterer of a proposition to an interpreter, and consists, in the first place, in the deliberate exercise, in uttering the proposition, of a force tending to determine a belief in it in the mind of the interpreter. Perhaps that is a sufficient definition of it; but it involves also a voluntary self-subjection to penalties in the event of the interpreter's mind (and still more the general mind of society) subsequently becoming decidedly determined to the belief at once in the falsity of the proposition and in the additional proposition that the utterer believed the proposition to be false at the time he uttered it.

A *judgment* is a mental act deliberately exercising a force tending to determine in the mind of the agent a belief in the proposition; to which should perhaps be added that the agent must be aware of his being liable to inconvenience in the event of the proposition's proving false in any practical aspect.

In order fully to understand the distinction between a proposition and an argument, it will be found important to class these acts, affirmation, etc., and ascertain their precise nature. The question is a purely logical one; but it happens that a false metaphysics is generally current, especially among men who are influenced by physics but yet are not physicists enough fully to comprehend physics, which metaphysics would disincline those who believe in it from readily accepting the purely logical statement of the nature of affirmation. I shall therefore be forced to touch upon metaphysics. Yet I refuse to enter here upon a metaphysical discussion; I shall merely hint at what ground it is necessary to take in opposition to a common doctrine of that kind. Affirmation is of the nature of a symbol. It will be thought that this cannot be the case since an affirmation, as the above analysis shows, produces real effects, physical effects. No sign, however, is a real thing. It has no real being, but only being represented. I might more easily persuade readers to think that affirmation was an index, since an index is, perhaps, a real thing. Its replica, at any rate, is in real reaction with its object, and it forces a reference to that object upon the mind. But a symbol, a word, certainly exists only in replica, contrary to the nature of a real thing; and indeed the symbol only becomes a sign because its interpreter happens to be prepared to represent it as such. Hence, I must and do admit that a symbol cannot exert any real force. Still, I maintain that every sufficiently complete symbol governs things, and that symbols alone do this. I mean that though it is not a force, it is a law. Now those who regard the false metaphysics of which I speak as the only clear opinion on its subject are in the habit of calling laws "uniformities," meaning that what we call laws are, in fact, nothing but common characters of classes of events. It is true that they hold that they are symbols, as I shall endeavor to show that they are; but this is to their minds equivalent to saying that they are common characters of events; for they entertain a very different conception of the nature of a symbol from mine. I begin, then, by showing that a law is not a mere common character of events. Suppose that a man throwing a pair of dice, which were all that honest dice are supposed to be, were to throw sixes a hundred times running. Every mathematician will admit that that would be no ground for expecting the next throw to turn up sixes. It is true that in any actual case in which we should see sixes thrown a hundred times running we should very rightly be confident that the next throw would turn up sixes likewise. But why should we do so? Can anybody sincerely deny that it would be because we should think the throwing of a hundred successive sixes was an almost infallible indication of there being some real connection between those throws, so that the series /was/ not merely a uniformity in the common character of turning up sixes, but something more, a result of a real circumstance about the dice connecting the throws? This example illustrates the logical principle that mere community of character between the members of a collection is no argument, however slender, tending to show that the same character belongs to another object not a member of that collection and not (as far as we have any reason to think) having any real connection with it, unless perchance it be in having the character in question. For the usual sup-position that we make about honest dice is that there will be no real connec-tion (or none of the least significance) between their different throws. I know that writer has copied writer in the feeble analysis of chance as consisting in our ignorance.[12] But the calculus of probabilities is pure nonsense unless it affords assurance in the long run. Now what assurance could there be con-cerning a long run of throws of a pair of dice, if, instead of knowing they were honest dice, we merely did not know whether they were or not, or if, instead of knowing that there would be no important connection between the throws, we merely did not know that there would be? That certain objects A, B, C, etc., are known to have a certain character is not the slightest reason for supposing that another object, Ξ, quite unconnected with the others so far as we know, has that character. Nor has this self-evident proposition ever been denied. A "law," however, is taken very rightly by everybody to be a reason for predicting that an event will have a certain character although the events known to have that character have no other real connection with it than the law. This shows that the law is not a mere uniformity but involves a real con-nection. It is true that those metaphysicians say that if A, B, C, etc., are known to have two common characters and Ξ is known to have one of these, this is a reason for believing that it has the other. But this is quite untenable. Merely having a common character does not constitute a real connection; and those very writers virtually acknowledge this, in reducing law to uniformity, that is, to the possession of a common character, as a way of denying that "law" implies any real connection. What is a law, then? It is a formula to which real events truly conform. By "conform," I mean that, taking the formula as a general principle, if experience shows that the formula applies to a given event, then the result will be confirmed by experience. But that such a general formula is a symbol, and more particularly, an asserted symbolical proposi-tion, is evident. Whether or not this symbol is a reality, even if not recog-nized by you or me or any generations of men, and whether, if so, it implies an Utterer, are metaphysical questions into which I will not now enter. One distinguished writer seems to hold that, although events conform to the for-mula, or rather, although /the formula/ conforms to the Truth of facts, yet it does not influence the facts.[13] This comes perilously near to being pure verbiage; for, seeing that nobody pretends that the formula exerts a compulsive force on the events, what definite meaning can attach to this emphatic denial of the law's "influencing" the facts? The law had such mode of being as it ever has before all the facts had come into existence, for it might already be experientially known; and then the law existing, when the facts happen there is agreement between them and the law. What is it, then, that this writer has in mind? If it were not for the extraordinary misconception of the word "cause" by Mill, I should say that the idea of metaphysical sequence implied in that word, in "influence," and in other similar words, was perfectly clear. Mill's singularity is that he speaks of the cause of a singular event. Everybody else speaks of the cause of a "fact," which is an element of the event. But, with Mill, it is the event in its entirety which is caused. The consequence is that Mill is obliged to define the cause as the totality of all the circumstances attending the event.[14] This is, strictly speaking, the Universe of being in its totality. But any event, just as it exists, in its entirety, is nothing else but the same Universe of being in its totality. It strictly follows, therefore, from Mill's use of the words, that the only *causatum* is the entire Universe of being and that its only cause is itself. He thus deprives the word of all utility. As everybody else but Mill and his school more or less clearly understands the word, it is a highly useful one. That which is caused, the *causatum*, is, not the entire event, but such abstracted element of an event as is expressible in a proposition, or what we call a "fact." The cause is another "fact." Namely, it is, in the first place, a fact which could, within the range of possibility, have its being without the being of the *causatum*; but, secondly, it could not be a real fact while a certain third complementary fact, expressed or understood, was realized, without the being of the *causatum*; and thirdly, although the actually realized *causatum* might perhaps be realized by other causes or by accident, yet the existence of the entire possible *causatum* could not be realized without the cause in question. It may be added that a part of a cause, if a part in that respect in which the cause is a cause, is also called a *cause*. In other respects, too, the scope of the word will be somewhat widened in the sequel. If the cause so defined is a part of the *causatum*, in the sense that the *causatum* could not logically be without the cause, it is called an *internal cause*; otherwise, it is called an *external cause*. If the cause is of the nature of an individual thing or fact, and the other factor requisite to the necessitation of the *causatum* is a general principle, I would call the cause a *minor*, or *individuating*, or perhaps a *physical cause*. If, on the other hand, it is the general principle which is regarded as the cause and the individual fact to which it is applied is taken as the understood factor, I would call the cause a *major*, or *defining*, or perhaps a *psychical cause*. The individuating internal cause is called the *material cause*. Thus the integrant parts of a subject or fact form its *matter*, or material cause. The individuating external cause is called the *efficient*, or *efficient cause*; and the *causatum* is called the *effect*. The defining internal cause is called the *formal cause,* or *form.* All these facts which constitute the definition of a subject or fact make up its form. The defining external cause is called the *final cause,* or *end.* It is hoped that these statements will be found to hit a little more squarely than did those of Aristotle and the scholastics the same bull's eye at which they aimed. From scholasticism and the medieval universities, these conceptions passed in vaguer form into the common mind and vernacular of Western Europe, and especially so in England. Consequently, by the aid of these definitions I think I can make out what it is that the writer mentioned has in mind in saying that it is not the law which influences, or is the final cause of, the facts, but the facts that make up the cause of the law. He means that the general fact which the law of gravitation expresses is composed of the special facts that this stone at such a time fell to the ground as soon as it was free to do so and its upward velocity was exhausted, that each other stone did the same, that each planet at each moment was describing an ellipse having the center of mass of the solar system at a focus, etc., etc.; so that the individual facts are the material cause of the general fact expressed by the law; while the propositions expressing those facts are the efficient cause of the law itself. This is a possible meaning in harmony with the writer's sect of thought; and I believe it is his intended meaning. But this is easily seen not to be true. For the formula relates to all possible events of a given description; which is the same as to say that it relates to all possible events. Now no collection of actual individual events or other objects of any general description can amount to all possible events or objects of that description; for it is possible that an addition should be made to that collection. The individuals do not constitute the matter of a general: those who with Kant,[15] or long before him, said that they *[do],* were wanting in the keen edge of thought requisite for such discussions. On the contrary, the truth of the formula, its really being a sign of the indicated object, is the defining cause of the agreement of the individual facts with it. Namely, this truth fulfills the first condition, which is that it might logically be although there were no such agreement. For it might be true, that is, contain no falsity, that whatever stone there might be on earth would have a real downward component acceleration even though no stone actually existed on earth. It fulfills the second condition, that as soon as the other factor (in this case the actual existence of each stone on earth) was present, the result of the formula, the real downward component of acceleration, would exist. Finally, it fulfills the third condition, that while all existing stones might be accelerated downwards by other causes or by an accidental concurrence of circumstances, yet the downward acceleration of every possible stone would involve the truth of the formula.

It thus appears that the truth of the formula, that is, the law, is, in the strictest sense, the defining cause of the real individual facts. But the formula, if a symbol at all, is a symbol of that object which it indicates as its object. Its truth, therefore, consists in the formula being a symbol. Thus a symbol may be the cause of real individual events and things. It is easy to see that nothing but a symbol can be such a cause, since a cause is by its definition the premiss of an argument; and a symbol alone can be an argument. Every sufficiently complete symbol is a final cause of, and "influences," real events, in precisely the same sense in which my desire to have the window open, that is, the symbol in my mind of the agreeability of it, influences the physical facts of my rising from my chair, going to the window, and opening it. Who but a Millian or a lunatic will deny that that desire influences the opening of the window? Yet the sense in which it does so is none other than that in which every sufficiently complete and true symbol influences real facts.

A symbol is defined as a sign which becomes such by virtue of the fact that it is interpreted as such. The signification of a complex symbol is determined by certain rules of syntax which are part of its meaning. A simple symbol is interpreted to signify what it does from some accidental circumstance or series of circumstances, which the history of any word illustrates. For example, in the latter half of the fifteenth century, a certain model of vehicle came into use in the town of Kots (pronounced, *kotch*) in Hungary. It was copied in other towns, doubtless with some modifications, and was called a *kotsi szeker,* or Kots cart. Copied in still other towns, and always more or less modified, it came to be called, for short, a *cotch*. It thus came about that the *coach* was used, first, for a magnificent vehicle to be drawn by horses for carrying persons in state and in such comfort as that state required; then, for a large and pretentious vehicle to be drawn by four or more horses for conveying passengers from one town to another; and finally, to any large vehicle for conveying passengers at a fare by the seat from one town to another. In all ordinary cases, it is, and must be, an accidental circumstance which causes a symbol to signify just the characters that it does; for were there any necessary, or nearly necessary, reason for it, it would be this which would render the sign a sign, and not the mere fact that so it would be interpreted, as the definition of a symbol requires. It will be well here to interpose a remark as to the identity of a symbol. A sign has its being in its adaptation to fulfill a function. A symbol is adapted to fulfill the function of a sign simply by the fact that it does fulfill it; that is, that it is so understood. It is, therefore, what it is understood to be. Hence, if two symbols are used, without regard to any differences between them, they are replicas of the same symbol. If the difference is looked upon as merely grammatical (as with *he* and *him*), or as merely rhetorical (as with *money* and *spondesime*[16]), or as otherwise insignificant, then logically they are replicas of one symbol. Hardly any symbol directly signifies the characters it signifies; for whatever it signifies it signifies by its power of determining another sign signifying the same character. If I write of the "sound of sawing," the reader will probably do little more than glance sufficiently at the words to assure himself that he could imagine the sound I referred to if he chose to do so. If, however, what *[I]* proceed to say about that sound instigates him to do more, a sort of auditory composite will arise in his imagination of different occasions when he has been near a saw; and this will serve as an icon of the signification of the phrase "sound of a saw." If I had used, instead of that phrase, the word "buzz," although this would have been less precise, yet, owing to the sound of the word being itself a sort of buzz, it would have more directly called up an iconic interpretation. Thus some symbols are far superior to others in point of directness of signification. This is true not only of outward symbols but also of general ideas. When a person remembers something, as for example in trying in a shop to select a ribbon whose color shall match that of an article left at home, he knows that his idea is a memory and not an imagination by a certain feeling of having had the idea before, which he will not be very unlikely to find has been somewhat deceptive. It is a sort of sense of similarity between the present and the past. Even if he had the two colors before his eyes, he could only know them to be similar by a peculiar feeling of similarity; because as two sensations they are different. But in the case supposed, it is not the mere general feeling of similarity which is required but that peculiar variety of it which arises when a present idea is pronounced to be similar to one not now in the mind at all, but formerly in the mind. It is clear that this feeling functions as a symbol. To call it an *icon* of the past idea would be preposterous. For instead of the present idea being serviceable as a substitute for the past idea by virtue of being similar to it, it is on the contrary only known to be similar to it by means of this feeling that it is so. Neither will it answer to call it an *index*. For it is the essence of an index to be in real connection with its object; so that it cannot be mendacious in so far as it is indexical; while this feeling is not infrequently deceptive; sometimes, in everybody's life, absolutely baseless. It is true that it is on the whole veracious; and veracity,—necessitated truth,—can belong to no sign except so far as it involves an index. But a symbol, if sufficiently complete, always involves an index, just as an index sufficiently complete involves an icon. There is an infallible criterion for distinguishing between an index and a symbol.[17] Namely, although an index, like any other sign, only functions as a sign when it is interpreted, yet though it never happen to be interpreted, it remains equally fitted to be the very sign that would be if interpreted. A symbol, on the other hand, that should not be interpreted, would either not be a sign at all, or would only be a sign in an utterly different way. An inscription that nobody ever had interpreted or ever would interpret would be but a fanciful scrawl, an index that some being had been there, but not at all conveying or apt to convey its meaning. Now imagine the feeling which tells us that a present idea has been experienced before not to be interpreted as having that meaning, and what would it be? It would be like any other feeling. No study of it could ever discover that it had any connection with an idea past and gone. Even if this should be discovered, and if it should further be discovered that that connection was of such a nature as to afford assurance that the present idea with which the feeling is connected is similar to that former idea, still this would be by an additional discovery, not involved in the sign itself; a discovery, too, of the nature of a symbol, since it would be the discovery of a general law. The only way in which an index can be a prop-osition is by involving an *icon*. But what *icon* does this feeling present? Does it exhibit anything similar to similarity? To suppose that the feeling in question conveys its meaning by presenting [in] a new idea a vague duplicate of the idea first present, gratuitous as this hypothesis would be, would not suffice to prove the feeling to be an index, since a symbol would be requisite to inform us that the first idea and the newly presented idea were similar; and even then there would be the element of preteritness to be conveyed, which no icon and consequently no index could signify. It is quite certain therefore that in this feeling we have a definite instance of a symbol which, in a certain sense, *neces-sarily* signifies what it does. We have already seen that it can only be by an accident, and not by inherent necessity, that a symbol signifies what it does. The two results are reconciled by the consideration that the accident in this case is that we are so constituted that that feeling shall be so interpreted by us. A little psychological examination will vindicate the first assertion. For although it is not a very rare experience to have a strong feeling of having been in a present situation before, when in fact one never was in such a situa-tion, yet everybody, unless he be a psychologist, is invariably deeply impressed by such an experience (or at least by his *first* experience of this sort), will not forget it for long years, and is importuned by the notion that he is here confronted with a phenomenon profoundly mysterious, if not super-natural. The psychologist may waive the matter aside, in his debonair satis-faction with the state of his science; but he seems to me to overlook the most instructive part of the phenomenon. This is, that though internal feelings generally are testimonies proverbially requiring to be received with reserve and caution, yet when this particular one plays as false, people feel as if the bottom had fallen out of the universe of being. Why should they take the mat-ter so seriously? It is that if we try to analyze what is *meant* by saying that a present idea "resembles" one that is past and gone, we cannot find that any-thing else is *meant* but that there is this feeling connected with it. From which it seems to result that for this feeling to be mendacious would be a self-contra-dictory state of things; in which case we might well say that the bottom had fallen out of Truth itself. Now a symbol which should by logical necessity sig-nify what it does would obviously have nothing but its own application, or predication, for its own signification as a predicate; or, to express the matter in abbreviation, would signify itself alone. For anything else that might be sup-posed to be signified by it might, by logical possibility, not be so signified. That such a symbol should be false would indeed involve a contradiction. Thus, the feeling of amazement at the "sense of pre-existence," as it has been called, amounts virtually to nothing more than the natural confusion of that which is necessary by virtue of the constitution of the mind with that which is logically necessary. The feeling under discussion is necessary only in the latter sense. Consequently, its falsity is not absurd but only abnormal. Nor is it its own sole signification, but only the sole signification recognizable without transcendental thought; because to say that a present idea is really similar to an idea really experienced in the past means that a being sufficiently informed would know that the effect of the later idea would be a revivification of the effect of the earlier idea, in respect to its quality of feeling. Yet it must be remarked that the only effect of a quality of feeling is to produce a memory, itself a quality of feeling; and that to say that two of those are similar is, after all, only to say that the feeling which is the symbol of similarity will attach to them. Thus, the feeling of recognition of a present idea as having been experienced has for its signification the applicability of a part of itself. The general feeling of similarity, though less startling, is of the same kind. All the special occurrences of the feeling of similarity are recognized as themselves similar, by the application to them of the same symbol of similarity. It is Kant's "I think," which he considers to be an act of thought, that is, to be of the nature of a symbol. But his introduction of the *ego* into it was due to his confusion of this with another element.

This feeling is not peculiar among feelings in signifying itself alone; for the same is true of the feeling "blue" or any other. It must not be forgotten that a feeling is not a psychosis, or state of mind, but is merely a quality of a psychosis, with which is associated a degree of vividness, or relative disturbance, or prominence, of the quality in the psychosis, as measured chiefly by after-effects. These psychoses are icons; and it is in being a symbol that the feeling of similarity is distinguished from other feelings. But the signification of the psychosis as a sign is that the percept to which it ultimately refers has the same quality, as determined by the symbol-feeling of similarity.

My principal object in drawing attention to this symbol of similarity is to show that the significations of symbols have various grades of directness up to the limit of being themselves their own significations. An icon is significant with absolute directness of a character which it embodies; and every symbol refers more or less indirectly to an icon.

An index is directly denotative of a real object with which it is in reaction. Every symbol refers more or less indirectly to a real object through an index. One goes into a shop and asks for a yard of silk. He wants a piece of silk, which has been placed (either by measurement or estimation depending on habits involving indices) into reactive comparison with a yardstick, which itself by successive reactions has been put into reaction with a certain real bar in Westminster. The word "yard" is an example of a symbol which is denotative in a high degree of directness. When we consider the successive comparisons more scientifically, we have to admit that each is subject to a probable error. The more pains we take to make the reaction significant, the more we are forced to recognize that each single act of comparison gives its own result; and a general inference which we make from a large number of these represents what each one would be if it could be performed more accurately. It is by the intervention of the inferential symbol that we virtually obtain a more intimate reaction. When a biologist labels a specimen, he has performed a comparison, as truly reactive in its nature as that of two standards of length, with an original "type-specimen," as he calls the prototype. His label thus involves something of the nature of an index, although less prominently than does the word "yard." It would be more scientific if in place of a single proto-type, comparisons were made with twenty-five different bars of different material and kept under different conditions, and that were called a "yard" which agreed with the mean of them all; and so in biology, there ought to be twenty-five type-specimens, exhibiting the allowable range of variation as well as the normal mean character. This more scientific proceeding is that of common sense in regard to ordinary names, except that instead of twenty-five instances, there are many more. I go into a furniture shop and say I want a "table." I rely upon my presumption that the shopkeeper and I have under-gone reactional experiences which though different have been so connected by reactional experiences as to make them virtually the same, in consequence of which "table" suggests to him, as it does to me, a movable piece of furni-ture with a flat top of about such a height that one might conveniently sit down to work at it. This convenient height, although not measured, is of the same nature as the yard of silk already considered. It means convenient for men of ordinary stature; and his reactive experience presumably agrees with mine as to what the ordinary stature is. I go into a shop and ask for butter. I am shown something, and I ask "Is this butter, or is it oleomargarine or some-thing of the sort?" "Oh, I assure you that it is, in chemical strictness, butter." "In chemical strictness, eh? Well, you know what the breed of neat cattle is, as well as I do. It is an individual object, of which we have both seen parts. Now I want to know whether this substance has been churned from milk drawn from the breed of neat cattle." That breed is known to us only by real reac-tional experience. What is gold? It is an elementary substance having an atomic weight of about 197¼.[18] In saying that it is elementary, we mean unde-composable in the present state of chemistry, which can only be recognized by real reactional experience. In saying that its atomic weight is 197¼, we mean that it is so compared with hydrogen. What, then, is hydrogen? It is an elementary gas 14½ times as light as air. And what is air? Why, it is this with which we have reactional experience about us. The reader may try instances of his own until no doubt remains in regard to symbols of things experienced, that they are always denotative through indices; such proof will be far surer than any apodictic demonstration. As to symbols of things not experienced it is clear that these must describe their objects by means of their differences from things experienced. It is plain that in the directness of their denotation, symbols vary through all degrees. It is, of course, quite possible for a symbol to represent itself, at least in the only sense in which a thing that has no *real being* but only *being represented*, and which exists in *replica*, can be said to be identical with a real and therefore individual object. A map may be a map of itself; that is to say one replica of it may be the object mapped. But this does not make the denotation extraordinarily direct. As an example of a symbol of that character, we may rather take the symbol which is expressed in words as "the Truth," or "Universe of Being." Every symbol whatever must denote what this symbol denotes; so that any symbol considered as denoting the Truth necessarily denotes that which it denotes; and in denoting it, it *is* that very thing, or a fragment of it taken for the whole. It is the whole taken so far as it need be taken for the purpose of denotation; for denotation essentially takes a part for its whole.

But the most characteristic aspect of a symbol is its aspect as related to its interpretant; because a symbol is distinguished as a sign which becomes such by virtue of determining its interpretant. An interpretant of a symbol is an outgrowth of the symbol. We have used the phrase, a symbol *determines* its interpretant. Determination implies a *determinandum*, a subject to be determined. What is that? We must suppose that there is something like a sheet of paper, blank or with a blank space upon it upon which an interpretant sign may be written. What is the nature of this blank? In affording room for the writing of a symbol, it is *ipso facto* itself a symbol, although a wholly vague one. In affording room for an interpretant of that particular symbol, it is already an interpretant of that symbol, although only a partial one. An *entire* interpretant should involve a replica of the original symbol. In fact, the interpretant symbol, so far as it is no more than an interpretant *is* the original symbol, although perhaps in a more developed state. But the interpretant symbol may be at the same time an interpretant of an independent symbol. A symbol is something which has the power of reproducing itself, and that essentially, since it is constituted a symbol only by the interpretation. This interpretation involves a power of the symbol to cause a real fact; and although I desire to avoid metaphysics, yet when a false metaphysics invades the province of logic, I am forced to say that nothing can be more futile than to attempt to form a conception of the universe which shall overlook the power of representations to cause real facts. What is the purpose of trying to form a conception of the universe if it is not to render things intelligible? But if this is to be done, we necessarily defeat ourselves if we insist upon reducing everything to a norm which renders everything that happens, essentially and *ipso facto* unintelligible. That, however, is what we do, if we do not admit the power of representations to cause real facts. If we are to explain the universe, we must assume that there was in the beginning a state of things in which there was nothing, no reaction and no quality, no matter, no consciousness, no space and no time, but just nothing at all. Not determinately nothing. For that which is determinately not *A* supposes the being of *A* in some mode. Utter indetermination. But a symbol alone is indeterminate. Therefore, Nothing, the indeterminate of the absolute beginning, is a symbol.[19] That is the way in which the beginning of things can alone be understood. What logically follows? We are not to content ourselves with our instinctive sense of logicality. That is logical which comes from the essential nature of a symbol. Now it is of the essential nature of a symbol that it determines an interpretant, which is itself a symbol. A symbol, therefore, produces an endless series of interpretants. Does anybody suspect all this of being sheer nonsense? *Distinguo*. There can, it is true, be no positive information about what antedated the entire Universe of being; because, to begin with, there was nothing to have information about. But the universe is intelligible; and therefore it is possible to give a general account of it and its origin. This general account is a symbol; and from the nature of a symbol, it must begin with the formal assertion that there was an indeterminate nothing of the nature of a symbol. This would be false if it conveyed any information. But it is the correct and logical manner of beginning an account of the universe. As a symbol it produced its infinite series of interpretants, which in the beginning were absolutely vague like itself. But the direct interpretant of any symbol must in the first stage of it be merely the *tabula rasa* for an interpretant. Hence the immediate interpretant of this vague Nothing was not even determinately vague, but only vaguely hovering between determinacy and vagueness; and *its* immediate interpretant was vaguely hovering between vaguely hovering between vagueness and determinacy and determinate vagueness or determinacy, and so on, *ad infinitum*. But every endless series must logically have a limit.[20]

Leaving that line of thought unfinished for the present owing to the feeling of insecurity it provokes, let us note, first, that it is of the nature of a symbol to create a *tabula rasa* and therefore an endless series of *tabulae rasae*, since such creation is merely representation, the *tabulae rasae* being entirely indeterminate except to be representative. Herein is a real effect; but a symbol could not be without that power of producing a real effect. The symbol represents itself to be represented; and that representedness is real owing to its utter vagueness. For all that is represented must be thoroughly borne out.

For reality is compulsive. But the compulsiveness is absolutely *hic et nunc*. It is for an instant and it is gone. Let it be no more and it is absolutely nothing. The reality only exists as an element of the regularity. And the regularity is the symbol. Reality, therefore, can only be regarded as the limit of the endless series of symbols.

A symbol is essentially a purpose, that is to say, is a representation that seeks to make itself definite, or seeks to produce an interpretant more definite than itself. For its whole signification consists in its determining an interpretant; so that it is from its interpretant that it derives the actuality of its signification.

A *tabula rasa* having been determined as representative of the symbol that determines it, that *tabula rasa* tends to become determinate. The vague always tends to become determinate, simply because its vagueness does not determine it to be vague (as the limit of an endless series). In so far as the interpretant is the symbol, as it is in some measure, the determination agrees with that of the symbol. But in so far as it fails to be its better self, it is liable to depart from the meaning of the symbol. Its purpose, however, is to represent the symbol in its representation of its object; and therefore, the determination is followed by a further development, in which it becomes corrected. It is of the nature of a sign to be an individual replica and to be in that replica a living general. By virtue of this, the interpretant is animated by the original replica, or by the sign it contains, with the power of representing the true character of the object. That the object has at all a character can only consist in a representation that it has so,—a representation having power to live down all opposition. In these two steps, of determination and of correction, the interpretant aims at the object more than at the original replica and may be truer and fuller than the latter. The very entelechy of being lies in being representable. A sign cannot even be false without being a sign and so far as it is a sign it must be true. A symbol is an embryonic reality endowed with power of growth into the very truth, the very entelechy of reality. This appears mystical and mysterious simply because we insist on remaining blind to what is plain, that there can be no reality which has not the life of a symbol.

How could such an idea as that of *red* arise? It can only have been by gradual determination from pure indeterminacy. A vagueness not determined to be vague, by its nature begins at once to determine itself. Apparently we can come no nearer than that to understanding the universe.

That is not necessarily logical which strikes me today as logical; still less, as mathematics amply exemplifies, is nothing logical except what appears to me so. That is logical which it is necessary to admit in order to render the universe intelligible. And the first of all logical principles is that the indeterminate should determine itself as best it may.

A chaos of reactions utterly without any approach to law is absolutely nothing; and therefore pure nothing was such a chaos. Then pure indeterminacy having developed determinate possibilities, creation consisted in mediating between the lawless reactions and the general possibilities by the influx of a symbol. This symbol was the purpose of creation. Its object was the entelechy of being which is the ultimate representation.

We can now see what *judgment* and *assertion* are. The man is a symbol. Different men, so far as they can have any ideas in common, are the same symbol. Judgment is the determination of the man-symbol to have whatever interpretant the judged proposition has. Assertion is the determination of the man-symbol to determining the interpreter, so far as he is interpreter, in the same way.

23

Ideas, Stray or Stolen, about Scientific Writing

MS 774. [First published by J. M. Krois in Philosophy and Rhetoric *11 (1978):147–55. Probably intending it for the* Popular Science Monthly, *Peirce wrote this article late in 1904, after he had published a negative review of a book by T. C. Allbutt on scientific writing (CN 3:179–81). Peirce planned a two-part essay on the rhetoric of scientific communications, the first to be general, and the second, special, but he only wrote the first one, whose complete title ended with "No. 1" here omitted.]* *Somewhat more popular in style than most of Peirce's writings, this short paper should be considered along with selections 20–22 as part of the first comprehensive statement of Peirce's "mature" general theory of signs. Here Peirce focuses on the third science of his semiotic trivium, rhetoric, which he has liberated from its traditional limitation to speech. The aim of his "speculative rhetoric" is to find out "the general secret of rendering signs effective," no matter what their kind. The range of semiotic effects taken to be legitimate interpretants is extended to include feelings and even physical results, in addition to thoughts and other symbols. Among the surprises of this paper, we learn that nothing can be represented unless it is of the nature of a sign and that ideas can only be communicated through their physical effects. Although brief, this paper provides a vivid snapshot of a broad terrain that still contains virgin territory for semioticians and language theorists.*

Scientific journals are publishing, nowadays, many discussions concerning two matters which the late enormous multiplication of true scientific workers has raised to vital importance; namely, the best vocabulary for one or another branch of knowledge, and the best types of titles for scientific papers. Both are plainly questions of rhetoric. To a good many persons of literary culture it has hitherto seemed that there was little or no room in scientific writings for any other rule of rhetoric than that of expressing oneself in the simplest and directest manner, and that to talk of the style of a scientific communication was somewhat like talking of the moral character of a fish. Nor can one fairly say that this view of the humanists has been a particularly narrow view, since by a good many persons trained to the scientific life a coupling of the ideas of rhetoric and of science would hitherto equally have been regarded as a typical example of incongruity. Yet now and here we come upon this phenomenon of two questions of rhetoric agitating the surface of the scientific deep; and looking a little beneath, we surprise the severest sciences doing homage to rules of expression as stringent and strange as any of those by which the excellence of compositions in Chinese or in Urdu is judged. A proposition of geometry, a definition of a botanical species, a description of a crystal or of a telescopic nebula is subjected to a mandatory form of statement that is artificial in the extreme. Evidently, our conception of rhetoric has got to be generalized; and while we are about it, why not remove the restriction of rhetoric to speech? What is the principal virtue ascribed to algebraical notation, if it be not the rhetorical virtue of perspicuity? Has not many a picture, many a sculpture, the very same fault which in a poem we analyze as being "too rhetorical"? Let us cut short such objections by acknowledging at once, as an *ens in posse*, a universal art of rhetoric, which shall be the general secret of rendering signs effective, including under the term "sign" every picture, diagram, natural cry, pointing finger, wink, knot in one's handkerchief, memory, dream, fancy, concept, indication, token, symptom, letter, numeral, word, sentence, chapter, book, library, and in short whatever, be it in the physical universe, be it in the world of thought, that, whether embodying an idea of any kind (and permit us throughout to use this term to cover purposes and feelings), or being connected with some existing object, or referring to future events through a general rule, causes something else, its interpreting sign, to be determined to a corresponding relation to the same idea, existing thing, or law. Whether there can be such a universal *art* or not, there ought, at any rate to be (and indeed there is, if students do not wonderfully deceive themselves) a science to which should be referable the fundamental principles of everything like rhetoric,—a *speculative rhetoric*, the science of the essential conditions under which a sign may determine an interpretant sign of itself and of whatever it signifies, or may, as a sign, bring about a physical result. Yes, a physical result; for though we often speak with just contempt of "mere" words, inasmuch as signs by themselves can exert no brute force, nevertheless it has always been agreed, by nominalist and realist alike, that general ideas are words,—or ideas, or signs of some sort. Now, by whatever machinery it may be accomplished, certain it is that somehow and in some true and proper sense general ideas do produce stupendous physical effects. For it would be a miserable logomachy to deny that a man's purpose of going down to his office causes him to go there; well, a purpose is a general idea, and his going is a physical fact. If it be objected that it is not the general ideas, but the men who believe in them, that cause the physical events, the answer is that it is the ideas that prompt men to champion them, that inspire those champions with courage, that develop their characters, and that confer upon them a magical sway over other men. It is necessary to insist upon the point for the reason that ideas cannot be communicated at all except through their physical effects. Our photographs, telephones, and wireless telegraphs, as well as the sum total of all the work that steam engines have ever done, are, in sober common sense and literal truth, the outcome of the general ideas that are expressed in the first book of the *Novum Organum*.[1]

The speculative rhetoric that we are speaking of is a branch of the analytical study of the essential conditions to which all signs are subject,—a science named *semeiotics*, though identified by many thinkers with logic. In the Roman schools, grammar, logic, and rhetoric were felt to be akin and to make up a rounded whole called the *trivium*. This feeling was just; for the three disciplines named correspond to the three essential branches of semeiotics, of which the first, called *speculative grammar* by Duns Scotus,[2] studies the ways in which an object can be a sign; the second, the leading part of logic, best termed *speculative critic*, studies the ways in which a sign can be related to the object independent of it that it represents; while the third is the speculative rhetoric just mentioned.

In a publication like this,[3] all scientifically thorough discussion of any but the smallest points would be out of place. We have no room for more, nor has the average reader,—reading the journal during his journey up town, let us suppose,—leisure for anything more than such ideas, serious or light, as might be struck out in conversation between two clever, but two probably tired and hungry, companions. Of the writer it is to be expected that he should have carried through as exhaustive a study as possible of every point he touches; and certes he should not make a secret of any truth merely because its study is difficult. Only, when he comes to deliver his ideas, good manners require that he should dismount from any high horse, and submit his conclusions as views that the reader is free to accept or reject, as may seem good to him. If the proposition that the circle cannot be squared happens to be pertinent to the matter in hand, by all means let him enunciate it. But, seeing that he cannot demonstrate it here, let him not have the air of denying the reader's perfect logical right to entertain the contrary hypothesis. Nor should the writer aver his own belief in the theorem, since the peculiar notions of an anonymous individual have no interest for the public. He may, at most, report that the impossibility of the circle's being squared is a proposition that has recommended itself to men generally esteemed competent; whereupon the reader of good sense will feel sure, as well he may, that no such intimation would have appeared in these columns unless the proposition had been a fruit ripened under the blaze of arduous investigation. But the day of editorial omniscience is past.

Of the three branches of semeiotics, the two first, the speculative grammar and critic, have been greatly elaborated. The speculative rhetoric has been comparatively neglected; yet enough has been done by two or three analysts to give results comparable in extent and value with the pure scientific contents of an ordinary textbook on logic,—enough, therefore, to afford no little guidance in forming opinions about ordinary rhetoric, and to give a notion of what the general character of its influence upon ordinary rhetoric is likely to be. It must not be supposed that there is anything of the nature of metaphysical speculation in this speculative rhetoric. "Speculative" is merely the Latin form corresponding to the Greek word "theoretical," and is here intended to signify that the study is of the *purely* scientific kind, not a practical science, still less an art. Its most essential business is to ascertain by logical analysis, greatly facilitated by the development of the other branches of semeiotics, what are the indispensable conditions of a sign's acting to determine another sign nearly equivalent to itself. A few examples have been remarked of artificial signs automatically reproducing themselves without being intended to do so. An engraving may make a vague copy of itself upon the tissue-paper guard placed over it. But these are confined to too narrow a class to illustrate anything more than the possibility of such a thing. The reproduction of signs in intended ways is, of course, common enough, but is as mysterious as the reciprocal action of mind and matter. Some of the requisites of communication which analysis has signalized are obvious enough; others are not so. Thus, it is said to be a necessary result of the analysis that the object represented by the sign, and whose characters are independent of such representation, should itself be of the nature of a sign, so that its characters are not independent of *all* representation. This is intelligible from the point of view of pragmatism, according to which the objects of which ordinary general propositions have to be true, if they are to be true at all, are the body of future percepts. But percepts are themselves signs, whether veracious or not. The fact that the characters of the future percepts are independent of what they have been expected to be does not in the least prevent their being signs. This result of analysis, that every object represented must be of the nature of a sign, is important (if accepted as true) for certain kinds of composition. Another remarkable result is that an entirely new sign can never be created by an act of communication, but that the utmost possible is that a sign already existing should be filled out and corrected. Thus, tell me that there is a diamond mine at a place I never heard of and of whose whereabouts I have not the slightest idea, and you tell me nothing; but tell me that I can find it by following out a path, the entrance to which I know well, and you are simply filling out my knowledge of that path. So you can convey no idea of colors to a man born blind; yet a certain optical investigator of high repute, domestic and foreign, is color-blind; and although the word red cannot have the same meaning to him that it has to the rest of us, yet he really knows more about the sensation than you and I are likely to do, in that he knows very exactly its relations to the sensations that he does possess. A writer who should lose sight of this principle would be in danger of becoming quite unintelligible. It is needless to go further to show that the sort of help that one who wishes to learn to write well can promise himself from the study of speculative rhetoric will not consist in any hitherto unheard of devices for conveying ideas to the reader's mind, but rather in clearer notions of the lineage and relationship of the different maxims of rhetoric, such notions carrying with them juster judgments of the several extents and limitations of those maxims.

It would be needless, we trust, to interpose any warning against inferring that a theory of rhetoric is false because a given advocate of it exhibits little grace, dexterity, or tact in the handling of language. For we all know how seldom an author treating of a particular kind of skill is found to be remarkably endowed himself with the skill he discourses about. Many a time, it has been precisely his consciousness of natural deficiency in that respect that has led him to study the art.

The general trend of the modifications that would be introduced into ordinary rhetoric by regarding it as a structure reared upon the foundation of the abstract study aforesaid would be determined in great part by the circumstance that the immediate basis of this ordinary rhetoric would be conceived to be merely one of a large number of special studies, or rather as one group of a large number of groups of special studies. For the specialization would be of three modes: first, according to the special nature of the ideas to be conveyed; secondly, according to the special class of signs to be interpreted,—the special medium of communication; and thirdly, according to the special nature of the class of signs into which the interpretation is to take place. The leading division of the first mode would be into a rhetoric of fine art, where the matter is of feeling mainly; a rhetoric of practical persuasion, where the chief matter is of the nature of a resolve; and a rhetoric of science, where the matter is knowledge. The rhetoric of science would be subdivided into a rhetoric of the communication of discoveries, a rhetoric of scientific digests and surveys, and a rhetoric of applications of science to special kinds of purposes. The rhetoric of communications of discoveries will vary again according as the discoveries belong to mathematics, to philosophy, or to special science; and further varieties, by no means insignificant, will result from the subdivision of the sciences. One principal kind of rhetoric resulting from the second mode of specialization would be the rhetoric of speech and language; and this again would differ for languages of different families. The rhetoric naturally adapted to a Shemitic tongue must be very different from a rhetoric well suited to Aryan speech. Moreover, each Aryan language has, or ought to have, its special rhetoric differing from that of even closely allied languages. German and English are marked instances of this. The rules of the common run of the books, based upon rules of Greek and Latin rhetoric, are adapted to English compositions of highly artificial styles alone. Fancy writing a fairy tale in periodic sentences! One effect of basing rhetoric upon the abstract science would be to take down the pretensions of many of the rhetorical rules and to limit their application to a particular dialect among the dialects of literary English,—that one which is founded on classical studies. At the same time, it would emphasize the necessity of the studies of Greek and Latin as the only way of gaining a mastery of an extremely important dialect of our language. The principal kind of rhetoric resulting from the third mode of specialization is the rhetoric of signs to be translated into human thought; and one inevitable result of basing rhetoric upon the abstract science that looks on human thought as a special kind of sign would be to bring into high relief the principle that in order to address the human mind effectively, one ought, in theory, to erect one's art upon the immediate base of a profound study of human physiology and psychology. One ought to know just what the processes are whereby an idea can be conveyed to a human mind and become embedded in its habits; and according to this doctrine, all the rules of ordinary rhetoric ought to be hinged upon such considerations and not upon the gratuitous assumption that men can only think according to a certain syntax-type of sentence that happens to be very common in the languages most familiar to most of us, but into which other sentences can be jammed only by Procrustean barbarities.

24

What Pragmatism Is

P 1078: The Monist *15 (April 1905):161–81. [Published in CP
5.411–37. Initially planned as a part of a review of Herbert Nichols's A*
Treatise on Cosmology, *this paper was composed in the middle of the
summer 1904. When it appeared in* The Monist, *it was supposed to be
followed by two additional papers, "The Consequences of Pragmaticism"
and "The Evidences for Pragmaticism," but this plan metamorphosed over
the following two years, and even though two more papers appeared, the
series was never concluded.] With this series, Peirce returns to his 1903
project to explain his pragmatism in a way that would distinguish it from
popular variants and facilitate the exposition of its proof. He renames it
"pragmaticism," a name "ugly enough to be safe from kidnappers," and
explores the underlying presuppositions, summing them up in the cryptic
admonition: "Dismiss make-believes." A key belief is that learning, or
mental development of any kind, has to begin with the "immense mass of
cognition already formed." In an imagined dialog between a pragmaticist
and a critic, Peirce addresses concerns about the purpose and consequences
of pragmaticism, emphasizing the importance of experimentation and explaining how the meaning of every proposition lies in the future. He concludes by arguing that while the pragmaticist regards Thirdness as an
essential ingredient of reality, it can only govern through action, and action cannot arise except in feeling. It is the dependence of Thirdness on action (Secondness) and feeling (Firstness) that distinguishes pragmaticism
from the absolute idealism of Hegel.*

The writer of this article has been led by much experience to believe that
every physicist, and every chemist, and, in short, every master in any department of experimental science, has had his mind molded by his life in the laboratory to a degree that is little suspected. The experimentalist himself can
hardly be fully aware of it, for the reason that the men whose intellects he
really knows about are much like himself in this respect. With intellects of
widely different training from his own, whose education has largely been a
thing learned out of books, he will never become inwardly intimate, be he on
ever so familiar terms with them; for he and they are as oil and water, and
though they be shaken up together, it is remarkable how quickly they will go
their several mental ways, without having gained more than a faint flavor
from the association. Were those other men only to take skillful soundings of
the experimentalist's mind,—which is just what they are unqualified to do, for

the most part,—they would soon discover that, excepting perhaps upon topics where his mind is trammelled by personal feeling or by his bringing up, his disposition is to think of everything just as everything is thought of in the laboratory, that is, as a question of experimentation. Of course, no living man possesses in their fullness all the attributes characteristic of his type: it is not the typical doctor whom you will see every day driven in buggy or coupé, nor is it the typical pedagogue that will be met with in the first schoolroom you enter. But when you have found, or ideally constructed upon a basis of observation, the typical experimentalist, you will find that whatever assertion you may make to him, he will either understand as meaning that if a given prescription for an experiment ever can be and ever is carried out in act, an experience of a given description will result, or else he will see no sense at all in what you say. If you talk to him as Mr. Balfour talked not long ago to the British Association, saying that "the physicist seeks for something deeper than the laws connecting possible objects of experience," that "his object is a physical reality" unrevealed in experiments, and that the existence of such nonexperiential reality "is the unalterable faith of science," to all such ontological meaning you will find the experimentalist mind to be color-blind.[1] What adds to that confidence in this which the writer owes to his conversations with experimentalists is that he himself may almost be said to have inhabited a laboratory from the age of six until long past maturity; and having all his life associated mostly with experimentalists, it has always been with a confident sense of understanding them and of being understood by them.

That laboratory life did not prevent the writer (who here and in what follows simply exemplifies the experimentalist type) from becoming interested in methods of thinking; and when he came to read metaphysics, although much of it seemed to him loosely reasoned and determined by accidental prepossessions, yet in the writings of some philosophers, especially Kant, Berkeley, and Spinoza, he sometimes came upon strains of thought that recalled the ways of thinking of the laboratory, so that he felt he might trust to them; all of which has been true of other laboratory-men.

Endeavoring, as a man of that type naturally would, to formulate what he so approved, he framed the theory that a *conception*, that is, the rational purport of a word or other expression, lies exclusively in its conceivable bearing upon the conduct of life; so that, since obviously nothing that might not result from experiment can have any direct bearing upon conduct, if one can define accurately all the conceivable experimental phenomena which the affirmation or denial of a concept could imply, one will have therein a complete definition of the concept, and *there is absolutely nothing more in it*. For this doctrine he invented the name *pragmatism*. Some of his friends wished him to call it *practicism* or *practicalism* (perhaps on the ground that πρακτικός is better Greek than πραγματικός). But for one who had learned philosophy out of Kant, as the writer, along with nineteen out of every twenty experimentalists who have turned to philosophy, had done, and who still thought in

Kantian terms most readily, *praktisch* and *pragmatisch* were as far apart as the two poles, the former belonging in a region of thought where no mind of the experimentalist type can ever make sure of solid ground under his feet, the latter expressing relation to some definite human purpose. Now quite the most striking feature of the new theory was its recognition of an inseparable connection between rational cognition and rational purpose; and that consideration it was which determined the preference for the name *pragmatism*.

* * *

Concerning the matter of philosophical nomenclature, there are a few plain considerations, which the writer has for many years longed to submit to the deliberate judgment of those few fellow-students of philosophy, who deplore the present state of that study, and who are intent upon rescuing it therefrom and bringing it to a condition like that of the natural sciences, where investigators, instead of contemning each the work of most of the others as misdirected from beginning to end, cooperate, stand upon one another's shoulders, and multiply incontestable results; where every observation is repeated, and isolated observations go for little; where every hypothesis that merits attention is subjected to severe but fair examination, and only after the predictions to which it leads have been remarkably borne out by experience is trusted at all, and even then only provisionally; where a radically false step is rarely taken, even the most faulty of those theories which gain wide credence being true in their main experiential predictions. To those students, it is submitted that no study can become scientific in the sense described, until it provides itself with a suitable technical nomenclature, whose every term has a single definite meaning universally accepted among students of the subject, and whose vocables have no such sweetness or charms as might tempt loose writers to abuse them,—which is a virtue of scientific nomenclature too little appreciated. It is submitted that the experience of those sciences which have conquered the greatest difficulties of terminology, which are unquestionably the taxonomic sciences, chemistry, mineralogy, botany, zoology, has conclusively shown that the only way in which the requisite unanimity and requisite ruptures with individual habits and preferences can be brought about is so to shape the canons of terminology that they shall gain the support of *moral principle* and of every man's sense of decency; and that, in particular (under defined restrictions), the general feeling shall be that he who introduces a new conception into philosophy is under an obligation to invent acceptable terms to express it, and that when he has done so, the duty of his fellow-students is to accept those terms, and to resent any wresting of them from their original meanings, as not only a gross discourtesy to him to whom philosophy was indebted for each conception, but also as an injury to philosophy itself; and furthermore, that once a conception has been supplied with suitable and sufficient words for its expression, no other *technical* terms denoting the same things, considered in the same relations, should be countenanced. Should this suggestion find favor, it might be deemed needful that the philosophians in congress assembled should adopt, after due deliberation, convenient canons to limit the application of the principle. Thus, just as is done in chemistry, it might be wise to assign fixed meanings to certain prefixes and suffixes. For example, it might be agreed, perhaps, that the prefix *prope-* should mark a broad and rather indefinite extension of the meaning of the term to which it was prefixed; the name of a doctrine would naturally end in *-ism*, while *-icism* might mark a more strictly defined acception of that doctrine, etc. Then again, just as in biology no account is taken of terms antedating Linnæus, so in philosophy it might be found best not to go back of the scholastic terminology. To illustrate another sort of limitation, it has probably never happened that any philosopher has attempted to give a general name to his own doctrine without that name's soon acquiring, in common philosophical usage, a signification much broader than was originally intended. Thus, special systems go by the names Kantianism, Benthamism, Comtianism, Spencerianism, etc., while transcendentalism, utilitarianism, positivism, evolutionism, synthetic philosophy, etc., have irrevocably and very conveniently been elevated to broader governments.

*   *   *

After awaiting in vain, for a good many years, some particularly opportune conjuncture of circumstances that might serve to recommend his notions of the ethics of terminology, the writer has now, at last, dragged them in over head and shoulders, on an occasion when he has no specific proposal to offer nor any feeling but satisfaction at the course usage has run without any canons or resolutions of a congress. His word "pragmatism" has gained general recognition in a generalized sense that seems to argue power of growth and vitality. The famed psychologist, James, first took it up, seeing that his "radical empiricism" substantially answered to the writer's definition of pragmatism, albeit with a certain difference in the point of view.[2] Next, the admirably clear and brilliant thinker, Mr. Ferdinand C. S. Schiller, casting about for a more attractive name for the "anthropomorphism" of his *Riddles of the Sphinx*, lit, in that most remarkable paper of his on "Axioms as Postulates,"[3] upon the same designation "pragmatism," which in its original sense was in generic agreement with his own doctrine, for which he has since found the more appropriate specification "humanism," while he still retains "pragmatism" in a somewhat wider sense.[4] So far all went happily. But at present, the word begins to be met with occasionally in the literary journals, where it gets abused in the merciless way that words have to expect when they fall into literary clutches. Sometimes the manners of the British have effloresced in scolding at the word as ill-chosen,—ill-chosen, that is, to express some meaning that it was rather designed to exclude. So then, the writer, finding his bantling "pragmatism" so promoted, feels that it is time to kiss his child goodbye and relinquish it to its higher destiny; while to serve the precise purpose of expressing the original definition, he begs to announce the birth of the word "pragmaticism," which is ugly enough to be safe from kidnappers.*

Much as the writer has gained from the perusal of what other pragmatists have written, he still thinks there is a decisive advantage in his original conception of the doctrine. From this original form every truth that follows from any of the other forms can be deduced, while some errors can be avoided into which other pragmatists have fallen. The original view appears, too, to be a more compact and unitary conception than the others. But its capital merit, in the writer's eyes, is that it more readily connects itself with a critical proof of its truth. Quite in accord with the logical order of investigation, it usually happens that one first forms an hypothesis that seems more and more reasonable the further one examines into it, but that only a good deal later gets crowned with an adequate proof. The present writer, having had the pragmatist theory under consideration for many years longer than most of its adherents, would naturally have given more attention to the proof of it. At any rate, in endeavoring to explain pragmatism, he may be excused for confining himself to that form of it that he knows best. In the present article there will be space only to explain just what this doctrine (which, in such hands as it has now fallen into, may probably play a pretty prominent part in the philosophical discussions of the next coming years) really consists in. Should the exposition be found to interest readers of *The Monist*, they would certainly be much more interested in a second article[5] which would give some samples of the manifold applications of pragmaticism (assuming it to be true) to the solution of problems of different kinds. After that, readers might be prepared to take an interest in a proof that the doctrine is true,[6]—a proof which seems to the writer to leave no reasonable doubt on the subject, and to be the one contribution of value that he has to make to philosophy. For it would essentially involve the establishment of the truth of synechism.[7]

The bare definition of pragmaticism could convey no satisfactory comprehension of it to the most apprehensive of minds, but requires the commentary to be given below. Moreover, this definition takes no notice of one or two other doctrines without the previous acceptance (or virtual acceptance) of which pragmaticism itself would be a nullity. They are included as a part of the pragmatism of Schiller, but the present writer prefers not to mingle different propositions. The preliminary propositions had better be stated forthwith.

The difficulty in doing this is that no formal list of them has ever been made. They might all be included under the vague maxim, "Dismiss make-believes." Philosophers of very diverse stripes propose that philosophy shall

---

*To show how recent the general use of the word "pragmatism" is, the writer may mention that, to the best of his belief, he never used it in copy for the press before today, except by particular request, in Baldwin's *Dictionary*. Toward the end of 1890, when this part of the *Century Dictionary* appeared, he did not deem that the word had sufficient status to appear in that work. But he has used it continually in philosophical conversation since, perhaps, the mid-seventies.

take its start from one or another state of mind in which no man, least of all a beginner in philosophy, actually is. One proposes that you shall begin by doubting everything, and says that there is only one thing that you cannot doubt, as if doubting were "as easy as lying."[8] Another proposes that we should begin by observing "the first impressions of sense," forgetting that our very percepts are the results of cognitive elaboration. But in truth, there is but one state of mind from which you can "set out," namely, the very state of mind in which you actually find yourself at the time you do "set out,"—a state in which you are laden with an immense mass of cognition already formed, of which you cannot divest yourself if you would; and who knows whether, if you could, you would not have made all knowledge impossible to yourself? Do you call it *doubting* to write down on a piece of paper that you doubt? If so, doubt has nothing to do with any serious business. But do not make believe; if pedantry has not eaten all the reality out of you, recognize, as you must, that there is much that you do not doubt, in the least. Now, that which you do not at all doubt, you must and do regard as infallible, absolute truth. Here breaks in Mr. Make Believe: "What! Do you mean to say that one is to believe what is not true, or that what a man does not doubt is *ipso facto* true?" No, but unless he can make a thing white and black at once, *he* has to regard what he does not doubt as absolutely true. Now you, *per hypothesis*, are that man. "But you tell me there are scores of things I do not doubt. I really cannot persuade myself that there is not some one of them about which I am mistaken." You are adducing one of your make-believe facts, which, even if it were established, would only go to show that doubt has a *limen*, that is, is only called into being by a certain finite stimulus. You only puzzle yourself by talking of this metaphysical "truth" and metaphysical "falsity," that you know nothing about. All you have any dealings with are your doubts and beliefs,* with the course of life that forces new beliefs upon you and gives you power to doubt old beliefs. If your terms "truth" and "falsity" are taken in such senses as to be definable in terms of doubt and belief and the course of experience (as for example they would be, if you were to define the "truth" as that to a belief in which belief would tend if it were to tend indefinitely toward absolute fixity), well and good: in that case, you are only talking about doubt and belief. But if by truth and falsity you mean something not definable in terms of doubt and belief in any way, then you are talking of entities of whose existence you can know nothing, and which Ockham's razor would clean shave off. Your problems would be greatly simplified, if, instead of saying that you want to know the "Truth," you were simply to say that you want to attain a state of belief unassailable by doubt.

Belief is not a momentary mode of consciousness; it is a habit of mind essentially enduring for some time, and mostly (at least) unconscious; and like

---

*It is necessary to say that "belief" is throughout used merely as the name of the contrary to doubt, without regard to grades of certainty nor to the nature of the proposition held for true, i.e. "believed."

other habits, it is (until it meets with some surprise that begins its dissolution) perfectly self-satisfied. Doubt is of an altogether contrary genus. It is not a habit, but the privation of a habit. Now a privation of a habit, in order to be anything at all, must be a condition of erratic activity that in some way must get superseded by a habit.

Among the things which the reader, as a rational person, does not doubt, is that he not merely has habits, but also can exert a measure of self-control over his future actions; which means, however, *not* that he can impart to them any arbitrarily assignable character, but, on the contrary, that a process of self-preparation will tend to impart to action (when the occasion for it shall arise) one fixed character, which is indicated and perhaps roughly measured by the absence (or slightness) of the feeling of self-reproach, which subsequent reflection will induce. Now, this subsequent reflection is part of the self-preparation for action on the next occasion. Consequently, there is a tendency, as action is repeated again and again, for the action to approximate indefinitely toward the perfection of that fixed character, which would be marked by entire absence of self-reproach. The more closely this is approached, the less room for self-control there will be; and where no self-control is possible there will be no self-reproach.

These phenomena seem to be the fundamental characteristics which distinguish a rational being. Blame, in every case, appears to be a modification, often accomplished by a transference, or "projection," of the primary feeling of self-reproach. Accordingly, we never blame anybody for what had been beyond his power of previous self-control. Now, thinking is a species of conduct which is largely subject to self-control. In all their features (which there is no room to describe here), logical self-control is a perfect mirror of ethical self-control,—unless it be rather a species under that genus. In accordance with this, what you cannot in the least help believing is not, justly speaking, wrong belief. In other words, for you it is the absolute truth. True, it is conceivable that what you cannot help believing today, you might find you thoroughly disbelieve tomorrow. But then there is a certain distinction between things you "cannot" do merely in the sense that nothing stimulates you to the great effort and endeavors that would be required, and things you cannot do because in their own nature they are insusceptible of being put into practice. In every stage of your excogitations, there is something of which you can only say, "I cannot think otherwise," and your experientially based hypothesis is that the impossibility is of the second kind.

There is no reason why "thought," in what has just been said, should be taken in that narrow sense in which silence and darkness are favorable to thought. It should rather be understood as covering all rational life, so that an experiment shall be an operation of thought. Of course, that ultimate state of habit to which the action of self-control ultimately tends, where no room is left for further self-control, is, in the case of thought, the state of fixed belief, or perfect knowledge.

Two things here are all-important to assure oneself of and to remember. The first is that a person is not absolutely an individual. His thoughts are what he is "saying to himself," that is, is saying to that other self that is just coming into life in the flow of time. When one reasons, it is that critical self that one is trying to persuade; and all thought whatsoever is a sign, and is mostly of the nature of language. The second thing to remember is that the man's circle of society (however widely or narrowly this phrase may be understood) is a sort of loosely compacted person, in some respects of higher rank than the person of an individual organism. It is these two things alone that render it possible for you,—but only in the abstract, and in a Pickwickian sense,[9]—to distinguish between absolute truth and what you do not doubt.

Let us now hasten to the exposition of pragmaticism itself. Here it will be convenient to imagine that somebody to whom the doctrine is new, but of rather preternatural perspicacity, asks questions of a pragmaticist. Everything that might give a dramatic illusion must be stripped off, so that the result will be a sort of cross between a dialogue and a catechism, but a good deal liker the latter,—something rather painfully reminiscent of Mangnall's *Historical Questions*.[10]

Questioner: I am astounded at your definition of your pragmatism, because only last year I was assured by a person above all suspicion of warping the truth,—himself a pragmatist,—that your doctrine precisely was "that a conception is to be tested by its practical effects." You must surely, then, have entirely changed your definition very recently.

Pragmaticist: If you will turn to Vols. VI and VII of the *Revue Philosophique*, or to the *Popular Science Monthly* for November 1877 and January 1878, you will be able to judge for yourself whether the interpretation you mention was not then clearly excluded. The exact wording of the English enunciation (changing only the first person into the second) was: "Consider what effects that might conceivably have practical bearings you conceive the object of your conception to have. Then your conception of those effects is the WHOLE of your conception of the object."[11]

Questioner: Well, what reason have you for asserting that this is so?

Pragmaticist: That is what I specially desire to tell you. But the question had better be postponed until you clearly understand what those reasons profess to prove.

Questioner: What, then, is the *raison d'être* of the doctrine? What advantage is expected from it?

Pragmaticist: It will serve to show that almost every proposition of ontological metaphysics is either meaningless gibberish,—one word being defined by other words, and they by still others, without any real conception ever being reached,—or else is downright absurd; so that all such rubbish being swept away, what will remain of philosophy will be a series of problems capable of investigation by the observational methods of the true sciences,—the truth about which can be reached without those interminable misunderstandings and disputes which have made the highest of the positive sciences a mere amusement for idle intellects, a sort of chess,—idle pleasure its purpose, and reading out of a book its method. In this regard, pragmaticism is a species of prope-positivism. But what distinguishes it from other species is, first, its retention of a purified philosophy; secondly, its full acceptance of the main body of our instinctive beliefs; and thirdly, its strenuous insistence upon the truth of scholastic realism (or a close approximation to that, well-stated by the late Dr. Francis Ellingwood Abbot in the Introduction to his *Scientific Theism*[12]). So, instead of merely jeering at metaphysics, like other prope-positivists, whether by long drawn-out parodies or otherwise, the pragmaticist extracts from it a precious essence, which will serve to give life and light to cosmology and physics. At the same time, the moral applications of the doctrine are positive and potent; and there are many other uses of it not easily classed. On another occasion, instances may be given to show that it really has these effects.

Questioner: I hardly need to be convinced that your doctrine would wipe out metaphysics. Is it not as obvious that it must wipe out every proposition of science and everything that bears on the conduct of life? For you say that the only meaning that, for you, any assertion bears is that a certain experiment has resulted in a certain way: Nothing else but an experiment enters into the meaning. Tell me, then, how can an experiment, in itself, reveal anything more than that something once happened to an individual object and that subsequently some other individual event occurred?

Pragmaticist: That question is, indeed, to the purpose,—the purpose being to correct any misapprehensions of pragmaticism. You speak of an experiment in itself, emphasizing *"in itself."* You evidently think of each experiment as isolated from every other. It has not, for example, occurred to you, one might venture to surmise, that every connected series of experiments constitutes a single collective experiment. What are the essential ingredients of an experiment? First, of course, an experimenter of flesh and blood. Secondly, a verifiable hypothesis. This is a proposition* relating to the universe environing the experimenter, or to some well-known part of it and affirming or denying of this only some experimental possibility or impossibility. The third indispensable ingredient is a sincere doubt in the experimenter's mind as to the truth of that hypothesis. Passing over several ingredients on which we need not dwell, the purpose, the plan, and the resolve, we come to the act of choice by which the experimenter singles out certain identifiable objects to be operated upon. The next is the external (or quasi-external) ACT by which he

---

*The writer, like most English logicians, invariably uses the word *proposition*, not as the Germans define their equivalent, *Satz*, as the language-expression of a judgment (*Urtheil*), but as that which is related to any assertion, whether mental and self-addressed or outwardly expressed, just as any possibility is related to its actualization. The difficulty of the, at best, difficult problem of the essential nature of a Proposition has been increased, for the Germans, by their *Urtheil*, confounding, under one designation, the mental *assertion* with the *assertible*.

modifies those objects. Next, comes the subsequent *reaction* of the world upon the experimenter in a perception; and finally, his recognition of the teaching of the experiment. While the two chief parts of the event itself are the action and the reaction, yet the unity of essence of the experiment lies in its purpose and plan, the ingredients passed over in the enumeration.

Another thing: in representing the pragmaticist as making rational meaning to consist in an experiment (which you speak of as an event in the past), you strikingly fail to catch his attitude of mind. Indeed, it is not in an experiment, but in *experimental phenomena*, that rational meaning is said to consist. When an experimentalist speaks of a *phenomenon*, such as "Hall's phenomenon," "Zeeman's phenomenon" and its modification, "Michelson's phenomenon," or "the chessboard phenomenon," he does not mean any particular event that did happen to somebody in the dead past, but what *surely will* happen to everybody in the living future who shall fulfill certain conditions.[13] The phenomenon consists in the fact that when an experimentalist shall come to *act* according to a certain scheme that he has in mind, then will something else happen, and shatter the doubts of sceptics, like the celestial fire upon the altar of Elijah.

And do not overlook the fact that the pragmaticist maxim says nothing of single experiments or of single experimental phenomena (for what is conditionally true *in futuro* can hardly be singular), but only speaks of *general kinds* of experimental phenomena. Its adherent does not shrink from speaking of general objects as real, since whatever is true represents a real. Now the laws of nature are true.

The rational meaning of every proposition lies in the future. How so? The meaning of a proposition is itself a proposition. Indeed, it is no other than the very proposition of which it is the meaning: it is a translation of it. But of the myriads of forms into which a proposition may be translated, what is that one which is to be called its very meaning? It is, according to the pragmaticist, that form in which the proposition becomes applicable to human conduct, not in these or those special circumstances, nor when one entertains this or that special design, but that form which is most directly applicable to self-control under every situation, and to every purpose. This is why he locates the meaning in future time; for future conduct is the only conduct that is subject to self-control. But in order that that form of the proposition which is to be taken as its meaning should be applicable to every situation and to every purpose upon which the proposition has any bearing, it must be simply the general description of all the experimental phenomena which the assertion of the proposition virtually predicts. For an experimental phenomenon is the fact asserted by the proposition that action of a certain description will have a certain kind of experimental result; and experimental results are the only results that can affect human conduct. No doubt, some unchanging idea may come to influence a man more than it had done; but only because some experience equivalent to an experiment has brought its truth home to him more intimately than before. Whenever a man acts purposively, he acts under a belief in some experimental phenomenon. Consequently, the sum of the experimental phenomena that a proposition implies makes up its entire bearing upon human conduct. Your question, then, of how a pragmaticist can attribute any meaning to any assertion other than that of a single occurrence is substantially answered.

Questioner: I see that pragmaticism is a thoroughgoing phenomenalism. Only why should you limit yourself to the phenomena of experimental science rather than embrace all observational science? Experiment, after all, is an uncommunicative informant. It never expatiates: it only answers "yes" or "no"; or rather it usually snaps out "No!" or, at best, only utters an inarticulate grunt for the negation of its "no." The typical experimentalist is not much of an observer. It is the student of natural history to whom nature opens the treasury of her confidence, while she treats the cross-examining experimentalist with the reserve he merits. Why should your phenomenalism sound the meagre Jew's harp of experiment rather than the glorious organ of observation?

Pragmaticist: Because pragmaticism is not definable as "thoroughgoing phenomenalism," although the latter doctrine may be a kind of pragmatism. The *richness* of phenomena lies in their sensuous quality. Pragmaticism does not intend to define the phenomenal equivalents of words and general ideas, but, on the contrary, eliminates their sential element, and endeavors to define the rational purport, and this it finds in the purposive bearing of the word or proposition in question.

Questioner: Well, if you choose so to make Doing the Be-all and the End-all of human life, why do you not make meaning to consist simply in doing? Doing has to be done at a certain time upon a certain object. Individual objects and single events cover all reality, as everybody knows, and as a practicalist ought to be the first to insist. Yet, your meaning, as you have described it, is *general.* Thus, it is of the nature of a mere word and not a reality. You say yourself that your meaning of a proposition is only the same proposition in another dress. But a practical man's meaning is the very thing he means. What do you make to be the meaning of "George Washington"?

Pragmaticist: Forcibly put! A good half dozen of your points must certainly be admitted. It must be admitted, in the first place, that if pragmaticism really made Doing to be the Be-all and the End-all of life, that would be its death. For to say that we live for the mere sake of action, as action, regardless of the thought it carries out, would be to say that there is no such thing as rational purport. Secondly, it must be admitted that every proposition professes to be true of a certain real individual object, often the environing universe. Thirdly, it must be admitted that pragmaticism fails to furnish any translation or meaning of a proper name, or other designation of an individual object. Fourthly, the pragmaticistic meaning is undoubtedly general; and it is equally indisputable that the general is of the nature of a word or sign. Fifthly, it must be admitted that individuals alone exist; and sixthly, it may be admitted that the very meaning of a word or significant object ought to be the very essence or reality of what it signifies. But when, those admissions having been unreservedly made, you find the pragmaticist still constrained most earnestly to deny the force of your objection, you ought to infer that there is some consideration that has escaped you. Putting the admissions together, you will perceive that the pragmaticist grants that a proper name (although it is not customary to say that it has a *meaning*) has a certain denotative function peculiar, in each case, to that name and its equivalents; and that he grants that every assertion contains such a denotative or pointing-out function. In its peculiar individuality, the pragmaticist excludes this from the rational purport of the assertion, although *the like* of it, being common to all assertions, and so, being general and not individual, may enter into the pragmaticistic purport. Whatever exists, *ex-sists*, that is, really acts upon other existents, so obtains a self-identity, and is definitely individual. As to the general, it will be a help to thought to notice that there are two ways of being general. A statue of a soldier on some village monument, in his overcoat and with his musket, is for each of a hundred families the image of its uncle, its sacrifice to the union. That statue, then, though it is itself single, represents any one man of whom a certain predicate may be true. It is *objectively* general. The word "soldier," whether spoken or written, is general in the same way; while the name "George Washington" is not so. But each of these two terms remains one and the same noun, whether it be spoken or written, and whenever and wherever it be spoken or written. This noun is not an existent thing: it is a *type*, or *form*, to which objects, both those that are externally existent and those which are imagined, may *conform*, but which none of them can exactly be. This is subjective generality. The pragmaticistic purport is general in both ways.

As to reality, one finds it defined in various ways; but if that principle of terminological ethics that was proposed be accepted, the equivocal language will soon disappear. For *realis* and *realitas* are not ancient words. They were invented to be terms of philosophy in the thirteenth century, and the meaning they were intended to express is perfectly clear. That is *real* which has such and such characters, whether anybody thinks it to have those characters or not. At any rate, that is the sense in which the pragmaticist uses the word. Now, just as conduct controlled by ethical reason tends toward fixing certain habits of conduct, the nature of which (as to illustrate the meaning, peaceable habits and not quarrelsome habits) does not depend upon any accidental circumstances, and *in that sense*, may be said to be *destined*; so, thought, controlled by a rational experimental logic, tends to the fixation of certain opinions, equally destined, the nature of which will be the same in the end, however the perversity of thought of whole generations may cause the postponement of the ultimate fixation. If this be so, as every man of us virtually assumes that it is, in regard to each matter the truth of which he seriously discusses, then, according to the adopted definition of "real," the state of things which will be believed in that ultimate opinion is real. But, for the most part, such opinions will be general. Consequently, *some* general objects are real. (Of course, nobody ever thought that *all* generals were real; but the scholastics used to assume that generals were real when they had hardly any, or quite no, experiential evidence to support their assumption; and their fault lay just there, and not in holding that generals could be real.) One is struck with the inexactitude of thought even of analysts of power, when they touch upon modes of being. One will meet, for example, the virtual assumption that what is relative to thought cannot be real. But why not, exactly? *Red* is relative to sight, but the fact that this or that is in that relation to vision that we call being red is not *itself* relative to sight; it is a real fact.

Not only may generals be real, but they may also be *physically efficient*, not in every metaphysical sense, but in the commonsense acception in which human purposes are physically efficient. Aside from metaphysical nonsense, no sane man doubts that if I feel the air in my study to be stuffy, that thought may cause the window to be opened. My thought, be it granted, was an individual event. But what determined it to take the particular determination it did was in part the general fact that stuffy air is unwholesome, and in part other *Forms*, concerning which Dr. Carus has caused so many men to reflect to advantage,[14]—or rather, *by* which, and the general truth concerning which Dr. Carus's mind was determined to the forcible enunciation of so much truth. For truths, on the average, have a greater tendency to get believed than falsities have. Were it otherwise, considering that there are myriads of false hypotheses to account for any given phenomenon, against one sole true one (or if you will have it so, against every true one), the first step toward genuine knowledge must have been next door to a miracle. So, then, when my window was opened, because of the truth that stuffy air is malsain, a physical effort was brought into existence by the efficiency of a general and nonexistent truth. This has a droll sound because it is unfamiliar; but exact analysis is with it and not against it; and it has, besides, the immense advantage of not blinding us to great facts,—such as that the ideas "justice" and "truth" are, notwithstanding the iniquity of the world, the mightiest of the forces that move it. Generality is, indeed, an indispensable ingredient of reality; for mere individual existence or actuality without any regularity whatever is a nullity. Chaos is pure nothing.

That which any true proposition asserts is *real*, in the sense of being as it is regardless of what you or I may think about it. Let this proposition be a general conditional proposition as to the future, and it is a real general such as is calculated really to influence human conduct; and such the pragmaticist holds to be the rational purport of every concept.

Accordingly, the pragmaticist does not make the *summum bonum* to consist in action, but makes it to consist in that process of evolution whereby the existent comes more and more to embody those generals which were just now said to be *destined*, which is what we strive to express in calling them *reasonable*.

In its higher stages, evolution takes place more and more largely through self-control, and this gives the pragmaticist a sort of justification for making the rational purport to be general.[15]

There is much more in elucidation of pragmaticism that might be said to advantage, were it not for the dread of fatiguing the reader. It might, for example, have been well to show clearly that the pragmaticist does not attribute any different essential mode of being to an event in the future from that which he would attribute to a similar event in the past, but only that the practical attitude of the thinker toward the two is different. It would also have been well to show that the pragmaticist does not make Forms to be the *only* realities in the world, any more than he makes the reasonable purport of a word to be the only kind of meaning there is. These things are, however, implicitly involved in what has been said. There is only one remark concerning the pragmaticist's conception of the relation of his formula to the first principles of logic which need detain the reader.

Aristotle's definition of universal predication,[16] which is usually designated (like a papal bull or writ of court, from its opening words) as the *Dictum de omni*, may be translated as follows: "We call a predication (be it affirmative or negative) *universal*, when, and only when, there is nothing among the existent individuals to which the subject affirmatively belongs, but to which the predicate will not likewise be referred (affirmatively or negatively, according as the universal predication is affirmative or negative)." The Greek is: λέγομεν δὲ τὸ κατὰ παντὸς κατηγορεῖσθαι ὅταν μηδὲν ᾖ λαβεῖν τῶν τοῦ ὑποκειμένου καθ᾽ οὗ θάτερον οὐ λεχθήσεται· καὶ τὸ κατὰ μηδενὸς ὡσαύτως. The important words "existent individuals" have been introduced into the translation (which English idiom would not here permit to be literal); but it is plain that existent individuals were what Aristotle meant. The other departures from literalness only serve to give modern English forms of expression. Now, it is well known that propositions in formal logic go in pairs, the two of one pair being convertible into [one] another by the interchange of the ideas of antecedent and consequent, subject and predicate, etc. The parallelism extends so far that it is often assumed to be perfect; but it is not quite so. The proper mate of this sort to the *Dictum de omni* is the following definition of affirmative predication: We call a predication *affirmative* (be it universal or particular) when, and only when, there is nothing among the sensational effects that belong universally to the predicate which will not be (universally or particularly, according as the affirmative predication is universal or particular) said to belong to the subject. Now, this is substantially the essential proposition of pragmaticism. Of course, its parallelism to the *Dictum de omni* will only be admitted by a person who admits the truth of pragmaticism.

* * *

Suffer me to add one word more on this point.[17] For if one cares at all to know what the pragmaticist theory consists in, one must understand that there is no other part of it to which the pragmaticist attaches quite as much importance as he does to the recognition in his doctrine of the utter inadequacy of action or volition or even of resolve or actual purpose, as materials out of which to construct a conditional purpose or the concept of conditional purpose. Had a purposed article concerning the principle of continuity and synthetizing the ideas of the other articles of a series in the early volumes of *The Monist* ever been written,[18] it would have appeared how, with thorough consistency, that theory involved the recognition that continuity is an indispensable element of reality, and that continuity is simply what generality becomes in the logic of relatives, and thus, like generality, and more than generality, is an affair of thought, and is the essence of thought. Yet even in its truncated condition, an extra-intelligent reader might discern that the theory of those cosmological articles made reality to consist in something more than feeling and action could supply, inasmuch as the primeval chaos, where those two elements were present, was explicitly shown to be pure nothing. Now, the motive for alluding to that theory just here is that in this way one can put in a strong light a position which the pragmaticist holds and must hold, whether that cosmological theory be ultimately sustained or exploded, namely, that the third category,—the category of thought, representation, triadic relation, mediation, genuine Thirdness, Thirdness as such,—is an essential ingredient of reality, yet does not by itself constitute reality, since this category (which in that cosmology appears as the element of habit) can have no concrete being without action, as a separate object on which to work its government, just as action cannot exist without the immediate being of feeling on which to act. The truth is that pragmaticism is closely allied to the Hegelian absolute idealism, from which, however, it is sundered by its vigorous denial that the third category (which Hegel degrades to a mere stage of thinking) suffices to make the world, or is even so much as self-sufficient. Had Hegel, instead of regarding the first two stages with his smile of contempt, held on to them as independent or distinct elements of the triune Reality, pragmaticists might have looked up to him as the great vindicator of their truth. (Of course, the external trappings of his doctrine are only here and there of much significance.) For pragmaticism belongs essentially to the triadic class of philosophical doctrines, and is much more essentially so than Hegelianism is. (Indeed, in one passage, at least, Hegel alludes to the triadic form of his exposition as to a mere fashion of dress.)

Postscript[19]

During the last five months, I have met with references to several objections to the above opinions, but not having been able to obtain the text of these objections, I do not think I ought to attempt to answer them. If gentlemen who attack either pragmatism in general or the variety of it which I entertain would only send me copies of what they write, more important readers they could easily find, but they could find none who would examine their arguments with a more grateful avidity for truth not yet apprehended, nor any who would be more sensible of their courtesy.

25

Issues of Pragmaticism

P 1080: The Monist 15 (October 1905):481–99. [Published in CP 5.438–63. Initially titled "The Consequences of Pragmaticism" as were several other earlier documents, Peirce changed the title in its last draft (MS 290). Only the last 44 pages of the 61-page manuscript, completed in June 1905, are today extant in the Open Court archives preserved at Southern Illinois University in Carbondale (Special Collections, The Morris Library). The text below reproduces pages 481–86 of the Monist article, and then follows the manuscript.] Peirce begins by restating his pragmatic maxim in semiotic terms, by identifying the meaning that pragmaticism seeks to enunciate as that of symbols rather than of conceptions. He devotes most of this article to a consideration of two long-held doctrines, now seen to be consequences of pragmaticism: critical common-sensism and scholastic realism. Peirce enumerates and discusses "six distinctive characters" of critical common-sensism, among them the important doctrine of vague ideas. He extends his realism to include the acceptance of "real vagues" and "real possibilities," and he points out that "it is the reality of some possibilities that pragmaticism is most concerned to insist upon." Because of this, Max Fisch has claimed that pragmaticism is pragmatism "purged of the nominalistic dross of its original exposition."

Pragmaticism was originally enounced* in the form of a maxim, as follows: Consider what effects, which might conceivably have practical bearings we conceive the object of our conception to have. Then, our conception of the effects is the whole of our conception of the object.

I will restate this in other words, since ofttimes one can thus eliminate some unsuspected source of perplexity to the reader. This time it shall be in the indicative mood, as follows: The entire intellectual purport of any symbol consists in the total of all general modes of rational conduct which, conditionally upon all the possible different circumstances and desires, would ensue upon the acceptance of the symbol.

Two doctrines that were defended by the writer about nine years before the formulation of pragmaticism may be treated as consequences of the latter belief.[1] One of these may be called Critical Common-Sensism. It is a variety of the Philosophy of Common Sense, but is marked by six distinctive characters, which had better be enumerated at once.

---

*Popular Science Monthly, XII, 293, for January 1878 [EP1:132, W3:266]. An introductory article opens the volume, in the number for November 1877 [EP1:109–23].

Character I. Critical Common-Sensism admits that there not only are indubitable propositions but also that there are indubitable inferences. In one sense, anything evident is indubitable; but the propositions and inferences which Critical Common-Sensism holds to be original, in the sense one cannot "go behind" them (as the lawyers say), are indubitable in the sense of being acritical. The term "reasoning" ought to be confined to such fixation of one belief by another as is reasonable, deliberate, self-controlled. A reasoning must be conscious; and this consciousness is not mere "immediate consciousness," which (as I argued in 1868, *Journal of Speculative Philosophy*)[2] is simple Feeling viewed from another side, but is in its ultimate nature (meaning in that characteristic element of it that is not reducible to anything simpler), a sense of taking a habit, or disposition to respond to a given kind of stimulus in a given kind of way. As to the nature of that, some *éclaircissements* will appear below and again in my third paper, on the "Basis of Pragmaticism."[3] But the secret of rational consciousness is not so much to be sought in the study of this one peculiar nucleolus, as in the review of the process of self-control in its entirety. The machinery of logical self-control works on the same plan as does moral self-control, in multiform detail. The greatest difference, perhaps, is that the latter serves to inhibit mad puttings forth of energy, while the former most characteristically insures us against the quandary of Buridan's ass.[4] The formation of habits under imaginary action (see the paper of January 1878)[5] is one of the most essential ingredients of both; but in the logical process the imagination takes far wider flights, proportioned to the generality of the field of inquiry, being bounded in pure mathematics solely by the limits of its own powers, while in the moral process we consider only situations that may be apprehended or anticipated. For in moral life we are chiefly solicitous about our conduct and its inner springs, and the approval of conscience, while in intellectual life there is a tendency to value existence as the vehicle of forms. Certain obvious features of the phenomena of self-control (and especially of habit) can be expressed compactly and without any hypothetical addition, except what we distinctly rate as imagery, by saying that we have an occult nature of which and of its contents we can only judge by the conduct that it determines, and by phenomena of that conduct. All will assent to that (or all but the extreme nominalist), but anti-synechistic thinkers wind themselves up in a factitious snarl by falsifying the phenomena in representing consciousness to be, as it were, a skin, a separate tissue, overlying an unconscious region of the occult nature, mind, soul, or physiological basis. It appears to me that in the present state of our knowledge a sound methodeutic prescribes that, in adhesion to the appearances, the difference is only relative and the demarcation not precise.

According to the maxim of Pragmaticism, to say that determination affects our occult nature is to say that it is capable of affecting deliberate conduct; and since we are conscious of what we do deliberately, we are conscious *habitualiter* of whatever hides in the depths of our nature; and it is presumable (and *only* presumable,* although curious instances are on record) that a sufficiently energetic effort of attention would bring it out. Consequently, to say that an operation of the mind is controlled is to say that it is, in a special sense, a conscious operation; and this no doubt is the consciousness of reasoning. For this theory requires that in reasoning we should be conscious, not only of the conclusion, and of our deliberate approval of it, but also of its being the result of the premiss from which it does result, and furthermore that the inference is one of a possible class of inferences which conform to one guiding principle. Now in fact we find a well-marked class of mental operations, clearly of a different nature from any others which do possess just these properties. They alone deserve to be called *reasonings*; and if the reasoner is conscious, even vaguely, of what his guiding principle is, his reasoning should be called a *logical argumentation*. There are, however, cases in which we are conscious that a belief has been determined by another given belief, but are not conscious that it proceeds on any general principle. Such is St. Augustine's "*cogito, ergo sum.*"⁶ Such a process should be called, not a reasoning but an *acritical inference*. Again, there are cases in which one belief is determined by another, without our being at all aware of it. These should be called *associational suggestions of belief*.

Now the theory of Pragmaticism was originally based, as anybody will see who examines the papers of November 1877 and January 1878, upon a study of that experience of the phenomena of self-control which is common to all grown men and women; and it seems evident that to some extent, at least, it must always be so based. For it is to conceptions of deliberate conduct that Pragmaticism would trace the intellectual purport of symbols; and deliberate conduct is self-controlled conduct. Now control may itself be controlled, criticism itself subjected to criticism; and ideally there is no obvious definite limit to the sequence. But if one seriously inquires whether it is possible that a completed series of actual efforts should have been endless or beginningless (I will spare the reader the discussion), I think he can only conclude that (with some vagueness as to what constitutes an effort) this must be regarded as impossible. It will be found to follow that there are, besides perceptual judgments, original (i.e., indubitable because uncriticized) beliefs of a general and recurrent kind, as well as indubitable acritical inferences.

It is important for the reader to satisfy himself that genuine doubt always has an external origin, usually from surprise; and that it is as impossible for a man to create in himself a genuine doubt by such an act of the will as would suffice to imagine the condition of a mathematical theorem, as it would be for him to give himself a genuine surprise by a simple act of the will.

I beg my reader also to believe that it would be impossible for me to put into these articles over two percent of the pertinent thought which would be necessary in order to present the subject as I have worked it out. I can

---

*But see the experiments of J. Jastrow and me: "On Small Differences of Sensation" in the *Memoirs of the National Academy of Sciences*. Vol. III *[*(1885): 75–83. W5: 122–35*]*.

only make a small selection of what it seems most desirable to submit to his judgment. Not only must all steps be omitted which he can be expected to supply for himself, but unfortunately much more that may cause him difficulty.

Character II. I do not remember that any of the old Scotch philosophers[7] ever undertook to draw up a complete list of the original beliefs, but they certainly thought it a feasible thing, and that the list would hold good for the minds of all men from Adam down. For in those days Adam was an undoubted historical personage. Before any waft of the air of evolution had reached those coasts how could they think otherwise? When I first wrote, we were hardly orientated in the new ideas, and my impression was that the indubitable propositions changed with a thinking man from year to year. I made some studies preparatory to an investigation of the rapidity of these changes, but the matter was neglected, and it has been only during the last two years that I have completed a provisional inquiry[8] which shows me that the changes are so slight from generation to generation, though not imperceptible even in that short period, that I thought to own my adhesion, under inevitable modification, to the opinion of that subtle but well-balanced intellect, Thomas Reid, in the matter of Common Sense (as well as in regard to immediate perception, along with Kant).*

Character III. The Scotch philosophers recognized that the original beliefs, and the same thing is at least equally true of the acritical inferences, were of the general nature of instincts. But little as we know about instincts, even now, we are much better acquainted with them than were the men of the eighteenth century. We know, for example, that they can be somewhat modified in a very short time. The great facts have always been known; such as that instinct seldom errs, while reason goes wrong nearly half the time, if not more frequently. But one thing the Scotch failed to recognize is that the original beliefs only remain indubitable in their application to affairs that resemble those of a primitive mode of life. It is, for example, quite open to reasonable doubt whether the motions of electrons are confined to three dimensions, although it is good methodeutic to presume that they are until some evidence to the contrary is forthcoming. On the other hand, as soon as we find that a belief shows symptoms of being instinctive, although it may seem to be dubitable, we must suspect that experiment would show that it is not really so; for in our artificial life, especially in that of a student, no mistake is more likely than that of taking a paper-doubt for the genuine metal. Take, for example, the belief in the criminality of incest. Biology will doubtless testify that the practice is unadvisable; but surely nothing that it has to say could warrant the intensity of our sentiment about it. When, however, we consider the thrill of horror which the idea excites in us, we find reason in that to consider it to be

---

*I wish I might hope, after finishing some more difficult work, to be able to resume this study and go to the bottom of the subject, which needs the qualities of age and does not call upon the powers of youth. A great range of reading is necessary; for it is the belief men *betray* and not that which they *parade* which has to be studied.

an instinct; and from that we may infer that if some rationalistic brother and sister were to marry, they would find that the conviction of horrible guilt could not be shaken off.

In contrast to this may be placed the belief that suicide is to be classed as murder. There are two pretty sure signs that this is not an instinctive belief. One is that it is substantially confined to the Christian world. The other is that when it comes to the point of actual self-debate, this belief seems to be completely expunged and ex-sponged from the mind. In reply to these powerful arguments, the main points urged are the authority of the Fathers of the Church and the undoubtedly intense instinctive clinging to life. The latter phenomenon is, however, entirely irrelevant. For though it is a wrench to part with life, which has its charms at the very worst, just as it is to part with a tooth, yet there is no *moral* element in it whatever. As to the Christian tradition, it may be explained by the circumstances of the early Church. For Christianity, the most terribly earnest and most intolerant of religions (see *The Book of Revelations of St. John the Divine*),—and it remained so until diluted with civilization,—recognized no morality as worthy of an instant's consideration except Christian morality. Now the early Church had need of martyrs, i.e., witnesses, and if any man had done with life, it was abominable infidelity to leave it otherwise than as a witness to its power. This belief, then, should be set down as dubitable; and it will no sooner have been pronounced dubitable, than Reason will stamp it as false.

The Scotch school appears to have no such distinction concerning[9] the limitations of indubitability and the consequent limitations of the jurisdiction of original belief.[10]

Character IV. By all odds, the most distinctive character of the Critical Common-Sensist, in contrast to the old Scotch philosopher, lies in his insistence that the acritically indubitable is invariably vague.

Logicians have been at fault in giving Vagueness the go-by, so far as not even to analyze it. The present writer has done his best to work out the Stechiology (or Stoicheiology), Critic, and Methodeutic of the subject, but can here only give a definition or two with some proposals respecting terminology.

Accurate writers have apparently made a distinction between the *definite* and the *determinate*. A subject is *determinate* in respect to any character which inheres in it or is (universally and affirmatively) predicated of it, as well as in respect to the negative of such character, these being the very same respect. In all other respects it is *indeterminate*. The *definite* shall be defined presently. A sign (under which designation I place every kind of thought,[11] and not alone external signs) that is in any respect objectively indeterminate (i.e., whose object is undetermined by the sign itself) is objectively *general* in so far as it extends to the interpreter the privilege of carrying its determination further.*

---

*Hamilton and a few other logicians understood the subject of a universal proposition in the collective sense; but every person who is well-read in logic is familiar with many passages in which the leading logicians explain with an iteration that would be superfluous if all readers were intelligent that such subject is distributively not collectively general. A term denoting a

Example: "Man is mortal." To the question, What man? the reply is that the proposition explicitly leaves it to you to apply its assertion to what man or men you will. A sign that is objectively indeterminate in any respect is objectively *vague* in so far as it reserves further determination to be made in some other conceivable sign, or at least does not appoint the interpreter as its deputy in this office. *Example:* "A man whom I could mention seems to be a little conceited." The *suggestion* here is that the man in view is the person addressed; but the utterer does not authorize such an interpretation or *any* other application of what she says. She can still say, if she likes, that she does *not* mean the person addressed. Every utterance naturally leaves the right of further exposition in the utterer; and therefore, in so far as a sign is indeterminate, it is vague, unless it is expressly or by a well-understood convention rendered general. Usually, an affirmative predication covers *generally* every essential character of the predicate, while a negative predication *vaguely* denies some essential character. In another sense, honest people, when not joking, intend to make the meaning of their words determinate, so that there shall be no latitude of interpretation at all. That is to say, the character of their meaning consists in the implications and non-implications of their words; and they intend to fix what is implied and what is not implied. They believe that they succeed in doing so, and if their chat is about the theory of numbers, perhaps they may. But the further their topics are from such presciss, or "abstract," subjects, the less possibility is there of such precision of speech. In so far as the implication is not determinate, it is usually left vague; but there are cases where an unwillingness to dwell on disagreeable subjects causes the utterer to leave the determination of the implication to the interpreter; as if one says, "That creature is filthy, in every sense of the term."

Perhaps a more scientific pair of definitions would be that anything is *general* in so far as the principle of excluded middle does not apply to it and is *vague* in so far as the principle of contradiction does not apply to it. Thus, although it is true that "Any proposition you please, *once you have determined its identity*, is either true or false"; yet *so long as it remains indeterminate and so without identity*, it need neither be true that any proposition you please is true, nor that any proposition you please is false. So likewise, while it is false that "A proposition *whose identity I have determined* is both true and false," yet until it is determinate, it may be true that a proposition is true and that a proposition is false.

In those respects in which a sign is not vague, it is said to be *definite*, and also with a slightly different mode of application, to be *precise*, a meaning probably due to *praecisus* having been applied to *curt* denials and refusals. It

---

collection is singular and such a term is an "abstraction" or product of the operation of hypostatic abstraction as truly as is the name of the essence. "Mankind" is quite as much an abstraction and *ens rationis* as is "humanity." Indeed, every object of a conception is either a signate individual or some kind of indeterminate individual. Nouns in the plural are usually distributive and general; common nouns in the singular are usually indefinite.

has been the well-established, ordinary sense of *precise* since the Plantagenets; and it were much to be desired that this word, with its derivates *precision, precisive*, etc., should, in the dialect of philosophy, be restricted to this sense. To express the act of *rendering precise* (though usually only in reference to numbers, dates, and the like), the French have the verb *préciser*, which, after the analogy of *décider*, should have been *précider*. Would it not be a useful addition to our English terminology of logic, to adopt the verb *to precide*, to express the general sense, to render precise? Our older logicians with salutary boldness seem to have created for their service the verb *to prescind*, the corresponding Latin word meaning only to "cut off at the end," while the English word means to suppose without supposing some more or less determinately indicated accompaniment. In geometry, for example, we "prescind" shape from color, which is precisely the same thing as to "abstract" color from shape, although very many writers employ the verb "to abstract" so as to make it the equivalent of "prescind." But whether it was the invention or the courage of our philosophical ancestors which exhausted itself in the manufacture of the verb "prescind," the curious fact is that instead of forming from it the noun *prescission*, they took pattern from the French logicians in putting the word *precision* to this second use. About the same time,* the adjective *precisive* was introduced to signify what *prescissive* would have more unmistakably conveyed (see Watts's *Logick*).[13] If we desire to rescue the good ship Philosophy for the service of Science from the hands of lawless rovers of the sea of literature, we shall do well to keep *prescind, presciss, prescission*, and *prescissive* on the one hand, to refer to dissection in hypothesis, while *precide, precise, precision*, and *precisive* are used so as to refer exclusively to an expression of determination which is either full or made free for the interpreter. We shall thus do much to relieve the stem "abstract" from staggering under the double burden of conveying the idea of prescission as well as the unrelated and very important idea of the creation of an *ens rationis* out of an ἔπος πτερόεν,[14]—to filch the phrase to furnish a name for an expression of non-substantive thought,— an operation that has been treated as a subject of ridicule,—this hypostatic abstraction,—but which gives mathematics half its power.

The purely formal conception that the three affections of terms, *determination, generality*, and *vagueness*, form a group dividing a category of what Kant calls "functions of judgment" will be passed by as unimportant by those who have yet to learn how important a part purely formal conceptions may play in philosophy. Without stopping to discuss this, it may be pointed out that the "Quantity" of propositions in logic, that is, the distribution of the *first* subject,† is either *singular* (that is, determinate, which renders it substantially

---

*But unfortunately it has not been in the writer's power to consult the *Oxford Dictionary* concerning these words; so that probably some of the statements in the text might be corrected with the aid of that work.[12]

†Thus returning to the writer's original nomenclature, in spite of *Monist* VII, 209, where an obviously defective argument was regarded as sufficient to determine a mere matter of terminology.[15] But the Quality of propositions is there regarded from a point of view which seems extrin-

negligible in formal logic), or *universal* (that is, general), or *particular* (as the medieval logicians say, that is, vague or *indefinite*). It is a curious fact that in the logic of relations it is the first and last quantifiers of a proposition that are of chief importance. To affirm of anything that it is a horse is to yield to it *every* essential character of a horse: to deny of anything that it is a horse is vaguely to refuse to it *some* one or more of those essential characters of the horse. There are, however, predicates that are unanalyzable in a given state of intelligence and experience. These are, therefore, determinately affirmed or denied. Thus, this same group of concepts reappears. Affirmation and denial are in themselves unaffected by these concepts, but it is to be remarked that there are cases in which we can have an apparently definite idea of a border line between affirmation and negation. Thus, a point of a surface may be in a region of that surface, or out of it, or on its boundary. This gives us an indirect and vague conception of an intermediacy between affirmation and denial in general, and consequently of an intermediate, or nascent state, between determination and indetermination. There must be a similar intermediacy between generality and vagueness. Indeed, in an article in the seventh volume of *The Monist*,[16] there lies just beneath the surface of what is explicitly said, the idea of an endless series of such *intermediacies*. We shall find below some application for these reflections.

Character V. The Critical Common-Sensist will be further distinguished from the old Scotch philosopher by the great value he attaches to doubt, provided only that it be the weighty and noble metal itself, and no counterfeit nor paper substitute. He is not content to ask himself whether he does doubt, but he invents a plan for attaining to doubt, elaborates it in detail, and then puts it into practice, although this may involve a solid month of hard work; and it is only after having gone through such an examination that he will pronounce a belief to be indubitable. Moreover, he fully acknowledges that even then it may be that some of his indubitable beliefs may be proved false.

The Critical Common-Sensist holds that there is less danger to heuretic science in believing too little than in believing too much. Yet for all that, the consequences to heuretics of believing too little may be no less than disaster.

Character VI. Critical Common-Sensism may fairly lay claim to this title for two sorts of reasons; namely, that on the one hand it subjects four opinions to rigid criticism: its own; that of the Scotch school; that of those who would base logic or metaphysics on psychology or any other special science, the least tenable of all the philosophical opinions that have any vogue; and that of Kant; while on the other hand it has besides some claim to be called Critical from the fact that it is but a modification of Kantism. The present writer was a pure Kantist until he was forced by successive steps into Pragmaticism. The Kantist has only to abjure from the bottom of his heart the

---

sic. I have not had time, however, to re-explore all the ramifications of this difficult question by the aid of existential graphs, and the statement in the text about the last quantifier may need modification.

proposition that a thing-in-itself can, however indirectly, be conceived; and then correct the details of Kant's doctrine, and he will find himself to have become a Critical Common-Sensist.

Another doctrine which is involved in Pragmaticism as an essential consequence of it, but which the writer defended (*Journal of Speculative Philosophy* 1868, and *North American Review* 1871)[17] before he had formulated, even in his own mind,[18] the principle of pragmaticism, is the scholastic doctrine of realism. This is usually defined as the opinion that there are real objects that are general, among the number being the modes of determination of existent singulars, if, indeed, these be not the only such objects. But the belief in this can hardly escape being accompanied by the acknowledgment that there are, besides, real *vagues*, and especially, real *possibilities*. For possibility being the denial of a necessity, which is a kind of generality, is vague like any other contradiction of a general. Indeed, it is the reality of some possibilities that pragmaticism is most concerned to insist upon. The article of January 1878 endeavored to glose over this point as unsuited to the exoteric public addressed; or perhaps the writer wavered in his own mind. He said that if a diamond were to be formed in a bed of cotton wool, and were to be consumed there without ever having been pressed upon by any hard edge or point, it would be merely a question of nomenclature whether that diamond should be said to have been hard or not. No doubt, this is true, except for the abominable falsehood in the word MERELY, implying that symbols are unreal. Nomenclature involves classification; and classification is true or false, and the generals to which it refers are either reals in the one case, or figments in the other. For if the reader will turn to the original maxim of pragmaticism at the beginning of this article, he will see that the question is, not what *did* happen, but whether it would have been well to engage in any line of conduct whose successful issue depended upon whether that diamond *would* resist an attempt to scratch it, or whether all other logical means of determining how it ought to be classed *would* lead to the conclusion which, to quote the very words of that article, would be "the belief which alone could be the result of investigation carried *sufficiently far*." Pragmaticism makes the ultimate intellectual purport of what you please to consist in conceived conditional resolutions, or their substance; and therefore, the conditional propositions, with their hypothetical antecedents, in which such resolutions consist, being of the ultimate nature of meaning, must be capable of being true, that is, of expressing whatever there be which is such as the proposition expresses, independently of being thought to be so in any judgment, or being represented to be so in any other symbol of any man or men. But that amounts to saying that possibility is sometimes of a real kind.

Fully to understand this, it will be needful to analyze modality, and ascertain in what it consists. In the simplest case, the most subjective meaning, if a person does not know that a proposition is false, he calls it *possible*. If, however, he knows that it is *true*, it is much more than possible. Restricting the word to its characteristic applicability, a state of things has the Modality of the possible,—that is, of the merely possible,—only in case the contradictory state of things is likewise possible, which proves possibility to be the vague modality. One who knows that Harvard University has an office in State Street, Boston, and has impression that it is at No. 30, but yet suspects that 50 is the number, would say "I think it is at No. 30, but it *may be* at No. 50," for "it *is possibly* at No. 50." Thereupon, another, who does not doubt his recollection, might chime in, "It *actually is* at No. 50," or simply "it *is* at No. 50," or "it *is* at No. 50, *de inesse*." Thereupon, the person who had first asked what the number was might say, "Since you are so positive, it *must be* at No. 50," or "I know the first figure is 5. So, since you are both certain the second is a 0, why 50 it *necessarily is*." That is to say, in this most subjective kind of Modality, that which is known by direct recollection is in the Mode of *Actuality*, the determinate mode. But when knowledge is indeterminate among alternatives, either there is one state of things which alone accords with them all, when this is in the Mode of *Necessity*, or there is more than one state of things that no knowledge excludes, when each of these is in the Mode of *Possibility*.

Other kinds of subjective Modality refer to a Sign or Representamen which is assumed to be true, but which does not include the Utterer's (i.e. the speaker's, writer's, thinker's, or other symbolizer's) total knowledge, the different Modes being distinguished very much as above. There are other cases, however, in which, justifiably or not, we certainly think of Modality as objective. A man says, "I *can* go to the seashore if I like." Here is implied, to be sure, his ignorance of how he will decide to act. But this is not the point of the assertion. It is that, the complete determination of conduct in the *act* not yet having taken place, the further determination of it belongs to the subject of the action regardless of external circumstances. If he had said "I *must* go where my employers may send me," it would imply that the function of such further determination lay elsewhere. In "You *may* do so and so," and "You *must* do so," the "may" has the same force as "can" except that in the one case freedom from particular circumstances is in question, and in the other freedom from a law or edict. Hence the phrase, "You *may* if you *can*." I must say that it is difficult for me to preserve my respect for the competence of a philosopher whose dull logic, not penetrating beneath the surface, leaves him to regard such phrases as misrepresentations of the truth. So an act of hypostatic abstraction which in itself is no violation of logic, however it may lend itself to a dress of superstition, may regard the collective tendencies to variableness in the world, under the name of Chance, as at one time having their way, and at another time overcome by the element of order; so that, for example, a superstitious cashier, impressed by a bad dream, may say to himself of a Monday morning, "*May be*, the bank has been robbed." No doubt, he recognizes his total ignorance in the matter. But besides that, he has in mind the absence of any particular cause which should protect his bank more than others that are robbed from time to time. He thinks of the variety in the universe as vaguely analogous to the indecision of a person, and borrows from that analogy the garb of his thought. At the other extreme stand those who declare as inspired (for they have no rational proof of what they allege) that an actuary's advice to an insurance company is based on nothing at all but ignorance.

Here is another example of objective possibility: "A pair of intersecting rays, i.e., unlimited straight lines conceived as movable objects, *can* (or *may*) move, without ceasing to intersect, so that one and the same hyperboloid shall be completely covered by the track of each of them." How shall we interpret this, remembering that the object spoken of, the pair of rays, is a pure creation of the Utterer's imagination, although it is required (and indeed, forced) to conform to the laws of space? Some minds will be better satisfied with a more subjective, or nominalistic, others with a more objective, realistic interpretation. But it must be confessed on all hands that whatever degree or kind of reality belongs to pure space belongs to the substance of that proposition, which merely expresses a property of space.

Let us now take up the case of that diamond which, having been crystallized upon a cushion of jewellers' cotton, was accidentally consumed by fire before the crystal of corundum that had been sent for had had time to arrive, and indeed without being subjected to any other pressure than that of the atmosphere and its own weight. The question is, Was that diamond *really* hard? It is certain that no discernible *actual* fact determined it to be so. But is its hardness not, nevertheless, a *real* fact? To say, as the article of January 1878 seems to intend, that it is just as an arbitrary "usage of speech"[19] chooses to arrange its thoughts, is as much as to decide against the reality of the property, since the real is that which is such as it is regardless of how it is, at any time, thought to be. Remember that this diamond's condition is not an isolated fact. There is no such thing; and an isolated fact could hardly be real. It is an unsevered, though presciss, part of the unitary fact of nature. Being a diamond, it was a mass of pure carbon, in the form of a more or less transparent crystal (brittle, and of facile octahedral cleavage, unless it was of an unheard-of variety), which, if not twinned after one of the fashions in which diamonds may be twinned, took the shape of an octahedron, apparently regular (I need not go into minutiae), with grooved edges, and probably with some curved faces. Without being subjected to any considerable pressure, it could be found to be insoluble, very highly refractive, showing under radium rays (and perhaps under "dark light" and X-rays) a peculiar bluish phosphorescence, having as high a specific gravity as realgar or orpiment,[20] and giving off during its combustion less heat than any other form of carbon would have done. From some of these properties hardness is believed to be inseparable. For like it they bespeak the high polymerization of the molecule. But however this may be, how can the hardness of all other diamonds fail to bespeak *some* real relation among the diamonds without which a piece of carbon would not be a diamond? Is it not a monstrous perversion of the word and concept *real* to say that the accident of the non-arrival of the corundum prevented the hardness of the diamond from having the *reality* which it otherwise, with little doubt, would have had?

At the same time, we must dismiss the idea that the occult state of things (be it a relation among atoms or something else) which constitutes the reality of a diamond's hardness can possibly consist in anything but in the truth of a general conditional proposition. For to what else does the entire teaching of chemistry relate except to the "behavior" of different possible kinds of material substance? And what does that behavior consist in, except that if a substance of a certain kind should be exposed to an agency of a certain kind, a certain kind of sensible result *would* ensue, according to our experiences hitherto. As for the pragmaticist, it is precisely his position that nothing else than this can be so much as *meant* by saying that an object possesses a character. He is therefore obliged to subscribe to the doctrine of a real Modality, including real Necessity and real Possibility.

A good question, for the purpose of illustrating the nature of Pragmaticism, is, What is Time? It is not proposed to attack those most difficult problems connected with the psychology, the epistemology, or the metaphysics of Time, although it will be taken for granted, as it must be according to what has been said, that Time is real. The reader is only invited to the humbler question of what we mean by Time, and not of every kind of meaning attached to Past, Present, and Future either. Certain peculiar feelings are associated with the three general determinations of Time; but those are to be sedulously put out of view. That the reference of events to Time is irresistible will be recognized; but as to how it may differ from other kinds of irresistibility is a question not here to be considered. The question to be considered is simply, What is the intellectual purport of the Past, Present, and Future? It can only be treated with the utmost brevity.

That Time is a particular variety of Objective Modality is too obvious for argumentation. The Past consists of the sum of *faits accomplis*, and this Accomplishment is the Existential Mode of Time. For the Past really acts upon us, and *that* it does, not at all in the way in which a Law or Principle influences us, but precisely as an Existent object acts. For instance, when a *Nova Stella* bursts out in the heavens, it acts upon one's eyes just as a light struck in the dark by one's own hands would; and yet it is an event which happened before the Pyramids were built. A neophyte may remark that its reaching the eyes, which is all we know, happens but a fraction of a second before we know it. But a moment's consideration will show him that he is losing sight of the question, which is not whether the distant Past can act upon us *immediately*, but whether it acts upon us just as any Existent does. The instance adduced (certainly a commonplace enough fact) proves conclusively that the mode of the Past is that of Actuality. Nothing of the sort is true of the Future, to compass the understanding of which it is indispensable that the reader should divest himself of his Necessitarianism,—at best, but a scientific theory,—and return to the Common-Sense State of Nature. Do you never say to yourself, "I *can* do this or that as well tomorrow as today"? Your Necessitarianism is a theoretical pseudo-belief,—a make-believe belief,—that such a sentence does not express the real truth. That is only to stick to proclaiming the unreality of that Time, of which you are invited, be it reality or figment, to consider the meaning. You need not fear to compromise your darling theory by looking out at its windows. Be it true in theory or not, the unsophisticated conception is that everything in the Future is either *destined*, i.e., necessitated already, or is *undecided*, the contingent future of Aristotle. In other words, it is not Actual, since it does not act except through the idea of it, that is, as a law acts; but is either Necessary or Possible, which are of the same mode since (as remarked above) Negation being outside the category of Modality cannot produce a variation in Modality. As for the Present instant, it is so inscrutable that I wonder whether no sceptic has ever attacked its reality. I can fancy one of them dipping his pen in his blackest ink to commence the assault, and then suddenly reflecting that his entire life is in the Present,—the "living present," as we say,—this instant when all hopes and fears concerning it come to their end, this Living Death in which we are born anew. It is plainly that Nascent State between the Determinate and the Indeterminate that was noticed above.

Pragmaticism consists in holding that the purport of any concept is its conceived bearing upon our conduct. How, then, does the Past bear upon conduct? The answer is self-evident: whenever we set out to do anything, we "go upon," we base our conduct on facts already known, and for these we can only draw upon our memory. It is true that we may institute a new investigation for the purpose; but its discoveries will only become applicable to conduct after they have been made and reduced to a memorial maxim. In short, the Past is the sole storehouse of all our knowledge. When we say that we know that some state of things exists, we mean that it used to exist, whether just long enough for the news to reach the brain and be retransmitted to tongue or pen, or longer ago. Thus, from whatever point of view we contemplate the Past, it appears as the Existential Mode of Time.

How does the Future bear upon conduct? The answer is that future facts are the only facts that we can, in a measure, control; and whatever there may be in the Future that is not amenable to control are the things that we *shall* be able to infer, or *should* be able to infer under favorable circumstances. There may be questions concerning which the pendulum of opinion never would cease to oscillate, however favorable circumstances may be. But if so, those questions are *ipso facto* not *real* questions, that is to say, are questions to which there is no true answer to be given. It is natural to use the future tense (and the conditional mood is but a mollified future) in drawing a conclusion or in stating a consequence. "If two unlimited straight lines in one plane are crossed by a third making the sum . . . then these straight lines *will* meet on the side, etc." It cannot be denied that acritical inferences may refer to the Past in its capacity as past; but according to Pragmaticism, the conclusion of a

Reasoning proper must refer to the Future. For its meaning refers to conduct, and since it is a reasoned conclusion must refer to deliberate conduct, which is controllable conduct. But the only controllable conduct is Future conduct. As for that part of the Past that lies beyond memory, the Pragmaticist doctrine is that the meaning of its being believed to be in connection with the Past consists in the acceptance as truth of the conception that we ought to conduct ourselves according to it (like the meaning of any other belief). Thus, a belief that Christopher Columbus discovered America really refers to the Future. It is more difficult, it must be confessed, to account for beliefs that rest upon the double evidence of feeble but direct memory and upon rational inference. The difficulty does not seem insuperable; but it must be passed by.

What is the bearing of the Present instant upon conduct? Introspection is wholly a matter of inference.[21] One is immediately conscious of his Feelings, no doubt; but not that they are feelings of an *ego*. The *self* is only inferred. There is no time in the Present for any inference at all, least of all for inference concerning that very instant. Consequently the present object must be an external object, if there be any objective reference in it. The attitude of the Present is either conative or perceptive. Supposing it to be perceptive, the perception must be immediately known as external,—not indeed in the sense in which a hallucination is *not* external, but in the sense of being present regardless of the perceiver's will or wish. Now this kind of externality is conative externality. Consequently, the attitude of the present instant (according to the testimony of Common Sense, which is plainly adopted throughout) can only be a Conative attitude. The consciousness of the Present is then that of a struggle over what shall be; and thus we emerge from the study with a confirmed belief that it is the Nascent State of the Actual.

But how is Temporal Modality distinguished from other Objective Modality? Not by any general character since Time is unique and *sui generis*. In other words there is only one Time. Sufficient attention has hardly been called to the surpassing truth of this for Time as compared with its truth for Space. Time, therefore, can only be identified by brute compulsion. But we must not go further.

26

The Basis of Pragmaticism
in Phaneroscopy

MS 908. [The last part of this document was published in CP 1.317–21.
Many versions of a text titled "The Basis of Pragmaticism" are extant;
they were written over a period of nine months starting in August 1905,
and they were all meant to become Peirce's third Monist *paper. The*
present text is Peirce's fifth attempt, probably written in December 1905.
The words "in Phaneroscopy" have been added to the title of this version.]
Peirce's original plan for this series of articles called for the third one to
present the proof of pragmaticism. In this selection and the one that fol-
lows, Peirce lays the foundation on which to erect his proof (but he later
decided that his best case needed to be made with the Existential Graphs).
His preliminary efforts offer important insights as to how deeply pragmat-
icism is embedded in his system of philosophy. The basis for pragmaticism
that Peirce develops here is his phaneroscopy and the doctrine of the valency
of concepts that derives from it. Peirce explains why it makes sense to expect
that experience will exhibit only three "indecomposable elements," and of-
fers an abbreviated proof of his reduction thesis. This article well exhibits
Peirce's intention to do what he can to make philosophy a science, toward
which end it is necessary to "abandon all endeavor to make it literary."
Still, Peirce concludes this draft with a poetic characterization of the cru-
cial interplay between the world of fancy, the rudeness of experience, and
our "garment of contentment and of habituation."

I have already given the reasons which convince me that if philosophy is to
be made a science, the very first price we must pay for it must be to abandon
all endeavor to make it literary. We must have a vocabulary in which every
word has a single meaning, whether definite or vague; and to this end we
must not shrink from inventing new words whenever they are really needed;
and if these words are disagreeable to writers of taste, that will only make
them the more suitable for our uses. It was in seeking to fulfill that condition
that I invented the word *pragmaticism* to denote precisely what I had formerly
invented *pragmatism* to mean; and since the latter had been employed, not
only by philosophists to express doctrines not covered by my original definition (as I was very much pleased by their doing), but also by elegant writers in
connections which I dare say convey some meaning to readers who share
their habits of mind, but which I could not comprehend without more labor

than I am willing to bestow; in view of these facts, thinking that possibly the wishes of the inventor of the word might have a certain weight, notwithstanding his neglect to take out a patent on it, or even to request that nobody should write or read it except himself, I ventured to recommend that this word should be used to denote that general opinion about the nature of the clear apprehension of thought which is shared by those whom all the world calls pragmatists, and who so call themselves, no matter how one or other of us might state the substance of that accord. After a good deal of reflection and careful rereading,* I have come to think that the common pragmatistic opinion aforesaid is that *every* thought (unless perhaps certain single ideas each quite *sui generis*) has a meaning beyond the immediate content of the thought itself, so that it is as absurd to speak of a thought in itself as it would be to say of a man that he was a husband in himself or a son in himself, and this not merely because thought always refers to a real or fictitious *object*, but also because it supposes itself to be interpretable. If this analysis of the pragmatistic opinion be correct, the logical breadth of the term *pragmatist* is hereby enormously enlarged. For it will become predicable not only of Mr. Royce (who, apart from this analysis, impresses me quite decidedly as a pragmatist), but also of a large section of the logical world,—perhaps the majority,—since ancient times. The usual opinion of modern logicians has been that a great proportion of concepts have a meaning beyond themselves; for they have followed Leibniz in so far as to admit a large class of "symbolical" cognitions, though they have no doubt differed as to the extension of non-symbolical, or "intuitive," thought. Indeed, nominalists, in so far as they adhere to the doctrine of their "venerable inceptor,"[1] must under this understanding be classed as pragmatists, since Ockham regarded all concepts as "terms," and distinctly spoke of them as mental signs.[2] Nor were the scholastic realists posterior to Aquinas particularly averse to this view. Indeed, Aristotle himself would be a pragmatist. If we wished to exclude the general body of such logicians from the ranks of this school, we should have to describe the latter, no longer as consisting of those who hold to the doctrine that every thought has a meaning beyond its immediate content, but as confined to those who specially insist upon certain consequences of this doctrine, when the unity of their opinion would lose its definiteness.

The contents of most logic books is a syncretistic hodgepodge, and it is difficult to detect any differences but those of detail between one book and another. It is certain, however, that there have been, and still are, many logicians who in regard to our more primary and simple thoughts would protest against the theory that they have any exterior meaning. "The meaning!" these logicians would exclaim, "That *is* precisely the concept!" The refutation of this opinion will make us pragmatists, according to my analysis. In order to

---

*But there has been much matter that circumstances have not placed within my reach, especially matter adverse to pragmatism, which is presumably what I most need to read. I should be most grateful for a copy of any refutation of pragmatism, or supposed refutation of it.

establish *pragmaticism*, it will be necessary further to show that if the ultimate interpretation of a thought relates to anything but a determination of conditional conduct, it cannot be of an intellectual quality and so is not in the strictest sense a *concept*.

I propose to use the word *Phaneron* as a proper name to denote the total content of any one consciousness (for any one is substantially any other), the sum of all we have in mind in any way whatever, regardless of its cognitive value. This is pretty vague: I intentionally leave it so. I will only point out that I do *not* limit the reference to an instantaneous state of consciousness; for the clause "in any way whatever" takes in memory and all habitual cognition. The reader will probably wonder why I did not content myself with some expression already in use. The reason is that the absence of any contiguous associations with the new word will render it sharper and clearer than any well-worn coin could be.

I invite the reader to join me in a little survey of the Phaneron (which will be sufficiently identical for him and for me) in order to discover what different forms of indecomposable elements it contains. On account of the general interest of this inquiry, I propose to push it further than the question of pragmaticism requires; but I shall be forced to compress my matter excessively. It will be a work of observation. But in order that a work of observation should bring in any considerable harvest, there must always be a preparation of thought, a consideration, as definite as may be, of what it is possible that observation should disclose. That is a principle familiar to every observer. Even if one is destined to be quite surprised, the preparation will be of mighty aid.

As such preparation for our survey, then, let us consider what forms of indecomposable elements it is possible that we should find. The expression "indecomposable element" sounds pleonastic; but it is not so, since I mean by it something which not only is elementary, since it seems so, and seeming is the only being a constituent of the Phaneron has, as such, but is moreover incapable of being separated by logical analysis into parts, whether they be substantial, essential, relative, or any other kind of parts. Thus, a cow inattentively regarded may perhaps be an element of the Phaneron; but whether it can be so or not, it is certain that it can be analyzed logically into many parts of different kinds that are not in it as a constituent of the Phaneron, since they were not in mind in the same way as the cow was, nor in any way in which the cow, as an appearance in the Phaneron, could be said to be formed of these parts. We are to consider what *forms* are possible, rather than what *kinds* are possible, because it is universally admitted, in all sorts of inquiries, that the most important divisions are divisions according to *form*, and not according to qualities of *matter*, in case division according to form is possible at all. Indeed, this necessarily results from the very idea of the distinction between *form* and *matter*. If we content ourselves with the usual statement of this idea, the consequence is quite obvious. A doubt may, however, arise whether any distinction of form is possible among indecomposable elements. But since a possibility is proved as soon as a single actual instance is found, it will suffice to remark that although the chemical atoms were until quite recently conceived to be, each of them, quite indecomposable and homogeneous, yet they have for half a century been known to differ from one another, not indeed in *internal* form, but in *external* form. Carbon, for example, is a tetrad, combining only in the form $^H_H C^H_H$ (marsh gas),[3] that is, with four bonds with monads (such as is H) or their equivalent; boron is a triad, forming by the action of magnesium on boracic anhydride, HB^H_H, and never combining with any other valency; glucinum is a dyad, forming $ClGCl$, as the vapor-density of this salt, corroborated by many other tests, conclusively shows, and it, too, always has the same valency; lithium forms LiH and LiI and Li_3N, and is invariably a monad; and finally helion, neon, argon, krypton, and xenon are medads, not entering into atomic combination at all. We conclude, then, that there is a fair antecedent reason to suspect that the Phaneron's indecomposable elements may likewise have analogous differences of external form. Should we find this possibility to be actualized, it will, beyond all dispute, furnish us with by far the most important of all divisions of such elements.[4]

I trust no reader will understand me to be capable of reasoning by analogy from the constitution of chemical substances to the logical constitution of thought. I know very well that much of the substance of the present article has a distinct resemblance to a certain species of demilunatic stuff of which there is so much in the world that it is likely to cumber the shelves of any elderly logician who does not take measures to get rid of it. I know furthermore that the world is full of minds of such a caliber that because a good deal of precious nonsense is of a certain type, they wish to know no more of anything that is of that type. I do not much regret it, because it is unlikely that a person who passes judgment in such fashion should possess that rare faculty of looking out of his own eyes and seeing what stares him in the face,—a faculty, however, that I desiderate in my reader, and feel confident of having in every attentive reader. But though I do not offer such a crude argument, it is certainly true that all physical science involves (I do not say *depends upon*) the postulate of a resemblance between nature's law and what it is natural for man to think, and moreover, the success of science affords overwhelming proof that that postulate is true; and consequently, sound logic does distinctly recommend that the hypothesis of the indecomposable elements of the Phaneron being in their general constitution like the chemical atoms be taken up as a hypothesis with a view to its being subjected to the test of an inductive inquiry.

There are further considerations, however, which warrant our expecting more confidently to find in elements of the Phaneron certain forms than to find certain others. Thus, unless the Phaneron were to consist entirely of elements altogether uncombined mentally, in which case we should have no idea of a Phaneron (since this, if we have the idea, is an idea combining all the rest), which is as much as to say that there would be no Phaneron, its *esse* being *percipi* if any is so; or unless the Phaneron were itself our sole idea, and were utterly indecomposable, when there could be no such thing as an interrogation and no such thing as a judgment (as will appear below), it follows that if there is a Phaneron (which would be an assertion), or even if we can ask whether there be or no, there must be an idea of *combination* (i.e., having *combination* for its object thought of). Now the general idea of a combination must be an indecomposable idea. For otherwise it would be compounded, and the idea of combination would enter into it as an analytic part of it. It is, however, quite absurd to suppose an idea to be a part of itself, and *not the whole*. Therefore, if there is a Phaneron, the idea of combination is an indecomposable element of it. This idea is a triad; for it involves the ideas of a whole and of two parts (a point to be further considered below). Accordingly, there will necessarily be a triad in the Phaneron. Moreover, if the metaphysicians are right in saying (those of them who do say so) that there is but one absolutely necessary idea, which is that of the Triune God, then this idea of the Triune God must in some way be identical with the simple idea of combination.

But out of triads exclusively it is possible to build all external forms, medads, monads, dyads, triads, tetrads, pentads, hexads, and the rest. The figure below suggests one way.

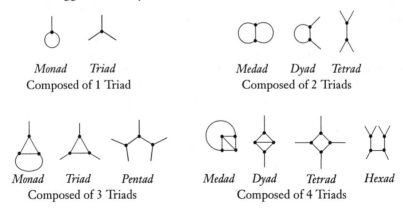

Monad	Triad		Medad	Dyad	Tetrad
Composed of 1 Triad			Composed of 2 Triads		

Monad	Triad	Pentad		Medad	Dyad	Tetrad	Hexad
Composed of 3 Triads				Composed of 4 Triads			

So far as our study has now gone, then, it appears possible that all elements of the Phaneron should be triads. But an obvious principle which is as purely *a priori* as a principle well can be, since it is involved in the very idea of the Phaneron as containing constituents of which some are logically unanalyzable and others analyzable, promptly reduces that subjective possibility to an absurdity. I mean the principle that whatever is logically involved in an ingredient of the Phaneron is itself an ingredient of the Phaneron; for it is in the mind even though it be only implicitly so. Suppose then a Triad to be in the Phaneron. It connects three objects, *A*, *B*, *C*, however indefinite *A*, *B*, and *C* may be. There must, then, be one of the three, at least, say *C*, which establishes a relation between the other two, *A* and *B*. The result is that *A* and *B* are in a dyadic relation, and *C* may be ignored, even if it cannot be supposed absent. Now this dyadic relation between *A* and *B*, without reference to any third, involves a Secundan. In like manner, in order that there may be a Secundan, so that *A* and *B* are in some sense opposed, and neither is swallowed up in the other,— or even if only one of them had such an independent standing, it must be capable of being regarded as more or less determinate and positive in itself, and so involves Primanity. This Primanity supposes a Priman element; so that the suggestion that no elements should be Primans is absurd, as is the suggestion that no elements should be Secundans.

This same principle may be applied in the same way to any Tetradic constituent of the Phaneron. But if we expect it to lead to an analogous conclusion we shall find ourselves out of that dead reckoning. Suppose a Tetrad in the Phaneron. Now just as the being of a Tertian consists precisely in its connecting the members of a triplet, so that two of them are united in the third, so the Quartanness of the tetrad will consist in its connecting the members of a quaternion, say *A*, *B*, *C*, *D*, and in nothing else. That is precisely its form. As the triad involves dyads, so likewise does the tetrad. Let *A*, *B* be the objects of such a dyad. The tetrad is more than a mere dyad for those objects. I mean that it not only makes one of them determine the other in some regard, after the manner of dyads, or,—to use the word which we are in the habit of using only in reference to the more characteristic kinds of dyads, but which I will extend for the nonce to all dyads, in order to call up my idea in the reader's mind,—the tetrad not only makes *A* to "act" upon *B* (or *B* upon *A*), but, like a triad, indeed as involving Tertianity (just as we have seen that a triad involves Secundanity), it puts together *A* and *B*, so that they make up a third object,— to continue my method of expression by stretching the extension of terms, I might say, so that they "create" a third, namely the pair, understood as involving all that the tetrad implies concerning these two prescinded from *C* and *D*. Moreover the tetrad involves a dyad, one of whose objects is this pair of *A* and *B*, while the other is either *C* or *D*, say *C*. Here again the tetrad makes the dyad more than a mere dyad, since it unites *C* to the pair of *A* and *B*, and makes them create a new object, *their* pair. And finally it unites this last pair to *D*. Thus, the entire function of the tetrad is performed by a series of Triads; and consequently, there can be no unanalyzable tetrad, nothing to be called a *quartan* element of the Phaneron. Plainly, the same process will exclude *quintanity, sextanity, septanity*, and all higher forms of indecomposable elements from the Phaneron.

To many a reader this reasoning will appear obscure and inconclusive. This effect is due to the argument's turning upon such a complex of prescissive abstractions; for an abstract concept is essentially indefinite. Now the reader would not have been a reader of this paper unless he had had the intellectual virtue of striving to give definite interpretations to concepts. But it often happens that this virtue being coupled with a particular natural turn of mind, breeds an intellectual vice, the bad habit of dropping all lines of study which largely introduce indefinite concepts, so that those who contract this habit never gain a proper training in handling such concepts. This is by no means the only difficulty of mathematics, which incessantly employs them, but it is perhaps the chief reason why we find among particularly able professional men, and even among thinkers, so many who are completely shut off from mathematics. But those whom this demonstration fails to reach may find themselves convinced by the facts of observation when we come to consider them.

Some will ask whether, if every tetrad can be built up out of triads, it must not be equally true that every triad can be built up out of dyads. The reason has already been stated, namely, that nothing can be built up out of other things without combining those other things, and combination is itself manifestly a triad. But those who do not see the force of this reason had better try to build up a chemical triad, that is, a connected group with three free bonds, out of chemical dyads, while observing the law of valency.

Much might be profitably added to this preliminary *a priori* study; but even with the greatest compression I shall cover too many of the valuable pages of the *Monist*.[5] We must hasten, then, to try how well or ill our *a priori* conclusions are supported by the actual examination of the contents of the Phaneron. Let us begin at once.

Can we find in the Phaneron any element logically indecomposable, which is such as it is, altogether otherwise than relatively, but positively, and regardless of aught else?

I answer, There are many such elements. I instance the color of a stick of countinghouse sealing wax which I had to use a few moments ago, and which still lies on my table in plain sight. This is an element, for I do not see it as composite. It is also logically indecomposable. It is true that I can take down my color wheel, analyze this color, and define it in an equation. But such an equation, far from expressing any logical analysis, does not even define the color-sensation. For an observer thoroughly trained to recognize his immediate feelings as they are felt, free from all the allowances which we naturally make for the circumstances of the experience, will perceive that when the stick of sealing wax be highly illuminated, the sensation is more scarlet, and that under a dim light it verges toward a dull vermillion hue; and yet the analysis by the color wheel will wholly fail to detect this. For a mere admixture of black with the color of the highly illuminated wax will make it a precise match for the feebly illuminated wax. Considerably more like a logical analysis is the ordinary description of a color in terms of its luminosity, chroma (or degree of departure from grey), and hue; as one might say that the color of this sealing wax is moderately luminous but extremely chromatic color, pretty nearly pure red in hue, yet decidedly leaning toward scarlet. But however much this may resemble a logical analysis, it *[is]* not what I mean by that term when I say that a Priman, a Secundan, or a Tertian is essentially indecomposable. For if a man possessed no other color-sensation but that excited by this sealing wax under good forenoon illumination from white clouds, indoors close to a window, he might devote his life to thinking about it, but he never would discover that there were those three respects: luminousness, chroma, and hue. They are not seen in the color taken by itself but only in the color as it appears in comparison with others. That is shown by the fact that in order to describe the color with tolerable accuracy, it is necessary to experiment by placing it in successive juxtaposition with others which are very much like it, one in luminosity, another in chroma, and a third in hue. This shows that though the description does not refer to the phenomena of mixture-experiments, it does refer to phenomena of experiments. If I am asked whether the same thing is not true of logical analyses, I admit that some analyses which are sometimes called logical are of that kind, but not the logical analyses meant when we speak of the Priman, Secundan, and Tertian being logically indecomposable. Consider, for example, the *word* "red." I mean the word "red" in that sense in which it is one and the same word, however often it be pronounced, and whether quite correctly or not. It has its being exclusively in governing this articulation (I leave writing out of account for simplicity) and the apprehension of Anglo-Saxons. The pronunciation varies enormously, the *r* from the *grassouillée* sound that most Frenchmen give to it, or did in my day, to the sound which is obtained by so much labor in the *Comédie française*, to the semi-articulate *r* of most of us, and to the "wred" of some people, the *e* also ranging over considerable variety, and finally the *d* being either of two sounds which are carefully distinguished in some languages, the dental *d* of the Latin races, and our alveolar *d*, and even an Arabic ض, Dhâd, or ظ, dhâ, if pronounced explosively, would be tolerated. All these variations are of the being of the word, for other, much smaller departures from the average pronunciation would render the vocable quite unintelligible. Therefore, whether it be apprehended as consisting of three sounds, or be not so apprehended, mere attention to the word itself will bring out that composition, without any comparison with other words; and such an analysis is what I rather inaptly style "logical" decomposition, because it is effected in the same way in which one would find a definition of a familiar word whose meaning one had never before analyzed. That the quality red is positive and wholly resident in itself regardless of aught else is obvious. Yet even this may be doubted. The legend of the music of the spheres at least *seems* to be based on the notion that sense-qualities are relative to each other. But even if everything in the world and in the Phaneron were precisely of this sealing-wax red, though we should not be *distinctly* aware of it, I suppose that it would tinge our disposition, and so be, in some sense, in the mind. If it would not, this would be merely a psychological fact: it would have nothing to do with the quality *red* in itself. Nor can it be said that red is relative to a surface. For though we cannot prescind redness from superficial extension, we can easily distinguish it from superficial extension, owing (for one thing) to our being able to prescind the latter from the former. Sealing-wax red, then, is a Priman.

So is any other quality of feeling. Now the whole content of consciousness is made up of qualities of feeling, as truly as the whole of space is made up of points or the whole of time of instants. Contemplate anything by itself,—

anything whatever that can be,[6] so contemplate it. Attend to the whole and drop the parts out of attention altogether. One can approximate nearly enough to the accomplishment of that to see that the result of its perfect accomplishment would be that one would have in his consciousness at the moment nothing but a quality of feeling. This quality of feeling would in itself, as so contemplated, have no parts. It would be unlike any other such quality of feeling. In itself, it would not even resemble any other; for resemblance has its being only in comparison. It would be a pure Priman. Since this is true of whatever we contemplate, however complex may be the object, it follows that there is nothing else in immediate consciousness. To be conscious is nothing else than to feel.

What room, then, is there for Secundans and Tertians? Was there some mistake in our demonstration that they must also have their places in the Phaneron? No, there was no mistake. I said that the Phaneron is made up entirely of qualities of feeling as truly as Space is entirely made up of points. There is a certain *protoidal* aspect,—I coin the word for the need,—under which Space is truly made up of nothing but points. Yet it is certain that no collection of points,—using the word collection to mean merely a plural, without the idea of the objects being brought together,—no collection of points, no matter how abnumerable its multitude, can in itself constitute Space. For Space has chorisy one, that is, is all one piece; its cyclosy and its periphraxy are each either zero or one,* that is, if it has room for a filament which could by no continuous deformation shrink indefinitely toward becoming a particle, a single simple superficial barrier would suffice to leave in the rest of Space no room for any such filament, and if it has room for any *film*, or deformable surface, which by no continuous deformation could shrink indefinitely toward becoming a filament, a single filamentary barrier would suffice to leave in the rest of Space no such room; and finally Space has an apeiry one, that is, it has room for a single solid which by no continuous deformation could shrink indefinitely toward becoming a film, but the barrier of a single particle would leave no room in the rest of Space for such unshrinkable solid.[7] Now none of these properties necessarily belongs to any mere plural of points, except that a *single* point has chorisy one. It is not the points, but the relations between the different points, which produce the chorisy, cyclosy, periphraxy, and apeiry of Space, as well as its being topically non-singular, that is, its containing no place of any dimensionality which a deformable object occupying it could quit in fewer or in more ways than it could quit innumerable other such places all about it. What is the nature of all these relations as well as those of time? They all result from complications of only two elements. One of these is the relation of a distributively general object, "any" something, to the single individual collection which embraces "any" such, and nothing else. The other is the relation of geometrical *betweenness*, upon which Kempe first did some considerable logical work,[8]

---

*In the space of quaternions both are zero; in the space of projective geometry both are one.

though I, and doubtless every other exact logician who had examined the subject, already well knew that the key of geometry lay in that. If we consider any portion of a line, this portion having two extremities, A and B, then any point, X, of that portion lies "between" A and B; and any second point, Y, of that portion is either "between" X and A, while X is "between" it and B, or else is "between" X and B, while X is "between" it and A. Of these two relations, that between the distributive and collective "all" is dyadic, that of betweenness is triadic. But these are not at all characteristic examples of the dyad and the triad. Either has a decided *protoidal* tinge. The characteristic color of the dyad,—if I may be allowed the metaphor,—is that of opposition. But the distributive and collective are the same thing differently expressed. To say that X is between A and B is to say that the place of X, in so far as it is not the place of A, is the place of B, and in so far as it is not the place of B, is the place of A. It is a sort of divided agreement.

But the Phaneron does contain genuine Secundans. Standing on the outside of a door that is slightly ajar, you put your hand upon the knob to open and enter it. You experience an unseen, silent resistance. You put your shoulder against the door and gathering your forces put forth a tremendous effort. Effort supposes resistance. Where there is no effort, there is no resistance; where there is no resistance, there is no effort, either in this world or in any of the worlds of possibility. It follows that an effort is not a feeling nor anything priman or protoidal. There are feelings connected with it; they are the sum of consciousness during the effort. But it is conceivable that a man should have it in his power directly to summon up all those feelings, or any feelings. He could not, in any world, be endowed with the power of summoning up an effort to which there did not happen to be a resistance all ready to exist. For it is an absurdity to suppose that a man could directly will to oppose that very will. A very little thinking will show that this is what it comes to. According to such psychological analysis as I can make, effort is a phenomenon which only arises when one feeling abuts upon another in time, and which then always arises. But my psychological pretensions are little if they exist at all, and I only mention my theory in order that contrast should impress the reader with the irrelevancy of psychology to our present problem, which is to say of what sort that is which is in our minds when we make an effort and which constitutes it an effort. We live in two worlds, a world of fact and a world of fancy. Each of us is accustomed to think that he is the creator of his world of fancy; that he has but to pronounce his fiat, and the thing exists, with no resistance and no effort; and although this is so far from the truth that I doubt not that much the greater part of the reader's labor is expended on the world of fancy, yet it is near enough the truth for a first approximation. For this reason we call the world of fancy the internal world, the world of fact the external world. In this latter, we are masters, each of us, of his own voluntary muscles, and of nothing more. But man is sly, and contrives to make this little more than he needs. Beyond that, he defends himself from the angles of hard fact by clothing himself with a garment of contentment and of habituation. Were it not for this garment, he would every now and then find his internal world rudely disturbed and his fiats set at naught by brutal inroads of ideas from without. I call such forcible modification of our ways of thinking, the influence of the world of fact, *experience*. But he patches up his garment by guessing what those inroads are likely to be and carefully excluding from his internal world every idea which is likely to be so disturbed. Instead of waiting for experience to come at untoward times, he provokes it when it can do no harm and changes the government of his internal world accordingly.

27

The Basis of Pragmaticism
in the Normative Sciences

MS 283. [Only a small part was published in CP 1.573–74, 5.448n, and 5.449–54. This paper, which was mostly composed in January 1906, is Peirce's sixth attempt at writing his third Monist *paper "The Basis of Pragmaticism." The words "in the Normative Sciences" have been added to the title of this version.] How does one do philosophy? A proof of pragmaticism will have to be understood from the perspective of our answer to this question. Peirce sets out to situate philosophy among the "heuretic" sciences, and to characterize its purpose and method. He returns to a consideration of experience, here characterized as a "male" intrusion into the mind, the "female" field of available consciousness. From this union, knowledge is born. This is Aristotle's idea of growth: first, the idea; second, the act; third, the life-giving principle. In selection 26, Peirce had considered why we should expect to find three fundamental elements in experience; here he examines why we should expect philosophy to separate naturally into three departments corresponding to the three kinds of experience. It is the second department, normative science, that becomes the main focus of this article, and the basis for Peirce's proof of pragmaticism. All three normative sciences—esthetics, ethics (practics), and logic—are essential, but it is logic, the general theory of signs, that is now seen to be the key to the proof.*

I. Introductory

§1. *The aim of this article* cannot be to set forth the argument for the truth of pragmaticism in full. A volume would be required for that; and it would be a volume requiring close study. One cannot communicate the substance of thirty years' energetic study in a few words. Having been invited to deliver six lectures on pragmaticism in Harvard University to trained students,[1] the author of this paper stretched the six to seven, and devoted them all to the development of this argument. He was most desirous that they should be printed, with interpolations, so that critics should be able to study the many different points at their leisure; but the friend upon whom the publication depended declined to recommend the matter for printing;[2] and it is certain that the writer would never be able to restate the argument with equal lucidity. [. . .][3]

§2. *The word "science"* has three principal acceptions, to wit:

Firstly, men educated in Jesuit and similar colleges often use the term in the sense of the Greek ἐπιστήμη, the Latin *scientia;* that is to say, to denote knowledge for certain. (Fuller explanations are given in the *Index Aristotelicus* of Bonitz.)[4]

Secondly, since the beginning of the nineteenth century, when Coleridge so defined it in the opening dissertation to the *Encyclopaedia Metropolitana,*[5] non-scientific people have generally understood "science" to mean systematized knowledge.

Thirdly, in the mouths of scientific men themselves "science" means the concrete body of their own proper activities, in seeking such truth as seems to them highly worthy of life-long devotion, and in pursuing it by the most critically chosen methods, including all the help both general and special that they can obtain from one another's information and reflection.

The present writer will call science in this third sense *heuretic science;* he will call science which differs from this in all the important respects which result from investigation being pursued, not because of the august nature of the truth sought, but for the sake of some anticipated utility of it to some man or men, *practical science,* and he will call science in the Coleridgian sense *retrospective science.*

It is to be remarked that although heuretic scientists look upon their work as purely theoretical, and many of them feel a utilitarian application, even of the highest kind, is comparatively lacking in the sacredness of pure science, they are nevertheless particularly given to thinking of their results as affording possible conditions for new experiments, if not in the narrower, then in the broader sense of the term,* although they may have the vaguest possible notions of what those experiments may be. This shows that regarding a truth as purely theoretical does not prevent its being regarded as a possible determinant of conduct.

§3. *Two meanings of the term "philosophy"* call for our particular notice. The two meanings agree in making philosophical knowledge positive, that is, in making it a knowledge of things real, in opposition to mathematical knowledge, which is a knowledge of the consequences of arbitrary hypotheses; and they further agree in making philosophical truth extremely general. But in other respects they differ as widely as they well could. For one of them, which is better entitled (except by usage) to being distinguished as *philosophia prima* than is ontology, embraces all that positive science which rests upon familiar experience and does not search out occult or rare phenomena; while the other, which has been called *philosophia ultima,* embraces all that truth which is derivable by collating the results of the different special sciences, but which is too broad to be perfectly established by any one of them. The former is

---

*An experiment in the narrow sense is where special conditions of experience are purposely created; but any observation made to test a hypothesis is an experiment in the broader sense. Such is an observation of an occultation to test the lunar tables.

well named by Jeremy Bentham's term *cenoscopy*[6] (κοινοσκοπιά, the lookout upon the common), the latter goes by the name of *synthetic philosophy*. Widely different as the two sciences are, /they are/ frequently confounded and intertangled; and when they are distinguished the question is often asked, "Which of these is the true philosophy?" as if an appreciation of one necessarily involved a depreciation of the other. In the writer's opinion each is an important study. Cenoscopy should be that department of heuretic science which stands next after Mathematics, and before Idioscopy, or special science; while Synthetic Philosophy, the subject upon which Francis Bacon, Auguste Comte, William Whewell, and Herbert Spencer have left us admirable works in their several ways, stands at the head of the Retrospective Sciences.

A sound methodeutic requires heuretic science to found its researches upon cenoscopy, passing with as slight a gap as possible from the familiar to the unfamiliar.

§4. *The method of cenoscopic research* presents a certain difficulty. In commencing it we are confronted with the fact that we already believe a great many things. These beliefs, or at least the more general of them, ought to be reconsidered with deliberation. This implies that it should be conducted according to a deliberate plan adopted only after the severest criticism. Indeed, nothing in cenoscopy should be embraced without criticism. Each criticism should wait to be planned, and each plan should wait for criticism. Clearly, if we are to get on at all, we must put up with imperfect procedure.

The only practicable method is that of the inductive sciences, the method of trying key after key until we find one that fits. Only, energy should not be wasted in even trying a key without a rational hope of its being the sound one. The reflective reader may find reason to suspect that the writer has bestowed no little thought upon this. In truth, such a world of different considerations jostle one another in his memory that it will be best to pass them all by in so brief a *résumé*. Let us rather ask what former thinkers had done toward setting our cogitations upon some smoothly running track of ratiocination.

§5. *The idea of growth*,—the stately tree springing from the tiny grain,— was the key that Aristotle brought to be tried upon this intricate grim lock. In such trials he came upon those wonderful conceptions, δύναμις and ἐνέργεια, ὕλη and μορφή or εἶδος,[7] or, as he might still better have said, τύπος, the blow, the *coup*. (*A propos* of what was said above about the way to read,[8] the sentence just set down is an instance of one beyond which a reader had better not proceed, until he pretty nearly understands the point of view from which the force of that remark appears.) This idea of Aristotle's has proved marvellously fecund; and in truth it is the only idea covering quite the whole area of cenoscopy that has shown any marked uberosity. Many and many a century is likely to sink in Time's flood, and be buried in the mud of Lethe, before the achievements of the nineteenth shall get matched. But of all those achievements, the greatest in the eye of reason, that of bringing to light the supremacy of the element of *Growth*, was, after all, nothing but a special application of Aristotle's pure vision.

Let us lose sight of no side of it; *Growth*,—the idea,—the act,—the lifegiving principle.

One special feature of growth has always received great attention; yet its lessons are far from having today been completely learned. It is that growth cannot proceed very far until those elements of it which constitute the functions of the two sexes get well separated. The female function, the function of the seed, has always been recognized as the δύναμις. The female is the general and essential sex; the male merely executes a hunch, the τύπος of the μορφή. It is the principle of unrest. But do not forget that the seed needs to be left to itself to grow as far as it can alone, before the *coup* of fertilization disturbs it. In order that it could so have grown alone, and indeed, in low organisms have reached the height of their attained potentiality, the female must have had an admixture of the restless. Pure femininity is not to be found even in the nucleus of the crystal of alum quietly growing out of its evaporating solution. Pure femininity can be conceived in a general way, but it cannot be realized even in consistent imagination. As for pure masculinity, it is an absurdity and nonsense, *vox et praeterea nihil.*[9]

Besides those two requisites of perfecting growth, there is a third, not implied in either of them, nor in both together. It is the congress of those two. It is something demonstrably additional to them. When this comes a new life begins.

Now apply these ideas to knowledge. Observe that this will itself [be] an act of copulation. There is nothing in the feminine conception of knowledge, nor in the masculine conception of sexuality, to prove that there will be any fruit for philosophy in bringing them together. An incomprehensible instinct urges us to it; nothing else.

The seed of knowledge is the mind, the field of available consciousness,—all that is present or that can be called up. The rude τύπος is experience. He who may not have felt quite sure of understanding why the entrance of the element of *Form* should be called [experience][10] will find enlightenment in thinking of the matter from this point of view.

II. Sketch of Cenoscopy

§6. *The business of cenoscopy* is to construct, as best one may, a true comprehension of the *omne*,—and if possible, of the *totum*,—of being and of nonbeing, and of the principal divisions of this *omne*.

How shall we lay out this business?

Let us not lose all possibility of advantage from the Aristotelian key merely because we cannot be quite sure, in advance of the essay, that it will fit.

Cenoscopy is not to resort to special experience, or only upon the most exceptional occasions, in order not to break the discussion of one question. There is no veritable exception. To say that cenoscopy is not to resort to special experience is to say that it is to be science in the seminal condition. Yet it could have no logic at all unless both of the sexual elements, together with the third that springs from their union, were all present.

Hence comes the suggestion that Cenoscopy should have three divisions,—a suggestion that further considerations, that cannot here be set forth, amply confirm. It will be well to state what these divisions are.

§7. *Metaphysics* is the proper designation for the third and completing department of cenoscopy, which in places welds itself into idioscopy, or special science. Its business is to study the most general features of reality and real objects. But in its present condition it is, even more than the other branches of cenoscopy, a puny, rickety, and scrofulous science. It is only too plain that those who pretend to cultivate it carry not the hearts of true men of science within their breast. Instead of striving with might and main to find out what errors they have fallen into, and exulting joyously at every such discovery, they are scared to look Truth in the face. They turn tail and flee her. Only a small number out of the great catalogue of problems which it is their business to solve have they ever taken up at all, and those few most feebly. Here let us set down almost at random a small specimen of the questions of metaphysics which press, not for hasty answers, but for industrious and solid investigation: Whether or no there be any real indefiniteness, or real possibility and impossibility? Whether or not there is any definite indeterminacy? Whether there be any strictly individual existence? Whether there is any distinction, other than one of more and less, between fact and fancy? Or between the external and the internal worlds? What general explanation or account can be given of the different qualities of feeling and their apparent connection with determinations of mass, space, and time? Do all possible qualities of sensation, including of course a much vaster variety of which we have no experience than of those which we know, form one continuous system, as colors seem to do? What external reality do the qualities of sense represent, in general? Is Time a real thing, and if not, what is the nature of the reality that it represents? How about Space, in these regards? How far, and in what respects, is Time external, or does it have immediate contents that are external? Are Time and Space continuous? What numerically are the Chorisy, Cyclosy, Periphraxy, and Apeiry of Space?[11] Has Time, or has Space, any limit or node? Is *hylozoism* an opinion, actual or conceivable, rather than a senseless vocable; and if so, what is, or would be, that opinion? What is consciousness or mind like; meaning, is it a single continuum like Time and Space, which is for different purposes variously broken up by that which it contains; or is it composed of solid atoms, or is it more like a fluid? Has Truth, in Kantian phrase, any "material" characteristics in general, by which it can with any degree of probability be recognized? Is there, for example, any general tendency in the course of events, any progress in one direction on the whole?

While a summary study of metaphysics will suffice to dispose of its problems, so far as they could disturb the course of ordinary scientific researches, there are sundry branches of science, and they are mostly particularly interesting branches to human curiosity,—psychology, for example, and psychical research, and on the other wing of idioscopy, molecular and corpuscular physics, radioactivity, physical geometry, and so on,—which cannot escape entirely.

§8. *Normative Science* forms the midportion of cenoscopy and its most characteristic part. In any adequate exposition of the *rationale* of pragmaticism, this present section, the eighth, would be particularly important, not so much for any especially definite ratiocination that it would have to unfold, as because it would serve to convey the reader into the intellectual clime, and for that matter to the very field where the operations of our argumentation are to be executed and our encounter with hard fact waged. He ought to be transported hither through the empyrean of pure thought as calmly as in the basket of a balloon, whence eye might sweep the general map of philosophy. It is a grievous shame and imposition that the reader should instead have to traverse this space, so full of marvels and of beauties, as in a night train, pent up in this cramped section, obscure and airless. It is much to be feared that it will prove to be more veritably a "sleeper" than any place of torment to which Pullman ever consigned him.

The topics which have mainly to be considered in this section suggest its division into three parts, as follows:

(A) Of Normative Science as an indispensable preliminary, propedeutic, and prolegomenon to Metaphysics.

(B) Of the hard dualism of Normative Science and whence it comes.

(C) Of the nature of Normative Science, as entirely distinct from Practical Science, though it tends to produce this, and as affording a basis for psychology and consequently in no degree itself resting upon psychology. In what sense it is a science of Mind, at all. Its approaches to Mathematics must also be discussed.

A. It would be folly to attack the fastnesses of the arcana of Metaphysics, with all their barbed wire entanglements, without having thoroughly considered beforehand the nature of the reasoning to be employed and the source of its validity. This is the most obvious reason for making one normative science antecede metaphysics; and also the most available reason and the one most suited to governing the dispositions of the elements of the research. It is not the strongest reason by a good deal. The strongest reason is that most of the metaphysical conceptions, such as Substance, Quality, Relation, Potentiality, Law, Causation, etc., are nothing but logical conceptions applied to real objects, and can only attain elucidation in logical study. But it is not convenient to prove this in advance, nor does it suggest the best arrangement until logic has actually been fathomed to its very bottom.

Logic regarded from one instructive, though partial and narrow, point of view, is the theory of deliberate thinking. To say that any thinking is deliberate is to imply that it is controlled with a view to making it conform to a purpose or ideal. Thinking is universally acknowledged to be an active operation. Consequently, the control of thinking with a view to its conformity to a standard or ideal is a special case of the control of action to make it conform to a standard; and the theory of the former must be a special determination of the theory of the latter. Now special theories should always be made to rest upon the general theories of which they are amplifications. The present writer takes the theory of the control of conduct, and of action in general, so as to conform to an ideal, as being the mid-normative science; that is, as the second of the trio, and as that one of the three sciences in which the distinctive characters of normative science are most strongly marked. He will not undertake to pronounce any other distribution of the matter of normative science to be wrong; but according to the dissection of that matter which seems to him to separate studies as they must be separated in research, such will be the mid-normative science. Since the normative sciences are usually held to be three, Esthetics, Ethics, and Logic, and since he, too, makes them three, he would term the mid-normative science ethics if this did not seem to be forbidden by the received acception of that term. He accordingly proposes to name the mid-normative science, as such (whatever its content may be), *Antethics*, that is, that which is put in place of ethics, the usual second member of the trio. It is the writer's opinion that this *antethics* should be the theory of the conformity of action to an ideal. Its name, as such, will naturally be *practics*. Ethics is not practics; first, because ethics involves more than the theory of such conformity; namely it involves the theory of the ideal itself, the nature of the *summum bonum*; and secondly, because, in so far as *ethics* studies the conformity of conduct to an ideal, it is limited to a particular ideal, which, whatever the professions of moralists may be, is in fact nothing but a sort of composite photograph[12] of the conscience of the members of the community. In short, it is nothing but a traditional standard, accepted, very wisely, without radical criticism, but with a silly pretense of critical examination. The science of morality, virtuous conduct, right living, can hardly claim a place among the heuretic sciences.

It has been a great, but frequent, error of writers on ethics to confound an ideal of conduct with a motive to action. The truth is that these two objects belong to different categories. Every action has a motive; but an ideal only belongs to a line of conduct which is deliberate. To say that conduct is deliberate implies that each action, or each important action, is reviewed by the actor and that his judgment is passed upon it, as to whether he wishes his future conduct to be like that or not. His ideal is the kind of conduct which attracts him upon review. His self-criticism followed by a more or less conscious resolution that in its turn excites a determination of his habit, will, with the aid of the sequelae, *modify* a future action; but it will not generally be a moving cause to action. It is an almost purely passive liking for a way of doing whatever he may be moved to do. Although it affects his own conduct, and nobody else's, yet the quality of feeling (for it is merely a quality of feeling) is just the same, whether his own conduct or that of another person real or imaginary is the object of the feeling, or whether it be connected with the thought of any action or not. If conduct is to be thoroughly deliberate, the ideal must be a habit of feeling which has grown up under the influence of a course of self-criticisms and of heterocriticisms; and the theory of the deliberate formation of such habits of feeling is what ought to be meant by *esthetics*. It is true that the Germans, who invented the word, and have done the most toward developing the science, limit it to *taste*, that is, to the action of the *Spieltrieb*,[13] from which deep and earnest emotion would seem to be excluded. But in the writer's opinion, the theory is the same whether it be a question of forming a taste in bonnets or of a preference between electrocution and decapitation, or between supporting one's family by agriculture or by highway robbery. The difference of earnestness is of vast practical moment; but it has nothing to do with heuretic science.

According to this view, Esthetics, Practics, and Logic form one distinctly marked whole, one separate department of heuretic science; and the question where precisely the lines of separation between them are to be drawn is quite secondary. It is clear, however, that esthetics relates to feeling, practics to action, logic to thought.

B. A *state of things* is an abstract constituent part of reality, of such a nature that a proposition is needed to represent it. There is but one *individual*, or completely determinate, state of things, namely, the all of reality. A *fact* is so highly a prescissively abstract state of things, that it can be wholly represented in a simple proposition, and the term "simple," here, has no absolute meaning, but is merely a comparative expression.

A *mathematical form* of a state of things is such a representation of that state of things as represents only the samenesses and diversities involved in that state of things, without definitely qualifying the subjects of the samenesses and diversities. It represents not necessarily all of these; but if it does represent all, it is the *complete* mathematical form. Every mathematical form of a state of things is the complete mathematical form of *some* state of things. The complete mathematical form of any state of things, real or fictitious, represents every ingredient of that state of things except the qualities of feeling connected with it. It represents whatever importance or significance those qualities may have; but the qualities themselves it does not represent.

Before any conclusion shall be made to rest upon this almost self-evident proposition, a way of setting it quite beyond doubt shall be explained. As at present enunciated, it is merely put forward as a private opinion of the writer's which will serve to explain the great interest he attaches to emphatic dualism of the three normative sciences, which may be regarded as being the sciences of the conditions of truth and falsity, of wise and foolish conduct, of attractive and repulsive ideas. Should the reader become convinced that the importance of everything resides entirely in its mathematical form, he, too, will come to regard this dualism as worthy of close attention. Meantime, that it exists, and is more marked in these sciences than in any others, is an indisputable fact. To what is this circumstance to be attributed? Skipping the easy reasoning by which it can be shown that this dualism cannot be due to any peculiar quality of feeling that may be connected with these sciences, nor to any intellectual peculiarity of them, which negative propositions will become obtrusively plain at a later stage of our reasoning, we may turn at once to the affirmative reason for attributing the dualism to the reference of the normative sciences to action. It is curious how this reason seems to seek to escape detection, by putting forward an apparent indication that it is not there. For it is evident that it is in esthetics that we ought to seek for the deepest characteristics of normative science, since esthetics, in dealing with the very ideal itself, whose mere materialization engrosses the attention of practics and of logic, must contain the heart, soul, and spirit of normative science. But that dualism which is so much marked in the True and False, logic's object of study, and in the Useful and Pernicious of the confessional of practics, is softened almost to obliteration in esthetics. Nevertheless, it would be the height of stupidity to say that esthetics knows no good and bad. It must never be forgotten that evil of any kind is none the less bad though *the occurrence of it* be a good. Because in every case the ultimate in some measure abrogates, and ought to abrogate, the penultimate, it does not follow that the penultimate ought not to have abrogated the antepenultimate in due measure. On the contrary, just the opposite follows.

Esthetic good and evil are closely akin to pleasure and pain. They are what would be pleasure or pain to the fully developed superman. What, then, are pleasure and pain? The question has been sufficiently discussed, and the answer ought by this time to be ready. They are secondary feelings or generalizations of such feelings; that is, of feelings attaching themselves to, and excited by, other feelings. A toothache is painful. It *is not* pain, but pain *accompanies* it; and if you choose to say that pain is an ingredient of it, that is not far wrong. However, the quality of the feeling of toothache is a simple, positive feeling distinct from pain; though pain accompanies it. To use the old consecrated terms, pleasure is the feeling that a feeling is "sympathetical," pain that it is "antipathetical." The feeling of pain is a symptom of a feeling which repels us; the feeling of pleasure is the symptom of an attractive feeling. Attraction and repulsion are kinds of action. Feelings are pleasurable or painful according to the kind of action which they stimulate. In general, the good is the attractive,— not to everybody, but to the sufficiently matured agent; and the evil is the repulsive to the same. Mr. Ferdinand C. S. Schiller informs us that he and James have made up their minds that the true is simply the satisfactory.[14] No doubt; but to say "satisfactory" is not to complete any predicate whatever. Satisfactory to what end?

That truth is the correspondence of a representation with its object is, as Kant says, merely the nominal definition of it.[15] Truth belongs exclusively to propositions. A proposition has a subject (or set of subjects) and a predicate. The subject is a sign; the predicate is a sign; and the proposition is a sign that the predicate is a sign of that of which the subject is a sign. If it be so, it is true.

But what does this correspondence, or reference of the sign to its object, consist in? The pragmaticist answers this question as follows. Suppose, he says, that the angel Gabriel were to descend and communicate to me the answer to this riddle from the breast of omniscience. Is this supposable; or does it involve an essential absurdity to suppose the answer to be brought to human intelligence? In the latter case, "truth," in this sense, is a useless word, which never can express a human thought. It is real, if you will; it belongs to that universe entirely disconnected from human intelligence which we know as the world of utter nonsense. Having no use for this meaning of the word "truth," we had better use the word in another sense presently to be described. But if, on the other hand, it be conceivable that the secret should be disclosed to human intelligence, it will be something that thought can compass. Now thought is of the nature of a sign. In that case, then, if we can find out the right method of thinking and can follow it out,—the right method of transforming signs,—then truth can be nothing more nor less than the last result to which the following out of this method would ultimately carry us. In that case, that to which the representation should conform is itself something in the nature of a representation, or sign,—something noumenal, intelligible, conceivable, and utterly unlike a thing-in-itself.

Truth is the conformity of a representamen to its object,—*its* object, ITS object, mind you. The *International Dictionary* at the writer's elbow, the *Century Dictionary* which he daily studies, the *Standard* which he would be glad sometimes to consult, all contain the word "yes"; but that word is not true simply because he is going to ask on this 8th of January, 1906, in Pike County, Pennsylvania, whether it is snowing. There must be an action of the object upon the sign to render the latter true. Without that, the object is not the representamen's object. If a colonel hands a paper to an orderly and says, "You will go immediately and deliver this to Captain Hanno," and if the orderly does so, we do not say the colonel told the truth; we say the orderly was obedient, since it was not the orderly's conduct which determined the colonel to say what he did, but the colonel's speech which determined the orderly's action. Here is a view of the writer's house; what makes that house to be the object of the view? Surely not the similarity of appearance. There are ten thousand others in the country just like it. No, but the photographer set up the film in such a way that according to the laws of optics, the film was forced to receive an image of this house. What the sign virtually has to do in order to indicate its object,—and make it its,—all it has to do is just to seize its interpreter's eyes and forcibly turn them upon the object meant; it is what a knock at the door does, or an alarum or other bell, a whistle, a cannon-shot, etc. It is pure physiological compulsion; nothing else.

So, then, a sign, in order to fulfill its office, to actualize its potency, must be compelled by its object. This is evidently the reason of the dichotomy of the true and the false. For it takes two to make a quarrel, and a compulsion involves as large a dose of quarrel as is requisite to make it quite impossible that there should be compulsion without resistance. So there are two parties, the compeller and the resister.

Thus, this subsection B seems pretty nearly to have accomplished its purpose, which was to outline a way of showing that it is the dualism of the normative sciences wherein is their quintessence. But no, the objector will say, you have perhaps shown that their dualism is an inevitable consequence of their normative character; but to show by any such argument that their normative character is involved in their dualism you would have to maintain that the number two always and everywhere means action and reaction, which, as a man supposed not yet to be clean daft, is a position you probably will not take. Nor would the objector be at one moment's loss if he were asked to say explicitly just wherein the untenability of that proposition would consist. One would be a victim of something much like a hallucination if one fancied that [that] mere skeleton of a conception, the number two, were clothed with all the warm flesh of perhaps the most living of all philosophical ideas, the idea of right and wrong. It would be to look at two dots on a sheet of paper, and instead of seeing two little dots, to dream that the eternal battle of life was there prepared, if not actually going on. Well, the writer must evidently abandon his contention if it involves the claim that two dots on a sheet of paper is a rich picture. At the same time, it will be interesting to inquire how the conception of *two* dots is composed. For the unity of apperception requires that that which we conceive should be conceived as one. These dots are to be exactly alike; for we should evidently be adding something to the concept of duality, if we were to conceive them as distinguished, as having severally in themselves different qualities each regardless of the other. But since it is thus manifest that duality consists in no quality of both or of either of the members of the pair concerned, it can only consist in a relation between them. To carry the discussion further, and to make out precisely in what that relation consists, requires a pretty thorough acquaintance with logic, since we are not only concerned with the logic of relations, which many of the ordinary treatises hardly touch, but also with the subtle doctrine of the indefinite, and at the same time with collective as opposed to distributive universality. For the relation between two individuals which *duality* implies,—the duality applying to the pair collectively,—is a relation between a single pair of individual objects. Only, this pair is *indefinite*. It is *some* pair. If A and B be taken to designate the two individuals, the relative term embodying the relation, when expressed in the writer's algebra of 1870 (substantially adopted by Schroeder)[16] is

$$A{:}B \;\dotplus\; B{:}A$$

This is, of course, an *equiparance;* that is, the relation of B to A is essentially the same as that of A to B, so far as the duality of the pair is concerned. But no equiparance whatever, with the exception of the very few that are necessary, such as *identity, coexistence,* etc., is a *logically simple relation.* In the case of those equiparances that are *opponencies*, or *juxtambilations*,[17] that is, relations in which something can stand to something else, this is easily shown. Yet even this comparatively facile analysis requires an intellect not without an edge. For considering a non-necessary equiparance in which one individual, *A*, stands to another, *B*, this supposes a contingent determination of *A* by virtue of which it is in some simple relation to *B*. But different individual objects being independent, this may be without *B* having a similar determination putting it into every possible such relation to *A*. Thus, there must be a possible such determination which does not necessarily imply the equiparance. Now to say that one term, say *u*, is *logically simpler* than another, say *w*, means precisely that the affirmation of *w* concerning any subject implies the affirmative truth of *u* concerning the same subject, while the affirmation of *u* does not reciprocally imply the affirmative truth of *w*; and it may be remarked, by the way, that *disquiparance* is thus necessarily involved in logical simplicity: but we need not argue from that principle. For the above considerations suffice to show that than any contingent equiparant opponency some other relation is logically simpler, and consequently no contingent equiparant opponency is perfectly simple logically; and perfectly simple is what simple means.

Duality is not simple because it involves a contingent equiparant opponency. The constituent elements of that relation will be elements of duality. The relation implied in duality is essentially and purely a dyadic relation. This proposition certainly ought not to pass unchallenged, although examination will sustain it. Are not two lines of this article truly *two*, although there is many another that there is as much reason [to consider]? Precisely that is the pertinent question; and little reflection is required to show that if anybody considers any two lines by themselves, although he may try to select them arbitrarily, there must not only be a reason, but an unmistaken reason why just those and no others are taken. It need not be recognized as such; and if the two lines are only vaguely individualized,—as *some* two,—the reason will be equally vague without thereby ceasing to exist. Nor does this proposition involve any matter of fact: it is a mere formula, that must hold in any universe. Let this proposition,—or rather, this formula, for it carries no positive truths,—be sufficiently considered, and then receive the reader's deliberate and formal assent. That given, he sees that the units of every two are the members of a set, like man and wife, teacher and pupil, the legs of a pair of dividers or of trousers, or the spring lamb and mint sauce, whose com-estion and con-coction were decreed before the Fiat Lux.

Relations are truly, though not very lucidly, said to be either relations of reason or relations *in re*. The latter expression the more obtrusively fails to hit its nail squarely on the head. It would be better to say that relations are either dicible or surd. For the only kind of relation which could be veritably described to a person who had no experience of it is a relation of reason. A relation of reason is not purely dyadic: it is a relation through a sign: that is why it is dicible. Consequently the relation involved in duality is not dicible, but surd; and duality must contain as an ingredient of it a surd disquiparance.

This sort of ratiocination by which we determine little by little the characters of the relation sought might be continued almost indefinitely; but after a time, the mind can no longer restrain itself from leaping to a conclusion. It becomes too clear that the real or conceived duality of anything, say of A and B, consists in the double fact that, really in case the duality is real, conceptually in case the duality is conceptual, the one, A, completes the other, B, and reciprocally the latter, B, completes the former, A. However, a very important modification of this statement must be made, since a conceptual duality is no true duality, inasmuch as it involves a reference to a third correlate, namely, to the conception. Therefore, in the analysis just given, all reference to conceptual relations must be struck out. True duality is a real or surd relation.

One of the most useful and at the same time one of the most arduous of the labors of cenoscopy consists in starting with a familiar but vague concept and searching out and defining the nearest definite concept of sufficient breadth for the purposes of metaphysics. Treating in this way the concept of *action*, and at the same time generalizing it so as not to confine it to temporal conditions, we get a concept which may very well be named *action* in the philosophical sense. It will be defined as a surd dyadic relation by which one correlate, the *patient*, receives a special determination, while the other correlate, the *agent*, receives *thereby*, or perhaps we should say *therein*, no special determination. The determination is *special* in the sense that in default of the relation the patient would not have been so determined. Thus, the completing of B by A is an action in the philosophical sense, in which A [is] the agent and B the patient. Duality consists in such action of A upon B together with a reciprocal action of the same completing nature of B upon A.

The double relation of equiparance which constitutes duality is surd. It may be described in words, but those words can only be understood by means of reference to certain experiences; just as a person may be told that a piece of textile fabric is a yard wide, yet can never know what is meant except through an experience immediate or mediate of a certain bar laid up in the Westminster palace. The experiences [that] acquaint us with action are of two varieties, experiences of active effort and experiences of passive surprise. By an experience of active effort is meant what is in the mind (and a less determinate phrase would be used if any were forthcoming) upon the contraction of a voluntary muscle, *minus* all idea of ulterior purpose, all sensations referred to the muscle that is contracted or to other parts of the body, and all that is otherwise plainly no part of the consciousness of effort. A person may opine that after those subtractions nothing will remain in consciousness; nor will he thereby by any means convict himself of being a bad observer. Nevertheless, such an opinion is erroneous. The sense of effort is the sense of an opposing resistance then and there present. It is entirely different from purpose, which is the idea of a possible general regarded as desirable together with a sense of being determined in one's habitual nature (in one's soul, if you like the expression; it is that part of our nature which takes general determinations of conduct) to actualize it. But the sense of effort is not an idea of anything general or of anything as possible, but of that which actually is; and it never again can be: it is the present. It is not a sensation of any kind; for that is a mere quality of feeling mixed with the sense of a present resistant, and is passive, not active. The sense of effort is a sense that the source of activity is within one's power. The sensation from the muscle is a sense that the source of a second concomitant activity is beyond one's control. Thus, the sense of active exertion is distinguished from both the concomitants with which even an excellent observer may confound it. The question is difficult, and agreement concerning it must await mature consideration. But the writer has been convinced by various experiments that the distinct character of the sense of active exertion must eventually be acknowledged on all hands. There are certain discriminations which all men make without paying any attention to them, and which perhaps are of no peculiar type, but [for] which the writer, at least, would be quite at a loss to suggest any probable explanation. One of these, for example, is the discrimination between an excitation of one nerve-terminal and a similar excitation of another terminal. Another is the discrimination between pairs of facts which may possibly be connected and pairs of facts which cannot be connected; although history shows that this power of discrimination is in part a very recent acquisition of civilized man. A third unexplained power is that of discriminating between fact and fancy, between the external and the internal worlds, that which we can, and that which we cannot, control *per nutum*. Possibly this power may be due to every external experience involving more or less genuine surprise. A dream cannot *really* surprise the dreamer: he may (contrary to common belief) *dream that* he is surprised; but the surprise in this case is a dream-illusion.

There are two kinds of surprise: the less passive and the more passive. The former takes place when a person has made an effort in anticipation of experiencing a definite result, and this result does not occur. Although what does occur may be more agreeable than what he had anticipated, still he has a sense of being overcome, since his effort had been made with a view of producing that effect. The more passive surprise is when a sensation of tremendous, or at least of decidedly great, intensity is forced upon his consciousness, overcoming his negative inertia, when he had made no effort to produce such an effect. The two kinds of surprise are often united, a person not only not producing the effect he had anticipated, but being met by a phenomenon which he had not contemplated at all. Thus, a person may wake up in the morning and go to look out of the window, expecting that this action will bring the sight of green fields; but he not only does not see what he did expect but sees what he had never thought of, a covering of snow over everything. The peculiar element in both kinds of surprise is a sense of being the object of a compelling force. "*Je suis saisi*," says the hellenoidal Frenchman. The English-speaker, with his reluctance to confess weakness, only admits, "I am amazed," or "I am flabbergasted" in extraordinary circumstances. His lighter ancestor was more ready to admit himself "astonied." These expressions bespeak one's sense of being in the hands of a power against which it would be hopeless to struggle.

Both active endeavor and passive surprise involve a sense of opposition to an external force. To describe what one is thus aware of is impossible. It is not a thing to be understood. For that which is intelligible is learned gradually in successive lessons, while this is given all at once, and once for all; nor is it any quality of feeling, although there is a feeling involved in surprise, and a feeling involved in the achievement of a difficulty. For a quality of feeling has no identity but resemblance, while this is an event that happens once, and once only. Effort and surprise are the only experiences from which we can derive the concept of action. This concept does not involve duality because *agent* and *patient* are not necessarily objects of the same universe. One may be a form, the other matter. But reciprocal action,—action and reaction,—give duality, however slight the energy of the action may be. For here are two objects which belong together in the sense of being such as they are only as acting upon, and being acted upon by, each other. All inhibition of action, or action upon action, involves reaction and duality. All self-control involves, and chiefly consists in, inhibition. All direction toward an end or good supposes self-control; and thus the normative sciences are thoroughly infused with duality.

C. Philosophers have always been very loose and inaccurate thinkers; and since Fechner's immortal publication of 1860[18] their minds have been so turned in the direction of psychology that when they have once found how any given element of thought affects the human consciousness, they feel as if they had touched bedrock and had got to the bottom of that element. But psychology is as special a science as physics is. It is the glory of the post-Fechnerian psychologists that they have made it so. Now to found the science of the general upon the science of the special is absurd.

Logic is no doubt a science of "thought"; but "thought," in that sense, is no more internal than it is external. Logic is the science of truth and falsity. But truth and falsity belong as much to propositions printed in books as to propositions in the human consciousness. The fact that a proposition is conscious or unconscious does not affect its truth or falsity.

But it may be said that logic is the theory of reasoning, and that reasoning can only be performed by a mind. That is certainly true, and must be true; for if anything could independently reason, it would be what we understand by a mind. But it does not follow that the phenomena that psychologists discover have any bearing upon the theory of reasoning. Compare logic with the theory of the behavior of a sailing vessel. A vessel can only sail upon a body of water, and no other liquid, and its sails must be exposed to currents of air, and no other gas. But it does not follow that the theory of sailing depends upon the chemistry of water and of air. But this comparison does not fully expose the impropriety of basing logic upon psychology, because the introduction of the study of the chemistry of air and water would have no worse effect than that of encumbering the science with irrelevant matter. The attempt to erect a theory of logic upon the work of the psychological laboratory does far worse, since it is extremely dangerous to reason at all about psychology without constant appeals to the science of logic. For example, Christoph Sigwart and others maintain that logical truth consists, in the last analysis, in a certain *feeling*,—he emphasizes its being a quality of feeling,—of logical gratification.[19] And to prove this he appeals to this conclusion of psychology, that in deciding whether a given consequence be logical or not we must always *trust* to that feeling. But if Sigwart and the others had made a sufficient study of exact logic, they would have seen that that principle cannot be a sound inference from observations made in their psychological laboratories. For we cannot trust a feeling as such, since a feeling as such neither is nor utters any proposition to be a subject of trust or distrust. We can only trust a feeling in so far as it is a sign of something else, namely, of a proposition. So, then, Sigwart's argument is that logical truth must consist in a feeling, because that feeling is a sign of something different from itself, namely, that truth.

But suppose he were to shift his ground and say that since this feeling always accompanies logical truth, we might as well identify it with logical truth. Then he may indeed boast that his psychological method has furnished him with an exceedingly simple theory of logic. It makes logic a pure question of feeling, of intellectual taste. *De gustibus non est disputandum.* A feeling is positively such as it is, regardless of aught else. It refers to nothing but itself. That which consists in feeling does not involve any comparison of feelings, or any synthesis of feelings. Properly speaking, because a feeling knows nothing but itself, no feeling can have, or even claim, any authority. It is true that to feeling is often joined passion, which claims autocracy over the whole world; but it is reason, thought, which alone can be the rightful head of government. The man who kindles a heap of shavings on his floor, and *feeling* that it is all right, locks his door and betakes himself to the theatre for the evening, may feel quite differently on his return. But one feeling is entitled to as much weight as another. The only system of logic which can in fact result from the principle that logical truth might as well be regarded as a quality of feeling, is, for the reasons just given, one which allows nothing but feeling to meddle at all with the decision as to what is materially true and what not; and on that principle it can only be said that the man's feeling before the theatre was logically sound for itself, and his contrary feeling on seeing the result of his conduct was equally sound logic for itself.

Logic includes a study of reasoning, it is true, and reasoning may be regarded,—not quite correctly, but we may waive that point,—as a psychical process. If we are to admit that, however, we must say that logic is not an all-round study of reasoning, but only of the conditions of reasoning being bad or good, and if good to what degree, and in what application. Now good reasoning is reasoning which attains its purpose. Its purpose is to supply a guide for conduct,—and thinking, being an active operation, is a species of conduct,—in case no percept from which a judgment could have been directly formed, is at hand. Its object is to say what the reasoner either *will* think when that percept occurs, or what he *would* think if it did occur. The psychological process of reasoning is wholly aside from the purpose of logic.

Logic, says Herbart, psychologist though he was, is a science of *concepts;* but a concept is that which is *conceived;* so that logic is a science of the result of conceiving and has nothing to do with the means whereby the conceiving is performed.[20] In these remarks of Herbart's, *thought* and *thinking* might be substituted for *concept* and *conceiving.* A concept is a symbol present to the imagination,—that is, more correctly speaking, of which a particular instance might be present to the imagination. But the imaginary character of the instance of the symbol has no importance for logic. Its rules hold equally for [the] symbol embodied in real existents. For it is with the symbol in its general mode of being and not with the individual embodiment of it with which logic has to do. The writer, in 1867, defined logic as the science of the formal laws of the relation of symbols to their objects.[21] But a more mature consideration of the nature of the limits between the different branches of science has convinced him that it is better to regard logic as the entire cenoscopic study of symbols, and not only of symbols but of all kinds of signs. It will be felt as a great objection to this view that a sign is not such unless it be interpreted and that it can only be interpreted by the human mind. The reply is that just as physiology explains all the operations of the animal organism purely and exclusively by the principles of general physics, as developed by experiment upon inorganic materials, although these operations cannot be performed without an organism, and an organism is something which cannot be put together by means of laboratory appliances, because it has a power of growth which cannot be conferred upon inorganic materials, and this circumstance does not invalidate the physiological explanation; so all the operations of reason can receive perfect logical explanation by principles which apply as much to real signs as to the imaginary signs called concepts, although it is quite true that we cannot make a machine that will reason as the human mind reasons until we can make a logical machine (logical machines, of course, exist) which shall not only be automatic, which is a comparatively small matter, but which shall be endowed with a genuine power of self-control; and we have as little hopes of doing that as we have of endowing a machine made of inorganic materials with life. Indeed, it shall be shown in a future article that these two attributes, *growth* and *self-control,* are confronted with closely analogous difficulties, and further that if we could endow a system of signs with self-control, there is very strong reason to believe that we should thereby have conferred upon it a *consciousness,* even more nearly like that of a man than is, for example, the consciousness of a fish. But although the proof, or quasi-proof, of that is certainly important, its importance is so far inferior to the matters that this series of papers is designed to discuss that it must wait for its turn to be taken up; and these papers have to be written in the spare time of a hard-driven worker.

What does it mean to speak of the "interpretation" of a sign? Interpretation is merely another word for translation; and if we had the necessary machinery to do it, which we perhaps never shall have, but which is quite conceivable, an English book might be translated into French or German without the interposition of a translation into the imaginary signs of human thought. Still, supposing there were a machine or even a growing tree which, without the interpolation of any imagination were to go on translating and translating from one possible language to a new one, will it be said that the function of signs would therein be fulfilled?

What are signs for, anyhow? They are to communicate ideas, are they not? Even the imaginary signs called thoughts convey ideas from the mind of yesterday to the mind of tomorrow into which yesterday's has grown. Of course, then, these "ideas" are not themselves "thoughts," or imaginary signs. They are some potentiality, some form, which may be embodied in external or in internal signs. But why should this idea-potentiality be so poured from one vessel into another unceasingly? Is it a mere exercise of the World-spirit's *Spiel-trieb,*—mere amusement? Ideas do, no doubt, grow in this process. It is a part, perhaps we may say the chief part, of the process of the Creation of the World. If it has no ulterior aim at all, it may be likened to the performance of a symphony. The pragmaticist insists that this is not all, and offers to back his assertion by proof. He grants that the continual increase of the embodiment of the idea-potentiality is the *summum bonum.* But he undertakes to prove by the minute examination of logic that signs which should be merely parts of an endless viaduct for the transmission of idea-potentiality, without any conveyance of it into anything but symbols, namely, into action or habit of action, would not be signs at all, since they would not, little or much, fulfill the function of signs; and further, that without embodiment in something else than symbols, the principles of logic show there never could be the least growth in idea-potentiality. These two propositions remain to be proved, although a mind of vigorous and healthy intellectual impulses may have to put on the brakes to restrain himself from rushing into the embrace of the former in advance of demonstration's sanction.

§9. *What is a sign?* This is a question of no ordinary difficulty, to which the answer must be sought by a well-considered method. To begin with, let us consider what the question means; and first, What is its general nature? We are not studying lexicography. It is the same sort of question as two which have already been considered, the questions, What is *two?* and, What is *action?* We all have a ragged-outlined notion of what we call a sign. We wish to replace that by a well-defined concept, which may exclude some things ordinarily called signs, and will almost certainly include some things not ordinarily so called. So that our new concept may have the highest utility for the science of logic, which is the purpose of the investigation, the terms of the definition must be strictly relevant to logic. As far as this condition will allow, it is to express that which is most essential in the vulgar notion of a sign or representamen. Now a sign as ordinarily understood is an implement of intercommunication; and the essence of an implement lies in its function, that is, in its purpose together with the general idea,—not, however, the plan,—of the means of attaining that purpose. The reader will perhaps have noted that the phrase "medium of communication"[22] is broader than the noun "sign," embracing for example a sentence in the imperative mood, which would be characterized as a "signal" rather than as a "sign." Whether or no such a thing as melody, regarded, not as a *symptom* of an emotion or other feeling, but as an *excitant* of the same, would be called a "medium of communication," it certainly would lie without the *Umfang*[23] of "sign." Now it is rather desirable that our sought concept should have a somewhat greater breadth than is strictly necessary for our purpose, on the principle that the surroundings of anything whatever aid to a comprehension of the surrounded object, and certainly in case of doubt we should prefer to include what may be needless rather than exclude anything needed. A too wide concept can do no harm whatever, provided that a careful division of it be made.

Let it be repeated that all the terms of the division must be strictly relevant to logic, and that consequently all accidents of experience, however universal, must be excluded. The result of this rule will necessarily be that the new concept of a "sign" will be defined exclusively by the forms of its logical relationships; and the utmost pains must be taken to understand those relations in a purely formal, or, as we may say, in a purely mathematical way.

At this point, some such question as the following may suggest itself: Is this new scientific concept of a Sign not to recognize the connection of every sign with two minds? The proper reply would first point out that two separate minds are not requisite for the operation of a sign. Thus the premises of an argument are a sign of the truth of the conclusion; yet it is essential to argument that the same mind that thinks the conclusion *as such* should also think the premises. Indeed, two minds in communication are, in so far, "at one," that is, are properly one mind in that part of them. That being understood, the answer to the question will go on to recognize that every sign,—or, at any rate, nearly every one,—is a determination of something of the general nature of a mind, which we may call the "quasi-mind." But the further consideration of the nature of this must be put off to the next section.

The writer knows no more handy phrase to describe the kind of analysis we are attempting than "logical analysis." It is a designation just tolerably apt. It is not accurate. For in this work we should wind ourselves up in apparent antinomies if we allowed dual distinctions to be as absolute as they are in the normative sciences. We are now in the realm of phaneroscopy, the first of the three main divisions of cenoscopy. It is not yet time to define it; but it approaches somewhat to the nature of mathematics. In mathematics, the negative of quantity is *zero;* but instead of being set over against quantity as its eternal foe, it is regarded as merely the limit of quantity, and in a sense as itself a special grade of quantity. This is no violation of the principle of contradiction: it is merely regarding the negative from another point of view. There are some languages in which two negatives make an affirmative. Those are the logical languages. The people who speak them ought, for consistency, to be hard, moral natures. In other languages, probably the majority, a double negative remains a negative, just as $0 \times 0 = 0$, none of none is none. These are quantitative languages. We should expect the people who speak them to be more humane and more highly philosophical. The fact is mentioned here merely to show that the quantitative view of negation, though it is not the view of the hard moralist, nor of the hard logician, does not really involve any bad reasoning. Did it ever occur to the gentle reader that in ordinary algebra we seldom write that one quantity is *unequal* to another: we simply write what else it equals? The general phenomenon throughout mathematics is that almost every strongly marked concept has border concepts which lose the strong characteristics but are included in a broader concept. Thus a conic curve, considered as a curve of the second order, includes as a case of it two intersecting rays, with which a hyperbola may indefinitely approach coincidence, and this figure again includes, and may indefinitely approximate to, one double ray with a nodal point upon it.[24] But a conic can equally well be conceived as a curve of the second class, and as such, it will not include the two intersecting rays, but will include a pair of points with the ray joining them, considered as a double tangent; and the tangents of a very narrow ellipse or hyperbola will indefinitely approach that as their envelope; and this figure again will indefinitely approach a double point with a ray through it; so that one line with one point upon it can be conceived either as a curve of the second order or as a curve of the second class. These colorless borders (if the expression be allowed) of highly colored concepts are, in mathematics, well called "degenerate forms." Not /that/ the two rays in a plane present any particular degeneracy; but when the pair is offered as a case of a conic, it is manifest that all the beautiful relations that characterize genuine conics have, in this form, quite petered out. The same phenomenon presents itself in the realm of phaneroscopy to such an extent that the only successful way of analyzing any of the concepts which belong peculiarly to this realm is not to begin by considering that concept in all its breadth, but rather to confine oneself, at first, to its highly characterized form, and when that has been thoroughly comprehended, to inquire by what modifications the bordering forms attach themselves to it. But this rule must not be understood as conflicting with the plan of examining the highest and most general concepts first. However, until special instances are before us, abstract descriptions can hardly be understood.

A sign is plainly a species of medium of communication, and medium of communication is a species of medium, and a medium is a species of third. A genuine third is something which differs from a first in one respect and from a second in another respect. If this other respect is a contrary respect, the third is a medium. Hence in Latin, where "medium" is a vernacular word, the distinction between it and "tertium" is slight. Thus the *principium exclusi medii* is indifferently, though more correctly, called *principium exclusi tertii*.

A triadic relation is most appropriately expressed in a proposition whose subject Nominative denotes the most active correlate, which we may call *N*, which acts upon a more or less similar correlate, *A*, denoted by the direct object or Accusative of the sentence, and at the same time upon something, *D*, of a different kind, denoted by the indirect object, which will be most appropriately put in the Dative. There will of course be three dyadic relations, between *N* and *A*, *N* and *D*, and *A* and *D*; but a genuine triadic relation does not consist in any or all of these. It may here be remarked that Combination is a triadic relation between the two elements (for every Combination results from successive couplings) and the result, and is in so far genuine that it cannot be analyzed into any Combination of dyadic relations. But Combination is not a thoroughly genuine triadic relation, since the different elements, the Combinants, are (as far as the mere relation of combination goes) in precisely the same relation to the result, the Combinate.

A medium of communication is something, *A*, which being acted upon by something else, *N*, in its turn acts upon something, *I*, in a manner involving its determination by *N*, so that *I* shall thereby, through *A* and only through *A*, be acted upon by *N*. We may purposely select a somewhat imperfect example. Namely, one animal, say a mosquito, is acted upon by the entity of a zymotic disease, and in its turn acts upon another animal, to which it communicates the fever. The reason that this example is not perfect is that the active medium is in some measure of the nature of a *vehicle*, which differs from a medium of communication in acting upon the transported object and determining it to a changed location, where, without further interposition of the vehicle, it acts upon, or is acted upon by, the object to which it is conveyed. A sign, on the other hand, just in so far as it fulfills the function of a sign, and none other, perfectly conforms to the definition of a medium of communication. It is determined by the object, but in no other respect than goes to enable it to act upon the interpreting quasi-mind; and the more perfectly it fulfills its function as a sign, the less effect it has upon that quasi-mind other than that of determining it as if the object itself had acted upon it. Thus, after an ordinary conversation, a wonderfully perfect kind of sign-functioning,[25] one knows what information or suggestion has been conveyed, but will be utterly unable to say in what words it was conveyed, and often will think it was conveyed in words, when in fact it was only conveyed in tones or in facial expressions.

It seems best to regard a sign as a determination of a quasi-mind; for if we regard it as an outward object, and as addressing itself to a human mind, that mind must first apprehend it as an object in itself, and only after that consider it in its significance; and the like must happen if the sign addresses itself to any quasi-mind. It must begin by forming a determination of that quasi-mind, and nothing will be lost by regarding that determination as the sign. So, then, it is a determination that really acts upon that of which it is a determination, although *genuine* action is of one thing on another. This perplexes us, and an example of an analogous phenomenon will do good service here. Metaphysics has been said contemptuously to be a fabric of metaphors. But not only metaphysics, but logical and phaneroscopical concepts need to be clothed in such garments. For a pure idea without metaphor or other significant clothing is an onion without a peel.

Let a community of quasi-minds consist of the liquid in a number of bottles which are in intricate connexion by tubes filled with the liquid. This liquid is of complex and somewhat unstable mixed chemical composition. It also has so strong a cohesion and consequent surface-tension that the contents of each bottle take on a self-determined form. Accident may cause one or another kind of decomposition to start at a point of one bottle producing a molecule of peculiar form, and this action may spread through a tube to another bottle. This new molecule will be a determination of the contents of the first bottle's contents which will thus act upon the contents of the second bottle by continuity. The new molecule produced by decomposition may then act chemically upon the original contents or upon some molecule produced by some other kind of decomposition, and thus we shall have a determination of the contents that actively operates upon that of which it is a determination, including another determination of the same subject.

But it is high time we insured ourselves against snares by determining the precise sense which we are to attach to the term *determination*, and to set in order the terminology of its mental vicinity. A few pages were given to this work in last October's *Monist*;[26] but those remarks require supplementation. Determination, in general, was not defined at all; and the attempt at defining the determination of a subject with respect to a character only covered (or seemed only to cover) explicit propositional determination. An incidental remark to the effect that words whose meaning should be determinate would leave "no latitude of interpretation" was more satisfactory,[27] since the context made it plain that there must be no such latitude either for the interpreter or for the utterer. The explicitness of the words would leave the utterer no room for explanations of his meaning. This definition has the advantage of being applicable to a command, to a purpose, to a medieval substantial form; in short to anything capable of indeterminacy.* Even a future event can only be determinate in so far as it is a consequent. Now the concept of a consequent is a logical concept. It is derived from the concept of the conclusion of an argument.

---

*That everything indeterminate is of the nature of a sign can be proved inductively by imagining and analyzing instances of the surdest description. Thus, the indetermination of an event which should happen by pure chance without cause, *sua sponte*, as the Romans mythologically said, *spontanément* in French (as if what was done of one's own motion were sure to be irrational), does not belong to the event,—say, an explosion,—*per se*, or as explosion. Neither is [it] by virtue of any real relation: it is by virtue of a relation of reason. Now what is true by virtue of a relation of reason is representative, that is, is of the nature of a sign. A similar consideration applies to the indiscriminate shots and blows of a Kentucky free fight.

But an argument is a sign of the truth of its conclusion; its conclusion is the rational *interpretation* of the sign. This is in the spirit of the Kantian doctrine that metaphysical concepts are logical concepts applied somewhat differently from their logical application. The difference, however, is not really as great as Kant represents it to be, and as he was obliged to represent it to be, owing to his mistaking the logical and metaphysical correspondents in almost every case.

Another advantage of this definition is that it saves us from the blunder of thinking that a sign is indeterminate simply because there is much to which it makes no reference; that, for example, to say, "C. S. Peirce wrote this article," is indeterminate because it does not say what the color of the ink used was, who made the ink, how old the father of the ink-maker /was/ when his son was born, nor what the aspect of the planets was when that father was born. By making the definition turn upon the interpretation, all that is cut off.

At the same time, it is tolerably evident that the definition, as it stands, is not sufficiently explicit, and further, that at the present stage of our inquiry /it/ cannot be made altogether satisfactory. For what is the interpretation alluded to? To answer that convincingly would be either to establish or to refute the doctrine of pragmaticism. Still some explanations may be made. Every sign has a single object, though this single object may be a single set or a single continuum of objects. No general description can identify an object. But the common sense of the interpreter of the sign will assure him that the object must be one of a limited collection of objects. Suppose, for example, two Englishmen to meet in a continental railway carriage. The total number of subjects of which there is any appreciable probability that one will speak to the other perhaps does not exceed a million; and each will have perhaps half that million not far below the surface of consciousness, so that each unit of it is ready to suggest itself. If one mentions Charles the Second, the other need not consider what possible Charles the Second is meant. It is no doubt the English Charles Second. Charles the Second of England was quite a different man on different days; and it might be said that without further specification the subject is not identified. But the two Englishmen have no purpose of splitting hairs in their talk; and the latitude of interpretation which constitutes the indeterminacy of a sign must be understood as a latitude which might affect the achievement of a purpose. For two signs whose meaning are for all possible purposes equivalent are absolutely equivalent. This, to be sure, is rank pragmaticism; for a purpose is an affection of action.

What has been said of subjects is as true of predicates. Suppose the chat of our pair of Englishmen had fallen upon the color of Charles II's hair. Now, that colors are seen quite differently by different retinas is known. That the chromatic sense is much more varied than it is positively known to be is quite likely. It is very unlikely that either of the travellers is trained to observe colors or is a master of their nomenclature. But if one says that Charles II had dark auburn hair, the other will understand him quite precisely enough for all their possible purposes; and it will be a determinate predication.

The October remarks made the proper distinction between the two kinds of indeterminacy, viz: indefiniteness and generality, of which the former consists in the sign's not sufficiently expressing itself to allow of an indubitable determinate interpretation, while the latter turns over to the interpreter the right to complete the determination as he pleases. It seems a strange thing, when one comes to ponder over it, that a sign should leave its interpreter to supply a part of its meaning; but the explanation of the phenomenon lies in the fact that the entire universe,—not merely the universe of existents, but all that wider universe, embracing the universe of existents as a part, the universe which we are all accustomed to refer to as "the truth,"—that all this universe is perfused with signs, if it is not composed exclusively of signs. Let us note this in passing as having a bearing upon the question of pragmaticism.

The October remarks,[28] with a view to brevity, omitted to mention that both indefiniteness and generality might primarily affect either the logical breadth or the logical depth of the sign to /which/ they belong. It now becomes pertinent to notice this. When we speak of the depth, or signification, of a sign, we are resorting to hypostatic abstraction, that process whereby we regard a thought as a thing, make an interpretant sign the object of a sign. It has been a butt of ridicule since Molière's dying week,[29] and the depth of a writer on philosophy can conveniently be sounded by his disposition to make fun of the basis of voluntary inhibition, which is the chief characteristic of mankind. For cautious thinkers will not be in haste to deride a kind of thinking that is evidently founded upon observation,—namely, upon observation of a sign. At any rate, whenever we speak of a predicate, we are representing a thought as a thing, as a *substantia*, since the concepts of *substance* and *subject* are one, its concomitants only being different in the two cases. It is needful to remark this in the present connection, because, were it not for hypostatic abstraction, there could be no generality of a predicate, since a sign which should make its interpreter its deputy to determine its signification at his pleasure would not signify anything, unless *nothing* be its significate. But hypostatic abstraction (the product of which may be termed a *hypostasis*) renders general classes of predicates possible, and classes of those classes, and so on, in a manner which the dull and lazy brood of modern logicians has failed to investigate sufficiently, not to say altogether. Oh, it maddens one to think how ignorant,—and in many respects, doubtless, far worse than ignorant,—their criminal neglect has left us. Only think what legions of good-for-nothing bummers have written logic books without bestirring themselves to repay their debt to the Greeks and to the medieval doctors by adding a single sentence of new truth to the science! It is not the fashion now even for our Platos to believe in a day of judgment; but remember, Reader, that if a logical talent has been given to you, you cannot maturely reflect upon your situation without coming to intend to deal with posterity as you would that your predecessors had dealt with you.*

*If the writer has fulfilled this duty, it has been no more an act of virtue than is the usual obedience to the common command in the 28th verse of Genesis.[30]

As an example, we may suppose that one of our two travellers informs the other that Charles II's hair was dark auburn. This would undoubtedly refer, not to the color, in the scientific sense, but to the color-*sensation*, and to this sensation as it becomes modified by unconscious quasi-judgments, that is, judgments unrecognized as modifying the immediate feeling; but it will be convenient to call this "color," as the Englishman himself, presuming him not to be a scientific man, would doubtless have done. The predicate "light auburn" would be sufficiently determinate. But had he said the hair was "colored," that would have been vague to the point of idiocy. Color has its hue, its chroma, or height of color, and its luminosity. A concept of color of any one hue, of any one chroma, or of any one luminosity is a concept of color somewhat indeterminate. As the predicate of a proposition concerning a colored object, it would be somewhat *vague;* in the predicate of an imperative sentence, as "paint this in a dark color," it would be *general,* since it leaves the interpreter free to give the other two coefficients of the color any determination that may suit him. As for hue, chroma, and luminosity, themselves, which we term *respects,* they are merely terms of second intention, somewhat like the biological words *variety, species, genus, family, order, class,* and *branch.* That is, any one of them describes the nature of the indeterminacy of a predicate. The biological words, in their only universally recognized significations, indicate the *relative quantity* of the indeterminacy of terms of first intention like pouter, dove, passerine, bird, vertebrate, etc., while the chromatic words express the *quality* of the indeterminacy of terms of first intention such as green, high color, tinted. Both series are of proper predicates of predicates. They agree also in that each has its tolerably close analogues through a wide range of predicates. A hierarchical series, more or less like the biological, is a necessary result of any eventful evolution of class-characters. Louis Agassiz argued with great force that the biological hierarchy expresses, or should express, the various stages of the execution of a purpose;[31] but whoever has read *The World and the Individual* will understand (despite the not unimportant logical slips of that work)[32] that purpose is the very fatherland of evolution. When, on the other hand, classification has a mathematical origin, as seems to be the case with that of the chemical elements, for example, cross-classifications are common, if not usual. Throughout a class of cases which could be logically defined, were there space for the discussion, but of which it will be sufficient to say that it embraces the qualities of each of our well-marked senses, there is a triad of respects analogous to luminosity, hue, and chroma. It will be remarked that in the *habitat* of a respect, or the general subject in which it is found, we have a logical concept of a different kind from any of those mentioned before.* We may formulate these chromatic respects by saying that the luminosity is the quantity, the more-or-less-ness,—meaning

---

*Only so much as seems pertinent to the business in hand is here given of a subject, one of a number equally extensive which have been worked out by the author; and the publication of his work, no matter what blunders he may have committed, must be of ultimate utility to human thought. But it will soon be too late to think of publication.

that whether the measurement be hyperbolic, parabolic, or elliptical is beside the meaning,—of the quality; that the hue is the *suchness* of the quality; and that the chroma is the *such-degree* of the quality. But these phrases are the merest ghosts, without explanation. In particular, the reader may well be at a loss to know what distinction can be made between quality and "suchness."

We are treading here the very littoral of our knowledge of logic. Every step has to be taken with caution for there are quicksands all about. Yet it is just the ground where many writers love to prance, overconfident and rash. If they did not speedily quit the subject, they would soon find how they had entrapped themselves, and would be drowned in the rising tide of the great ocean of doubt and ignorance. No satisfactory account has ever been given of the logical nature of a hypostasis. Take, as an example, a very precise abstract term; say, *hardness*. One may hesitate to say whether the single object denoted by this term, that is, the quality of hardness, is a capacity or a habit; the *possibility* that its subject should sustain the moderate pressure of a knife-edge drawn over it without being scratched, or the *impossibility* of its being scratched by the moderate pressure of the knife-edge. For having no experience of substances whose rasibility is as uncertain as the throw of a die, we can appeal to no instance to show whether we should call such an object hard or not. But one illuminating phenomenon we can note; namely, that *hard* is one of a whole category of predicates which appear to be invariably true under circumstances capable of being generally described, and are invariably false when that general condition is not fulfilled. The opinion that this phrase "appear to be" ought to read "are," and that it is not a category of predicates but all predicates whatever of which this holds good, is held by very many logicians, and especially by nominalists, who are, oddly enough, most unwarrantably addicted to universal assertions, for all their maintaining that universality is a mere figment or, at best, a mere subjective appearance.

Nobody, however, has ever found any law, reason, or rhyme according to which such and such points of the heavens are occupied with stars, or for any other fact of existence. Existence can be traced back to a metamorphosis, but the existence did not begin with the metamorphosis; and there is no single instance in which any law has ever been found to regulate with precision the when and where of existence. That the chemical elements of the atmosphere should have low atomic weights and that elements of high atomic weights should be rare in the earth's crust is roughly true, as a mere consequence of the association of specific weight with atomic weight; but to suppose that there is any exact law as to arrangements of existents is a well-recognized mark of a mind not sanely loyal to truth of fact. Men's minds are confused by a looseness of language and of thought which leads them to talk of the causes of single events. They ought to consider that it is not the single actuality, in its identity, which is the subject of a law, but an ingredient of it, an indeterminate predicate. Consequently, the question is, not whether each and every event is precisely caused, in one respect or another, but whether every predicate of that event is caused. For instance, a man bets upon the toss of a coin.

He wins his bet. Now the question is whether there was any circumstance about the toss of that coin which necessitated this character of it; namely, its accordance with his bet. There are those who believe that such predicates are precisely determinate; but rational proof fails them. The majority of men call such things uncaused; and this opinion is powerfully supported by the utter failure of every attempt to base predictions of such occurrences upon any specified law. The class of predicates is one of which every man on earth for several thousand years has had multiplied hourly experience; and since in no case has there been any promising appearance of approach to a law, we are more than justified in saying that precise dependence upon general conditions appears to be limited to a category of predicates, without undertaking to say what category that is.

28

Pragmatism

MS 318. [A highly complex and multi-layered manuscript, MS 318 contains five intermingled versions of an article initially conceived as a long "letter to the editor." The article was rejected by both the Nation *and the* Atlantic Monthly. *All versions share the same beginning—the "introduction" below, also found in CP 5.11–13 and 464–66. Other portions are published in CP 1.560–62 and 5.467–96. "Variant 1" below is the third version, composed in March–April 1907, and "Variant 2" the fifth, composed a few months later.] In this selection, Peirce comes closer than in any other to fully expressing his brand of pragmatism and to giving a clearly articulated proof. He begins by reaffirming that pragmatism (pragmaticism) is not a doctrine of metaphysics, nor an attempt to determine the truth of things, but is only a method of ascertaining the meanings of hard words and abstract concepts. By this time, Peirce has thoroughly integrated his pragmatism with his semiotics, and he bases his proof in his theory of signs (rather than in his theory of perception as he had for the 1903 proof in his Harvard Lectures). His semiotic proof begins with the premiss that every concept and every thought beyond immediate perception is a sign, and works its way to the proposition that a logical interpretant must be of the nature of a habit. "Consequently," Peirce concludes, "the most perfect account of a concept that words can convey will consist in a description of that habit which [it] is calculated to produce. But how else can a habit be described than by a description of the kind of action to which it gives rise." Since Peirce's conclusion amounts to a paraphrase of his definition of pragmatism, his proof is complete.*

[Introduction]

Mr. Editor:

The philosophical journals, the world over, are just now brimming over, as you know, with pragmatism and antipragmatism. The number of *Leonardo* that reaches me this morning has an admirable piece on the subject by a writer of genius and of literary skill, Giovanni Papini.[1] Yesterday brought news of discussions along the same line in New Zealand.[2] Often, however, one hears glib utterances that betray complete misunderstanding of this new ingredient of the thought of our time; so that I gladly accept your invitation to explain what pragmatism really is, how it came into being, and whither it is tending. Any philosophical doctrine that should be completely new could hardly fail to prove completely false; but the rivulets at the head of the river of pragmatism are easily traced back to almost any desired antiquity.

Socrates bathed in these waters. Aristotle rejoices when he can find them. They run, where least one would suspect them, beneath the dry rubbish-heaps of Spinoza. Those clean definitions that strew the pages of the *Essay concerning Humane Understanding*[3] (I refuse to reform the spelling) had been washed out in these same pure springs. It was this medium, and not tar-water, that gave health and strength to Berkeley's earlier works, his *Theory of Vision* and what remains of his *Principles*.[4] From it the general views of Kant derive such clearness as they have. Auguste Comte made still more,—much more,—use of this element; as much as he saw his way to using. Unfortunately, however, both he and Kant, in their rather opposite ways, were in the habit of mingling these sparkling waters with a certain mental sedative to which many men are addicted,—and the burly businessmen very likely to their benefit,—but which plays sad havoc with the philosophical constitution. I refer to the habit of cherishing contempt for the close study of logic.

So much for the past. The ancestry of pragmatism is respectable enough; but the more conscious adoption of it as *lanterna pedibus* in the discussion of dark questions, and the elaboration of it into a method in aid of philosophic inquiry came, in the first instance, from the humblest *souche* imaginable. It was in the earliest seventies that a knot of us young men[5] in Old Cambridge, calling ourselves, half-ironically, half-defiantly, "The Metaphysical Club,"—for agnosticism was then riding its high horse, and was frowning superbly upon all metaphysics,—used to meet, sometimes in my study, sometimes in that of William James. It may be that some of our old-time confederates would today not care to have such wild-oats-sowings made public, though there was nothing but boiled oats, milk, and sugar in the mess. Mr. Justice Holmes, however, will not, I believe, take it ill that we are proud to remember his membership; nor will Joseph Warner Esq. Nicholas St. John Green was one the most interested fellows, a skillful lawyer and a learned one, a disciple of Jeremy Bentham. His extraordinary power of disrobing warm and breathing truth of the draperies of long worn formulas was what attracted attention to him everywhere. In particular, he often urged the importance of applying Bain's definition of belief,[6] as "that upon which a man is prepared to act." From this definition, pragmatism is scarce more then a corollary; so that I am disposed to think of him as the grandfather of pragmatism. Chauncey Wright, something of a philosophical celebrity in those days, was never absent from our meetings. I was about to call him our corypheus; but he will better be described as our boxing-master whom we,—I, particularly,—used to face to be severely pummelled. He had abandoned a former attachment to Hamiltonianism to take up with the doctrines of Mill, to which, and to their cognate, agnosticism, he was trying to weld the really incongruous ideas of Darwin. John Fiske and, more rarely, Francis Ellingwood Abbot, were sometimes present, lending their countenances to the spirit of our endeavors, while holding aloof from any assent to their success. Wright, James, and I were men of science, rather scrutinizing the doctrines of the metaphysicians on their scientific side than regarding them as very momentous spiritually. The type of our thought was decidedly British. I, alone of our number, had come upon the threshing-floor of philosophy through the doorway of Kant, and even my ideas were acquiring the English accent.

Our metaphysical proceedings had all been in winged words (and swift ones, at that, for the most part) until at length, lest the club should be dissolved without leaving any material *souvenir* behind, I drew up a little paper expressing some of the opinions that I had been urging all along under the name of pragmatism.[7] This paper was received with such unlooked-for kindness, that I was encouraged, some half-dozen years later, on the invitation of the great publisher, Mr. W. H. Appleton, to insert it, somewhat expanded, in the *Popular Science Monthly* for November 1877 and January 1878, not with the warmest possible approval of the Spencerian editor, Dr. Edward Youmans. The same paper appeared the next year in a French redaction in the *Revue Philosophique*.[8] In those medieval times, I dared not in type use an English word to express an idea unrelated to its received meaning. The authority of Mr. Principal Campbell weighed too heavily upon my conscience.[9] I had not yet come to perceive, what is so plain today, that if philosophy is ever to stand in the ranks of the sciences, literary elegance must be sacrificed,—like the soldier's old brilliant uniforms,—to the stern requirements of efficiency, and the philosophist must be encouraged,—yea, and required,—to coin new terms to express such new scientific concepts as he may discover, just as his chemical and biological brethren are expected to do. Indeed, in those days, such brotherhood was scorned, alike on the one side and on the other;—a lamentable but not surprising state of scientific feeling. As late as 1893, when I might have procured the insertion of the word pragmatism in the *Century Dictionary*, it did not seem to me that its vogue was sufficient to warrant that step.

It is now high time to explain what pragmatism is. I must, however, preface the explanation by a statement of what it is not, since many writers, especially of the starry host of Kant's progeny, in spite of pragmatists' declarations, unanimous, reiterated, and most explicit, still remain unable to "catch on" to what we are driving at, and persist in twisting our purpose and purport all awry. I was long enough, myself, within the Kantian fold to comprehend their difficulty; but let it go. Suffice it to say once more that pragmatism is, in itself, no doctrine of metaphysics, no attempt to determine any truth of things. It is merely a method of ascertaining the meanings of hard words and of abstract concepts. All pragmatists of whatsoever stripe will cordially assent to that statement. As to the ulterior and indirect effects of practicing the pragmatistic method, that is quite another affair.

All pragmatists will further agree that their method of ascertaining the meanings of words and concepts is no other than that experimental method by which all the successful sciences (in which number nobody in his senses would include metaphysics) have reached the degrees of certainty that are severally proper to them today;—this experimental method being itself nothing but a particular application of an older logical rule, "By their fruits ye shall know them."[10]

Beyond these two propositions to which pragmatists assent *nem. con.*, we find such slight discrepancies between the views of one and another declared adherents as are to be found in every healthy and vigorous school of thought in every department of inquiry. The most prominent of all our school and the most respected, William James, defines pragmatism as the doctrine that the whole "meaning" of a concept expresses itself either in the shape of conduct to be recommended or of experience to be expected.[11]

[Variant 1]

Between this definition and mine there certainly appears to be no slight theoretical divergence, which, for the most part, becomes evanescent in practice; and though we may differ on important questions of philosophy,—especially as regards the infinite and the absolute,—I am inclined to think that the discrepancies reside in other than the pragmatistic ingredients of our thought. If pragmatism had never been heard of, I believe the opinions of James on one side, of me on the other, would have developed substantially as they have; notwithstanding our respective [ways of] connecting them at present with our conception of that method. The brilliant and marvellously human thinker, Mr. F. C. S. Schiller, who extends to the philosophic world a cup of nectar stimulant in his beautiful *Humanism*, seems to occupy ground of his own, intermediate, as to this question, between those of James and mine.

I understand pragmatism to be a method of ascertaining the meanings, not of all ideas, but only of what I call "intellectual concepts," that is to say, of those upon the structure of which arguments concerning objective fact may hinge. Had the light which, as things are, excites in us the sensation of blue, always excited the sensation of red, and *vice versa*, however great a difference that might have made in our feelings, it could have made none in the force of any argument. In this respect, the qualities of hard and soft strikingly contrast with those of red and blue; because while red and blue name mere subjective feelings only, hard and soft express the factual behavior of the thing under the pressure of a knife-edge. (I use the word "hard" in its strict mineralogical sense, "would resist a knife-edge.") My pragmatism, having nothing to do with qualities of feeling, permits me to hold that the predication of such a quality is just what it seems, and has nothing to do with anything else. Hence, could two qualities of feeling everywhere be interchanged, nothing but feelings could be affected. Those qualities have no intrinsic significations beyond themselves. Intellectual concepts, however,—the only sign-burdens that are properly denominated "concepts,"—essentially carry some implication concerning the general behavior either of some conscious being or of some inanimate object, and so convey more, not merely than any feeling, but more, too, than any existential fact, namely, the "*would-act*s" of habitual behavior; and no agglomeration of actual happenings can ever completely fill up the meaning of a "would be." But that the *total* meaning of the predication of an intellectual concept consists in affirming that, under all conceivable circumstances of a given kind, the subject of the predication would (or would not) behave in a certain way,—that is, that it either would, or would not, be true that under given experiential circumstances (or under a given proportion of them, taken *as they would occur* in experience) certain facts would exist,—*that* proposition I take to be the kernel of pragmatism. More simply stated, the whole meaning of an intellectual predicate is that certain kinds of events would happen, once in so often, in the course of experience, under certain kinds of existential circumstances.

But how is this pregnant principle to be proved true? For it seems to be in violent contrast to what one will read, let us say, for example, in Mr. Bradley's *Appearance and Reality*,[12] and in the other works of the high metaphysicians; as it no less decidedly conflicts with the simpler doctrines of Haeckel, Karl Pearson, and other nominalists. I might offer half a dozen different demonstrations of the pragmatist principle; but the very simplest of them would be technical and lengthy. It would not be such as a reader of this journal, a student of current literature, could be expected to undertake critically to examine. Such a reader would like to know the color of the thought that supports the positive assertion of pragmatism, without entering too minutely into details. Just such desire I shall endeavor to satisfy, though the smallest sufficient measure of detail will scare away some readers who if they were to persevere would find the detail interesting.

To begin with, every concept and every thought beyond immediate perception is a sign. So much was well made out by Leibniz, Berkeley, and others about two centuries ago. The use of the word λόγος shows that the Greeks, before the development of the science of grammar, were hardly able to think of thought from any other point of view. Let anybody who may desire evidence of the truth of what I am saying just recall the course of what passed in his mind during some recent sincere and fervid self-deliberation. If he is a good introspector, he will remark that his deliberations took a dialogic form, the arguer of any moment appealing to the reasonableness of the *ego* of the succeeding moment for his critical assent. Now, it is needless to say that conversation is composed of signs. Accordingly, we find the sort of mind that is least sophisticated and is surest to betray itself by its language is given to such expressions as "I says to myself, says I," or even to audibly talking to himself, like Launcelot Gobbo,[13] according to the subtle psychologist who created him. Oh, I am confident the reader will grant that every thought is a sign.

Now how would you define a *sign*, Reader? I do not ask how the word is ordinarily used. I want such a definition as a zoologist would give of a fish, or a chemist of a fatty body, or of an aromatic body,—an analysis of the essential nature of a sign, if the word is to be used as applicable to everything which the most general science of sēmeio´tic must regard as its business to study; be it of the nature of a significant quality, or something that once uttered is gone forever, or an enduring pattern, like our sole definite article; whether it professes to stand for a possibility, for a single thing or event, or for a type of things or of truths; whether it is connected with the thing, be it truth or fiction, that it represents, by imitating it, or by being an effect of its object, or by a convention or habit; whether it appeals merely to feeling, like a tone of voice, or to action, or to thought; whether it makes its appeal by sympathy, by emphasis, or by familiarity; whether it is a single word, or a sentence, or is Gibbon's *Decline and Fall*;[14] whether it is interrogatory, imperative, or assertory; whether it is of the nature of a jest, or is sealed and attested, or relies upon artistic force; and I do not stop here because the varieties of signs are by any means exhausted. Such is the definitum which I seek to fit with a rational, comprehensive, scientific, structural definition,—such as one might give of "loom," "marriage," "musical cadence"; aiming, however, let me repeat, less at what the definitum conventionally does mean, than at what it were best, in reason, that it should mean.

Everybody recognizes that it is no inconsiderable art, this business of "phaneroscopic" analysis by which one frames a scientific definition. As I practice it, in those cases, like the present, in which I am debarred from a direct appeal to the principle of pragmatism, I begin by seizing upon that predicate which appears to be most characteristic of the definitum, even if it does not quite apply to the entire extension of the definitum. If the predicate be too narrow, I afterward seek for some ingredient of it which shall be broad enough for an amended definitum and, at the same time, be still more scientifically characteristic of it.

Proceeding in that way with our definitum, "sign," we note, as highly characteristic, that signs mostly function each between two minds, or theatres of consciousness, of which the one is the agent that *utters* the sign (whether acoustically, optically, or otherwise), while the other is the *patient* mind that *interprets* the sign. Going on with my account of what is characteristic of a sign, without taking the least account of exceptional cases, for the present, I remark that, before the sign was uttered, it already was virtually present to the consciousness of the utterer, in the form of a thought. But, as already remarked, a thought is itself a sign, and should itself have an utterer (namely, the ego of a previous moment), to whose consciousness it must have been already virtually present, and so back. Likewise, after a sign has been interpreted, it will virtually remain in the consciousness of its interpreter, where it will be a sign,—perhaps, a resolution to apply the burden of the communicated sign,—and, as a sign should, in its turn have an interpreter, and so on forward. Now it is undeniably conceivable that a beginningless series of successive utterers should all do their work in a brief interval of time, and that so should an endless series of interpreters. Still, it is not likely to be denied that, in some cases, neither the series of utterers nor that of interpreters forms an infinite collection. When this is the case, there must be a sign without an utterer and a sign without an interpreter. Indeed, there are two pretty conclusive arguments on these points that are likely to occur to the reader. But why argue, when signs without utterers are often employed? I mean such signs as symptoms of disease, signs of the weather, groups of experiences serving as premisses, etc. Signs without interpreters less manifestly, but perhaps not less certainly, exist. Let the cards for a Jacquard loom[15] be prepared and inserted, so that the loom shall weave a picture. Are not those cards signs? They convey intelligence,—intelligence that, considering its spirit and pictorial effect, cannot otherwise be conveyed. Yet the woven pictures may take fire and be consumed before anybody sees them. A set of those models that the designers of vessels drag through the water may have been prepared; and with the set a complete series of experiments may have been made; and their conditions and results may have been automatically recorded. There, then, is a perfect representation of the behavior of a certain range of forms. Yet if nobody takes the trouble to study the record, there will be no interpreter. So the books of a bank may furnish a complete account of the state of the bank. It remains only to draw up a balance sheet. But if this be not done, while the sign is complete, the human interpreter is wanting.

Having found, then, that neither an utterer, nor even, perhaps, an interpreter is essential to a sign, characteristic of signs as they both are, I am led to inquire whether there be not some ingredient of the utterer and some ingredient of the interpreter which not only are so essential, but are even more characteristic of signs than the utterer and the interpreter themselves. We begin with seeking the essential ingredient of the utterer. By calling this quaesitum an *ingredient* of the utterer, I mean that where this quaesitum is absent the utterer cannot be present; and further that where there is no utterer, it cannot be that this quaesitum together with all the others of a certain body of "ingredients" should all be present. This latter clause, however, has so little importance and is so nearly self-evident that I need not insist upon it. A fact concerning our quaesitum, which we can know in advance of all study, is that, because this quaesitum will function as a sort of substitute for an utterer, in case there be no utterer, or at any rate fulfills nearly the same, but a more essential, function, it follows that since it is not the sign that constructs or voices or represents the utterer, but, on the contrary, the utterer that constructs, voices, and sets forth the sign, therefore, although *ex hypothesi* the quaesitum is something quite indispensible to the functioning of the sign, yet it cannot be fully revealed or brought to light by any study of the sign alone, as such. Knowledge of it must come from some previous or collateral source. Moreover, since it is conceived to act upon the sign, it must be conceived as singular, not general. But perhaps this is not very clear and needs illustration.

Example 1. Suppose I chance to overhear one man at a club say to another "Ralph Pepperill has bought that mare Pee Dee Kew." Never having heard before either of Ralph Pepperill or of Pee Dee Kew, it means to me only that some man has bought some famous trotter; and since I knew already that some men do make such purchases, it does not interest me. But the next day I hear somebody inquire where he can find a copy of Steven's edition of Plato;[16] to which reply is made that Ralph Pepperill says he has a copy. Now although I never was knowingly acquainted with any purchaser of crack trotting-horses, yet I should not have supposed that such a person would be aware of possessing an old edition of Plato whose chief value is due to the circumstance that modern citations from the Dialogues usually refer to it. After this, I begin to pay attention to what I hear of Ralph Pepperill; until, at length, that which the name means to me probably represents pretty fairly what it would mean to an acquaintance of the man. This imparts, not merely an interest, but also a *meaning* to every little scrap of new information about him;—to scraps that would have conveyed no information whatsoever, had they first introduced his name to my ears. Yet the name itself will remain a designation devoid of essential signification, and so much of the accidental kind as it may at any time have acquired will not have been derived, in however slight measure, from the utterer of any sentence which it may furnish with informatory interest;—at least, not from him in his capacity as utterer of that sentence.

Example 2. I remember a blazing July noon in the early sixties when a fellow-student in the chemical laboratory, in whose company I was crossing the Harvard "College Yard," while the grass shone like emeralds, and the red-brick buildings, not red enough by nature for the taste of the curator, were blazing in a fresh coat of something like vermillion,—when this fellow student casually remarked upon the pleasing harmony of color between the grass, the foliage, and the buildings. With eyes feeling as if their balls were being twisted by some inquisitor, I at first understood the remark as a sorry joke, like the gibes of some Indian captive at the want of skill of his tormentors. But I soon found that it was the utterance of a sincere feeling, and then, by a series of questions, soon discovered that my friend was blind to the red element of color. A man may have learned that he is color-blind; but it is impossible that he should be conscious of the stupendous gulf between his chromatic impressions and those of ordinary men; although it is needful to take account of this in all interpretations of what he may say about colors. In the course of my examination of that young gentleman, which occupied several days, I learned a more general lesson, worth multiples of the time it lost me from the laboratory.

Example 3. Toward the end of a sultry afternoon, three young gentlemen are still lounging together; one in a long chair, one supine upon a lounge, the third standing by the open casement that looks down seven stories upon the Piazza di Spagna from its Pincian side,[17] and seems to be half glancing at the newspaper that has just been brought to him. His is one of those natures that habitually hold themselves within the limits of extreme calm, because they too well know the terrible expense of allowing themselves to be stirred. In a few moments, he breaks the silence with the words, "Verily, it is a terrible fire." What does he mean? The other twain are too lazy to ask. The long-chaired one thinks the utterer was looking at the newspaper when he made his exclamation, and concludes that there has been a conflagration in Tehe-ran, in Sydney, or in some such place, appalling enough to be flashed round the globe. But the couched man thinks the utterer was looking out of the win-dow, and that there must be a fire down in the Corso, or in that direction. Here is another case in which the whole burden of the sign must be ascer-tained, not by closer examination of the utterance, but by collateral observa-tion of the utterer.

Example 4. I find (let us suppose) among my books, a quarto volume among the leaves of which an old manuscript letter has got bound, which gives some details about a fire,—apparently a considerable conflagration, since the writer speaks of it as "the fire," as if the addressee could not possibly misidentify it, and since different houses being consumed are mentioned as small details. If it refers to the great fire of London,[18] it is certainly of remark-able interest. But how am I to know whether it does so or not? I need not say that the binder in trimming the edges has cut off the date; since the oath of their trade, as it would seem, must oblige binders to do this whenever the margins carry matter of special interest. I can, therefore, only submit the manuscript to some experts in diplomatics who can pronounce on the date of the writing and of the paper. In this case, again, the whole significance of the sign depends upon collateral observation.

Example 5. Pronouns are words whose whole object is to indicate what kind of collateral observation must be made in order to determine the signifi-cance of some other part of the sentence. "Which" directs us to seek the quaesitum in the previous context; the personal pronouns to observe who is the speaker, who the hearer, etc. The demonstrative pronouns usually direct this sort of observation to the circumstances of the utterance (perhaps to the way a finger points) rather than to the words.

Since the most acute minds, in dealing with conceptions unfamiliar to them, will blunder in ways that astonish those who are habituated to such dealings, I will propose, as an additional example, that of a weathercock. Now a weathercock is one of those natural signs, like a *[ny]* sign of the weather, which depend upon a physical connection between the sign and that of which it is the sign. But a weathercock having been devised, as everyone knows, to show which way the wind blows, itself signifies to what it refers; and conse-quently it may be argued that no collateral observation is called for to com-plete its significance. But this reasoning commits two faults. In the first place, it confuses two incompatible ways of conceiving of a weathercock: as a natu-ral sign, and therefore as having no utterer; and as a human contrivance to show the direction of the wind, and as such, uttered by its original inventor (for I speak of the weathercock,—the type, not the single instance). In the second place, the reasoning overlooks the obvious truth that when thoughts are determined or revealed by a sign, the sign exists first (virtually, at any rate), and those thoughts subsequently. Hence, thoughts applied to devise a weathercock cannot be revealed by the weathercock, but come under the head of "previous or collateral" information. To this all-sufficient reply, it may be added, by way of surplusage, that prudent persons, in consulting a weathercock, watch it to see whether it veers, as a security against the possibility of its being jammed by rust or otherwise, and against its being deflected by any other force than that of the wind.

It is now easy to see that the *requaesitum* which we have been seeking is simply that which the sign "stands for," or the idea of that which it is calculated to awaken. We now have a clearer idea of the *requaesitum* than we had, at first, of the "object of the sign." Our remarks may be regarded as attempts to analyze the idea of "standing for" or "representing." The *requaesitum*, when there are both an utterer and an interpreter, is that which the former has in mind, but which it does not occur to him to express, because he well knows that the interpreter will understand that he refers to that, without his saying so. I am speaking of cases in which the sign stands alone without any context. Thus if the utterer says "Fine day!" he does not dream of any possibility of the interpreter's thinking of any mere *desire* for a fine day that a Finn of the North Cape might have entertained on April 19, 1776. He means, of course, to refer to the actual weather, then and there, where he and the interpreter are alike influenced by the fine weather, and have it near the surface of their common consciousness. Marine fossils found on a mountain, considered as a sign of the sea level having been higher than the levels of deposit of those fossils, refers to a distant but indefinite date. Here, there is no utterer; but this is what might have remained unexpressed in the mind of the utterer, though essential to the significance of the sign, if that sign had been devised and constructed to give the human race a first lesson in geology. Where the sign is only a part of another sign, so that there is a context, it is in that context that the *requaesitum* is likely, in part at least, to be found; though it is not absolutely necessary that it should be found in any part of the sign.

This *requaesitum* I term the *Object* of the sign;—the *immediate* object, if it be the idea which the sign is built upon, the *real* object, if it be that real thing or circumstance upon which that idea is founded, as on bedrock.

The Object of a Sign, then, is necessarily unexpressed in the sign, taken by itself. Indeed, we shall soon see that whatever is so expressed comes under quite a different category. But the above examples show that that idea which though essential to the functioning of a sign can only be attained by collateral observation is the idea of a strictly individual thing, or individual collection or series, or an individual event, or an individual *ens rationis*. This sufficiently proves the truth of the proposition. There are deeper causative reasons that cannot be given here. The proposition does not amount to so much as it has the air of doing, since whatever actually exists is an individual. For a finite plural is nothing but the singular of an indefinite collective noun; while the endlessness of an infinite collection is of a hypothetical, or ideal, nature, and lacks completed existence. The object of a sign, though singular, may nevertheless be multiple, and may even be infinitely so. Take a verb in the indicative mood out from its context, and what is its object? What, for example, is the object of "runs"? *Answer:* it is something, a runner. What is the object of "kills"? *Answer:* it is a pair of indesignate individuals, the one a killer, the other killed by him. So "gives" has for its object a triplet of related indesignate singulars, a giver, a gift, a recipient of that gift from that giver. "Buys" is predicated of a quartette composed of the seller, the buyer, the legal right that is transferred from the former to the latter, and the price. The different members of the set which is the object of a verb,—its *partial* objects, as they may be called,—often have distinctive characters which are the same for large numbers of verbs. Thus, the partial objects of an ordinary transitive verb are an agent and a patient. These distinctive characters have nothing to do with the form of a verb, as a sign, but are derived from the form of the fact signified. By taking note of this, one may avoid some perplexity when the verb itself expresses the functioning of a sign. For example, one of the partial objects of the verb "expresses" is of course the thing expressed, which in some drowsy moment might seem an instance refuting the principle that the object of a sign cannot be expressed by the sign itself. To avoid the puzzle, one need but note that the verb "expresses" not only *is* a sign, and expresses something, but also signifies the action of a sign, or expresses its expressing something. Its accusative is the object of the outer sign, but not of the other, inner, sign which this outer sign implies.

It should be mentioned that though a sign cannot express its Object, it may describe, or otherwise indicate, the kind of collateral observation by which that Object is to be found. Thus, a proposition whose subject is distributively universal (not plural or otherwise collectively universal), such as "Any man will die," allows the interpreter, after collateral observation has disclosed what single universe is meant, to take any individual of that universe as the Object of the proposition, giving, in the above example, the equivalent "If you take any individual you please of the universe of existent things, and if that individual is a man, it will die." If the proposition had been, "Some Old Testament character was translated," the indication would have been that the individual must be suitably selected, while the interpreter would have been left to his own devices to identify the individual.

Now that we have attained, you and I, Reader, as I hope, a pretty clear notion of what, in strictness of speech, must be meant by the Object of a sign, it becomes pertinent to inquire how far such strictness of speech is practicable and convenient. Of the two loosely synonymous terms, "individual" and "singular," the former translates Aristotle's τὸ ἄτομον, the latter his τὸ καθ᾽ ἕκαστον.[19] "Individual" is usually and well defined as that which is absolutely determinate; the "singular" is that which is absolutely determinate as long as the time is so, or to generalize this definition, is variable only in two precisely opposite and converse ways of varying. Now it is quite impossible that any collateral observations, however they might be eked out by imagination or thought, should ever approach a *positive* idea of a singular, let alone an individual; that is, that we should actually think it as determinate in each one of the more than millions of respects in which things may vary. Suppose, for example, that it is visible; and consider only the outline of a single aspect of it. Even though this outline were restricted to being one of a family of curves, say ellipses, the different possible shapes between any two limiting shapes are more than innumerable; for there is a continuum of them. It would be impossible to complete our collateral observation, aided though it were by imagination and thought, even in this one, almost insignificant, respect. It is plainly impracticable, therefore, to restrict the meaning of the term "object of a sign" to the Object strictly so called.

For, after all, collateral observation, aided by imagination and thought, will usually result in some idea, though this need not be particularly determinate; but may be indefinite in some regards and general in others. Such an apprehension, approaching, however distantly, that of the Object strictly so called, ought to be, and usually is, termed the "immediate object" of the sign in the intention of its utterer. It may be that there is no such thing or fact in existence, or in any other mode of reality; but we surely shall not deny to the common picture of a phoenix or to a figure of naked truth in her well[20] the name of a "sign," simply because the bird is a fiction and Truth an *ens rationis*.

If there be anything *real* (that is, anything whose characters are true of it independently of whether you or I, or any man, or any number of men think them as being characters of it, or not) that sufficiently corresponds with the immediate object (which, since it is an apprehension, is not real), then whether this be identifiable with the Object strictly so called or not, it ought to be called, and usually is called, the "real object" of the sign. By some kind of causation or influence it must have determined the significant character of the sign.

So much for the object, or that by which the sign is essentially determined in its significant characters in the mind of its utterer. Corresponding to it there is something which the sign in its significant function essentially determines in its interpreter. I term it the "interpretant" of the sign. In all cases, it includes feelings; for there must, at least, be a sense of comprehending the meaning of the sign. If it includes more than mere feeling, it must evoke some kind of effort. It may include something besides, which, for the present, may be vaguely called "thought." I term these three kinds of interpretant the "emotional," the "energetic," and the "logical" interpretants.

If a sign has no interpreter, its interpretant is a "would be," i.e., is what it *would* determine in the interpreter if there were one. In its general nature, the interpretant is much more readily intelligible than the object, since it includes all that the sign of itself expresses or signifies. But there is some difficulty in defining the three kinds of interpretant. It may possibly be, for example, that I am taking too narrow a conception of the sign in general in saying that its initial effect must be of the nature of feeling, since it may be that there are agencies that ought to be classed along with signs and yet that at first begin to act quite unconsciously. But since this error, if it be one, does not seem to have anything to do with the subject of pragmatism, I do not now stop to consider it. A much more serious question, especially in the present connection, concerns the nature of that logical interpretant, the conveyed thought, which we easily assure ourselves that some signs have, though we do not straightway discern in what it consists.

I am now prepared to risk an attempt at defining a sign,—since in scientific inquiry, as in other enterprises, the maxim holds, *Nothing hazard, nothing gain*. I will say that a sign is anything, of whatsoever mode of being, which mediates between an object and an interpretant; since it is both determined by the object *relatively to the interpretant*, and determines the interpretant *in reference to the object*, in such wise as to cause the interpretant to be determined by the object through the mediation of this "sign."

The object and the interpretant are thus merely the two correlates of the sign; the one being antecedent, the other consequent of the sign. Moreover, the sign being defined in terms of these correlative correlates, it is confidently to be expected that object and interpretant should precisely correspond, each to the other. In point of fact, we do find that the immediate object and emotional interpretant correspond, both being apprehensions, or are "subjective"; both, too, appertain to all signs without exception. The real object and energetic interpretant also correspond, both being real facts or things. But to our surprise, we find that the logical interpretant does not correspond with any kind of object. This defect of correspondence between object and interpretant must be rooted in the essential difference there is between the nature of an object and that of an interpretant; which difference is that the former antecedes, while the latter succeeds the sign. The logical interpretant must, therefore, be in a relatively future tense.

To this may be added the consideration that it is not all signs that have logical interpretants, but only intellectual concepts and the like; and these are all either general or intimately connected with generals, as it seems to me. This shows that the species of future tense of the logical interpretant is that of the conditional mood, the "*would-be*."

At the time I was originally puzzling over the enigma of the nature of the logical interpretant, and had reached about the stage where the discussion now is, being in a quandary, it occurred to me that if I only could find a moderate number of concepts which should be at once highly abstract and abstruse, and yet the whole nature of whose meanings should be quite unquestionable, a study of them would go far toward showing me how and why the logical interpretant should in all cases be a conditional future. I had no sooner framed a definite wish for such concepts, than I perceived that in mathematics they are as plenty as blackberries.[21] I at once began running through the explications of them, which I found all took the following form: Proceed according to such and such a general rule. Then, if such and such a concept is applicable to such and such an object, the operation will have such and such a general result; and conversely. Thus, to take an extremely simple case, if two geometrical figures of dimensionality N should be equal in all their parts, an easy rule of construction would determine, in a space of dimensionality N containing both figures, an axis of rotation, such that a rigid body that should fill not only that space but also a space of dimensionality $N+1$ containing the former space, turning about that axis, and carrying one of the figures along with it, while the other figure remained at rest, the rotation would bring the movable figure back into its original space of dimensionality N, and when that event occurred, the movable figure would be in exact coincidence with the unmoved one, in all its parts; while if the two figures were not so equal, this would never happen.

Here was certainly a stride toward the solution of the enigma. For the treatment of a score of intellectual concepts on that model, only a few of them being mathematical, seemed to me to be so refulgently successful as fully to convince me that to predicate any such concept of a real or imaginary object is equivalent to declaring that a certain operation, corresponding to the concept, if performed upon that object, would (certainly, or probably, or possibly, according to the mode of predication) be followed by a result of a definite general description.

Yet this does not quite tell us just what the nature is of the essential effect upon the interpreter, brought about by the sēm ī ō´sis of the sign, which constitutes the logical interpretant. (It is important to understand what I mean by *semiosis*. All dynamical action, or action of brute force, physical or psychical, either takes place between two subjects,—whether they react equally upon each other, or one is agent and the other patient, entirely or partially,—or at any rate is a resultant of such actions between pairs. But by "semiosis" I mean, on the contrary, an action, or influence, which is, or involves, a cooperation of *three* subjects, such as a sign, its object, and its interpretant, this tri-relative influence not being in any way resolvable into actions between pairs. Σημείωσις in Greek of the Roman period, as early as Cicero's time, if I remember rightly, meant the action of almost any kind of sign; and my definition confers on anything that so acts the title of a "sign."[22])

Although the definition does not require the logical interpretant (or, for that matter, either of the other two interpretants) to be a modification of consciousness, yet our lack of experience of any semiosis in which this is not the case leaves us no alternative to beginning our inquiry into its general nature with a provisional assumption that the interpretant is, at least, in all cases, a sufficiently close analogue of a modification of consciousness to keep our conclusion pretty near to the general truth. We can only hope that, once that conclusion is reached, it may be susceptible of such a generalization as will eliminate any possible error due to the falsity of that assumption. The reader may well wonder why I do not simply confine my inquiry to psychical semiosis, since no other seems to be of much importance. My reason is that the too frequent practice, by those logicians who do not go to work without any method at all, of basing propositions in the science of logic upon results of the science of psychology,—as contradistinguished from commonsense observations concerning the workings of the mind, observations well known even if little noticed, to all grown men and women that are of sound minds,—that practice is to my apprehension as unsound and insecure as was that bridge in the novel of *Kenilworth* that, being utterly without any sort of support, sent the poor Countess Amy to her destruction;[23] seeing that, for the firm establishment of the truths of the science of psychology, almost incessant appeals to the results of the science of logic,—as contradistinguished from natural perceptions that one relation evidently involves another,—are peculiarly indispensable. Those logicians continually confound *psychical* truths with *psychological* truths, although the distinction between them is of that kind that takes precedence over all others as calling for the respect of anyone who would tread the strait and narrow road that leadeth unto exact truth.

Making that provisional assumption, then, I ask myself, since we have already seen that the logical interpretant is general in its possibilities of reference (i.e., refers or is related to whatever there may be of a certain description), what categories of mental facts there be that are of general reference. I can find only these four: conceptions, desires (including hopes, fears, etc.), expectations, and habits. I trust I have made no important omission. Now it is no explanation of the nature of the logical interpretant (which, we already know, is a concept) to say that it is a concept. This objection applies also to desire and expectation, as explanations of the same interpretant; since neither of these is general otherwise than through connection with a concept. Besides, as to desire, it would be easy to show (were it worth the space) that the logical interpretant is an effect of the energetic interpretant, in the sense in which the latter is an effect of the emotional interpretant. Desire, however, is cause, not effect, of effort. As to expectation, it is excluded by the fact that it is not conditional. For that which might be mistaken for a conditional expectation is nothing but a judgment that, under certain conditions, there would be an expectation: there is no conditionality in the expectation itself, such as there is in the logical interpretant after it is actually produced. Therefore, there remains only habit, as the essence of the logical interpretant.

Let us see, then, just how, according to the rule derived from mathematical concepts (and confirmed by others), this habit is produced; and what sort of a habit it is. In order that this deduction may be rightly made, the following remark will be needed. It is not a result of scientific psychology, but is simply a bit of the catholic and undeniable common sense of mankind, with no other modification than a slight accentuation of certain features.

Every sane person lives in a double world, the outer and the inner world, the world of percepts and the world of fancies. What chiefly keeps these from being mixed up together is (besides certain marks they bear) everybody's well-knowing that fancies can be greatly modified by a certain nonmuscular effort, while it is muscular effort alone (whether this be "voluntary," that is, preintended, or whether all the intended endeavor is to inhibit muscular action, as when one blushes, or when peristaltic action is set up on experience of danger to one's person) that can, to any noticeable degree, modify percepts. A man can be durably affected by his percepts and by his fancies. The way in which they affect him will be apt to depend upon his personal inborn disposition and upon his habits. Habits differ from dispositions in having been acquired as consequences of the principle, virtually well known even to those whose powers of reflection are insufficient to its formulation, that multiply reiterated behavior of the same kind, under similar combinations of percepts and fancies, produces a tendency,—the *habit*,—actually to behave in a similar way under similar circumstances in the future. Moreover,—*here is the point*,—every man exercises more or less control over himself by means of modifying his own habits; and the way in which he goes to work to bring this effect about in those cases in which circumstances will not permit him to practice reiterations of the desired kind of conduct in the outer world shows that he is virtually well acquainted with the important principle that *reiterations in the inner world,—fancied reiterations,—if well-intensified by direct effort, produce habits*, just as do reiterations in the outer world; *and these habits will have power to influence actual behavior in the outer world*; especially, if each reiteration be accompanied by a peculiar strong effort that is usually likened to issuing a command to one's future self.*

(I here owe my patient reader a confession. It is that when I said that those signs that have a logical interpretant are either general or closely connected with generals, this was not a scientific result, but only a strong impression due to a life-long study of the nature of signs. My excuse for not answering the question scientifically is that I am, as far as I know, a pioneer, or rather a backwoodsman, in the work of clearing and opening up what I call *semiotic*, that is, the doctrine of the essential nature and fundamental varieties of possible semiosis; and I find the field too vast, the labor too great, for a first-comer. I am, accordingly, obliged to confine myself to the most important questions. The questions of the same particular type as the one I answer on the basis of an impression, which are of about the same importance, exceed four hundred in number; and they are all delicate and difficult, each requiring much search and much caution. At the same time, they are very far from being among the most important of the questions of semiotic. Even if my answer is not exactly correct, it can lead to no great misconception as to the nature of the logical interpretant. There is my apology, such as it may be deemed.)

*I well remember when I was a boy, and my brother Herbert, now our minister at Christiania,[24] was scarce more than a child, one day, as the whole family were at table, some spirit from a "blazer," or "chafing-dish," dropped on the muslin dress of one of the ladies and was kindled; and how instantaneously he jumped up, and did the right thing, and how skillfully each motion was adapted to the purpose. I asked him afterward about it, and he told me that since Mrs. Longfellow's death[25] he had often run over in imagination all the details of what ought to be done in such an emergency. It was a striking example of a real habit produced by exercises in the imagination.

It is not to be supposed that upon every presentation of a sign capable of producing a logical interpretant, such interpretant is actually produced. The occasion may either be too early or too late. If it is too early, the semiosis will not be carried so far, the other interpretants sufficing for the rude functions for which the sign is used. On the other hand, the occasion will come too late if the interpreter be already familiar with the logical interpretant, since then it will be recalled to his mind by a process which affords no hint of how it was originally produced. Moreover, the great majority of instances in which formations of logical interpretants do take place are very unsuitable to serve as illustrations of the process, because in them the essentials of this semiosis are buried in masses of accidental and hardly relevant semioses that are mixed with the former. The best way that I have been able to hit upon for simplifying the illustrative example which is to serve as our matter upon which to experiment and observe is to suppose a man already skillful in handling a given sign (that has a logical interpretant) to begin now before our inner gaze for the first time seriously to inquire what that interpretant is. It will be necessary to amplify this hypothesis by a specification of what his *interest* in the question is supposed to be. In doing this, I by no means follow Mr. Schiller's brilliant and seductive humanistic logic,[26] according to which it is proper to take account of the whole personal situation in logical inquiries. For I hold it to be very evil and harmful procedure to introduce into scientific investigation an unfounded hypothesis, without any definite prospect of its hastening our discovery of the truth. Now such a hypothesis Mr. Schiller's rule seems to me, with my present lights, to be. He has given a number of reasons for it; but, to my estimate, they seem to be of that quality that is well calculated to give rise to interesting discussions, and is consequently to be recommended to those who intend to pursue the study of philosophy as an entertaining exercise of the intellect, but is negligible for one whose earnest purpose is to do what in him lies toward bringing about a metamorphosis of philosophy into a genuine science. I cannot turn aside into Mr. Schiller's charming lane. When I ask what the interest is in seeking to discover a logical interpretant, it is not my fondness for strolling in paths where I can study the varieties of humanity that moves me, but the definite reflection that unless our hypothesis be rendered specific as to that interest, it will be impossible to trace out its logical consequences, since the way the interpreter will conduct the inquiry will greatly depend upon the nature of his interest in it.

I shall suppose, then, that the interpreter is not particularly interested in the theory of logic, which he may judge by examples to be profitless; but I shall suppose that he has embarked a great part of the treasures of his life in the enterprise of perfecting a certain invention; and that, for this end, it seems to him extremely desirable that he should acquire a demonstrative knowledge of the solution of a certain problem of reasoning. As to this problem itself, I shall suppose that it does not fall within any class for which any general method of handling is known, and that indeed it is indefinite in every respect which might afford any familiar kind of handle by which any image fairly representing it could be held firmly before the mind and examined; so that, in short, it seems to elude reason's application or to slip from its grasp.

Various problems answering this description might be instanced; but to fix our ideas, I will specify one of them, and will suppose that this is the very one which our imaginary inventor wishes to solve. It shall be the following "map-coloring problem": Let a globular body be bored through in two wide holes; and, though it is unnecessary, the edge at each end of each tunnel shall be smoothly rounded off. Then the problem is, supposing its utterer is free to divide the whole surface of this body,—including the surfaces of the bores,—into regions in any way he likes (no region consisting of separated pieces), and supposing that it will then fall to the interpreter to color the whole area of each region in one color, but never giving to two regions that abut along a common boundary-line the same color; required to ascertain what will be the least number of different colors that will always suffice, no matter how the surface may have been divided.

Under the high stimulus of his interest in this problem, and with that practical knack that we have supposed him to possess in coloring maps without too frequently being obliged to go back and alter the colors he had assigned to given regions, we need not doubt that our inquirer will be thrown into a state of high activity in the world of fancies, in experimenting upon coloring maps, while trying to make out what subconscious rule guides him, and renders him as successful as he usually is; and in trying, too, to discover what rule he had violated in each case where his first coloration has to be changed. This activity is, logically, an energetic interpretant of the interrogatory he puts to himself. Should he in this way succeed in working out a determinate rule for coloring every map on the two-tunnelled (or, what is the same thing, the two-bridged) everywhere unbounded surface with the fewest possible colors, there will be good hope that a demonstration may tread upon the heels of that rule, in which case, the problem will be solved in the most convenient form. But while he may very likely manage to formulate his own usually successful way of coloring the regions, it is very unlikely that he will obtain an unfailing rule for doing so. For after some of the first mathematicians in Europe had found themselves baffled by the far simpler problem, to prove that every map upon an ordinary sheet can be colored with four colors, one of the very first logico-mathematicians of our age, Mr. Alfred B. Kempe, proposed a proof of it, somewhat, though not exactly, of the kind we are supposing our imaginary inventor to be aiming at. Yet I am informed that many years later a fatal flaw was discovered in Mr. Kempe's proof.[27] I do not remember that I ever knew what the fallacy was. We may assume with confidence, then, that our imaginary interpreter will, at length, come to despair of solving the problem in that way. What way shall I imagine him to try next?

It will be very natural for him to pass from endeavoring to define a uniformly successful rule of procedure, to endeavoring either, first, to define the topical conditions under which two different regions must be colored alike, if the colors are not to exceed a given number; whence he will deduce the conditions under which two regions that do not abut must be colored differently; or else, first to define the conditions under which two regions cannot, by being stretched out, be brought into abuttal along a boundary, and thence to define the conditions under which two regions must be colored alike. Either of these methods is more promising than the one with which he began; and yet were either capable of being perfected without some very peculiar *aperçu*, the easier task of demonstrating that four colors suffice for every map on an ordinary limited sheet or globular surface must long ago have been brought to completion, which never has been accomplished, I believe, in print. We may assume, then, that he will, at length, come to abandon every such method. Meantime, he cannot fail to have noticed several obvious propositions that will be useful in his further inquiries. One of these will be that by minute alterations of the boundaries between regions, which alterations can neither diminish nor increase the number of colors that will in all cases just suffice, he can get rid of all points where four or more regions concur, and thus render the number of points of concurrence two-thirds as many as the number of boundaries, so that the latter number will be divisible by three, and the former by two, unless fewer colors are required than are generally necessary. He will also have remarked that there must for each color be at least one region of that color which abuts upon regions of all the other colors, that for each of these other colors there must be at least one region that besides abutting upon the first region abuts upon regions of all the remaining colors, etc.

I shall suppose that it now occurs to him that it not only makes no difference what the proportionate dimensions either of the whole surface or of any of the regions are, but that it is equally indifferent whether any part of the whole surface be flat, convex, concave, curved, or broken by angles, or whether any boundaries are straight, curved, or broken by angles, and are convex or concave to either of the regions it bounds; whence it will follow that the problem belongs neither to Metrical, nor to Graphical (or Projective) Geometry, but to Topical Geometry, or Geometrical Topics. This is the most fundamental, and no doubt, in its own nature, much the easiest of the three departments of geometry. For just as metrics is but a special problem in the easier graphics, as Cayley showed;[28] so quite obviously graphics is a special problem in the easier topics. For there is no other possible way of defining unlimited planes and rays, than by the topical statement (which does not fully define them) that the unbounded planes are a family of surfaces in three-dimensional space of which any two contain one common line only, which is a *ray*, and of which any three that do not all contain one common ray have one point and only one in common; and further, any two points are both contained in one and in only one ray, while any three points not all in one ray are contained in one and only one unbounded plane.*

*This supposes the unbounded three-dimensional space to have a peculiar shape. For if it had the simplest shape possible (or what seems to me such, and what Listing assumed to be the real shape of space), every unbounded surface in it would separate it into two parts, and the

But though Topics must be the easiest kind of geometry, yet geometers were so accustomed to rely on considerations of measure and of flatness, that when they were deprived of these, they did not know how to handle problems; so that, apart from mere enumerations of forms, such as knots, we are still in possession of only one general theorem of Topics, Listing's census-theorem.[29] Consequently, our imagined investigator, as soon as he remarks that he has a problem in topical geometry before him, will infer that he must utilize that sole known theorem of topics; albeit it is sufficiently obvious that that theorem of itself is not adequate to furnishing a solution of his problem. I will state the census-theorem of Listing with some sacrifice of exactitude to perspicuity, in so far as it applies to the map-coloring problem. The surface which is divided into regions may be bounded by a line or unbounded. If it be unbounded and separates [a] solid into two parts, I call it *artiad*; if it does not, I call it *perissid*. The *Cyclosy*, or ringiness, of the surface of a body unpierced by any tunnel (i.e. not bridged over by an unbounded bridge) is *zero*; and every tunnel through the body adds *two* to the cyclosy of its surface. The cyclosy of the simplest perissid surface, such as an unbounded plane, is *one*, and every tunnel connecting two parts of it in an additional way (or every cylindrical bridge, which will be a tunnel on the other side of the surface) adds *two* to the cyclosy. A region, or an uninterrupted boundary that does not return into itself (as I will assume is the case with all regions and boundaries between two regions), has *zero* cyclosy. I will further assume that there is more than one region on the surface. Under these circumstances, the census-theorem takes this form, supposing all points of concurrence of regions are points where three regions and no more run together: One third of the number of boundaries from one point of concurrence to the next diminished by the number of regions is equal to one less than the cyclosy of the whole surface, if this be bounded, or to two less than the cyclosy, if the surface be unbounded. In the case of the surface of a body pierced by two tunnels, the surface is unbounded, and its cyclosy is 4. The investigator will see at once that the number of colors must be at least seven, and is likely to be more. For were the body pierced by but one tunnel, let the number of regions each abutting upon all the rest be x. Then, the number of boundaries would be $\frac{1}{2}x(x-1)$; and the census-theorem applied to this case would be $\frac{1}{6}x(x-1) - x = 2 - 2$. That is, $x^2 - 7x = 0$, or $x = 7$. Since, then, even with but one tunnel seven colors might be required, at least that number will be required for the case of two tunnels. On the other hand, were two tunnels made in a projective plane, where the cyclosy would be 5, instead of 4, only nine regions could touch one another; so that it is likely that for a surface of cyclosy 4, the requisite number

---

unbounded line common to two surfaces would cut any third unbounded surface in an even number of points, since this line would pass alternately from one to the other of the two parts into which the first surface had cut the unbounded solid space. The peculiar shape of the solid space is that of "projective space."

of colors is less than nine. The investigator will, therefore, only have to ascertain whether eight, and if so whether nine, colors can be required. He is still not very near his solution, but he is not hopelessly removed from it.

In every case, after some preliminaries, the activity takes the form of experimentation in the inner world; and the conclusion (if it comes to a definite conclusion) is that under given conditions, the interpreter will have formed the habit of acting in a given way, whenever he may desire a given kind of result. The real and living logical conclusion *is* that habit; the verbal formulation merely expresses it.

I do not deny that a concept, proposition, or argument may be a logical interpretant. I only insist that it cannot be the final logical interpretant, for the reason that it is itself a sign of that very kind that has itself a logical interpretant. The habit alone, though it may be a sign in some other way, is not a sign in that way in which the sign of which it is the logical interpretant is a sign. The habit conjoined with the motive and the conditions has the action for its energetic interpretant; but action cannot be a logical interpretant, because it lacks generality. The concept which is a logical interpretant is only imperfectly so. It somewhat partakes of the nature of a verbal definition, and is as inferior to the habit, and much in the same way, as a verbal definition is inferior to the real definition. The deliberately formed, self-analyzing habit,—self-analyzing because formed by the aid of analysis of the exercises that nourished it,—is the living definition, the veritable and final logical interpretant. Consequently, the most perfect account of a concept that words can convey will consist in a description of the habit which that concept is calculated to produce. But how otherwise can a habit be described than by a description of the kind of action to which it gives rise, with the specification of the conditions and of the motive?

If we now revert to the psychological assumption originally made, we shall see that it is already largely eliminated by the consideration that habit is by no means exclusively a mental fact. Empirically, we find that some plants take habits. The stream of water that wears a bed for itself is forming a habit. Every ditcher so thinks of it. Turning to the rational side of the question, the excellent current definition of habit, due, I suppose, to some physiologist (if I can remember my bye-reading for nearly half a century unglanced at, Brown-Sequard much insisted on it in his book on the spinal cord),[30] says not one word about the mind. Why should it, when habits in themselves are entirely unconscious, though feelings may be symptoms of them, and when consciousness alone,—i.e., feeling,—is the only distinctive attribute of mind?

What further is needed to clear the sign of its mental associations is furnished by generalizations too facile to arrest attention here, since nothing but feeling is exclusively mental. But while I say this, it must not be inferred that I regard consciousness as a mere "epiphenomenon"; though I heartily grant that the hypothesis that it is so has done good service to science. To my apprehension, consciousness may be defined as that congeries of non-relative predicates, varying greatly in quality and in intensity, which are symptomatic of the interaction of the outer world,—the world of those causes that are exceedingly compulsive upon the modes of consciousness, with general disturbance sometimes amounting to shock, and are acted upon only slightly, and only by a special kind of effort, muscular effort,—and of the inner world, apparently derived from the outer, and amenable to direct effort of various kinds with feeble reactions, the interaction of these two worlds chiefly consisting of a direct action of the outer world upon the inner and an indirect action of the inner world upon the outer through the operation of habits. If this be a correct account of consciousness, i.e., of the congeries of feelings, it seems to me that it exercises a real function in self-control, since without it, or at least without that of which it is symptomatic, the resolves and exercises of the inner world could not affect the real determinations and habits of the outer world. I say that these belong to the outer world because they are not mere fantasies but are real agencies.

I have now outlined my own form of pragmatism; but there are other slightly different ways of regarding what is practically the same method of attaining vitally distinct conceptions, from which I should protest from the depths of my soul against being separated. In the first place, there is the pragmatism of James, whose definition[31] differs from mine only in that he does not restrict the "meaning," that is, the ultimate logical interpretant, as I do, to a habit, but allows percepts, that is, complex feelings endowed with compulsiveness, to be such. If he is willing to do this, I do not quite see how he need give any room at all to habit. But practically, his view and mine must, I think, coincide, except where he allows considerations not at all pragmatic to have weight. Then there is Schiller, who offers no less than seven alternative definitions of pragmatism.[32] The first is that pragmatism is the doctrine that "truths are logical values." At first blush, this seems far too broad; for who, be he pragmatist or absolutist, can fail to prefer truth to fiction? But no doubt what is meant is that the objectivity of truth really consists in the fact that, in the end, every sincere inquirer will be led to embrace it;—and if he be not sincere, the irresistible effect of inquiry in the light of experience will be to make him so. This doctrine appears to me, after one subtraction, to be a corollary of pragmatism. I set it in a strong light in my original presentation of the method.[33] I call my form of it "conditional idealism." That is to say, I hold that truth's independence of individual opinions is due (so far as there is any "truth") to its being the predestined result to which sufficient inquiry *would* ultimately lead. I only object that, as Mr. Schiller himself seems sometimes to say, there is not the smallest scintilla of logical justification for any assertion that a given sort of result will, as a matter of fact, either *always* or *never* come to pass; and consequently we cannot know that there *is* any truth concerning any given question; and this, I believe, agrees with the opinion of Monsieur Henri Poincaré,[34] except that he seems to insist upon the nonexistence of any absolute truth for *all* questions, which is simply to fall into the very same error on the opposite side. But practically, we know that questions do generally get settled in time, when they come to be scientifically investigated; and that is practically and pragmatically enough. Mr. Schiller's second definition is Captain Bunsby's that "the 'truth' of an assertion depends on its application,"[35] which seems to me the result of a weak analysis. His third definition is that pragmatism is the doctrine that "the meaning of a rule lies in its application,"[36] which would make the "meaning" consist in the energetic interpretant and would ignore the logical interpretant; another feeble analysis. His fourth definition is that pragmatism is the doctrine that "all meaning depends on purpose." I think there is much to be said in favor of this, which would, however, make pragmatists of many thinkers who do not consider themselves as belonging to our school of thought. Their affiliations with us are, however, undeniable. His fifth definition is that pragmatism is the doctrine that "all mental life is purposive." His sixth definition is that pragmatism is "a systematic protest against all ignoring of the purposiveness of actual knowing." Mr. Schiller seems habitually to use the word "actual" in some peculiar sense. His seventh definition is that pragmatism is "a conscious application to epistemology (or logic) of a teleological psychology, which implies, ultimately, a voluntaristic metaphysics." Supposing by "psychology" he means *not* the science so called, but a critical acceptance of a sifted common sense of mankind regarding mental phenomena, I might subscribe to this. I have myself called pragmatism "critical common-sensism"; but, of course, I did not mean this for a strict definition.[37]

Signor Giovanni Papini goes a step beyond Mr. Schiller in maintaining that pragmatism is indefinable.[38] But that seems to me to be a literary phrase. In the main, I much admire Papini's presentation of the subject.

There are certain questions commonly reckoned as metaphysical, and which certainly are so, if by metaphysics we mean ontology, which as soon as pragmatism is once sincerely accepted, cannot logically resist settlement. These are for example, What is reality? Are necessity and contingency real modes of being? Are the laws of nature real? Can they be assumed to be immutable or are they presumably results of evolution? Is there any real chance, or departure from real law? But on examination, if by metaphysics we mean the broadest positive truths of the psycho-physical universe,—positive in the sense of not being reducible to logical formulae,—then the very fact that these problems can be solved by a logical maxim is proof enough that they do not belong to metaphysics but to "epistemology,"—an atrocious translation of *Erkenntnislehre*. When we pass to consider the nature of Time, it seems that pragmatism is of aid, but does not of itself yield a solution. When we go on to the nature of Space, I boldly declare that Newton's view that it is a real entity is alone logically tenable; and that leaves such further questions as, Why should Space have three dimensions?, quite unanswerable for the present. This, however, is a purely speculative question without much human interest. (It would, of course, be absurd to say that tridimensionality is without practical consequences.) For those metaphysical questions that have such interest,—the question of a future life and especially that of One Incomprehensible but Personal God, not immanent in but creating the universe,—I, for one, heartily admit that a Humanism that does not pretend to be a science but only an instinct, like a bird's power of flight, but purified by meditation, is the most precious contribution that has been made to philosophy for ages.

[Variant 2]

If this definition were to be interpreted as the same words ought to be interpreted if they came from me, I should certainly say that the term "pragmatism" has a marked difference of meaning for him and for me.[39] But though I seldom am able to attach a very distinct signification to any statement by Professor James, least of all in philosophy, yet I have sufficiently studied the, to me, very difficult dialect of his thought to be satisfied that a minute analysis of a formal definition is not the right way to ascertain what he means. Without being able to make out exactly what he means by "pragmatism," I think there is the best of evidence, in the principal applications he makes of it, that it does not differ very widely from the signification I attach to the same word. Even where he deduces very different consequences from his pragmatism from those which I should draw from mine, it by no means follows that this is due to a divergence in our pragmatistic faith. I was bred in a scientific and particularly in a mathematical atmosphere. I insist upon starting from definite concepts, and on drawing up statements that strictly follow the rules of grammar and logic, making room, however, for familiar metaphors, and for such enormous generalizations as physicists, and still more, mathematicians are accustomed to make. I know very well that such a thing as an absolutely definite concept is beyond the power of the human mind; but I insist upon rendering the initial concepts as definite as they can be made. How Professor James, on the other hand, communes with himself, I cannot presume to say. I can only say that by processes I cannot comprehend he arrives at much the same practical conclusions that I should. Professor James's eloquence and his recognized eminence as a psychologist have caused the word "pragmatism" to be identified with such interpretations as have been put upon his doctrines; and the consequence has been that many thinkers whom I should reckon among pragmatists have appeared as opponents of pragmatism.

I shall endeavor, first, to give an idea of pragmatism as I understand it; and shall afterward give some very brief notices of the doctrines of other professed pragmatists.

I understand pragmatism to be a method of ascertaining the meanings, not of all ideas, but only of such as I term "intellectual concepts," that is to say, of those upon the structure of which arguments concerning objective fact may hinge. But an example will answer better than this baffling and not altogether accurate definition. Had the light of the wavelength that excites in our consciousness, as things actually are, the sensation of blue, had the property of exciting in us, in the same measure, the sensation of red instead of blue, and *vice versa*, however great a difference that might have made in our feelings, it could have made none in the force of any argument not relating to feeling. In this respect, the qualities of hard and soft strikingly contrast with those of red and blue; because while *blue* and *red* signify nothing but subjective feelings, *hard* (taking the term in its strict mineralogical sense of capable of resisting a knife-edge), with its contrary *soft*, express factual behavior of material surfaces. Pragmatism, or my variety of it, at any rate, has nothing to say to mere qualities of feeling, and so leaves me untrammelled to hold, as I do, that the reality of such a quality is just what it seems to be, without preventing others from holding (with Locke, if I remember rightly)[40] from pronouncing these so-called "secondary" qualities to be false appearances, or from straddling the question by simply saying that they are relative to human sense. But arguments may turn upon such a quality as hardness, for the reason that its meaning has structure. It implies that its forces of elasticity and cohesion do not break down under so small an external force as do those of soft bodies; so that it may, for example, be argued that solids expanded by heat will, other things being equal, be softer than the same bodies at a lower temperature, and that the skin of a body brought by cooling, and contraction, to the solid state, since it will cool more rapidly than the interior, and thus be stretched, will be harder than the inner parts. Accordingly, two such qualities, say, for example, hardness and specific heat, could not be interchanged, as we have supposed the feelings of blue and red to be interchanged, without considerable (in fact, without enormous) disturbance of the general condition of nature, as well as of a revolution in chemical physics, and other physical theories.

How is the truth of the doctrine of pragmatism to be proved? Two distinct bodies of thinkers declare against it. The one is the army of so-called absolutists, the Bradleys and the Taylors,[41] toward whose main proposition of a unitary entirety in the universe I decidedly lean, myself, while I think that the reputation of the present representatives of that school, though they have, of course, corrected some of the errors of their predecessors, is somewhat inflated, and that in real power of thought they are far below some /representatives/ of the so-called German romanticist school. On the other hand, pragmatism is opposed by some positivistic nominalists, Haeckel and Karl Pearson,[42] who rank, in my esteem, a good deal higher than do the present absolutists, as being, up to a certain point, sound and useful men of science; although I have not the same disposition to find truth in their philosophical positions that I have in the case of the absolutists. What of real decisive weight is to be said for the pragmatism that on two such opposite sides meets with denial and disdain? If I were content to bring against those two bodies of argument, counter-arguments, honest and free from fallacy, and a good deal stronger and more telling than they, I flatter myself that my readers would be well content and would see reason on the side of pragmatism. But I have a scruple that forbids it.

The great majority of those who interest themselves in "philosophy," as it is now called, "moral philosophy" as it used to be called, when physics and chemistry were reckoned as branches of philosophy, are (as I suppose, for I have no statistics to support the surmise) of two classes. The larger I take to consist of those who study philosophy in the hopes of finding therein support for religion, without perceiving how poor a religion it must be that rests on the feeble and cold support of metaphysics. To such, pragmatism cannot appeal, because it must honestly acknowledge the uncertainty of metaphysical doctrine, while religion calls for an entire belief of the whole soul. It cannot rest on metaphysics without an entire falsification of the security of metaphysical argument, to which pragmatism utterly refuses to lend itself. (I beg leave to say, by the way, that I am myself a miserably unworthy follower of Jesus, and that I am far from approving any religion that rests on mere gush.) The other and smaller of the two principal classes of students of philosophy is composed, as I imagine, of those who read ethics, "epistemology" (atrocious translation of *Erkenntnislehre*), and other branches of philosophy, not because they anticipate any extraordinary gain of moral or mental strength from their studies, but because they find the subtle swordplay of reason amazingly entertaining, as it certainly is, and because they deem it in every way an improving amusement, in which I concur. I imagine the number of those to be insignificant who, like myself, are so deeply interested in doing what in them lies toward rendering philosophy truly scientific that they are unwilling to take part in any controversies in the spirit of controversy (though I confess with shame that in one article I was, many years ago, provoked into far too much of this),[43] or to advance any arguments except such as would appeal to a sincere searcher for the truth.

Even of arguments for pragmatism of this cool and disinterested kind, and which seem to me to be conclusive, I know of two or three. They rest mostly upon the same considerations, yet are independent arguments. Unfortunately, they are one and all of a pretty intricate structure, as much so, for example, as is that of Euclid for his 47th proposition (the Pythagorean theorem), and what is worse, are decidedly "technical," that is to say, call for as exact thought as do the average of the major theorems of mathematics, which in some respects they considerably resemble. In addition to that inconvenience, the very briefest of them is intolerably long. It is needless to say that they are, one and all, utterly unfit for presentation in a literary journal; and for that reason, the writing of this letter has halted at this point for several months,[44] while I made experiments in this and that manner of continuing it. I have finally decided that the best way is not to attempt to present any considerable part of the argument itself, but simply to give an outline sketch of how I was myself brought to a conviction of the truth of pragmatism.

Before I came to man's estate, being greatly impressed with Kant's *Critic of the Pure Reason*, my father, who was an eminent mathematician, pointed out to me lacunae in Kant's reasoning which I should probably not otherwise have discovered. From Kant, I was led to an admiring study of Locke, Berkeley, and Hume, and to that of Aristotle's *Organon*, *Metaphysics*, and psychological treatises, and somewhat later derived the greatest advantage from a deeply pondering perusal of some of the works of medieval thinkers, St. Augustine, Abelard, and John of Salisbury, with related fragments from St. Thomas Aquinas, most especially from John of Duns, the Scot (Duns being the name of a then not unimportant place in East Lothian), and from William of Ockham. So far as a modern man of science can share the ideas of those medieval theologians, I ultimately came to approve the opinions of Duns, although I think he inclines too much toward nominalism. In my studies of Kant's great *Critic*, which I almost knew by heart, I was very much struck by the fact that, although, according to his own account of the matter, his whole philosophy rests upon his "functions of judgment," or logical divisions of propositions, and upon the relation of his "categories" to them, yet his examination of them is most hasty, superficial, trivial, and even trifling, while throughout his works, replete as they are with evidences of logical genius, there is manifest a most astounding ignorance of the traditional logic, even of the very *Summulae logicales*, the elementary school-book of the Plantagenet era. Now although a beastlike superficiality and lack of generalizing thought spreads like a pall over the writings of the scholastic masters of logic, yet the minute thoroughness with which they examined every problem that came within their ken renders it hard to conceive in this twentieth century how a really earnest student, goaded to the study of logic by the momentous importance that Kant attached to its details, could have reconciled himself to treating it in the debonair and *dégagé* fashion that he did. I was thus stimulated to an independent inquiry into the logical support of the fundamental concepts called categories.

The first question, and it was a question of supreme importance requiring not only utter abandonment of all bias, but also a most cautious yet vigorously active research, was whether or not the fundamental categories of thought really have that sort of dependence upon formal logic that Kant asserted. I became thoroughly convinced that such a relation really did and must exist. After a series of inquiries, I came to see that Kant ought not to have confined himself to divisions of propositions, or "judgments," as the Germans confuse the subject by calling them, but ought to have taken account of all elementary and significant differences of form among signs of all sorts, and that, above all, he ought not to have left out of account fundamental forms of reasonings. At last, after the hardest two years' mental work that I have ever done in my life, I found myself with but a single assured result of any positive importance. This was that there are but three elementary forms of predication or signification, which as I originally named them (but with bracketed additions now made to render the terms more intelligible) were *Qualities* [of feeling], [dyadic] *Relations, and* [predications of] *Representations*. It must have been in 1866 that Professor De Morgan honored the unknown beginner in philosophy that I then was (for I had not earnestly studied it for more than ten years, which is a short apprenticeship in this most difficult of subjects) by sending me a copy of his memoir "On the Logic of

Relations, etc."[45] I at once fell to upon it; and before many weeks had come to see in it, as De Morgan had already seen, a brilliant and astonishing illumination of every corner and every vista of logic. Let me pause to say that no decent semblance of justice has ever been done to De Morgan, owing to his not having brought anything to its final shape. Even his personal students, reverent as they perforce were, never sufficiently understood that his was the work of an exploring expedition, which every day comes upon new forms for the study of which leisure is, at the moment, lacking, because additional novelties are coming in and requiring note. He stood indeed like Aladdin (or whoever it was), gazing upon the overwhelming riches of Ali Baba's cave, scarce capable of making a rough inventory of them.[46] But what De Morgan, with his strictly mathematical and indisputable method, actually accomplished in the way of examination of all the strange forms with which he had enriched the science of logic was not slight and was performed in a truly scientific spirit not unanimated by true genius. It was quite twenty-five years before my studies of it all reached what may be called a near approach toward a provisionally final result (absolute finality never being presumable in any universal science); but a short time sufficed to furnish me with mathematical demonstration that indecomposable predicates are of three classes; first, those which, like neuter verbs, apply but to a single subject; secondly, those which like simple transitive verbs have two subjects each, called in the traditional nomenclature of grammar (generally less philosophical than that of logic) the "subject nominative" and the "object accusative," although the perfect equivalence of meaning between "A affects B" and "B is affected by A" plainly shows that the two things they denote are equally referred to in the assertion; and thirdly, those predicates which have three such subjects, or correlates. These last (though the purely formal, mathematical method of De Morgan does not, as far as I see, warrant this) never express mere brute fact, but always some relation of an intellectual nature, being either constituted by action of a mental kind or implying some general law. Now law is distinguished from brute fact, either, as the nominalists say, by being a product of the human mind, or, as the realists say, by being a real intellectual ingredient of the universe. That it is true that triadic predicates are uniformly of this intellectual sort could not be made to appear in the space at my disposal. I must confine myself to two examples. If A gives B to C, he performs, not a mechanical, but a legal act; now human law is certainly a creation of the mind. If A fastens B to C, either what he does to B is unconnected with the fact that B remains in contact with C, in which case the fact is a compound one, and does not fall within my assertion, or else what he does is the *cause* of B's adhesion to C; now the action of a cause is essentially a case of the operation of a law, and implies a law. That no indecomposable predicate can have four or more subjects is easily proved mathematically. I regret that the clumsiness of ordinary language prevents my giving any idea of how it is proved. No doubt, it could be expressed; but few would have the patience to read it,—I among the last. The number of triads required to compose a higher predicate is usually very considerable.

When we inquire precisely how many they are, certain important difficulties arise, in which Kempe and Royce have taken one side and I the other, which, as they have not yet been cleared up, I shall not go into. I wish particularly to say, however, that the last proposition but one, that triadic predicates always have an intellectual basis, cannot be proved by merely formal logic, and rests, for the present, upon inductive evidence, which is always liable to be defective in generalization. For that reason I prefer to content myself with terming such predicates, which certainly express something more than mere physical force or brutal making, *triadic*, meaning that they are intellectual (as the great majority of them certainly are), or else something like it. A suspicion that not all triadic predicates are intellectual [may arise]. There are certain physical phenomena which certainly cannot be explained by any supposed mechanical forces. Those of them that are understood are explained by the doctrine of chances. The viscosity of gases is an example. Since the molecules of gases of which there is every reason to think that there are trillions (i.e., millions of millions or millions) in a tumblerful, are supposed to move rectilinearly and indiscriminately in all directions, it is practically certain that they will pass one way and the other between two layers of gas having different average velocities, thus tending to equalize these mean velocities; and the laws of the phenomenon deducible from the hypothesis accord with observations. But there are other phenomena neither explicable by force nor, so far as appears, by the doctrine of chances. Thus, elaterists, or students of elasticity, seem to have come to the conclusion that the elastic properties of crystals cannot be accounted for by any mere attractions and repulsions between pairs of free particles. It naturally suggests itself that there is some elementary inanimate action that involves more than pairs, contrary to all our notions of dynamics. But the subject is still too obscure to render this a very formidable objection as yet. Another and more familiar phenomenon is the fact that some vines insist upon twisting to the right and others to the left. I believe some dynamical explanation of this has been proposed. But I cannot help doubting it, because it is impossible to state the difference between a right-handed and a left-handed screw without mention of four places on each. A very similar phenomenon in the mineral kingdom (though always originating, so far as is known, in living organisms, unless one, like Pasteur, picks out the right-handed and left-handed crystals one by one under a microscope)[47] is that of the unsymmetrical carbon atom. A carbon atom has four bonds, or links, by which other atoms can be connected with it. If it has distinguishable atoms at all four bonds, the compound will generally turn the plane of polarized light passing through it either to the right or to the left, and there are always two varieties of the compound which differ not at all in their ordinary physical properties nor in their reactions with ordinary chemical bodies, but which turn the plane of polarization by exactly equal amounts in opposite directions, and behave altogether differently toward other bodies containing unsymmetrical carbon atoms. The formation in equal amounts of the right-handed and left-handed varieties is well accounted for by chance. Their separation is said to be due to organisms that feed on one and not on the other; and this must be explained by their own substance being of a right-handed or left-handed composition. How this is to be accounted for, unless by some chance in the course of the evolution of their race, I cannot guess. On the whole, I suppose we must provisionally add chance to intelligence as one of the possible sources of triads, though how that chance can operate I am unable to guess. If we might trust to human instinct, which we must ultimately trust in all our reasonings, just as a bird trusts to its wings without understanding the principles of aerodynamics according to which it flies, and which show why its wings may be trusted, we might venture to say that there must be an intelligence behind that chance; but restrained as we are to scientific procedure, we must say no more than that we do not know how there come to be those divergencies of triadic phenomena.

A predicate may be described as a blank form of proposition from which when each blank has been filled with a proper name, a proposition, or assertion, however nonsensical, will result. Only, since the proposition will be different when two of the proper names are interchanged, it is proper to distinguish the blanks from one another, as for example by putting either $*$, $\dagger$, $\ddagger$, etc., into each. This view of the matter renders it plain that a triadic predicate involves three dyadic predicates and three monadic predicates; while a dyadic predicate involves two monadic predicates. Thus, "$*$____ gives $\dagger$____ to $\ddagger$____" involves the possibility of "$*$____ gives $\dagger$____ to Z," of "$*$____ gives Y to $\ddagger$____," and of "X gives $\dagger$____ to $\ddagger$____," which last is precisely equivalent to "$\ddagger$____ gift-wise from X receives $\dagger$____."

To assert a predicate of certain subjects (taking these all in the sense of forms of words) means,—intends,—only to create a belief that the real things denoted by those subjects possess the real character or relation signified by that predicate. The word "real," *pace* the metaphysicians, whose phrases are sometimes empty, means, and can mean, nothing more nor less. Consequently, to the three forms of predicates there must correspond three conceptions of different categories of characters: namely, of a character which attaches to its subject regardless of anything else such as that of being hard, massive, or persistent; of a character which belongs to a thing relatively to a second regardless of any third, such as an act of making an effort against a resistance; and of a character which belongs to a thing as determining a relation between two others, such as that of being transparent or opaque or of coloring what is seen through it. Moreover, turning from the three kinds of predicates to their subjects, since by the "mode of being" of anything can be meant only the kinds of characters which it has, or is susceptible of taking, corresponding to the three kinds of characters, there must be three categories of things: first, those which are such as they are regardless of anything else, like the living consciousness of a given kind of feeling, say of red; secondly, those which are such as they are by virtue of their relation to other things, regardless of any third things, which is the case with the existence of all bodies, whose reality consists in their acting on each other, in pairs; thirdly, those which are such as they are by virtue of bringing two others into relation, as signs of all sorts are such only so far as they bring their significations to bear upon the objects to which they are applied.

I have followed out this trichotomy into many other ramifications, and have uniformly found it to be a most useful polestar in my explorations into the different branches of philosophy. There is no fallacy in it; for it asserts nothing, but only offers suggestions. It has preserved me, in innumerable cases, from one-sided opinions. It has had me search in directions that it has indicated for points of view that I should otherwise have overlooked. I do not claim that it is a novelty;—or rather, to express myself more frankly, I do not confess that it is a novelty. For it is my conviction that any philosophical idea that in this age of the world is altogether novel is subject to a *prima facie* presumption of falsity. My trichotomy is plainly of the family stock of Hegel's three stages of thought,—an idea that goes back to Kant, and I know not how much further. But the arbitrariness of Hegel's procedure, utterly unavoidable at the time he lived,—and presumably, in less degree, unavoidable now, or at any future date,—is in great measure avoided by my taking care never to miss the solid support of mathematically exact formal logic beneath my feet. I am thus, for example, rescued from the one-sidedness of allowing one member of my trichotomy to supersede the other two. On the contrary, I am obliged to acknowledge that indecomposable predicates of only one subject, and others of only two, are just as true as those of three; just as minerals and vegetables are as real as animals, though they may perhaps be in different stages of existence. I may say that my much too insufficient study of Hegel (insufficient because I found it unprofitable) left me with the impression that he was a man unqualified for the supremely difficult task of giving an entirely candid account of his reflections upon philosophy, and that the two works of his that I had examined, his *Phänomenologie* and his *Logik*, while overgrown with brambles of self-deception, yet beneath these were replete with the most profound analyses, which it was yet next to impossible to get at so as to understand them, much more to judge of them, until one had by oneself substantially accomplished the same analyses. With this remark, I close the introductory chapter of my account of how I was led to the pragmatistic faith.

I have already mentioned that after more than a dozen years' devotion to the study of philosophy, I was unable to convince myself what, if indeed anything at all, was meant by some of the formulas upon which metaphysicians have the most insisted. I never was more of a nominalist than the incomparable Duns, and am now still less so; yet I cannot but acknowledge that Ockham, Leibniz, and Berkeley (I omit the perverse Hobbes) have laid down some of the soundest maxims of thought (such as Ockham's razor), and among these I would include this, that thoughts ought to be regarded as signs. Let anybody call to mind some recent earnest self-deliberation, and I think he will acknowledge that it took a dialogic form, every reasoning appealing to the self of the near following moment of time for assent and confirmation. But I do not believe you readers will hesitate to admit that concepts are signs.

Now a sign is something which functions triadically. A proposition which may be said to have been universally admitted for over seven hundred years, since John of Salisbury in the third quarter of the twelfth century mentions it as a thing "*quod fere in omnium ore celebre est,*"[48] is that any common noun, whether substantive or adjective, on the one hand signifies something and on the other hand names something else. All modern logicians have made much of this distinction; and many of them have pointed out that the term of its very essence signifies what it does, while that which it is intended to name must be ascertained not from the term itself but by observation of the context or other attendant circumstances of its utterance. But we need not restrict the proposition to nouns. It may be generalized, so as to be true of any sign whatsoever. For every sign, in functioning as such, produces a mental effect. How shall we name the entire mental effect which a sign by itself is calculated, in its proper significative function, to produce? The word *signification* is somewhat too narrow, since, as examples will soon show, this mental effect may be of the nature of an emotion or of that of an effort. No existing word is sufficiently appropriate. Permit me to call this total proper effect of the sign taken by itself the *interpretant* of the sign. But merely producing a mental effect is not sufficient to constitute an object a sign; for a thunder-clap or avalanche may do that without conveying any meaning at all. In order that a thing may be a true sign, its proper significate mental effect must be *conveyed* from another object which the sign is concerned in indicating and which is by this conveyance the ultimate cause of the mental effect. In order to be the cause of an effect,—or *efficient cause*, as the old phrase was,—it must either be an existent thing or an actual event. Now such things are only known by observation. It cannot be itself any part of the mental effect, and therefore can only be known by collateral observation of the context or circumstances of utterance, or putting forth, of the sign. But the sign may describe the kind of observation that is appropriate and even indicate how the right object is to be recognized. The meaning of the sign is not conveyed until not merely the interpretant but also this object is recognized. But although the full realization of the meaning requires the actual observation, direct or indirect, of the object, yet a close approach to this may be made by imagining the observation. If the sign is not a *true*, but only a *fictitious* sign, it is the mere semblance of a sign. If, however, it be so far true as to profess to be in certain respects fictitious, the conditions of a true sign hold, though somewhat modified.

From this point on the argument calls for more and more active attention and criticism on the part of a mind that would follow it; for no argument is really comprehended unless every step of it has been criticized. Should it have occurred to the reader before reaching this point that there has been a certain resemblance to mathematics in the argument, he will find this resemblance diminished in one respect as it draws to a close. For now subdivision upon subdivision has to be drawn (most of which shall here pass unnoticed) and as the objects of thought thus become specialized, not only will they depart from mathematical abstractions, but reasoning about them will appeal more to experience of phenomena presented in signs and in mental life. At the same time, the reasoning will grow more like that of difficult mathematics in calling for perfect distinctness and exactitude of thought. It also resembles mathematics more than it does the usual philosophical discourse, in that it can be illustrated by concrete examples all along, never soaring high above *terra firma*.

It is easy to see that there are three kinds of interpretants of signs. Our categories suggest this; and we have only to run over in our minds a sufficient variety of remembered signs, with a slight examination of each, to gain ample confirmation of the division. Namely, the interpretant may be a feeling. Thus, an air for a guitar, if considered as meant to convey the genuine or feigned musical emotions of its composer, can only fulfill this function by exciting responsive feelings in the listener. But in the second place, the interpretant may be an effort. Thus, when a drill-officer gives a company of infantry the word of command, "Ground arms!", if this is really to act as a sign and not in a purely "physiological" way (I use this inaccurate distinction, rather than waste time in explanations), there must first be, as in all action of signs, a feeling-interpretant,—a sense of apprehending the meaning,—which in its turn at once stimulates the soldiers to the slight effort required to perform the motion. This effect caused by the sign in its significative capacity is, by the definition, an interpretant of it. In the third place, our categories lead us to credit ourselves, in expectation, with a kind of interpretant of a triadic character, while our acquaintance with signs enters upon the debit side of the account a kind of interpretant not included in either of the enumerated two, but which is, we know, the interpretant *par excellence*, I mean of course the intellectual apprehension of the meaning of a sign. We cannot but be tempted to this debit entry as balancing the credit entry, that is to say, at once, that is the triadic interpretant that the categories authorize us to look for. But we now tread so close upon the essence of pragmatism that we must walk warily lest we assume some position not authorized by full proof; and we cannot identify the two until we have more closely scrutinized the characters of each.

It is evident that a definition, even if it be imperfect owing to vagueness, is an intellectual interpretant of the term it defines. But it is equally evident that it cannot be the *ultimate* intellectual interpretant, inasmuch as it is itself a sign, and a sign of the kind that has itself an intellectual interpretant, which is thereby an intellectual interpretant of the term defined. This consideration compels us to seek elsewhere than among signs, or among concepts, since they are all signs, for ultimate intellectual interpretants. This same consideration cuts off from searching among desires, expectations, etc., for ultimate intellectual interpretants, since such intellectual character as desires, etc., possess is due solely to their referring to concepts. At the same time, the ultimate intellectual interpretants must be some kind of mental effects of the signs they interpret. Now after an examination of all varieties of mental phenomena, the only ones I have been able to find that possess the requisite generality to interpret concepts and which fulfill the other conditions are habits.[49]

This is a good, sound argument; but, as it stands, it has hardly sufficient solidity to support the weight of so momentous a conclusion as that of the doctrine of pragmatism. Not that the induction is too loose; for the enumeration of mental phenomena was sufficiently careful to give it rather the character of an argument from enumeration than that of what is properly called an induction; but because it may be necessary, in order to render the conclusion true, to take the term "habit" in a much wider sense than that in which it is requisite that it should be understood in order that our conclusion should imply the truth of pragmatism. Just this turns out to be the truth of the matter. That it is so will be illustrated by my sole reply to a possible objection to our conclusion, which, though I am not sure that either the author of that important work *The World and the Individual*[50] or anybody else would, as a fact, be disposed to consider it to be an objection, yet I think I had better take occasion to answer. The supposed objection is that, besides habits, another class of mental phenomena of a general nature is found in *purposes*. My reply is that while I hold all logical, or intellectual, interpretants to be habits, I by no means say that all habits are such interpretants. It is only *self-controlled* habits that are so, and not all of them, either. Now a purpose is only the special character (and what is, strictly speaking, special, as contradistinguished from individual, is essentially general) of this or that self-controlled habit. Thus, if a man has a general purpose to render the decorations of a house he is building beautiful, without yet having determined more precisely what they shall be, the normal way in which the purpose was developed, of which all other ways are probably inessential variations, was that he actually made decorations in his inner world, and on attention to the results, in some cases experienced feelings which stimulated him to endeavors to reproduce them, while in other cases the feelings consequent upon contemplation of the results excited efforts to avoid or modify them, and by these exercises a habit was produced, which would, we know, affect not only his actions in the world of imagination, but also his actions in the world of experience; and this habit being self-controlled, and therefore recognized, his conception of its character joined to his self-recognition, or adoption, of it, constitute what we call his *purpose*. It is to be noted that in calling a habit "self-controlled," I do not mean that it is in the power of the man who has it to cast it off,—to cease, in the example just given, to try to make his decorations beautiful; for we well know that he has no such power,—but what I mean is that it has been developed under the process just described in which critical feelings as to the results of inner or outer exercises stimulate to strong endeavors to repeat or to modify those effects. I may mention that I do not recognize pleasure and pain as specific feelings but only as being whatever feelings may stimulate efforts, in the one case to reproduce or continue them, or, as we say, "attractive" feelings, and in the other case to annul and avoid them, or, as we say, "repulsive" feelings.

The only way of attaining any satisfactory general knowledge of experiential truth is by the inductive testing of theories. This is, therefore, the only way to ascertain the meaning of a current concept; and there are few fields of inquiry to which that method adapts itself so readily. Remembering that a concept has meaning only as it is predicated, one need only create in the imagination as great a variety of examples of objects to which would be applicable the supposed meaning as may seem desirable, and then try whether or not the concept would be applicable to each of them. One thus pursues a strict experimental method. It may turn out that the meaning lies in a feeling, or in some single thing or event. But in so far as either of these results are found, it will be shown thereby that the concept is not an intellectual one, though it may have other ingredients which are intellectual. In so far as it has an intellectual character, the experimental investigation will show that to believe the concept in question is applicable to anything is to be prepared under certain circumstances, and when actuated by given motives, to act in a certain way. This is quite clearly the case with all mathematical concepts. To say that a collection consists of seventeen single members involves, if thought out to its ultimate meaning, the act of counting in the imagination, and, of course, the action must be generalized into a habit connected with the predication of seventeen. A geometrical idea supposes one goes through the operation of making the figure. In these cases, and one will find in Berkeley's *Theory of Vision* more particular proofs, ideas of space all involve effort. Now when those ideas are general, the effort must be generalized; and the generalization of effort is habit. The same thing is more easily seen to be true of physical concepts, since the doctrine of the French psychologists of the early nineteenth century that the idea of force has at its foundation that of effort, is abundantly confirmed by analyses more exact than they were equal to making. As for psychical concepts, the same truth is much more easily ascertained and confirmed.

But while it is to me indubitable, and I think to anyone who may sufficiently think the matter out in concrete inner experiments, that every general predicate may have the intellectual part of its meaning analyzed into habits of conduct on the part of him who predicates it, yet I do not recommend carrying the analysis so far, in other than exceptional cases. My original exposition of pragmatism, which those who seek to depreciate it limit to one article in the *Popular Science Monthly* of January 1878, although I have, whenever such statements were brought to my attention, protested to each one of them personally that the argument is incomplete and insufficient without the article of November 1877 in the same journal,—but such persons are, for the most part, incapable of any exact thought,—in this original exposition, I laid down, in the very first place, the doctrine of Common Sense; namely, that there are some propositions that a man, as a fact, does not doubt; and what he does not doubt, he can, at most, make but a futile pretense to criticize. The test of doubt and belief is conduct. No sane man doubts that fire would burn his fingers; for if he did he would put his hand in the flame, in order to satisfy his doubt. There are some beliefs, almost all of which relate to the ordinary conduct of life, such as that ordinary fire burns the flesh, /which,/ while pretty vague, are beyond the reach of any man's doubt. When the analysis of the meaning of a concept has carried us to such a "practical" matter, it is idle to go further in analyzing it into a habit of conduct. But along with such "instinctive" beliefs, as we may call them, because, however they came about, they resemble the instincts of the lower animals, there are a good many formulae, almost universally accepted, which mean nothing, or, at any rate, nothing indubitable. For example, one often hears it said, "I could no more doubt that than I doubt of my own existence." But, after all, what does a man mean when he says that he exists? By what concrete experiments in the imagination will he exemplify his meaning? I will not stop to discuss this particular proposition. I will only say that if we are to admit that some propositions are beyond our powers of doubt, we must not admit any specified proposition to be of this nature without severe criticism; nor must any man assume with no better reason than because he cannot doubt it, that another man cannot do so. These remarks give some idea of what is meant by critical common sense, without which the doctrine of pragmatism amounts to very little. But perhaps a little illustration may aid the comprehension of what I am saying. When one seeks to know what is meant by a physical force, and finds that it is a real component acceleration of defined amount and direction that would exist whatever were the original velocity, it is possible to press the question further and inquire what the meaning of acceleration is; and the answer to this must show that it is a habit of the person who predicates an acceleration, supposing him to use the term as others do. For ordinary purposes, however, nothing is gained by carrying the analysis so far; because these ordinary commonsense concepts of everyday life, having guided the conduct of men ever since the race was developed, are by far more trustworthy than the exacter concepts of science; so that when great exactitude is not required they are the best terms of definition.

29

A Neglected Argument for the Reality of God

MS 841 and P 1166: The Hibbert Journal 7 *(October 1908):90–112.*
*[Published in CP 6.452–91. In April 1908, Peirce was invited by his
mathematician friend Cassius J. Keyser to contribute an article to the*
Hibbert Journal. *Peirce accepted and spent the next three months diligently writing and rewriting his celebrated paper. The final version was
sent in toward the end of June 1908.] This is one of Peirce's most enigmatic writings. He outlines an "argument" that is forceful in bringing anyone
who practices musement to a belief in the reality of God, a belief that is
exhibited in changed conduct; but it turns out that this "argument" is not
a matter of reasoning at all. It is more like an instinctive response to the
very idea of God. In his addendum, Peirce calls this the "Humble Argument." The Neglected Argument, it seems, is an "argumentation" to demonstrate how the reality of God can be proved from the effectiveness of the
Humble Argument. The neglect is on the part of theologians, who have
taken surprisingly little interest in why the mere contemplation of the idea
of God leads to belief. A key question is why our "instinct" for guessing—
Galileo's il lume naturale—is so successful. In section IV, Peirce gives a
good account of the three stages of scientific inquiry, but its application to
the preceding argument(s) is left mostly to the reader. Whether this paper
is an elaboration of or an offense against pragmaticism is an unsettled
question.*

I

The word "God," so "capitalized" (as we Americans say), is *the* definable
proper name, signifying *Ens necessarium:* in my belief Really creator of all
three Universes of Experience.

Some words shall herein be capitalized when used, not as vernacular, but
as terms defined. Thus, an "idea" is the substance of an actual unitary thought
or fancy; but "Idea,"—nearer Plato's ideas of ἰδέα,—denotes anything whose
Being consists in its mere capacity for getting fully represented, regardless of
any person's faculty or impotence to represent it.

"Real" is a word invented in the thirteenth century to signify having Properties, i.e. characters sufficing to identify their subject, and possessing these
whether they be anywise attributed to it by any single man or group of men,
or not. Thus, the substance of a dream is not Real, since it was such as it was,

merely in that a dreamer so dreamed it; but the fact of the dream is Real, if it was dreamed; since if so, its date, the name of the dreamer, etc., make up a set of circumstances sufficient to distinguish it from all other events; and these belong to it, i.e., would be true if predicated of it, whether *A, B,* or *C* Actually ascertains them, or not. The "Actual" is that which is met with in the past, present, or future.

An "Experience" is a brutally produced conscious effect that contributes to a habit, self-controlled, yet so satisfying, on deliberation, as to be destructible by no positive exercise of internal vigor. I use the word "self-controlled" for "controlled by the thinker's self," and not for "uncontrolled" except in its own, i.e., automatic, self-development, as Professor J. M. Baldwin uses the word.[1] Take for illustration the sensation undergone by a child that puts its forefinger into a flame with the acquisition of a habit of keeping all its members out of all flames. A compulsion is "Brute" whose immediate efficacy nowise consists in conformity to rule or reason.

Of the three Universes of Experience familiar to us all, the first comprises all mere Ideas, those airy nothings to which the mind of poet, pure mathematician, or another *might* give local habitation and a name within that mind.[2] Their very airy-nothingness, the fact that their Being consists in mere capability of getting thought, not in anybody's Actually thinking them, saves their Reality. The second Universe is that of the Brute Actuality of things and facts. I am confident that their Being consists in reactions against Brute forces, notwithstanding objections redoubtable until they are closely and fairly examined. The third Universe comprises everything whose Being consists in active power to establish connections between different objects, especially between objects in different Universes. Such is everything which is essentially a Sign,—not the mere body of the Sign, which is not essentially such, but, so to speak, the Sign's Soul, which has its Being in its power of serving as intermediary between its Object and a Mind. Such, too, is a living consciousness, and such the life, the power of growth of a plant. Such is a living institution,—a daily newspaper, a great fortune, a social "movement."

An "Argument" is any process of thought reasonably tending to produce a definite belief. An "Argumentation" is an Argument proceeding upon definitely formulated premises.

If God Really be, and be benign, then, in view of the generally conceded truth that religion, were it but proved, would be a good outweighing all others, we should naturally expect that there would be some Argument for His Reality that should be obvious to all minds, high and low alike, that should earnestly strive to find the truth of the matter, and further that this Argument should present its conclusion, not as a proposition of metaphysical theology, but in a form directly applicable to the conduct of life, and full of nutrition for man's highest growth. What I shall refer to as the N.A.,—the Neglected Argument,—seems to me best to fulfill this condition, and I should not wonder if the majority of those whose own reflections have harvested belief in God must bless the radiance of the N.A. for that wealth. Its persuasiveness is no less than extraordinary; while it is unknown to nobody. Nevertheless, of all those theologians (within my little range of reading) who, with commendable assiduity, scrape together all the sound reasons they can find or concoct to prove the first proposition of theology, few mention this one, and they most briefly. They probably share those current notions of logic which recognize no other Arguments than Argumentations.

There is a certain agreeable occupation of mind which, from its having no distinctive name, I infer is not as commonly practiced as it deserves to be; for, indulged in moderately,—say through some five to six percent of one's waking time, perhaps during a stroll,—is refreshing enough more than to repay the expenditure. Because it involves no purpose save that of casting aside all serious purpose, I have sometimes been half-inclined to call it *rêverie*, with some qualification; but for a frame of mind so antipodal to vacancy and dreaminess, such a designation would be too excruciating a misfit. In fact, it is Pure Play. Now, Play, we all know, is a lively exercise of one's powers. Pure Play has no rules, except this very law of liberty. It bloweth where it listeth.[3] It has no purpose, unless recreation. The particular occupation I mean,—a *petite bouchée* with the Universes,—may take either the form of esthetic contemplation, or that of distant castle-building (whether in Spain or within one's own moral training), or that of considering some wonder in one of the Universes or some connection between two of the three, with speculation concerning its cause. It is this last kind,—I will call it "Musement" on the whole,—that I particularly recommend, because it will in time flower into the N.A. One who sits down with the purpose of becoming convinced of the truth of religion is plainly not inquiring in scientific singleness of heart, and must always suspect himself of reasoning unfairly. So, he can never attain the entirety even of a physicist's belief in electrons, although this is avowedly but provisional. But let religious meditation be allowed to grow up spontaneously out of Pure Play without any breach of continuity; and the Muser will retain the perfect candor proper to Musement.

If one who had determined to make trial of Musement as a favorite recreation were to ask me for advice, I should reply as follows: The dawn and the gloaming most invite one to Musement; but I have found no watch of the nychthemeron that has not its own advantages for the pursuit. It begins passively enough with drinking in the impression of some nook in one of the three Universes. But impression soon passes into attentive observation, observation into musing, musing into a lively give-and-take of communion between self and self. If one's observations and reflections are allowed to specialize themselves too much, the Play will be converted into scientific study; and that cannot be pursued in odd half-hours.

I should add: adhere to the one ordinance of Play, the law of liberty. I can testify that the last half-century, at least, has never lacked tribes of Sir Oracles, colporting brocards to bar off one or another roadway of inquiry; and a Rabelais would be needed to bring out all the fun that has been packed in their airs of infallibility. Auguste Comte, notwithstanding his having apparently produced some unquestionably genuine thinking, was long the chief of such a band. The vogue of each particular maxim of theirs was necessarily brief. For what distinction can be gained by repeating saws heard from all mouths? No bygone fashion seems more grotesque than a *panache* of obsolete wisdom. I remember the days when a pronouncement all the rage was that no science must borrow the methods of another: the geologist must not use a microscope, nor the astronomer a spectroscope. Optics must not meddle with electricity, nor logic with algebra. But twenty years later, if you aspired to pass for a commanding intellect, you would have to pull a long face, and declare that "It is not the business of science to search for origins." This maxim was a masterpiece, since no timid soul, in dread of being thought naïve, would dare inquire what "origins" were, albeit the secret confessor within his breast compelled the awful self-acknowledgment of his having no idea into what else than "origins" of phenomena (in some sense of that indefinite word) man can inquire. That human reason can comprehend some causes is past denial; and once we are forced to recognize a given element in experience, it is reasonable to await positive evidence before we complicate our acknowledgment with qualifications. Otherwise, why venture beyond direct observation? Illustrations of this principle abound in physical science. Since, then, it is certain that man is able to understand the laws and the causes of some phenomena, it is reasonable to assume, in regard to any given problem, that it would get rightly solved by man, if a sufficiency of time and attention were devoted to it. Moreover, those problems that at first blush appear utterly insoluble receive, in that very circumstance,—as Edgar Poe remarked in his "The Murders in the Rue Morgue,"—their smoothly-fitting keys.[4] This particularly adapts them to the Play of Musement.

Forty or fifty minutes of vigorous and unslackened analytic thought bestowed upon one of them usually suffices to educe from it all there is to educe, its general solution. There is no kind of reasoning that I should wish to discourage in Musement; and I should lament to find anybody confining it to a method of such moderate fertility as logical analysis. Only, the Player should bear in mind that the higher weapons in the arsenal of thought are not play-things, but edge-tools. In any mere Play they can be used by way of exercise alone; while logical analysis can be put to its full efficiency in Musement. So, continuing the counsels that had been asked of me, I should say, "Enter your skiff of Musement, push off into the lake of thought, and leave the breath of heaven to swell your sail.[5] With your eyes open, awake to what is about or within you, and open conversation with yourself; for such is all meditation." It is, however, not a conversation in words alone, but is illustrated, like a lecture, with diagrams and with experiments.

Different people have such wonderfully different ways of thinking that it would be far beyond my competence to say what courses Musements might not take; but a brain endowed with automatic control,—as man's indirectly is,—is so naturally and rightly interested in its own faculties that some psychological and semi-psychological questions would doubtless get touched; such, in the latter class, as this: Darwinians, with truly surprising ingenuity, have concocted, and with still more astonishing confidence have accepted as proved, one explanation for the diverse and delicate beauties of flowers, another for those of butterflies, and so on; but why is all nature,—the forms of trees, the compositions of sunsets,—suffused with such beauties throughout,—and not nature only, but the other two Universes as well? Among more purely psychological questions, the nature of pleasure and pain will be likely to attract attention. Are they mere qualities of feeling, or are they rather motor instincts attracting us to some feelings and repelling others? Have pleasure and pain the same sort of constitution, or are they contrasted in this respect, pleasure arising upon the formation or strengthening of an association by resemblance, and pain upon the weakening or disruption of such a habit or conception?

Psychological speculations will naturally lead on to musings upon metaphysical problems proper,—good exercise for a mind with a turn for exact thought. It is here that one finds those questions that at first seem to offer no handle for reason's clutch, but which readily yield to logical analysis. But problems of metaphysics will inevitably present themselves that logical analysis will not suffice to solve. Some of the best will be motived by a desire to comprehend universe-wide aggregates of unformulated but partly experienced phenomena. I would suggest that the Muser be not too impatient to analyze these, lest some significant ingredient be lost in the process; but that he begin by pondering them from every point of view, until he seems to read some truth beneath the phenomena.

At this point, a trained mind will demand that an examination be made of the truth of the interpretation; and the first step in such examination must be a logical analysis of the theory. But strict examination would be a task a little too serious for the Musement of hour-fractions, and if it is postponed, there will be ample remuneration even in the suggestions that there is not time to examine; especially, since a few of them will appeal to reason as all but certain.

Let the Muser, for example, after well appreciating, in its breadth and depth, the unspeakable variety of each Universe, turn to those phenomena that are of the nature of homogeneities of connectedness in each; and what a spectacle will unroll itself! As a mere hint of them I may point out that every small part of space, however remote, is bounded by just such neighboring parts as every other, without a single exception throughout immensity. The matter of Nature is of the same elementary kinds in every star, and (except for variations of circumstance) what is more wonderful still, throughout the whole visible universe, about the same proportions of the different chemical elements prevail. Though the mere catalogue of known carbon-compounds alone would fill an unwieldy volume, and perhaps, if the truth were known, the number of amino-acids alone is greater yet, it is unlikely that there are in all more than about 600 elements, of which 500 dart through space too swiftly to be held down by the earth's gravitation, coronium being the slow-est-moving of these.[6] This small number bespeaks comparative simplicity of structure. Yet no mathematician but will confess the present hopelessness of attempting to comprehend the constitution of the hydrogen-atom, the simplest of the elements that can be held to earth.

From speculations on the homogeneities of each Universe, the Muser will naturally pass to the consideration of homogeneities and connections between two different Universes, or all three. Especially, in them all we find one type of occurrence, that of growth, itself consisting in the homogeneities of small parts. This is evident in the growth of motion into displacement, and the growth of force into motion. In growth, too, we find that the three Universes conspire; and a universal feature of it is provision for later stages in earlier ones. This is a specimen of certain lines of reflection which will inevitably suggest the hypothesis of God's Reality. It is not that such phenomena might not be capable of being accounted for, in one sense, by the action of chance with the smallest conceivable dose of a higher element; for if by God be meant the *Ens necessarium*, that very hypothesis requires that such should be the case. But the point is that that sort of explanation leaves a mental explanation just as needful as before. Tell me, upon sufficient authority, that all cerebration depends upon movements of neurites that strictly obey certain physical laws, and that thus all expressions of thought, both external and internal, receive a physical explanation, and I shall be ready to believe you. But if you go on to say that this explodes the theory that my neighbor and myself are governed by reason, and are thinking beings, I must frankly say that it will not give me a high opinion of your intelligence. But however that may be, in the Pure Play of Musement the idea of God's Reality will be sure sooner or later to be found an attractive fancy, which the Muser will develop in various ways. The more he ponders it, the more it will find response in every part of his mind, for its beauty, for its supplying an ideal of life, and for its thoroughly satisfactory explanation of his whole threefold environment.

II

The hypothesis of God is a peculiar one, in that it supposes an infinitely incomprehensible object, although every hypothesis, as such, supposes its object to be truly conceived in the hypothesis. This leaves the hypothesis but one way of understanding itself; namely, as vague but as true so far as it is definite, and as continually tending to define itself more and more, and without limit. The hypothesis, being thus itself inevitably subject to the law of growth, appears in its vagueness to represent God as so, albeit this is directly contradicted in the hypothesis from its very first phase. But this apparent attribution of growth to God, since it is ineradicable from the hypothesis, cannot, according to the hypothesis, be flatly false. Its implications concerning the Universes will be maintained in the hypothesis, while its implications concerning God will be partly disavowed, and yet held to be less false than their denial would be. Thus, the hypothesis will lead to our thinking of features of each Universe as purposed; and this will stand or fall with the hypothesis. Yet a purpose essentially involves growth, and so cannot be attributed to God. Still it will, according to the hypothesis, be less false to speak so, than to represent God as purposeless.

Assured as I am from my own personal experience that every man capable of so controlling his attention as to perform a little exact thinking will, if he examines Zeno's argument about Achilles and the tortoise, come to think as I do that it is nothing but a contemptible catch, I do not think that I either am or ought to be less assured, from what I know of the effects of Musement on myself and others, that any normal man who considers the three Universes in the light of the hypothesis of God's Reality, and pursues that line of reflection in scientific singleness of heart, will come to be stirred to the depths of his nature by the beauty of the idea and by its august practicality, even to the point of earnestly loving and adoring his strictly hypothetical God, and to that of desiring above all things to shape the whole conduct of life and all the springs of action into conformity with that hypothesis. Now to be deliberately and thoroughly prepared to shape one's conduct into conformity with a proposition is neither more nor less than the state of mind called Believing that proposition, however long the conscious classification of it under that head be postponed.

III

There is my poor sketch of the N.A., greatly cut down to bring it within the limits assigned to this article. Next should come the discussion of its logicality; but nothing readable at a sitting could possibly bring home to readers my full proof of the principal points of such an examination. I can only hope to make the residue of this paper a sort of table of contents, from which some may possibly guess what I have to say, or to lay down a series of plausible points through which the reader will have to construct the continuous line of reasoning for himself. In my own mind the proof is elaborated, and I am exerting my energies to getting it submitted to public censure. My present abstract will divide itself into three unequal parts. The first shall give the headings of the different steps of every well-conducted and complete inquiry, without noticing possible divergences from the norm. I shall have to mention some steps which have nothing to do with the N.A. in order to show that they add no jot nor tittle to the truth which is invariably brought just as the N.A. brings it. The second part shall very briefly state, without argument (for which there is no room), just wherein lies the logical validity of the reasoning characteristic of each of the main stages of inquiry. The third part shall indicate the place of the N.A. in a complete inquiry into the Reality of God, and shall show how well it would fill that place, and what its logical value is, supposing the inquiry to be limited to this; and I shall add a few words to show how it might be supplemented.

Every inquiry whatsoever takes its rise in the observation, in one or another of the three Universes, of some surprising phenomenon, some experience which either disappoints an expectation, or breaks in upon some habit of expectation of the *inquisiturus;* and each apparent exception to this rule only confirms it. There are obvious distinctions between the objects of surprise in different cases; but throughout this slight sketch of inquiry such details will be unnoticed; especially since it is such upon which the logic books descant. The inquiry begins with pondering these phenomena in all their aspects, in the search of some point of view whence the wonder shall be resolved. At length a conjecture arises that furnishes a possible Explanation,—by which I mean a syllogism exhibiting the surprising fact as necessarily consequent upon the circumstances of its occurrence together with the truth of the credible conjecture, as premises. On account of this Explanation, the inquirer is led to regard his conjecture, or hypothesis, with favor. As I phrase it, he provisionally holds it to be "Plausible"; this acceptance ranges, in different cases,— and reasonably so,—from a mere expression of it in the interrogative mood, as a question meriting attention and reply, up through all appraisals of Plausibility, to uncontrollable inclination to believe. The whole series of mental performances between the notice of the wonderful phenomenon and the acceptance of the hypothesis, during which the usually docile understanding seems to hold the bit between its teeth and to have us at its mercy,—the search for pertinent circumstances and the laying hold of them, sometimes without our cognizance, the scrutiny of them, the dark laboring, the bursting out of the startling conjecture, the remarking of its smooth fitting to the anomaly, as it is turned back and forth like a key in a lock, and the final estimation of its Plausibility,—I reckon as composing the First Stage of Inquiry. Its characteristic formula of reasoning I term Retroduction, i.e., reasoning from consequent to antecedent. In one respect the designation seems inappropriate; for in most instances where conjecture mounts the high peaks of Plausibility,—and is *really* most worthy of confidence,—the inquirer is unable definitely to formulate just what the explained wonder is; or can only do so in the light of the hypothesis. In short, it is a form of Argument rather than of Argumentation.

Retroduction does not afford security. The hypothesis must be tested. This testing, to be logically valid, must honestly start, not as Retroduction starts, with scrutiny of the phenomena, but with examination of the hypothesis, and a muster of all sorts of conditional experiential consequences which would follow from its truth. This constitutes the Second Stage of Inquiry. For its characteristic form of reasoning our language has, for two centuries, been happily provided with the name Deduction.

Deduction has two parts. For its first step must be, by logical analysis, to Explicate the hypothesis, i.e. to render it as perfectly distinct as possible. This process, like Retroduction, is Argument that is not Argumentation. But unlike Retroduction, it cannot go wrong from lack of experience, but so long as it proceeds rightly must reach a true conclusion. Explication is followed by Demonstration, or Deductive Argumentation. Its procedure is best learned from Book I of Euclid's *Elements,*—a masterpiece which in real insight is far superior to Aristotle's *Analytics*,—and its numerous fallacies render it all the more instructive to a close student. It invariably requires something of the nature of a diagram; that is, an "Icon," or Sign which represents its Object in resembling it. It usually, too, needs "Indices," or Signs which represent their Objects by being actually connected with them. But it is mainly composed of "Symbols," or Signs which represent their Objects essentially because they will be so interpreted. Demonstration should be *Corollarial* when it can. An accurate definition of Corollarial Demonstration would require a long explanation; but it will suffice to say that it limits itself to considerations already introduced or else involved in the Explication of its conclusion; while *Theorematic* Demonstration resorts to more complicated processes of thought.

The purpose of Deduction, that of collecting consequents of the hypothesis, having been sufficiently carried out, the inquiry enters upon its Third Stage, that of ascertaining how far those consequents accord with Experience, and of judging accordingly whether the hypothesis is sensibly correct, or requires some inessential modification, or must be entirely rejected. Its characteristic way of reasoning is Induction. This Stage has three parts. For it must begin with Classification, which is an Inductive Non-Argumentational kind of Argument, by which general Ideas are attached to objects of Experience; or rather by which the latter are subordinated to the former. Following this, will come the testing-argumentations, the Probations; and the whole inquiry will be wound up with the Sentential part of the Third Stage, which, by Inductive reasonings, appraises the different Probations singly, then their combinations, then makes self-appraisal of these very appraisals themselves, and passes final judgment on the whole result.

The Probations, or direct Inductive Argumentations, are of two kinds. The first is that which Bacon ill described as "*inductio illa quae procedit per enumerationem simplicem.*"[7] (So, at least, he has been understood.) For an enumeration of instances is not essential to the argument that, for example, there are no such beings as fairies, or no such events as miracles. The point is that there is no well-established instance of such a thing. I call this Crude Induction. It is the only Induction which concludes a logically Universal Proposition. It is the weakest of arguments, being liable to be demolished in a moment, as happened toward the end of the eighteenth century to the opinion of the scientific world that no stones fall from the sky. The other kind is Gradual Induction, which makes a new estimate of the proportion of truth in the hypothesis with every new instance; and given any degree of error there will *sometime* be an estimate (or would be, if the Probation were persisted in,) which will be absolutely the last to be infected with so much falsity. Gradual Induction is either Qualitative or Quantitative, and the latter either depends on measurements, or on statistics, or countings.

IV

Concerning the question of the nature of the logical validity possessed by Deduction, Induction, and Retroduction, which is still an arena of controversy,

I shall confine myself to stating the opinions which I am prepared to defend by positive proofs. The validity of Deduction was correctly, if not very clearly, analyzed by Kant.[8] This kind of reasoning deals exclusively with Pure Ideas attaching primarily to Symbols and derivatively to other Signs of our own creation; and the fact that man has a power of Explicating his own meaning renders Deduction valid. Induction is a kind of reasoning that may lead us into error; but that it follows a method that, sufficiently persisted in, will be Inductively Certain (the sort of certainty we have that a perfect coin, pitched up often enough, will *sometime* turn up heads) to diminish the error below any predesignate degree, is assured by man's power of perceiving Inductive Certainty. In all this, I am inviting the reader to peep through the big end of the telescope: there is a wealth of pertinent detail that must here be passed over.

Finally, comes the bottom question of logical Critic, what sort of validity can be attributed to the First Stage of inquiry? Observe that neither Deduction nor Induction contributes the smallest positive item to the final conclusion of the inquiry. They render the indefinite definite: Deduction Explicates; Induction evaluates: that is all. Over the chasm that yawns between the ultimate goal of science and such ideas of Man's environment as, coming over him during his primeval wanderings in the forest, while yet his very notion of error was of the vaguest, he managed to communicate to some fellow, we are building a cantilever bridge of induction, held together by scientific struts and ties. Yet every plank of its advance is first laid by Retroduction alone, that is to say, by the spontaneous conjectures of instinctive reason; and neither Deduction nor Induction contributes a single new concept to the structure. Nor is this less true or less important for those inquiries that self-interest prompts.

The first answer we naturally give to this question is that we cannot help accepting the conjecture at such a valuation as that at which we do accept it; whether as a simple interrogation, or as more or less Plausible, or, occasionally, as an irresistible belief. But far from constituting, by itself, a logical justification such as it becomes a rational being to put forth, this pleading, that we *cannot help* yielding to the suggestion, amounts to nothing more than a confession of having failed to train ourselves to control our thoughts. It is more to the purpose, however, to urge that the strength of the impulse is a symptom of its being instinctive. Animals of all races rise far above the general level of their intelligence in those performances that are their proper function, such as flying and nest-building for ordinary birds; and what is man's proper function if it be not to embody general ideas in art-creations, in utilities, and above all in theoretical cognition? To give the lie to his own consciousness of divining the reasons of phenomena would be as silly in a man as it would be in a fledgling bird to refuse to trust to its wings and leave the nest, because the poor little thing had read Babinet, and judged aerostation to be impossible on hydrodynamical grounds.[9] Yes; it must be confessed that *if we knew* that the impulse to prefer one hypothesis to another really were analogous to the instincts of birds and wasps, it would be foolish not to give it play, within the bounds of reason; especially, since we must entertain some hypothesis, or else forgo all further knowledge than that which we have already gained by that very means. But is it a fact that man possesses this magical faculty? Not, I reply, to the extent of guessing right the first time, nor perhaps the second; but that the well-prepared mind has wonderfully soon guessed each secret of nature, is historical truth. All the theories of science have been so obtained. But may they not have come fortuitously, or by some such modification of chance as the Darwinian supposes? I answer that three or four independent methods of computation show that it would be ridiculous to suppose our science to have so come to pass. Nevertheless, suppose that it can be so "explained," just as that any purposed act of mine is supposed by materialistic necessitarians to have come about. Still, what of it? Does that materialistic explanation, supposing it granted, show that reason has nothing to do with my actions? Even the parallelists[10] will admit that the one explanation leaves the same need of the other that there was before it was given; and this is certainly sound logic. There is a reason, an interpretation, a logic, in the course of scientific advance; and this indisputably proves to him who has perceptions of rational, or significant, relations, that man's mind must have been attuned to the truth of things in order to discover what he has discovered. It is the very bedrock of logical truth.

Modern science has been builded after the model of Galileo, who founded it on *il lume naturale*. That truly inspired prophet had said that, of two hypotheses, the *simpler* is to be preferred;[11] but I was formerly one of those who, in our dull self-conceit fancying ourselves more sly than he, twisted the maxim to mean the *logically* simpler, the one that adds the least to what has been observed, in spite of three obvious objections: first, that so there was no support for any hypothesis; secondly, that by the same token we ought to content ourselves with simply formulating the special observations actually made; and thirdly, that every advance of science that further opens the truth to our view discloses a world of unexpected complications. It was not until long experience forced me to realize that subsequent discoveries were every time showing I had been wrong,—while those who understood the maxim as Galileo had done, early unlocked the secret,—that the scales fell from my eyes and my mind awoke to the broad and flaming daylight that it is the simpler hypothesis in the sense of the more facile and natural, the one that instinct suggests, that must be preferred; for the reason that unless man have a natural bent in accordance with nature's, he has no chance of understanding nature, at all. Many tests of this principal and positive fact relating as well to my own studies as to the researches of others have confirmed me in this opinion; and when I shall come to set them forth in a book,[12] their array will convince everybody. Oh no! I am forgetting that armor, impenetrable by accurate thought, in which the rank and file of minds are clad! They may, for example, get the notion that my proposition involves a denial of the rigidity of the laws of association: it would be quite on a par with much that is current. I do not mean that logical simplicity is a consideration of no value at all, but only that its value is badly secondary to that of simplicity in the other sense.

If, however, the maxim is correct in Galileo's sense, whence it follows that man has, in some degree, a divinatory power, primary or derived, like that of a wasp or a bird, then instances swarm to show that a certain altogether peculiar confidence in a hypothesis, not to be confounded with rash cocksureness, has a very appreciable value as a sign of the truth of the hypothesis. I regret I cannot give an account of certain interesting, and almost convincing cases. The N.A. excites this peculiar confidence in the very highest degree.

V

We have now to apply these principles to the evaluation of the N.A. Had I space, I would put this into the shape of imagining how it is likely to be esteemed by three types of men; the first of small instruction with corresponding natural breadth, intimately acquainted with the N.A. but to whom logic is all Greek; the second, inflated with current notions of logic, but prodigiously informed about the N.A.; the third, a trained man of science who, in the modern spirit, has added to his specialty an exact theoretical and practical study of reasoning and the elements of thought; so that psychologists account him a sort of psychologist, and mathematicians a sort of mathematician.

I should, then, show how the first would have learned that nothing has any kind of value in itself,—whether esthetic, moral, or scientific,—but only in its place in the whole production to which it appertains; and that an individual soul with its petty agitations and calamities is a zero except as filling its infinitesimal place and accepting its little utility as its entire treasure. He will see that though his God would not "*really*" (in a certain sense) adapt means to ends, it is nevertheless quite true that there are relations among phenomena which finite intelligence must interpret, and truly interpret, as such adaptations; and he will macarize himself for his own bitterest griefs, and bless God for the law of growth, with all the fighting it imposes upon him,—Evil, i.e., what it is man's duty to fight, being one of the major perfections of the Universe. In that fight he will endeavor to perform just the duty laid upon him, and no more. Though his desperate struggles should issue in the horrors of his rout, and he should see the innocents who are dearest to his heart exposed to torments, frenzy and despair, destined to be smirched with filth, and stunted in their intelligence, still he may hope that it be best *for them*, and will tell himself that in any case the secret design of God will be perfected through their agency; and even while still hot from the battle, will submit with adoration to His Holy will. He will not worry because the Universes were not constructed to suit the scheme of some silly scold.

The context of this, I must leave the reader to imagine.[13] I will only add that the third man, considering the complex process of self-control, will see that the hypothesis, irresistible though it be to first intention, yet needs Probation; and that though an infinite being is not tied down to any consistency, yet man, like any other animal, is gifted with power of understanding sufficient for the conduct of life. This brings him, for testing the hypothesis, to taking his stand upon Pragmaticism, which implies faith in common-sense and in instinct, though only as they issue from the cupel-furnace of measured criticism. In short, he will say that the N.A. is the First Stage of a scientific inquiry, resulting in a hypothesis of the very highest Plausibility, whose ultimate test must lie in its value in the self-controlled growth of man's conduct of life.[14]

Additament

A nest of three arguments for the Reality of God has now been sketched, though none of them could, in the limits of a single article, be fairly presented. The first is that entirely honest, sincere, and unaffected, because unprepense, meditation upon the Idea of God, into which the Play of Musement will inevitably sooner or later lead, and which by developing a deep sense of the adorability of that Idea, will produce a Truly religious Belief in His Reality and His nearness. It is a reasonable argument, because it naturally results in the most intense and living determination (*Bestimmung*) of the soul toward shaping the Muser's whole conduct into conformity with the hypothesis that God is Real and very near; and such a determination of the soul in regard to any proposition is the very essence of a living Belief in such proposition. This is that "humble argument," open to every honest man, which I surmise to have made more worshippers of God than any other.

The second of the nest is the argument which seems to me to have been "neglected" by writers upon natural theology, consisting in showing that the humble argument is the natural fruit of free meditation, since every heart will be ravished by the beauty and adorability of the Idea, when it is so pursued. Were the theologians able to perceive the force of this argument, they would make it such a presentation of universal human nature as to show that a latent tendency toward belief in God is a fundamental ingredient of the soul, and that, far from being a vicious or superstitious ingredient, it is simply the natural precipitate of meditation upon the origin of the Three Universes. Of course, it could not, any more than any other theological argumentation, have the value or the religious vitality of the "Humble Argument"; for it would only be an apology,—a vindicatory description,—of the mental operations which the Humble Argument actually and actively lives out. Though this is properly the neglected argument, yet I have sometimes used the abbreviation "the N.A." for the whole nest of three.

The third argument of the nest consists in a study of logical methodeutic, illuminated by the light of a first-hand acquaintance with genuine scientific thought,—the sort of thought whose tools literally comprise not merely Ideas of mathematical exactitude, but also the apparatus of the skilled manipulator, actually in use. The student, applying to his own trained habits of research the art of logical analysis,—an art as elaborate and methodical as that of the chemical analyst,—compares the process of thought of the Muser upon the

Three Universes with certain parts of the work of scientific discovery, and finds that the "Humble Argument" is nothing but an instance of the first stage of all such work, the stage of observing the facts, of variously rearranging them, and of pondering them until, by their reactions with the results of previous scientific experience, there is "evolved" (as the chemists word it), an explanatory hypothesis. He will note, however, that this instance of Retroduction, undeniable as this character is, departs widely from the ordinary run of instances, especially in three respects. In the first place, the Plausibility of the hypothesis reaches an almost unparalleled height among deliberately formed hypotheses. So hard is it to doubt God's Reality, when the Idea has sprung from Musements, that there is great danger that the investigation will stop at this first stage, owing to the indifference of the Muser to any further proof of it. At the same time, this very Plausibility is undoubtedly an argument of no small weight in favor of the truth of the hypothesis.

In the second place, although it is a chief function of an explanatory hypothesis (and some philosophers say the only one), to excite a clear image in the mind by means of which experiential consequences of ascertainable conditions may be predicted, yet in this instance the hypothesis can only be apprehended so very obscurely that in exceptional cases alone can any definite and direct deduction from its ordinary abstract interpretation be made. How, for example, can we ever expect to be able to predict what the conduct would be even of any omniscient being governing no more than one poor solar system for only a million years or so? How much less if, being also omnipotent, he be thereby freed from all experience, all desire, all intention! Since God, in His essential character of *Ens necessarium*, is a disembodied spirit, and since there is strong reason to hold that what we call consciousness is either merely the general sensation of the brain or some part of it, or at all events some visceral or bodily sensation, God probably has no consciousness. Most of us are in the habit of thinking that consciousness and psychic life are the same thing and otherwise greatly to overrate the functions of consciousness.*

The effects of the second peculiarity of the hypothesis are counteracted by a third, which consists in its commanding influence over the whole conduct of life of its believers. *[. . .]*

Since[15] I have employed the word *Pragmaticism*, and shall have occasion to use it once more, it may perhaps be well to explain it. About forty years ago, my studies of Berkeley, Kant, and others led me, after convincing myself that all thinking is performed in Signs, and that meditation takes the form of a dialogue, so that it is proper to speak of the "meaning" of a concept, to conclude that to acquire full mastery of that meaning it is requisite, in the first place, to learn to recognize the concept under every disguise, through extensive familiarity with instances of it. But this, after all, does not imply any true understanding of it; so that it is further requisite that we should make an abstract

---

* See James's paper "Does 'Consciousness' Exist?" in *Journal of Philosophy, Psychology, and Scientific Method* 1 (1 September 1904):477–91. But the negative reply is, in itself, no novelty.

logical analysis of it into its ultimate elements, or as complete an analysis as we can compass. But, even so, we may still be without any living comprehension of it; and the only way to complete our knowledge of its nature is to discover and recognize just what general habits of conduct a belief in the truth of the concept (of any conceivable subject, and under any conceivable circumstances) would reasonably develop; that is to say, what habits would ultimately result from a sufficient consideration of such truth. It is necessary to understand the word "conduct," here, in the broadest sense. If, for example, the predication of a given concept were to lead to our admitting that a given form of reasoning concerning the subject of which it was affirmed was valid, when it would not otherwise be valid, the recognition of that effect in our reasoning would decidedly be a habit of conduct.

In 1871, in a Metaphysical Club in Cambridge, Mass.,[16] I used to preach this principle as a sort of logical gospel, representing the unformulated method followed by Berkeley, and in conversation abo ɪ it I called it "Pragmatism." In November 1877 and January 1878, I set forth the doctrine in the *Popular Science Monthly;* and the two parts of my essay were printed in French in the *Revue Philosophique*, volumes 6 and 7.[17] Of course, the doctrine attracted no particular attention, for, as I had remarked in my opening sentence, very few people care for logic. But in 1897, Professor James remodelled the matter, and transmogrified it into a doctrine of philosophy,[18] some parts of which I highly approved, while other and more prominent parts I regarded, and still regard, as opposed to sound logic. About the time Professor Papini discovered, to the delight of the Pragmatist school, that this doctrine was incapable of definition,[19] which would certainly seem to distinguish it from every other doctrine in whatever branch of science, I was coming to the conclusion that my poor little maxim should be called by another name; and accordingly, in April 1905, I renamed it *Pragmaticism.*[20] I had never before dignified it by any name in print, except that, at Professor Baldwin's request, I wrote a definition of it for his *Dictionary of Psychology and Philosophy.*[21] I did not insert the word in the *Century Dictionary*, though I had charge of the philosophical definitions of that work; for I have a perhaps exaggerated dislike of *réclame.*

It is that course of meditation upon the three Universes which gives birth to the hypothesis and ultimately to the belief that they, or at any rate two of the three, have a Creator independent of them, that I have throughout this article called the N.A., because I think the theologians ought to have recognized it as a line of thought reasonably productive of belief. This is the "humble" argument, the innermost of the nest. In the mind of a metaphysician it will have a metaphysical tinge; but that seems to me rather to detract from its force than to add anything to it. It is just as good an argument, if not better, in the form it takes in the mind of the clodhopper.

The theologians could not have *presented* the N.A.; because that is a living course of thought of very various forms. But they might and ought to have *described* it, and should have defended it, too, as far as they could, without going into original logical researches, which could not be justly expected of them. They are accustomed to make use of the principle that that which convinces a normal man must be presumed to be sound reasoning; and therefore they ought to say whatever can truly be advanced to show that the N.A., if sufficiently developed, will convince any normal man. Unfortunately, it happens that there is very little established fact to show that this is the case. I have not pretended to have any other ground for my belief that it is so than my assumption, which each one of us makes, that my own intellectual disposition is normal. I am forced to confess that no pessimist will agree with me. I do not admit that pessimists are, at the same time, thoroughly sane, and in addition are endowed in normal measure with intellectual vigor; and my reasons for thinking so are two. The first is, that the difference between a pessimistic and an optimistic mind is of such controlling importance in regard to every intellectual function, and especially for the conduct of life, that it is out of the question to admit that both are normal, and the great majority of mankind are naturally optimistic. Now, the majority of every race depart but little from the norm of that race. In order to present my other reason, I am obliged to recognize three types of pessimists. The first type is often found in exquisite and noble natures of great force of original intellect whose own lives are dreadful histories of torment due to some physical malady. Leopardi is a famous example. We cannot but believe, against their earnest protests, that if such men had had ordinary health, life would have worn for them the same color as for the rest of us. Meantime, one meets too few pessimists of this type to affect the present question. The second is the misanthropical type, the type that makes itself heard. It suffices to call to mind the conduct of the famous pessimists of this kind, Diogenes the Cynic, Schopenhauer, Carlyle, and their kin with Shakespeare's Timon of Athens, to recognize them as diseased minds.[22] The third is the philanthropical type, people whose lively sympathies, easily excited, become roused to anger at what they consider the stupid injustices of life. Being easily interested in everything, without being overloaded with exact thought of any kind, they are excellent raw material for *littérateurs:* witness Voltaire. No individual remotely approaching the calibre of a Leibniz is to be found among them.

The third argument, enclosing and defending the other two, consists in the development of those principles of logic according to which the humble argument is the first stage of a scientific inquiry into the origin of the three Universes, but of an inquiry which produces, not merely scientific belief, which is always provisional, but also a living, practical belief, logically justified in crossing the Rubicon with all the freightage of eternity. The presentation of this argument would require the establishment of several principles of logic that the logicians have hardly dreamed of, and particularly a strict proof of the correctness of the maxim of Pragmaticism. My original essay, having been written for a popular monthly, assumes, for no better reason than that real inquiry cannot begin until a state of real doubt arises and ends as soon as Belief is attained, that "a settlement of Belief," or, in other words, a state of *satisfaction*, is all that Truth, or the aim of inquiry, consists in. The reason I gave for this was so flimsy, while the inference was so nearly the gist of Pragmaticism, that I must confess the argument of that essay might with some justice be said to beg the question. The first part of the essay, however, is occupied with showing that, if Truth consists in satisfaction, it cannot be any *actual* satisfaction, but must be the satisfaction which *would* ultimately be found if the inquiry were pushed to its ultimate and indefeasible issue. This, I beg to point out, is a very different position from that of Mr. Schiller and the pragmatists of today. I trust I shall be believed when I say that it is only a desire to avoid being misunderstood in consequence of my relations with pragmatism, and by no means as arrogating any superior immunity from error which I have too good reason to know that I do not enjoy, that leads me to express my personal sentiments about their tenets. Their avowedly undefinable position, if it be not capable of logical characterization, seems to me to be characterized by an angry hatred of strict logic, and even some disposition to rate any exact thought which interferes with their doctrines as all humbug. At the same time, it seems to me clear that their approximate acceptance of the Pragmaticist principle, and even that very casting aside of difficult distinctions (although I cannot approve of it), has helped them to a mightily clear discernment of some fundamental truths that other philosophers have seen but through a mist, and most of them not at all. Among such truths,—all of them old, of course, yet acknowledged by few,—I reckon their denial of necessitarianism; their rejection of any "consciousness" different from a visceral or other external sensation; their acknowledgment that there are, in a Pragmatistical sense, Real habits (which Really *would* produce effects, under circumstances that may not happen to get actualized, and are thus Real generals); and their insistence upon interpreting all hypostatic abstractions in terms of what they *would* or *might* (not actually *will*) come to in the concrete. It seems to me a pity they should allow a philosophy so instinct with life to become infected with seeds of death in such notions as that of the unreality of all ideas of infinity and that of the mutability of truth, and in such confusions of thought as that of active willing (willing to control thought, to doubt, and to weigh reasons) with willing not to exert the will (willing to believe).[23]

30

A Sketch of Logical Critics

MS 675. [In the spring of 1909, J. W. Slaughter and G. F. Stout, two friends of Victoria Lady Welby, decided to honor her with a collection of essays on "Significs," and eagerly sought a contribution from Peirce. He was glad to accept, but ill health slowed him down until a reminder from Slaughter, in April 1911, revived his impetus. MS 675, probably written in August 1911, is one of the more polished versions of Peirce's eventually unsuccessful attempt to complete his assignment. Maybe as a consequence, the collection of essays was never published.] Although this writing is at most only a fragment of the paper Peirce had in mind, it contains important clarifications and sheds much light on the late trajectory of Peirce's thought. By "logical critics," Peirce means "the theory of the kinds and degrees of assurance that can be afforded by the different ways of reasoning." This is, for Peirce, a semiotic question, and one that exercised him a great deal in his later years. Although he never really reaches the question here, he does come to discuss "precisely" what we mean by "reasoning," and points out that it is only one of two ways that knowledge is acquired, the other being experience. Belief acquired through reasoning must be justified by what preceded it in our minds; but belief gained from experience needs no justification. Peirce discusses two faults with his 1877–78 pragmatism papers: his definition of "belief," and his failure to see that "a true would-be is as real as an actuality." He concludes with a call for a cooperative scientific attack on the "problems of the nature, properties, and varieties of Signs."

An[1] American revisiting London after an absence of twenty or thirty years is struck with so many modes of speech that he is confident he never heard before on either side of the Atlantic, that in his journal, if we could search it and find it kept regularly and full, we should be pretty sure to find that on some night he had been moved to set down affectation as one of the traits of John Bull.[2] It would be an inference equally natural and fallacious;—which, of course, is not to say that the English are absolutely immune to this particular variety of pedantry or whatever other kind of snobbery it may be. As an instance, ask our American what he would call these five things: firstly, the examination of any performance, with a view to evaluating the peculiar qualities and degrees of its excellences and peccancies; secondly, a writing setting forth the judgment resulting from such an examination; thirdly, the general theory, or science, of the principles upon which any such examination ought to be founded and conducted; fourthly, a treatise setting forth that doctrine; and fifthly, the author of the examination, the account of it, the theory, or the treatise aforesaid. If the American spoke "good United-States," my own impression is that he would call the first,—i.e., the examining act,—"criticism"; the second,—the expression of his judgment,—"a critique," or "a criticism," the noun carrying one or other article; the third,—the science,—"critics" rather than "critic," accented on the first syllable; the fourth,—the treatise,—"a critics," distinguishing it from the third only by attaching an article to the substantive; the fifth,—the author,—"a critic," distinguished from the fourth by the absence of the final "s." An Englishman, on the other hand, as I gather from a small number of observations, would be more likely to call the fourth, like the second, "a critique," and the third "critique," without the article, imitating the French (as closely as he would think it befitting the dignity of an Englishman to do) in pronunciation as in spelling. Undoubtedly it is a habit of relative antiquity in England, as old as Johnson's *Dictionary*,[3] at least, which was published in 1755, though Locke wrote "critick" for the theory (sense three).[4] Our American, however, would be almost ready to swear that when he was in London before, everybody spoke as he did. Probably the truth was that the word never had happened to turn up at that time in his hearing. Perhaps he had something about him to suggest his being of the "scientific" sort, and repelling *littérateurs*, or preventing their talking to him about the doctrine of literary critics. His chronology would certainly have been out by more than a century. He would have been on surer ground had he contented himself with insisting that his own usage was much the more convenient, distinguishing as it does the five things that need to be distinguished, if only for the reason that our vocabulary, by marking such distinctions in all other cases, gives one a right to expect them to be marked here, and makes a stumbling block for the American in interpreting the Englishman's speech. Those who hold, as some lexicographers seem to do, that if a writing whose intention is to discuss the literary merit of a particular book is to be called "a critique," then it will go without saying that a discussion of the principles of literary criticism in general may, with equal propriety, be so called,—those who take this position, I say, ought, upon precisely the same principle (and not merely by a converse principle, as a hasty reasoner might at first think), to have no hesitation in calling an almanac "an astronomy," the ledger of a commercial house "an arithmetic," or the prayer that bursts from the heart of a shipwrecked sailor "a theology." Some will, perhaps justly, find fault with us Americans as being inconsistent in, after all, resorting to the French form to express sense two, or the special writing, for which "a criticism" would do as well as "a critique;" but it is hardly worth while to split philological hairs in adapting our vernacular to scientific uses. There is a similarly microscopic question as to whether we shall prefer "critics" or "critic." To whatever could be alleged in the way of rational defense for our traditional plural forms of the names of sciences in -ic, in general, may here be added the convenience of having distinct forms to denote sense four, the treatise, and sense five, its author.

In the third sense, the noun "critic," or "critics," seems to have been introduced into English by Hobbes,* who wrote it substantially in that sense, if not in quite the generality of the above definition, in the year 1657.[5] Some high authorities, as far back as Johnson's time, have supposed the word, in that third sense, to have been borrowed from the French. Possibly it really was so; but the French spelling and pronunciation were not, as a matter of history, the *cause,* but the *effect,* of adhesion to that hypothesis. The real cause, I believe, was an honest admiration of French elegance. But, considering that Hobbes was a hellenist, an enthusiast over Thucydides and translator of his difficult prose; considering moreover that he used the plural form, "criticks," in English,—like "ethicks," and other names of sciences that in Greek are adjectives agreeing with βιβλιῶν,—while only the singular form ever was in French vogue; considering, too, that Hobbes would have remembered the passage of Plato's *Politicus* where the word occurs in substantially the same sense,[6] can one refrain from thinking that those who adopt the hypothesis of Hobbes's having followed a supposed Paris fashion in using it, bestow a too liberal gratuity upon a beggarly postulate? I am not aware of any evidence that there existed in 1657 any Paris fashion of expressing sense three as "la critique." Those who seem to think there is such evidence refer us, a little vaguely, to Molière and to Boileau Despréaux.[7] The latter at the date in question was a sickly youth, under twenty-one years of age, whose entire catalogue of literary works more than three years later was as follows: Songs, 2; Sonnet, 1; Ode, 1. I am unable to assert that "la critique" in sense three is not to be found among these works. It belongs to those who talk of Boileau as supporting the hypothesis of the English being here indebted to the French to find the word in one of those five pieces. With Molière I am not quite so ignorant. Among his productions not later than 1657, being two farces in addition to the truly comical *Étourdi* and the not uninteresting *Dépit amoureux,* the word "critique" does not occur in any sense. Such small acquaintance as I have with French literature hardly entitles me even to a private opinion. If it did, I should opine that the use of "la critique" in sense three was considerably later. I have at hand no means of informing myself further.

By "logical critics," I mean the theory of the kinds and degrees of assurance that can be afforded by the different ways of reasoning.

But[8] what, precisely, shall we take "reasoning" to mean here? And what shall "assurance" mean? In order to answer such questions in the manner that shall render our critics as useful as possible, we have to shape our thoughts to the general facts of human life. There is a moment when the child awakes to

---

*This impression appears to be consistent with the quotations of the *Oxford Dictionary,* although in one point I venture to draw a different inference from that of so high an authority as Dr. Murray.

the business of self-government, and when he has many questions to ask himself about himself. It is he himself who has to train himself, after this moment has come; and then, for a time, the best teacher he can have is the one that has the skill to insinuate suspicion of meaningless and mistaken phrases, to suggest those questions that have a real meaning, and to put him on the road to their practical solution. Although this is not at all what we are to do here, where we are to be occupied with pure theory, yet it will be well that we should square our definitions so that they may fit in with those main facts of human nature and human life that each of us has learned.

The[9] definition and the utility of a definition require it to specify everything essential, and to omit all that is inessential, to its *definitum*: though it may be pardoned for calling special attention to an omission in order to show that it was not inconsiderate. By *"Reasoning"* shall here be meant any change in thought that results in an appeal for some measure and kind of assent to the truth of a proposition called the *"Conclusion"* of the reasoning, as being rendered *"Reasonable"* by an already existing cognition (usually complex) whose propositional formulation shall be termed the *"Copulate Premiss"* of the reasoning. The reader will remark, as the point where this definition most markedly breaks with actual usage, that it refuses the name of reasoning to the synthesis into one recognition of the major and minor premisses of a syllogism. The considerations that move me to this heresy are these: the essential difference between the two ways in which we gain knowledge,—as we know, not by any psychological research, but by indefeasible common sense,—is that in learning by reasoning, each new accretion to our belief is *justified*, to our eyes, *by what was in our minds just before*, while what we are taught by experience is not *justified* at all: on the contrary, the less it is like previous knowledge, the more valuable an information it is, other things being equal. We are simply compelled to admit it. Now if at one time one fact was brought to one's mind, and at another time another, then on the first occasion on which the two facts are brought to mind in their relation to each other, in which case one has suggested the other, this complex recognition is not justified by anything that ever, once, was in one's mind, and though more like an acquisition by experience than like an acquisition by reasoning, it is rather to be regarded as an intermediate type of acquisition; and the more one considers the immense illuminating power there often is in such co-recognition,[10] the more one will be disposed to admit the intermediacy of this mode of acquisition, which must not be mistaken for memory. It is easy to see what it is *psychologically*; it is a slightly complicated variety of suggestion due to association by resemblance,*—which, it is to be noted, is no *actual* association, at all. Thus, from

---

*I[11] follow the usage of the early associationalists, Gay, Hartley, etc.,[12] in confining the term "association" to the storing away, in our spiritual or physical organisms, [of] ideas that, when so stored away, are in the potential mode of being, and in terming the agency of ideas in calling forth others from such potential, into actual being, *suggestion*,—a word of which the hypnotists ought not to be allowed the monopoly.

the pure psychological point of view, it would seem to belong to the class of dreams. From the logical point of view, it is certainly not a true reasoning, since the fact first in the mind does not make the thought of the suggested fact *reasonable*, nor does it incline us to admit the reality of the latter. But since in treating of reasoning one has occasion to refer to this mental process, it will be convenient to adopt a designation for it; and it may very properly be called "*syllogistic recollection.*"

The second character to be noted in the definition of reasoning here adopted,—and here the writer has ample support from others,—is that no feebleness in the recommendation that a reasoning offers for trust in its conclusion will prevent its being called a "reasoning" by anybody who adopts this definition. If an acknowledged fact only makes a conclusion to be thought a little less inadmissible rationally than it would have been but for that fact, the passage from the fact to this acknowledgment is a "reasoning," according to this definition.

There remains a third point that I could not blamelessly leave wholly unexpressed, although I shall not undertake in this essay to bring readers to see its full importance. Namely, I have referred to reasoning as a process, or change, "of thought."[13] I have not said "of thinking," since if, for example, there be a certain fossil fish, certain observations upon which, made by a skilled paleontologist, *[and]* taken in connection with chemical analyses of the bones and of the rock in which they were embedded, will one day furnish that paleontologist with the keystone of an argumentative arch upon which he will securely erect a solid proof of a conclusion of great importance, then, in my view, in the true logical sense, that thought has already all the reality it ever will have, although as yet the quarries have not been opened that will enable human minds to perform that reasoning. For the fish is there, and the actual composition of the stone already in fact determines what the chemist and the paleontologist will one day read in them; and they will not read into them anything that is not there already recorded, although nobody has yet been in condition to translate it. It is, therefore, true, in the logician's sense of the words, although not in that of the psychologist, that the thought is already expressed there. It surely is so, if God designedly left things to be so understood. It remains, then, unconditionally true,—design or no design: this last point will sustain pondering.

In order to render the meaning of the word "Reasoning" thoroughly distinct, there are one or two other conceptions that need to be analyzed; and especially these two: *Belief* and *Reality*. At an early stage of my studies of logic,—though it is humiliating, indeed, to reflect upon the amount of labor I had already bestowed upon the subject while yet liable to such manifest errors as I am about to record,—I published in the *Popular Science Monthly* for November 1877 and January 1878 an essay on these matters (substantially written five years before)[14] that defines "Belief," at least, tolerably, provided two great *errata* be corrected. The first of these,[15] though it betrays an illogical obstinacy, is easily corrected. Namely, in the first fascicule of the essay, on page 5, I said of Belief that it is "a calm and satisfactory state which we do not wish to avoid, *or to change to a belief in anything else*";[16] and then, having met with persons who expressed a wish that they could believe differently from what they were forced to believe (an idle regret that does not prove that they *would* reverse their belief if they actually could), I added in a footnote, "I am not speaking of secondary effects occasionally produced by the interference of other impulses." But this does not meet the point. Either there are persons so weak and inconsistent that they would reverse their belief if they could, or there are not. If there are not, that is sufficient. If there are, it proves that an unwillingness to reverse one's belief is not an essential character of belief, and should not have been stated as such. I should now content myself with the following statement: Belief, once attained, removes all the discontent inherent in doubt; and moreover the believer well knows that there is no different belief that could long maintain itself in his mind, while he remains sane, unless, indeed, he should discover that the real state of facts was quite contrary to his belief. It follows that no thoroughly sane man will desire that the matter of his belief should be changed unless by some such discovery. We find, however, some half-distracted souls who, finding they can do nothing to remedy a state of things that causes them great misery, express a longing to believe what they know to be false; in other words, they think they would desire to become insane in that one respect. To such a one I would say, "You are, already, so near being a subject for a psychiatrist, in expressing so base and shameful a wish, that I have hardly any doubt that, if you will go to work with an intelligent will, you will soon be able to superinduce upon yourself the very sort of insanity you so much desire; and perhaps you will even be able to conceal your idiosyncrasy from others. If you really desire it, you certainly will do all that lies in your power to actualize what you desire; and let me assure you that it will be a far easier task than you imagine; for everybody but yourself perceives that there remains only a little lacking for you to be in possession of the bliss you so much hanker after. You will have no need of alcohol or cocaine or anything else that might make you a more complete fool than you care to be."

The other fault of that essay [which] is infinitely more serious than the first, though perhaps it is not so great a stupidity, is that I apparently allowed the conception of mechanical forces as unceasingly actual component accelerations, even when they are counterbalanced by equal and opposite components, to carry me to the generalization that there is no reality in any habit, or lasting state in which something *would* happen in case a certain condition should be fulfilled, unless that condition sometime actually *is* fulfilled, instead of reading in the phenomenon of mechanical equilibrium the lesson that a true "*would be*" is as real as an actuality. For what is it for a thing to be Real? The concept is rightly analyzed in the second part of that very essay. To say that a thing is *Real* is merely to say that such predicates as are true of it, or some of them, are true of it regardless of whatever any actual person or persons might think concerning that truth. Unconditionality in that single respect constitutes what we call Reality. Consequently, any habit, or lasting state that consists in the fact that the subject of it *would*, under certain conditions, behave in a certain way, is *Real*, provided this be true whether actual persons think so or not; and it must be admitted to be a *Real Habit*, even if those conditions never actually do get fulfilled. In that second part, I call "truth" the predestinate opinion,[17] by which I ought to have meant that which *would* ultimately prevail if investigation were carried sufficiently far in that particular direction. Yet, although it ought to have been sufficiently obvious that the further investigation is pushed, the greater will be the multiplication of unsettled questions, I nevertheless talked,—except perhaps in a single sentence,—as if, for example, it was at least questionable whether any Real flower was ever "born to blush unseen, and waste its sweetness on the desert air."[18] But, beyond question, such there are, which would have been found if inquiry could have been, and had been, sufficiently pushed in the right direction, although, in fact, it was not; and of things in which we rightly but vaguely believe, the immense majority are similarly unknown; and this majority grows relatively (and not merely numerically) larger the further inquiry is pushed, and we cannot, in any sense, look forward to a state of things in which such beliefs as that any stone let fall from the hand would drop to the earth are to be replaced by such a knowledge as that every stone that has been let loose has dropped.

The purpose of that essay, on account of the suggestions of which it may be useful to the reader even at this late day, was to show that the real meaning of a purely theoretical statement or word, though assuredly it does not lie in any possible practical application, yet does precisely lie in the conceivability, quite regardless of the practicability, of such applications. It was this doctrine with its corollaries that I had been preaching to my fellow-members of a little "Metaphysical Club," in Cambridge, Massachusetts, since the last months of the year 1871, under the name of "pragmatism."[19] I had the signal good fortune to be born at a date and into a circle where I could follow understandingly every important incident of that scientific development of which the first that I recollect was Helmholtz's paper *Ueber die Erhaltung der Kraft*;[20] and it was about five years after the appearance of *The Origin of Species*[21] and the introduction of the spectroscope that all of us, students of philosophy, were stirred to our depths by Mill's *Examination of Sir William Hamilton*,[22] as no metaphysical eloquence ever did stir us before or has since stirred us. I have always fathered my "pragmaticism" (as I have called it since James and Schiller made the word imply "the will to believe," the mutability of truth, the soundness of Zeno's refutation of motion, and pluralism generally)[23] upon Kant, Berkeley, and Leibniz, and have rated J. S. Mill by the fatal inaccuracy of his reasoning, as decidedly inferior to his father. But those opinions only oblige me the more to acknowledge the great power of his *Examination*, and the probability that it aided me to discern the whole indebtedness of our cognitive to our conative functions.

If ever there were a genuine and conscientious thinker, it was Auguste Comte; and detestable as his queer Romanism is to us, I find it difficult to esteem a writer to whom no delight seems greater than to detect Comte plagiarizing, since every original mind will appear to plagiarize from the point of view of the infinitely little. After a hundred writers had tried to classify the sciences to no advantage, Comte succeeded in making all the world appreciate a very simple principle of arranging them; namely, that which places above any given science those which lend it principles, and places below it those which lend it new applications.

I will now give as good an account as I summarily can of the place of Logical Critics among the sciences. Some such knowledge is requisite to understanding the doctrine of Logical Critics itself. It involves a general scheme or arrangement of the sciences, and the one here to be proposed has been found by me sufficiently satisfactory. Viewed from a higher standpoint,—I mean in a more general way,—I confess I am not altogether satisfied with it, without being sure that it would be possible greatly to improve it. I submit it to the reader because, without occupying much space, it will serve to draw his attention to some useful truths, and will aid me in explaining myself.

Let all science be divided into first, *Heuretic Science;* second, Science of Review, or *Science of Science;* and third, *Practical Science,* which embraces whatever scientific inquiry is conducted with a view to some ulterior end. Let science of review include all handbooks and digests, all such works as those *[of]* Comte, Whewell, and Spencer, all classifications and all histories of science, etc.

Let Heuretic Science be divided into, first, *Mathematics,* which assumes no responsibility for the truth of its premises, but only for its conclusions necessarily following from those premises; second, *Philosophy,* or, as Bentham calls it, Cenoscopy,[24] which makes no new observations, but merely draws such conclusions as it can from universally undoubted truths and universally admitted phenomena; and thirdly, *Special Science,* Bentham's Idioscopy, which is chiefly occupied with bringing to light phenomena hitherto unnoticed. In idioscopy two wings must be recognized; one *Psychical* or Humanistic, the other *Physical.* In each wing alike we find three orders of sciences: first, the Nomological, or *Sciences of Laws;* second, the Classificatory, or *Sciences of Kinds;* third, the Descriptive and Explanatory, or *Sciences of Individual Objects.* There is more or less parallelism in the subdivisions of these Orders in the two wings. As under Nomological Physics, we find the general science of Dynamics and the special branches of Physics, Molar, Molecular, and Etheric, these again subdivided according to the different kinds of training and of opportunity they call for, so under Nomological Psychics we find

General Psychology as sharply distinguished from General Politics, Economics, the general science of Law, etc., and these subdivided by similar causes to those of the subdivision of Physics. We further observe, in both wings alike, that the Descriptive Sciences, such as Biography on the Psychic wing, Astronomy on the Physic, as the objects studied multiply, tend to become, or rather to procreate, Classificatory Sciences. The classificatory sciences strive to become nomological; while the nomological sciences have shown occasional aspirations toward a metaphysical character. Under Philosophy, we shall find ourselves again forced,—unless we wrench matters,—to make a trichotomy; recognizing first, Phenomenology; second, the Critical, or Normative, Sciences, and third, Metaphysics, the science of Reality. Of the Normative Sciences, three are generally recognized, relating respectively to how our Feelings, our Energies, and our Thoughts should be self-directed. But of these three ideas of sciences, one only can be said as yet actually to have been born into the world, if we mean by a "science" what scientific men themselves mean when they talk with one another; namely, if we mean by a science the total activity of a social group whose members devote their whole being to finding out and to helping one another to find out the truth in a certain department into which they are peculiarly equipped to search; and are doing this for no ulterior object whatsoever beyond that of making the holy truth known; and who are in substantial accord as to the general method proper for prosecuting such inquiries, and as to what has, in fact, already been discovered in their field,—I say, if we were to take the word "science" in this professional sense, a sense manifestly too restricted for ordinary use (and particularly distressing to me), then Ethics is the only one of the Critical, or Normative, Sciences that can be said, with propriety, to have yet been born into the world of actualities; and even that one, creditable as its history is, is not yet mature enough fully to comprehend its own purposes. It still sticks to the obsolete pretense of teaching men what they are "bound" to do. From a shelf measuring just five feet, filled exclusively with treatises on this subject, the majority of them nineteenth-century works of importance, I picked out the third in order of intelligence, in order to make sure that this conception still prevails; and sure enough, on page 5 I found this very statement without qualification. No wonder young men are wild! Shame upon them if they did not resent such a pretension. God has created every man *free*, and not "bound" to any kind of conduct but that which he freely selects. It is true that he finds he cannot be satisfied without a firm and stiff government over his impulses; but then it is a self-government, instituted by himself to suit himself;—copied, it is true, largely from the government his parents wielded when he was a child, but only continued because he finds it answers HIS OWN purposes, and not in the least because he is "bound" in any proper sense whatever; unless, indeed, he be one of those feeble-minded individuals who are shocked at the idea of their venturing openly to hold opinions about personal conduct differing from those of the estimable helpmeet of good deacon

Grundy.[25] In some communities there will be more than a sprinkling of such young men; but those who form the majority, and the *best* part, too, will pay such tax to the lady as it is convenient to pay, without being bound or pretending to be bound in any respect,—as long as they live in a country where free they can be. Middle-class mothers will, of course, prevent their daughters from seeing much of young men of bad lives; and this will strongly influence any young man whose mind is not deranged. Still, this does not *bind* him; neither is it, *directly*, of the nature of a moral influence, at all. Any pretension to "morally binding" men is, however, a moral influence, and one cast squarely in the direction of bad living. Yet it is not so strong as is supposed. What most influences men to self-government is intense disgust with one kind of life and warm admiration for another. Careful observation of men will show this; and those who desire to further the practice of self-government ought to shape their teachings accordingly.

Meantime, instead of a silly science of Esthetics, that tries to bring us enjoyment of sensuous beauty,—by which I mean all beauty that appeals to our five senses,—that which ought to be fostered is meditation, ponderings, day-dreams (under due control), concerning ideals—oh, no, no, no! "ideals" is far too cold a word! I mean rather passionate admiring aspirations after an inward state that anybody may hope to attain or approach, but of whatever more specific complexion may enchant the dreamer. Our contemporary religious doubt will prove a terrible calamity indeed, if the sort of meditations I mean are to be weakened, lying as they do at the very bottom, the very lowest hold of the ship that carries all the hopes of humanity. One should be careful not to repress day-dreaming too absolutely. Govern it,—*à la bonne heure!*—I mean, see that *self*-government is exercised; but be careful not to do violence to any part of the anatomy of the soul.*

I have permitted myself this unrestrained expression of my sentiments (contrasting in that respect, but not otherwise, with a comparison of motives in the *Popular Science Monthly* for January 1901)[27] because the space for a discussion was more than I could give, while the sentiments themselves are too intimately related to my logical opinions to permit anything like concealment of them.

Now what is Logic? I early remarked that it is quite indifferent whether it be regarded as having to do with thought or with language, the wrapping of thought, since thought, like an onion, is composed of nothing but wrappings. That led me to think that logic has to do with some kind of signs. But, I had observed that the most frequently useful division of signs is by trichotomy into firstly Likenesses, or, as I prefer to say, *Icons*, which serve to represent their

---

*Three books from the study of which I have profited concerning morality and otherwise are Henry James the First's *Substance and Shadow, The Secret of Swedenborg*, and *Spiritual Creation*.[26] The fact that I have been unable to agree with much, not to say *most*, of the author's opinions, while not quite confident of my own, has, no doubt, increased their utility to me. Much that they contain enlightened me greatly.

objects only in so far as they resemble them in themselves; secondly, *Indices*, which represent their objects independently of any resemblance to them, only by virtue of real connections with them, and thirdly *Symbols*, which represent their objects, independently alike of any resemblance or any real connection, because dispositions or factitious habits of their interpreters insure their being so understood. Of sensuous qualities and, indeed, of Feelings generally, Icons are the sole possible *ultimate* signs. But an ordinary yardstick, which is nothing but a representative of the yard that is supposed to be walled up in Westminster Palace, is not a mere Likeness in itself of that prototype, since all lengths, as far as we know, are precisely alike in themselves,—and this illustrates why I prefer to call signs of this class "Icons." The yardstick represents the standard yard, not in the least because it is like that standard, but because if it were to be brought into a certain actual physical relation, called *comparison*, with the standard,—as in point of fact it must have been brought, mediately, if not immediately,—neither of the two sole conceivable *positive* sensible results would occur,—i.e., it would neither be found sensibly too long nor sensibly too short. We can easily see that this truth is general, and that the presence or absence of falsity can only be ultimately and directly assured by an Index, and can only be ultimately and directly brought to mind by an Icon of an Index. But what is plainer still is that if one's desire is neither to excite an idea nor to record a fact but to make a rational appeal, the only sort of sign that can possibly answer the purpose is that which represents its object by virtue of the disposition of the interpreter,—that is to say, a Symbol. Since, therefore, the conduct of reasoning is the ultimate aim of the logician, as such, I used to think that he should recognize the Symbol as the object of his study, and this only as regards its relation to the object it represents. But now I have come to opine that while it is possible that some thousands of years hence, men may know so much more than we of today do, and with that increase of knowledge problems may have multiplied,—in somewhat such a way as a number is increased as a consequence of an increment to its logarithm,—so that the study of the necessary relations of symbols in general to their objects may afford sufficient occupation for a scientific group, yet today I do not think that the whole investigation of signs in general is too much. Besides, this general study must be done by somebody; and I do not see what other group there is that can do it. Of course, psychologists ought to make, as in point of fact they are making, their own invaluable studies of the sign-making and sign-using functions,—invaluable, I call them, in spite of the fact that they cannot possibly come to their final conclusions, until other more elementary studies have come to their first harvest,—studies that it is natural for the psychologist to regard (which is not saying that every psychologist does regard) with something of the same disdain as he may naturally bestow upon the still more vacuous studies of the pure mathematician,—or would, if mathematics were not so old a science that its rich granaries command respect. Logic, too, is said to be an old science. Yes; but let a diligent student of its immense literature be asked a question calculated to reveal the degree of his respect for the way in which its devotees have used their time, if before the question be put, some pressing engagement have not compelled him to take his leave with genuine chagrin upon his countenance.

Would it not, at any rate, in the present state of science, be good scientific policy, for those who have both a talent and a passion for eliciting the truth about such matters, to institute a cooperative cenoscopic attack upon the problems of the nature, properties, and varieties of Signs, in the spirit of twentieth-century science. For my part, although I have had sundry universal propositions concerning Signs under anxious advisement for many years, I have been unable to satisfy myself as to a single one of them. (N.B. Having made this explicit avowal it will be needless for me to express my doubts again.) This is not because of any definite reason for hesitation, but simply that having been unable to urge my argument upon any mind but my cautious self, I cannot help having a vague question whether a fresh intelligence, uncramped by long dwelling on the same questions, might not start objections that have escaped my own fagged understanding on account of their very obviousness, just as in my fatigue I very frequently think I have mislaid some familiar instrument or utensil and lose the better part of an hour searching for it and finally discover it very prominently placed just where it always is and ought to be, but where the very absence of any feature to which I am not accustomed has prevented its attracting my attention. I think it most likely that my doubts about all universal predications concerning signs are mostly quite gratuitous, but still my having no second person to whom to appeal as to the reasonableness of my doubts prevents their being laid to rest.[28]

31

An Essay toward Improving Our Reasoning in Security and in Uberty

MS 682. [This text, composed in September–October 1913, a few months before Peirce's death, belongs to a series of unfinished papers on reasoning.] Written in a retrospective mood, this unfinished work shows Peirce continuing to assess the completeness of his logic and the scope of his pragmatism. We learn that reasoning involves a trade-off between security and uberty (rich suggestiveness), and that, not surprisingly, deductive reasoning provides the most security, but little uberty, while abduction provides much uberty but almost no security. Pragmatism, it seems, falls in on the side of security: "[it] does not bestow a single smile upon beauty, upon moral virtue, or upon abstract truth; — the three things that alone raise Humanity above Animality." Peirce objects strongly to Francis Bacon's pessimistic claim that nature is beyond human understanding and repeats his long-held conviction that psychology can offer no significant aid to logic. The essay ends with a reminder that the connection between words and thought is as intimate as that between body and mind.

When it happens that a new belief comes to one as consciously generated from a previous belief,—an event which can only occur in consequence of some third belief (stored away in some dark closet of the mind, as a habit of thought) being in a suitable relation to that second one,—I call the event an *inference*, or a *reasoning*. And your Honor, the Reader, will please observe that any decided leaning toward a belief is or involves a full belief; namely, the full belief that the substance of the belief to which one leans is probable, or promising, or has some other title to intellectual honor. I express these things as yet in rough-and-ready fashion, subject [to] amendment in the sequel, my present purpose being merely to apprise the reader that this essay is limited to an examination of *Reasoning* only in a pretty broad sense of that word. For of course it will be necessary in the course of our study to scrutinize what passes through our minds during the incubation and birth of beliefs very closely and critically.

I address the Reader as "your Honor," simply because I sincerely do honor anybody who is disposed to undertake a sustained endeavor to train himself to reason in such ways as to miss as little as possible of such truth as it concerns him to know, while at the same time, as far as circumstances permit, avoiding risks of error; and I address him in the second person because I think of him as a real person, with all the instincts of which we human beings are so sublimely and so responsibly endowed.

I have postponed writing this essay for nearly fifty years in order that I might prepare myself to do so as little unworthily of the reader's attention as the limitations of my life and of my talent would allow. I shall assume that You, too, are willing to exert yourself to consider what I shall urge and to verify or correct what I may assert to be observable. I shall not assume that the reader has any training in making precise observations of any kind, nor that he has any acquaintance with the distinctions or laws of any science, unless vulgar arithmetic and the most elementary algebraic notation be called sciences. But I cannot deny that some experience in analyzing his ideas would facilitate the formation of a judgment on many points, very much.*

Reasoning-power, or *Ratiocination,* called by some *Dianoetic Reason,*[4] is the power of drawing inferences that tend toward the truth, when their premisses or the virtual assertions from which they set out are true. I regard this power as the principal of human intellectual instincts; and in this statement I select the appellation "instinct" in order to profess my belief that the reasoning-power is related to human nature very much as the wonderful instincts of ants, wasps, etc., are related to their several natures. Should I be asked for a more explicit statement of what I mean by an "instinct," I should [define it], after premising that while action may, in the first place, be purely physical and open to outward inspection, it may also, in the second place, be purely mental and knowable (by others, at any rate, than the actor) only through outward symptoms or indirect effects, and thirdly it may be partly inward and partly outward, as when a person talks, involving some expenditure of potential energy,—that premised, I say, I should define what I mean by an "instinct" as a way of voluntary acting prevalent almost universally among

---

*I do not know that it might not be well for him to have read, as critically as he could, the first one hundred and thirty *aphorisms* of Francis Bacon's *Novum Organum,* without allowing himself to be overawed by the high-stepping gait of its language and thought. One can have a profound respect and gratitude for this benefactor of us all without losing sight of his faults,— his contemptuous tone toward the physical science of his day, including all that Galileo, Kepler, Gilbert, and Harvey had done (Aph. viii); nor of the absurd extravagance of a part of what he says and fails to say; as in Aph. x [and] xxiv, where we ask what can be definitely meant by *subtilitas naturae;* in Aph. xxx, which condemns the method by which all the discoveries of the greatest difficulty have been first suggested; in Aph. xlix, where Bacon seems to think that there are irremediable defects in human intellect, which can nevertheless be nullified by an artificial contrivance, somewhat like a method of bookkeeping; and especially in Aph. xlviii, where he implies that of those two of the Aristotelean "causes" (αἰτίαι) that would still be called causes in modern speech, the *final* cause is a mere fiction as far as the external world goes, and the *efficient,* i.e., the antecedent cause, alone is to be accepted. Now what is a "final" cause? It is merely a tendency to produce some determinate kind of effect having some relation to the *destiny* of things. But is not such a tendency abundantly manifest in the whole life-process of plants? It is true that the biologists assume (far in advance of anything like proof) that this is only a derivative effect. But what if it be so? That does not make it *unreal,* in the least; and all the admirable labors of hundreds of men specially adapted to such work, during more than half a century have not done more than to leave the weight of argument directly over the fulcrum of a well-balanced mind.

otherwise normal individuals of at least one sex or other unmistakable natural part of a race (at some stage, or during recurring periods of their lives), which action conduces to the probable perpetuation of that race, and which, in the present stage of science, is not at once satisfactorily and fully explicable as a result of any more general way of mental action.

Here it is but fair to the Reader, lest he should be seduced unawares into assent to a disputable doctrine, that I should at once avow that in my endeavor to meet the exigencies of verifiable thought in science, I have long ago come to be guided by this maxim: that as long as it is *practically certain that we cannot* directly, nor with much accuracy even indirectly, observe what passes in the consciousness of any other person, while it is far from certain that we can do so (and accurately record what *[we]* can even glimpse at best but very glibberly)[5] even in the case of what shoots through our own minds, it is much safer to define all mental characters as far as possible in terms of their outward manifestations. In the case of any consciousness of the nature of Thought, I shall show that there appears to be an even more imperative reason for following the maxim than that methodological, or prudential, one just given, though this ought to be sufficient to determine us.

That maxim is, roughly speaking, equivalent to the one that I used in 1871 to call the rule of "pragmatism."[6] It certainly aids our approximation to *[the] security* of reasoning. But it does not contribute to the *uberty* of reasoning, which far more calls for solicitous care.[7] For reasoning must be strangely perverse if it habitually gives falsity rather than truth, while we know but too well from history that in any one field it may remain completely sterile through one millennium after another. Yet the maxim of Pragmatism does not bestow a single smile upon beauty, upon moral virtue, or upon abstract truth;—the three things that alone raise Humanity above Animality.

The Reader may suppose, in taking up this essay, that while it may effect some improvement in the practice of an inexperienced reasoner, it cannot profit him in any respect more than would the study of modern science. But I undertake to show him that even the most admirable of modern reasoners,

---

And note that when in most enthusiastic and profound sincerity I call their labors *"admirable,"* I mean that they are so *except* in their determination to work toward a preconceived conclusion,—which is testimony to the power of final causation from those who are trying with all their might to prove there is no such thing. Even gravity might without falsity be conceived as a final cause, since it certainly destines things ultimately to approach the center of the earth. But since Galileo's illuminating *Discorsi* (Vol. xiii of Alberi's edition, 1855, of *Le Opere di Galileo Galilei*), not to speak of his *Sermones de motu gravium* (Vol. xi),[1] which, though not in print at the date (1620) of the *Novum Organum*, had long been widely circulated, it has proved extremely difficult for physicists to conceive of effects only being separated by a lapse of time from their causes, unless a motion of matter or some change of its character occupies that interval of time. But perhaps the Lord Chancellor[2] had a difficulty in putting his mind into the attitude of a physicist. Such strictures leave quite untouched the impressive grandeur of his *liber primus* and the noble peculiarity of its expression, as well as the instructive example that *liber secundus* puts before us of how the crudest observations, skillfully used, may anticipate by two centuries the conclusions of minuter science.[3]

and in those kinds of reasoning in which they are at their very best, occasionally draw inferences that *[are] utterly* unfounded, but which more or less tinge all their subsequent teachings. Yet considering modern science as a whole, I believe its positively wrong conclusions are of small moment compared with its neglect systematically to consider possibilities among which there are likely to be keys to undiscovered treasuries of truth. My reasons for this opinion shall be submitted to the judgment of the reader in due time.

A reasoner of the sixteenth century (or even in the century following) might very well have objected (and very likely did in fact, although I do not now recall any such passage), "If you purpose arraigning the very principles of human Ratiocination itself before the bar of judgment, how can they ever be vindicated? Reasoning cannot be allowed to pass judgment in favor of itself!" But now that we have learned that whatever has vitality, whatever is to be called *good*, has been in process of development doubtless from a rudiment further back than any vestige now remains for us, and is still presumably to develop further, we ought to see that although it is more than true that no single act of reasoning "can be allowed to" pass judgment upon itself, since it would be powerless to do so even if it had every conceivable permission, since it is past and gone before any doubt of it can arise, yet there appears no reason why, provided reasoning at all tends to be true, in a more developed stage of growth of the reasoning-power, a former reasoning should not be put on trial and be convicted of weakness or utter irrationality. But even the idea of any growth of knowledge about unchanging conditions is almost confined to modern times. Any inspiring and well-grounded hope of that sort blossomed only in the breasts of an elect few,—Petrus Peregrinus, Roger Bacon,[8] and some half-crazed successors until our blessed Galileo Galilei and then the shrewd John Kepler lit their torches and passed on the flame; for even Koppernyk only took courage to publish his embarrassed theory because he understood it had been taught by Pythagoras. No such glad tidings had been published since the Gospels; and no doubt Francis Bacon helped a good deal to spread the news, somewhat in the role of St. Paul. The latter, however, never tried to steal the credit for the message.

Since Galileo, the progress of science has been accelerated more; and the question cannot be suppressed: "What are we to anticipate in this respect?" I do not myself believe that we have any tolerable reason for any answer to that question. I once thought the indications were that the human race would become extinct before any great number of future centuries. But in the first place further consideration has pretty nearly balanced that inclination of judgment; and in the next place, if it be so, I incline toward guessing that another and more intelligent race may supplant us to advantage, though this is the merest dream. Francis Bacon, laying down his decisions "after the manner of a Lord Chancellor" (as the great physiologist Harvey is reported to have remarked),[9] categorically asserted that "The subtilty of Nature far exceeds the subtilty of the human mind."*[10] If this has any meaning whatsoever, it must be

---

*Aph. x. *Subtilitas naturae subtilitatem sensus et intellectus multis partibus superat*; etc.

that there are phenomena in nature which no man will ever be able even approximately to describe in general terms. Supposing this to be true, one would like to know how Bacon ever found it out. It was probably by some very different process from that of which he gives us an account in the *Novum Organum*. So far, the difficulties of explanatory science have rather been of the contrary kind; that is, that different and inconsistent hypotheses would equally account for the observed facts. The only case in which there has been any serious difficulty in conceiving of any hypothesis has been that of Morley and Michelson's celebrated experiment, which has, however, now received one exact possible explanation based on a hypothesis which there was already reason to surmise might be true.[11] And it would not surprise me if other explanations of the same general character made their appearance. Certainly I can hardly imagine how Bacon's despairing belief can ever be justified.

So, then, when one fact puts a person in mind of another, but related, fact, and on considering the two together, he says to himself, "Hah! Then this third is a fact," though I say that it is by *instinct* that he draws the inference, I nevertheless admit that he may be very much mistaken, just as such animals as dogs and ants are sometimes betrayed by their instincts. It is true that neither man nor beast has any immediate appeal from a judgment rendered by his instinct. Yet the instincts of the more intelligent mammals, birds, and insects, sometimes undergo modification under new experience. It is said that a swarm of honeybees, carried to the West Indies, will soon abandon the practice of storing up honey; and I myself once had pointed out to me by Professor Evangelinos Apostolides Sophocles,[12]—who was a curious observer of many other things than the habits of aorist infinitives,—a certain toad who used to come out at dusk upon a certain walk to capture ants, etc., with his swift tongue, but who, having lost one eye, was in great apparent danger of starvation after that accident, owing to his then invariably striking to a certain side of the insect; but a week or so later, Sophocles showed me that the one-eyed toad was picking up again and looking quite cheerful, and was now as sure of his aim as ever,—at least during the hour or so through which we watched him. Some people are so inobservant as to suppose that the training of dogs and horses is simply forced upon them from without, and consequently that very rude conduct on the part of the trainer must be persisted in. But it is quite the other way. When they once understand what is wanted they try to learn until fatigued. My wife has a black poodle (named Zola, after the humane advocate of Dreyfus)[13] who has learned a great many "tricks" under affectionate treatment exclusively; but those of them that do not seem to him to have any practical or moral purpose he is not very fond of doing, unless, indeed, a stranger is present, before whom he can show off. He seems to have a nice sense of genuine grace of manners in people; but that is so common in dogs of pedigree as not to be worth mention. When his mistress puts his plate with his one daily meal on the hearth, she says (being a French woman), "A table, Zola," and he sits before it, and waits for the next word. Sometimes it has happened that she has been called away at this stage of the business, and returning after a couple of hours, has found him still sitting alone in the room, with the water running down from his chaps. But when she says "Zola est servi," the plate is emptied almost instantaneously.

Now if the vital instincts of beasts are so much modified by human companionship, it is surely to be anticipated that the instincts of mankind, owing to the vastly greater range of our ideas, as well as to the gift of more articulate speech and the power of recording, and that multiply, whatever flits through consciousness, should prove more mutable by far; and this anticipation is not merely confirmed but more deeply and sharply engraved into our conviction by facts. For although there is as much reason to believe in the unity of origin of humankind as there is in that of the dogs, the parrots, or the finches,—which I instance as being among the families whose mental constitutions strike us as most like our own,—yet the extraordinary variety of languages, customs, institutions, religions, as well as the many revolutions /these/ have undergone in the brief half-dozen of millennia to which our acquaintance with them is as yet limited, as compared with the almost insignificant anatomical variations,—these facts, I say, make the old-fashioned notion that because there is no immediate appeal from instinctive ratiocinative conviction there can therefore be no improvement or growth in fundamental ratiocinative procedure, appear to a modern a good deal in the attitude of a schoolboy perched on a stool with a fool's cap on his head.

It is a state of mind now so outgrown that I believe no reader will blame me for merely indicating, as I have done, the kinds of consideration that refute it.

It seems to me sufficiently likely that among my Readers there may be one or more to whom the subject of this essay is almost or altogether new; and since of these, those, at least, whose youth brings them into this class are worthy of particular honor from me as being possibly among those who are destined to advance future knowledge and understanding, I am going to address the rest of the present paragraph particularly to them. I have read or examined an enormous number of books that seemed to me to have been written because their authors thought either that they would sell, or would advance their reputations, or would render them popular with certain classes. There is nothing morally wrong about such motives *in themselves;* but nevertheless they have always been most repugnant to me, because I am of opinion that men's unavowed motives influence the effects of their doings far more than the doers ever suspect, and that books in the writing of which such motives were not completely overwhelmed under the weight of others,—such, for example, as the impulse to give utterance to what it was almost killing the man to keep in,—were not worth to the reader the cost, in time and attention, of reading them, and thus were, in effect, swindles, whatever their authors' intentions may have been. I readily admit that my feelings on this subject are perhaps more extreme than reasonably ought to be. But such as they are, I think it is proper that /they/ should not be concealed; especially they have had three main effects, as follows: first, that I have never published a complete volume of my own, but only detached articles; second, that I have never published anything except to record my observations of facts, or to present reasonings that I had long and critically considered; and third, that I have never put forth anything in my own name unless it was either quite new, as far as I was aware, or else gave new reasons for believing what others had denied. Now this concerns the young reader in this way: that since of course my opinions, however cautiously I may have examined them, cannot be infallible, and presumably are denied by some writers, he is not to place any *implicit* faith in them, but only in so far as they recommend themselves to his own judgment, taking due account both of my fallibility and of his own inexperience in judging of such matters. I can only say that I have held this publication up for very many years of constant reconsideration, until approaching senility warned that I must either publish "or else forever hold my peace."[14] But please understand, Young Reader, to whom I have addressed this last long sentence, that though I thought myself under an implied obligation to put you on your guard against my possible mistakes, that you should not infer from what I have said that I have myself any positive misgiving as to any doctrine of this essay. It would be impossible, I suppose, to convey to any naïve young thinker any accurate idea of the state of belief of a hoary-headed student who has considered and turned over in his mind through near two generations a difficult question, always schooling himself to distrust his own reasonings as long as there remains any part of it where closer scrutiny might perhaps detect a weakness; but maybe a comparison will convey an idea of it which, vague as it must be, nevertheless perhaps may not prove useless to you as time goes on. Close to my house (i.e., my wife's) and parallel to the front of it, runs a broad grass-grown gravel walk about a quarter of a mile long and very substantially constructed with solid foundation of boulders, good ditches on both sides, etc. But what chiefly makes me delight in it is the fine view from it. For the ground slopes down or rather descends by three short jumps, and a pretty lofty one, to the picturesque Delaware River, beyond which one sees two ridges parallel to the river and to my walk. They are of markedly different shades of green, the further and brighter (five or six miles away) being what subsists, in this latitude of proud Blue Ridge, which in the South reaches heights of six and seven thousand feet above sea level but at this fag-end little exceeds two thousand at its highest point, which is the center of the view I am so fond of. Five roads run over the ridge, and one has a private branch leading to that summit. It is a charming spot looking far and wide over a smiling and civilized-looking country; and all but at the very tip-top lies a most poet-inspiring tarn that makes one weep for joy to catch sight of. So a man of wealth has established a large house there,[15] and apparently very near the house has erected a sort of less ambitious *tour d'Eiffel*, which stands up above my skyline with very good effect indeed. I have never examined it with a field glass, for I feared descrying some feature that would break the tower's charm. Now suppose I went out on walk with writing materials and were there to sit and write out as accurate, and detailed, and careful a description of the high point, and house, and tower as I possibly could, and then were to induce a score of other people whose eyes were as good as my own, one by one separately to do the same. I know by other experiences that among the twenty records there would be discrepancies utterly confounding. Very likely I should find some detail in which the majority would conflict with my account, and yet on careful and oft repeated reexamination I might remain satisfied that mine correctly described the appearance. Still, I should have to acknowledge to myself that it was possible that I had been wrong on this point and the others right. Now this supposed case seems to me not unlike that of the relation between the assertions that I make in this essay and the conflicting views of other inquirers into the same subject.

I now come a little nearer to that subject. Because we often reason wrongly, so that it requires much care to avoid doing, and it is harder yet so to reason as to gain all the truth we might from it, it is very important that we should know just what passes in our minds in reasoning and how it differs from other states of mind. And the fact that it is an instinctive performance, that is to say, is such that we can only correct it by doing more of the same kind of work, and not by doing something of an altogether different nature *without reasoning*, so that what reasoning does for us can absolutely not be accomplished without it, furnishes an additional motive for finding out, if we can, just what it is that makes the difference between genuine reasoning and other things that pass through the mind. (I may notice, by the way, that when I was a child I was told by my teachers, or understood them so, that only human beings reason, while only the other animals have incomprehensible instincts; but I suppose that today only benighted persons any longer believe either of these two assertions. No animals reason so much as men or about such intricate subjects; but to say that an intelligent dog, or horse, or parrot, or magpie, or canary bird does not reason at all, or only in such ways as humans have taught him, can have no definite meaning. On the other hand, to say that man has no incomprehensible instincts would be to talk without reflection and from surprisingly slight or else shockingly untilled experience.)

Now there is a science of what passes in the mind, called psychology. The English eighteenth-century philosophers, Hobbes, Locke, Hume, Berkeley, Gay, Hartley, Reid, and others, did good work in it. But following the *Origin of Species* by less than a year came another most remarkable work by a very singular man, Gustav Theodor Fechner's *Elemente der Psychophysik*,[16] consisting of experimental researches concerning the relations and reactions of the material and mental worlds. Fechner's work was followed within two years by Wilhelm Wundt's *Beiträge zur Theorie der Sinneswahrnehmung*,[17] in my opinion quite the most solid piece of work that eminent leader ever did; and just one year later came his fascinating and stimulating *Vorlesungen über die Menschen- und Thier-Seele*, which begot the race of devotees of modern psychology. His *Grundzüge der physiologischen Psychologie* has been the standard encyclopedia of the science. I beseech my readers to make no mistake as to my enthusiastic rejoicing over the great light this new psychology has brought. Of course I do not think it is the final word to be said about the mind; for such finality is not yet known, thank God, in any modern science; should such ever take possession of scientific minds, it will forebode either the speedy extinction of the human race, or else an era of intellectual epilepsy. So, it in no degree conflicts with my admiration of modern psychology that I at once express the opinion that (at least, as far as I am acquainted with it) it can afford no aid whatever in laying the foundation of a sane philosophy of reasoning, albeit it has been and can still be of the most precious service in planning and executing the observations on which the reasonings depend and from which they spring.

The grounds of this opinion are as follows. First, although *Observation*, as distinguished from mere *Sensation*, certainly produces *items of Knowledge*, no amount of it ever can constitute what we all call *Science*. Even an "item of knowledge" involves more than Sensation, as I shall, I trust, soon help the Reader to see for himself. For it involves *Attention*, which is something radically different from *Mere Sensation*. But even Attentive Sensation, though one might, in ordinary parlance, call it "observation,"—that is to say *Noticing*,—would not make up the whole of a *Scientific Observation*; of which *Thought* is an essential ingredient, as I shall soon show. But, furthermore, no mere aggregate of even Scientific Observation can constitute a Science. To say that it can constitute even a *part* of a science would amount to mere logomachy; for it would not be such a part that, added to others like it, would go to make up *a Science*. Scientific Observation is, unquestionably, the whole foundation of every Science; even of pure mathematics. Training in Observation is essential to the business of a man of science, and has been pretty much the sum total of the professional training of many very celebrated naturalists, unless we reckon, as part of their professional training, that rhetorical training which enabled them to impress other minds with their ideas. But it will lead to clearer ideas if we agree to call the whole work of Scientific Observation together with all the labor of preparation for it, such as experimentation *et cetera et cetera*, as merely laying the foundation for Science, and agree to consider the processes of collecting and grouping results of Observation and of Reasoning from them as alone constituting the operation of erecting the Science itself; so that Science itself, when this word is used in the sense of that sort of *information* that it is the function of men of science to supply to practical men, will consist in what those men have concluded from their reasonings about observations. I say that in my judgment this conception of Science as something erected upon a foundation of Observation, but distinct from that foundation, will contribute to clearness of thought; but however this may be in other cases, I am quite as sure as I can be of anything I shall have to say, that the Reader and I shall be obliged to draw that distinction,—since our study, in this essay, will be confined to Reasoning. We shall find occasion to inquire whether or not the reasonings of scientific men are sound, and we shall not in every case be led to reply in the affirmative. No doubt, observations are more often bad than reasonings are; but that is a subject so entirely distinct and remote from that of fallacious reasoning that the two cannot conveniently be treated in the same essay. Should somebody here whip out his lead pencil in order to note on the margin of the page that no such immiscibility attaches to the subjects of the *fruitfulness* of observations and that *[of]* reasonings, I hope he will pause long enough to reflect that I can hardly be supposed to have selected the unusual word "uberty" instead of "fruitfulness" merely because it is spelled with half as many letters. Observations may be as *fruitful* as you will, but they cannot be said to be *gravid* with young truth in the sense in which reasoning may be, not because of the nature of the subject it considers, but because of the manner in which it is supported by the ratiocinative instinct.

We are obliged, then, for our purposes to consider the work of science proper to consist in the operation of reasoning.

Second, of the two questions with which this essay is to concern itself, the first, and, on the whole, the more fundamental, relates to the degree of confidence that we ought to have in conclusions reached by different ways of reasoning, while the other question is how far we ought to resort to ways of reasoning that, although they are hazardous, may put us upon the track of important truths that no safer ways of reasoning could ever suggest to us, and which, once suggested, may be supported by such a multitude of independent lines of reasoning that must every one have been false unless their common conclusion is true, that reason commends that common conclusion to us, as less dangerous than to reject it, or even than to act as if it did not exist.

Third, what I am *aware* of, or, to use a different expression for the same fact, what I am *conscious* of, or, as the psychologists strangely talk, the "contents of my consciousness" (just as if what I am conscious of and the fact that I am conscious were two different facts, and as if the one were inside the other), this same fact, I say, however it be worded, is evidently the entire universe, so far as I am concerned. At least, so it would seem. Yet there is a wonderful revelation for me in the phenomenon of my sometimes becoming conscious that I have been in error, which at once shows me that if there can be no universe, as far as I am concerned, except the universe I am aware of, still there are differences in awareness. I become aware that though "universe" and "awareness" are one and the same thing, yet somehow the universe will go on in some definite fashion after I am dead and gone, whether I shall be the least aware of it, or not.

Please understand, Reader, that I do not in the least mean to represent that it is at all in this way that we actually do come to this conclusion; for our natural rational instinct (for Reason *is* a sort of instinct) makes us pretty well aware of it all in advance of any such reflections. I only sketch in the vaguest outline how we *might* come to the truth of the matter, even though we were in the most hardened state of cecity to the just authority of instinct. Tut, tut! Have I, at my time of life, been betrayed into talking of "the just authority of instinct"? What can that phrase mean? The word "Instinct" itself is but a generalization of abstractions,—one of the brood of language or of thought: there is no great difference between the two, as we shall see. When an animal responds to a stimulus in much the same way as almost any other individual of the same species or division of that species (such as a sex, for example), and does so not, so to speak, mechanically (as when a well man's kneepan is struck), but voluntarily, and when the response is of such a kind as generally to have a beneficial effect upon that same animal or its progeny, which effect, however, the animals that act so can hardly be supposed to have divined or, at any rate not to have ascertained by reasoning from any other facts within their knowledge, then we call the action "instinctive," while the general habit of behavior, regarded as appertaining to the animal's consciousness, we call "an instinct." It will thus be seen that one "instinct" of an animal may be a special determination of a more general "instinct" of the same animal; so that the former can be said in one sense to be a "part" of the latter, while in another sense the latter may be called a "part" of the former. The sense in which the special is regarded as a part of the general is called the "extensive" sense, and the other the "intensive" sense. Of course, this "intensiveness" has nothing to do with the *intensity* of a sensation, any more than this "extensiveness" has to do with spatial *extension*. It is more congenial to other phrases that have naturally grown up in such few intellectual vernaculars as I am acquainted with, to speak of intensive muchness,—the more characters that one expression implies than another does, so that a definition of it must specify items of its meaning which the definition of the other should not mention,—to call this, with Sir W. Hamilton, the *depth*, while the other muchness, by which one expression is applicable to all the kinds of things or of states of things to which another is applicable, and still more besides, to call this the superior *breadth* or *width* of the former.[18] Thus, in our own language, we may say of a man that he has a wide acquaintance with animals or with plants, however superficial that acquaintance may be; or we may say that though a man's linguistic acquirements may be somewhat narrow, yet those languages that [he] pretends to know, he knows to their very bottom (or that he is deeply versed in them). Or in French, "Celui-ci possède une connaissance étendue mais peu profonde; celui-là est bien de son village, mais du peu d'affaires dont il s'est instruit il sait le fond et le tréfonds."[19] There are similar idioms in Latin; and it was from the Greek that Hamilton drew the suggestion of calling the two "quantities" *breadth* and *depth*. De Morgan, though a remarkably accurate thinker, even among mathematicians (which is far enough from being true of Hamilton), certainly blundered in proposing to substitute for *breadth* the word "scope," which is not vernacular itself nor has any vernacular kindred;[20] and his proposal to substitute "force" for *depth* was much worse still. J. S. Mill used the words "denote" and "connote."[21] The former, as representing the equivalent Latin *notare*, was accurate though not at all vernacular; but "connote" is unpardonably bad, because it had a quite different exact signification in the science of reasoning, and the only real utility of his suggestion was that his attempt to make out that he was only following Ockham's usage served to exhibit his extraordinary faculty for deceiving himself. He ought to have seen that the stem *nota* was to be avoided in speaking of *Depth*, while there were plenty of ways already in English for expressing what he meant by *connote*; such as *to mean, signify, express, imply, import, include, involve, comprehend, convey*, etc. Perhaps the best of these is *import*, although it is perhaps too psychological. It might, at first blush, seem inaccurate to speak of Depth and Breadth, in these senses, as Quantities, since they do not in the least imply any equivalence in their parts. But no more do ordinal numbers. Nor do cardinal numbers either; for to speak of two men does not imply that the two units are at all equal. So the algebraic *plus* carries not the slightest implication that the terms added are at all comparable as to equality or inequality. There is no valid reason why we should not add a distance to an interval of time, just as we are accustomed to write $a + b\sqrt{-1}$. For although we have hitherto only had occasion to do this in cases in which they can be brought into comparison by rotation amounting to a right angle, Lorentz has already shown us such a convenience in considering a time, if not exactly as a dimension of time-space, at least as that fourth unit that Hamilton adds to the three dimensions of space to make up a quaternion;[22] and indeed one may say that, from the point of view of matrices, three-dimensional space appears as not altogether comprehensible without a fourth. Consequently, as science now is, it seems to me imprudent to insist upon including in our conception of quantity that of the metrical comparability of parts.

Now I know that a considerable part of my readers, and that the very part for which I care the most, since it is they to whom I can be of most service, since they have the most to learn about reasoning, will be getting very impatient at so much talk about mere words. I also fully realize that in these times and as long as I shall live, it is those who know the least and who can least continue /to be/ patient who are to decide how matters shall be conducted. But I hope, too, that I shall have some reader, if it be but one, who either already knows, or else will try whether I can convince him, that, the connection between words and thought being as intimate as that between body and mind, it is impossible to make reasoning really understood without saying a good deal, especially in the introductory part, about words; and after all, the only reader to whom I can be of any service at all is the one who will read what I write and will carefully and critically reflect upon it. Him, and him alone, I am absolutely certain of benefitting, though he conclude that I am in the wrong from beginning to end.[23]

APPENDIX:

SEMIOTICS FROM LATE CORRESPONDENCE

32

Excerpts from Letters to Lady Welby

*L 463 and Welby Collection, York University. [The first excerpt comes
from L 463:98–102, a letter-draft composed in the early spring of 1906;
it was published in* Semiotics and Significs, *pp. 196–97. The second
comes from a letter dated 23 December 1908, also published in* Semiotics
and Significs, *pp. 80–85. The third comes from L 463:132–46, a letter-
draft begun a few days before Christmas 1908; published in CP 8.342–
76.] Peirce's letters to Lady Welby are among the richest records of the
evolution of his semiotic thought. In the first excerpt, we learn that there
are two semiotic objects and three interpretants, and we meet with the
striking idea of the* commens, *that fused mind of utterer and interpreter
without which there can be no communication. We also learn that the dynamic object, the object of experience, though not in the sign, is not outside
the mind. In the 1908 segments, Peirce delivers his famous "sop to Cerberus"—his insertion of the phrase "upon a person" in his definition of
"Sign"—and builds the case for his ten trichotomies. In the final postscript
he diagrams a ten-fold classification of signs based on the modalities of
Idea, Occurrence, and Habit.*

Spring 1906

I use the word "*Sign*" in the widest sense for any medium for the communication or extension of a Form (or feature).[1] Being medium, it is determined
by something, called its Object, and determines something, called its Interpretant or Interpretand. But some distinctions have to be borne in mind in
order rightly to understand what is meant by the Object and by the Interpretant. In order that a Form may be extended or communicated, it is necessary
that it should have been really embodied in a Subject independently of the
communication; and it is necessary that there should be another Subject in
which the same Form is embodied only in consequence of the communication. The Form (and the Form is the Object of the Sign), as it really determines the former Subject, is quite independent of the sign; yet we may and
indeed must say that the object of a sign can be nothing but what that sign
represents it to be. Therefore, in order to reconcile these apparently conflicting truths, it is indispensable to distinguish the *immediate* object from the
dynamical object.

The same form of distinction extends to the interpretant; but as applied to
the interpretant, it is complicated by the circumstance that the sign not only

determines the interpretant to represent (or to take the form of) the *object*, but also determines the interpretant to represent the sign. Indeed in what we may, from one point of view, regard as the principal kind of signs, there is one distinct part appropriated to representing the object, and another to representing how this very sign itself represents that object. The class of signs I refer to are the dicisigns. In "John is in love with Helen," the object signified is the pair, John and Helen. But the "is in love with" signifies the form this sign represents itself to represent John-and-Helen's Form to be. That this is so is shown by the precise equivalence between any verb in the indicative and the same made the object of "I tell you": "Jesus wept" = "I tell you that Jesus wept."

There is the *Intentional* Interpretant, which is a determination of the mind of the utterer; the *Effectual* Interpretant, which is a determination of the mind of the interpreter; and the *Communicational* Interpretant, or say the *Cominterpretant*, which is a determination of that mind into which the minds of utterer and interpreter have to be fused in order that any communication should take place.[2] This mind may be called the *commens*. It consists of all that is, and must be, well understood between utterer and interpreter, at the outset, in order that the sign in question should fulfill its function. This I proceed to explain.

No object can be denoted unless it be put into relation to the object of the *commens*. A man, tramping along a weary and solitary road, meets an individual of strange mien, who says, "There was a fire in Megara." If this should happen in the Middle United States, there might very likely be some village in the neighborhood called Megara. Or it may refer to one of the ancient cities of Megara, or to some romance. And the time is wholly indefinite. In short, nothing at all is conveyed, until the person addressed asks, "Where?"—"Oh about half a mile along there" pointing to whence he came. "And when?" "As I passed." Now an item of information has been conveyed, because it has been stated relatively to a well-understood common experience. Thus the Form conveyed is always a determination of the dynamical object of the *commind*. By the way, the dynamical object does not mean something out of the mind. It means something forced upon the mind in perception, but including more than perception reveals. It is an object of actual *Experience*.

23 December 1908

I define a Sign as anything which is so determined by something else, called its Object, and so determines an effect upon a person, which effect I call its Interpretant, that the latter is thereby mediately determined by the former. My insertion of "upon a person" is a sop to Cerberus, because I despair of making my own broader conception understood. I recognize three Universes, which are distinguished by three Modalities of Being.[3]

One of these Universes embraces whatever has its Being in itself alone, except that whatever is in this Universe must be present to one consciousness, or be capable of being so present in its entire Being. It follows that a member of this universe need not be subject to any law, not even to the principle of contradiction. I denominate the objects of this Universe *Ideas*, or *Possibles*, although the latter designation does not imply capability of actualization. On the contrary as a general rule, if not a universal one, an Idea is incapable of perfect actualization on account of its essential vagueness if for no other reason. For that which is not subject to the principle of contradiction is essentially vague. For example, geometrical figures belong to this Universe; now since every such figure involves lines which can only be *supposed* to exist as boundaries where three bodies come together, or to be the place common to three bodies, and since the boundary of a solid or liquid is merely the place at which its forces of cohesion are neither very great nor very small, which is essentially vague, it is plain that the idea is essentially vague or indefinite. Moreover, suppose the three bodies that come together at a line are wood, water, and air, then a whole space including this line is at every point either wood, water, or air; and neither wood and water, nor wood and air, nor water and air can together occupy any place. Then plainly the principle of contradiction, were it applicable, would be violated in the idea of a place where wood, water, and air come together. Similar antinomies affect all Ideas. We can only reason about them in respects which the antinomies do not affect, and often by arbitrarily assuming what upon closer examination is found to be absurd. There is this much truth in Hegel's doctrine, although he is frequently in error in applying the principle.

Another Universe is that of, first, Objects whose Being consists in their Brute reactions, and of, second, the Facts (reactions, events, qualities, etc.) concerning those Objects, all of which facts, in the last analysis, consist in their reactions. I call the Objects, Things, or more unambiguously, *Existents*, and the facts about them I call Facts. Every member of this Universe is either a Single Object subject, alike to the Principles of Contradiction and to that of Excluded Middle, or it is expressible by a proposition having such a singular subject.

The third Universe consists of the co-being of whatever is in its Nature *necessitant*, that is, is a Habit, a law, or something expressible in a universal proposition. Especially, *continua* are of this nature. I call objects of this universe *Necessitants*. It includes whatever we can know by logically valid reasoning. I note that the question you put on the first page of your letter as to whether a certain proposition is "thoroughly tested" and supports the test, or whether it is "logically proved," seems to indicate that you are in some danger of enlisting in that army of "cranks," who insist on calling a kind of reasoning "logical" which leads from true premises to false conclusions, thus putting themselves outside the pale of sanity. People, for example, who maintain that the reasoning of the "Achilles" (and the tortoise) is "logical," though they cannot state it in any sound syllogistic or other form acknowledged by sane reasoners. I knew a gentleman who had mind enough to be a crack chess-player, but who insisted that it was "logical" to reason

It either rains or it doesn't rain,
Now it rains;
∴ It doesn't rain.

This is on a perfect level with saying that [the] contemptible Achilles catch is "logical." The truth is that an inference is "logical," if, and only if, it is governed by a habit that would in the long run lead to the truth. I am confident you will assent to this. Then I trust you do not mean to lend any countenance to notions of logic that conflict with this. It is a part of our duty to frown sternly upon immoral *principles;* and logic is only an application of morality. Is it not?

A Sign may *itself* have a "possible" Mode of Being; e.g., a hexagon inscribed in or circumscribed about a conic. It is a Sign in that the collinearity of the intersections of opposite sides shows the curve to be a conic, if the hexagon is inscribed; but if it be circumscribed, the copunctuality of its three diameters (joining opposite vertices)[shows the curve to be a conic]. Its Mode of Being may be Actuality: as with any barometer. Or Necessitant: as the word "the" or any other in the dictionary. For a "possible" Sign I have no better designation than a *Tone,* though I am considering replacing this by "Mark." Can you suggest a really good name? An Actual sign I call a *Token;* a Necessitant Sign a *Type.*

It is usual and proper to distinguish two Objects of a Sign, the Mediate without, and the Immediate within the Sign. Its Interpretant is all that the Sign conveys: acquaintance with its Object must be gained by collateral experience. The Mediate Object is the Object outside of the Sign; I call it the *Dynamoid* Object. The Sign must indicate it by a hint; and this hint, or its substance, is the *Immediate* Object. Each of these two Objects may be said to be capable of either of the three Modalities, though in the case of the Immediate Object, this is not quite literally true. Accordingly, the Dynamoid Object may be a Possible,—when I term the Sign an *Abstractive,* such as the word Beauty; and it will be none the less an Abstractive if I speak of "the Beautiful," since it is the ultimate reference, and not the grammatical form, that makes the sign an *Abstractive.* When the Dynamoid Object is an Occurrence (Existent thing or Actual fact of past or future), I term the Sign a *Concretive;* any one barometer is an example, and so is a written narrative of any series of events. For a Sign whose Dynamoid Object is a Necessitant, I have at present no better designation than a *Collective,* which is not quite so bad a name as it sounds to be until one studies the matter: but for a person, like me, who thinks in quite a different system of symbols to words, it is so awkward and often puzzling to translate one's thought into words! If the Immediate Object is a Possible, that is, if the Dynamoid Object is indicated (always more or less vaguely) by means of its Qualities, etc., I call the Sign a *Descriptive;* if the Immediate [Object] is an Occurrence, I call the Sign a *Designative;* and if the Immediate Object is a Necessitant, I call the sign a *Copulant;* for in that case the Object has to be so identified by the Interpreter that the Sign may represent a necessitation. My name is certainly a temporary expedient.

It is evident that a Possible can determine nothing but a Possible; it is equally so that a Necessitant can be determined by nothing but a Necessitant. Hence it follows from the Definition of a Sign that since the Dynamoid Object determines the Immediate Object,

> which determines the Sign itself,
>
> which determines the Destinate Interpretant,
>
> which determines the Effective Interpretant,
>
> which determines the Explicit Interpretant,

the six trichotomies, instead of determining 729 classes of signs, as they would if they were independent, only yield 28 classes; and if, as I strongly opine (not to say almost prove) there are four other trichotomies of signs of the same order of importance, instead of making 59,049 classes, these will only come to 66. The additional four trichotomies are undoubtedly first,

Icons*	Indices	Symbols

and then three referring to the Interpretants. One of these I am pretty confident is into:

Suggestives	Imperatives	Indicatives

where the Imperatives include Interrogatives. Of the other two I *think* that one must be into Signs assuring their Interpretants by

Instinct	Experience	Form.

The other I suppose to be what, in my *Monist* exposition of Existential Graphs, I called

Semes	Phemes	Delomes.[5]

24–28 December 1908

The publishers of the *Britannica* have given an unequivocal earnest of their determination to make every edition of their encyclopaedia maintain its supereminence in employing editors who would enlist you for an epitome of your exploration of "significs." It greatly encourages me in my endeavors, since, as well as I can make out, what you call "significs" is equivalent to the study that I entitle logic. In my paper of 1867 May 14 *(Proceedings of the American Academy of Arts and Sciences)* I said, "We come to this, that logic

---

*Or Simulacra, Aristotle's ὁμοιωμάτα, caught from Plato, who I guess took it from the Mathematical school of logic, for it earliest appears in the *Phaedrus* which marks the beginning of Plato's being decisively influenced by that school. Lutoslawski is right in saying that the *Phaedrus* is later than the *Republic* but his date 379 B.C. is about 8 years too early.[4]

treats of the reference of symbols in general to their objects. In this view it is one of a trivium of conceivable sciences. The first would treat of the formal conditions of symbols having meaning, that is of the reference of symbols in general to their grounds, or imputed characters; and this might be called formal grammar (the *grammatica speculativa* of Duns). The second, logic, would treat of the formal conditions of the truth of symbols. The third would treat of the formal conditions of the force of symbols, or their power of appealing to a mind, that is, of their reference in general to interpretants, and this might be called formal rhetoric."[6] I should still opine that in the future there probably will be three such sciences. But I have learned that the only natural lines of demarcation between nearly related sciences are the divisions between the social groups of devotees of those sciences; and for the present the cenoscopic studies (i.e., those studies which do not depend upon new special observations) of all signs remain one undivided science,—a conclusion I had come to before I made your acquaintance, but which the warm interest that you and I have in each other's researches, in spite of the difference in their lines, decidedly confirms.

It seems to me that one of the first useful steps toward a science of *semeiotic* (σημειωτική), or the cenoscopic science of signs, must be the accurate definition, or logical analysis, of the concepts of the science. I define a *Sign* as anything which on the one hand is so determined by an Object and on the other hand so determines an idea in a person's mind, that this latter determination, which I term the *Interpretant* of the Sign, is thereby mediately determined by that Object. A Sign, therefore, has a triadic relation to its Object and to its Interpretant. But it is necessary to distinguish the *Immediate Object*, or the Object as the Sign represents it, from the *Dynamical Object*, or really efficient but not immediately present Object. It is likewise requisite to distinguish the *Immediate Interpretant*, i.e., the Interpretant represented or signified in the Sign, from the *Dynamic Interpretant*, or effect actually produced on the mind by the Sign; and both of these from the *Normal Interpretant*, or effect that would be produced on the mind by the Sign after sufficient development of thought. On these considerations I base a recognition of ten respects in which Signs may be divided. I do not say that these divisions are enough. But since every one of them turns out to be a trichotomy, it follows that in order to decide what classes of Signs result from them, I have 3^{10}, or 59,049, difficult questions to carefully consider; and therefore I will not undertake to carry my systematical division of Signs any further, but will leave that for future explorers.

The ten respects according to which the chief divisions of signs are determined are as follows: first, according to the Mode of Apprehension of the Sign itself; second, according to the Mode of Presentation of the Immediate Object; third, according to the Mode of Being of the Dynamical Object, fourth, according to the Relation of the Sign to its Dynamical Object, fifth, according to the Mode of Presentation of the Immediate Interpretant, sixth, according to the Mode of Being of the Dynamical Interpretant, seventh, according to the Relation of the Sign to the Dynamical Interpretant, eighth, according to the Nature of the Normal Interpretant, ninth, according to the Relation of the Sign to the Normal Interpretant, tenth, according to the Triadic Relation of the Sign to the Dynamical Object and to its Normal Interpretant.

The ten divisions appear to me to be all Trichotomies; but it is possible that some of them are not properly so. Of these Ten Trichotomies, I have a clear apprehension of some (which I mark δ for $\delta\tilde{\eta}\lambda o\varsigma$), an unsatisfactory and doubtful notion of others (which I mark α for $\tilde{\alpha}\delta\eta\lambda o\varsigma$), and a tolerable but not thoroughly tried conception of others (which I mark μ for $\mu\acute{\epsilon}\tau\rho\iota o\varsigma$, σ for $\sigma\chi\epsilon\delta\acute{o}\nu$, almost clear, χ for $\chi\alpha\lambda\epsilon\pi\tilde{\omega}\varsigma$, hardly better than α).[7]

The Ten Main Trichotomies of Signs
(as they are apprehended by me 1908 December 24)

I. A Sign is necessarily in itself present to the Mind of its Interpreter. Now there are three entirely different ways in which Objects are present to minds:

First, in themselves as they are in themselves. Namely, Feelings are so present. At the first instant of waking from profound sleep when thought, or even distinct perception is not yet awake, if one has gone to bed more asleep than awake in a large, strange room, with one dim candle. At the instant of waking the *tout ensemble* is felt as a unit. The feeling of the skylark's song in the morning, of one's first hearing of the English nightingale.

Secondly, the sense of something opposing one's Effort, something preventing one from opening a door slightly ajar; which is known in its individuality by the actual shock, the Surprising element, in any Experience which makes it *sui generis.*

Thirdly, that which is stored away in one's Memory; Familiar, and as such, General.

Consequently, Signs, in respect to their Modes of possible Presentation, are divisible (σ) into:

A. *Potisigns,* or Objects which are Signs so far as they are merely possible, but felt to be positively possible; as for example the seventh ray that passes through the three intersections of opposite sides of Pascal's hexagram.[8]

B. *Actisigns,* or Objects which are Signs as Experienced *hic et nunc;* such as any single word in a single place in a single sentence of a single paragraph of a single page of a single copy of a Book. There may be repetition of the whole paragraph, this word included, in another place. But that other occurrence is not *this* word. The book may be printed in an edition of ten thousand; but THIS word is only in my copy.

C. *Famisigns,* familiar signs, which must be General, as General signs must be familiar or composed of Familiar signs. (I speak of signs which are "general," not in the sense of *signifying* Generals, but as being *themselves* general;

just as *Charlemagne* is general, in that it occurs many times with one and the same denotation.)

I think I might as well have marked this division δ instead of σ, except that perhaps the question may arise whether I ought not to have recognized a division according as the sign is a *natural sign*, which has no party to the dialogue as its author, or whether it be an *uttered sign*, and in the latter case, is the very sign that is getting uttered or another. But it seems to me that this division turns upon the question of whether or not the sign uttered is a sign of a sign as its Object. For must not every sign, in order to become a sign, get uttered?

II. 1908 December 25. *[. . .]* Objects may be presented in three ways, thus:

First, as mere Ideas, or what might be if things were not as they are; such as a geometrical Surface, or an absolutely definite or distinct notion.

Second, as Brutely compelling attention.

Third, as Rationally recommending themselves, or as Habitudes to which one is already reconciled.

Adopting this enumeration as a basis of a division of Signs, I obtain:

A. *Descriptives*, which determine their Objects by stating the characters of the latter.

B. *Designatives* (or *Denotatives*), or *Indicatives, Denominatives*, which like a Demonstrative pronoun, or a pointing finger, brutely direct the mental eyeballs of the interpreter to the object in question, which in this case cannot be given by independent reasoning.

C. *Copulants*, which neither describe nor denote their Objects, but merely express universally the logical sequence of these latter upon something otherwise referred to. Such, among linguistic signs, as "If _____ then _____," "_____ is _____," "_____ causes _____," "_____ would be _____," "_____ is relative to _____ for _____," "Whatever," etc.

Shall I appoint this famous distinction (as I have stated it, or modified) to the governance of my Second way of dividing Signs, or shall I yield this place to a distinction prominent in every language on earth, that between the three "persons," *amo, amas, amat?* If *I* and *Thou* are the Objects, we say *We*; if *Thou* and *He* are the Objects, we say *Ye*. But if *I* and *He* are the Objects to the exclusion of *Thee*, I know no other linguistic form than the French expression "*Nous autres.*" *I, Thou,* and *He* can be expressed by the Tri-al and *Quadral* numbers of Polynesian languages; in English we can only say "*We all of us.*" Thus there ought, logically, one would say, to be *seven* grammatical persons, if any at all. But none at all are needed, if we have the Designative pronouns *I, Thou, He.* But hold! When I say there are only seven persons I forget the differences between Thou and I are Anglo-Saxon. Thou and I are correspondents. Thou and I are endurer and endured. Thou and I are admired and admirer. Thou, He, and I are accuser to and of, accuser of and to, accused by and to, accused to and by, informed of by, informed by of. In short this distinction does not require any special form of sign, nor could any form be adequate without numerous variations.

On the other hand, /there is/ the distinction of *Designatives* such as concrete subjects of signs or essentially nominative signs, /and/ *Descriptives* such as Predicates and Predicative Signs (such as a portrait with a legend designating the person represented), with Abstract nouns to be reckoned among Descriptives. The *Copulants* are likewise indispensable and have the property of being *Continuant*. What I mean is that the sign "*A* is red" can be decomposed so as to separate "is red" into a Copulative and a Descriptive, thus: "*A* possesses the character of redness." But if we attempt to analyze "possesses the character" in like manner, we get "*A* possesses the character of the possession of the character of Redness"; and so on *ad infinitum*. So it is, with "*A* implies *B*," "*A* implies its implication of *B*," etc. So with "It rains and hails," "It rains concurrently with hailing," "It rains concurrently with the concurrence of hailing," and so forth. I call all such signs Continuants. They are all Copulants and are the only *pure* Copulants. These signs *cannot be explicated*: they must convey Familiar universal elementary relations of logic. We do not derive these notions from observation, nor by any sense of being opposed, but from our own reason. This trichotomy, then, sustains criticism and must be marked (*μ*) at least. I would mark it (*δ*) if I were satisfied with the distinction between Descriptives and Denominatives.

Before proceeding to the third trichotomy, let /us/ inquire what relations, if any, are found between the two that have been brought to light. What I mean precisely by *between these relations* is whether or not the three members of the first trichotomy, which we may for the moment denote as 11, 12, 13, are or are not independent of the three members of the second, which we may denote by 21, 22, 23; so that they form nine classes, which if we use a dot to mean "which is," will be denoted by

$$11 \cdot 21 \quad 11 \cdot 22 \quad 11 \cdot 23$$
$$12 \cdot 21 \quad 12 \cdot 22 \quad 12 \cdot 23$$
$$13 \cdot 21 \quad 13 \cdot 22 \quad 13 \cdot 23$$

The inquiry ought, one would expect, to be an easy one, since both trichotomies depend on there being three Modes of Presence to the mind, which we may term

The Immediate,—The Direct,—The Familiar

Mode of Presence.

The difference between the two trichotomies is that the one refers to the Presence to the Mind of the Sign and the other to that of the Immediate Object. The Sign may have any Modality of Being, i.e. may belong to any one of the three Universes; its Immediate Object must be in some sense, in which the Sign need not be, Internal.

To begin, then, it is evident that an Actisign, or one that belongs to the Universe of Experience, which Brutely acts on the person, can also be a Denominative, that is, that its Immediate Object is represented as belonging to the same Universe; so that 12·22, the central class of our block of nine, is possible. Indeed, a pointing finger is a familiar example of a Sign of that class. Let us next ask whether all the four corner classes of the block are possible. We fully expect to find that a Potisign can be Descriptive and that a Famisign can be Copulant. But we may well doubt whether a Potisign can be Copulant or a Famisign can be Descriptive. Let us see.

Before taking up the cases, let me notice a source of possible confusion. By a "General Sign," or a "General Term," we do not, in the ordinary language of Logic, mean, as might be supposed, a Famisign. For we do not mean that the Sign *itself* is General: we only mean that its Object is so.

The Northern United States are full of I know not how many thousand "villages," as they are called in the State of New York, "towns" as they are called in New England, which are governed in a simple way by "town meetings" or otherwise; and in Pennsylvania "boroughs," whose head is a "chief burgess"; and there are also countless little places somewhat larger (especially in the West) called "cities." In the middle of any one of these where one might wander he would find a small green of an acre or two and in the middle of this will be a stone statue, often of granite, representing a common soldier standing in his regulation overcoat and resting on his grounded musket. Nothing imaginable could be more devoid of imagination, less idealized, less artistically beautiful. They are eyesores to all cultivated people; but not to me. For I know that that means that almost every family in that place,—vulgar people, though not quite so vulgar as the lower-middle classes of England, but small shopkeepers and the like, living upon profits made out of dealings with the surrounding farmers in a way just short of dishonesty,—every such family had in the war of the southern rebellion sent its flower, who had no military instinct whatever, much less any hatred for southern people, to the war, bitterly contrary to all his instincts but simply from a sense of duty; and only a fraction of them came back. The very fact of their vulgarity, which the statue proclaims above all else, makes this universal self-sacrifice on the altar of the abstraction which we call the "general government" pathetically sublime. To each such family, that very realistic statue represents the mourned one who fell in the war. That statue is one piece of granite, and not a Famisign. Yet it is what we call a "General" sign, meaning that it is *applicable* to many singulars. It is not *itself* General: it is its Object which is taken to be General. And yet this Object is not truly Universal, in the sense of implying a truth of the kind of "Any S is P"; it only expresses "Some S is P." This makes it *not* a //Copulant/Copulative// but only a *Descriptive*. This needs to be borne in mind. And this warning having been noticed, we can proceed to inquire about the corners of our block of supposed classes, which I will designate according to the usual map that has N above, S below, E to the right, W to the left.

As to the NW corner, a geometrical diagram is always capable of being *imagined*, seldom or never of *existing*; since the limits of solid bodies are the loci at which forces of cohesion are neither very great nor very small, which, being vague, has not the character of a geometrical surface. The diagram is therefore a *Potisign*. It is clearly Descriptive; and therefore 11·21 is possible.

The verbal expression "If ____, then ____" is a Famisign, as all words are (in the sense in which two that are just alike are the very same "word"). It is also a Copulative since it expresses a universal sequence, "If A, then C" meaning that in every state of things whatever, either *not-A* or *is-C* is true. So that the SE corner 13·23 is possible.

"Given any four rays in space; then either there can be only two rays, at most, that cut them all, or there can be any number." True or not, this is a Copulant; and any single expression of it is an Actisign. It is also expressible in Existential Graphs in the form of a geometrical diagram, which is a Potisign. Therefore, the NE corner 11·23 is possible.

But can a Famisign be Descriptive? Everybody will make haste to cry, "Of course, it can: of course, a description can be expressed in words, when even a universal can." Yet, while I am more than usually sensible of the danger of my being mistaken, I venture, for the present, the opinion that it is not so. The proper way to pursue the inquiry is to start from the definition already given of the triadic relation of Sign-Object-Interpretant. We thus learn that the Object determines (i.e., renders definitely to be such as it will be) the Sign in a particular manner. Now it is of the essence of the Sign to determine certain Ideas, i.e., certain Possibles; and it is the essence of any Tendency to determine Occurrences. Therefore, an Actisign or a Potisign may be a Copulative. But no Occurrence or collection of Occurrences can logically determine a Habit or other Tendency. Thus, if wishing to test a *die* to see whether it is loaded (whether intentionally or not) I throw it say 900 times. If the different faces come up with as equal frequency as they could be expected to do, what can I infer? Only that *as long as the habit or tendency of the die remains what it is*, it will probably not bring the different faces up so unequally as to show decisively in 900 throws. That is, I base my inference on the assumption that *there is some habit*. Or take a simpler case. If I positively knew (what I cannot *know*) that a certain shilling had a habit when pitched to turn up *heads* and *tails* with equal frequency, then I should positively know that if it were pitched often enough, it would *sometime* turn up "heads." For if it would *always* turn up tails, that would constitute a habit contrary to the habit supposed to be known. That known habit may be defined thus: Let a tally be kept of the heads as they occur and another of the tails; and after each throw let the exact quotient of the number of heads divided by the number of tails be calculated. Then, given any positive number (not zero therefore), there will *certainly* come a time after which none of the quotients will differ by as much as that number from 1, the value 1 being the only one about which the values of the quotients will never cease to oscillate. Thus the tendency consists entirely in what *will be*; and what *has been* has nothing to do with it. But what *will be* is not an Actual Occurrence. It is true that physiological and some other habits are determined by what has been done; but not by those occurrences *of themselves*, but only because there is a *special Tendency* by virtue of which what has been done *will be* done oftener than what has not been done. In general, it is of the essence of a Real Tendency that no Actual Occurrence can of itself determine it in any way. Whence a Denominative cannot be a Famisign. Whence the middle of the S side of the block 13·22 is impossible. But an Actual Occurrence always determines the Possibility of its character; whence no Descriptive can be a Famisign; i.e., the SW corner of the block 13·21 is impossible. As an example of this, no number of Descriptive propositions of the type "Some *S* is *P*" can ever determine the truth of a Copulative Proposition "Any *S* is *P*." It is, if possible, still more obvious that Possibility can never determine Actuality and therefore a Descriptive cannot be an Actisign, i.e., the middle of [the] W side of the block 12·21 is impossible. The remaining six classes are possible, i.e.,

Copulative Potisigns

Denominative Potisigns   *Copulative Actisigns*

Descriptive Potisigns   *Denominative Actisigns*   *Copulative Famisigns*

There are four objections that would probably be raised against my doctrine; but I will not lengthen this letter with the refutations of them. I have carefully considered them and have found them to be unsound.

From the summer of 1905 to the same time in 1906, I devoted much study to my ten trichotomies of signs.[9] It is time I reverted to the subject, as I know I could now make it much clearer. But I dare say some of my former names are better than those I now use. I formerly called

a *Potisign*	a *Tinge* or *Tone*
an *Actisign*	a *Token*
a *Famisign*	a *Type*
a *Descriptive*	an *Indefinite* (but this was bad)
a *Denominative*	a *Designation*
a *Copulative* (which is bad)	a *Distributive* (which is much better)

I think

	Potisign	*Actisign*	*Famisign*
might be called			
	Mark	*Token*	*Type* (?)
while			
	Descriptive	*Denominative*	*Copulative*
might be called			
	Descriptive	*Denominative*	*Distributive*

I have now given as much time to this letter as I can afford and I cannot now reexamine the remaining Trichotomies, although I must do so as soon as possible. So I just give them as they stood two years and more ago. In particular, the relations I assumed between the different classes were the wildest guesses and cannot be altogether right I think.

III. In respect to the Nature of their Dynamical Objects, Signs I found to be either

> 1. Signs of Possibles. That is, *Abstractives* such as Color, Mass, Whiteness, etc.
>
> 2. Signs of Occurrences. That is, *Concretives* such as Man, Charlemagne.
>
> 3. Signs of Collections. That is, *Collectives* such as Mankind, the Human Race, etc.

By *Abstractives* I meant signs of *immediate* abstractions; but was in some doubt what to do with abstractions resulting from experiment. I thought it would be requisite to study subdivisions of these classes but never went into that research.

I was of the opinion that if the Dynamical Object be a mere Possible the Immediate Object could only be of the same nature, while if the Immediate Object were a Tendency or Habit then the Dynamical Object must be of the same nature. Consequently an Abstractive must be a Mark, while a Type must be a Collective, which shows how I conceived Abstractives and Collectives.

IV. The fourth Trichotomy is the one which I most frequently use

| *Icon* | *Index* | *Symbol.* |

All the remaining six trichotomies have to do with the Interpretants, which you have, I imagine, studied much more thoroughly than I have done.

V. As to the nature of the Immediate (or Felt?) Interpretant, a sign may be

| *Ejaculative*
or merely giving
utterance to feel-
ing | *Imperative*
including of
course Interroga-
tives | *Significative.* |

But later I made this the seventh Trichotomy and for the fifth substituted—with great hesitation

| *Hypothetic* | *Categorical* | *Relative.* |

VI. As to the Nature of the Dynamical Interpretant

Sympathetic or *Congruentive*	*Shocking* or *Percussive*	*Usual.*

VII. As to the Manner of Appeal to the Dynamic Interpretant

Suggestive	*Imperative*	*Indicative.*

VIII. According to the Purpose of the Eventual Interpretant

Gratific	*To produce action*	*To produce self-control.*

IX. As to the Nature of the Influence of the Sign

Seme like a simple sign	*Pheme* with Antecedent and Consequent	*Delome* with Antecedent, Consequent, and principle of sequence.

X. As to the Nature of the Assurance of the Utterance

Assurance of Instinct	*Assurance of Experience*	*Assurance of Form.*

I don't know whether these trichotomies will suggest anything to you or not. No doubt you have studied relations to Interpretants in some directions much further than I. *[. . .]*

P.S. 1908 December 28. Well, dear Lady Welby, you deserve this infliction, for having spoken of my having "always been kindly (!!!) interested in the work to which my life is devoted," when I have myself been entirely absorbed in the very same subject since 1863, without meeting, before I made your acquaintance, a single mind to whom it did not seem very like *bosh*. I add some scraps.

Signs divided into Ten Classes.

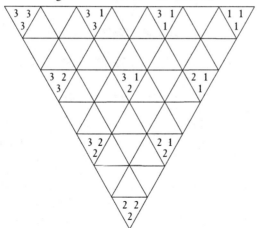

The Number above to the left describes the Object of the Sign. That above to the right describes its Interpretant. That below describes the Sign itself.

> 1 signifies the Possible Modality, that of an Idea.
>
> 2 signifies the Actual Modality, that of an Occurrence.
>
> 3 signifies the Necessary Modality, that of a Habit.

33

Excerpts from Letters to William James

L 224 and William James Papers, Houghton Library. [The four excerpts below were written in 1909. The first comes from pp. 6–14 of a long letter Peirce began on 26 February but did not send (L 224:90–98, CP 8.177–85 with some omissions, and NEM 3:839–44). This unwieldy letter was replaced with two shorter ones sent on March 9 and 14. The second excerpt consists of pages 6–10 of the 14 March letter, partly published in CP 8.314. The third excerpt includes pages 19–22 of a letter sent on 1 April, and published in CP 8.315. The last extract consists of the first eight pages of a letter begun on Christmas day; NEM 3:867–71.] Peirce's effort to establish a "commens" with James resulted in interesting and sometimes unusual presentations of his semiotic ideas. Nearly all of the technical terms of Peirce's semiotics, including "sign," are well worked over in these excerpts. Not surprisingly, Peirce makes sure to let James know that "the Final Interpretant does not consist in the way in which any mind does act but in the way in which every mind would act." In the final segment, Peirce outlines his "System of Logic," a book on semiotics he was working on, and provides one of the last summary accounts of his theory. Among other things, we learn that "every conceivable thing is either a May-be, an Actual, or a Would-be." Peirce admits that there may be more than ten trichotomies of signs, but his ten "exhibit all the distinctions that are generally required by logic." In his discussion of "Critic," Peirce describes the kind of warrant that applies to each of the three types of reasoning.

26 February 1909

A Sign is a Cognizable that, on the one hand, is so determined (i.e., specialized, *bestimmt*) by something *other than itself*, called its Object (or, in some cases, as if the Sign be the sentence "Cain killed Abel," in which Cain and Abel are equally Partial Objects, it may be more convenient to say that that which determines the Sign is the Complexus, or Totality, of Partial Objects. And in every case the Object is accurately the Universe of which the Special Object is member, or part), while, on the other hand, it so determines some actual or potential Mind, the determination whereof I term the Interpretant created by the Sign, that that Interpreting Mind is therein determined mediately by the Object.

This involves regarding the matter in an unfamiliar way. It may be asked, for example, how a lying or erroneous Sign is determined by its Object, or how if, as not infrequently happens, the Object is brought into existence by the Sign. To be puzzled by this is an indication of the word "determine" being taken in too narrow a sense. A person who says Napoleon was a lethargic creature has evidently his mind determined by Napoleon. For otherwise he could not attend to him at all. But here is a paradoxical circumstance. The person who interprets that sentence (or any other Sign whatsoever) must be determined by the Object of it through collateral observation quite independently of the action of the Sign. Otherwise he will not be determined to [the] thought of that object. If he never heard of Napoleon before, the sentence will mean no more to him than that some person or thing to which the name "Napoleon" has been attached was a lethargic creature. For Napoleon cannot determine his mind unless the word in the sentence calls his attention to the right man and that can only be if, independently, [a] habit has been established in him by which that word calls up a variety of attributes of Napoleon the man. Much the same thing is true in regard to any sign. In the sentence instanced Napoleon is not the only Object. Another Partial Object is Lethargy; and the sentence cannot convey its meaning unless collateral experience has taught its Interpreter what Lethargy is, or what that is that "lethargy" means in this sentence. The Object of a Sign may be something to be created by the Sign. For the Object of "Napoleon" is the Universe of Existence so far as it is determined by the fact of Napoleon being a Member of it. The Object of the sentence "Hamlet was insane" is the Universe of Shakespeare's Creation so far as it is determined by Hamlet being a part of it. The Object of the Command "Ground arms!" is the immediately subsequent action of the soldiers so far as it is affected by the molition[1] expressed in the command. It cannot be understood unless collateral observation shows the speaker's relation to the rank of soldiers. You may say, if you like, that the Object is in the Universe of things desired by the Commanding Captain at that moment. Or since the obedience is fully expected, it is in the Universe of his expectation. At any rate, it determines the Sign although it is to be created by the Sign by the circumstance that its Universe is relative to the momentary state of mind of the officer.

Now let us pass to the Interpretant. I am far from having fully explained what the Object of a Sign is; but I have reached the point where further explanation must suppose some understanding of what the Interpretant is. The Sign creates something in the Mind of the Interpreter, which something, in that it has been so created by the Sign, has been, in a mediate and *relative* way, also created by the Object of the Sign, although the Object is essentially other than the Sign. And this creature of the Sign is called the Interpretant. It is created by the Sign; but not by the Sign *quâ* member of whichever of the Universes it belongs to; but it has been created by the Sign in its capacity of bearing the determination by the Object. It is created in a Mind (how far this mind must be real we shall see). All that part of the understanding of the Sign which the Interpreting Mind has needed collateral observation for is outside the Interpretant. I do not mean by "collateral observation" acquaintance with the system of signs. What is so gathered is *not* COLLATERAL. It is on the contrary the prerequisite for getting any idea signified by the Sign. But by collateral observation, I mean previous acquaintance with what the Sign denotes. Thus if the Sign be the sentence "Hamlet was mad," to understand what this means one must know that men are sometimes in that strange state; one must have seen madmen or read about them; and it will be all the better if one specifically knows (and need not be driven to *presume*) what Shakespeare's notion of insanity was. All that is collateral observation and is no part of the Interpretant. But to put together the different subjects as the Sign represents them as related,—that is the main of the Interpretant-forming. Take as an example of a Sign, a *genre* painting. There is usually a lot in such a picture which can only be understood by virtue of acquaintance with customs. The style of the dresses, for example, is no part of the *significance*, i.e., the deliverance, of the painting. It only tells what the *subject* of it is. *Subject* and *Object* are the same thing except for trifling distinctions (and the German fashion of making them mark a great cleavage in thought is either a great blunder or it is a shocking instance of disregard of the morals of science,—which in fact they are apt not to "give a damn" for). But that which the painter aimed to point out to you, presuming you to have all the requisite collateral information, that is to say, just the quality of the sympathetic element of the situation, generally a very familiar one,—a something you probably never did so clearly realize before,—*that* is the Interpretant of the Sign,—its "significance."

Now all this is, so far, very muddled for the lack of certain distinctions which I proceed to point out, though it will be hard to make them fully comprehended.

In the first place, it should be observed that so far as the Sign denotes its Object, it calls for no particular *intelligence* or *Reason* on the part of its Interpreter. To read the Sign at all, and distinguish one Sign from another, what is requisite is delicate perceptions and acquaintance with what the usual concomitants of such appearances are, and what the conventions of the systems of signs are. To know the Object, what is requisite is previous experience of that Individual Object. The Object of every Sign is an Individual, usually an Individual Collection of Individuals. Its *Subjects*, i.e., the Parts of the Sign that denote the Partial Objects, are either *directions for finding the Objects* or are *Cyrioids*, i.e. signs of single Objects. (I form the word from κύριον ὄνομα, Proper Name, literally the *regular, legitimate, literal* name, from κῦρος, authority; which Liddell and Scott says is with all its cognates entirely post-Homeric, in spite of the fact that the root is the same as that of Latin *fortis*. But it seems very doubtful whether it has anything to do with Latin *fortis* = *forctis*.) Such for example are all *abstract* nouns, which are names of single characters, the personal pronouns, and the demonstrative and relative pronouns, etc. By directions for finding the Objects, for which I have as yet invented no other word than "*Selectives*," I mean such as "Any" (i.e., any you please), "Some" (i.e., one properly selected), etc. To know the Interpretant, which is what the Sign itself expresses, may require the highest power of reasoning.

In the second place, to get more distinct notions of what the Object of a Sign in general is, and what the Interpretant in general is, it is needful to distinguish two senses of "Object" and three of "Interpretant." It would be better to carry the division further; but these two divisions are enough to occupy my remaining years. Others must carry the study further when I am gone, which will be, I fear, all too soon for me to explain what work I have done. (Indeed, there are some studies of years of which I never expect to be able to say a word: I can only pick out what few I can. If the Carnegie[2] or some such rich institution would put me in the position in which happier students are placed it would be different. It is most irksome to me to feel myself dependent on persons who need all their money themselves. And at the same time, I cannot deny that it is a deep happiness to feel that I have the warm friendship of such a soul as you; while I wish I could dispense with putting you to unknown amounts of trouble and expense and annoyance.)

As to the Object, that may mean the Object as cognized in the Sign and therefore an Idea, or it may be the Object as it is regardless of any particular aspect of it, the Object in such relations as unlimited and final study would show it to be. The former I call the *Immediate* Object, the latter the *Dynamical* Object. For the latter is the Object that Dynamical Science (or what at this day would be called "Objective" science) can investigate. Take, for example, the Sentence "the Sun is blue." Its Objects are "the Sun" and "blueness." If by "blueness" be meant the Immediate Object, which is the quality of the sensation, it can only be known by Feeling. But if it means that "Real," existential condition, which causes the emitted light to have short mean wavelength, Langley[3] has already proved that the proposition is true. So the "Sun" may mean the occasion of sundry sensations, and so is [the] Immediate Object, or it may mean our usual interpretation of such sensations in terms of place, of mass, etc., when it is the Dynamical Object. It is true of both Immediate and of Dynamical Object that acquaintance cannot be given by a Picture or a Description, nor by any other sign which has the Sun for its Object. If a person points to it and says, "See there! *That* is what we call the 'Sun'," the Sun is *not* the Object of that sign. It is the *Sign* of the sun, the *word* "sun" that his declaration is about; and that *word* we must become acquainted with by collateral experience. Suppose a teacher of French says to an English-speaking pupil, who asks "Comment appelle-t-on ça?" pointing to the Sun, "C'est le soleil"; he begins to furnish that collateral experience by speaking in French of the Sun itself. Suppose, on the other hand, he says "Notre mot est 'soleil'," then, instead of expressing himself in language and *describing* the word, he offers a pure *Icon* of it. Now the Object of an Icon is entirely indefinite, equivalent to "something." He virtually says "our word is like this:" and makes the sound. He informs the pupil that the word (meaning, of course, a certain *habit*) has an effect which he *pictures* acoustically. But a pure picture without a legend only says "*something* is like this." True he attaches what amounts to a legend. But that only makes his sentence analogous to a portrait we will say of Leopardi with Leopardi[4] written below it. It conveys its information to a person who knows who Leopardi was, and to anybody else it only says "something called Leopardi looked like this." The pupil is in the state of a person who was pretty sure there was a man Leopardi; for he is pretty sure there must be a word in French for the sun and thus is already acquainted with it, only he does not know how it sounds when spoken nor how it looks when written. I think by this time you must understand what I mean when I say that no sign can be understood,—or at least that no *proposition* can be understood,—unless the interpreter has "collateral acquaintance" with every Object of it. As for a mere *substantive*, it must be borne in mind that it is not an indispensable part of speech. The Semitic languages seem to be descendants of a language that had no "common nouns." Such a word is really nothing but a *blank form* of proposition and the Subject is the blank, and a blank can only mean "something" or something even more indefinite. So now I believe I can leave you to consider carefully whether my doctrine is correct or not.

As to the Interpretant, i.e., the "signification," or "interpretation" rather, of a sign, we must distinguish an Immediate and a Dynamical, as we must the Immediate and Dynamical Objects. But we must also note that there is certainly a third kind of Interpretant, which I call the Final Interpretant, because it is that which *would* finally be decided to be the true interpretation if consideration of the matter were carried so far that an ultimate opinion were reached. My friend Lady Welby has, she tells me, devoted her whole life to the study of *significs*, which is what I should describe as the study of the relation of signs to their interpretants; but it seems to me that she chiefly occupies herself with the study of words. She also reaches the conclusion that there are three senses in which words may be interpreted. She calls them *Sense, Meaning*, and *Significance*. Significance is the deepest and most lofty of these, and thus agrees with my *Final Interpretant;* and Significance seems to be an excellent name for it. *Sense* seems to be the logical analysis or definition, for which I should prefer to stick to the old term *Acception* or *Acceptation*. By *Meaning* she means the *intention* of the utterer. But it appears to me that all symptoms of disease, signs of weather, etc., have no utterer. For I do not think we can properly say that God *utters* any sign when He is the Creator of all things. But when she says, as she does, that this is connected with Volition, I at once note that the volitional element of Interpretation is the *Dynamical Interpretant*. In the Second Part of my Essay on Pragmatism, in the *Popular Science* of November 1877 and January 1878, I made three grades of Clearness of Interpretation.[5] The first was such Familiarity as gave a person familiarity with a sign and readiness in using it or interpreting it. In his consciousness he seemed to himself to be quite *at home* with the sign. In short, it is Interpretation *in Feeling*. The second was Logical Analysis = Lady Welby's *Sense*. The third was Pragmaticistic Analysis *[and]* would seem to be a Dynamical Analysis, but *[is]* identified with the Final Interpretant.

14 March 1909

A *Sign* is anything of either of the three Universes which, being *bestimmt* by something other than itself, called its *Object*, in its turn *bestimmt* the mind of an interpreter to a notion which I call the *Interpretant; and does this in such a manner* that the Interpretant is, thereby and therein, determined mediately by the Object. This definition is, perhaps, not easy to grasp. It was not so to me, at any rate. It is necessary to see that a sentence about something, though it be utterly false, is nevertheless determined by the subject-thing which it misrepresents. If it weren't, it would not even *mis*-represent it: It wouldn't have anything to do with it. A thing may determine another to disagreement with itself as well as to agreement with itself.* The being determined by its Object, i.e., the Determination by its Object, is what we call the *Denotation* of a concept, and the collection which consists of the aggregate of whatever Objects it permits its Interpreter to refer it to, is its *Umfang*, its *Extension*.

On the other hand, its *Interpretant* is the *Signification* of the concept, its *Inhalt*, its "connotation" (to use a bad term). As John of Salisbury, a clear and elegant writer of the twelfth century, a disciple of Abelard, said, the distinction (though frequently confused) is nevertheless "quod fere in omnium ore

---

*You will probably object that *bestimmt*, to your mind, means "causes" or "*caused*." Very well, so it does to mine. But, you may suggest, to take as an example the old-fashioned hygrometer in the form of a house from which the goodman emerges while the goodwife retreats when the interpreter of the instrument is to expect a storm and *vice versa* when it ought to clear up, although both man and wife are apt to be procrastinate in their movements, especially after a long storm, is it not a little forced to say that the *future* weather *causes* these antecedent movements? How can a cause *act* before it exists? It is conceivable that, before the morrow whose weather the instrument professes to predict comes, the Three Universes may collapse, and Time with them; so that nothing at all shall come into being to be the Dynamic Object of the sign. Can absolute Nothing be a cause in any recognized sense? Recognized or not, I reply, it is accurately *so*. An object does not need to be Real in order to have predicates, since to be Real means to have predicates independently of what you or I or any individual mind or collections of minds may opine, imagine, or otherwise represent. Now predicates so independent are a particular class of predicates, and a Figment is an Object that does not possess these, but *does* possess such Predicates as it was fabricated to have. Such fabricated predicates cannot *Really* cause real changes, but they can cause a mind to fabricate some further notions, which may cause it to create a hygrometer to be a predictor of weather. And thus, the Unreal Object,—or the Object which may be unreal, viz. *whatever weather there may be next after any day when this Hygrometer may be consulted,* may in that indirect manner *cause* (though not *really* cause) this Real hygrometer to predict (though not *really* to predict, and perhaps not even *truly* to predict) that that hypothetical weather will *really* have certain definite and designate predicates. Yes, I hear you confess, this is certainly as lucid as it could possibly be. There may perhaps be some room to regret that it couldn't be still more lucid,—say, as lucid as a bottle of ink. But perhaps it answers its purpose better as it is.

celebre est, aliud scilicet esse quod appellativa (i.e., adjectives and common nouns *he* means, but *I* say ANY signs; for otherwise they would fail of *being* signs) *significant*, et aliud esse quod *nominant*. Nominantur singularia, sed universalia significantur."[6] It is very true that this *fere in omnium ore celebre est*, as truly, at least, in the twentieth century as in the twelfth and much earlier, hideously as the distinction is apt to be confused.

But now it is absolutely indispensable that we should carry the distinction one step further, *at least*. We must distinguish between the Immediate Object,—i.e., the Object as represented in the Sign,—and the Real (no, because perhaps the Object is altogether fictive, I must choose a different term; therefore:), say rather the Dynamical Object, which, from the nature of things, the Sign *cannot* express, which it can only *indicate* and leave the interpreter to find out by *collateral experience*. For instance, I point my finger to what I mean, but I can't make my companion know what I mean, if he can't see it, or if seeing it, it does not, to his mind, separate itself from the surrounding objects in the field of vision. It is useless to attempt to discuss the genuineness and possession of a personality beneath the histrionic presentation of Theodore Roosevelt with a person who recently has come from Mars and never heard of Theodore before. A similar distinction must be made as to the Interpretant. But in respect to *that* Interpretant, the dichotomy is not enough by any means. For instance, suppose I awake in the morning before my bedfellow, and that afterwards she wakes up and inquires, "What sort of a day is it?" *This* is a Sign, whose Object, as expressed, is the weather at that time, but whose Dynamical Object is the *impression which I have presumably derived from peeping between the window curtains*. Whose Interpretant, as expressed, is the quality of the weather, but whose Dynamical Interpretant is *my answering her question*. But beyond that, there is a *third* Interpretant. The *Immediate Interpretant* is what the Question expresses, *all* that it immediately expresses, which I have imperfectly restated above. The *Dynamical Interpretant* is the actual effect that it has upon me, its interpreter. But the Significance of it, the *Ultimate*, or *Final*, *Interpretant* is her *purpose* in asking it, what effect its answer will have as to her plans for the ensuing day. I reply, let us suppose: "It is a stormy day." Here is another sign. Its *Immediate Object* is the notion of the present weather so far as this is common to her mind and mine,—not the *character* of it, but the *identity* of it. The *Dynamical Object* is the *identity* of the actual and *Real* meteorological conditions at the moment. The *Immediate Interpretant* is the *schema* in her imagination, i.e., the vague Image or what there is in common to the different Images of a stormy day. The *Dynamical Interpretant* is the disappointment or whatever actual effect it at once has upon her. The *Final Interpretant* is the sum of the *Lessons* of the reply, Moral, Scientific, etc. Now it is easy to see that my attempt to draw this three-way, "trivialis," distinction, relates to a real and important three-way distinction, and yet that it is quite hazy and needs a vast deal of study before it is rendered perfect. Lady Welby has got hold of the same real distinction in her "Sense, Meaning, Significance,"[7] but conceives it as imperfectly as I do, but imperfectly in other ways. Her *Sense* is the *Impression* made or normally to be made. Her *Meaning* is what is intended, its purpose. Her *Significance* is the real upshot.

1 April 1909

Let me give a *little* fuller explanation of my distinction between the Immediate, the Dynamical, and the Final Interpretants; because from what you say, it does not seem to me that you quite catch the idea that I put upon this trichotomy. The Dynamical Interpretant is whatever interpretation any mind actually makes of a sign. This Interpretant derives its character from the Dyadic category, the category of Action. This has two aspects, the Active and the Passive, which are not merely opposite aspects but make relative contrasts between different influences of this Category as More Active and More Passive. In psychology this category marks Molition in its active aspect of a force and its passive aspect as a resistance. When an imagination, a daydream, fires a young man's ambition or any other active passion, that is a more Active variety of his Dynamical Interpretation of the dream. When a novelty excites his surprise,—and the scepticism that goes along with surprise,—this is a more Passive variety of Dynamical Interpretant. I am not speaking of the *feelings* of passion or of surprise as *qualities*. For those *qualities* are no part of the Dynamic Interpretant. But the *agitations* of passion and of surprise are the actual Dynamic Interpretants. So surprise again has its Active and its Passive variety;—the former when what one perceives positively *conflicts* with expectation, the latter when, having no positive expectation but only the absence of any suspicion of anything out of the common, something quite unexpected occurs,—such as a total eclipse of the sun which one had not anticipated. Any surprise involves a resistance to accepting the fact. One rubs one's eyes, as Shaler[8] used to do, determined not to admit the observation until it is plain one will be compelled to do so. Thus every actual interpretation is dyadic. As pragmaticism says,—what I mean is one part of pragmaticism for Pragmaticism is not exclusively an opinion about the Dynamic Interpretant,—but it says, for one thing, that the meaning of any sign for anybody consists in the way he reacts to the sign. When the captain of infantry gives the word "Ground arms!" the Dynamic Interpretant is in the thump of the muskets on

the ground, or rather it is the Act of their Minds. In its more $\begin{Bmatrix} \text{Active} \\ \text{Passive} \end{Bmatrix}$

forms, the Dynamical Interpretant indefinitely approaches the character of

the $\begin{Bmatrix} \text{Final} \\ \text{Immediate} \end{Bmatrix}$ Interpretant; and yet the distinction is absolute. The Final

Interpretant does not consist in the way in which any mind does act but in the way in which every mind would act. That is, it consists in a truth which might be expressed in a conditional proposition of this type: "If so and so were to happen to any mind, this sign would determine that mind to such and such *conduct*." By "conduct," I mean *action* under an intention of self-control. No event that occurs to any mind, no action of any mind, can constitute the truth of that conditional proposition. The Immediate Interpretant consists in the *Quality* of the Impression that a sign is fit to produce, not to any actual reaction. Thus the Immediate and Final Interpretants seem to me absolutely distinct from the Dynamical Interpretant and from each other. And if there be any fourth kind of Interpretant on the same footing as those three, there must be a dreadful rupture of my mental retina, for I can't see it at all.

25 December 1909

Since I promised to say something about my System of Logic, I will do so. It is to regard Logic as the theory of Signs in general; and will consist of three books. Book I treats of the essential nature of a Sign, and of the different main classes of *possible* Signs. If I were making a natural history of such signs as exist, I should have to recognize irregularity in the divisions, just as I do, in some measure, in classifying the Sciences. My classification of the Sciences is however intended to be useful in the future, and therefore is not absolutely confined to what exists. Indeed, I found it quite impossible to state the relations between the sciences without, on the one hand, relying exclusively upon what the members of the different groups have said,—in which case the ideas governing my classification would be antiquated beyond what one would suppose before he tried that method,—or else one must speculate upon what seems to be in the atmosphere of science but has perhaps never yet been uttered. Scientific *ideas* do not get uttered until long after they have been influential. The consequence is that I found I could make a useful classification only by adopting as a skeleton of it my own notions of how the sciences *ought* to be related. My classification of signs, however, is intended to be a classification of *possible* signs and therefore observation of existing signs is only of use in suggesting and reminding one of varieties that one might otherwise overlook. And our notions of what is Possible are necessarily drawn largely from our Innate Ideas. In this first book I shall analyze and define and classify all the concepts of Logic so far as I know them. I start by defining what I mean by a Sign. It is something determined by something else, its Object, and itself influencing some person in such a way that that person becomes thereby mediately influenced or determined in some respect by that Object. This being what I mean by a Sign, I must classify signs according first to their natures in themselves, second in relation to their Objects and third in their relation to their *Interpretants*, i.e., the effects on the interpreter. You see here the triplet is absolutely forced upon me by the nature of my concept of a Sign. Then in dividing Signs in the first respect, I must recognize that some are actual occurrences or are definite existing things. But other signs, such as the word "the," in the sense in which "the" is a single word, consist, each of them, in something being possible. I call such things (whether they be signs or not) "May-be's," perhaps better "Can-be's." Still other signs are neither Actuals nor May-be's. For example Greek syntax is a sign,—a medium by which my knowledge is determined by things that Plato or Sextus Empiricus have written; and yet it is neither an actual individual occurrence or thing nor does it consist in a mere possibility. It consists rather more truly in *impossibilities*, for example in the impossibility that a Greek would express certain ideas in other than certain ways. I call things of this kind (whether Signs or not) "Would-be's." A Sign then may be a Would-be. Now it is plain that every conceivable thing is either a May-be, an Actual, or a Would-be. If it is not at once plain, it will become so on considering that "may be," "can be," and "might be" are but various applications of one idea; "may be" suggesting insufficient knowledge, "can be" insufficient action of the Subject (in grammar), and "might be" insufficiency of the circumstances. Now applying these ideas to the copula of a proposition, if "*S* may be *P*" and *no more*, then certainly "*S* may be non-*P*" so that nothing prevents both *P* and not-*P* /from/ being predicated under this Mode /and the principle of Contradiction does not apply to it/. On the other hand, both "*S* would be *P*" and "*S* would be non-*P*" may be false; so that the principle of Excluded Middle does not apply under the Mode of Would-be; while both /principles/ apply under the Mode of Actuality. Thus, the only fourth Mode there could be would be one in which neither the principle of Contradiction nor that of Excluded Middle would apply. A state in which one neither knows that *S* is *P* nor that *S* is not *P* nor that *S* is not both nor that *S* is one or the other is a total absence of knowledge as to *S* being *P*; and similarly a state of *being* that neither makes *S* *P* nor prevents it, nor lets it be one or the other, nor prevents it from being one or the other is not a state of being at all as to *S* being *P*. I make ten distinctions, and they are all trichotomies *because of my* making a classification of May-be's or Can-be's. I might have drawn more than ten distinctions; but these ten exhibit all the distinctions that are generally required in logic; and since investigation of these involved my consideration,—virtually at least,— of 59,049 questions, still leaving me on the portico of logic, I thought it wise to stop with these.

Book II, on Critic, discusses the warrant for each of the different kinds of reasoning. Throughout this Book and Book I, I do not allow myself to accept any discovery of "Psychology Proper," by which I mean the Empirical Science of the Modes of Functioning of finite Minds. For example, the modes of Association, its formation, suggestions through it, etc., Fatigue,—and in short the Physiology of the Mind. For in my opinion, excepting Metaphysics, there is no science that is more in need of the science of Logic than Psychology Proper is. On the other hand, I found Logic largely on a study which I call Phaneroscopy, which is the keen observation of and generalization from the direct Perception of what we are immediately aware of. I find there are three kinds of possible warrant for a Belief. Here is this distressing number 3 again, against which you seem to have sworn eternal enmity, but which *will* turn up again and again. I don't think you are willing to believe that space has three dimensions, are you? None of the three warrants is Positively Infallible although one of them is so in a Pickwickian sense. The first kind of warrant consists in the reasoner's being *disposed to believe* in his proposition. This goes toward warranting the belief, since the very undertaking to find out a truth one does not directly perceive assumes that things conform in a measure to what our reason thinks they should. In other words our Reason is akin to the Reason that governs the Universe; we must assume that or despair of finding out anything. Now despair is always illogical, and we are warranted in thinking so, since otherwise all reasoning will be in vain. If it be so, a strong inward impulse to Believe a given proposition tends to show that proposition to be true; and if it be not so, we never can discover what we don't directly perceive, do what we may.

[. . .] The second warrant is in case one's inference is from some state of things capable of expression in a proposition (generally a copulative proposition of some complexity) and when every state of things not denied by this proposition is a state of things in which the conclusion is true. Such inference is Deduction, or Necessary Inference. There are two kinds of Deduction; and it is truly significant that it should have been left for me to discover this. I first found, and subsequently *proved*, that every Deduction involves the observation of a Diagram (whether Optical, Tactical, or Acoustic) and having drawn the diagram (for I myself always work with Optical Diagrams) one finds the conclusion to be represented by it. Of course, a diagram is required to comprehend any assertion. My two genera of Deductions are first those in which any Diagram of a state of things in which the premisses are true represents the conclusion to be true and such reasoning I call *Corollarial* because all the corollaries that different editors have added to Euclid's *Elements* are of this nature. Second kind. To the Diagram of the truth of the Premisses something else has to be added, which is usually a mere May-be, and then the conclusion appears. I call this *Theorematic* reasoning because all the most important theorems are of this nature. [. . .]

The third kind of warrant is that which justifies the use of a method of inference provided it be carried out to the end consistently. There are three kinds of inference of this kind. They are all inferences from random samples. The strongest is that which is a sample (that is, a collection) of units. In that case, the theory of errors is applicable. The second kind is where there are no definite multitudes but where, as the sample is enlarged, the inference becomes stronger and stronger. The third kind, which is the weakest of all forms of Induction, is where the only defence is that if the conclusion is false, its falsity will *sometime* be detected if the method of inference be persisted in long enough. For example, if we infer from the fact that so closely as we have been able to measure, the sum of the angles of a triangle is 180°, therefore it is exactly so, the only warrant for this inference is that if we go on making our errors of measurement less and less, then if the sum be not exactly 180°, we shall ultimately find out that it is more or less if we persist in making the measurements. No inductive inference can be weaker than that and have any warrant at all.

My Book III treats of methods of research.

N O T E S*

1. IMMORTALITY IN THE LIGHT OF SYNECHISM

1. The root verb for συνεχισμός is συνέχω, to hold or keep together, to continue, to preserve. Peirce's surgical etymology does not appear prominently in Liddell and Scott's *Greek-English Lexicon*, which gives many examples related to the continuity of space, time, numbers, and arguments. The edition of the *Lexicon* Peirce most likely used only indicates that ὁ συνεχισμός is a form of ἡ συνέχεια encountered in medical writers (a more recent edition identifies two authors, but without specifying the context). This is apparently the only basis for Peirce's claim that the word meant, as he put it in a draft, "'the establishment of continuity' in a surgical sense" (MS 946:5).

2. "The Law of Mind," *The Monist* 2 (July 1892): 533–59; EP1:312–33.

3. This is a paraphrase of Peirce's pragmatic maxim, first expressed in print in his 1878 paper "How to Make Our Ideas Clear" (EP1:132), but anticipated in earlier publications, including the 1868 "Cognition series" (EP1:11ff.). Other expressions are found throughout this volume; see for instance selection 8, p. 96, selection 10, pp. 134–35, and selection 24, pp. 340–41.

4. From Parmenides' poem Περί φύσεως, fragment 6, lines 1–2. Peirce miswrote the last word as εἶναι; it is here corrected into ἔστιν.

5. The hymn, according to MS S70:7, is from the beginning of *The Metaphysics of the Upanishads, or Vichar Sagar*, a work by Niscaladasa (d. c.1863), originally titled *Vicarasagara*; translated by Lala Sreeram (Calcutta: Heeralal Dhole, 1885; New Delhi: Asian Publication Services, 1979).

6. Edward Stanton Huntington (1841–1895) wrote, under the pseudonym Edward Stanton, *Dreams of the Dead* (Boston, 1892). The *Nation* published a review by Peirce on 8 September 1892: see CN 1:165–66 (a partial draft is in MS 1513).

7. Gustav Freytag (1816–1895), German writer, published *Die verlorene Handschrift*, a novel of university life, in 1864. The novel was translated and serialized in *The Open Court* in the late 1880s, and published in book form as *The Lost Manuscript: A Novel* (Chicago: Open Court Pub. Co., 1890).

2. WHAT IS A SIGN?

1. Section numbers, which in the manuscript begin with §31, here begin with §1, since the first chapter of Peirce's projected book is not included.

2. Book II of Jonathan Swift's *Gulliver's Travels* opens on a fanciful map of Brobdingnag merged into a map of the North American Pacific coast.

3. Peirce wrote "signs" instead of "indices," a mistake given the preceding context. Some early writings, however, do refer to indices as "signs" (see EP1:7).

4. *De interpretatione*, II.16a.12.

5. Peirce wrote "in Greek" rather than "in Greece" because he is working through the list of alternative translations provided by Liddell and Scott's *Greek-English Lexicon* under the entry σύμβολον.

6. Cf. William of Ockham's *Summa totius logicae*, part I, ch. 14.

*Bibliographic abbreviations used in these notes are identified in the Preface on page xv.

7. "Every symbol follows from a symbol."

8. Peirce often quotes this verse from the fourteenth stanza of Emerson's poem "The Sphinx" (*Dial*, Jan. 1841).

3. Of Reasoning in General

1. Archibald Henry Sayce (1845–1933). As Peirce noted in parentheses here removed, Sayce's article is in the ninth edition of the *Encyclopaedia*, 6:43.b.

2. Joseph H. Allen and James B. Greenough, *Allen and Greenough's Latin Grammar for Schools and Colleges, Founded on Comparative Grammar* (Boston: Ginn and Co., 1884), 131n.

3. Horace, *Odes*, I.2.

4. Priscian (fl. c. A.D. 500), best known of all the Latin grammarians, author of the influential *Institutiones grammaticae*.

5. Four paragraphs have here been omitted; they present a long discussion of certain logico-grammatical features of Egyptian and other languages.

6. Despite Peirce's claim, Martin Grabmann showed in 1922 that the *Tractatus*, found in the first volume of Duns Scotus's *Opera Omnia* (1639), was written by Thomas von Erfurt (first half of fourteenth century).

7. Siger de Brabant (c.1235–c.1284), radical Aristotelianist who taught at the University of Paris. Peirce may be confounding him with Siger de Courtrai, however, who was also a master of arts in Paris around 1309, and the author of a *Summa modorum significandi*. Michel de Marbais is one of many lesser known authors of similar treatises *De modis significandi*. Albert of Saxony (d. 1390), German Ockhamist philosopher, was rector of the universities of Paris and Vienna, and the author of many works of logic, physics, and mathematics.

8. That other chapter was not written, but selection 8 probably discusses many of the points Peirce would have made. See also his "Note on the Theory of the Economy of Research" (W4:72–78).

9. Thomas Davidson (1840–1900), *Aristotle and Ancient Educational Ideals* (New York: Scribner's Sons, 1892). Davidson, born in Scotland, moved to the United States in 1867 where he was highly respected as an independent philosopher, scholar, and teacher by a circle of friends that included Peirce and William James.

10. A composite photograph, according to a *Century Dictionary* definition, is a single photographic portrait produced from more than one person. The negatives taken from each person show the faces as nearly as possible of the same size and lighting, and in the same position. The negatives are then printed in superposition on the same sheet of paper, and are each exposed to light for an equal amount of time. Study of such photographs was thought to manifest general types of countenance and other traits.

11. William de la Mare (d. c.1290), English philosopher and Franciscan theologian, leading critic of Thomas Aquinas, and author of *Correctorium fratris Thomae* (1278; "Corrective of Brother Thomas"). William Ware (d. after 1300), also a Franciscan, very probably a teacher of Duns Scotus at Oxford. Scholars are divided on whether the two Williams were the same person.

12. No such chapter was written, and Peirce does not appear to have treated of compound icons elsewhere.

13. Shakespeare, *The Tempest*, act 4, scene 1, line 151. This appears to have been a favorite line of Peirce's parents (see W5:xlvii).

4. PHILOSOPHY AND THE CONDUCT OF LIFE

1. Peirce alludes, among others, to Eduard Zeller and Christian August Brandis (see notes 4 and 10 below).

2. See selection 8, "On the Logic of Drawing History from Ancient Documents."

3. *Theaetetus*, 174a.

4. Eduard Zeller (1814–1908), *A History of Greek Philosophy: From the Earliest Period to the Time of Socrates*, tr. S. F. Alleyne (London: Longmans, Green, and Co., 1881), 1:213n.2.

5. *A History of Greek Philosophy*, 2:4n.1 and 2:213n.1.

6. Diogenes of Sinope (4th century B.C.), prototype of the Cynics. Zeller's statement comes from his *Socrates and the Socratic Schools*, tr. Oswald J. Reichel (London: Longmans, Green, and Co., 1885), 288.

7. *Socrates and the Socratic Schools*, 288n.1. Zeller says "so greatly exaggerated by tradition."

8. Pyrrho of Elis (c.360–c.272 B.C.), the founder of Skepticism.

9. Timon of Phlius (c.320–c.230 B.C.); his works, which have survived in fragments only, preserved and propagated Pyrrho's teaching.

10. Christian August Brandis (1790–1867), German historian of classical philosophy, editor of Aristotle and author of, among other works, *Geschichte der Entwickelungen der griechischen Philosophie und ihrer Nachwirkungen im romischen Reiche.*

11. The "arduous madness of the learned Lucretius"—author of the celebrated Epicurean poem *De rerum natura*.

12. *Republic*, VII.532a–534e; *Phaedrus*, 276–277a.

13. Aristotle's father, Nicomachus, was a member of the medical guild of Asclepiadae, "the descendants of Asclepius" (the god of healing)—physicians whose school was located in the island of Cos (Hippocrates's home), and who took their name from the Homeric Ἀσκληπιαδαί.

14. Peirce refers to a set of eight lectures on the "Logic of Events," which he described in an 18 December 1897 letter to William James.

15. The "word" came from William James, in a letter to Peirce dated 22 December 1897: "I am sorry you are sticking so to formal logic. . . . Now be a good boy and think a more popular plan out. . . . You are teeming with ideas—and the lectures need not by any means form a continuous whole. Separate topics of a vitally important character would do perfectly well."

16. Peirce wrote a number of lectures on "Detached Ideas on Vitally Important Topics"; they are found in MSS 435–36, 438–40.

17. Peirce probably refers to a letter from William James, dated January 23, 1898, to which he responded three days later.

18. The next lecture is "Types of Reasoning" (MS 441), in RLT 123–42.

19. At first Peirce had written: "Such men are intellectual *petits crevés*, nice to have around"; he then deleted it.

20. By "the fly on the wheel" Peirce means a device that regulates the rotation of a wheel, such as is used in clockwork and other machinery; also called a flywheel.

21. The Greek expression (found in Thucydides, *The Peloponnesian War*, I.22) means "a possession for all time." Used by Carus in his *Fundamental Problems* (Chicago: Open Court, 1891), 22.

22. "Everyone believes it is difficult to die. I believe it as well. But I see that once we reach that moment, everyone can do it." (The author has not been identified.)

23. Auguste Comte, *Cours de philosophie positive* (Paris, 1835), 2nd lesson.

24. As Peirce explains later, Heraclitus's two "errors" are that the continuous is transitory (or that the eternal is not continuous), and that the being of the Idea is potential.

25. Roger Joseph Boscovich (1711–1787), Jesuit natural philosopher, mathematician, physicist, astronomer, geodesist, engineer, and poet. Boscovichian points are centers of force interacting with each other according to an oscillatory law.

26. Peirce is referring to Wincenty Lutoslawski's *The Origin and Growth of Plato's Logic*, which had appeared the year before (New York: Longmans, Green, and Co., 1897). Lutoslawski determined that the *Sophist* belonged to the late dialogues through a stylometric study (see table pp. 178–79 in his book). See selection 13, note 2.

27. *Metaphysics*, 987b20–30; *De anima*, 404b19–26.

28. In 1903, if not earlier, Peirce changed his mind and made ethics the second branch of the normative sciences (after esthetics and before logic), themselves the second branch of philosophy, between phenomenology and metaphysics.

29. The eighth and last lecture was "The Logic of Continuity" (MS 948); in RLT 242–68.

30. *Metaphysics*, 988a7–14.

31. Alexander Pope (1688–1744). Fulke Greville (1554–1628), first Baron Brooke, born in Beauchamp Court (Warwickshire, England), philosophical poet. Sir John Davies (1569–1626), English jurist and poet.

32. Peirce is probably referring, not to the "Book of the Dead," but to a fragment of writing known as the Ebers papyrus, written about 1600 B.C. and found in 1862 by Edwin Smith. The Ebers papyrus includes a large collection of prescriptions for numerous ailments, interspersed with magical spells and incantations. A number of other Egyptian medical texts had been found but not published by the time of Peirce's lecture.

33. Attributed to Thucydides by Dionysius of Halicarnassus (*Ars rhetorica* xi.2): "The contact with manners then is education; and this Thucydides appears to assert when he says history is philosophy learned from examples."

34. Sir William Herschel (1738–1822), British astronomer, noted especially for his discovery of Uranus; praised as the father of the new astronomy in Peirce's 1901 review of a Herschel biography (CN 3:21).

35. Sir Francis Galton (1822–1911), English scientist, studied heredity and intelligence, and founded the science of eugenics. Galton's work influenced Peirce's study of great men. Alphonse de Candolle (1806–1893), Swiss botanist, was also known for his bio-bibliographical study *Histoire des sciences et des savants depuis deux siècles* (Geneva: H. Georg, 1873).

36. Dmitry Ivanovich Mendeleyev (1834–1907), Russian chemist who in 1869 formulated the periodic law that allowed him to classify and tabulate the chemical elements. Alexander William Williamson (1824–1904), English chemist, known for work on reversible reactions, dynamic equilibrium, and catalysis.

37. This is an allusion to the last two verses of Alfred Tennyson's poem *Will* (1855), which read "Sown in a wrinkle of the monstrous hill, | The city sparkles like a grain of salt."

38. On 30 January 1898 Peirce wrote to William James: "I have now finished my first lecture and I have no doubt that when you hear it you will admit that it is far superior to the one on the First Rule of Logic. Every trace of personal vexation as well as of condemnation has been completely erased. One sentence of 5 words 'There is a lesson there' is all I utter in recommendation of the cultivation of mathematics."

39. Arthur Cayley (1821–1895), "Sixth Memoir Upon Quantics," *Philosophical Transactions of the Royal Society of London* 149 (1860):61–90. "A Memoir on the Theory

of Matrices," ibid., 148 (1858):17–37. "A Memoir on Abstract Geometry" (1870), in *Collected Mathematical Papers* (Cambridge, Eng.: The University Press, 1889–97), 6:456–69. In the manuscript, Peirce mistakenly wrote "Memoir on Absolute Geometry."

40. Felix Klein (1849–1925), German mathematician, famous for his contribution to non-Euclidean geometry and for his *Erlanger Programm* which presented connections between geometry and group theory.

41. Georg Friedrich Bernhard Riemann (1826–1866) and Johann Benedikt Listing (1808–1882), German mathematicians. Riemann initiated a general non-Euclidean system of geometry and contributed to the theory of functions. Listing was a naturalistic geometer, a founder of topology, and the author of *Vorstudien zur Topologie* (Göttingen, 1848; reprinted from the *Göttingen Studien*, 1847) and of the memoir "Der Census raümlicher Complexe" (*Abhandlungen der K. Gesellschaft der Wissenschaft zu Göttingen*, vols. 9–10, part II (1861):97–180), which greatly influenced Peirce.

5. The First Rule of Logic

1. An exact reference has not been found, but some statements by Aristotle approaching this idea can be found in *Prior Analytics*, bk. 1, chapters 12–14, bk. 2, ch. 27, and in *Posterior Analytics*, bk. 1, chapters 13, 10, 13–14, 24 and 33.

2. By "in a Pickwickian sense" Peirce usually means "in a sense that has no effect" (CP 8.277). The phrase originates in Dickens's *The Pickwick Papers*.

3. Peirce reviewed *Phantasms of the Living*, by Edmund Gurney, Frederic William Henry Myers, and Frank Podmore (London: Society for Psychical Research, 1886) in the *Proceedings of the American Society for Psychical Research* 1 (December 1887):150–56.

4. See J. L. Adams, "On the Secular Variation of the Moon's Mean Motion," *Philosophical Transactions of the Royal Society of London*, 143 (1853):397–406.

5. The *pons asinorum* (asses' bridge) is the fifth proposition of the first book of Euclid, so named from its figure resembling a bridge, and from the difficulty many experience in getting over it. John Stuart Mill, *A System of Logic, Ratiocinative and Inductive* (London: Longmans, Green, and Co., 1865), bk. 2, ch. 4, §4, pp. 247–51. See Peirce's "The 'Pons Asinorum' Again" in *New York Daily Tribune* (6 January 1891), and HP 1:568–69.

6. See the third lecture, "The Logic of Relatives," in RLT 151–56, where Peirce provides an example of how the construction of diagrams according to the rules of his Existential Graphs illustrates logical inference in a way suggested by his theory of categories. For a full discussion of Existential Graphs see Don D. Roberts, *The Existential Graphs of Charles S. Peirce* (The Hague and Paris: Mouton, 1973).

7. William Whewell, *Novum Organum Renovatum*, 3rd ed. (London: John W. Parker & Son, 1858), II, iv.

8. This passage is followed in the manuscript by the deleted sentence: "I am happy to find this point receives valuable confirmation of an entirely independent thinker, whose care and thoroughness gives weight to all he says, Dr. Francis Ellingwood Abbot."

9. See Peirce's paper "Logical Machines" in *The American Journal of Psychology* 1 (November 1887):165–70, reprinted in *Modern Logic* 7 (1997):71–77.

10. *Republic*, VII.532c (ἐπανάγωγή); *Republic*, VII.526d (συναγωγή); *Prior Analytics*, bk. 2, ch. 23, 68b15 (ἐπαγωγή).

11. William Whewell (1794–1866), *Architectural Notes on German Churches* (Cambridge: J. and J. J. Deighton, 1835).

12. William Whewell, *History of the Inductive Sciences: From the Earliest to the Present Time* (London: J.W. Parker, 1837).

13. The Greek phrase is explained in note 21 of selection 4.

14. To shorten reading time, Peirce deleted the passage ending here in the manuscript, from "But, then, Whewell" to "utterly exploded."

15. Alexander Dumas (1802–1870), *Impressions de voyage* (Paris: Revue des Deux Mondes, 1834).

16. Peirce deleted the end of this paragraph to save time, from "I have been reading Alexandre Dumas" to "befalls it."

17. Peirce cites the three most prominent English mathematicians of his time. Arthur Cayley (1821–1895) developed the theory of algebraic invariants together with James Joseph Sylvester (1814–1897), who taught at Johns Hopkins while Peirce taught logic. Peirce had a high regard for Sylvester, the first editor of the *American Journal of Mathematics*, though Peirce claimed that Sylvester failed to properly recognize Peirce's priority for certain algebraic results. William Kingdon Clifford (1845–1879), also an English mathematician and philosopher, known for the theory of biquaternions and for his work on non-Euclidean space and topology; for Peirce's review of Clifford's best known work, see W5:254–56.

18. This passage is followed in the manuscript by the following crossed-out paragraph:

> Since I myself am in no sense a teacher, but only a learner, and at the very foot of my class at that, for the reproach made against me is a just one that I am all the time modifying my doctrines, it is only to please you and not by any means myself that I have elected to address you upon topics of vital importance. To me no subject could possibly be more distasteful. For I know nothing about matters of vital importance. All I *think* I know concerns things which I hope may prove of subsidiary importance. As to topics of vital importance I have nothing to inculcate but sentiments. True, I am a sentimentalist in theory. I believe sentiment is far more deeply important than science. But by my training I am nothing /but/ a scientific man myself and am quite out of my element in talking about things vitally important. My only excuse for attempting it is my desire to conform to your wishes. But I find that struggle as I may and do, I cannot keep dry details altogether out of my lectures. For if I did I should have nothing to say.

It is likely that Peirce decided to tuck in, at the precise location of this deleted paragraph which hinges between two pages in the manuscript, three additional leaves written later (located in MS 825); they contain the seven paragraphs that begin with "Upon this first, and in one sense this sole, rule of reason" and end with "denial of an unusual phenomenon." Other editors, however, have concluded differently.

19. Peirce's strong interest in the economy of research is manifested in his 1879 paper "Note on the Theory of the Economy of Research" (W4:72–78).

20. This is the Academy founded by Plato c.387 B.C., which lasted until A.D. 529.

21. *Cours de philosophie positive*, 19th lesson.

22. In 1897 Salomon August Andrée (b. 1854), a Swedish engineer, died in an attempt to fly in a balloon to the North Pole from Spitzbergen.

23. Reported in Sir David Brewster's *Memoirs of the Life, Writings, and Discoveries of Sir Isaac Newton* (Edinburgh : T. Constable and Co., 1855), vol. 2, ch. 27.

24. Listing's theorem, formulated in 1847, gives, for a geometrical configuration, a relation between the numbers of its points, lines, surfaces, and spaces. Though he is counted as a founder of topology (the name he coined), Listing's work in this area has been largely supplanted by other approaches. Peirce devised more general "Listing numbers" that applied to a wider range of configurations, including ones that were not confined to three dimensions as were Listing's. See chapter 9 in Murray Murphey's *The Development of Peirce's Philosophy* (1961) and Hilary Putnam's commentary in RLT 99–101 and 279n.70–271n.75, and the last note to the previous selection.

25. The rest of this paragraph (beginning with "In favor") and the beginning of the next one (up to the sentence ending with "and nothing more.") was deleted by Peirce in the manuscript to save time.

26. Peirce's reference to Captain Edward Cuttle ("a kind-hearted, salt-looking" old retired sailor in Charles Dickens's *Dombey and Son*) alludes to the nautical origins of the phrase, meaning "in one direction and another."

27. Paul Charles Morphy (1837–1884), American chess player, world's chess master (1857–1859). Wilhelm Steinitz (1836–1900), born in Prague, naturalized American in 1884; world's chess champion from 1866 to 1894.

28. The beginning of this paragraph, from "Passing to" to "application," was deleted by Peirce to save time.

29. *Philosophiae naturalis principia mathematica*, bk. 3, general scholium. "I frame no hypotheses."

30. Hilary Putnam has called these last three sentences "the first really anti-foundationalist metaphor," in Giovanna Borradori's *The American Philosopher* (University of Chicago Press, 1994, p. 62). He added, in RLT 73, that "the idea that knowledge does not need to start with a *foundation* in the traditional epistemological sense has rarely been more beautifully expressed." Peirce's metaphor stands comparison with Otto Neurath's famous "ship metaphor" (in his 1921 *Anti-Spengler*).

31. Peirce deleted the entire last paragraph in the manuscript (here restored), either to save time, or, as H. William Davenport has suggested, at the possible urging of William James, who might have advised Peirce against criticizing Paul Carus publicly. (James recommended Peirce's lectures to Carus for publication, but Carus did not pay heed.)

32. Peirce refers to Paul Carus's paper "The Founder of Tychism, His Methods, Philosophy, and Criticisms: In Reply to Mr. Charles S. Peirce" in *The Monist* 3 (July 1893):571–622. The passage alluded to is pp. 592–93.

33. Peirce may be misquoting Duns Scotus (he wrote the same phrase on interleaf 395 of his copy of the *Century Dictionary*). Consulted sources have "ille maledictus Averroes" instead. See John Duns Scotus, *Philosophical Writings*, tr. by Allan Wolter (Indianapolis & Cambridge: Hackett Pub. Co., 1987), 138 (*Opus oxoniense*, IV, dist. XLIII, q. ii).

6. PEARSON'S *GRAMMAR OF SCIENCE*

1. Karl Pearson (1857–1936), British scientist and philosopher of science, professor of geometry, applied mathematics, and mechanics (mostly at University College, London). A friend of Francis Galton, he applied statistics to biological problems, and was one of the founders of modern statistical theory and biometry. Appointed to the chair of eugenics in 1911, he was for a time the editor of the *Annals of Eugenics*. His main philosophical work is contained in *The Ethic of Freethought, a Selection of Essays and Lectures* (London: T. F. Unwin, 1888), and in *The Grammar of Science* (second edition here reviewed; London: Adams and Charles Black, 1900). Of the latter work, Peirce also reviewed the first edition (London: Walter Scott, 1892) for *The Nation* in July 1892 (CN 1:160–61). Peirce regarded Pearson as a champion of contemporary nominalism.

2. *Multiplicamini:* from the biblical injunction for mankind to be fruitful and "multiply" (Genesis 1:28).

3. *The Grammar of Science*, ch. 1, §3.

4. "Dr. Karl Pearson . . . declares that the only valid excuse for the encouragement of scientific activity lies in its tending to maintain 'the stability of society.' This is truly

a British phrase, meaning the House of Lords and vested rights and all that" (Peirce's review of *Clark University, 1889–1899: Decennial Celebration,* published in *Science,* new series 11 (20 April 1900):620).

5. This idea of the mind reflecting or mirroring the cosmos is one of the major tenets of Peirce's philosophy. See for instance MS 900, "The Logic of Mathematics," where Peirce says: "Under the third clause, we have, as a deduction from the principle that thought is the mirror of being, the law that the end of being and highest reality is the living impersonation of the idea that evolution generates" (CP 1.487, c.1896). This recalls Peirce's use of the Shakespearian phrase "man's glassy essence," which Richard Rorty set out to shatter in his *Philosophy and the Mirror of Nature* (Princeton University Press, 1979).

6. See also Peirce's classification of "motives from which a man may act" in MS 1434:21–28.

7. Josiah Royce, *The World and the Individual, Gifford Lectures Delivered before the University of Aberdeen. First Series: The Four Historical Conceptions of Being* (New York: Macmillan, 1899). Peirce's review of the first series appeared in *The Nation* 70 (5 April 1900):267; see CP 8.100–116 and CN 2:239–41.

8. Leslie Stephen (1832–1904), English critic, biographer, and editor of the *Dictionary of National Biography.* Peirce refers to Stephen's *Science of Ethics* (1882).

9. In MS 641:17 (6 November 1909), Peirce explained this sentence thus: "I meant by this expression that something in my consciousness made me virtually aware that I could not directly will the appearance down."

10. Commenting on this passage (beginning with "I see an inkstand") in 1909, Peirce wrote (MS 641:18–19, "Significs and Logic," 6 Nov. 1909):

Thus, the Signs of the Reality of an appearance are, 1st, its Insistency (of which Sign its Vividness is again a Sign), 2nd, its sameness to all witnesses, except for differences that are but corroborative, and 3rd, its physical reactions; and the Reality is that which these Signs go toward proving; so that we have only to ask what they do prove, and the answer to that question will be the Definition *of a Percept.*

What they prove as thoroughly as any Actual Fact can be proved, is that genuine Percepts represent, both in their qualities and their occasions, Facts concerning Matter as independent of themselves, the Perceptions.

11. Chapter 3 in Pearson's book is entitled "The Scientific Law."

12. Francis Bacon (1561–1626), *Novum Organum (The New Organon,* 1620).

13. "The Order of Nature," in *Popular Science Monthly* 13 (June 1878):208; EP1:175–76, W3:311–12.

14. *The Grammar of Science,* ch. 3, §3.

15. *Hamlet,* act 1, scene 5.

16. Chapter 4 in Pearson's book is entitled "Cause and Effect—Probability."

7. LAWS OF NATURE

1. Augustus De Morgan (1806–1871). See article "Logic" in the *English Cyclopaedia* (1860), *Essay on Probabilities* (1838), *Formal Logic, or the Calculus of Inference, Necessary and Probable* (1847).

2. Also called the Titius-Bode Law, from German astronomers Johann Daniel Titius (who announced it in 1766) and Johann Elert Bode (who popularized it in 1772), it is a formula giving the approximate distances of planets from the sun. It has the form $d = 0.4 + 0.3 \times 2^n$ where d is the distance (in astronomical units) of a planet from

the sun, and *n* takes the values $-\infty$, 0, 1, 2, 3, etc. Though approximately correct for the first seven planets, the law fails for the eighth planet, Neptune, giving a result that roughly equals the distance of Pluto.

3. Nicholas Amhurst (1697–1742), English poet and publicist, was expelled from Oxford for Whig sympathies. *Terrae Filius* (1721–26) is a series of satirical papers about the university.

4. In MS 870:43 Peirce attributes this view to Ralph Cudworth (1617–1688): "Cudworth in particular advocated this doctrine [of the plastic nature] in his *True Intellectual System of the Universe* published in 1678." Peirce may also be alluding to Alexander Pope's *Essay on Man*, whose third epistle contains the verse "Plastic Nature working to this end."

5. The quoted phrase follows the full title of Fulke Greville's book *Certaine Learned and Elegant Workes of the Right Honorable Fulke Lord Brooke* (London: Henry Seyle, 1633), and the verses come from stanza 74 of the "Treatie of Humane Learning." Philip Sidney (1554–1586) was an English poet and politician.

6. Francis Hutcheson (1694–1746), Scottish philosopher, author of *Inquiry into the Original Ideas of Beauty and Virtue* (1725) and *System of Moral Philosophy* (1755).

7. William Wollaston (1659–1724), English philosopher, author of *The Religion of Nature Delineated* (1722), of which there had been eight editions by 1750.

8. Pierre Gassendi (1592–1655), French scientist, mathematician, and Epicurean philosopher, author of *Disquisitio Metaphysica* (1644), an expansion of his skeptical objections against Descartes's *Meditations*, and *Syntagma Philosophicum*, posthumously published in his *Opera Omnia* (1658). The "perfected form" in which Peirce reawakened Gassendi's theory is the metaphysics blending tychism and synechism that he began to conceive in his 1884 lecture on "Design and Chance" (EP1:215–24). Gassendi was an Epicurean, and the main difference Peirce sees between the Epicurean and the evolutionist view of the development of the universe is described both in "A Guess at the Riddle" (EP1:251) and in "The Architecture of Theories" (EP1:294–95). For the Epicurean, the development of the universe proceeds forever without tending toward anything unattained, while for Peirce the universe sprang from a chaos in the infinitely distant past to tend toward something different in the infinitely distant future.

9. Ralph Cudworth, *The True Intellectual System of the Universe* (London: Thomas Tegg, 1845), 2:599. The "atomic Atheist" mentioned in the quote is Gassendi. The last sentence, shortened by Peirce, ends with the following words in the original: "or else being, by the mere necessity of things, at length forced so to move, as they should have done, had art and wisdom directed them."

8. ON THE LOGIC OF DRAWING HISTORY FROM ANCIENT DOCUMENTS

1. In the second half of MS 690, not published here, Peirce discusses at great length three examples illustrating how solid hypotheses can be made to reconcile the facts reported in ancient testimonies. The first example (published in CP 7.232–55) attempts to show that Strabo's historical account of the transmission of Aristotle's manuscripts can be trusted on the basis of a careful examination both of the reasonableness of the reported facts and of the texts themselves as presented in their Berlin edition. Special focus is given to the second book of *Prior Analytics*, in which Peirce detects misplaced chapters and two corrupt passages, one of which involves changing a word in order to improve (or restore) Aristotle's account of abduction (see selection 14, note 11). In the second example (in HP 2:763–91) Peirce attempts to determine the chronology of Plato's life, including his birth date (late in June of 428 B.C.), the

question of whether Plato ever went to Megara, and the dating of the dialogues. The third example (in HP 2:791–800) attempts to discern what is believable in the various accounts of Pythagoras's life, including where and when he might have travelled, whether he was a mystical person, and why the Pythagoreans made such a mystery of their doctrine.

2. Section x in Hume's *Enquiry Concerning Human Understanding* is titled "Of Miracles" (1748).

3. Peirce is referring here to three key works in the early history of probability. Abraham De Moivre (1667–1754) was a French mathematician who emigrated to England. The first edition of *The Doctrine of Chances: or, a Method of Calculating the Probabilities of Events in Play* appeared in 1718 and not 1716 as Peirce had it (London: printed by W. Pearson); the second edition appeared in 1738, and not 1735 as Peirce had it (London: printed by H. Woodfall). Pierre Rémond de Montmort (1678–1719) was also a French mathematician; the dates Peirce gives for Montmort's *Essay d'analyse sur les jeux de hazard* (Paris: J. Quillau) are correct. Jakob Bernoulli (1654–1705), Swiss mathematician, died before completing his posthumously published *Ars conjectandi* (Basilae: Impensis Thurnisiorum, 1713).

4. Peirce alludes notably to Eduard Zeller and Christian August Brandis (see selection 4), and maybe also to George Grote (1794–1871), Carl Steinhart (1801–1872), Carl M. W. Schaarschmidt (1822–1909), Wilhelm Windelband (1848–1915), and Wincenty Lutoslawski (1863–1954).

5. Richard Bentley (1662–1742), English philologist and critic, whose editions of classical writers were renowned for their scholarship.

6. The remaining long part of this paragraph has been omitted in this edition; it consists first of Peirce's answer to F. Y. Edgeworth's objection that Peirce confuses testimonies with arguments, and second of the illustration of a confusion of thought that might lead to the idea that the theory of the probability of testimonies cannot be applicable to arguments in general.

7. Christoph Sigwart (1830–1904), German philosopher and logician, author of a two-volume *Logik* (1873 and 1878), a treatise about the theory of knowledge translated by Helen Dendy as *Logic* (London, 1890). Peirce frequently criticizes Sigwart's psychologism in his later writings (and thus throughout this volume).

8. Eduard Zeller (*A History of Greek Philosophy*, 1:338n.4) cites more than three authorities: Aristotle (according to both Aelian and Apollonius), Plutarch, Diogenes Laertius, and Nicomachus (according to both Porphyry and Iamblichus).

9. Diogenes Laertius states merely that "there is a story that once, when he [Pythagoras] was disrobed, his thigh was seen to be of gold" (*Lives of Eminent Philosophers*, 8.11).

10. These authorities include Plato (*Theaetetus*, 174a), Aristotle (*Nicomachean Ethics*, bk. 6, ch. 7, 1141b3), and Diogenes (*Lives*, 1.34).

11. Eduard Zeller, *A History of Greek Philosophy*, 1:212n.2.

12. From this point on in this volume, the spelling "premiss(es)" replaces that of "premise(s)" found in the earlier selections. In the article "premiss" he wrote for Baldwin's *Dictionary* in 1901, Peirce insisted that the word's etymology demanded that it be so spelled, a practice he followed consistently afterward. See selection 21, pp. 293–94 for a similar argument.

13. Johannes Kepler, *Astronomia Nova* (1609).

14. At the time Peirce was composing this essay, he had also begun to write a book titled "Minute Logic" (MSS 425–34), of which selection 9 is a part, with the financial support of his friend Francis Lathrop. Peirce contended that the study of logic requires minute analysis in a manner analogous to the physical sciences.

15. Peirce deleted the second half of the sentence, after "successfully": "and they may be supplemented by a sketch of how, if the reasons for it were given, one might embrace the whole of logic in one comprehensive, unitary conception, in which the method here advocated for treating ancient historical documents shall find its native and fitting place."

16. Peirce addressed the question of miracles in an earlier set of papers (see MSS 692 and 869–73, and the Smithsonian manuscript of which selection 7 is a part). Some of this material has been published in *Charles S. Peirce: Selected Writings (Values in a Universe of Chance)*, ed. by Philip P. Wiener (New York: Dover Publications, 1966), ch. 18, pp. 275–321.

17. The "St. Petersburg problem" was first discussed by Nicholas Bernoulli in a paper published posthumously in the journal of the St. Petersburg Academy in 1713. What is the equitable fee Paul should pay to enter the following game of chance: Peter promises to pay him one dollar if a fair coin lands heads on the first toss, two dollars if it lands heads on the second toss, and in general 2^{n-1} dollars if it first lands heads on the nth toss? If we agree with Bernoulli that the fair price for a game is its moral expectation, the formula derived from the standard theory leads to the paradoxical answer that Paul should pay an infinite amount for the privilege of playing.

18. Samuel Butler (1612–1680), *Hudibras*, part 3, canto 3. The original reads "He that complies against his will, | Is of his own opinion still."

19. The Italian medical professor Luigi Galvani (1737–1798) is credited with initiating the study of electricity in animals. Accounts of the discovery state that his wife, for whom he was preparing a frog-leg soup, called his attention to the violent convulsions she had observed in a skinned frog lying on a table when its legs were accidentally touched by a scalpel while sparks were being mechanically generated nearby.

20. Paul Carus, "The Idea of Necessity, Its Basis and Scope," *The Monist* 3 (Oct. 1892):68–96 (especially p. 86 in the section "Necessity and Chance").

21. The great earthquake of Lisbon occurred on 1 November 1755.

22. John Venn (1834–1923), *The Principles of Empirical or Inductive Logic* (London: Macmillan, 1889), 492–93.

23. Ibid., 495.

24. See Raymond Clare Archibald's account of the discovery of Uranus in his *Benjamin Peirce, 1809–1880* (Oberlin: The Mathematical Association of America, 1925), 14.

25. Venn, *Empirical or Inductive Logic*, 494, 498.

26. Ibid., 492–93.

27. *System of Positive Polity* (Paris: L. Mathias, 1851), 1:421–22.

28. Lewis Carroll, *The Hunting of the Snark (An Agony, in Eight Fits)* (London: Macmillan, 1876), Fit II, "The Bellman's Speech," stanza 16 (the first line in Peirce's quotation blends the last line of st. 15 and the first line of st. 16).

29. *Critique of Pure Reason*, A7, 303–5; B11, 360–61.

30. The primary example of the reform of mathematical reasoning at this time for Peirce is probably the work of Ernst Schröder who in his *Vorlesungen über die Algebra der Logik*, vol. 3 (1895), §23 and §31, used a form of Peirce's logical algebra to recast Richard Dedekind's work in the foundations of mathematics (see note 32 below).

31. At this point in the typescript Peirce inserted a very long handwritten text titled "Note on Collections" which, in spite of its great interest, cannot be reproduced here for lack of space. Most of it has been printed in HP 2:737–42.

32. C. S. Peirce, "On the Logic of Number," in *American Journal of Mathematics* 4 (1881):85–95, W4:299–309. Richard Dedekind, *Was sind und was sollen die Zahlen?* (Braunschweig: F. Vieweg, 1888). See also selection 12, note 1.

33. Peirce gave this "definition" of convergence in his manuscript; it is equivalent to the Cauchy criterion for convergence of a sequence. In his typescript, instead of the last inequality Peirce had " $(x_n - x) < \varepsilon$," which would be the more "common definition" of convergence provided it is changed into $(x_n - x)^2 < \varepsilon^2$ or $|x_n - x| < \varepsilon$.

34. The manuscript and the typescript provide two different figures: in the TS, the figure is 28½, while in the MS it is 27, followed by an illegible fraction which might be either ½, ⅓, or ⅛. Here we follow the MS and take the figure to be 27½. It is interesting to note that Peirce used the same illustration two years later, in the seventh Lowell lecture of 1903, where the number appears to be a round 27 (CP 7.122). Peirce identifies in neither place the probability function he has used.

35. Lambert Adolphe Quetelet (1796–1874), Belgian mathematician and sociologist; *Lettres sur la théorie des probabilités,* third letter.

36. See Peirce and Joseph Jastrow's 1884 paper "On Small Differences of Sensation" in W5:122–35. The word "Differenzschwelle," or "Unterschiedsschwelle," means "differential threshold," and Peirce's denial that there is any such threshold is a criticism of G. T. Fechner's theory.

37. Ole Römer (1644–1710), Danish astronomer noted for the discovery of the finite speed of light, which he estimated, in 1676, at 140,000 miles per second.

38. Boyle's law is that the pressure of a gas, at constant temperature, is inversely proportional to its volume. See EP1:196–97.

39. In the table, "O – C" means "Observation minus Calculation." Peirce starts with Potassium (K), leaving out the first eighteen elements (from Hydrogen to Argon). Most of the atomic weights listed in the "Obs" rows are wrong by today's standards, and the difference O – C is often a little larger than shown in the table. The notion of atomic number, which is more fundamental than that of atomic weight, as well as the notion of isotopes of elements, were not yet known.

40. It has since been discovered that instead of "sixteen consecutive elements" there are just twelve, eleven of which belong to the Lanthanide series (the first three, Ce, Pr, and Nd, are in the table; those missing are Pm, Sm, Eu, Gd, Tb, Dy, Ho, Er, Tm, Yb, and Lu), and the last, coming before Ta, is Hf (Hafnium). The missing element between Mo and Ru is Tc (Technetium), and between W and Os is Re (Rhenium). The three elements after Bi are Po (Polonium), At (Astatine), and Rn (Radon).

41. Peirce's figures are very close to today's figures: he has 127.5 for Te (today: 127.6), and 137.4 for Ba (today: 137.33).

9. On Science and Natural Classes

1. This first paragraph is the second one in the manuscript; the opening paragraph has been skipped in this volume because it relates to matters not printed here.

2. Ernest Cushing Richardson, *Classification, Theoretical and Practical* (New York: Charles Scribner's Sons, 1901). Part I of the book is titled "The Order of the Sciences," and part II "The Classification of Books." Peirce reviewed the book for *The Nation,* 27 February 1902 (CN 3:61–62).

3. Louis Agassiz (1807–1873), *An Essay on Classification* (London: Longman, Brown, Green, Longmans, & Roberts, 1859). The essay appeared for the first time in 1857 as an introduction to a larger work, *Contributions to the Natural History of the United States.*

4. Carl Auer, Freiherr von Welsbach (1858–1929), Austrian chemist and engineer who invented the gas mantle, a device consisting of a fabric impregnated with a mixture of thorium nitrate and cerium nitrate which glowed brightly when heated by a gas flame.

5. William Matthew Flinders Petrie (1853–1942), English egyptologist. The title of Petrie's work is *Naukratis*, part I, 1884–85, Third Memoir of the Egypt Exploration Fund (London: Trübner & Co., 1886). Chapter 9 is titled "The Weights of Naukratis."

6. Not printed here is a long statistical and historical discussion of the distribution of weights among the kets (or kats) supporting Peirce's last statement.

7. The "long digression" refers to the omitted text. Peirce apparently did not fulfill his intention of studying the theory of errors: no such discussion has been found in this or surrounding documents. It was, however, a subject of importance to Peirce, especially in his work for the U. S. Coast Survey; he gave a general account, making use of his logic of relations, in his paper, "On the Theory of Errors of Observations," *Report of the Superintendent of the United States Coast Survey, 1870* (Washington, D.C.: Government Printing Office, 1873), 200–24; W3:114–60.

8. *De partibus animalium*, 639b12–15.

9. The year 1860 is probably meant to mark the year following the publication of Darwin's *Origin of Species*. August Weismann and Francis Galton are two other scientists mentioned by Peirce in this volume who have shaped the notion of heredity. Peirce was evidently not acquainted with the genetic theory that Gregor Mendel developed earlier in the nineteenth century and that did not become known before 1900. An appraisal of Peirce's treatment of evolutionary theory can be found in Arthur W. Burks, "Logic, Learning, and Creativity in Evolution," *Studies in the Logic of Charles Sanders Peirce*, ed. Nathan Houser et al. (Bloomington: Indiana University Press, 1997), 497–534.

10. William Cullen Bryant (1794–1878), *The Battle-Field* (1839), stanza 9.

11. Volapük is an artificial international language constructed in 1880 by Johann Martin Schleyer, a German cleric. It was popular until Esperanto supplanted it.

12. In the *Century Dictionary* Peirce defined "vortex" as "a portion of fluid in rotational motion inclosed in an annular surface which is a locus of vortex-lines. . . . In a perfect fluid, which can sustain no distorting stress even for an instant, the velocity of a rotating particle cannot be retarded any more than if it were a frictionless sphere; and, in like manner, no such velocity can be increased. Consequently, a vortex, unlike a wave, continues to be composed of the same identical matter." A "wave," Peirce defined as a "form assumed by parts of a body which are out of equilibrium, such that as fast as the particles return they are replaced by others moving into neighboring positions of stress, so that the whole disturbance is continually propagated into new parts of the body while preserving more or less perfectly the same shape and other characters."

13. The conception of vortices as a fundamental component of the world can be found most prominently in René Descartes. Peirce, in his *Century Dictionary* definition, makes a distinction between the discredited Cartesian theory and the modern physical theory of vortex-rings which were posited as a foundation for a new atomic theory.

14. Shakespeare's characterization of the rebel "Hotspur" Henry Percy (1366–1403) in *Henry IV*, part 1, lines 1597–98, remains the epitome of a rash, impetuous, hot-headed man.

15. The manganate should be $K_2 Mn O_4$ (obtained when a manganese compound is fused with potassium nitrate ($K N O_3$)). The rutheniate should be $K_2 Ru O_4$.

16. These are the names Peirce gives to the Listing numbers. See selection 4, note 41, and selection 5, note 24.

17. Peirce attached the following page numbers to the sentences quoted from Agassiz's book (referenced in note 3 above): p. 145 for the quotation after *Classes;* p. 151 after *Orders;* and pp. 159 and 160 after *Families.*

18. Pierre de Fermat (1601–1665), French mathematician, whose famous last theorem (that the equation $x^n + y^n = z^n$, where x, y, and z are positive integers, has no solution if n is an integer greater than 2) has only been proved in 1996. John Wilson (1741–1793), English mathematician. Wilson's theorem is that, if p is a prime number, then $1 + (p - 1)!$ is divisible by p.

19. See selection 5, note 17.

20. Sir Joseph Norman Lockyer (1836–1920), English astronomer, whose book *The Dawn of Astronomy* Peirce reviewed in *The Nation* in 1894 (CN 2:48–53).

21. Peirce's text continues in the manuscript for 120 pages (two-thirds of the document) and provides a very detailed classification of the sciences.

10. The Maxim of Pragmatism

1. Peirce may be referring to any number of pragmatists, but certainly to both William James and F. C. S. Schiller.

2. "How to Make Our Ideas Clear," *Popular Science Monthly* 12 (Jan. 1878):286–302; EP1:124–41; W3:257–76.

3. Peirce introduced the term "pragmatism" in its modern use in conversations held with the members of the Metaphysical Club in the early 1870s (see selection 28, note 5), and kept using it informally thereafter. It was William James who both officialized the word and recognized Peirce's paternity of it in his 26 August 1898 address on "Philosophical Conceptions and Practical Results" delivered before the Philosophical Union at Berkeley. Praising Peirce, James wrote: "The principle of practicalism— or pragmatism, as [Peirce] called it, when I first heard him enunciate it at Cambridge in the early '70's—is the clue or compass by following which I find myself more and more confirmed in believing we may keep our feet upon the proper trail" (in *Pragmatism* (Cambridge: Harvard University Press, 1975), Appendix 1, p. 258).

4. *Revue Philosophique* 7 (Jan. 1879):47; W3:363–64. English version in EP1:131 and W3:265. Peirce fails to cite the last important sentence of the French paragraph: "Il n'y a pas de nuance de signification assez fine pour ne pouvoir produire une différence dans la pratique" ("there is no distinction of meaning so fine as to consist in anything but a possible difference of practice").

5. *Revue Philosophique* 7 (Jan. 1879):48; W3:365.

6. See above, pp. 135–36.

7. "Entities [or beings] must not be multiplied beyond necessity."

8. Simon Newcomb (1835–1909), American astronomer and mathematician. No trace of the particular discussion Peirce refers to has been found in their correspondence. Peirce often noticed that Newcomb did not keep himself well informed of the latest advances in mathematics, and could not see any sense in the mathematics of infinities.

9. On the difference between commensurability and incommensurability, see "Reason's Rules" (MS 596, c.1902), in CP 5.539 and 541. See also selection 8, p. 86, selection 11, p. 146, and selection 16, pp. 237–38.

10. Karl Pearson, *The Grammar of Science*, Introduction, pp. 26–27. See selection 6, p. 57.

11. Henry Rutgers Marshall (1852–1927), architect, psychologist and novelist, interested mainly in aesthetics. The quotation is from *Instinct and Reason; An Essay Concerning the Relation of Instinct to Reason, with Some Special Study of the Nature of Religion* (New York and London: Macmillan and Co., 1898), 569.

12. Peirce owned a copy of the second enlarged edition of G. W. F. Hegel's *Encyklopädie der philosophischen Wissenschaften im Grundrisse* (Heidelberg: August Osswald, 1827).

13. Hegel's "three stages of thought" consist of thesis, antithesis, and synthesis.

11. On Phenomenology

1. Five documents related to the second lecture are extant: the first two treat of mathematics (see note 3 below), and the last three discuss phenomenology. Of the latter Peirce rejected the first one (MS 304, published in HL 139–50) with the self-injunction "to be rewritten and compressed." This leaves MS 305, the second draft, with which Peirce was also dissatisfied—he wrote "This won't do; it will have to be rewritten"—and MS 306, labeled "3rd Draught" and titled "On Phenomenology, or the Categories." MS 306 is incomplete: it is only twelve pages long, and despite Peirce's intention to begin with a discussion of the third category (see note 23 below), it barely touches on the matter. Since MS 305 discusses only the first two categories, the practical solution is to conjoin the two documents. MS 306 begins with the header section "III," but there is no such header in MS 305. In order to distinguish the two documents clearly, the header "I" has been inserted at the beginning of the lecture, and the number "II" has been substituted for "III" to indicate the start of the second document. It is likely that Peirce composed yet another text for the second lecture, similar in content but more polished and complete, which has unfortunately disappeared. Supporting evidence consists of remarks made in the third lecture about points made in the second lecture that cannot be found there, and also of the fact that Peirce made the text of the lecture available to people who had misssed its presentation, and that he sent it later to William James. The surviving drafts are textually so confused that it is difficult to imagine Peirce lending them to anyone.

2. See EP1:132, and the previous lecture in this volume, p. 135.

3. Peirce's first plan for the second lecture had been to discuss mathematics and to show how an analysis of mathematical reasoning could lend support to pragmatism. He wrote the first two versions of the lecture toward that end (MSS 302–3, published in HL 123–38), but then realized he could not afford the time needed to do justice to such a formidable subject. Although Peirce says here that he is restricted to six lectures, arrangements were soon made so he could give a seventh lecture. The eighth lecture he gave on "Multitude and Continuity" the day after the seventh is sometimes counted as part of the series, but Peirce would later refer to his "seven lectures."

4. Jeremy Bentham (1748–1832), *Chrestomathia; Part II* (London: Payne and Foss, 1817), 177–79. Bentham preferred the spelling "coenoscopic."

5. Peirce owned Edward William Lane's 1840 translation of the collection of Arabic tales entitled *Thousand and One Nights* or *Arabian Nights* which are strung together by Scheherazade, the reputed story-teller who hopes to save her life by entertaining her husband, the king of Samarkand.

6. Peirce's derivation of the universal categories occurs in his 1867 paper "On a New List of Categories" (EP1:1–10). In many manuscripts composed between 1859 and 1864 Peirce strove to generate long lists of particular categories systematically, mostly founded on Kant's categories, with additional ones of Peirce's own, to which he applied different rules of combination and recurrence.

7. The predicaments are Aristotle's well-known ten categories. The predicables are the five classes of predicates (*quinque voces* or *modi praedicandi*) distinguished by

Porphyry in his *Isagoge:* genus, species, difference, *proprium,* and accident. They come from Aristotle's older distinction of four classes: *proprium,* definition, genus, and accident (*Topics,* I, ch. 4, 101b17–25). Peirce is suggesting that the predicables would be Aristotle's universal categories.

8. *Critique of Pure Reason,* A80, B106.

9. *Encyclopedia of the Philosophical Sciences,* part 1, "The Science of Logic," ch. VI, section 79.

10. Peirce returns to the seven systems of metaphysics in the third and fourth Harvard lectures, pp. 164–65 and 179–81.

11. *Philosophiae naturalis principia mathematica* (1687), bk. 1, def. 4.

12. This first party is identified in the next lecture as that of Condillac and the Associationalists. The second party is that of the Hegelianists.

13. *Νοῦς* is the Greek word for spirit, mind, intelligence.

14. The first five sentences of this paragraph, from "In the course" to "Exact Logician," were written by Peirce to replace three sentences, only the last two of which he crossed out:

> I shall have to content myself with giving some hints as to how I would meet this second double-headed objection, leaving the first to your own reflexions. I will only say that in order to refute that first objection it is by no means necessary to oppose any psychological theory that the adversaries of the category may find reason to entertain. Let it be true, if you will, that the sense of effort and resistance is a sort of instinctive hypothesis which arises within us in the attempt to comprehend certain feelings connected with contractions of the muscles.

The editors chose to omit the first of these three sentences since Peirce immediately addresses the first objection.

15. Paul Carus, "Mr. Charles S. Peirce's Onslaught on the Doctrine of Necessity," *The Monist* 2 (July 1892). Carus titled the first section of his paper "David Hume Redivivus" (pp. 561–65).

16. Peirce had made studies of psychical research since at least 1887 and in a manuscript of 1903, titled "Telepathy and Perception," Peirce addressed the scientific standing of telepathy (CP 7.597–688).

17. The passage from "I would not have anybody accept" to "about the truth" was not read by Peirce when he delivered his lecture. The beginning of it replaces a deleted passage that followed "Exact Logician":

> You may depend upon it that I am not in the habit of adopting logical doctrines without the most searching and impartial criticism. I would not have anybody accept any doctrine of logic because I hold to it. But I do say that when I have given my very closest examination to a logical question and have become entirely confident as to what the true answer to it is, a mere pooh-poohing of my opinion on the part of a person who has never studied the question in a minute and thorough manner, ought not to be sufficient.

18. The Latin means "lightning striking blindly."

19. Aristotle, *De anima,* bk. 3, ch. 4, 430a1; Thomas Aquinas, *Quaestiones disputatae de anima* VIII, ad Resp.; *Summa theologica* I, 89, 1, 3°; John Locke, *Essay concerning Human Understanding* II, 1.

20. See especially the seventh Harvard lecture, pp. 226–33, for Peirce's theory of perception.

21. Bartolomé Esteban Murillo (1618–1682), a popular Spanish painter of religious subjects.

22. Peirce probably refers to "occasionalism," a theory of causation held by a number of seventeenth-century Cartesian philosophers, including Nicolas Malebranche.

In its extreme version it states that God is the only true causal agent, directly responsible for bringing about all phenomena.

23. This paragraph ends MS 305, and the next one begins a new notebook, MS 306, which opens with the following red-inked note: "I begin by making a first draught of what I intend to say about the third category; and what I say of the first two will have to be compressed into so much of the hour as this leaves unoccupied." This is followed by a quotation from Shakespeare, revealing Peirce's frustration: "'Tis true 'tis pity | And pity 'tis 'tis true" (*Hamlet*, act 2, scene 2, lines 97–98). The roman section number "III" that precedes the text has been changed to "II". See note above.

24. Peirce is referring to Georg Cantor (1845–1918) because of the pioneer work this German mathematician accomplished on continuity, which characterizes a fundamental form of Thirdness.

25. Ernst Heinrich Haeckel (1834–1919), German zoologist and monistic philosopher, author of *Die Welträtsel: Gemeinverstandliche Studien über monistische Philosophie* (Stuttgart: A. Kroner, 1899).

26. The words "as objects" stem from an incomplete authorial alteration: Peirce interlined at first the words "as real objects," then he wrote "as" over the end of "real" but failed to cross out "as real," here interpreted as having been implicitly deleted by the overwriting.

27. One year earlier, Peirce had written the following in the second chapter of his "Minute Logic" (CP 7.380; MS 427:246–47, 29 March 1902):

Still, it would seem that Progressive minds must have, in some mysterious way, probably by arrested development, grown from Instinctive minds; and they are certainly enormously higher. The Deity of the *Théodicée* of Leibniz is as high an Instinctive mind as can well be imagined; but it impresses a scientific reader as distinctly inferior to the human mind. It reminds one of the view of the Greeks that Infinitude is a defect; for although Leibniz imagines that he is making the Divine Mind infinite, by making its knowledge Perfect and Complete, he fails to see that in thus refusing it the powers of thought and the possibility of improvement he is in fact taking away something far higher than knowledge. It is the human mind that is infinite.

28. Robert Boyle (1627–1691), *The Origin of Forms and Qualities According to the Corpuscular Philosophy* (1666).

29. Rudolf Clausius stated in 1850 the first law of thermodynamics, that energy can be transformed from one form to another but is neither created nor destroyed.

30. J. M. Baldwin's *Dictionary of Philosophy and Psychology* (New York: Macmillan Co., 1901–2) defines psychophysical parallelism as "the affirmation that conscious process varies concomitantly with synchronous process in the nervous system, whether the two processes have a direct causal relation or not." Psychophysics is the branch of psychology concerned with the measurement of the psychological effects of sensory stimulation; it is the oldest branch of experimental psychology, said to have begun with the publication of Gustav Fechner's *Elemente der Psychophysik* (Leipzig: Breitkopf & Härtel, 1860). In MS 329 (1904), Peirce views Wilhelm Wundt as the chief propagator of psychophysical parallelism, "roughly, the doctrine that mind and matter are the two sides of one shield."

31. Charles Darwin's *Origin of Species* appeared in 1859, thus when Peirce was twenty years old.

32. Chauncey Wright (1830–1875) was a mathematician, zoologist, and philosopher, and a member of the Metaphysical Club to which Peirce belonged in the early 1870s (see selection 28, note 5).

33. Asa Gray (1810–1888), American botanist, professor of natural history at Harvard. Gray corresponded with Darwin and brought his evolutionary theories to the attention of Americans.

34. Associationism is the psychological theory, initiated by David Hartley (1705–1757) and defended by James Mill and others, that makes mental development consist mainly in the combination of simple constituents of consciousness according to certain laws of association.

35. Herbert Spencer (1820–1903), English philosopher whose major work, *First Principles* (half-titled in vol. 1 as *A System of Synthetic Philosophy*), was heavily criticized by Peirce. Edward L. Youmans (1821–1887), editor of the journal *Popular Science Monthly*.

36. Matthew 13:57. Peirce left a blank on the page, which has here been filled with the usual continuation of the phrase. Jesus said more, however, adding "in his own country and in his own house."

37. From Mark Twain's story "Jim Smiley and His Jumping Frog" (1865), also published as "The Notorious Jumping Frog of Calaveras County" (1867), in which someone tells Jim Smiley "Well, I don't see no p'ints about that frog that's any better'n any other frog."

12. THE CATEGORIES DEFENDED

1. Cf. the article "Multitude" by Peirce and H. B. Fine in Baldwin's *Dictionary*:

The multitude of all the different finite multitudes is the smallest infinite multitude. It is called the *denumeral* multitude. (Cantor uses a word equivalent to *denumerable*; but the other form has the advantage of being differentiated from words like *enumerable*, *abnumerable*, which denote classes of multitudes, not, like *denumeral*, a single multitude.) Following upon this is a denumeral series of multitudes called by C. S. Peirce the *first*, *second*, etc. *abnumerable* multitudes. Each is the multitude of possible collections formed from the members of a collection of the next preceding multitude. They seem to be the same multitudes that are denoted by Cantor as *Alephs*.

One of Peirce's most important treatments of this subject is in MS 25, "Multitude and Number" (c.1897; CP 4.170–226); see also selection 8, pp. 99–100. The last clause of the paragraph, "than which no conception yet discovered is higher," alludes to the formulation of St. Anselm's proof of the existence of God.

2. This point about singulars and individuals is implicit rather than explicit in the second lecture, but it may be that Peirce emphasized it more explicitly during the actual talk.

3. The American philosopher George Santayana (1863–1952) attended this lecture and was influenced by its ideas. He later recalled that Peirce had just been dining with William James and his family "and his evening shirt kept coming out of his evening waistcoat. He looked red-nosed and disheveled, and a part of his lecture seemed to be *ex-tempore* and whimsical" (letter to Justus Buchler, 15 Oct. 1937, quoted in Buchler, "One Santayana or Two?" *The Journal of Philosophy* 51 (1954):54).

4. The word between "speck" and "any" reads "on" in the manuscript, a reading here retained. But Peirce may have meant the conjunction "or" instead: "no speck or any grain of sand"; the parallel passage in the draft (MS 307) does not mention the speck: "a representation of every grain of sand on the soil of the country."

5. In the earlier draft Peirce explains: "Those of you who have read Prof. Royce's Supplementary Essay will have remarked that he avoids this result, which does not suit his philosophy, by not allowing his map to be continuous. But to exclude continuity is to exclude what is best and most living in Hegel" (MS 307:13). Royce's "Supplementary Essay," which is titled "The One, the Many, and the Infinite," is found at the end of the first volume of *The World and the Individual* (see selection 6, note 7). Royce discusses the example of the map in the essay's third section, pp. 502–7. Royce imagines

a perfect map drawn upon a part of the surface of the very region that is to be mapped; such a map must contain as a part of itself a representation of its own contour and contents, which latter representation must also contain its own representation, and so on ad infinitum. "We should now, indeed, have to suppose the space occupied by our perfect map to be infinitely divisible, even if not a *continuum*" (p. 505). A note attached to the latter statement says: "Continuity implies infinite divisibility. The converse does not hold true" (p. 505n). See also Peirce's *Nation* review of the second volume of *The World and the Individual*, in CN 3:83 (31 July 1902), and CP 8.122, 125.

6. What 1873 paper Peirce might be referring to is unclear. The analogy of the map is used, though not in the same connection, in Peirce's 1869 "Grounds of Validity of the Laws of Logic" (EP1:62, W2:249). Or Peirce might be referring to some Metaphysical Club conversation.

7. To illustrate the stemmas of thirdness, Peirce drew three alternate figures on the facing verso leaf in the notebook; the topmost version is the one used here.

8. Horatio Greenough (1805–1852) designed the tall obelisk constructed in 1842 at the Bunker Hill Revolutionary War site in Boston, Massachusetts. He wrote: "The obelisk has to my eye a singular aptitude, in its form and character; to call attention to a spot memorable in history. It says but one word, but it speaks loud. If I understand its voice, it says, Here! It says no more. For this reason it was that I designed an obelisk for Bunker Hill" ("Aesthetics in Washington," in *A Memorial of Horatio Greenough*, ed. by Henry T. Tuckerman (New York: G. P. Putnam, 1853), 82).

9. Peirce skipped this second section when he gave the lecture. It reappears with some modifications in the next lecture.

10. Étienne Bonnot de Condillac (1715–1780), French philosopher, author of *Traité des sensations* (*Treatise on Sense Perception*, 1754).

11. The law of Parsimony is equivalent to Ockham's razor. In Baldwin's *Dictionary*, Peirce explains the law by saying that "it is bad scientific method to introduce, at once, independent hypotheses to explain the same facts of observation."

12. Ernst Schröder had died one year earlier, on 16 June 1902. The first volume of his *Vorlesungen über die Algebra der Logik: Exakte Logik* (Leipzig: Teubner, 1890) contained much praise of Peirce and numerous references to his work. The first part of the second volume appeared in 1891, the first part of the third volume in 1895, and the second part of the second volume posthumously in 1905.

13. See selection 8, note 7 on Sigwart.

14. Charles Rollin (1661–1741), French historian, known especially for his *Histoire ancienne* (1730–38). Comte George Louis Leclerq de Buffon (1707–1788), French naturalist, co-author of *Histoire naturelle* (1749–89). Joseph Priestley (1733–1804), English theologian, philosopher, and scientist, who discovered oxygen in 1771, and founded associational psychology with David Hartley. Jean Baptiste Biot (1774–1862), French physicist and astronomer, whose most important work was in optics (chromatic polarization and corpuscular theory of light).

15. *De interpretatione*, ch. 7, 17a.

16. Since this point is not one made in writing in the extant manuscripts of the second lecture, we assume Peirce made it only during his presentation.

17. Alfred Bray Kempe (1849–1922), English barrister and mathematician. "A Memoir on the Theory of Mathematical Forms," *Philosophical Transactions of the Royal Society of London* 177 (1886):1–70.

18. "Optical geometry" is Peirce's term for projective geometry and the "ten-ray theorem" is known also as the theorem of Desargues: If the lines joining corresponding vertices of two triangles pass through a point, then the points of intersection of corresponding sides lie on a line. Karl Georg Christian von Staudt's proof is given in

his *Geometrie der Lage* (Nürnberg: Korn, 1847), theorem 90, p. 41. Kempe drew a figure similar to Peirce's rendition of the ten-ray theorem in his 1886 memoir, p. 63, para. 357, theorem 1 and fig. 67.

19. Peirce drew this same graph and two others in his personal copy of Kempe's memoir, around Kempe's own graph (his "fig. 13"), with the comment "the same in more obvious shape." Kempe explained: "The graphical units may be taken to represent either the ten straight lines of the theorem, or the ten points of intersection; the form is the same in either case. Taking the former case, the pairs of graphical units which are joined by links correspond to pairs of lines whose points of intersection are points other than the ten considered in the theorem" (p. 11).

20. At this point in the lecture Peirce wrote out, on pp. 40–45 in the notebook, his second and third responses to Kempe; afterward, however, he decided to skip this part of the text ("Skip to Page 46. I must pass by my other two answers, although one of them is extremely interesting"), but replaced it with a summary that follows directly in the text ("My other two answers . . ."). We have followed Peirce's instruction. Interested readers will find the skipped passage in HL 183–85.

21. Kempe drew a similar geometrical figure, as a rendition of the nine-ray theorem, in his 1886 memoir, p. 63, para. 357, theorem 2 and fig. 68. The three-triangle graph is found in Kempe's memoir p. 40, para. 249, fig. 48. But an important difference is that the letters Kempe associates with the vertex points each correspond to an intersection of three lines, while the numbers in Peirce's graph represent the lines.

22. "Symbolic logic" in Baldwin's *Dictionary* 2:645–50; also in CP 4.372–93.

23. Peirce's definition of "hyperboloid" in the *Century Dictionary* reads:

a quadric surface having a center not at infinity, and some of its plane sections hyperbolas. There are two kinds of hyperboloid, those of one and of two sheets. The hyperboloid of one sheet has a real intersection with every plane in space; that of two sheets has only imaginary intersections with some planes. In either case all the plane sections perpendicular to one of the axes are ellipses, and those perpendicular to either of the others are hyperbolas.

13. The Seven Systems of Metaphysics

1. Pages 1 to 11 of Peirce's notebook contain the draft of two sections, numbered I and II, which Peirce replaced on facing pages with the present much shorter single section (numbered I by the editors). Page 12 in the notebook begins a new second section numbered II, the one printed here.

2. Wincenty Lutoslawski (1863–1954), Polish philosopher, author of *The Origin and Growth of Plato's Logic* (a book Peirce studied very carefully); his "unpronounceable master" is Adam Mickiewicz (1798–1855), Poland's greatest romantic poet and advocate of Polish national freedom. The doctrine referred to may be that of Polish messianism combined with some brand of mysticism.

3. Peirce first wrote "except my own" and then replaced it with "or very little."

4. Peirce originally inserted "except perhaps Schelling's & mine" after "modern philosophy"; he then apparently changed his mind, crossed out the insertion, and added instead the word "substantially" earlier in the sentence.

5. Aristotle's two grades of being are δύναμις (potentiality) and ἐνέργεια (actuality). As regards the two kinds of actualities, see for instance *Metaphysics*, bk. 9, ch. 8, 1050a22–23: "For activity (ἔργον) is the end, and the actuality (ἐνέργεια [energy]) is the activity; hence the term 'actuality' is derived from 'activity', and tends to have the meaning of 'complete reality' (ἐντελέχεια [entelechy])." The distinction is thus between the action being accomplished (the process of actualization) and the accomplished result of this action.

6. Hegel's "doctrine of *Wesen*" (of essence) forms a chapter of his *Science of Logic*, itself a part of his *Encyclopedia of the Philosophical Sciences*.

7. "A general is that whose expression naturally suits many things." Petrus Hispanus wrote similarly: "Praedicabile est quod aptum natum est praedicari de pluribus." See Aristotle, *De interpretatione*, ch. 7, 17a38.

8. Patrick Henry (1736–1799); the quotation comes from his famous Virginia Convention speech of 23 March 1775 in which he said "Give me liberty or give me death."

9. From Peirce's *Century Dictionary* definition: Individuation is "the determination or contraction of a general nature to an individual mode of existence," and "the principle of individuation is the (supposed) general cause of such transformation of the general into the individual."

10. The text beginning here and ending ten paragraphs later (at "the reverse.") is found on facing verso pages in the notebook and forms a complete rewriting of an earlier and quite different presentation of the same argument made on the recto pages. The length of this earlier version prevents its publication here, and in lieu of it the following summary is provided. Peirce wants to show that reasoning with mathematical accuracy about infinity is no longer difficult. The idea of an enumerable collection of discrete objects, where each object is in a unique relation r to any other object, is easy to admit. Since such a collection can always be enlarged by adding a new object to it, it follows that for every enumerable multitude there is always another one greater by one. Thus there is an endless series of enumerable multitudes, which series is a collection whose grade of multitude is called a *denumeral*. Peirce explains that a collection of denumeral multitude is not increased either by the addition of, or the multiplication by, a collection of any multitude not larger than itself. He then attempts a demonstration that $2^x > x$ where, for a collection of multitude x, 2^x is the multitude of all possible collections that can be formed from that collection.

11. Peirce's offer was heard, and he was invited to give a special lecture on "multitude and continuity" the day that followed the seventh lecture on pragmatism, on 15 May 1903. Sketchy notes for that supplementary lecture survive in MS 316a. See selection 11, note 3.

12. Peirce's example of this spiral recurs many times in his writings. It is the third of three spirals described in MS 427:125–27 ("Minute Logic": ch. 2, sect. 1, "Classification of the Sciences," February-March 1902; also CP 1.276 ; the three spirals were drawn by Peirce on graph paper and are located in MS S13). We find it again in a letter to William James of 12 June 1902 (CP 8.274), and elsewhere. The equations that accompany them are never fully identical, but all produce similar results.

13. Peirce drew a very rough diagram of the spiral in his manuscript. The one given here was generated from his equation using $P = 8$ and $Q = 2$. The limiting circle of radius 5 is also indicated. Peirce was aware that the spiral does not cross the circle. The circle corresponds to the precise point where the value of θ may be said to pass through infinity.

14. The next three paragraphs (from "As for Hertz's" to "fundamental character") were skipped by Peirce at reading time, but are here restored. They replaced the following shorter passage:

The Physicist prides himself on being a Specialist. He would not have it supposed that he busies himself with a *Weltanschauung*, not even a general conception of the physical universe. He is experimenting upon a certain phenomenon and confines himself to making out the relation of that phenomenon to phenomena that are well known. The consequence of this is that when time comes to enunciate any very general principle,—such as that of the Conservation of Energy,—you find there are a dozen physicists who have been long convinced of it, but probably thought it derogatory to say so,—or their Academy or Poggendorff refused to publish their memoir,—

and very likely it will turn out that the earliest discoverable enunciation of it belonged to some obscure person outside the ranks of the professional physicists. That is probably less true today than it was fifty years ago. At any rate, it certainly ought to be the duty of some class of physicists to study the general question.

What has led me to this remark is the phenomenon of right and left. It is only when a third dimension enters into the phenomenon,—as in the case of a screw,—that there is any difference of right and left.

15. Heinrich Rudolf Hertz (1857–1894), in *The Principles of Mechanics* (1894, transl. 1899), put forward a "fundamental law" that summarized the connection between the three basic concepts of time, space, and mass, without using the concepts of either force or energy: "Every natural motion of an independent material system consists herein, that the system follows with uniform velocity one of its straightest paths."

16. Ludwig Boltzmann (Austrian physicist, 1844–1906) thought we could not entirely eliminate metaphysical assumptions from theories in favor of bare equations: physics ought to build a coherent picture of reality, and not simply discover equations. Jules Henri Poincaré (French mathematician, 1854–1912), on the other hand, thought that competing theories are each true only to the extent to which their equations agree, because these represent the real relations between things in the world. Both Poincaré and Boltzmann, however, held similar views about conventionalism in the sciences.

17. *Cours de philosophie positive* (Paris, 1835), 2:8, 19th lesson.

18. In contrast with *logica docens*, which stands for scientific or theoretical logic, Peirce writes elsewhere (MS 428, "Minute Logic," ch. 2, sect. 2, "Why Study Logic," April 1902; CP 2.186):

Now a person cannot perform the least reasoning without some general ideal of good reasoning; for reasoning involves deliberate approval of one's reasoning; and approval cannot be deliberate unless it is based upon the comparison of the thing approved with some idea of how such a thing ought to appear. Every reasoner, then, has some general idea of what good reasoning is. This constitutes a theory of logic: the scholastics called it the reasoner's *logica utens*.

19. At this point, which corresponds to a transition between two notebooks, Peirce made significant changes to his text, one result of which was that he dropped the remainder of this paragraph. Originally it continued, after "Wickedness" and a semicolon, as follows:

just as this d' inction of Righteousness and Wickedness amounts, in the last analysis, to nothing but a particular application of the most general distinction of Esthetic Goodness and Badness. To say this is not to pronounce for hedonism; for the hedonist, on the contrary, instead of admitting that Goodness and Badness is founded on Qualities of Feeling in their multitudinous variety,—admits only one, Discomfort and its absence; and to admit but one quality of feeling is at bottom not to admit any Quality at all. The Hedonist makes the mistake of supposing Gratification to be a mere Quality of Feeling; but the truth is that gratification is at bottom an affair of reaction having a quality of feeling dependent on it just as all sorts of conscious operations have their indescribable feelings. Since therefore the Hedonist bases Morality on Gratification alone, he bases it on that which is really and principally Reaction and not on Quality of Feeling, the inseparable nature of which it is to be multitudinous.

20. Théodore Simon Jouffroy (1796–1842), French philosopher, translator of Dugald Stewart and Thomas Reid. Peirce may be referring to Jouffroy's *Introduction to Ethics*. Dr. James Walker (1794–1874), president of Harvard University and professor of moral and intellectual philosophy. Peirce probably refers to William Whewell's *The Elements of Morality, Including Polity* (London, 1845).

21. This was in connection with his research for the *Century Dictionary*, for which Peirce wrote hundreds of philosophical definitions, including the entries for "ethics" and "moral."

22. Peirce circled the last two sentences of this paragraph in red ink, presumably as a reminder to give them special emphasis at reading time.

23. Peirce instructed himself to skip the text that follows "Oh, yes;" and to resume the reading in the middle of the first sentence of the next paragraph, which he altered to ease the transition. The skipped passage has been here restored, and Peirce's alterations to the transitional sentence have been ignored. Had Peirce's instructions been followed, the passage would have read as follows: "Oh yes. Among artists I have known more than one case of downright hallucinatory imaginations at the beck and call of these ποιηται."

24. Peirce may be referring to one of two painters who were his close friends: either Albert Bierstadt (1830–1902), German-born painter of the American West, or Francis A. Lathrop (1849–1909).

25. Peirce skipped this sentence at reading time. It is here restored.

26. Peirce inserted here a remark indicating that he skipped the rest of this long paragraph, as well as the two paragraphs that come next (down to "conceptions of the Universe"), at reading time. The text has been restored. His note reads: "Well I will skip this. Suffice it to say that there is no reason for suspecting the veracity of the senses; and the presumption is that the physics of the future will find out that they are more real than the present state of scientific theory admits of their being represented as being."

27. Peirce may have had a painting by Claude Monet in mind (cf. CP 5.508).

28. This may have been the original ending of the lecture text, and it is possible that Peirce decided *in fine* to add a new section titled "The Reality of Secondness" because lack of time had prevented him from presenting the matter in the second lecture (which has a parallel discussion); he may have hoped that enough time would remain to let him read this supplementary section.

14. The Three Normative Sciences

1. The text that begins here corresponds to the second section of Peirce's lecture. The first section, which Peirce decided not to read, consists of the following fascinating description of his exacting research methodology. Since a condensed version of it appears at the end of the lecture, the section has not been restored in the main text.

Ladies and Gentlemen:

You may perhaps gain some useful hints if I describe to you how I go to work in studying philosophy. I shall merely sketch the outline of the proceeding without going into details. I mostly work pen in hand and although important steps are taken while I am away from my writing-table, they are recorded at once. A given question in philosophy comes up for discussion, never mind how. I begin by writing out a Collation upon it. That is, I begin by setting down briefly yet sufficiently and as formally as possible all the arguments which I have seen used on the one side or which seem to me likely to be used on that side; and then I do the same for the other side. Such of the arguments as admit of ready refutation, I at once set down the refutations of. Next, without going into the merits of the case, I draw up a list of the general methods in which a solution of the problem might be sought. If some of them appear to be quite futile, I draw up brief formal statements of the reasons of this futility. One of the methods will appear to me to be the one which ought to be decisive, and I carefully set down the reason why, keeping a good look out for special circumstances which might annul this reason. Other methods may appear to me to have a secondary utility and I further set down the reasons for this and for my estimate of just how far and where those methods are valuable. Search is made for objections to all these reasons, and any that seem considerable are formally set down and refuted. But if, in this course of this part of the discussion or at a later stage, it appears that the question in hand depends upon another which I have never submitted to any systematic examination or concerning which, since my last examination of it, any considerable grounds of doubt have been found, I put aside the first examination until this other question shall have been at least provisionally settled in my mind. If no such interruption takes place, I take up first the principal method and afterwards the subsidiary or secondary methods and apply them with the severest critical scrutiny of which I am master, setting down always brief and formal but sufficient statements of all the steps of the argumentation, and disposing of all objections either by assent or refutation. I also dispose, in the same way, of all the arguments which have not already been disposed of. Having this brief drawn up I study it with the minutest care to detect any loopholes, and sometimes amend it more or less radically, even giving the question itself a new and broader turn, and this is sometimes done three or four times over, before I am satisfied with the discussion. I then put the paper away and dismiss the matter from my mind. Sometimes I do so in despair of being able at the time to obtain any clear light on the subject; for when such light is not at hand my experience is that hard thinking is of very little use. There is nothing to be done but wait until the light comes from some other source. But even when my discussion does seem satisfactory at first, yet my experience of my own stupidity is such that I always mutter to my intellect, "Very well, you have only to possess yourself in patience and the inadequacy of your present ideas will appear plainly enough in due time." In fact, after a long time, something or other flashes a new light on the old question, and only too often I find that strenuous as was my scrutiny of the previous arguments, I have committed some horrible stupidity. At last, my ideas seem ripe for a new setting of them in order; and I make a second collation of the question without looking at the first but endeavoring to proceed quite as if the question were a new one. This second collation is drawn up just as the first one was; only, when it is complete, I get out the first and compare the two with minute criticism, both where they differ and where they agree. It may seem to me best to allow the matter to go over for a third collation; but commonly I consider that I am now well started upon the right track; or at any rate all that can be done in this way has been done. I impress the cardinal considerations on my mind, and perhaps draw up a note of anything difficult to bear in mind exactly; and I then look upon all the labor so far performed as a mere exercise of no value except in the parts which have impressed me. It now remains to treat my conception of the problem like a seedling tree, which must have water, nutriment, sunlight, shade, and air and frequent breaking of the ground about it, in order that it may grow up into something worthy of respect. These operations I also carry out, pen in hand, with intervals of digestion; and by drawing up new statements at irregular intervals according to the state of my reflections, but probably averaging a year in length, after I have made from half a dozen to a dozen of these, I begin to feel that I have carried the discussion about as far as I am likely ever to do. There is no single logical point in the present lectures, for example, however small, which has not undergone at least four such digestions, and most of them a dozen or more.

That, gentlemen, is my way of philosophizing in which I have learned to place much confidence. The expression "swift as thought" ought to gain for you a new meaning as applied to my thought. It becomes equivalent to "agile as a slime-mould." Anybody who knows how I think as I myself do must be impressed by my awful stupidity. But I am fortunately capable of a vast amount of drudgery, and I never lose confidence that I shall ultimately accomplish any intellectual task that I set myself provided I live long enough. In that particular I will pose as a model to young philosophers.

But what I particularly wanted to come to in speaking of my way of philosophizing was to point out to you that it is nothing if not minute. I certainly endeavor to generalize as far as I can find support for generalization; but I depend on the sedulous care with which I scrutinize every point. What is commonly called "breadth of treatment" of philosophical questions is my soul's abhorrence. My analysis is so detailed and minute, that it would be impossible in these lectures to give you any specimen of it. I can really do nothing more than to state some of the chief conclusions to which I have been led, with the merest hints of the nature of the arguments by which

I have been led to them, especially since I cannot assume that you have any acquaintance with the real logic of modern thought as I conceive it. While I have the warmest admiration for the great metaphysicians and psychologists of this university who are among the world's leaders in their departments, I cannot but think it deeply lamentable that true, modern, exact, non-psychological logic, which ought to form the background of a liberal education, does not receive sufficient attention here to be at all in evidence. As time goes on the consequences of this neglect will be deeply graven.

To return to my necessarily superficial treatment of my subject in this course of lectures, you will not, I am sure, so utterly misunderstand me as to suppose that I would have you accept any proposition in logic because I say so. Indeed, that would be impossible; for one does not know what the proposition in logic means until one fully comprehends the arguments for it. But my object in describing my way of philosophizing has been chiefly to show you that if I seem to be treating these questions in what is called a "broad way," that is merely the effect of the extreme compression which is necessary, and to warn you that the propositions to which I am able to bring little support, if they be not as true as I hold them, at least are matters worthy of careful study, and are not to be assumed to be so superficially adopted as they must seem to be from the manner in which I am here forced to treat them.

2. The explanation is found in the second Harvard lecture, selection 11, p. 146.

3. Gaspard Coriolis (1792–1843), French mathematician and physicist, author of *Théorie mathématique des effets du jeu de billard* (Paris: Carilian-Gœury, 1835).

4. In Descartes's treatise on the *Passions of the Soul*.

5. In the first 1898 Cambridge lecture in this volume ("Philosophy and the Conduct of Life"), Peirce stated explicitly that ethics was not one of the normative sciences. He seems to imply here that he changed his mind about this matter as early as 1899.

6. Between 1855 and 1857 Peirce made an independent study of Friedrich von Schiller's *Briefe über die ästhetische Erziehung des Menschen* (*Letters on the Aesthetic Education of Man*, 1794–95), which was his first real philosophical reading, one that made an indelible impression upon him.

7. Kant's *Groundwork of the Metaphysics of Morals* (1785), second section.

8. Euripides, *Fragments*, 1024; *Menander*, 218.

9. John Stuart Mill, *A System of Logic*, bk. 1, ch. 2, §5.

10. "On the Natural Classification of Arguments," in W2:23–48 and CP 2.461–514.

11. See selection 8, note 1. The matter of the "illegibility of a single word" in *Prior Analytics* (bk. 2, ch. 25, 69a30–36) is treated by Peirce in the first of three illustrations discussed in MS 690 (but not published in this volume). Peirce suggests that a passage where Aristotle illustrates a case of abduction (ἀπαγωγή) contains a corrupt reading. The passage in question reads as follows: "Let Δ be capable of being squared (τετραγωνίζεσθαι); E, rectilinear; Z, the circle. If there is only one middle to EZ, that the circle is equal to a rectilinear figure, then the circles being equal by lunes to a rectilinear figure, is near to being known" (69a31–34). Peirce argues:

The reference plainly is to the discovery of Hippocrates of Chios that certain lunes, or figures bounded by two arcs of circles, were equal to rectilinear figures and capable of being squared; and Aristotle plainly meant that this fact justified the hope, which we know was entertained on this ground, that the circle could be squared. There was "only one middle," or remove from knowledge, concerning the circle's being equal to a constructible rectilinear figure, since it is evidently equal to some square. . . . It is likely, however, that [Aristotle] understood the argument to be the inference of the minor premiss of the following syllogism from its other two propositions:

> Whatever is equal to a constructible rectilinear figure is equal to a sum of lunes;
> The circle is equal to a constructible rectilinear figure;
> ∴ The circle is equal to a sum of lunes.

To make this out, we have to change just one word of the text. In place of saying that the major term is τετραγωνίζεσθαι we have to put ἴσον μηνίσκοις. This change of a single word of the text, not only renders the whole chapter intelligible; but gives it the very meaning which it ought to have in the development of Aristotle's doctrine. Such a singular corruption of the text as I suppose could hardly have taken place without an Apellicon; but with him, it was easy enough. (CP 7.250–51)

Apellicon (d. c.84 B.C.), an Athenian bibliophile, acquired the libraries of Aristotle and Theophrastus from Neleus and brought them back to Athens. The papers had much suffered from a century and a half of neglect, and were in places illegible. Apellicon published them with many corrections.

12. The remaining paragraphs were written on verso pages in the notebook, replacing four paragraphs in which Peirce discusses the wavering history of his work on the three categories and the three kinds of inference. He explains that the division of the three inferences is better supported by evidence than that of the three categories, and that the connection between the two triads remains obscure. Peirce believed early on that there was a link between Firstness, Icon, and Abduction, between Secondness, Index, and Induction, and between Thirdness, Symbol, and Deduction, and that, following the logic of categorial subdivisibility, there was one kind of Abduction, two of Induction, and three syllogistic figures. In ensuing years, however, Peirce began to hesitate about such conclusions; at one time he confounded Abduction with the second kind of Induction, at another he stated the rationale of Induction in terms more suitable to Abduction, and later on he represented a connection between Deduction and Secondness and between Induction and Thirdness. But now Peirce thinks his original opinion may be sounder, though he will leave the question undecided. He adds that such hesitations show how unusually free he is from favoring his own opinions. But one idea he still strongly holds to is that, although Abduction and Induction are not reducible to Deduction, their rationale must be Deductive, so that the ultimate ground of any reasoning is that in which the validity of mathematical (deductive) reasoning consists.

13. For a detailed description of Peirce's research methodology, see note 1 above.

14. In "Prolegomena for an Apology to Pragmaticism," *The Monist* 16 (1906):492–546 (CP 4.571ff.), Peirce gives such an analysis, using existential graphs.

15. See selection 5, note 5.

15. THE NATURE OF MEANING

1. Aristotle, *De interpretatione*, ch. 7, 17a38. Peirce first provided the Latin form, "quod aptum natum est praedicari de pluribus" (traceable to Abelard and others), but then replaced it with the Greek form.

2. See selection 11, note 5.

3. Jeremy Bentham in his *Introduction to the Principles of Morals and Legislation* (1789) made "the greatest good for the greatest number" the highest goal of human commerce.

4. Peirce refers mainly to Christoph Sigwart (see selection 8, note 7).

5. See selection 5, "The First Rule of Logic": "Precisely those three things are all that enter into the experiment of any deduction—colligation, iteration, erasure."

6. See selection 12, note 22.

7. Julius Adolph Stöckhardt (1809–1886), *Die Schule der Chemie, oder erster Unterricht in der Chemie, versinnlicht durch einfache Experimente* (Braunschweig: F. Vieweg, 1850), part I, §6. Peirce's uncle, Charles Henry Peirce (1814–1855), translated Stöckhardt's book, *The Principles of Chemistry, Illustrated by Simple Experiments* (Cambridge:

Bartlett, 1851), which became a very popular textbook at Harvard. Peirce studied it in his undergraduate years, if not before since it was his uncle who introduced him to chemistry at an early age.

8. See selection 8, note 35.

9. Francis Ysidro Edgeworth (1845–1926), British economist and logician.

10. Poincaré thought that all physical theories, besides having a mathematical, experimental, and hypothetical dimension, were also partly conventional, since any number of hypotheses can be selected, and their selection often rests on economical conventions. Since we do not know a priori whether our selected hypotheses will fit reality, it is unreasonable to think that they are true.

11. Perceptive judgment or perceptual judgment: Peirce uses these two phrases interchangeably (see especially the next lecture, where both are found together).

12. *Critique of Pure Reason*, A7, B10–11.

13. Christian Wolff (1679–1754), influential German rationalist philosopher. Among Wolffians are such names as L. O. Thümmig, G. B. Bilfinger, A. G. Baumgarten, H. F. Meier, Martin Knutzen, and J. H. Lambert.

14. *Critique of Pure Reason*, A656, B684.

15. Kant thought that all syllogisms were reducible to syllogisms in Barbara (the first figure), a point he made in his 1762 memoir *On the False Subtlety of the Four Syllogistic Figures*. Peirce's first major logical discovery was that every such reduction takes the logical form of an argument in the figure from which the reduction is made. See his 1866 *Memoranda Concerning the Aristotelean Syllogism* (W1:505–14).

16. Adrien Legendre (1752–1833), French mathematician, author of *Théorie des nombres* (1830). Carl Friedrich Gauss (1777–1855), German mathematician and astronomer, author of *Disquisitiones Arithmeticae* (1801), a work that had a profound impact on Peirce and his father. Peirce said of Gauss that he was the greatest geometer.

17. Gottfried Ploucquet (1716–1790), German philosopher and logician, author of a symbolic logic that made use of diagrams. Peirce owned his *Commentationes philosophicae* (1781).

18. Leonhard Euler (1707–1783) illustrated syllogisms by means of embedded circles in the second volume of his *Lettres à une Princesse d'Allemagne* (1772).

19. Johann Heinrich Lambert (1728–1777), *Neues Organon* (1764) pt. I, pp. 111ff. In a document dated c.1903 (MS 479:12–13, "On Logical Graphs"), Peirce wrote, touching the history of graphical logic (CP 4.353):

Eight years before Euler's publication appeared the *Neues Organon* of John Henry Lambert . . . in which the author made the same use of the stretches of parallel lines essentially as Euler did of the areas of circles, with an additional feature of dotted lines and extensions of lines. Lambert, however, does not seem to aim at any mathematical accuracy of thought in using his lines. He certainly does not attain it; nor could he do so as long as he failed to perceive that the only purpose such diagrams could subserve is that of representing the necessity with which the conclusion follows from the premisses of a necessary reasoning, and that that necessity is not a compulsion in thinking (although there is such a compulsion) but is a relation between the *facts* represented in the premisses and the facts represented in the conclusion.

20. Ernst Schröder, *Vorlesungen über die Algebra der Logik (Exakte Logik)*, vol. 3, lesson 12, §31 (Leipzig: B. G. Teubner, 1895). Richard Dedekind, *Was sind und was sollen die Zahlen?* (Braunschweig: F. Vieweg, 1888).

21. "On the Logic of Number," in *American Journal of Mathematics* 4 (1881):85–95; W4:299–309.

22. Karl Prantl finds the name "copula" first in Abelard, though with traces of earlier usage (*Geschichte der Logik im Abendlande*, II, 196). From Psellus and Petrus Hispanus, the name passed into the technical vocabulary of logic.

23. The Greek word means "nothing"; hence the word "medad," indicating that there is "no" blank left in the proposition.

24. Peirce wrote the word "indicative" above the deleted "indexical."

25. Theodore Roosevelt knew enough of Peirce's abilities to have been one of those who recommended him to the Carnegie Institution. The "club" is probably the New York-based Century Club, of which Peirce was a member from 1877 to the early 1890s.

26. Claude Bernard (1813–1878), one of the leading physiologists of the century, *Leçons de pathologie expérimentale*, second lesson (Paris: Baillière, 1872).

27. Louis Pasteur (1822–1895), French chemist, in the mid-century discovered the basic characteristics of bacteria, while the German scientist Robert Koch (1843–1910) established in the 1880s that bacteria were the cause of many infectious diseases. August Weismann (1834–1914), German biologist, author of the theory of "germ plasm" (hereditary elements carried by sex cells, as opposed to "somatoplasm"—the rest of the body). He published in 1892 *Das Keimplasma, eine Theorie der Vererbung* (translated as *The Germ-Plasm; a Theory of Heredity*, 1893).

28. These three truths are the three "cotary propositions" Peirce discusses at greater length in the final lecture (the next selection).

29. Peirce is using the word "quodlibetical" in its literal meaning: "any individual you please," without restriction of any sort. The quodlibetical subject is called the hypothetical subject earlier in the lecture (pp. 209–10), while the indesignate is called the indesignative.

30. *Cours de philosophie positive*, 28th lesson.

31. Peirce wrote "probimetric" in the notebook, but the better form "probametric" occurs in the draft of this lecture (MS 313:16–17), where it is explained as follows:

If, however, in place of a deductive argument we are dealing with an inductive argument, by which I mean a course of experimentation and reflection designed to put a theory to the test, the case is different because we have [a] different end in view. We are now no longer considering hypothetical states of things. We want to know how nearly a given theory represents the facts, and the answer to this question, from the nature of things, must have the well-known character which I have hitherto expressed by calling it "probable and approximate." This, however, is a clumsy and inexact expression. A single word is wanted. Suppose we call it *probametric*, meaning that the answer will be a quantity whose value has been so chosen that the probability of its having an error not exceeding a variable magnitude will vary, according to the doctrine of chances, in a convenient manner. The inductive procedure will be sound or otherwise according as it is or is not calculated according to the principles of probability, to reduce the probable error indefinitely as the experimentation is carried further and further.

16. Pragmatism as the Logic of Abduction

1. Peirce knew Horace's work well, and may be alluding to verses 304–5 of his *Ars poetica*: "ergo fungar vice cotis, acutum | reddere quae ferrum valet exsors ipsa secandi" ("I will thus perform the function of a whetstone, which is able to restore sharpness to iron, though itself unable to cut"). Peirce at first coined the adjective "cossal" from the Latin nominative and used it throughout the lecture. Upon revision, he substituted the word "cotary" (from the genitive) everywhere, missing only two that have been here corrected.

2. "Nothing is in the intellect which was not previously in the senses." This is a scholastic idea derived from Aristotle (*Posterior Analytics*, bk. 2, ch. 19, 100a,b); see Thomas Aquinas, *De veritate*, qu. 26, art. 6, 2nd answer to contrary difficulties, and *Summa theologica*, bk. 1, qu. 84, art. 6. For a modern perspective, see Descartes's "Sixth Meditation."

3. *De anima*, bk. 3, ch. 8, 432a3–8.

4. George Berkeley, *A Treatise Concerning the Principles of Human Knowledge*, Introduction, §13 (where Berkeley disagrees with Locke on this very point). See EP1:48 and 97.

5. The passage from this sentence to the end of the first section was added later by Peirce.

6. Peirce may here be recalling his father's third Smithsonian lecture on "Potential Algebra" (from a series of six, titled "Potential Physics"), delivered on Friday, 23 January 1857, and of which a review appeared in the *National Intelligencer* the following Monday. The following excerpt from the fourth paragraph of the unsigned review alludes to the drawing:

The learned lecturer [i.e., Benjamin Peirce] next showed, by tracing a continuous line in such a way as to look anything but linear, but exactly similar to a batch of loaves of bread or a heap of stones, how apt we are to be deceived by our months and years and centuries about the idea of continuity, properly considered. This illustration was very obvious and striking, and drew down the acknowledgments of the audience. The error in human thought here arises from the prevalence of the law of discontinuity over continuity.

7. Peirce sketched eight examples of his father's serpentine line. A slightly stylized version of the more finely drawn one is used here. The reader can be confident that the entire drawing consists of just one continuous line. Compare with the figure in selection 2, p. 6.

8. This optical illusion is the equivocal figure known as Schröder's Stair, originally noticed in *Annalen der Physik und Chemie* 105 (1858):298–311. The "two or three dozen" visual illusions mentioned in the next paragraph may be those that are illustrated under "Optical Illusions" in Baldwin's *Dictionary* (vol. 2, plates I–IV, after p. 208).

9. John Stuart Mill, *An Examination of Sir William Hamilton's Philosophy* (London: Longmans, etc., 1865). See chapters IV, V, and especially VI, on "The Philosophy of the Conditioned." Peirce bought Mill's *Examination* as soon as it was published and read it with great care. Although he rejected Mill's psychologism entirely, the book much contributed to clarify his own opinions. See selection 30, p. 457, and Max Fisch's "A Chronicle of Pragmaticism, 1865–1879" in *Peirce, Semeiotic, and Pragmatism* (Bloomington: Indiana University Press, 1986), 115–16, 124–25.

10. Peirce made a note to himself to skip the rest of this paragraph (beginning with "At the same time") and the first four sentences of the next paragraph (ending with "a logical fallacy."). He replaced them with the following remark: "I should easily show you that this difficulty, however formidable theoretically, amounts practically to little or nothing for a person skilled in shaping such inquiries. But this is unnecessary, since the objection founded upon it has no logical force whatever."

11. When Peirce first wrote this paragraph, he stated only the first two objections. He added the third objection later, and made a number of textual alterations to accommodate the change, including the addition of a long two-paragraph response to it, inserted at the end of the second section of this lecture.

12. The next two large paragraphs (beginning with "I have argued" and ending with "so excluded.") were written on facing verso pages, replacing a longer text Peirce decided to skip, but of which a few significant excerpts are reproduced below.

The maxim of Pragmatism, if it is sound, or whatever ought to replace it, if it is not sound, is nothing else than the logic of abduction.

A mass of facts is before us. We go through them. We examine them. We find them a confused snarl, an impenetrable jungle. We are unable to hold them in our minds. We endeavor to set them down upon paper; but they seem to be so multiplex intricate that we can neither satisfy ourselves that what we have set down represents the facts, nor can we get any clear idea of what it is that we have set down. But suddenly, while we are poring over our digest of the facts and are endeavoring to set them into order, it occurs to us that if we were to assume something to be true that we do not know to be true, these facts would arrange themselves luminously. That is *abduction*. . . .

Now, as I remarked in a former lecture, anything is *good* in so far, and only in so far, as it conforms to its *end*.

The question is, then, what can come of an abductive theory. Someone may say that it is a grand and adorable idea just as it is. That may be. Its contemplation may fill the soul with a sort of music. But that is esthetic goodness. Our inquiry relates, however, to cognitive goodness. What can the theory teach us. I should make the same reply if anybody said that there was some sort of mysterious result to be expected from certain theories. It is not necessary to deny that there are mysterious agencies in ideas. It is sufficient to say that it is not rational cognitive goodness. To have that goodness the theory must lead to some further knowledge. It must be the basis of some advance in reasoning.

If it embody clear and definite ideas of relationship, it may be the foundation of a lofty edifice of mathematical developments, which may be good in various ways, esthetically (for the esthetic element in mathematics is intense), educationally in training the mind to deal with analogous ideas, and cognitively in teaching us its lesson of the world of ideas.

But those modes of goodness of the theory it would possess just the same if there were no anticipation of its proving actually true of the real world, and therefore independently of its having the character of an abduction. If it is to be good as an abduction it must subserve the end of abduction. Now the end of abduction is that the deductive consequences of it may be tested by induction. So alone is any application made of its essential anticipatory character. Consequently the good of abduction, as such, that is, its adaptation to its end, will consist of its being of such a character that its deductive consequences may be experimentally tested. . . .

It is plain that a man cannot consistently engage in this discussion or in any discussion unless he admits that there is a distinction between truth and falsity. It is also plain that to admit this distinction is to admit that there is something whose characters are what they are independently of what he may think that they are; and further the words "truth" and "falsity" are not appropriate unless he wishes to make his opinions conform to that object and thinks that in some measure he can do so. Neither is it what we mean to wish to satisfy some man, or body of men, or other being or beings with his opinions. We must mean by the real that which has such characters as it has independently of what any particular mind or minds may think those characters may be. At the same time, these characters of the real must be of the nature of thoughts or sufficiently so to impart some sense to our talking of thoughts conforming to those characters. But this thought or quasi-thought in which the characters of the real consist cannot be any existential happening or being. Thus suppose we were to say that the real is what men will ultimately come to think. Then the real fact that they will so come to think would have to consist in their coming to think that they would come so to think and this again would consist in their coming to think that they would come to think that so they would come to think, and so on *ad infinitum*, and it is plain that this would not be making the reality consist in the existential coming to pass of anything. I am forced to say that that which thought conforms to has a representational mode of being which does not consist in any reactional existence. At the same time, it will be too manifestly false for me to say that the redness of a red thing consists in anything but the immediate positive quality itself. Neither can I deny that when I make an effort it is then and there that the event takes place, however it is represented. I must thus acknowledge the distinctness of the three categories, and at the same time that Thirdness is continuous up to the other two as limits before I can have any clear notion of truth and falsity; and without such clear notion I have no basis for any discussion of the maxim of abduction.

13. "On the Natural Classification of Arguments" in W2:23–48, and "On a New List of Categories" in EP1:1–10 and W2:49–59.

14. *Cours de philosophie positive*, 28th lesson.

15. See previous selection, p. 216.

16. This is the lecture on "Multitude and Continuity" Peirce delivered the next evening, on Friday, May 15, 1903. Preparatory notes for this lecture are in MS 316a. See selection 11, note 3.

17. Peirce deleted the following sentence at the end of this paragraph: "I will mention tomorrow a way in which these logicians might conceivably be able to escape this difficulty."

18. See selection 10, note 9, and p. 141.

19. Peirce gave one of his more extensive treatments of continuity in his 1898 Cambridge Conferences lecture series, which is published in RLT with explanatory comments by Hilary Putnam.

20. "Thirty years ago," taken literally, brings us back to 1873 and possibly alludes to informal conversations held at the Metaphysical Club rather than to a specific writing (the sentence first read, before Peirce altered it, "I went about among philosophers telling them . . ."). See selection 28, note 5.

21. This idea is already implicit in the "New List of Categories" (1867) and becomes most explicit in the "Description of a Notation for the Logic of Relatives" (1870).

22. Gustav Robert Kirchhoff (1824–1887), German physicist, takes the view in his *Vorlesungen über mathematische Physik: Mechanik* (Leipzig: B. G. Teubner, 1876) that it is the task of mechanics to describe the motions that take place in nature and not their causes. Hence he does not find it useful to try to fully define force and energy.

23. Peirce wrote "abduction" instead of "induction," an apparent error that has been here corrected. The second attitude or position defined two paragraphs earlier holds that thirdness is inferable by induction and is not directly perceived, which means that it is not apprehended by way of a perceptual judgment (abduction). The editors of the *Collected Papers* have suggested alternatively that the word "induction" in the earlier statement of the second position be replaced with "abduction" (CP 5.209), but the accompanying assertion that thirdness is "experimentally verifiable" works against that reading.

17. What Makes a Reasoning Sound?

1. The "thorough and formal refutation of the fallacy" has not been identified. Peirce makes the same claim of having written it out in one of the drafts (MS 453). One remote possibility is that the second notebook containing the present lecture text, MS 449 (see note 5 below), was attached, not to MS 448 as here surmised, but to yet another no longer extant notebook, and that the combination of that missing notebook and of MS 449 would have constituted the formal refutation.

2. The "more obvious" objection, which Peirce did not enunciate in previous drafts either, is probably that the argument would easily allow contrary propositions to be true simultaneously. For instance, one person could have the "logical feeling" that the proposition "there is no distinction between good and bad reasoning" was true, and another that it was false, and they would equally be right.

3. The 324-foot (99-metre) Campanile in St. Mark's Square, constructed from the tenth through the sixteenth centuries, collapsed on 14 October 1902, its structure having been eroded by the sirocco winds. It was rebuilt in 1912.

4. *Elements of Philosophy* (1655), part I, "Computation or Logic," ch. 1, sect. 2: "By ratiocination, I mean computation." In *The English Works of Thomas Hobbes of Malmesbury*, translated by Sir William Molesworth (London: John Bohn, 1839), 1:3.

5. The end of this paragraph corresponds to the point on p. 37 in the first note-book (MS 448) where Peirce appears to have decided to skip the remaining pages (38–48) and to resume with the text found in the next notebook (MS 449), whose first page is also numbered 37. The transition appears to be solid, since the "great fallacy" men-tioned at the beginning of the next paragraph is the belief that there is no factual dis-tinction between good and bad reasoning.

6. Four days after this lecture, an anonymous listener sent Peirce the following question: "If not inconvenient for you, will you be kind enough to give tonight a sum-mary—however brief—of your answer to the question 'What makes a Reasoning Sound?'" Peirce prepared a response that he read at the beginning of the third lecture. This response, found in MS 465, is as follows:

My first duty this evening is to reply to a note which asks me to give an explanation at my last lecture. The letter did not come to hand until the following morning. The question asked is what my answer in the first lecture was to the question "What makes a Reasoning to be sound?" I had no intention of answering that question in my first lecture, because I dislike to put forth opinions until I am ready to prove them; and I had enough to do in the first lecture to show what does *not* make reasoning to be sound. Besides in this short course it seems better to skip such purely the-oretical questions. Yet since I am asked, I have no objection to saying that in my opinion what makes a reasoning sound is the real law that the general method which that reasoning more or less consciously pursues does tend toward the truth. The very essence of an argument,—that which distinguishes it from all other kinds of signs,—is that it professes to be the representative of a general method of procedure tending toward the truth. To say that this method tends toward the true is to say that it is a real law that existences *will* follow. Now if that profession is true, and the conclusions of that method really will be true, to the extent and in the manner in which the argument pretends that they will, the argument is sound; if not, it is a false pretension and is un-sound. I thus make the soundness of argument *consist* in the facts of the case and not at all in whether the reasoner feels confidence in the argument or not. I may further say that there are three great classes of argument, Deductions, Inductions, and Abductions; and these profess to tend toward the truth in very different senses, as we shall see. I suppose this answers the question intended. However, it is possible that my correspondent did not intend to ask in what I think the soundness of reasoning consists, but by the question "What makes reasoning sound?" he may mean "What causes men to reason right?" That question I did substantially answer in my first lecture. Namely, to begin with, when a boy or girl first begins to criticize his inferences, and until he does that he does not reason, he finds that he has already strong prejudices in favor of certain ways of arguing. Those prejudices, whether they be inherited or acquired, were first formed un-der the influence of the environing world, so that it is not surprising that they are largely right or nearly right. He, thus, has a basis to go upon. But if he has the habit of calling himself to ac-count for his reasonings, as all of us do more or less, he will gradually come to reason much bet-ter; and this comes about through his criticism, in the light of experience, of all the factors that have entered into reasonings that were performed shortly before the criticism. Occasionally, he goes back to the criticism of habits of reasoning which have governed him for many years. That is my answer to the second question.

7. Robert Grosseteste, Bishop of Lincoln (c.1168–1253), initiator of the English scientific tradition and commentator of the newly recovered works of Aristotle. He believed that our discovery of the cause of what experiment reveals is the basis of sense knowledge, which itself is the basis of all knowledge.

8. Peirce reviewed Lady Welby's *What is Meaning?* (London and New York: Mac-millan, 1903) in the *Nation* 77 (15 Oct. 1903):308–9; CN 3:143–45.

9. See selection 3, note 6.

10. The last paragraph of this lecture has been omitted since it refers to a text not published here. It reads: "In the next lecture I shall introduce you to a system of signs

which I have invented as an aid in the study of logic." Much of this system of signs is found in selections 20 and 21, two sections of the "Syllabus."

18. An Outline Classification of the Sciences

1. *Cours de philosophie positive*, 2nd lesson.

2. Peirce constructed a detailed classification of the sciences in a large section of his projected book "Minute Logic." See MS 427, "Chapter II. Prelogical Notions. Section I. Classification of the Sciences" (1902; CP 1.203–83).

3. In the original document, the majority of the letters and numbers here found between parentheses were instead between commas. The style has been modified and modernized for the sake of greater legibility. Peirce's capitalization and italicization of names of sciences have also been made more consistent. Names of sciences are capitalized only when they are either defined or placed precisely within the classification. They are italicized only when they are within the classification and at a level higher than that indicated by arabic numbers, with the only exception of the three branches under Logic.

4. Alexander von Humboldt (1769–1859) popularized science with his *Kosmos: Entwurf einer physischen Weltbeschreibung* (Stuttgart and Tübingen: Cotta, 1845–62). Herbert Spencer published an essay titled *The Classification of the Sciences: To Which are Added Reasons for Dissenting from the Philosophy of M. Comte* (London: Williams and Norgate, 1864; New York: Appleton, 1870). His *First Principles*, also known as *A System of Synthetic Philosophy*, appeared in several revised editions between 1862 and 1896.

5. Elaterics is the theory of elasticity.

6. Peirce's elaborate classification of the practical sciences is in MS 1343, "Of the Classification of the Sciences. Second Paper. Of the Practical Sciences" (1902).

19. The Ethics of Terminology

1. In Kant's *Critique of Pure Reason*, see for instance Axvii, B139–40, 142.

2. On this matter, see the closely related document titled "A Proposed Logical Notation" (MS 530, 1904).

3. Quincy Hall is a private dormitory for Harvard students built in 1891.

20. Sundry Logical Conceptions

1. In Hermann Diels's *Fragmente der Vorsokratiker*, vol. 1, p. 171, fragment 91; cited from Plutarchus. See also fragments 12 (p. 154) and 49a (p. 161).

2. Peirce prepared the definition of "precision" in Baldwin's *Dictionary* 2:323–24; see also selection 25, "Issues of Pragmaticism," p. 351–52.

3. "On a New List of Categories," EP1:2–3; W2:50–51.

4. *A Treatise Concerning the Principles of Human Knowledge* (Dublin, 1710), §88.

5. The text here was much altered by the editors of the *Collected Papers*. Peirce's original statement has been restored. In the next section of the Syllabus (selection 21), Peirce adds a third trichotomy to the two described here, that of Qualisign, Sinsign, and Legisign, and makes it the first of the three. Peirce's semiotic theory is thus here at an important point of development.

6. Peirce will use the word "seme" in a very different sense in his 1906 *Monist* paper "Prolegomena to an Apology for Pragmaticism," where it becomes the first term

of the trichotomy "Seme, Pheme, Delome," a generalization of the third trichotomy "Rheme (Term), Proposition, Argument." See CP 4.538–540.

7. This second trichotomy will become the third one in the next selection.

8. If "one of them" refers to either individual in the pair, then Peirce means presumably that if the interpreter singles out either the father or the mother from the unit "two parents," the predicate "son of" remains true of the dyad.

9. In the *Century Dictionary*, Peirce defines "exponible proposition" as follows: "an obscure proposition, or one containing a sign not included in the regular forms of propositions recognized by logic. Such are, Man alone cooks his food; Every man but Enoch and Elijah is mortal." The word "exponible" can be defined as "admitting, or requiring, an exposition or explanation."

10. Karl Prantl, *Geschichte der Logik im Abendlande*, 1:580–81. "Thus there are two species of propositions, just as there are of the conclusions themselves: one is predicative, which is also a simple proposition; as when we say, *He who reigns is happy;* the other is substitutive, or conditional, which is also a compound proposition; as when you say: *he who reigns, if he is wise, is happy.* You are indeed laying down a condition, which is that unless he is wise, he will not be happy."

11. John of Salisbury, bishop of Chartres (d. 1180), spoke of "that which is well known to nearly everyone, namely that what common names [i.e. adjectives] signify is one thing, and what they name is another. They name particulars [i.e. existent individual things and facts], but they signify universals [i.e. Firstnesses]." *Ioannes Saresberiensis Metalogicus, e codice ms. academiae Cantabrigiensis* (Parisiis: Apud Hadrianum Beys, 1610).

12. "Upon Logical Comprehension and Extension," W2:70–86.

13. *Fulget:* "it's lightning"; *lucet:* "it is light."

14. Kant, *Critique of Pure Reason*, A70, 74–75; B95, 100. See the large entry that Peirce wrote for "modality" in Baldwin's *Dictionary*, 2:89–93 (CP 2.382–90).

15. "Billingsgate": the word derives from, and is here used by Peirce to indicate, the coarse vituperative language for which the old London fish market known as Billingsgate was famous.

16. Lucius Apuleius of Madaura (fl. c.150), Platonist philosopher and rhetorician.

17. On the difference between negative and infinite, see MS 921:65–66 (July 1859), and also Kant's *Critique of Pure Reason*, A72, B97. Also relevant are Peirce's definitions of "quality," "negation," and "limitative" in Baldwin's *Dictionary* (CP 2.374–81).

18. Dionysius Thrax (fl. 100 B.C.), Greek grammarian whose *Art of Grammar* defined the field (Leipzig: G. Uhlig, 1883) 638.3–4. "A verb is a word without cases, admitting tenses, persons, and numbers, displaying either activity or passivity."

19. Karl Prantl, *Geschichte der Logik im Abendlande*, 1:696.

20. *Prior Analytics*, bk. 1, ch. 1, 24b16. "I call a term that into which the premiss is resolved, i.e. both the predicate and that of which it is predicated."

21. The term "syncathegreuma," so spelled, is found at the beginning of Petrus Hispanus's *Summulae logicales*, but this may have been a fifteenth-century printer's error, since the word "sincathegoreumatic" occurs at the end of the treatise (the fourth letter being alternately a "c" or a "k"). Peirce added at the end of this sentence a footnote which is not reproduced here: a Latin quotation from Ockham distinguishing two kinds of terms, the "cathegreumata" and the "sincathegreumata." The quotation is followed by a remark about the nominalists's peculiar use of the Latin language.

22. Three long paragraphs, amounting to eleven manuscript pages, have been omitted at this point. They discuss the origin of the three terms "deduction," "induction," and "abduction."

23. Oscar Howard Mitchell, "On a New Algebra of Logic," in *Studies in Logic* (Boston, 1883), 72–106. The "master" is of course Peirce himself, who taught Mitchell at Johns Hopkins University in the early 1880s.

21. Nomenclature and Divisions of Triadic Relations

1. This trichotomy is here formulated for the very first time by Peirce. The word "Sinsign" is interlined above the deleted word "Sesign," which was Peirce's first coinage for the second type of sign (it is found in several drafts).

2. The word "Dicent" is only used as an adjective; an earlier variant was "Dicisignal" (MS 799:4). The word "Dictor" is also found in one place (MS S104:92).

3. Henry Peter Brougham, first Baron Brougham and Vaux (1778–1868), British statesman, orator, jurist, and scientist.

4. Richard Whately (1787–1863), English logician and theologian. Whately's *Elements of Logic* was the book that introduced Peirce to logic when he was twelve (see W1:xviii–xix). Isaac Watts (1674–1748), English theologian and hymn writer, author of *Logic, or The Right Use of Reason in the Inquiry after Truth* (London: J. Buckland et al., 1790; J. Haddon, 1813).

5. A short paragraph that followed this sentence has been omitted because Peirce repeated its content two paragraphs down (beginning with "In the course of").

22. New Elements (Καινὰ στοιχεῖα)

1. The Greek title is Peirce's, and the English title is supplied by the editors. Peirce added the subtitle "Preface" under his title, indicating that the entire manuscript was to serve as a preface to a book that he never finished writing. The subtitle has here been omitted. Research shows that Peirce intended to write a book that would have revisited the epistemic grounds of mathematics, following a rigorous methodology in the manner of Euclid.

2. The book referred to here survives in MSS 164–66, most of which was composed in 1895.

3. The only publisher Peirce is known to have submitted his "New Elements of Mathematics" to is Edwin Ginn, of Ginn & Co., with whom he had extensive correspondence in the first half of 1895. No evidence has been found that Peirce submitted his manuscript to Macmillan, even though it was Macmillan that published the "treatise on geometry" Peirce refers to three sentences later. The treatise is J. Humphrey Spanton's *Science and Art Drawing: Complete Geometrical Course. . .* (New York: Macmillan, 1895), which Peirce reviewed negatively in *The Nation* (CN 2:126–27) in January 1896.

4. Maybe Peirce misplaced the manuscript and thought he had lost it. Carolyn Eisele published MS 165 in her well-known *New Elements of Mathematics*.

5. Here begins the description of the second of the "three distinct ways" in which the sign is connected with the "Truth."

6. The Port-Royalists are Antoine Arnauld (1612–1694) and Pierre Nicole (1625–1695). Though Peirce recognized the major importance of the Port-Royalists in modern logic, in a draft version of the third Harvard Lecture he stated: "Arnauld, for example, was a thinker of considerable force, and yet *L'Art de penser*, or the *Port-Royal Logic*, is a shameful exhibit of what the two and a half centuries of man's greatest achievements could consider as a good account of how to think" (CP 5.84).

7. In "Upon Logical Comprehension and Extension," *Proceedings of the American Academy of Arts and Sciences* 7 (published 1868; presented 13 November 1867); W2:83–84.

8. *De interpretatione*, 17a, 19b.

9. The difference between the two Latin clauses is that the first is in direct, and the second in indirect discourse: it is an infinitive clause, implicitly assuming an utterer: "Someone says that Socrates is wise."

10. James Stanley Grimes (1807–1903), Bostonian phrenologist and speculative amateur scientist. Peirce seems to refer to Grimes's *Etherology, and the Phreno-Philosophy of Mesmerism and Magic Eloquence* (New York, Boston: Saxton and Miles, Saxton, Peirce, & Co., etc., 1845; second edition revised, Boston: J. Munroe & Co., 1853). Grimes uses "credenciveness" to designate a specific mental organ located in the brain, whose function is to make people act out what is asserted about them (the matter is discussed in his book, pp. 142–54). In a 1898 *Nation* review of Boris Sidis's *Psychology of Suggestion*, Peirce wrote (CN 2:166):

> This faculty [of suggestibility], or state of mind, was first assigned as the main secret of the ordinary phenomena of hypnotism as long ago as 1845 by the American itinerant lecturer Grimes. But he was not an academic person, and was naturally ignored. . . . We may add that, by reducing Consciousness to the rank of a special faculty, Grimes paved the way to the modern doctrine of the subconscious mind. . . . The word "credenciveness" is not particularly apt, because it does not obviously imply a tendency to action, although it was so understood by Grimes.

11. "The Fixation of Belief," in EP1:109–23, and W3:242–57.

12. Paul Carus has been cited by Peirce as one who appears to base chance on ignorance ("Reply to the Necessitarians," *The Monist* 3 (1893):543; CP 6.602). Elsewhere Peirce refers to John Venn as having refuted in his *Logic of Chance* many logic texts that hold that view (CP 6.74). One of the early writers Peirce may have been thinking of is Laplace, who claims that probabilities arise from ignorance.

13. For some reason, Peirce did not identify the "distinguished writer" whom he refers to several times. One good hypothesis points to Karl Pearson. The last two paragraphs of Peirce's review of Pearson's *Grammar of Science* (selection 6) address precisely the nominalistic ("Pearsonist") view that the formula is a human device that conforms to the facts.

14. *System of Logic*, vol. 1, bk. 3, ch. 5, §§ 2–3.

15. See *Critique of Pure Reason*, A652, B 680.

16. The word "spondesime" is not found in the *Oxford English Dictionary* or any other dictionary consulted by the editors. The closest word is "spondulics," defined in the *Century Dictionary* as an American slang word meaning "originally, paper money; now, any money; funds."

17. The manuscript reading for "a symbol" is "an icon," which appears to be an accidental repetition of the final words of the previous sentence. Subsequent context ("A symbol, on the other hand") makes it clear that Peirce is distinguishing between an index and a symbol.

18. The atomic weight of gold is 196.9665. The *Century Dictionary* says 196.7.

19. This statement brings to mind Peirce's favorite Evangelist: "In the beginning was the Word" (John 1:1).

20. Mathematically not every endless series need have a limit, but it is a tenet of Peirce's mathematical-logical reasoning that they do have a limit. Judging from examples of series he gives elsewhere, Peirce evidently means by series a succession of distinct entities that are ordered by some relation. By limit Peirce means "an object which comes after all the objects of that series, but so that every *other* object which

comes after all those objects comes after the limit also" (1898, CP 6.185). "Thus, the series of whole numbers is an increasing endless series. Its limit is the denumerable multitude" (1897, CP 4.213).

23. IDEAS, STRAY OR STOLEN, ABOUT SCIENTIFIC WRITING

1. See selection 6, note 12.
2. See selection 3, note 7.
3. It is unclear in which journal Peirce wanted to publish this essay; it could have been the *Popular Science Monthly*, whose editor asked Peirce in September 1904 to contribute an article—which Peirce decided to forgo when he realized the journal could not afford to pay him.

24. WHAT PRAGMATISM IS

1. Arthur James Balfour, Earl of Balfour (1848–1930), *Reflections Suggested by the New Theory of Matter*, Presidential Address, British Association for the Advancement of Science, 17 August 1904 (New York: Longmans, Green and Co., 1904).
2. For William James's first use of "pragmatism," see selection 10, note 3. James defined "radical empiricism" at the beginning of his preface to *The Will to Believe* (Dec. 1896) as a philosophical attitude that regards its most assured conclusions concerning matters of fact, including monism, as hypotheses liable to modification in the course of future experience. He defined it further in his 1904 essay "A World of Pure Experience" (see the 1976 Harvard edition of *Essays in Radical Empiricism*, pp. 22–23). At the end of his preface to *Pragmatism* (the Lowell Lectures of 1906–7), James warned: "To avoid one misunderstanding at least, let me say that there is no logical connexion between pragmatism, as I understand it, and a doctrine which I have recently set forth as 'radical empiricism.' The latter stands on its feet. One may entirely reject it and still be a pragmatist."
3. F. C. S. Schiller (1864–1937), *Riddles of the Sphinx: a Study in the Philosophy of Evolution, by a Troglodyte* (London: S. Sonnenschein, 1891). Schiller's paper "Axioms as Postulates" is the second essay in *Personal Idealism: Philosophical Essays by Eight Members of the University of Oxford*, ed. by Henry Cecil Sturt (New York: Macmillan, 1902), especially p. 63.
4. See Schiller's *Humanism: Philosophical Essays* (London: Macmillan, 1903, 1912; second edition reprinted by Greenwood Press, 1970). In the preface to the first edition (p. xxv), Schiller wrote: "Pragmatism itself is in the same case with Personal Idealism, Radical Empiricism and Pluralism. It is in reality only the application of Humanism to the theory of knowledge. . . . Great, therefore, as will be the value we must claim for Pragmatism as a method, we must yet concede that man is greater than any method he has made, and that our Humanism must interpret it." Schiller also published, at the same time as Peirce's own paper appeared, a short article, "The Definition of 'Pragmatism' and 'Humanism,'" in *Mind* 14 (April 1905):235–40, a copy of which he sent to Peirce.
5. The second article here referred to is not "Issues of Pragmaticism" (which Peirce did not have in mind yet), but "The Consequences of Pragmaticism" (MSS 288–89); it may also include MS 326, "Some Applications of Pragmaticism."
6. Peirce did not write the third paper mentioned here, which he had planned to title "The Evidences for Pragmaticism," as he told William James in a letter dated 28 September 1904.

7. On synechism, see "The Law of Mind" in EP1:312–33, and selection 1.

8. Shakespeare, *Hamlet*, act 3, scene 2 (Hamlet beseeches Guildenstern to play the recorder: "'Tis as easy as lying.")

9. See selection 5, note 2.

10. Richmal Mangnall (1769–1820), an English schoolmistress, wrote *Historical and Miscellaneous Questions, For the Use of Young People.* Known as "Mangnall's Questions," it appeared first in 1800 and was much used in the education of English girls in the first half of the nineteenth century.

11. See EP1:109–41 (quotation p. 132), or W3:242–76 (quotation p. 266) and 338–74 (French text).

12. F. E. Abbot (1836–1903), *Organic Scientific Philosophy: Scientific Theism* (Boston: Little, Brown & Co., 1885). Abbot defines his "Relationism" or "Scientific Realism" in the introduction (pp. 11–12, 23, and 25–29).

13. The Hall effect (after American physicist Edwin Hall) is the development of an electric field in a solid placed in a magnetic field. The Zeeman effect (after Dutch physicist Pieter Zeeman) is the splitting of spectral lines of elements into two or more components of different frequency when the light source is placed in a strong magnetic field. By the Michelson phenomenon, Peirce probably means an effect that occurs in the Michelson-Morley experiment (see selection 31, note 11). The chessboard phenomenon may possibly refer to one of the checkerboard optical illusions depicted in Baldwin's *Dictionary* (see selection 16, note 8).

14. Paul Carus, "The Foundations of Geometry," in *The Monist* 13 (1903):370.

15. Here ends the conversation between the Questioner and the Pragmaticist.

16. *Prior Analytics*, bk. 1, ch. 1, 24b27–30.

17. The paragraph that begins here was added at the end of September 1904, about two weeks after the article was finished.

18. This is the *Monist* metaphysical series of 1891–93, the first five articles of which are published in EP1:285–371, and the sixth one, "Reply to the Necessitarians," is in CP 6.588–618. The sentence here was rewritten by Peirce who had originally phrased it in a way that offended Paul Carus, for it suggested unfairly that Carus had discouraged Peirce from writing the "purposed article" on continuity.

19. This postscript was added in February 1905.

25. ISSUES OF PRAGMATICISM

1. See the *Journal of Speculative Philosophy* "cognition series" of 1868–69 (EP1:11–82; W2:193–272).

2. "Some Consequences of Four Incapacities," *Journal of Speculative Philosophy* 2 (1868):140–57. See especially EP1:41–44, or W2:226–29.

3. Several manuscripts titled "The Basis of Pragmaticism" survive (MSS 279–84, 908), two of which are published in this volume (selections 26 and 27). None of them became the "third paper," however: they were replaced by "Prolegomena to an Apology for Pragmaticism," in *The Monist* 16 (Oct. 1906):492–546.

4. Jean Buridan (1300–1358), Aristotelian philosopher and logician. "Buridan's ass" refers to the dilemma of having to decide between two equally attractive choices: how will an ass choose between two identical bales of hay placed at equal distance before him? One solution holds that he must choose at random, another that he will die of starvation. The dilemma, similar to Aristotle's hungry man in *De Caelo* 295b32, is not found in Buridan's works, but was probably used to refute his idea that choice is always delayed until reason decides in favor of one course of action against another.

5. Peirce indicated "p. 290 at the top," referring to the original publication of "How to Make Our Ideas Clear" (EP1:128, lines 16–29; W3:262, lines 5–19).

6. *De trinitate*, XV, 12, 21; *De civitate Dei*, XI, 26; the latter has "Si enim fallor sum."

7. Peirce refers to the Scottish common sense philosophy, developed by Thomas Reid (1710–1796), James Beattie (1735–1803), James Oswald (d. 1793), and Dugald Stewart (1753–1828).

8. Which documents the "preparatory studies" and "provisional inquiry" might refer to have not been determined.

9. The first seventeen pages of Peirce's manuscript, which served as printer's copy for the *Monist* compositors, are lost. The surviving portion starts here at mid-word ("concern-|ing") and continues to the end of the article. Thus from this point on, the manuscript serves as copy-text.

10. In a draft of a letter to Mario Calderoni (c. July 1905), Peirce wrote (L 67:4; CP 8.208):

In an article which should have appeared in the July *Monist* but which seems to have been crowded out by matters of superior importance, magic squares and the like, I specify six errors which I find in the Scotch doctrine of common sense, of which the most important is that those philosophers failed to remark the extreme vagueness of our indubitable beliefs. For example, everybody's actions show that it is impossible to doubt that there is an element of order in the world; but the moment we attempt to define that orderliness we find room for doubt.

11. Peirce inserted an asterisk after the word "thought" in the manuscript, intending to add a footnote he had attached in the draft (MS 290) to the following asterisked words: "To say with Kant that Time is but the form of human thought*. . . ." Peirce eventually dropped the footnote, but forgot to delete the asterisk. The relevant portion from the footnote in the draft follows here:

This expression slips from my pen, and I think as well expresses in English terminology Kant's theory as any equally brief expression can. . . . Yet the use in philosophical English of the word "thought" to express the absolute irrevocable imposition of an intuitive form upon the matter of inward experience, and thus upon all intelligence, seems to me correct enough. It is not Kantian terminology, of course, but I believe it to be good English terminology.

12. The *O.E.D.* has definitions for the words Prescission, Prescind, and Prescindent. Prescissive has no entry but is mentioned under Precisive. Under the verb to Prescind, three definitions are offered: 1. *trans.* To cut off beforehand, prematurely, or abruptly; to cut away or remove at once. 2. To cut off, detach, or separate from; to abstract. 3. *intr.* (for refl.) with from: a. To withdraw the attention from; to leave out of consideration. b. To separate itself, withdraw from (*obs.*).

13. Isaac Watts (1674–1748), English theologian and hymn writer. Peirce refers to Watts's *Logick: or, The Right Use of Reason in the Enquiry After Truth, with a Variety of Rules to Guard Against Error in the Affairs of Religion and Human Life, as well as in the Sciences* (London, 1724): I, vi, 9 *ad fin.* "This Act of Abstraction is . . . either Precisive or Negative. Precisive Abstraction is when we consider those Things apart which cannot really exist apart; as when we consider a Mode without considering its Substance and Subject" (this quotation, already found in the *Imperial Dictionary*, was chosen by Peirce for the *Century Dictionary*, and from there it made its way into the *O.E.D.* under "Precisive"—with the added remark "apparently for prescissive").

14. The Greek means "winged word."

15. In "The Logic of Relatives," *The Monist* 7 (January 1897):208–9, Peirce wrote: "In former publications I have given the appellation of *universal* or *particular* to a proposition according as its *first* quantifier is Π or Σ. But the study of substantive logical possibility has led me to substitute the appellations *negative* and *affirmative* in this sense, and to call a proposition *universal* or *particular* according as its *last* quantifier is Π or Σ" (CP 3.532).

16. "The Logic of Relatives," ibid., 205–17. These pages correspond to the thirteenth section of the paper, subtitled "Introduction to the Logic of Quantity" (CP 3.526–52).

17. Peirce indicated "p. 155 *ad fin.*" in the original publication of "Some Consequences of Four Incapacities"; EP1:53–55 and W2:240–42. The second paper is Peirce's 1871 review of A. C. Fraser's edition of *The Works of George Berkeley*, in *North American Review* 113 (1871):449–72; EP1:83–105 and W2:462–87.

18. Peirce had first written "(in his own mind, in 1873)."

19. At EP1:132 and W3:267.

20. Orpiment is a yellow compound of two equivalents of arsenic and three of sulphur (arsenic trisulphid). Realgar is red orpiment, and combines an equal number of sulphur and arsenic atoms (arsenic disulphid).

21. See EP1:22–23 and W2:205–7.

26. The Basis of Pragmaticism in Phaneroscopy

1. *Summa totius logicae*, part I, ch. 1. William of Ockham became known as the "venerable inceptor" not because he was the founder of nominalism but because his academic career at Oxford was interrupted while he was an *inceptor*, i.e., a scholar who has completed the requirements for the degree of master of theology and has yet to receive a teaching chair.

2. Peirce inserted here a footnote which has been omitted, because it refers to a long technical note ("a defense of the strict doctrine of valency in chemistry") found at the end of the document but not published here.

3. Peirce's "planar" representation of methane has been retained, although today's representation would either be a variation of his planar form, or more often the three-dimensional stereoscopic form that gives the true tetrahedral shape of the molecule. His notational representation of lithium compounds is also left untouched.

4. Peirce inserted here another footnote which is omitted for the same reason as above. One interesting part of it says that "there is a denumerable multitude of compounds of triads of any given valency, so that a complete enumeration of them singly is not possible."

5. Peirce intended to publish this manuscript (the fifth in a long series of variant drafts) as the third article in his "Pragmaticism series," but decided against it. It was first replaced by the next selection, which was itself superseded by "Prolegomena to an Apology for Pragmaticism," published in *The Monist*.

6. Peirce did not insert a comma here, but one seems necessary, and it can be placed either before or after "so"—which yields two different readings. This edition chose to insert the comma before "so" on account of Peirce's insistence (shown in the next three sentences) on the manner in which one needs to contemplate anything. Another possibility, one that does not call for a comma, is that, instead of "contemplate it," Peirce could have meant "contemplated."

7. Chorisy, cyclosy, periphraxy, and apeiry are the names Peirce assigns to the four Listing or census numbers. See selection 4, note 41, and selection 5, note 24.

8. Alfred B. Kempe (see selection 12, note 17) discusses geometrical betweenness in "On the Relation between the Logical Theory of Classes and the Geometrical Theory of Points," *Proceedings of the London Mathematical Society* 21 (1891):147–182, especially 176–79.

27. THE BASIS OF PRAGMATICISM IN THE NORMATIVE SCIENCES

1. The seven Harvard lectures of 1903: see selections 10 to 16.

2. The friend is William James, but James's negative recommendation was more nuanced than here acknowledged. On 5 June 1903, he wrote to Peirce: "You spoke of publishing these lectures, but not, I hope, *tels quels*. They need too much mediation by more illustrations, at which you are excellent (non-mathematical ones if possible) and by a good deal of interstitial expansion and comparison with other modes of thought. What I wish myself is that you might *revise these lectures* for your Lowell course, possibly confining yourself to fewer points. . . . As things stand, it is only highly skilled technicians and professionals who will sniff the rare perfume of your thought, and *after you are dead*, trace things back to your genius. You ought to gain a bigger audience when living."

3. The bracketed ellipsis indicates a gap of four missing manuscript leaves, numbered 3 to 6, equivalent to thirty-two handwritten lines. A remark in §5 of the text suggests that Peirce may have discussed, among other things, the proper "way to read" his article.

4. Hermann Bonitz (1814–1888), *Index Aristotelicus* (Berlin: G. Reimer, 1870; Graz: Akademische Druck- und Verlagsanstatt, 1955), 278–80.

5. Samuel Taylor Coleridge wrote the general introduction, entitled "A Preliminary Treatise on Method," to this influential British encyclopedia which was first published in 1818.

6. See selection 11, note 4.

7. The Greek words mean, respectively, potentiality, act or activity, matter, and form. The passage that begins here appears to draw its inspiration from the beginning of the second book of Aristotle's *De anima*.

8. See note 3 above.

9. "A voice, and nothing beyond that" (a phrase attributed to Seneca).

10. Peirce dropped a word here as he moved to a new manuscript sheet. The immediate context suggests that "experience" is the missing word.

11. See previous selection, note 7.

12. See selection 3, note 10.

13. This *Spieltrieb* (or play instinct) refers to Friedrich Schiller's theory of the three instincts (the other two being those of matter and form) as explained in his *Aesthetische Briefe*. See selection 14, note 6, and Peirce's early essay on the *Aesthetic Letters* in W1:10–12.

14. The precise location of this remark of F. C. S. Schiller has not been identified. Peirce might be referring to a no longer extant letter from the English philosopher. The connection between truth and satisfaction is made by Schiller in different places. James, too, makes the same connection: "Truth in science is what gives us the maximum possible sum of satisfactions, taste included, but consistency both with previous truth and with novel fact is always the most imperious claimant" (*Pragmatism*, Lecture VI, "Pragmatism's Conception of Truth" (New York: Longmans, Green and Co., 1907), 217). James also ascribes such a view to both Schiller and Dewey: "[Truth] means, they say, nothing but this that ideas (which themselves are but part of our experience) become true just in so far as they help us to get into satisfactory relation with other parts of our experience" (Ibid., Lecture II, "What Pragmatism Means," p. 58). Peirce criticizes such a view pointedly in CP 5.555–64 (a c.1906 manuscript entitled "Reflexions upon Pluralistic Pragmatism and upon Cenopythagorean Pragmaticism," which seems to have disappeared from the Harvard collection of Peirce's papers).

15. *Critique of Pure Reason*, A58, B82.

16. On Schröder, see selection 12, note 12. The symbol of aggregation used by Peirce in the formula is not one found in his 1870 paper (see W2:418–19), where he uses +, for the operation of logical addition. The present symbol stems from Peirce's modification of an aggregation sign devised by Stanley Jevons in 1869, which was two dots separated by a vertical stroke. Peirce added a curved line to connect the two dots and started to use this new aggregation sign around 1894. It appears frequently in his 1897 *Monist* paper "The Logic of Relatives," a review of Schröder's work.

17. Peirce in his 1903 paper "Nomenclature and Divisions of Dyadic Relations" (the fourth section of the "Syllabus," MS 539:2–29, CP 3.571–608) defines "juxtambilation" and explains his terminology; see especially CP 3.575, 584–85.

18. See selection 11, note 30, on Fechner.

19. See selection 8, note 7, on Sigwart.

20. Johann Friedrich Herbart (1776–1841), *Lehrbuch zur Einleitung in die Philosophie* (Königsberg: August Wilhelm Unger, 1813). Reprinted in Herbart's *Sämmtliche Werke*, ed. by G. Hartenstein (Leipzig: Leopold Voss, 1850), vol. 1, part 1, sect. 2, ch. 1, §34.

21. "On a New List of Categories," EP1:8 and W2:57.

22. The conception of a sign as a medium of communication becomes very prominent in Peirce's 1906 writings. It appears for instance in his Logic Notebook (MS 339:526, 30 Jan. 1906) and in a spring 1906 letter to Lady Welby (see selection 32 in the Appendix). In MS 793, which appears to be a draft of the present selection, Peirce writes:

> For the purpose of this inquiry a Sign may be defined as a Medium for the communication of a Form. It is not logically necessary that anything possessing consciousness, that is, feeling of the peculiar common quality of all our feeling, should be concerned. But it is necessary that there should be two, if not three, *quasi-minds*, meaning things capable of varied determination as to forms of the kind communicated.
>
> As a *medium*, the Sign is essentially in a triadic relation, to its Object which determines it, and to its Interpretant which it determines. In its relation to the Object, the Sign is *passive*; that is to say, its correspondence to the Object is brought about by an effect upon the Sign, the Object remaining unaffected. On the other hand, in its relation to the Interpretant the Sign is *active*, determining the Interpretant without being itself thereby affected.
>
> But at this point certain distinctions are called for. That which is communicated from the Object through the Sign to the Interpretant is a Form. It is not a singular thing; for if a singular thing were first in the Object and afterward in the Interpretant outside the Object, it must thereby cease to be in the Object. The Form that is communicated does not necessarily cease to be in one thing when it comes to be in a different thing, because its being is a being of the predicate. The Being of a Form consists in the truth of a conditional proposition. Under given circumstances, something would be true. The Form is in the Object, entitatively we may say, meaning that that conditional relation, or following of consequent upon reason, which constitutes the Form, is literally true of the Object. In the Sign the Form may or may not be embodied entitatively, but it must be embodied representatively, that is, in respect to the Form communicated, the Sign produces upon the Interpretant an effect similar to that which the Object itself would under favorable circumstances.

23. Peirce often translates *Umfang* by "sphere" (logical breadth or extension), or even "circuit."

24. Peirce's *Century Dictionary* definition of "conic section" is helpful:
a curve formed by the intersection of a plane with a right circular cone. If the plane is more inclined to the axis of the cone than is the side of the cone (fig. 3), the intersection is oval and is called an *ellipse*. The circle is one limit of the ellipse—that, namely, in which the plane becomes

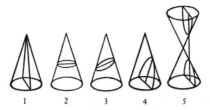

perpendicular to the axis of the cone (fig. 2). If the plane is less inclined to the axis of the cone than is the side of the cone, it will also cut the second sheet of the cone on the other side of the vertex (fig. 5), and the twofold curve thus generated is a *hyperbola*. A particular case of the hyperbola, produced when the plane becomes tangent to the surface of the cone, is that of two intersecting straight lines, called a *degenerate conic* (fig. 1). Intermediate between the ellipse and the hyperbola is the case where the plane is parallel to the side of the cone (fig. 4), and the curve thus produced is a *parabola*. The degenerate form of the ellipse is a point, that of the parabola a straight line. The degenerate forms are not true conics, because they are of the first class, the conics being of the second class.

25. The notion of "perfect sign" is explained in the draft as follows (MS 283:279–83):

Consider then the aggregate formed by a sign and all the signs which its occurrence carries with it. This aggregate will itself be a sign; and we may call it a *perfect* sign, in the sense that it involves the present existence of no other sign except such as are ingredients of itself. Now no perfect sign is in a statical condition: you might as well suppose a portion of matter to remain at rest during a thousandth of a second, or any other long interval of time. The only signs which are tolerably fixed are non-existent abstractions. We cannot deny that such a sign is real; only its mode of reality is not that active kind which we call existence. The existent acts, and whatsoever acts changes. . . .

Every real ingredient of the perfect sign is aging, its energy of action upon the interpretant is running low, its sharp edges are wearing down, its outlines becoming more indefinite.

On the other hand, the perfect sign is perpetually being acted upon by its object, from which it is perpetually receiving the accretions of new signs, which bring it fresh energy, and also kindle energy that it already had, but which had lain dormant.

In addition, the perfect sign never ceases to undergo changes of the kind we rather drolly call *spontaneous*, that is, they happen *sua sponte* but not by *its* will. They are phenomena of growth.

Such perfect sign is a quasi-mind. It is the sheet of assertion of Existential Graphs. . . .

This quasi-mind is an object which from whatever standpoint it be examined, must evidently have, like anything else, its special qualities of susceptibility to determination. Moreover, the determinations come as events each one once for all and never again. Furthermore, it must have its rules or laws, the more special ones variable, others invariable.

26. "Issues of Pragmaticism," *The Monist* 15 (Oct. 1905):487–90; selection 25, pp. 350–53.

27. See selection 25, p. 351.

28. Ibid.

29. Molière died on 17 February 1673, while performing the leading role in his play *Le malade imaginaire*. In the third intermède at the end of the play, a young doctor about to be admitted to the profession answered the question "quare opium facit dormire?" with the ridiculed "quia est in eo vertus dormitiva, cujus est natura sensus assoupire." See Peirce's related comments in CP 5.534.

30. "Be fruitful, and multiply, and replenish the earth, and subdue it" (Genesis 1:28).

31. On Louis Agassiz, see selection 9, note 3.

32. A book by Josiah Royce; see selection 6, note 7.

28. PRAGMATISM

1. The Italian philosopher Giovanni Papini (1881–1956) founded the Florentine pragmatist journal *Leonardo* which was issued from 1903 to 1907 (its contributors included Mario Calderoni, G. Vailati, Giuseppe Prezzolini, and F. C. S. Schiller). Peirce is referring to Papini's article "Introduzione al Pragmatismo" which appeared in February 1907 in *Leonardo* and was translated by Katharine Royce under the title "What Pragmatism Is Like," *Popular Science Monthly* 71 (1907):351–68. On 10 April 1907 Peirce sent Papini a description of the contents of his *Atlantic Monthly* article, which had been submitted to the editor Bliss Perry two days earlier.

2. Peirce received a letter from Frederick William Frankland (1854–1916) on 25 February 1907. In one of the preliminary drafts Peirce wrote (MS 320:38):

> There lives in New Zealand a gentleman of very exact and interesting thought, Frederick William Frankland, who is just about publishing two volumes of *Collected Essays and Citations* [(Foxton, N.Z.: G. T. Beale, 1907)]. He does not profess to be a pragmatist; but his opinion upon one point that concerns pragmatism is so clear and definite, that it will furnish an instance of a possible variety of pragmatism. . . . Mr. Frankland holds that there is only one infinite collection. He thinks there is no such thing as continuity, and that time consists of discrete instants of which a fixed number goes to a second.

3. This is John Locke's work of 1689.

4. George Berkeley (1685–1753), *An Essay Towards a New Theory of Vision* (1709) and *A Treatise Concerning the Principles of Human Knowledge* (1710). The medicinal use of a cold infusion of tar was once quite popular. Berkeley's last major philosophical writing was entitled *Siris: A Chain of Philosophical Questions and Inquiries Concerning the Virtues of Tar-Water, and Divers Other Subjects Connected Together and Arising One from Another* (1744). Berkeley's *Principles* can be regarded as incomplete since he designated it as "Part I" and elsewhere indicated the intention of producing a second part.

5. About the evidence attesting the existence of the Metaphysical Club, see Max Fisch's "Was There a Metaphysical Club?" in *Studies in the Philosophy of Charles Sanders Peirce*, second series, ed. Edward C. Moore and Richard S. Robin (Amherst: The University of Massachusetts Press, 1964), 3–23. Fisch concluded that Peirce founded the Club some time in the spring or fall of 1871; that it counted among its members, besides Peirce and the six others mentioned below, William James and Francis G. Peabody; that the meetings were held fortnightly during the most active period (1871–72); and that the Club lasted at least until the winter of 1874–75, before it was reorganized into a new form. Oliver Wendell Holmes (1841–1935), United States Supreme Court justice, collaborated with the lawyer Joseph Bangs Warner (1848–1923) on a commentary upon common law. Nicholas St. John Green (1830–1876) taught law at Harvard University. John Fiske (1842–1901), historian and philosopher, was a graduate of Harvard Law School. On Wright see selection 11, note 32, and on Abbot see selection 24, note 12.

6. Alexander Bain (1818–1903), Scottish philosopher and psychologist; *The Emotions and the Will* (London: J. W. Parker and son, 1859; 3d ed. London: Longmans & Green, 1875; New York: Appleton, 1876), ch. 11, p. 505.

7. The "little paper" has not survived, unless it is buried in the notes Peirce left for a projected book on logic: see W2:14–60, especially the chapters on belief and reality (1872). It is probably the paper Peirce read at a November 1872 meeting of the

Metaphysical Club, and which Thomas Sergeant Perry hoped to publish in the *North American Review*.

8. "The Fixation of Belief" in *Popular Science Monthly* 12 (Nov. 1877):1–15, *Revue Philosophique* 6 (Dec. 1878):553–69, EP1:109–23, and W3:242–57, 338–55. "How to Make Our Ideas Clear" in *Popular Science Monthly* 12 (Jan. 1878):286–302, *Revue Philosophique* 7 (Jan. 1879):553–69, EP1:124–41 and W3:257–76, 355–74.

9. George Campbell (1719–1796), principal of Marischal College in Aberdeen, Scotland, was the author of *The Philosophy of Rhetoric* which appeared in many editions through the nineteenth century and was used as a textbook at Harvard College.

10. Matthew 7:20.

11. This comes from a paragraph James wrote for the entry "Pragmatic and Pragmatism" in Baldwin's *Dictionary* (1902), 2:321–22:

The doctrine that the whole "meaning" of a conception expresses itself in practical consequences, consequences either in the shape of conduct to be recommended, or in that of experiences to be expected, if the conception be true; which consequences would be different if it were untrue, and must be different from the consequences by which the meaning of other conceptions is in turn expressed. If a second conception should not appear to have other consequences, then it must really be only the first conception under a different name. In methodology it is certain that to trace and compare their respective consequences is an admirable way of establishing the differing meanings of different conceptions.

12. Francis Herbert Bradley (1846–1924), *Appearance and Reality: A Metaphysical Essay* (London: S. Sonnenschein; New York: Macmillan, 1893).

13. Launcelot Gobbo is the clown servant to Shylock in Shakespeare's *The Merchant of Venice*, act 2, scene 2.

14. Edward Gibbon (1737–1794), *The History of the Decline and Fall of the Roman Empire* (London: Printed for W. Strahan and T. Cadell, 1776–88).

15. A device developed in 1804–5 in France by Joseph-Marie Jacquard, which used punched cards to control the weaving of the cloth so that intricate patterns could be obtained automatically.

16. Henri Stephanus (or Estienne, or Stephens; 1528–1598) published the 1578 edition of Plato's works, *Platonis opera quae extant omnis*.

17. The Piazza di Spagna in Rome, here viewed from the direction of the Pincian Hill, has been a popular stop for tourists since the sixteenth century, especially for students, artists, and young aristocrats making the Grand Tour of Europe.

18. The fire occurred in 1666.

19. *Categories*, ch. 5, 3a34–35: "It is the mark of substances and of differentiae that, in all propositions of which they form the predicate, they are predicated univocally. For all such propositions have for their subject either the individual (τὸ ἄτομον) or the species." *Prior Analytics*, bk. 1, ch. 27, 43a25–28: "Of all the things which exist some are such that they cannot be predicated of anything else truly and universally, e.g. Cleon and Callias, i.e. the individual and sensible (τὸ καθ' ἕκαστον καὶ αἰσθητόν), but other things may be predicated of them (for each of these is both man and animal)."

20. The saying "Truth lies at the bottom of a well" has been attributed to a number of ancient authors, including Heraclitus, Cleanthes, and Democritus.

21. *Henry IV*, part I, act 2, scene 4, Falstaff: "Give you a reason on compulsion! If reasons were as plentiful as blackberries I would give no man a reason upon compulsion, I."

22. Liddell and Scott's *Greek-English Lexicon* lists the following meanings under σημείωσις: indication, notice (Plutarch), inference from a sign (Philodemus), observing of symptoms (Galen), and visible sign or token (Psalms).

23. Peirce apparently had in mind the scene in the last chapter of the novel *Kenil-worth* (1821) by Sir Walter Scott in which Countess Amy falls to her death through a trap-door whose supports had been deliberately removed.

24. Christiania was the name given to Norway's capital Oslo from the seventeenth century to 1925. After the separation of Norway from Sweden Peirce's younger brother, Herbert Henry Davis Peirce (1849–1916), was appointed on 22 June 1906, as the first envoy extraordinary and minister plenipotentiary of the United States to Norway.

25. Henry Wadsworth Longfellow's second wife died in 1861 after she accidentally set her dress on fire.

26. F. C. S. Schiller, *Studies in Humanism* (London and New York: Macmillan, 1907), especially part III: "The Relations of Logic and Psychology."

27. Alfred B. Kempe, "On the Geographical Problem of the Four Colors," *American Journal of Mathematics* 2 (1879):193–200 and "How to Colour a Map with Four Colours," *Nature* 21 (1880):399–400. The Four Color Conjecture, that a plane map needs no more than four colors to distinguish the regions, was not proven correct until 1977. The flaw in Kempe's work was revealed by P. J. Heawood in 1890 ("Map Colour Theorem," *Quarterly Journal of Mathematics* 24 (1890):332–38). Peirce's bored globular body is topologically equivalent to a sphere with two handles or a teacup with two handles: each of these surfaces can be smoothly deformed into the other (assuming that the second "wide" hole does not pass through the first). Peirce was apparently unaware of Heawood's paper, which also presented a general formula for the minimum number of colors for surfaces of this type with any number of handles (the number is eight for Peirce's example). Though his formula was correct, Heawood's argument was shown to be inadequate in 1891 and an acceptable proof was not given until 1968.

28. Arthur Cayley, "A Sixth Memoir upon Quantics," *Philosophical Transactions of the Royal Society of London* 149 (1860):61–90, esp. §230.

29. See selection 4, note 41, and selection 5, note 24.

30. Charles-Edouard Brown-Sequard (1817–1894), *Experimental and Clinical Researches on the Physiology and Pathology of the Spinal Cord and Some Other Parts of the Nervous Centres* (Richmond: Colin & Nowlan, 1855).

31. James's most succinct definition of pragmatism appears in Baldwin's *Dictionary* 2:321 (printed after Peirce's own definition). See note 11 above.

32. Schiller gives the seven definitions in his paper "The Definition of 'Pragmatism' and 'Humanism,'" in *Mind* 14 (April 1905):235–40; republished in *Studies in Humanism* (London: Macmillan and Co., 1912), 1–21. The definitions are found on pp. 7–12.

33. See note 8 above.

34. In the introduction to the first part of his *Électricité et optique: cours de physique mathématique* (Paris: G. Carré, 1890–91), Poincaré states some of the tenets of his conventionalism. See selection 13, note 16, and selection 15, note 10.

35. Captain Bunsby is Captain Cuttle's friend in Charles Dickens's *Dombey and Son* (1848): "'If so be,' returned Bunsby, with unusual promptitude, 'as he's dead, my opinion is he won't come back no more. If so be as he's alive, my opinion is he will. Do I say he will? No. Why not? Because the bearings of this observation lays in the application on it'" (ch. 39). Schiller remarks that Alfred Sidgwick has "justly laid stress" on the second formulation of pragmatism in his *The Application of Logic* (London: Macmillan, 1910), p. 272 and ch. 9, §43.

36. Schiller writes that Sidgwick regarded this third definition as "the essence of the pragmatic method" (*Studies in Humanism*, p. 9).

37. Critical common-sensism is discussed in selection 25, "Issues of Pragmaticism."

38. "What Pragmatism is Like," *Popular Science Monthly* 71 (1907):351.

39. This sentence follows directly after the last sentence of the "Introduction" above. The definition referred to is that of William James (see note 11).

40. In his *Essay Concerning Human Understanding* (1689), bk. 2, ch. 23, §11, Locke argues that secondary qualities would disappear if we could perceive primary qualities.

41. Like Bradley (see note 12 above), Alfred Edward Taylor (1869–1945) was a British neo-Hegelian philosopher. Peirce may have read F. C. S. Schiller's extensive critique of Bradley, "Truth and Mr. Bradley," in *Mind* 13 (Oct. 1904), reprinted in *Studies in Humanism*, pp. 114–40. Schiller also reviewed A. E. Taylor's *Elements of Metaphysics* in "Empiricism and the Absolute," *Mind* 14 (July 1905), reprinted in *Studies* pp. 224–57.

42. On Haeckel see selection 11, note 25, and on Pearson see selection 6, note 1.

43. Peirce may have been referring to his "Reply to the Necessitarians" (*The Monist* 3 (July 1893):526–70), a long response to Paul Carus's "Mr. Charles S. Peirce's Onslaught on the Doctrine of Necessity" (ibid., 2 (1892):560–82).

44. The "several months" refer to a period following April 1907, when Peirce had finished writing the first three versions of the present "letter to the editor" (all signed "Charles Santiago Sanders Peirce").

45. "On the Syllogism, No. IV, and on the Logic of Relations," *Transactions of the Cambridge Philosophical Society* 10 (1864):331–58. The three categories, Qualities, Relations, and Representations, were so named by Peirce in the "New List of Categories" (EP1:6) in 1867 and in several texts written the previous year (W1:476 and 520, for instance).

46. Peirce confuses two stories from *The Arabian Nights:* "Aladdin; Or, the Wonderful Lamp" and "Ali Baba and the Forty Thieves." It was Ali Baba who discovered by chance the thieves' cave full of treasure. Aladdin, on the other hand, found a magic lamp that contained a genie which granted him wishes.

47. Louis Pasteur, *Oeuvres de Pasteur: Dissymétrie Moléculaire* (Paris: Masson, 1922), 1:83.

48. See selection 20, note 11.

49. Peirce scribbled an interesting but rough note on habit in MS 318:183–84. It is reproduced below with some punctuation corrections.

Habit. Involuntary habits are not meant, but voluntary habits, i.e., such as are subject in some measure to self-control. Now under what conditions is a habit subject to self-control? Only if what has been done in one instance with the character, its consequents, and other circumstances, can have a triadic influence in strengthening or weakening the disposition to do the like on a new occasion. This is as much as to say that voluntary habit is conscious habit. For what is consciousness? In the first place feeling is conscious. But what is a feeling, such as blue, whistling, sour, rose-scented? It is nothing but a quality, character, or predicate, which involves no reference to any other predicate or other thing than the subject in which it inheres, but yet positively is. We may suppose a crystal to have such a quality, and if we suppose it to be no otherwise different from a crystal as ordinarily conceived, this quality will be forever unknown to itself, to the crystal, and to every other thing or mind. In what then will it differ from another crystal that does not possess that quality? Is it not a quality of pure moonshine and empty verbiage? Our own feelings, if there were no memory of them for any fraction of a second, however small, if there were no triadic time-sense to testify with such assurance to their existence and varieties, would be equally unknown to us. Therefore, such a quality may be utterly unlike any feeling we are acquainted with; but it would have all that distinguish all our feelings from everything else. In the second place, effort is conscious. It is at once a sense of effort on the part of the being who wills and is a sense of resistance on the part of the object upon which the effort is exerted. But these two are one and the same consciousness. Otherwise, all that has been said of the feeling consciousness is true of the effort consciousness. It, like the feeling consciousness, is guaranteed by a triadic consciousness; and to say that this is veracious means less if possible than to say that a thing is whatever it may be.

There is, then, a triadic consciousness which does not supersede the lower order, but goes bail for them and enters bonds for their veracity.

Experiment upon inner world must teach inner nature of concepts as experiment on outer world must teach nature of outer things.

Meaning of a general physical predicate consists in the conception of the habit of its subject that it implies. And such must be the meaning of a psychical predicate.

The habits must be known by experience which however exhibits singulars only.

Our minds must generalize these. How is this to be done?

The intellectual part of the lessons of experimentation consists in the consciousness or purpose to act in certain ways (including motive) on certain conditions.

50. See selection 6, note 7.

29. A Neglected Argument for the Reality of God

1. James Mark Baldwin, *Thought and Things: a Study of the Development and Meaning of Thought or Genetic Logic* (London: Sonnenschein, 1906), 1:261.

2. Shakespeare, *A Midsummer Night's Dream*, act 5, scene 1: "And as imagination bodies forth | The forms of things unknown, the poet's pen | Turns them to shapes and gives to airy nothing | A local habitation and a name."

3. "The wind bloweth where it listeth, and thou hearest the sound thereof, but canst not tell whence it cometh, and whither it goeth: so is every one that is born of the Spirit" (John 3:8).

4. Edgar Allen Poe (1809–1849) has his detective, Monsieur Dupin, say "It appears to me that this mystery is considered insoluble for the very reason which should cause it to be regarded as easy of solution. I mean the outré character of its features." "The Murders in the Rue Morgue" (first published in 1841), *The Complete Works of Edgar Allan Poe*, ed. by James A. Harrison (New York: Thomas Y. Crowell and Co., 1902), vol. 4.

5. "But oars alone can ne'er prevail | To reach the distant coast, | The breath of heaven must swell the sail, | Or all the toil is lost." William Cowper (1731–1800), "Human Frailty," in *The Works of William Cowper: Comprising His Poems, Correspondence, and Translations. With a Life of the Author, by the Editor, Robert Southey* (London: Baldwin and Cradock, 1835–37).

6. Current estimates of the maximum number of elements are closer to 200 than to Peirce's figures.

7. Francis Bacon contrasts "that induction which proceeds by simple enumeration" with "scientific induction" in his *Novum Organum* (see especially book I, aphorism 105).

8. *Critique of Pure Reason*, A154–58, B193–97.

9. Jacques Babinet (1794–1872), French physicist known for his work in meteorology, optics, and hydrodynamics; author of *Résumé complet de la physique des corps impondérables* (Paris, 1825).

10. See selection 11, note 30.

11. See "Dialogues Concerning the Two Great Systems of the World," in *Mathematical Collections and Translations of Thomas Salisbury* (London, 1661), 1:301.

12. It is evident that this book was not written.

13. In the original, Peirce added the following explanation after this sentence: "It is strictly pertinent. I am exceeding the limits of my article."

14. The manuscript ends here at the end of the fifth section. At the end of July 1908, the *Hibbert* editor, L. P. Jacks, let Peirce know (through their common friend Cassius J. Keyser) that he found Peirce's contribution to be of "permanent value," but that, because of the paper's complexity, he wanted Peirce "to summarize the article in a concluding page or two, to be added to the article, in order to forestall careless cavillers who might say, 'what, then, precisely, is your neglected argument?'" Peirce wrote two versions of his addendum, wich he called "Additament." Jacks published the second one without title, a mere blank line serving to separate it from the end of the article. Peirce was surprised that the addendum was printed entirely, because, as he told William James later, he thought it was somewhat distasteful and he had asked Jacks to pick out "a small passage that was neither egotistical nor offensive to anybody," thinking that such an injunction would ensure "the rejection of the whole." The "Additament" published in the present edition combines the first five paragraphs of Peirce's first version of the text (found in MS 844) with the full text of the second version. The reason for this amalgamation is that only in the first version did Peirce clearly identify "a nest of three arguments" that is then referred to in the second version.

15. The full text of the second "Additament" begins here with this paragraph. The bracketed ellipsis at the end of the previous paragraph indicates that the text of the first "Additament" continues beyond that sentence (for three pages and a half) but has not been included here to avoid both a rough transition and an overlap. The first omitted sentence reads as follows: "According to that logical doctrine which the present writer first formulated in 1873 and named Pragmatism, the true meaning of any product of the intellect lies in whatever unitary determination it would impart to practical conduct under any and every conceivable circumstance, supposing such conduct to be guided by reflection carried to an ultimate limit." The reader will notice that when Peirce rewrote the "Additament," he pushed back the year of his fathering of pragmatism from 1873 to 1871.

16. See selection 28, note 5.

17. See selection 28, note 8.

18. William James, *The Will to Believe and Other Essays in Popular Philosophy* (Cambridge: Harvard University Press, 1979; first edition 1897).

19. See selection 28, notes 1 and 38.

20. In his *Monist* paper "What Pragmatism Is" (selection 24).

21. See the entry "Pragmatic and Pragmatism" in Baldwin's *Dictionary* (1902), 2:321–22; also in CP 5.1–4.

22. The hunch-backed Italian poet Giacomo Leopardi (1798–1837) was known for his scholarship as well as his lyric verses. Peirce's misanthropes are: the unconventional Greek cynic philosopher Diogenes of Sinope (c.410–c.320 B.C.); the philosopher Arthur Schopenhauer (1788–1860), who lived most of his life in Germany in retirement; the British man of letters Thomas Carlyle (1795–1881); and Timon, known as the Misanthrope of Athens (5th century B.C.), on whom Shakespeare based his play *Timon of Athens*.

23. Allusion to William James's book *The Will to Believe* (New York: Longmans, Green & Co., 1897) and its first chapter by the same title (an address published in 1896). On the mutability of truth, see for instance James's lecture "What Pragmatism Means" in his book *Pragmatism*.

30. A SKETCH OF LOGICAL CRITICS

1. In several places in the first half of the manuscript, and beginning just above this first line, Peirce interlined outline subheadings in brown ink. The first one reads "Discussion of the term 'critics.'" These subheadings have not been incorporated into the text, in accordance with Peirce's instruction found in a variant text (MS 674:2): "I shall write all directions to the printer in green and everything else that is not to appear in print in other colors."

2. John Bull is the name traditionally used to epitomize or caricature the typical Englishman.

3. Samuel Johnson (1709–1784), *A Dictionary of the English Language* (London: W. Strahan, 1755).

4. See for example John Locke's *An Essay Concerning Humane Understanding* (London: Thomas Bassett, 1690), bk. 4, ch. 21, para. 4.

5. Thomas Hobbes, *Stigmai ageometrias. . .* (first published in 1657), in *The English Works of Thomas Hobbes of Malmesbury* (London: J. Bohn, 1839–45), 7:389.

6. *Statesman* 260c: "And now, in which of these divisions shall we place the king? Is he a judge and kind of spectator *(ἀρ' ἐν τῇ κριτικῇ, καθάπερ τινὰ θεατήν)*?"

7. Nicolas Boileau Despréaux (1636–1711), French poet and literary critic, famous for his *Art poétique* (1674), which strongly influenced Samuel Johnson.

8. Peirce interlined the subheading "The Budding of Reason" above this paragraph.

9. Peirce interlined the subheading "Sense in which 'reasoning' is here used" above this paragraph.

10. Peirce inserted the subheading "Syllogistic Recollection" above this line.

11. This footnote is preceded by the interlined subheading "The word 'suggestion.'"

12. The English philosopher and psychologist David Hartley (1705–1757) gives credit to his fellow Englishman John Gay (1699–1745) for asserting the importance of psychological association. In MS 318:37 Peirce wrote:

The great founders of associationalism and of scientific psychology (after Aristotle), the Rev. Mr. Gay and Dr. David Hartley, usefully limited the term "association" to the process whereby one idea acquires the power to attract another from the depths of memory to the surface of consciousness, and to the habit resulting from this process. An association having once been established, that act by which, in accordance with it, one idea calls up another, they called *suggestion.*

13. Peirce inserted the subheading "Unthought thought" above this line.

14. See selection 28, notes 7 and 8.

15. Peirce inserted the subheading "Belief essentially a satisfaction, but not necessarily pleasant" above this line.

16. EP1:114; W3:247.

17. EP1:138–39; W3:273.

18. "Full many a flower is born to blush unseen, | And waste its sweetness on the desert air." Thomas Gray, "Elegy Written in a Country Churchyard," stanza 14. See W2:104, and EP1:139 or W3:274. The "single sentence" in which Peirce did not make it questionable whether any real flower was born to blush unseen may be the following (EP1:139–40):

To this I reply that, though in no possible state of knowledge can any number be great enough to express the relation between the amount of what rests unknown to the amount of the known, yet it is unphilosophical to suppose that, with regard to any given question (which has any clear meaning), investigation would not bring forth a solution of it, if it were carried far enough.

19. See selection 28, note 5.

20. Hermann Ludwig Ferdinand von Helmholtz (1821–1894), German physicist, anatomist, and physiologist. *Über die Erhaltung der Kraft* (Berlin: G. Reimer, 1847) is his classic paper in which he formulated the philosophical and physical basis of the principle of the conservation of energy.

21. Concerning Darwin, see selection 11, note 31. Peirce in his photometric work at Harvard beginning in 1875 was one of the first scientists in the United States to make extensive use of the spectroscope.

22. See selection 16, note 9.

23. See selection 29, note 23.

24. See selection 11, note 4.

25. The English playwright Thomas Morton first created the off-stage character of Mrs. Grundy in *Speed the Plough* (produced in 1798). Concern for "What would Mrs. Grundy think?" came to represent the tyranny of social convention.

26. Henry James, Sr. (1811–1882), *Substance and Shadow: or, Morality and Religion in Their Relation to Life: An Essay on the Physics of Creation* (Boston: Ticknor and Fields, 1863); *The Secret of Swedenborg: Being an Elucidation of His Doctrine of the Divine Natural Humanity* (Boston: Fields, Osgood & Co., 1869); *Spiritual Creation* (unfinished) included in *The Literary Remains of the Late Henry James*, ed. William James (Boston: Houghton Mifflin Co., 1884).

27. For Peirce's review of Pearson's *Grammar of Science*, see selection 6.

28. The manuscript continues here for another five pages before coming to an unfinished end; this last portion is not included because of its incompleteness.

31. An Essay toward Reasoning in Security and Uberty

1. Galileo Galilei (1564–1642), *Le opere di Galileo Galilei. Prima edizione completa, condotta sugli autentici manoscritti palatini*, edited by Eugenio Alberi (Firenze, Italy: Societa Editrice Fiorentina, 1842–56), 15 v. in 16.

2. Francis Bacon served as Lord Chancellor of England from 1618 to 1621 in the reign of James I.

3. This passage was originally part of the main text, but Peirce later instructed the typesetter to turn it into a new paragraph in smaller type. Given its notational nature, it has here been transformed into a footnote.

4. One example Peirce may have in mind is William Hamilton, *Lectures on Metaphysics and Logic*, edited by H. L. Mansel and J. Veitch (Boston: Gould and Lincoln, 1860), 2:350, where Hamilton uses the word dianoetic "to denote the operations of the discursive, elaborative, or comparative faculty" (quoted by Peirce in the *Century Dictionary*).

5. Peirce apparently coined this adverb himself, from the rare dialectal word "glibber" meaning either "worn smooth" or "slippery"—so that the adverb may be read "with all edges worn smooth" or "in slippery fashion."

6. See selection 1, note 3, selection 16, note 20, and selection 29, note 15.

7. In a letter to Frederic Adams Woods, written in the fall of 1913, Peirce wrote: "I think logicians should have two principal aims: first, to bring out the amount and kind of *security* (approach to certainty) of each kind of reasoning, and second, to bring out the possible and esperable *uberty*, or value in productiveness, of each kind" (CP 8.384).

8. Around 1893 Peirce attempted, unsuccessfully, to publish a proposed translation of a work by the thirteenth-century French scholar, *The Treatise of Petrus Peregrinus on the Lodestone*. Peirce claims to have been the first person to completely decipher

and transcribe the manuscript (MS 1310 and HP 1:39–95). The English scholastic Roger Bacon (c.1220–1292) was a student of Peregrinus.

9. This is reported by John Aubrey (1626–1697) in his chapter on William Harvey (1578–1657), in *Brief Lives, chiefly of contemporaries, set down by John Aubrey, between the years 1669 & 1696*, ed. by Andrew Clark (Oxford: Clarendon Press, 1898), 1:299. Aubrey reports that Harvey "had been physician to the Lord Chancellor Bacon, whom he esteemed very much for his wit and style, but would not allow him to be a great Philosopher. Said he to me, *He writes Philosophy like a Lord Chancellor*, speaking in derision; *I have cured him*."

10. Francis Bacon's tenth aphorism says: "The subtilty of nature far exceeds the subtilty of the senses and understanding; so that the specious meditations, speculations, and theories of mankind are but a kind of insanity, only there is no one to stand by and observe it."

11. In their experiments beginning in 1887, A. A. Michelson and E. W. Morley were unable to detect expected variations in the speed of light. Peirce was acquainted with the explanation of the Nobel laureate in physics, Hendrik Antoon Lorentz (1853–1928), namely that the speed of light appeared to be constant in vacuum because the measuring instruments contract in the direction of their motion. Peirce seems not to have taken note of the then less well-known Albert Einstein who posited the universal constancy of the speed of light in his 1905 paper that established the special theory of relativity.

12. Evangelinos Apostolides Sophocles (1807–1883) was professor of Greek at Harvard.

13. In the Dreyfus Affair the French novelist Émile Zola (1840–1902) published his "J'accuse" against the anti-Dreyfus contingent in 1898.

14. Allusion to a phrase commonly used in Protestant wedding ceremonies: "If any man can show just cause, why they may not lawfully be joined together, let him now speak, or else hereafter for ever hold his peace" (*The Book of Common Prayer*, "Solemnization of Matrimony," p. 300).

15. On 7 January 1913 Peirce wrote to Alice H. James the following description, which might be related:

We had a little outing the other day, when a friend came in his auto and took us over a famous road called the "Hawk's Nest Road" which I had never been over before, though Juliette had the year we first came to Milford. It goes up 1000 feet above the Delaware river which is vertically below the parapet of the drive. When we got up we went to a place where nine millionaires have houses of gorgeous magnificence. Mr. Chapin formerly of Springfield Mass. is one of them.

The Peirces also often visited the Norman-style mansion, called "Grey Towers," of James W. Pinchot and his son Gifford; their wives were good friends of Peirce's wife, Juliette. The chateau, now a National Historic Landmark building, overlooks the Delaware River and Milford.

16. See selection 8, note 36, and selection 11, note 30.

17. Wilhelm Max Wundt (1832–1920), *Beiträge zur Theorie der Sinneswahrnehmung* (Leipzig: C. F. Winter, 1862); *Vorlesungen über die Menschen- und Thierseele* (Leipzig: L. Voss, 1863); *Grundzüge der physiologischen Psychologie* (Leipzig: W. Engelmann, 1874).

18. William Hamilton, *Lectures on Logic*, edited by Henry L. Mansel and John Veitch (Boston: Gould and Lincoln, 1859), Lecture viii, §24. See also his *Discussions on Philosophy and Literature, Education and University Reform* (New York: Harper & Brothers, 1853), 699.

19. "This one has an extended, though not very deep, knowledge; that other one is very much of his village, but of the few things he has learned on his own, he knows the bottom and the deeper bedrock."

20. Augustus De Morgan, *Syllabus of a Proposed System of Logic* (London: Walton and Maberly, 1860), §212.

21. See selection 14, note 9.

22. Presumably Peirce is picturing the complex number $a + b\sqrt{-1}$ in the standard fashion in a plane coordinate system where a and b are represented as distances along the two perpendicular x and y axes respectively. William Rowan Hamilton (1805–1865) in his futile attempt to find the three-dimensional, spatial equivalent to the complex numbers (which was later shown not to exist) discovered the quaternions, a four-unit generalization of the complex number. Lorentz made use of time as, in effect, a fourth dimension in his "Electromagnetic Phenomena in a System Moving with Velocity Smaller Than That of Light," *Proceedings of the Academy of Sciences of Amsterdam* 6 (1904):809–31.

23. The last sentence in the manuscript, which follows the last sentence here, has been omitted, since it alludes to a continuation Peirce never wrote. That sentence reads:

Nevertheless, considering how much more numerous the others will be, to whom I have considerable hope of not being entirely useless, I will endeavor, even in this introductory part of my essay, not to be insufferably prolix about words; and perhaps they, on their side, may find some advantage in considering the merits and defects of my method of ascertaining the meanings of words.

32. Excerpts from Letters to Lady Welby

1. See selection 27, note 22.

2. In the Logic Notebook (MS 339:531, 533, 541–44), the Intentional Interpretant is also called the Intended, Impressional, or Initial Interpretant; the Effectual Interpretant is also called the Factual, Middle, or Dynamic Interpretant; and the Communicational Interpretant is also called the Normal, Habitual, or Eventual Interpretant.

3. The three universes are explained in selection 29. See also Peirce's definition of "universe" in Baldwin's *Dictionary* 2:742, and "Prolegomena to an Apology for Pragmaticism," *The Monist* 16 (Oct. 1906):514–17 (CP 4.546–47).

4. The text of this footnote comes from a remark Peirce wrote in the margin. Plato's use of the Greek word appears in *Phaedrus* 250b and *Sophist* 266d; Aristotle's is in *Rhetoric*, 1356a31. Lutoslawski dates the *Phaedrus* 379 B.C. in his *Origin and Growth of Plato's Logic*, p. 358 (see selection 4, note 26), but on p. 176 of his copy of the book Peirce wrote the date 373 B.C. (as opposed to that of 371 B.C. suggested in the footnote).

5. "Prolegomena to an Apology for Pragmaticism," *The Monist* 16 (Oct. 1906):506–7 (CP 4.538).

6. "On a New List of Categories," *Proceedings of the American Academy of Arts and Sciences* 7 (1868):295; EP1:8 and W2:57.

7. The Greek words mean "clear, manifest" (δῆλος), "obscure" (ἄδηλος), "moderately" (μέτριος), "approximately, more or less" (σχεδόν), and "hardly, with difficulty" (χαλεπῶς).

8. Pascal's Theorem states that if six points of a conic are regarded as vertices of a hexagon, then the three points of intersection of opposite sides lie on a line.

9. Much of this work is recorded in the Logic Notebook, MS 339:489–550.

33. EXCERPTS FROM LETTERS TO WILLIAM JAMES

1. In his letter to James of 17 December 1909 Peirce defined "molition" as "volition minus all desire and purpose, the mere consciousness of *exertion* of any kind" (CP 8.303).

2. The Carnegie Institution, founded in 1902 in Washington, D.C., rejected Peirce's grant application in May 1903.

3. The American astronomer, flight pioneer, and friend of Peirce, Samuel Pierpont Langley (1834–1906), made fundamental discoveries concerning the nature of the sun's radiation. See "The Solar and the Lunar Spectrum," in *Memoirs of the National Academy of Sciences* 4 (1888):159–70, and *The New Spectrum* (New Haven, 1901). As Secretary of the Smithsonian Institution Langley engaged Peirce for a number of writing assignments, including many translations of scientific articles.

4. See selection 29, note 22.

5. While Peirce refers here to his first two papers of 1877 and 1878 (see selection 28, note 8), it is the second one, "How to Make Our Ideas Clear," that contains the distinction between the three grades of clearness. The first grade (familiarity) is described in EP1:124–25 and 136; the second grade (logical analysis), in EP1:125–26, 136; and the third grade is the pragmatic maxim itself, enunciated in EP1:132. See also Peirce's 1897 *Monist* paper on "The Logic of Relatives," which has the following passage (CP 3.457):

Now there are three grades of clearness in our apprehensions of the meanings of words. The first consists in the connection of the word with familiar experience. In that sense, we all have a clear idea of what reality is and what force is—even those who talk so glibly of mental force being correlated with the physical forces. The second grade consists in the abstract definition, depending upon an analysis of just what it is that makes the word applicable. . . . The third grade of clearness consists in such a representation of the idea that fruitful reasoning can be made to turn upon it, and that it can be applied to the resolution of difficult practical problems.

6. *Metalogicus*, bk. 2, ch. 20. See selection 20, note 11.

7. Lady Welby made this triple distinction in her article "Significs" in the *Encyclopaedia Britannica*, 11th edition (1911), 25:78–81, reproduced in *Semiotics and Significs* pp. 167–75. She sent a copy of it to Peirce at the end of January 1909. Welby had also published a two-part paper, "Sense, Meaning and Interpretation" in *Mind* 5 (Jan. 1896):24–27 and (Apr. 1896):186–202.

8. Nathaniel Southgate Shaler (1841–1906) was an American geologist and naturalist, and a professor of paleontology at Harvard. He was the head of the Atlantic Coast division of the U. S. Geological Survey (1884–1900). Peirce and Shaler observed the solar eclipse of 7 August 1869 together in Kentucky (W2:291–92).

INDEX

Knowledge *(continued)*
science's purpose, xxiii, 94; starting-point of, 87–88; the theory of its advancement, xxxiii, 256–57
Koch, Robert, 222, 530*n*27

Lamare, William, 21, 504*n*11
Lambert, Johann Heinrich, 219–20, 529*n*19
Lane, Edward William, 517*n*5
Langley, Samuel Pierpont, 67, 495, 556*n*3
Language: act of, 278, 292, 312–13; American vs. British English, 451–52; Arabic, 220, 221; Aryan, 17, 18, 20, 220–21, 309, 309*n*, 329; Basque, 285, 309, 309*n*; Chinese, 326; Egyptian, 7, 16*n*, 220, 221; Eskimo, 12, 16*n*; Gaelic, 170, 309*n*; good, 263; Greek, 17*n*, 221, 282, 308–9, 310, 329; Indo-European, 12; Latin, 17*n*, 282, 309*n*, 310, 329; vs. logic, 16*n*, 18, 221, 285, 309; looseness of, 396; Polynesian, 484; quantitative, 390; Semitic, 309, 329, 496; its symbolic nature, 307; and thought, 460; Urdu, 326
Laplace, Pierre Simon de, 50, 215, 538*n*12; *Mécanique céleste*, 44
Lathrop, Francis A., 75, 512*n*14, 525*n*24
Law: active, 197; in argument, 293; cause of facts, 316–17; court-sheriff analogy, 120–21, 122, 152, 245; its essence, 58–59; vs. fact, 425; vs. force, 120–21; formula for events to conform to, 314–16; and legisign, 291; not part of secondness, 160; reality of, 269, 313–16; regularity of indefinite future, 274; and symbol, 274–75, 313, 314, 316–17; third correlate, 290; and thirdness, 271; truth of, 316–17; as uniformity, 313–14
Law of nature: and action and reaction, 152–53; breach of, 53; in contemporary science, 73; definition of, 68; history of its conception, 69–71; influencing matter, 184; its metaphysical essence, 73; nominalistic vs. realistic view of, 153; as objective fact, xxiii, 74; Pearson about, 63–64, 66; reality of, 63–64, 66, 72*n*, 181–83; its representation, 181–83; resembling law of thought, 363; resolution in a deity's mind, 184–85; Scotistic view of, 68–69; shaping events, 72*n*; two characters of, 67–68
Leading principle: in inference, 24
Learning, xxviii; in animals, 467–68; desire for, 47, 48, 56, 130–31; from experience, 454; by reasoning, 454; sense of, 5; spurred by sense of ignorance, 48; vs. teaching, 49, 50; will to learn, xxi, 47
Legendre, Adrien, 207, 219, 529*n*16
Legisign: definition of, 291; its different kinds, 294–95
Leibniz, Gottfried Wilhelm, xviii, 215, 361, 402, 428, 449, 457; denying reason to God, 157, 519*n*27; modern nominalist, 157; pre-

established harmony, 155; on space and time, 187
Leibnizianism, 180
Lemma: definition of, 96
Leopardi, Giacomo, 449, 496, 551*n*22
Letter: designation in logic, 303
Leverrier, Urbain, 93
Liberty: compulsion to make one's life more reasonable, 248; in pure play, 436
Life: moral vs. intellectual, 347; and thirdness, 271. *See also* Conduct, of life
Likelihood: antecedent, 80; arguments in favor of theory, 78–79; danger of, 108–9; of hypothesis, 108–9; objections against the theory, 79–84; vs. probability, 287; subjective, 114; theory of balancing —s, 77–79
Likeness: and capacity for experience, 8; examples of, 5–6; and icon, 13, 460–61; and imitation, 6–7; and indication, 8; not conveying information, 6–7; its oneness, 9; and symbol, 10; three kinds of, 6–7. *See also* Icon
Limit, 538*n*20; of endless series of symbols, 323
Linguistics, 261, 285
Lisbon, earthquake of, 89, 513*n*21
Listing, Johann Benedikt, 40, 416*n*, 507*n*41; his census theorem, 417, 508*n*24
Listing numbers, 50, 125, 417, 508*n*24, 515*n*16, 542*n*7; applied to space, 368
Listing's theorem, 417, 508*n*24
Liszka, James Jakób, xxx, xxx*n*28
Locke, John, 47, 70, 422, 423, 452, 470, 549*n*40; as pragmatist, 399
Lockyer, Joseph Norman, 130
Logic, 198; analogous to moral self-control, 169; application of ethics, xxv, 142, 188–89, 200–201, 253, 272, 337, 480; as art of reasoning, 11; its business, 18; as classification of arguments, 200; in classification of sciences, 36, 260; coeval with reasoning, 200; as Critic, 256; as critic of arguments, 188, 200; as criticism of conscious thought, 169; defined in the "New List," 481–82; definition of, xxiv, 36, 200, 309, 376; dualism in, 379; vs. epistemology, 257; exactitude of thought, 265; formal, 18, 31; general theory of signs, 272, 500; German, 252; vs. grammar, 221, 425; guided by mathematics, 36; as heuretic science, 378; of history, 54–55; vs. language, 18, 309; in liberal education, 527*n*1; and man's ultimate aim, 252–53; its mathematical principles, 214; of mathematics, xxiii, 301, 302; vs. mathematics, 311; vs. matter of taste, 27; maxim of, 188; vs. metaphysics, 30–31, 36, 257; as methodeutic, 256; minute, 85, 512*n*14; modal, xxx; as normative science, xxv; object of its method, 85; part of trivium, 19, 327; its preference for theory, 304–5; of propositions, 311–12; vs. psychology, 189, 210, 217, 232, 256–57,